HANDBOOK FOR Human Sexuality COUNSELING

A Sex Positive Approach

edited by
Angela M. Schubert
Mark Pope

American Counseling Association
2461 Eisenhower Avenue, Suite 300 • Alexandria, VA 22331
www.counseling.org

American Counseling Association
2461 Eisenhower Avenue, Suite 300
Alexandria, VA 22331

Publisher • Carolyn C. Baker

Digital and Print Development Editor • Nancy Driver

Senior Production Manager • Bonny E. Gaston

Cover and text design by Bonny E. Gaston

Library of Congress Cataloging-in-Publication Data

Names: Schubert, Angela M., editor. | Pope, Mark, 1952– editor.
Title: Handbook for human sexuality counseling : a sex positive approach / edited by Angela M. Schubert and Mark Pope.
Description: Alexandria, VA : American Counseling Association, [2022] | Includes bibliographical references and index
Identifiers: LCCN 2022020487 | ISBN 9781556203985 (paperback)
Subjects: LCSH: Sex counseling.
Classification: LCC HQ60.5 .H36 2022 | DDC 306.76—dc23/eng/20220604
LC record available at https://lccn.loc.gov/2022020487

Dedication

Thank you to my mama, friends, and dear mentors for all your support.
And a very special thank you to my wildlings and lovies for
teaching me the greatest lesson of all—
to love with courage and an open heart.

—*Angela M. Schubert*

Table of Contents

Preface

To set the tone of this book, we wish to share a clinical vignette to demonstrate the power of a sex positive approach. To do so, coauthor and coeditor Dr. Angela Schubert asked permission from her client to share his personal perspective of what brought him to counseling and the poem that was birthed from the ashes of his personal sexual script—one that was informed by religion, disability, identity loss, and the internal conflict that occurred as each of those aspects challenged the very essence of his sexual being. We give you Henry, in his own words.

Henry's Voice

One of the main reasons I finally went to therapy was because I felt I had no identity. I was no longer in high school, no longer defined by school pride or religion, or by the characters I had been inhabiting during high school as a means of survival. I felt like a gray blob: unnamed, uncharacterized, unworthy. I hoped I had identities in me; I certainly had questions about what identities I could claim and what claiming an identity meant. I started with what felt most pressing and uncomfortable: disability. I live with epidermolysis bullosa, a genetic skin condition that causes my skin to be as fragile as a butterfly's wings. I have always lived as a disabled person, but only through therapy was I able to comfortably claim and identify as disabled.

This poem tackles the intersectionality of disability and sex. It tells my story of how I grappled with sex as a disabled person raised in a Catholic school system that taught purity culture and denied the questions I had about my own human desire. A denial that ultimately pushed me to pornography as an alternative sex educator. Pornography is, of course, a shit teacher and only heightened my anxieties and worries that manifested over the years. Therapy has been tremendously helpful because it provides the space and safety to explore, unlearn, and craft identities. Self-love has been one of the constant areas of exploration for me to unlearn self-hatred, to challenge incorrect ideas, and, most importantly, to grow and craft and claim the identities I want to live.

My One Regret

Henry DeAngelis

I audibly choked
Swallowing the hopeless taste
Of purity culture.
"No, I don't have any questions."

My one regret.
My one moment I cannot forget.
The beginning of my emotional debt.

Fuck purity culture.
Fuck it until it restores to me
What should have always been mine:
A curious exploration of my body.
My sexuality.
My sexiness.

Oh yes.
Fuck purity culture.
Fuck it until it lets me ask those questions again.
Fuck it until it has a better answer than
"you shouldn't be thinking about it."
(nasally)

Purity culture pushed me away.
Purity culture threatened to
Tell my parents
All my embarrassing questions
Threatened to shame me for wondering how sex worked with disability.
Shame me for wondering how I could be loved, when I was taught not to love myself;

Wondering how I could be desired, when I was taught disabled people were
Undesirables.

Wondering how my crip hands could unclasp a button or bra.

How my tied tongue could french kiss,
How my coarse hands could soothe,
And stumpy fingers pleasure,
And fragile skin be touched.
Or even how to open the heavy door at the restaurant
Or have my date be seen as my date and not my nurse
Or have my date not pity me
And people not call my date a hero for going out with me

These are the questions purity culture
pushed down my throat

to the very bottom of my stomach
From there it jumped up to my mind

And scolded me for wondering about my own human desire
And before it left
It whispered one final thing into my ear

Shame.

Shame for thinking about sex.
Shame for thinking about one day having children.
Shame for not being the asexual person
purity culture believes I should be.

And with that purity's damage was wrought
And it left me content with its knowledge
That I would forever shame myself
For my own human desire.

My one regret.
My one moment I can't forget.
The beginning of my emotional debt.

As in that moment,
Purity.
Pushed.
Me. To.
Pornography.

Angela Schubert's Voice

Henry was fearless in his pursuit to find his own truth and narrate his own story. His story and reliance on sexually explicit material, also known as pornography, for sex education is not unique to Henry. Considering the utter void of comprehensive sex education across all social fronts, it is no wonder sexually explicit materials have become the sex educator for all who are interested. This is not to say that sexually explicit material is to blame for existing and thriving as the default sex educator, but rather that the finger is pointed at the gap that allows sexually explicit material to be the default educator in people's lives.

Henry chose counseling as a means to explore his own path as a sexual being with desires and needs, to challenge his own assumptions and biases, and to redefine his own sexual script. Henry took the path toward awareness, acceptance, and self-love, and I humbly held the lantern to shine a light on the path. My foundation as a counselor educator and sex therapist is rooted in the firm belief that everyone is deserving of their sexual story, and everyone is capable of narrating their own sexual script. Throughout this book, you will find the term "sexual script" repeated. A *sexual script* is the result of embedded cultural beliefs, social messaging, biology, personal experiences, and any formal/informal education about sexuality a person has received over their lifetime.

In the counseling session, counselors are gifted the opportunity to support a person as they come into their awareness of themselves and, sometimes, awareness of their sexual script. As mental health professionals, we are absolutely capable of facilitating therapeutic conversations to help clients better understand how their upbringing and personal experiences have crafted a view of their sexual selves. We are in the perfect place to illuminate the path as they begin to explore their sexuality, their sexual essence, and as a result, honor the parts of sexuality they wish to keep and release the parts that no longer work for them.

This book is an attempt to help mental health professionals and budding mental health students understand how to approach specific issues with clients yearning to explore their sexual story—without judgment and full of radical acceptance.

Why We Created This Book

Human sexuality counseling is an area rarely addressed directly in either the human sexuality literature or the professional counseling literature. Human sexuality textbooks generally consist of the fundamentals of sexuality, specifically the physiological aspects. The 2016 Council for Accreditation of Counseling and Related Educational Programs (CACREP) Standards now address the need for educating counseling students about human sexuality counseling, specifically in clinical rehabilitation counseling (CACREP, 2016, Section 5, Standard D.2.m.); marriage, couple, and family counseling (Section 5, Standard F.2.e.); and rehabilitation counseling (Section 5, Standard H.2.h.).

Furthermore, there is a belief by some that "information is enough." According to this approach, all that needs to be covered in sex education classes in secondary schools are basic and introductory facts and data. That approach may then carry over through a counseling student's undergraduate coursework too. By the time that the counseling student reaches graduate school, they too may have integrated into their own belief system that information is enough. Researchers have found, however, time and time again that training in sexuality-related pathology is too limited and that information alone is not enough in terms of which topics are addressed in counseling related to sexuality (Blount et al., 2017). It is, therefore, ethically imperative for counselor education curriculum to include an affirmative and expansive training in known pathologies wherein sexual arousal is attributed directly to typical and atypical (or nonmajority/nonrepronormative/nonheteronormative) fantasies, behaviors, or partners that cause danger, distress, or dysfunction (Blount et al., 2017).

Understanding and comprehensive application of effective treatment approaches associated with sexuality is absolutely necessary for the wellness of the counseling clients. Many people with sexuality-related concerns that are discovered in a medical setting are often referred to a mental health professional in conjunction with pharmacological interventions. For example, the American Urological Association (Burnett et al., 2018) guidelines for treating erectile difficulties recommend that urologists connect patients with a mental health professional to enhance communication about sexual concerns and to reduce performance anxiety. Furthermore, practicing urologists see an average of 70 patients per week, or 3,360 patients per year, and the types of cases they serve also include erectile dysfunction, pelvic floor, urinary tract concerns, penile rehabilitation following prostate cancer, reproduction, ejaculatory dysfunction, hypogonadism, penile implants, and sexually transmitted diseases—to name a few. Specifically, Burnett et al. (2018) explained that "psychotherapy and psychosexual counseling focus on helping patients and their partners improve communication about sexual concerns, reduce anxiety related to entering a sexual situation and during a sexual situation, and discuss strategies for integrating ED [erectile dysfunction] treatments into their sexual relationship" (p. 14).

Furthermore, physiological sexual dysfunctions in women are predominantly treated by pelvic floor therapists. Pelvic floor therapists are physiotherapists and occupational therapists who specialize in pelvic health. Berghmans (2018) identified a psychosomatic element in cases of female sexual dysfunction that cannot be treated with pelvic floor therapy alone. Instead, Berghmans advocated for a biopsychosocial approach that includes mental health treatment in conjunction with physiotherapy. Counselors need to be prepared to have these conversations with clients struggling with physiological disturbances in their sexuality and sexual expression to enhance the client's quality of life.

The *Handbook for Human Sexuality Counseling: A Sex Positive Approach* is a straightforward, honest, and positive book on human sexuality counseling. This book consists of much more than the fundamentals of sexuality and gender. It is a book that steers away from the older views of human sexuality and that eschews pathology and "othering" approaches that pathologize and discriminate against sexual behaviors and expressions that are not heteronormative, repronormative, or cisnormative. Sexuality is part of the human experience; however, it is often disregarded in both counselor training and the actual process of counseling (Reissing & Giulio, 2010). Ultimately, students and counseling professionals alike are left with resources that address the basic concepts of sexuality and gender many times from a narrow cisgender, heteronormative, and pathological framework. The foundation of each of the mental health professions' codes of ethics is a nonjudgmental approach to issues of counseling. A sex positive approach to sexuality in counseling is a perfect integration of these issues as it challenges pathology and emphasizes nonjudgmental openness, sexual freedom, and liberation of sexual expression (Donaghue, 2015).

This book will be useful for both undergraduate and graduate students, as well as counselors and other mental health professionals. It is designed for those whose work will bring them into contact with clients of all types of sexual backgrounds and experiences. Most books try to broadly cover sexuality and gender-related topics in hopes to be generalizable, but the material is foundational at best. In this book, we selected expert authors to write on a variety of diverse topics related to sexuality. Our aim was to be both fun and sex positive in the book's approach to human sexuality.

As counselor educators with a combined 40 years of experience training counselors, we find that counseling students still complain of a lack of training in working with clients regarding sex. Many graduate programs provide only a cursory treatment of human sexuality counseling as part of their multicultural counseling course or as a small part of their foundational counseling courses, with school counselors especially noting a lack of knowledge and skills in this particular area. We believe that this book is a critical resource in bridging that gap in the training of counselors and other mental health professionals.

Sex Positive Counseling

The task of sex positive human sexuality counseling is to view all people and their sexuality as central and self-defining, rather than as marginal and defined by cisgender and heterosexual norms (Morrow, 2000). Sex positive human sexuality counseling is geared to the creative enhancement of an individual's sexual and cultural identities. To be effective in their work, counselors must understand their own sexual orientation; have an appreciation for gender diversity; and understand their own sexuality, sexual beliefs, and values.

The bottom line is that clinicians of any theoretical framework can practice sex positive counseling, as long as they have examined their own heterosexism, homonegativity, or bi-negativity and the oppressive messages around transgenderism and clients who are questioning (Ritter & Terndrup, 2002). Therefore, it is our perspective that experience and expertise are more important than the counselor's sexual orientation when practicing affirming human sexuality counseling with clients.

In the core traditions of the counseling profession, this book includes a strengths-based, developmentally appropriate, psychoeducational, and sex positive approach to human sexuality counseling. This approach permeates each chapter.

As Phillips (2000) stated, "Students with little experience are especially appreciative if they are given examples of what . . . therapists tend to do and say and what they tend not to do and say" (p. 349). Since training in this area is limited, it is not only students who are hungering for concrete examples of human sexuality counseling. Counseling professionals who are many times already licensed and practicing are also eager to understand what they should be doing and what they should be considering when working with clients addressing issues of their sexuality (Dworkin & Pope, 2012). In addition, both students and professionals need a constant reminder about how important it is to get in touch with and stay in touch with biases, stereotypes, and the negative messages from religion, society, and even parents.

Rather than simply reviewing the literature about therapy with a given population, each chapter in this book integrates current research and clinical practice by providing examples of evidence-based, sex positive, and practical treatment planning and implementation. Each individual chapter author, or group of authors, addresses their topic with a modern, empowering approach and provides a specific protocol to follow in the treatment of clients.

Written from a multidisciplinary perspective, this book uses expert narratives to address treatment approaches for the sexual issues that many individuals and couples are facing today. The chapter authors provide examples of inclusive and affirming language to use in counseling, as well as describing the attitudes and behaviors counselors should exhibit when addressing clients' sexuality. Many of the authors have included a case example illustrating a sex positive approach to working with a fictional client. Some provide answers to questions readers may have "always wanted to ask" about their topic, and some take a personal stance, offering their personal and professional perspectives.

Chapter Highlights

The chapters in this book are organized into eight sections providing a comprehensive view of the human sexual experience:

- Foundations
- Physiological and psychological
- Attraction, orientation, and gender
- Sexual wellness
- Sexual agency
- Approaches to sexual divergence
- Relationships
- Education

Part 1: Foundations

Chapter 1 expands on current issues in mental health, explains the distinction between a sexual wellness and a medical framework, and provides a radically informed sex positive approach to sexual issues.

Chapter 2 provides an intersectional perspective on the history of sex, including cultural taboos around the world, contributions of religion to sexuality, and cultural differences in sexual norms. This chapter also addresses the politics of sex, including issues of sexual rights, reproductive rights, and the medicalization of sex.

Chapter 3 expands on the intersecting realities that exist in relation to ethical practices, decision-making, and sexual concerns. This chapter addresses common ethical and professional pitfalls specific to sexuality, including the professional obligation to identify personal biases, assumptions, and belief systems regarding sexuality and sexual concerns, as well as the need to ensure competency for any given sexuality topic and the process of referring to a sex therapist or other professional in cases where the sexual concern is beyond the competency of the counselor. This chapter provides an informative matrix, the knowledge-based decision-making matrix, to evaluate clinical competency.

Part 2: Physiological and Psychological

Chapter 4 provides readers with medical information associated with the reproductive systems of the human body as well as the physiology of sex in human beings, including the role of hormones and how human anatomy affects sexual expression. This chapter also describes the ways that a person's physical body interacts with their psyche to promote or inhibit sexual health and response to therapeutic psychological interventions.

Chapter 5 examines the role of the brain during arousal and desire and in human beings. The chapter further elaborates on research that has used advanced brain imaging, such as functional MRI and positron-emission tomography (i.e., PET) scans, during sexual activity. The chapter uses illustrations to elaborate on sexual functioning, sexual response, and arousal in hopes to provide education on how clinicians may better understand how to overcome barriers to sexual wellness.

Chapter 6 explores the perception and act of orgasm through an intersectional lens. It also addresses misconceptions, myths, and prescriptions around orgasm and how they influence a person's perception of themself as a sexual being. This chapter also examines techniques and strategies to clinically treat and support the orgasm explorations of clients from a therapeutic standpoint.

Chapter 7 explores the messages humans receive and communicate about sex and sexuality and addresses how these messages (implicit and explicit) affect the perception of oneself as a sexual being, such as with internalized anxiety around performance, faking interest and climax, and comparing one's performance to sexual behavior that is depicted in commercial pornography.

Part 3: Attraction, Orientation, and Gender

Chapter 8 addresses the multidimensional role of sexual attraction in human sexual expression and how expression may change over time. Addressing the role of sexual attraction from a multiculturally responsive perspective, the chapter debunks myths related to sexual attraction and highlights the nuances of attraction and affectional identities.

Chapter 9 explores the sexuality orientation spectrum, including sexual and romantic attraction, straight, gay, lesbian, bisexual, pansexual, and asexual. This chapter also addresses constructs of sexual attraction that fall outside of these labels, such as men who have sex with men.

Chapter 10 reviews the spectrum of gender identity and gender expression. Topics include cisgender and transgender, sex role stereotyping, intersex, agender; masculinity and femininity explored; derailing the binary, trans people of color, hijra; two-spirited; eunuch; and more.

Part 4: Sexual Wellness

Chapter 11 reviews historical and current literature on the health benefits of masturbation and helps to familiarize counselors on how to support and empower clients to begin to see themselves as the protagonist of their sexual story. Myths surrounding masturbation are critiqued and factual explanations are provided. A sex positive approach is described to assist clinicians with this conversation with future clients.

Chapter 12 addresses information on how counselors can assist survivors of sexual harassment, assault, trauma, and trafficking. Of those who have experienced sexual trauma of any sort, many become disconnected from their sexual selves and, as a result, the very personal definitions of sexuality, sexual safety, and sexual script. The chapter also explores the consequences for victims of sexual abuse or exploitation and how this may affect their later sexual health or functioning.

Chapter 13 addresses the physical and psychological impact of chronic illness and pain on sexual attitudes and desire. This chapter also helps counselors understand the reality and possibility of sexual expression after diagnoses.

Chapter 14 describes the most common sexually transmitted infections (STIs) and how mental health professionals can approach clinical work with individuals with HIV and other STIs.

Part 5: Sexual Agency

Chapter 15 explores aging sexuality from a sex positive framework by first addressing the barriers and myths surrounding older adult sexuality. This chapter expands on how adults change and adapt to their bodies and sexual functioning, and how vitality and resiliency support sexual needs and expression.

Chapter 16 provides readers with the opportunity to experience a "person first" approach to disability and sexuality. Counselors will learn how to support clients to embrace both their sexuality and their disability. This chapter also introduces sex surrogacy and describes potential mental health and physical benefits of receiving sex surrogacy treatment.

Chapter 17 takes a unique approach to exploring the narrative of Black sexuality and sexual expression. Through their individual narratives, the authors reveal the ways in which Black bodies have been sexualized, objectified, and vilified. This chapter will help counselors explore their own implicit and explicit biases surrounding the intersection of race/ethnicity and sexuality as well as the role that the constructs of race and ethnicity play in attraction and desire.

Chapter 18 provides a comprehensive review of sexuality as it pertains to the most common religious groups. The chapter will explore the role of religion in sexuality and the taboos associated with certain religions. This chapter will help counselors better understand how to support sexual discussion within the confines of one's religious values.

Part 6: Approaches to Sexual Divergence

Chapter 19 will explore alternative sexual activities such as kink, swinging, BDSM, fetishes, and consensual objectification. This chapter helps readers become acquainted with the current literature on sexual behaviors and activities that are focused on multiple definitions of pleasure and are not necessarily reproduction centered. Counselors will be confronted with many different aspects of sexual behavior in their counseling practice, and through exposure to such topics, this chapter seeks to increase comfort with addressing these topics.

Chapter 20 takes a sex positive approach to sexual divergence in relation to the paraphilic section of the *Diagnostic and Statistical Manual of Mental Disorders, Text Revision* (5th ed.; *DSM-5-TR*; American Psychiatric Association, 2022). The authors challenge the criteria of each of the paraphilic diagnoses and offer a sex positive approach to treatment by addressing the presence and severity of distress, dysfunction, and/or danger.

Chapter 21 explores the neuroscience of pleasure and healthy sexual behavior. This chapter challenges the medicalized framework used to approach frequent sexual proclivities and potentially troublesome sexual behaviors and offers a sex positive approach to treat hypersexual behaviors. This chapter will help counselors understand and treat clients who struggle with problematic sexual behavior.

Part 7: Relationships

Chapter 22 addresses modern love, dating, and hookup culture. Additionally, values are explored in terms of how people understand and engage in cyber dating, hooking up, and gamers and cyber love. Counselors will be better prepared to evaluate their own values on love, sex, and intimacy after reading this chapter.

Chapter 23 addresses how infidelity impacts relationships and how counselors can best help couples heal after infidelity. This chapter will define infidelity and provide current literature on how infidelity impacts emotional well-being and the relational dynamic of both the individual and couple. The chapter also provides a step-by-step approach to helping the couple process the infidelity and move toward a place of compassion and healing.

Part 8: Education

Chapter 24 examines current laws and policies regarding K–12 sexual education in the United States and other countries. This chapter reviews the research results of both comprehensive sex education and abstinence-only sex education with respect to teen pregnancy, reported abstinence, and sexual engagement. The chapter also identifies implications of comprehensive sex education on decreasing rape and sexual assault, increasing sex positivity and body image, decreasing mental health concerns, and normalizing healthy sexual behavior. These implications are examined in terms of how they may surface in the counseling session.

Chapter 25 provides a rationale for sex education and counselor training across all states and all programs. This chapter addresses clinician ethical responsibilities and examines the current literature on counselors' and counselor educators' perceived comfort when addressing sexuality in both the counseling session and the counseling classroom. The chapter also addresses how specific sexuality counseling training will enhance comfort level and competency among counselors, increase clinical efficacy, and further enhance the professional role of the counselor in professional interactions with other mental health fields.

References

American Psychiatric Association. (2022). *Diagnostic and statistical manual of mental disorders* (5th ed., text rev).

Berghmans, B. (2018). Physiotherapy for pelvic pain and female sexual dysfunction: An untapped resource. *International Urogynecology Journal, 29*(5), 631–638. https://doi.org/10.1007/s00192-017-3536-8

Blount, K. C., Booth, C., Webb, T., & Liles, R. G. (2017). Integration of sex and sexuality into counseling programs. *VISTAS Online*, Article 50. https://www.counseling.org/knowledge-center/vistas/by-subject2/vistas-physical-health-and-counseling-issues/docs/default-source/vistas/integration_of_sex_and_sexuality

Burnett, A. L., Nehra, A., Breau, R. H., Culkin, D. J., Faraday, M. M., Hakim, L. S., Heidelbaugh, J., Khera, M., McVary, K. T., Miner, M. M., Nelson, C. J., Sadeghi-Nejad, H., Seftel, A. D., & Shindel, A. W. (2018). *Erectile dysfunction: AUA guideline.* American Urological Association. https://www.auanet.org/guidelines/erectile-dysfunction-(ed)-guideline

Council for Accreditation of Counseling and Related Educational Programs. (2016). *2016 CACREP standards.* http://www.cacrep.org/for-programs/2016-cacrep-standards/

Donaghue, C. (2015). *Sex outside the lines: Authentic sexuality in a sexually dysfunctional culture.* BenBella Books.

Dworkin, S. H., & Pope, M. (Eds.). (2012). *Casebook for counseling lesbian, gay, bisexual, and transgender persons and their families.* American Counseling Association.

Morrow, S. L. (2000). First do no harm: Therapist issues in psychotherapy with lesbian, gay and bisexual clients. In R. M. Perez, K. A. DeBord, & K. J. Bieschke (Eds.), *Handbook of counseling and psychotherapy with gay, lesbian, and bisexual clients* (pp. 137–156). American Psychological Association.

Phillips, J. C. (2000). Training issues and considerations. In R. M. Perez, K. A. DeBord, & K. J. Bieschke (Eds.). *Handbook of counseling and psychotherapy with gay, lesbian, and bisexual clients* (2nd ed., pp. 337–358). American Psychological Association.

Reissing, E. D., & Giulio, G. D. (2010). Practicing clinical psychologists' provision of sexual health care services. *Professional Psychology: Research and Practice*, *41*, 57–63. https://doi.org/10.1037/a0017023

Ritter, K. Y., & Terndrup, A. I. (2002). *Handbook of affirmative psychotherapy with lesbians and gay men*. Guilford Press.

About the Editors

Angela M. Schubert, PhD, LPC, NCC, BC-TMH, is a clinical practitioner and associate professor for the Council for Accreditation of Counseling and Related Educational Programs (CACREP)-accredited clinical mental health counseling program at Central Methodist University. A member of the American Counseling Association (ACA), Association for Counselor Education and Supervision (ACES), Sexuality and Aging Consortium, American Association of Sexuality Educators, Counselors, and Therapists (AASECT), and the Society for the Scientific Study of Sexuality, Schubert served for 6 years as Missouri state chair for AASECT. She currently serves on the editorial board for the *Journal of Counseling Sexology & Sexual Wellness.* Dr. Schubert is the past president of the Association of Counseling Sexology and Sexual Wellness (ACSSW) and cohost of the *Let's Get Uncomfortable* podcast. Her research interest focuses on intersectionality of culture, gender, age, and sexuality through a relational-cultural theoretical lens. She has continued to act as expert consultant on sexuality-related topics such as sexual wellness, aging sexuality, sexual consent, sexual assault, and body image. She is currently undergoing supervision to become an AASECT-certified sex therapist.

Mark Pope, EdD, NCC, CCC, MAC, ACS, is Curators' Distinguished Professor Emeritus and Thomas Jefferson Fellow in the CACREP-accredited counseling and family therapy programs at the University of Missouri–St. Louis. He is the author/editor of 11 books, more than 100 other professional publications, as well as more than 150 keynote addresses, research symposia, and workshops at international, national, regional, and state venues from 1978 to 2021. From Dr. Pope's first publication in 1990 on the sexual behavior and attitudes of midlife and aging gay men to his most recent article on the trials that lesbian, gay, bisexual, and transgender international students face as they study in the United States, his work has been groundbreaking in the counseling literature. Through his scholarly work and leadership, he has been instrumental in bringing to the forefront of the counseling profession broadly and the career counseling field in particular the special issues that lesbian and gay individuals face in American society. Dr. Pope has served as president of ACA; the National Career Development Association; the Association for Lesbian, Gay, Bisexual, and Transgender Issues in Counseling; and the Society for the Psychology of Sexual Orientation and Gender Diversity (Division 44 of the American Psychological Association). He was also editor of *The Career Development Quarterly*, the preeminent professional journal in career counseling and development, and senior associate editor of the *Journal of Counseling & Development* (the flagship journal of ACA) and the *Psychology of Sexual Orientation and Gender Diversity* (the primary journal of the Society for the Psychology of Sexual Orientation and Gender Diversity, Division 44 of the American Psychological Association).

About the Contributors

Aninda B. Acharya, MD, is a neurologist at Saint Louis University School of Medicine, Department of Neurology, in Saint Louis. He is part of SLUCare Physician Group. He is board-certified in neurology and vascular neurology and holds a master's degree in public health. Dr. Acharya has expertise in general clinical neurology, rehabilitation medicine, and stroke, as well as migraine and other headache disorders. Dr. Acharya was recognized by *St. Louis Magazine* as one of the Best Doctors of Saint Louis.

James P. Ahearn, JD, MEd, LPC, is currently pursuing a PhD in counselor education and supervision at the University of Missouri–St. Louis. He also works as an adjunct instructor at local universities and serves on the board of Psychotherapy Saint Louis.

M. N. Barringer, PhD, (she/her) is an assistant professor of sociology at the University of North Florida. Her research interests include sexualities, gender, religion, and applied sociology. She has used quantitative data to examine gender and sexual minorities' religious identities, subjective well-being, and attitudes toward American mainline religious traditions. Her academic articles also cover religiosity, religious identity, and birth cohort attitudes. Her work has been published in journals such as *Social Currents*, *Journal of Homosexuality*, and *Sociological Inquiry*.

Caitlyn McKinzie Bennett, PhD, LMHC (FL), LMFT (FL), LPC (TX), NCC, (she/her/hers) is an assistant professor of counseling at Rollins College in Winter Park, Florida. Dr. Bennett's clinical specialty focuses on anxiety, stress, family-of-origin issues, sexuality, gender, and sexual and gender minority experiences for adolescents, young adults, and couples. Dr. Bennett's research agenda has focused on neuro-informed counseling approaches (i.e., neurofeedback training) to mitigate experiences of anxiety, stress, and depression.

Nicole Woodcox Bolden, MSW, LCSW, is a therapist, trainer, family support specialist, and cofounder of Thriving With Baby LLC, a clinical service in Chicago. Bolden specializes in supporting birthing people in creating and adjusting to their new role as a parent through therapy, childbirth education, and pregnancy and family wellness coaching services.

Laurie Bonjo, PhD, is an associate professor in the Department of Counseling and School Psychology at Southern Connecticut State University and program coordinator of the doctoral program in counselor education and supervision. Dr. Bonjo's research interests include clinical applications with members of groups at risk for marginalization and disenfranchisement particularly by attending to destigmatization, decolonization, and liberation in clinical practice.

Ethan L. Bratt, MS, LMFT, CST, (he/his) is a licensed marriage and family therapist and certified sex therapist. Having treated clients since 2007, in 2012 Bratt established Pivotal Counseling, a group practice specializing in relationship and sexual health issues that serves clients throughout Colorado and southeast Wyoming. He also works with many individuals and couples struggling to reconcile their religiosity and sexuality or seeking to reclaim and heal their sexuality after damaging religious experiences.

Roseina Britton, PhD, is originally from Queens, New York, and has a master's degree in clinical mental health from North Carolina Agricultural and Technical State University. She earned her PhD in counselor education and supervision from the University of Iowa in 2019. As a licensed professional counselor in Illinois, Dr. Britton specializes in researching, educating, and alleviating the stigma and related hardships associated with contracting and living with HIV/AIDS in the United States.

H. L. Brostrand, PhD, LPCC, is a counselor at Contra Costa County Behavioral Health Services and adjunct faculty at Napa Valley College in California.

Lexx Brown-James, PhD, (she/her/hers) is a best-selling author on Amazon, a licensed marriage and family therapist, and certified sexuality educator and supervisor who specializes in sex therapy. Dr. Lexx provides individual and group therapy, coaching, and supervision. Dr. Lexx also provides mental health workshops on adolescent sexual development, sex positive parenting, sexuality educator antiracist training, parenting, sexting, and porn, and on utilizing her sexual intervention model with Black women. In classrooms and training, Dr. Lexx uses experiential pedagogy coupled with affective-based learning to challenge attitudes and support learners in being able to apply knowledge and skills.

Anastasia Canfield, MA, MT-BC, LPCC, NCC, specializes in music therapy with mental health populations across the life span, as well as children and young adults with developmental disabilities, intellectual disabilities, and autism spectrum disorders. Canfield recently completed her clinical training at Brightside Counseling as an intern under Dr. Angela Schubert, while she pursued a second master's degree in mental health counseling from Northwestern University, earning dual licensure as a licensed professional counselor and a board-certified music therapist.

Christian D. Chan, PhD, NCC, (he, him, his) is an assistant professor in the Department of Counseling and Educational Development at The University of North Carolina at Greensboro, past president of the Association for Adult Development and Aging, and a proud queer person of color. As a scholar-activist, his interests revolve around intersectionality; multiculturalism in counseling practice, supervision, and counselor education; social justice and activism; career development; critical research methodologies; and couple, family, and group modalities with socialization/communication of cultural factors.

Michael P. Chaney, PhD, is an associate professor in the Department of Counseling at Oakland University in Rochester, Michigan, and a licensed professional counselor and approved clinical supervisor. He has held several leadership positions, including president of the Society for Sexual, Affectional, Intersex, and Gender Expansive Identities (SAIGE). He currently serves as editor-in-chief for the *Journal of LGBTQ Issues in Counseling* and as an editorial board member for the *Journal of Addictions & Offender Counseling* and *Journal of Counseling Sexology & Sexual Wellness.* He has numerous publications in prestigious peer-reviewed journals and regularly gives presentations and workshops nationally and internationally in the areas of substance use disorders; sexual compulsivity; lesbian, gay, bisexual, transgender, queer, plus other identities (LGBTQ+) issues; male body image; and social justice and advocacy in counseling.

Barbara M. Chuback, MD, is an assistant professor of urology at the Icahn School of Medicine at Mount Sinai, New York, where she specializes in the diagnosis and treatment of sexual dysfunction for all patients, regardless of sex, gender, orientation, or congenital condition. In addition to her training in medicine and surgery, she holds master's degrees in the history of medicine and bioethics and applies all of these disciplines to clinical care, research, and teaching. She is an active member and regularly invited speaker for several professional organizations focused on sexual medicine, both within the United States and internationally.

L. Allen Crosby, LMHCA, LPSC, earned her master's degree in clinical mental health counseling from Trinity Washington University in Washington, DC, and is currently a counselor education and supervision doctoral candidate at Walden University. Her research is focused on the empowerment of Black women, trauma-informed schools, Black mental health, and Black sexuality.

V. A. Dansereau, MA, is a qualified mental health professional and a student of clinical psychology at The Chicago School of Professional Psychology in Washington, DC, with a dissertation on the etiology of violent sexual fantasy. She holds master's degrees in both forensic and clinical psychology and is kink and poly-allied. She primarily works with populations that are court involved.

Leslie E. Davis, MA, LPC, CST, is a private practice counselor who is obtaining her PhD in counselor education and certificate in university teaching from the University of Missouri–St. Louis. Her specializations and research interests in counseling include trauma, sexuality and disability, somatic experiencing, polyvagal theory, eye movement desensitization and reprocessing (EMDR), BDSM, addiction, spiritual trauma, and trauma-informed teaching.

lore m. dickey, PhD, a board-certified counseling psychologist, is retired. A long-time member of Girl Scouts of the USA for over 50 years, dickey has taught over 25 different courses for undergraduate and graduate students; has more than 65 publications, including three books; and has presented more than 135 times throughout the world. He has been recognized numerous times for his commitment to making the world a safe place for transgender and gender diverse people.

Molly Eames, MEd, LPC, is a sex educator and wellness consultant at Molly Eames Counseling in St. Louis, with more than a decade of professional experience and certification in sex therapy and sex education from the University of Michigan.

Cheryl A. Faber, MD, is a board-certified neurologist in Saint Louis. Part of BJC Medical Group, Dr. Faber has been recognized by *St. Louis Magazine* as one of the Best Doctors of Saint Louis.

Melissa Franzen, PhD, LPC, received her doctorate in counselor education and supervision at Walden University. Dr. Franzen is a student development professional at Lincoln Land Community College. Her research interests include sexual wellness, play therapy, and supervision.

Sharon Gerstein, LMFT, is a self-employed marriage and family therapist in Long Beach, California, who has specialized in mental health and clinical supervision since 1990.

Hannah Glusenkamp, (she/her/hers) is pursuing a master of science in clinical mental health counseling with a certificate in animal-assisted therapy in counseling from the University of North Florida. As a graduate-level counseling intern, she has provided community mental health counseling at a sexual violence advocacy center and at a no-cost community clinic in Jacksonville, Florida. Prior to counseling, she taught comprehensive sexual health education in community and school settings. Glusenkamp, who strives to be a holistic, trauma-focused, sex positive, antiracist, and growth-oriented counselor, has interests that include mindfulness and narrative, somatic, nature-based, and creative arts therapies and healing modalities.

Reginald W. Holt, PhD, NCC, MAC, LPC, is assistant professor and clinical program coordinator in the Department of Counselor Education and Family Therapy at Central Connecticut State University. He completed a PhD in counseling/counselor education at the University of Missouri–St. Louis, an MA in clinical psychology at East Tennessee State University, and a 2-year postgraduate training program in advanced psychodynamic psychotherapy at the St. Louis Psychoanalytic Institute. Dr. Holt is recognized by the Connecticut Certification Board as an advanced alcohol and drug counselor and by the International Certification and Reciprocity Consortium as an internationally certified advanced alcohol and drug counselor. In addition to operating his own private practice, he has had an extensive clinical career that included work in behavioral health care hospitals, the correctional system, and a Fortune 500 managed care organization.

Kim Lee Hughes, PhD, served as the 2020–2021 president for the Association of Multicultural Counseling and Development, a division of ACA. She served as a tenure-track assistant professor in the Department of Mental Health Counseling at Clark Atlanta University and The University of Texas at San Antonio. Dr. Lee Hughes's research centers on the expansion of social justice and cultural responsivity within counseling and related professions, women of color across the life span, the impact and efficacy of group practices based on positionality, women in leadership, collaboration in counselor education, queer communities and social mobility, and best practices in qualitative methodology in counselor education.

J. Richelle Joe, PhD, NCC, is an associate professor in the Department of Counselor Education and School Psychology at the University of Central Florida (UCF). Her scholarship and service focus on culturally responsive services for underserved and marginalized clients and communities and includes an emphasis on the experiences of individuals of color and the mental health and wellness implications of HIV for individuals and families. Dr. Joe has written extensively about HIV, with publications that address the ethics of counseling clients living with HIV, the importance of using stigma-free language in counseling, and the value of relationally and culturally informed therapeutic approaches for women affected by HIV and intimate partner violence. At UCF, she leads the HIV Education, Awareness, and Research Team, known as HEART, which collaborates with university and community organizations in their efforts to provide HIV education and prevention programming.

Theresa L. Keown, PhD, LPC, NCC, is an associate professor, program director, and Park Hills coordinator for the master of science in clinical counseling program at Central Methodist University's College of Graduate and Extended Studies. She is currently trained in EMDR and Applied Suicide Intervention Skills Training and is dialectical behavior therapy (DBT) informed. Her research interests include group therapy, community mental health, and marriage and family counseling.

Stacey Diane Arañez Litam, PhD, LPCC-s, NCC, CCMHC, (she, her, hers) is an assistant professor of counselor education at Cleveland State University. Dr. Litam is an award-winning and nationally recognized researcher, educator, clinical counselor, and social justice advocate on topics related to human sexuality, sex trafficking, and Asian American and Pacific Islander concerns. She is an immigrant and identifies as a Chinese and Filipina American woman. As a researcher and scholar, Dr. Litam's work has been published in prestigious journals such as *Journal of Counseling & Development*, *The Professional Counselor*, *The International Journal for the Advancement of Counselling*, *Counseling Outcome Research and Evaluation*, *The Journal of Sexual Aggression*, *Journal of Counseling Sexology & Sexual Wellness*, and *Journal of Child Sexual Abuse.* Dr. Litam has published in over 20 academic journals and facilitated over 100 presentations at international, national, regional, and state levels, and she has served as a content expert for National Public Radio, podcasts, media and news outlets, and within legislative arenas.

Frances L. McClain, PhD, LCPC, NCC, received her PhD in counselor education and supervision from The Chicago School of Professional Psychology and her master's in counseling from Governors State University. She is a director of clinical training in counseling psychology at The Chicago School of Professional Psychology in Chicago. She specializes in working with individuals with co-occurring illnesses, trauma, and sexuality-related issues and those in LGBTQ+ and other sexual minoritized communities.

Virginia Ogletree, PsyD, graduated from Wright State University School of Professional Psychology in 2019 after many educational, vocational, and personal detours, then finally finding her calling in a community college classroom during an introductory psychology class. As a survivor of childhood maltreatment, her professional interests are focused on the stress and growth that result from trauma. As a person who experiences both privilege and oppression, she aligns with the oppressed peoples of the world in seeking and working toward liberation.

Karen O'Hearn, MEd, LSC, (she/her) is a retired high school teacher and counselor in St. Louis and retired associate professor of counseling at the University of Missouri–St. Louis and Saint Louis University. Her counseling coursework and research focus is career development and adolescent sexual health and wellness. Since retirement, she promotes comprehensive sexuality education by speaking at school district and community resource board meetings in St. Charles, Missouri.

Jun Park, MA, P-LPC, is in clinical practice in Texas. His prior work includes being a clinical assistant at an eating disorders treatment and research facility and as a behavioral therapist for children with autism. His interests include researching culturally marginalized groups, providing empirically based therapeutic treatment, and social justice advocacy in counseling.

Faith Ponti, is a second-year master's student in the clinical mental health counseling program at the University of North Florida in Jacksonville, Florida. A counseling intern at both Volunteers in Medicine Jacksonville and Child Guidance Center, Faith is interested in advocacy and public policy, community education, and working with adolescents and emerging adults. Her research interests include gender and sexuality, social inequality, and the effect of social media on mental health. Faith is a passionate advocate of social justice, which is reflected in much of her professional and educational pursuits.

Sarah Richards, MA, LPC, studied international disaster psychology at the University of Denver. Her clinical training has primarily been with children who have experienced trauma and childhood adversity. Much of her work has focused on childhood bereavement and how to support grieving children. She uses a trauma-informed care lens to support her clients and meets them where they are. She has experience working with people of all ages and uses individual, play, family, couples, and group therapy.

Jared S. Rose, PhD, LPCC-S, NCC, EMDRC, is an assistant professor and program coordinator for Bowling Green State University's clinical mental health and school counseling programs and owner of a private practice. His areas of clinical practice, research, and teaching include sex and sexual health; human trafficking; LGBTQ+ and trans/gender expansive issues; HIV and AIDS; and advocacy and social justice in the counseling profession.

Lisa Salvadore, MSW, LCSW, LCPC, CADC, received her master's degree in social work from Aurora University. She is a full-time lecturer at the Jane Addams College of Social Work at University of Illinois–Chicago and an adjunct assistant professor at The Chicago School of Professional Psychology. She has presented at state and national conferences and provided trainings on topics related to compassion fatigue, motivational interviewing, working with adult offenders, and human sexuality.

Samuel Sanabria, PhD, is a professor of counseling at Rollins College, Winter Park, Florida. He has specialized in multicultural and social justice with a specific focus on prejudicial development toward LGBTQ+ and Latinx communities. He is a licensed mental health counselor, Florida-qualified clinical supervisor, nationally certified counselor, and certified sex therapist.

Tanisha N. Sapp, LPC, CST, NCC, ACS, CPCS, is an assistant professor of counseling at Liberty University. She currently serves as the secretary for Chi Sigma Iota International Counseling Honor Society and the treasurer for ACSSW. Dr. Sapp is an AASECT-certified sex therapist and the owner of Tanisha Sapp, where she provides professional development training, clinical supervision, and individual and couples sex therapy. Dr. Sapp's areas of research and interest include counselor professional identity and ethics; social justice for Black, Indigenous, and people of color; sexual health and wellness; and professional advocacy in leadership.

Shannon Shoemaker, PhD, is an assistant professor at Hood College. She earned her MEd in counselor education at Bridgewater State College and a doctorate in counselor education and supervision from The Pennsylvania State University. She has over 10 years of clinical experience in school systems; community counseling services; and working with adults, adolescents, and families. Dr. Shoemaker has presented at local, national, and international counseling conferences. She is the secretary of ACSSW and a member of ACA, ACES, SAIGE, and the Association of Creativity in Counseling.

Megan Speciale, PhD, is an associate professor in the counseling department at Palo Alto University in California who has worked as a professional counselor and advocate in a variety of community settings, focusing primarily on sexual wellness and on lesbian, gay, bisexual, transgender, queer, intersex, and asexual children, adolescents, adults, and families. Her research explores the intersection of sexual, mental, and relational health and focuses on such topics as kink/BDSM, sexual shame, sexual and gender identity, sex education, and sex work. She is also the current editor-in-chief for *The Thoughtful Counselor* podcast and the associate editor for the *Journal of Counseling Sexology & Sexual Wellness.*

John T. Super, LMFT, NCC, is a faculty member in the University of Central Florida's counselor education program and directs the operations at the university's community counseling clinic. He earned his master's degree in marriage, couples, and family counseling and his doctorate in counselor education. He has worked in and developed a clinical private practice with a focus on helping LGBTQ+ couples with relational issues, often focusing on or around sexuality and intimacy. As an educator, he helps prepare master's- and doctoral-level students for their future professional roles as marriage, couples, and family counselors, mental health counselors, school counselors, and counselor educators.

Jessica Z. Taylor, PhD, LPC, NCC, BC-TMH, is an associate professor and director of assessment for the CACREP-accredited master's-level clinical counseling program at Central Methodist University. Dr. Taylor obtained a PhD in counselor education and certificate in university teaching from the University of Missouri–St. Louis and an MS in nonprofit management from Johnson & Wales University. A board-certified telemental health provider, she is a member of ACA and ACES. Her professional counseling-related specializations and research interests include psychosocial aspects of medical illness and disability, allergies and anaphylaxis, crisis intervention, emotional regulation, DBT, EMDR, counselor education pedagogy, trauma-informed teaching, college counseling, research self-efficacy, and program assessment and evaluation.

Cheryl D. Walker, MA, NCC, APC, is an associate professional counselor and a candidate to become a certified sex therapist. She is currently pursuing a master's in clinical mental health and counseling at Argosy University in Atlanta, Georgia. Over the past 15 years, she has been an active volunteer for several nonprofit organizations as well as local school communities. Cheryl believes that sexuality is a crucial component of mental wellness and that the absence of an authentic and educated exploration of sexual values and sexual behaviors creates a degradation of the human spirit. She is currently a sex therapist with GlobeCoRe in Atlanta and conducts sex positive psychoeducational groups with women throughout the city.

Joy S. Whitman, PhD, LPC, LCPC, recently retired as clinical full professor at the Family Institute of Northwestern University in the master's Counseling@Northwestern program. She has served as a past president of SAIGE, a division representative on the ACA Governing Council, and a member of the ACA ethics committee. She is a board member of the International Academy for LGBT+ Psychology and Related Fields and an editorial board member of the *Journal of LGBTQ Issues in Counseling.* She has coedited several books on LGBTQ and counselor education topics, has presented on affirmative counseling with and training of affirmative therapy with LGBTQ+ clients, and maintains a private practice focused on LGBTQ+ communities.

Julie Lynn Williams, PsyD, APBB, is a full professor at Wright State University School of Professional Psychology and clinical psychology supervisor at an integrated medical care facility. Her areas of interest include disability and rehabilitation psychology, social justice, liberation theory, and health disparities. She is an active participant in the disability community and is the cocreator of the intersectional disability justice project Breaking Silences in Ohio. She has authored publications and book chapters, particularly on teaching and providing diversity inclusive care within psychology and health care settings. She is an active scholar and presenter at national and international conferences addressing disability issues, mental health, and culture regarding the lives of LGBTQ+, gender nonbinary, and people of color.

Ilene Wong, MD, FACS, is a general urologist and award-winning novelist in the greater Philadelphia area. Her essays and features have appeared in *The Washington Post*, *San Francisco Chronicle*, *Newsweek*, *Scientific American*, *New York Daily News*, *San Jose Mercury News*, and *Journal of General Internal Medicine*. A graduate of Yale Medical School, she has lectured on intersex awareness at medical schools across the country and is a board member at interACT Advocates: Advocates for Intersex Youth.

James A. Young, MD, is a resident in the Department of Urology at the David Geffen School of Medicine at the University of California, Los Angeles. He attended the cross-disciplinary Brown-RISD Dual Degree Program, whereby he studied illustration at the Rhode Island School of Design and science and society at Brown University and has worked as a medical illustrator on several books. He graduated with distinction from the Icahn School of Medicine at Mount Sinai. His work has included videos on novel techniques for gender-affirming genital surgery, an online learning module on transgender health care for medical schools, and presentations for national and international professional organizations. His current research interests include reconstructive urology, andrology, medical education, and health disparities.

Robert J. Zeglin, PhD, NCC, CST, LMHC, (he/him) is an associate professor and program director for clinical mental health counseling at the University of North Florida. His area of research is human sexuality, particularly human sexuality counselor competencies, HIV/AIDS, sexual health and wellness, and LGBTQ+ health. He is founding editor of the *Journal of Counseling Sexology & Sexual Wellness*, director of the Community Sexual Health Education and Research Initiative, and past president of ACSSW. In addition to teaching and research, Dr. Zeglin continues his clinical work with clients at the Jacksonville Center for Sexual Health.

PART 1
Foundations

Ain't No Shame in This Game: The Foundation of a Radically Informed Sex Positive Approach

Angela M. Schubert

> *Sex lies at the root of life, and we can never learn to reverence life until we know how to understand sex.*
>
> —Havelock Ellis, *Studies in the Psychology of Sex*

I once had the wonderful opportunity to attend a sexual health training presented by Emily Nagoski, author of the 2015 bestselling book *Come as You Are: The Surprising New Science That Will Transform Your Sex Life.* She was incredibly insightful and perfectly nerdy about all things related to sexual and mental health. One thing she said that really stood out for me was "When you were born, you were deeply and gloriously satisfied with each and every part of your body. And from the time you became aware of your body, you began to receive negative messages about your body and your sexuality. As such, our sex becomes our first shame" (E. Nagoski, personal communication, October 17, 2019). Our first shame—tying this idea to the shame work of researcher and educator Brené Brown, it is conceivable that people internalize sex negative messages toward self and the world from the onset of their sexual awareness. According to Brown (2012), guilt is defined as "I did something bad," whereas shame is defined as "I am bad." Combining the two, it may be that we are all at risk of internalizing the message "I am bad because I am a sexual being (or not a sexual being)."

We start off perfectly content with our sexual selves and with each message received, we begin to chip away at our sexual awesomeness . . . into something more palatable for others. And yet, sexuality is ever complex and inherently individual. Sexuality may be best represented by the umbrella tip—it is the overarching construct of all things tethered to one's sexual script and it is influenced by environment, genetics, experiences, culture, and time. As such, it is one of the most complicated constructs created by the human species. As humans, we have evolved over time because of our sexual proclivity and yet, we continue to question, both passively and actively, the importance of sexuality in a person's life. Human sexuality as an aspect of wellness is met with contention, confusion, and negativity.

Sex negativity manifests as a result of shame, sadness, and guilt and derives from discrimination, power, control, unhealthy relationships, puritanical beliefs about reproduction, and lack of representation (Ivanski & Kohut, 2017). We perpetuate the belief system of sex negativity in the way we live, raise our children, navigate social conversations, create and uphold law, honor religion, and participate in discrimination. People die, kill, cheat, loathe, and berate others over sexuality. Laws are made to condemn sexuality. Policies are constructed to discriminate on the basis of sexuality. Throughout history, wars in the home and across lands have been enacted as a result of sexuality. But is sexuality exclusively negative and condemnable? Absolutely not. So how might the mental health field play a part in facilitating healthy, meaningful conversations about sexuality? With a sex positive approach.

As a mental health clinician for over a decade and an advocate for a sex positive approach, I see this as THE reason why we as counselors are in a critical position to *level up* and approach human sexuality with as much candidness and open-mindedness as we do depression, suicide, alcohol use, and the day-to-day struggle—with radical respect. Unlike those who subscribe to a reductionist, medication-orientation view of mental health, a wellness orientation and a sex positive framework allow for a person to be treated as a whole person, rather than being reduced to symptoms and behaviors. Because counseling programs support a wellness approach to mental health, we counselors are perfectly located within the mental health field to approach human sexuality from a sex positive approach—if we consider human sexuality as a core domain of counselor training and an integral part of mental wellness. As a field, where does the counseling profession stand regarding human sexuality?

Counselor Education and Training

Clinicians support the belief that sexuality is an important aspect of the human sexual experience (Buehler, 2017; Cupit, 2010; Haboubi & Lincoln, 2003; Zimmerman, 2012), and yet, research suggests clinicians do not feel appropriately trained to address the sexual concerns of their clients (Haboubi & Lincoln, 2003; Mallicoat, 2013; Sanabria & Murray, 2018; Speciale, 2020; Zeglin et al., 2018). Why is this?

There is a widely held belief within the mental health field—including psychology, social work, psychiatry, counseling psychology, and counseling—that human sexuality falls into a specialized domain (Binik & Meana, 2009). This belief is reinforced not only by the educational systems training mental health professionals but also by the states that license them. Although requirements for licensed professional counselors vary from state to state, most states do not require a course in human sexuality. Currently, Florida and California require a course in sexuality, and Florida is the only state that licenses sex therapists and therefore is the only state that protects the title "sex therapist." Most counseling programs abide by their respective state's licensure requirements and, as a result, do not require students to take a human sexuality course. This belief is further supported by the Council for Accreditation of Counseling and Related Educational Programs (CACREP), which accredits counselor education programs nationally. As it stands today, CACREP (2016) has only two standards that address human sexuality, both of which are located under specialty domains in Section 5. One of these falls within the Clinical Rehabilitation

Counseling standards (see Standard 5.D.2.m.) and the other in the Marriage, Couple, and Family Counseling standards (see Standard 5.F.2.e.; CACREP, 2016).

What does this say about the counseling profession and the mental health field as a whole? It might suggest that sexuality is not considered a core aspect of human identity, not only by the mental health field but also by those in a position to create and implement the education and licensure requirements. Consequently, when sexuality is not considered a key aspect of human identity by the counseling field, then counseling professionals, students, practitioners, and educators alike are left to navigate client concerns primarily through their own personal experiential lens. Such experience may include personal sexual interactions and observations; familial, societal, and institutional messages; instilled values, biases, and assumptions; and maybe one or two sex education classes during middle school or high school (at least in the United States).

Beyond the contradictory notion that somehow counselors are to be free of biases without proper training or education on the topic of sexuality, it is even more troublesome when considering the historical state of sex education curriculum provided in primary and secondary education systems in the United States. According to a Guttmacher (2022) report on sex and HIV education, 26 states and the District of Columbia mandate sex education and HIV education; two states mandate only sex education; 11 states mandate only HIV education; 18 states require program content to be medically accurate; 26 states and the District of Columbia require instruction to be appropriate for the student's age; nine states require the program to provide instruction that is appropriate for a student's cultural background and that is not biased against any race, sex, or ethnicity; three states prohibit the program from promoting religion; and 11 states require the program to cover the importance of consent to sexual activity.

Considering most people in this country have never had the opportunity to receive adequate sex education (if any at all), we as a field should be addressing the real possibility that most of our master's-level students have also not received formal sex education. Considering where we are with sex education in the United States and the lack of training offered in counseling programs, how comfortable are counselors when it comes to sexual issues and concerns?

Counselor Comfort With Sexual Issues

When I ask students about their comfort with sexual issues in my Introduction to Human Sexuality in Counseling class, the majority of the class laughs uncomfortably. This is expected. Why? People do not talk about sex in general, let alone in formal education settings. So, I engage students in a little icebreaker to encourage community rapport and assess overall comfort with the topic. I ask students to provide slang and other terms for genitalia, which may include, for example, penis, pecker, cockmeat, johnson, woody, dick, vagina, clit, queen, vajajay, vajeen, cunt, or pearl. There is a catch. As students are saying these terms, they are asked to repeat each word and increase their speaking volume. You may have experienced this type of icebreaker yourself, or you might be asking yourself "Why?" There is a method here. The power of the word is slowly defused as a result of saying it out loud; no longer are terms such as vulva whispered—at least in my class. The approach can also be seen in narrative therapy and trauma-informed approaches to sexual trauma. When we are able to release what is in our head and say it out loud or write it down, we take away the emotional power it holds on our psyche. The icebreaker activity is just one of many used in class, and it marks the beginning of the student's growth and development as it pertains to comfort around addressing sexual concerns. Counselors who have little to no education on the topic of human sexuality also lack confidence and are less comfortable in their ability to broach sexual concerns, assess sexual concerns, and treat sexual concerns in an ethical and timely fashion (Cupit, 2010; Miller & Byers, 2009; Zeglin et al., 2018).

Moreover, discomfort in addressing a client's sexual concerns can seriously impair the therapeutic relationship and negatively influence the client's growth and development (Hipp & Carlson, 2019; Speciale, 2020). Preparing to address challenging sexual topics such as sex work or sexual exploitation, Litam (2019) explained, "counselors must reflect on whether they hold stigmatizing beliefs about individuals who have engaged in commercial sex work or who have survived forced sexual exploitation" (p. 411). Bloom et al. (2016) found that as a result of counselor discomfort, proper and timely assessments and subsequent treatment may be missed entirely. To the contrary, education and training that encourage counselors to explore comfort, biases, and assumptions can enable them to better "integrate a thorough cultural assessment at intake, as well as to attend to the specific ways clients' cultural worldviews shape attitudes and knowledge about sexual practices" (Burnes et al., 2017, p. 478).

Harris and Hays (2008) found that licensed marriage and family therapists who received formal education and supervision in human sexuality were more likely to feel comfortable and confident in approaching the topic of sexuality with clients. Similarly, when Kazukauskas and Lam (2010) administered a modified version of the Knowledge, Comfort, Approach and Attitude Towards Sexuality Scale to 199 rehabilitation counselors, they found that knowledge was a significant predictor of comfort when approaching sexual issues with clients. Moreover, they identified a more positive attitude about human sexuality and disability as a primary contributor to counselor comfort.

Such research findings support the need to expand counselor education to require a comprehensive human sexuality course, regardless of which path the counselor eventually lands on, whether that is marriage and family, rehabilitation, mental health, school counseling, or career counseling. This is especially important considering that clients are less inclined to address sexual issues themselves (Kazukauskas & Lam, 2010; Schubert & Pope, 2020). Counselors are trained to not rely on their client to inform or educate them on aspects of the client's story. The same stands for sexuality concerns of clients. This aspect is critical. If counselors do not ask the questions, then who will? Let's consider what sexual issues might be addressed in counseling.

Sexual Issues

When it comes to the nature of sexual issues, the possibilities are endless. It makes sense there would be some concern, confusion, and discomfort in knowing how to best approach sexual issues in counseling. For the most part, counseling students receive limited education on sexual orientation, gender identity and expression, and sexual dysfunction; yet, sexual concerns are far more expansive. Sexual issues can be tied to age, gender, psychological health, cognitive ability, physical ability, illness, race, ethnicity, career, culture, spirituality/religion, economics, politics, laws, family, and history. Sexual issues can present as primary issues, secondary issues, or unrelated issues that come up as a result of continued counseling.

Sexual concerns presented in session are not always just about sexual dysfunction, "doing it" or "not doing it." The role of the counselor may vary from giving the client permission to speak freely about their sexual concerns to needing to take a more integrative approach to the sexual concern, with input from other professionals who are working with the client. An integrative team might include a general physician, a psychologist, a psychiatrist, or a couples counselor.

The nature of sexuality is multifaceted, and the possible sexual concerns that may be presented by clients are extensive. Despite this reality, we counselors are indeed capable of approaching sexual concerns with clients if trained properly, and especially if we approach human sexuality in the same way we do with every other aspect of counselor development, by addressing biases and assumptions about sex and considering sex as a critical aspect of mental wellness.

Sexual Wellness

Although human sexuality is not identified as a key element in most wellness models, it is still considered a critical aspect of overall health and wellness (Mallicoat, 2014). When we look at the definition of human sexuality, we can see how one's expression and experiences of sexuality influence mental wellness. *Human sexuality* can be broadly defined as the ways in which people experience and express themselves as sexual beings (Cavendish, 2010; Schubert, 2015). Human sexuality is woven into the fabric of the individual human experience and is influenced by biology, psychology, ability, illness, society, history, economics, politics, culture, laws, and spirituality. Human sexuality is far more expansive than reproduction and sexual orientation. It includes arousal, pleasure, eroticism, sexual identities and expressions, gender identities and expressions, attraction, and sexual agency (Cavendish, 2010; Schubert, 2020; World Health Organization, 2006). When it comes to understanding how to navigate concerns with clients, it is important to understand how all of these aspects of human sexuality support and/or oppress sexual wellness.

The Association of Counseling Sexology & Sexual Wellness (ACSSW) defines *sexual wellness* as follows:

> The unique, subjective experience of physical, emotional, mental, and social well-being in relation to sexuality is essential to overall wellness. While sexual wellness can include the absence of disease, dysfunction, or infirmity, the holistic and subjective nature of sexual wellness extends beyond one's physical health status to include a positive and respectful approach to sexuality and sexual relationships, as well as the possibility of having pleasurable and safe sensual experiences, free of coercion, discrimination, and violation. Sexual wellness encompasses diversity in both expression and influences, respecting, protecting, and fulfilling the sexual rights of all persons. (ACSSW, n.d., para. 3)

As we move forward in our conceptualization of sexual wellness, we can advance the narrative by locating wellness within the counselor education program accreditation standards. According to CACREP (2016), the counseling curriculum should include "ethical and culturally relevant strategies for promoting resilience and optimum development and wellness across the lifespan" (Section 2, Standard F.3.i.). Human sexuality is complex and rich and ever gray; however, this reality does not necessarily require specialization. What better way to promote resilience and optimal development and wellness than to approach clients from a sex positive approach?

A Sex Positive Framework to Sexual Wellness Counseling

An ethically informed sexual wellness counseling approach is inherently sex positive and located within the scope of counseling as it integrates key elements of the counselor's roles and responsibilities, including ethics, social justice, advocacy, and radical respect, and embraces the intersectional reality of the human experience (see Figure 1.1).

Figure 1.1
Radically Informed Sex Positive Framework

Ethical Responsibility

According to the *ACA Code of Ethics* (American Counseling Association [ACA], 2014), counselors are responsible for the safety and care of their clients. This responsibility can be met in a variety of ways. When preparing to care for the complex needs (including the sexual concerns) of clients, it is critical for counselors to look first at their own story. Specific curriculum is dedicated to helping budding counselors explore their own personal narratives and potential barriers. Engaging in such reflection is a means to prevent any imposition of the counselor's values, beliefs, and attitudes on clients (ACA, 2014, Standard A.4.b.). Moreover, although counseling students and counselors are not expected to be competent in everything, they are challenged to enhance their own knowledge and understanding of a given topic, rather than simply referring the client to another provider (ACA, 2014, Standard C.2.a.). This challenge is imperative when we look at the sexual concerns of clients.

One popular way to assess competency and client needs in relation to sexual issues is to use Jack Annon's (1976) PLISSIT model for introducing sex into a therapeutic conversation. The acronym comprises

P for permission giving,
LI for limited information,
SS for specific suggestions, and
IT for intensive treatment.

The PLISSIT model offers counselors a way to assess and treat clients' sexual concerns while remaining ethically within their scope of practice. Using the model, clinicians can engage clients in a dialogue that is fundamentally open and inclusive, with a nonjudgmental attitude toward sexuality and sexual expression (Donaghue, 2015). It is responsive to clients' need to know "Am I normal?" when it comes to their sexual concerns.

Counselors are capable of offering the therapeutic space for clients to express their concerns without fear of judgment or negative attitude. With proper clinical training, counselors are in an optimal position to offer limited information and specific suggestions related to sexual concerns and how to approach and treat said concerns. When it comes to intensive treatment, we counselors need to honestly examine the degree to which we are competent to support our client. Chapter 3 has a phenomenal knowledge-based, decision-making matrix using the PLISSIT model. Engaging a client's needs from a sex positive framework in counseling allows counselors to uphold their ethical codes and, at the same time, seek guidance and training when deemed necessary to evaluate for potential referral.

There is some contention about what *sex positive* means and whether it is ethical to promote a sex positive framework with all clients. To be clear, sex positive does not mean a sexual free-for-all. It does not mean clinicians who subscribe to a sex positive approach are in support of clients having sex with everyone and anyone, regardless of their personal comfort, desire, or interest. It also does not mean that clients are assumed to be capable of having the capacity to be sexual or desirous at any given time. An ethically sex positive framework is founded upon an individual's *sexual agency*, which is the ability to act independently and make free choices related to sexuality and intimate expression. Sexual agency is paramount to personal liberation as it intersects with one's overall mental well-being and quality of life.

By engaging in a sex positive framework, clinicians are better able to encourage clients to speak freely about their sexuality, sexual expression, and sexual concerns and process their own narratives in a developmentally human-centered way. (Of course, regardless of clinical framework or openness, before providing services, counselors are ethically obligated to explain to mandated clients the limitations of client confidentiality [ACA, 2014, Section A.2.e.], which include knowledge of situations involving harm to self/others, child abuse, and elder abuse.) Importantly, clinicians who work from a sex positive framework are better able to assist those who have been hurt, marginalized, and/or discriminated against because of their sexuality.

Advocacy

Advocacy simply means to assist. There are those who believe counselors should not engage or support clients outside of the session. To the contrary, I believe it is our ethical duty to support and assist our clients in developing the changes they seek. A sex positive approach to counseling allows for counselors to honor such responsibilities, regardless of the sexual concern. Advocacy ultimately promotes sexual autonomy and safe, consensual relationships with self and others as well as within the client's community.

Advocacy on behalf of the client's sexual autonomy can best be done in session by engaging clients in an exploration of their own sexual script. *Sexual scripts* are internalized norms constructed and cultivated through the individual lens of the person as they experience and engage in sociocultural contexts (Rutagumirwa & Bailey, 2018). Sexual scripts typically develop during childhood and adolescence (Nagoski, 2015; Wiederman, 2015) and so are heavily influenced by family and community. Familial and community messages surrounding cultural norms, masculinity, femininity, relationships, affection, and sexuality are all part of one's sexual script (Simon & Gagnon, 1986; Wiederman, 2015). Such messages are used as standards by which to assess an individual's sexual experiences and evaluate whether their thoughts, emotions, or behaviors are "appropriate" (Simon & Gagnon, 1986).

Counselors can help clients explore their sexual script by examining how their narrative developed over the course of their lifetime and evaluating which aspects will be honored and which need a "rewrite." For example, older adults are typically viewed by society as no longer desiring, or as asexual, and may even be mocked for sexual expression (Schubert & Pope, 2020). This stigma tends to be perpetuated by the older adults themselves as they internalize such messages as truth. Despite the stigma, research has shown that desire fluctuates across the life span, and although sexual functioning and traditional ways of sexual expression may change because of age, older adults continue to desire sexual intimacy until the end of life (Pope, 1997; Schubert & Pope, 2020; Syme & Cohn, 2016). Counselors in this position can offer their older adult clients the opportunity to explore what they enjoy about their bodies and their partner(s) and what they wish to honor when it comes to their own sexual desires. Counselors might also advocate for their older adult clients by preparing them to have conversations with their physician about testing for sexually transmitted infections (STIs), about medications to assist with erections and hormone balance, or about any health conditions that might warrant assessment prior to sexual engagement.

Taking it one step further, counselors might also advocate on behalf of their clients by advocating within the community. This can be done by promoting comprehensive sexual education in their school districts and the school districts of their clients. Similar to older adults, adolescents and young adults are also likely to have their rights infringed upon by society. Promoting sexual autonomy at a young age through comprehensive sexual education might also prevent future internalized ageism as they grow into older adulthood. Furthermore, comprehensive sex education when done properly can advocate for gender equality and power relations that might also prevent sexual assault, sexual abuse, and intimate partner violence. Counselors can advocate for their younger clients by providing comprehensive sex education and informing them of their rights as sexual beings—for example, by educating a teenage client on when and how to ask about STIs. Given the increase in hookup culture, it is imperative for younger folks to know how to navigate possibly tricky conversations, such as asking about STI status and how to be regularly tested.

Social Justice

As helping professionals, counselors have an ethical responsibility to address mental health disparities and marginalization that are rooted in oppression as well as inequities at the individual, group, societal, and institutional levels (Ratts et al., 2010). Ethically and when appropriate, counselors are expected to address any potential barriers and obstacles that inhibit access and/or the growth and development of clients (ACA, 2014, Section A.7.a.). To help clients therapeutically explore the marginalization, counselors must first recognize the power dynamic that exists within the therapeutic relationship (Sanabria & Murray, 2018). As counselors, we have an incredible amount of power and privilege compared with our clients; after all, clients are coming to us for help. When we consider our clients, it is therefore important to acknowledge their reality and start the work from their point of view.

Identified by Ratts (2009) as the fifth force of counseling, *social justice counseling* uses ethically and culturally appropriate advocacy strategies to enhance the voices of the marginalized and the oppressed at the interpersonal, intrapersonal, and institutional level. Consider Maslow's (1987) hierarchy of human needs. Individuals generally seek to satisfy those needs that are lower down in the hierarchy before they can attend to needs higher up, with needs ranging from basic (physiological to safety) to psychological (love and belonging to self-esteem) to self-fulfillment (self-actualization). For example, it is a challenge to consider how to best help your client "come out" as a trans woman at their workplace (satisfying a psychological need) if doing so may result in termination (loss of a basic need). Or for the same client, how might they feel safe in the world if trans women of color are being murdered without cause, policed at a much higher rate than others, or misgendered in police reports and newspapers?

The National Transgender Discrimination Survey (Grant et al., 2011) received nearly 6,500 responses from the trans and gender-nonconforming communities. The survey found that 54% of trans and gender-nonconforming respondents had contact with the police, 46% reported feeling "uncomfortable" seeking police support, 29%–38% of trans people of color reported police harassment, 20% reported being denied equal services, 6% reported being physically assaulted by police officers, and 7% of African American trans folx reported being sexually assaulted by police officers. Again, how do we best help our clients be their most authentic selves and encourage self-actualization when their basic physiological and psychological needs are not being met?

Out of fear of being perceived as sexually deviant or criminal, those who engage in sexual activity or have sexual desires socially considered taboo might also refrain from being their authentic self in counseling. Examples of such groups might include those who identify as having a paraphilia or paraphilic disorder (see Chapter 20). Because atypical sexual desires are so stigmatized, we know very little about them. For example, most data on paraphilic disorders such as pedophilia are drawn from forensic settings (Krueger, 2010). Such data were used to inform the *Diagnostic and Statistical Manual of Mental Disorders* (5th ed.; *DSM-5*; American Psychiatric Association, 2013). To best support those with distress as a result of sexual desires perceived as nonnormophilic, counselors need to be aware of the limited knowledge that has informed the paraphilic disorders described by the diagnostic criteria.

Berer (2004) described how social justice often fails citizens in life critical ways:

> Ensuring social justice on the part of governments in relation to sexuality means ensuring that public and economic policies, and public services and education, prevent discrimination and abuse in relation to sexuality, and promote sexual health and rights. Social justice is denied in forced and other non-consensual marriages, in discrimination against homosexual men and women because of their sexual orientation, in the acceptance of so-called honour killings as crimes of passion, and in arguments that cruel and life-threatening punishments such as stoning of women on grounds of adultery are religiously-sanctioned. Issues of social justice arise in discrimination against pregnant adolescents, such as expelling them from school, or denying single mothers social benefits for themselves and their children as a judgement on them for having sexual relations. (pp. 8–9)

To pursue social justice in counseling would mean to take action against such discrimination in both the community and the counseling field itself. Doing so requires us as counselors to acknowledge our own biases and assumptions as they pertain to our own intersecting identities, our own power and privilege, and all the ways in which we experience marginalization. Engaging in this type of reflection allows for counselors to better understand the power differential that exists within the therapeutic relationship and how human sexuality is influenced, discriminated against, or compounded by the intersecting realties and identities of our clients.

Intersectional Lens

Intersectionality, a term originally coined by Kimberlé Crenshaw, has evolved from a position on the ways in which women of color have been, and still are, systemically and politically oppressed, to what she described in an interview with Columbia Law School (2017) as "a lens through which you can see where power comes and collides, where it interlocks and intersects" (para. 2) as it pertains to identities and the systems located to oppress and privilege individuals based on such identities. When we explore our clients' narratives associated with their sexuality, it is critical to consider all the ways in which their identities, such as age, ability, race, ethnicity, gender, sexual orientation, socioeconomic status, and religion, support or oppress their individual sexual experience. One way of doing this is to recognize the pervasive binary ideologies that exist in our communities and the way we all tend to "other." Patricia Hill Collins (2004) wrote in *Black Sexual Politics: African Americans, Gender, and the New Racism* how ideologies of racism and heterosexism are perpetuated by social systems that ultimately impact our clients:

> It views race through two oppositional categories of Whites and Blacks, gender through two categories of men and women, and sexuality through two oppositional categories of heterosexuals and homosexuals. A master binary of normal and deviant overlays and bundles together these and other lesser binaries. In this context, ideas about "normal" race (whiteness, which ironically, masquerades as racelessness), "normal" gender (using male experiences as the norm), and "normal" sexuality (heterosexuality, which operates in a similar hegemonic fashion) are tightly bundled together. In essence, to be completely "normal," one must be White, masculine, and heterosexual, the core hegemonic White masculinity. This mythical norm is hard to see because it is so taken-for-granted. (pp. 96–97)

Counselors who engage in the introspective work might find themselves exploring all the ways in which they other and are othered. Othering exists within individuals themselves as well as for groups of people, across communities and systems. When it comes to the intersectional reality of humans, it is imperative for us as counselors to approach our clients and their respective identities with an openness that allows for such identities to be seen, heard, validated, and honored, and with full recognition that we too have our own experiences related to our many identities.

As we explore sexual concerns of our clients, addressing identities and worldviews will be of great importance. Table 1.1 includes several examples of client concerns related to sexuality. As you review each of the examples, consider where your comfort is and how you might best proceed to support each of the clients and their concerns. How might othering exist within each sexual concern described? How might individual identities influence other aspects of the sexual concern addressed?

Although this is not an exhaustive list, there are multiple ways in which sexual concerns may come up. You might also notice that the mentioned concerns are reflective of intersecting realities and identities and that such realities cannot be simply isolated from each other. As an example, trans women of color experience multiple marginalizations compared with White trans women, and discrimination can be seen in many safety forms, such as negative interactions with police, familial abandonment, and isolation, and in economic forms, such as housing, health care, employment, and education (Grant et al., 2011). The reality of trans women of color is reflective of Crenshaw's (1996) theory of *structural intersectionality*, defined as "the ways in

Table 1.1
Intersectional Factors and Client Concerns Related to Sexuality

Client Factor	*Examples of Client Concerns*
Age	"Is there something wrong with my 4-year-old daughter—she's always playing with herself 'down there'?" "Am I too old to have sex?"
Gender	"My mother always told me to never touch myself, but my friends talk about masturbating all the time. Where do I even begin?" "Every time I have a period, I am reminded of my female reproductive system and I become really depressed."
Psychological	"I haven't been able to 'get it up' since my wife died, but I desire to be intimate with another woman again." "It takes so much effort for me to want to have sex. Once I start, I am usually OK, but until then, I get 'all in my head' about it."
Cognitive ability	"My partner has dementia. Can we still make love?" "How can I best support the sexual needs of my teenager who has Down syndrome?"
Physical ability	"I have back pain and my partner wants me to have sex, but I have low desire and sex sounds painful and too much work. How do I stay connected to them?" "My wheelchair feels like a barrier to exploring sex, but it seems like other folks are figuring it out. Can I be intimate?"
Illness	"I have sickle cell disease, and one of the side effects is priapism. I can't imagine even thinking sexual thoughts because the pain of it all is too much." "My Parkinson's disease seems to be taking over my body. I can no longer get into the sexual positions I want. In my head I feel like a strong, beautiful man, but my body is failing me now."
Race	"Trans women of color are DYING out there! Just for being themselves! We can't go to the cops. Newspapers don't care about us. Where is our justice?" "I am Ojibwe and two spirit. I believe I am gifted, but I am bullied at school for it."
Career	"My boss made a pass at me, and I am having a hard time getting intimate with my spouse now." "My work team made a big 'to-do' about Cheryl's pregnancy, but I just got married to my partner and no one said anything."
Culture	"My child is gay. I believe I must disown him." "In my heart of hearts, I am poly. But my family doesn't understand. My spouse reminds me of our vows. What do I do?"
Spirituality/ religion	"I married into a Mormon family. We aren't allowed to masturbate. I miss touching myself, but I don't want to break our religious rules." "My ex-husband asked for an annulment. I am so angry. I feel like the annulment makes me a whore and my children are now bastards."
Economics	"My father would sell me for sexual acts as a child to anyone who would give him a bottle of whiskey. We were poor. But it doesn't make it right." "I enjoy being a sex worker. I like the hours, making fast money, the free time, and making up my own rules. But my partner wants me to quit."
Politics	"It causes me a lot of distress knowing my reproductive organs are always up for political debate. When I speak openly about my abortion, people call me a 'baby killer.' The abortion was difficult enough but to be verbally assaulted. It is too much." "My lover was killed. They didn't even use her correct name or pronoun in the newspaper. They called her Reginald. They don't even see us as real people."
Laws	"I'm attracted to minors, but I haven't acted. How do I even tell my partner? I don't feel like I can tell anyone out of fear they will call me in and convict me for my thoughts." "My work fired me after I came out as trans. They say it was because of my work performance. But I have stellar records."
Historical trauma	"I was molested by my stepfather for years. My husband doesn't know." "Everybody that I have ever dated has cheated on me. I don't even know how to begin to trust."
Family	"Every family member in my life has gone through a divorce. I don't even know how to fight for my marriage or know if it is worth it." "My grandma said men aren't worth a wooden nickle, they ain't worth a dime. And my mother said 'always take care of you and yours.' How am I to trust relationships with these messages?"

which the location of women of color at the intersection of race and gender makes our actual experience of domestic violence, rape, and remedial reform qualitatively different from that of white women" (p. 94). It would be difficult to consider how to effectively address the intersectional reality of the client or how to ethically and competently advocate on behalf of the client without considering the counselor's capacity to hear the story of the client.

Radical Respect

Such capacity requires radical respect by the counselor; it is something not to be earned but rather to be freely given. Radical respect can best be defined as the belief that people are inherently worthy of trust and dignity and to be approached with openness and free from contempt or judgment (Walker, 2004).

Radical respect honors the story of the human experience and upholds the belief that every story deserves to be heard. The key to being radically respectful is to hold unconditional positive regard and empathy for the client's worldview, their context of joy and suffering, how they came to make meaning in their life, and the ways in which they have survived and thrived—ultimately, to see the human first.

I'd like to invite you to consider which population you are or were most concerned to serve. I ask this question quite often. The population typically identified is that of child offenders. The conversation usually evolves into a reflective exploration of the term "child offender" and distinguishing sex offender typologies from pedophilia, as most offenders who sexually assault children are not diagnosed with pedophilia. So, how can one counsel someone they are fearful of? I invite you to imagine that client (the one who is struggling with a topic you are concerned about) and what they were like as a child, envisioning them at 7 or 10 years old. In most cases, I imagine it would be challenging to be fearful of or truly angry at a 7-year-old child. What was that child's life like? Were they exposed to love, affection, and connection? How did they come to understand the world as a result? Asking these questions can sometimes allow a counselor to cultivate compassion toward the client. To be radically respectful does not mean that we agree with the actions, thoughts, or beliefs of our clients, but it does mean that we acknowledge their existence and their worldview as their truth. Clinicians are ethically obligated to refrain from imposing values or biases on to clients. Engaging in radical respect offers counselors the ability to create the therapeutic space necessary for the client to be heard (Schubert & Taylor, 2020).

Other ways to engage in radical respect include using language that is person centered, affirming, and sex positive. Becoming comfortable with sexual language is important not only in how you address but also in how you assess clients. For example, counselors may share their own pronoun and ask which pronouns a client uses, such as they, ze, she, or he. Honoring pronouns demonstrates respect to the client. It is important to acknowledge that pronouns are not considered a preferred decision but a critical aspect of a person's identity. Neglecting to acknowledge and accurately identify a client's pronoun increases the risk of harming the client and irrevocably damaging the therapeutic relationship. Counselors might also ask clients how they label their relationship status (e.g., dating, partnered, thruple, polycule). Counselors who honor the diverse interpersonal and sexual connections that may exist for their client might prevent any negative influence on the client-therapist relationship (Burnes et al., 2017).

Radical respect also acknowledges that not everyone is going to be comfortable discussing the sexual topic in depth despite it being an addressed concern in session.

It is important for the counselor to proactively assess client comfort discussing the topic with regular check-ins. For example, you have a client who wishes to learn more about their own sexuality and how to please themselves. The conversation may include a client's perception of body image, knowledge of and comfort with masturbation, and/or attitudes toward self as a sexual being and self-pleasure. This might also include how messages of all kinds have influenced their perception of self, their worldview of sexuality, and their attitude toward intimacy.

In the end, what are we looking at when considering what is required of counselors and other mental health professionals to work from a sex positive framework such as this? My guess is that we are looking at a focus on humanity in the most expansive and inclusive way. Acknowledge the personal script and move through the discomfort experienced in the presence of differences. There are no others, there is just the human experience. Yet, to truly understand and support clients, we as mental health professionals must acknowledge that othering is real. Similarly, as mental health professionals we are not expected to have all the answers or to have our own personal stuff completely worked out, nor are we entitled to bestow our opinion or personal script onto someone else. How do you know you are working from a sex positive framework?

You know you are working from a radically informed sex positive framework if you

- consider your ethical obligation to lean in to any discomfort surrounding your personal beliefs, assumptions, and values surrounding human sexual expression;
- empower and support the client's perception of sexual agency;
- ethically evaluate client concerns using the PLISSIT model;
- advocate on behalf of those who have been hurt, marginalized, and/or discriminated against as a result of their sexuality;
- understand that sex positivity does not mean a free-for-all and that consent is essential;
- acknowledge that human sexuality cannot be pathologized;
- target the distress, dysfunction, and danger associated with the sexual concern not the sexuality itself; and
- critically challenge historical systems such as the *DSM-5* when addressing diagnosis and treatment with clients whose concerns are not heteronormative, repronormative, or normophilic;
- approach clients and their respective intersecting identities with an openness that allows for such identities to be seen, heard, validated, and honored; and
- engage in radical respect.

It's that simple.

Conclusion

How do we get there? How do we get to a place where we are fully working from a sex positive framework? As stated in this chapter, there are no counselor education or state licensure requirements (except in Florida and California) regarding education and training in human sexuality. We know that counselors with training are less likely to cause pain or harm to their clients. We know that mental health is inclusive of sexual health. We need to acknowledge first that human sexuality is a key element of human identity and, therefore, human wellness. Second, we need to support associations such as ACSSW and others lobbying for inclusion of human sexuality as a domain within counselor education and other mental health education curriculum. Third, we must do our due diligence and seek out the necessary education and training to best support our clients.

Let's consider how each component of this sex positive framework might look in a case example. As you read through the case scenario, consider what you are personally feeling and thinking about the client and how you might approach treatment.

Case Example

Kye is a 21-year-old, gender-nonconforming, demisexual individual of Filipino descent. Kye reported that they were in a car accident that left them with a traumatic brain injury. Kye came to counseling initially to discuss better ways to communicate with their partner Roz. Kye and Roz have been together since Kye was 19 years old. Kye explained that Roz was in the vehicle when the accident occurred. Kye reported that they have difficulty communicating feelings with Roz and carries resentment toward Roz for "coming out of the accident totally OK."

After slowly developing the therapeutic rapport, the counselor, Jasmine, explored other ways in which the relationship has been affected by the incident. Kye reported that they have difficulty staying connected to their body during sex and feels like they are burdening their partner: "Roz puts up with all of my shit. She is probably better off without me." Jasmine spent time validating the frustration and sadness expressed by Kye and asked them to expand on how they felt disconnected to their body. Kye explained that prior to the accident, they were physically fit, quick to joke, and loved their body. They loved having sex with Roz and "going really slow." After the accident, Kye described multiple surgeries to fix their leg, physical therapy sessions, and speech and language therapy for the following year.

Kye explained that they are quick tempered when an argument ensues between they and Roz. They want to go "slow" again when it comes to sexual activities, but their mind and their body still have a difficult time communicating with each other. At the end of the session, Kye explained that they yearn to communicate effectively again with Roz: "Roz is the only person I have ever felt emotionally connected to. To lose Roz would be to lose everything." Kye also explained that they would like to learn how to reconnect with their body.

Reflections About the Case Example

After reading this case example, consider the following questions:

1. What ethical and safety considerations might you need to explore as a counselor moving forward with Kye?
2. How might you best explore the sexual script of Kye (possibly grieving the lost sense of sexual self, redefining the new sexual script)?
3. In what ways can you advocate and engage in social justice on behalf of Kye?
4. What are the intersecting identities of Kye and how might they work to oppress and/or support Kye?
5. In what ways can you engage in radical respect with Kye?

Questions You Always Wanted to Ask

Questions you always wanted to ask may include the following:

1. **What is the first step I need to take to become a sex positive counselor?** Start within. Yes, this has been repeated in this chapter, but it cannot be said enough. My entire world is sex focused, and I still find myself surprised and in awe of the complex nature of the human sexual experience. The best way to approach your own "stuff" as it pertains to sexuality is to take a sexual attitude reassessment (SAR) program. A SAR can range from a 1-day intensive workshop to a week(s)-long intensive program. Although the details may vary from trainer to trainer, the overall purpose of a SAR is to help participants deeply explore their own personal narrative of their story and examine all the ways in which biases, values, and assumptions influence the sexual worldview of the participant. The SAR also focuses on clinical training and explore a variety of sexual behaviors, experiences, and ways of life. My warning to you: Not all SARs are created equal. They are time-consuming and expensive, so be sure to research beforehand and find a SAR that resonates with you and meets your expectations. I personally researched SARs that clearly outlined a focus on reproductive justice, social justice, intersectional exploration, current data, and inclusive language that suggested no "yum" would be "yucked."

   Be prepared to do some internal work. I am naturally a crier (I LOVE "feels"), but dang, I was not expecting childhood sexual experiences to be a group conversation. As painfully embarrassing as it was, I loved it. Hell, I needed it. I left my SAR with a strengthened sense of support and love for my child self and all of her sexually curious adventures.
2. **How do I get connected to the world of sexuality and mental health?** There are wonderful professional associations dedicated to human sexuality. ACSSW is the only association entirely dedicated to the field of counseling and counseling sexology. ACSSW offers members access to training webinars, sexuality curriculum, a quarterly email, and the *Journal of Counseling Sexology & Sexual Wellness*. Other associations include

   - American Association of Sexuality Educators, Counselors, and Therapists
   - American College of Sexologists
   - The Association of Black Sexologists and Clinicians
   - European Society for Sexual Medicine
   - Gay and Lesbian Medical Association
   - International Academy of Sex Research
   - International Society for Sexual Medicine
   - International Society for the Study of Women's Sexual Health
   - Planned Parenthood
   - Sexual Medicine Society of North America
   - Society for Sex Therapy and Research
   - Society for the Scientific Study of Sexuality
   - Society for Women's Health Research
   - World Association for Sexual Health
   - World Professional Association for Transgender Health

3. **My program doesn't offer a human sexuality counseling course. Where do I go for more information?**
I suggest going "grassroots" on this! When I first started in my master's program, there was not a course on human sexuality. Faculty and programs alike typically develop course electives that are meaningful to them, but you are the consumer. If you are interested in taking a human sexuality counseling course, ask your faculty if they would be interested in teaching the course. Survey your peers to assess if they would like to take a human sexuality course. If the program has Chi Sigma Iota, the counseling professional honorary, ask them if they would like to sponsor a guest lecturer to teach a human sexuality workshop. When I started my doctoral program, there was no human sexuality course offered. I took this as an opportunity to develop a course curriculum on human sexuality counseling as part of my doctoral internship. Fortunately, I had the support of faculty who allowed me to teach the course as an elective. All this to say, your voice is powerful—use it!

References

American Counseling Association. (2014). *ACA code of ethics*. https://www.counseling.org/resources/aca-code-of-ethics.pdf

American Psychiatric Association. (2013). *Diagnostic and statistical manual of mental disorders* (5th ed.). https://doi.org/10.1176/appi.books.9780890425596

Annon, J. S. (1976). The PLISSIT model: A proposed conceptual scheme for the behavioral treatment of sexual problems. *Journal of Sex Education and Therapy, 2*(1), 1–15. https://doi.org/10.1080/01614576.1976.11074483

Association of Counseling Sexology & Sexual Wellness. (n.d.). *What is sexual wellness?* https://www.counselingsexology.com/

Berer, M. (2004). Sexuality, rights and social justice [Editorial]. *Reproductive Health Matters, 12*(23), 6–11. https://doi.org/10.1016/S0968-8080(04)23130-5

Binik, Y. M., & Meana, M. (2009). The future of sex therapy: Specialization or marginalization? *Archives of Sexual Behavior, 38*(6), 1016–1027. https://doi.org/10.1007/s10508-009-9475-9

Bloom, Z. D., Guiterrez, D., Lambie, G. W., & Ali, S. (2016). Counselors' comfort with sexuality, attitudes towards pornography, and propensity to assess and treat client issues related to pornography use. *Journal of Mental Health Counseling, 38*(4), 327–345. https://doi.org/10.17744/mehc.38.4.04

Brown, B. (2012). *Listening to shame* [Video]. TED Conferences. https://www.ted.com/talks/brene_brown_listening_to_shame

Buehler, S. (2017). *What every mental health professional needs to know about sex* (2nd ed.). Springer Publishing.

Burnes, T. R., Singh, A. A., & Witherspoon, R. G. (2017). Sex positivity and counseling psychology: An introduction to the major contribution. *Counseling Psychologist, 45*(4), 470–486. https://doi.org/10.1177/0011000017710216

Cavendish, M. (2010). *Sex and society*. Cavendish Square.

Collins, P. H. (2004). *Black sexual politics: African Americans, gender, and the new racism*. Routledge.

Columbia Law School. (2017, June 8). Kimberlé Crenshaw on intersectionality, more than two decades later. *News From Columbia Law*. https://www.law.columbia.edu/news/archive/kimberle-crenshaw-intersectionality-more-two-decades-later

Council for Accreditation of Counseling and Related Educational Programs. (2016). *2016 CACREP standards.* http://www.cacrep.org/for-programs/2016-cacrep-standards/

Crenshaw, K. W. (1996). Mapping the margins: Intersectionality, identity politics, and violence against women of color. In M. A. Fineman & R. Mykitiuk (Eds.), *The public nature of private violence* (pp. 93–120). Routledge.

Cupit, R. W. (2010). *Counselors' comfort levels and willingness to discuss sexual issues with couples they counsel* [Doctoral dissertation, University of New Orleans]. University of New Orleans Theses and Dissertations. https://scholarworks.uno.edu/td/1150

Donaghue, C. (2015). *Sex outside the lines: Authentic sexuality in a sexually dysfunctional culture.* Benbella Books.

Grant, J. M., Mottet, L. A., & Tanis, J. (with Harrison, J., Herman, J. L., & Keisling, M.). (2011). *Injustice at every turn: A report of the National Transgender Discrimination Survey.* National Center for Transgender Equality & National Gay and Lesbian Task Force. http://transequality.org/PDFs/NTDS_Report.pdf

Guttmacher Institute. (2022). *Sex and HIV education.* https://www.guttmacher.org/state-policy/explore/sex-and-hiv-education

Haboubi, N. H., & Lincoln, N. (2003). Views of health professionals on discussing sexual issues with patients. *Disability and Rehabilitation, 25*(6), 291–296. https://doi.org/10.1080/0963828021000031188

Harris, S. M., & Hays, K. W. (2008). Family therapist comfort with and willingness to discuss client sexuality. *Journal of Marital and Family Therapy, 34*(2), 239–250. https://doi.org/10.1111/j.1752-0606.2008.00066.x

Hipp, C. J., & Carlson, R. G. (2019). Comfort in treating sexual problems: Current training and counselor self-efficacy. *The Family Journal, 27*(2), 105–114. https://doi.org/10.1177/1066480719835342

Ivanski, C., & Kohut, T. (2017). Exploring definitions of sex positivity through thematic analysis. *Canadian Journal of Human Sexuality, 26*(3), 216–225. https://doi.org/10.3138/cjhs.2017-0017

Kazukauskas, K. A., & Lam, C. S. (2010). Disability and sexuality: Knowledge, attitudes, and level of comfort among certified rehabilitation counselors. *Rehabilitation Counseling Bulletin, 54*(1), 15–25. https://doi.org/10.1177/0034355209348239

Krueger, R. B. (2010). The *DSM* diagnostic criteria for sexual sadism. *Archives of Sexual Behavior, 39*(2), 325–345.

Litam, S. D. A. (2019). She's just a prostitute: The effects of labels on counselor attitudes, empathy, and rape myth acceptance. *The Professional Counselor, 9*(4), 396–415. https://doi.org/10.15241/sdal.9.4.396

Mallicoat, W. D. (2013). *A constructivist examination of counselors' conceptualization of "sexuality": Implications for counselor education* [Doctoral dissertation, University of South Carolina]. University of South Carolina Theses and Dissertations. https://scholarcommons.sc.edu/etd/829/

Mallicoat, W. D. (2014). Counselors' perception of sexuality in counseling: A pilot study. *The Practitioner Scholar: Journal of Counseling Professional Psychology, 3*, 63–81.

Maslow, A. H. (1987). *Motivation and personality* (3rd ed.). Pearson Education.

Miller, S. A., & Byers, E. S. (2009). Psychologists' continuing education and training in sexuality. *Journal of Sex & Marital Therapy, 35*(3), 206–219. https://doi.org/10.1080/00926230802716336

Nagoski, E. (2015). *Come as you are: The surprising new science that will transform your sex life*. Simon & Schuster Paperbacks.
Pope, M. (1997). Sexual issues for older lesbians and gays. *Topics of Geriatric Rehabilitation, 12*(4), 53–60.
Ratts, M. J. (2009). Social justice counseling: Toward the development of a fifth force among counseling paradigms. *The Journal of Humanistic Counseling, Education and Development, 48*(2), 160–172. https://doi.org/10.1002/j.2161-1939.2009.tb00076.x
Ratts, M. J., Toporek, R. L., & Lewis, J. A. (Eds.). (2010). *ACA advocacy competencies: A social justice framework for counselors*. American Counseling Association.
Rutagumirwa, S. K., & Bailey, A. (2018). "The heart desires but the body refuses": Sexual scripts, older men's perceptions of sexuality, and implications for their mental and sexual health. *Sex Roles, 78*(9), 653–668. https://doi.org/10.1007/s11199-017-0822-3
Sanabria, S., & Murray, T. L., Jr. (2018). Infusing human sexuality content and counseling in counselor education curriculum. *American Journal of Sexuality Education, 13*(2), 190–204. https://doi.org/10.1080/15546128.2018.1457461
Schubert, A. M. (2015). *Attitudes toward aging sexual expression in nursing homes: An exploration of the older adult resident phenomenon* [Doctoral dissertation, University of Missouri–St. Louis]. University of Missouri–St. Louis Institutional Repository Library. https://irl.umsl.edu/dissertation/191/
Schubert, A. (2020, April 16). Sexual agency inherent in self exploration and mental wellness among women. *ACA Member Blogs*. https://www.counseling.org/news/aca-blogs/aca-member-blogs/aca-member-blogs/2020/04/16/sexual-agency-inherent-in-self-exploration-and-mental-wellness-among-women
Schubert, A., & Pope, M. (2020). Sexuality beyond young adulthood: Affordances and barriers to sexual expression in the nursing home. *Journal of Counseling Sexology & Sexual Wellness, 2*(1), 35–47. https://doi.org/doi:10.34296/02011022
Schubert, A., & Taylor, J. Z. (2020). Teaching radical respect: Increasing empathy for stigmatized groups through a relational-cultural theoretical lens. In M. Pope, M. Gonzalez, E. R. N. Cameron, & J. S. Pangelinan (Eds.), *Social justice and advocacy in counseling: Experiential activities for teaching* (p. 51). Routledge.
Simon, W., & Gagnon, J. H. (1986). Sexual scripts: Permanence and change. *Archives of Sexual Behavior, 15*, 97–120. https://doi.org/10.1007/BF01542219
Speciale, M. (2020). Negotiating sexual values in counselor education: A qualitative case exploration. *Journal of Counseling Sexology & Sexual Wellness, 2*(1), 10–21. https://doi.org/doi:10.34296/02011032
Syme, M. L., & Cohn, T. J. (2016). Examining aging sexual stigma attitudes among adults by gender, age, and generational status. *Aging & Mental Health, 20*(1), 36–45. https://doi.org/10.1080/13607863.2015.1012044
Walker, M. (2004). How relationships heal. In M. Walker & W. Rosen (Eds.), *How connections heal: Stories from relational-cultural therapy* (pp. 3–21). Guilford Press.
Wiederman, M. (2015). Sexual script theory: Past, present, and future. In J. DeLamater & R. Plante (Eds.), *Handbook of the sociology of sexualities* (pp. 7–22). Springer International Publishing.
World Health Organization. (2006). *Defining sexual health: Report of a technical consultation on sexual health, 28–31 January 2002*.

Zeglin, R. J., Van Dam, D., & Hergenrather, K. C. (2018). An introduction to proposed human sexuality counseling competencies. *International Journal for the Advancement of Counselling, 40*(2), 105–121. https://doi.org/10.1007/s10447-017-9314-y

Zimmerman, K. J. (2012). Clients in sexually open relationships: Considerations for therapists. *Journal of Feminist Family Therapy, 24*(3), 272–289. https://doi.org/10.1080/08952833.2012.648143

CHAPTER 2

Adam and Eve/Steve/Pat and the History of Sexual Behavior: From Sin to Illegal to Deviance to Difference

Mark Pope

The history of sexual behavior begs for limits, specifically limits of geography (only in the United States?), of time (from the birth of the universe to 1950?), of species (only homo sapiens?), of behaviors (only heterosexual?), of attitudes (free love?), or any of a number of variables that might be used to limit the exploration of this topic to a page-limited chapter. Otherwise, it just gets too long. I have chosen therefore a more broad-brush approach that gives you a little bit of what I consider seminal points in time that got us to where we are now historically.

As the title of this chapter suggests, it might have all started with the Christian biblical allegory of Adam and Eve—you know, the Garden of Eden, the snake, the apple, and all of that. It's a morality tale of how the world was born. Every culture has one. It's not meant to be scientific. It's meant to make a point and to introduce the traditional values of a religion or of a people to others of that group (i.e., something that we can all agree on, a shared point of view) or even to others of the world. But, even way back then, the story was about sexual images like apples, fig leaves, naked people, and a snake. The story doesn't mention a "cigar," but I'm sure you get the point.

Sexual behavior has been a part of being human from the beginning. The idea of sex, on the other hand, has taken some quite bold zigs and zags from then to now, and that's the story of the evolution of sexual behavior—including sexual attitudes. From the basic functional semiclonal creation of another human being to the boundaries provided by the religions of the world, with sex as sin at the center and their clergy as arbiters, to the passage of laws providing parameters to what sexual behaviors were acceptable and therefore legal, and what was unacceptable and therefore illegal, enforced by police and courts and, early on, the king, to a disease model of human sexual behavior, with psychiatrists as the provider of the cure, to the reconstruction of sexual behavior as a basic human need as pleasurable and fun and passionate, and to variations in sexual behavior as mere differences and the victims of previous stages as activists in the transition process, we have gone through some changes as a species.

Sexual permissiveness and repression, however, wax and wane over time and from culture to culture on our planet. What is taboo in one culture is not in another, and what is taboo in one culture at one point in time is not in that same culture at a different point in time. Martin Luther King Jr. (1968) told us that the arc of the moral universe is long, but it bends toward justice and progress. The one constant in all of this is change.

There has been a reticence to study sexual behavior, and historians have, however, been quite reluctant until more recently in human history to delve into this (Bullough, 1972, 1985). "It is not only sex in the biological sense that has been avoided but such aspects of sexual behavior as courtship, marriage, and child rearing have also been ignored" (Bullough, 1972, p. 101). A lot changed in the 1960s and 1970s in the United States and around the world, bringing—along with the great civil rights and liberation movements of those times—more light into these sometimes quite hushed discussions that seemed to occur only in rather dark corners. Since then, we have had an explosion of interest in topics such as sexual behavior and sexuality in the counseling, psychology, psychiatry, and social work literature as well as in the more general medical and nursing fields. You now get to benefit from all this.

This is, however, not an exercise in presenting "truth," merely that of describing evidence of what has been. You are both permitted and requested to make your own interpretations. Here we go. Hang on, because as Bette Davis, the famous American actor, once stated in her delicious role in the movie *All About Eve* (Mankiewicz, 1951): "Fasten your seat belts; it's going to be a bumpy night."

First

But first, we must discuss the limitations of the reporters of histories of sexual behavior and attitudes so that you have more context for all this. First, such histories have been previously written by men who were European or American, White, and with a distinctly Jewish or Christian point of view.

Bullough (1971) reported that "there is still another problem, and one that plagued the historian of sexual attitudes until comparatively recent times: almost all of the writing was done by men" (p. 190) and later that "the general Judaic Christian orientation of historians and translators make[s] the question of sexual life . . . difficult to reconstruct and fraught with uncertainties" (p. 190). Vern Bullough met these criteria himself, and such self-criticism made his writings even more powerful. Such a practice is always useful for scientists and researchers, in particular.

Second, human beings are great at telling others to "do as I say, not as I do":

> Ethical behavior in any age can be divided into two categories: the standards actually practiced among the mass of the population, and the ideals proclaimed by the thinkers and the prophets. The degree of divergence between these two standards differs from age to age and even within one period urban and rural customs for example, may not be uniform. (Bullough, 1971, p. 187)

The effects of culture, diversity, religion, and politics on sexual practices and attitudes have generally been reported through such lenses—less so now, but more so in the 1970s. Such is simply another piece of the puzzle, for your contemplation.

Animals as Analogues

As an admittedly ardent evolutionist and scientist, I must begin all this with a brief look at animals generally as analogues to human sexual behavior but also to allow you to see from where we have evolved in our own sexual behaviors (as best we can reconstruct it from historical evidence).

Vaginas and Penises

First, vaginas and penises are generally a good place to start when discussing animal, primate, and human sexuality. Where did they come from? Does every animal have them? Are human beings different from other animals? The answers to this and other such questions require your forbearance for a biological explanation.

Vaginas (by the way, the word "vagina," used for the channel from a female's cervix to the outside of her body, was not in use until the 1680s) provide a path for the internal fertilization of the egg (as opposed to external fertilization practiced especially by fish and frogs). From the female's viewpoint, internal fertilization gives her more control over who does the fertilizing and when. When a female frog or fish jettisons eggs into the water, any number of males can release clouds of sperm over them. With internal fertilization, females have the means to exclude the wrong sort of males. Various kinds of insect, snail, and other invertebrate females have long, complicated vaginas that are defended with flanges, flaps, sphincters, twists, and curves that exclude males of the wrong species. This reduces the likelihood of a female mating with a male of the wrong species and wasting her eggs in producing hybrid and unviable offspring (Forsyth, 2001). This must have been a quite useful adaptation in humans (and our cousins).

As for penises (or *penes*, which is the Latin plural for penis),

> as soon as females evolve[d] some mechanisms to put some distance between their eggs and the males that would fertilize them, a situation is created in which the male placing his sperm closest to the eggs has an advantage. Hence, some males have evolved a penis with penis bone, muscles, ligaments, and expandable pressurized sinuses to support it. (Forsyth, 2001, p. 18)

For human males, however, there is no penis bone (or baculum) now; however, the common ancestor of primates and carnivores had a baculum. It appears that the penis bone has disappeared, and all human males have left is spongy tissue that fills with blood during an erection (Brindle & Opie, 2016). That seems to be enough for us as placental mammals.

Bonobos and Chimpanzees

Next, consider bonobos and chimpanzees. I like bonobos and chimpanzees because the ways that they have organized their communities represent two of the ways that we humans have also chosen to organize ourselves. I'm sure it's just random. Nothing to do with evolution, except that bonobos (*Pan paniscus*) and chimpanzees (*Pan troglodytes*) are our closest genetic relatives sharing 99.6% of our genes (Gibbons, 2012). Bonobos and chimpanzees are considered to be "great apes" and diverged geographically 1 million years ago when the two groups were physically separated by the Congo River in Africa—bonobos lived on the southern side, chimpanzees on the northern. Bonobos are sometimes referred to as "pygmy chimpanzees" because of their smaller stature.

One important difference is their social organization, as bonobos live in female-dominated groups while chimpanzees live in male-dominated groups. Sexually, they are especially different, with chimpanzees' sexual life dominated by high-ranking males monopolizing and guarding females during their estrus cycles (a recurring period of sexual receptivity and fertility around ovulation, popularly known as "heat" such as "that chimpanzee is in heat"). Sexual behavior for bonobos is, however, ubiquitous and is used for many purposes other than simple procreation, such as greeting, social bonding, conflict resolution, reduction of tension, and eliciting social or food benefits. Pair bonding in bonobos can include any age and biological sex combination with frequent same-sex sexual interactions, especially in females (Frandsen, 2016). I'm pretty sure there's a message in there to we humans.

Sex and Prehistory Evidence

The earliest evidence of sexual behavior in animals is a 165-million-year-old artifact—a fossil of two insects (froghoppers) mating—found at a northern China archeological site near Daohugou, Inner Mongolia. (Please pause here and take some time to imagine how such a fossil came to exist.) Researchers believe the pair were in the process of mating when they were killed by toxic gases released by a volcanic eruption. They were then blown by the wind into a lake where they were buried, and ultimately protected, for millions of years. They were found in the sediment, face-to-face, with the male sex organ visibly inserted inside the female (Li et al., 2013).

For humans, the first evidence was in cave paintings of vulvas (external opening of the vagina) from some 37,000 years ago in the Abri Castanet cave in southern France (Balter, 2012). Other ancient depictions of penises, vulvas, and human sexual behavior have been found in China, Egypt, England, France, Germany, Greece, India, Italy, Japan, Mesopotamia (Sumer, Assyria), Persia, Peru, and other places all over the world.

Ancient Philosophical and Religious Contributions

The relationship between religion and sex is a complex one. Sometimes sex was part of the religion. Witness the sacred prostitutes (where money was given) and sacred or ritual sex (where no money was required) found in a number of religions throughout history, usually as part of a fertility rite (Cutner, 1940; Frazer, 1894). Sometimes sex was encouraged by a religion, but only under certain circumstances. According to the Puritans (one of the founding religious sects in the United States), sex was to be limited to marriage between a man and a woman and only for procreation (D'Emilio & Freedman, 1988). And sometimes sex was punished, with certain kinds of sex (especially sodomy and sex with animals) punishable by death (Trexler, 1995). I told you it was complicated.

Taoism and Male Orgasm in Ancient China

Taoism is one of the most ancient philosophical traditions in the world. In ancient China (fourth century BCE), a Taoist tenet was that male orgasm creates an energy "leak." As Lister (2020) explains it, "a key belief within Taoism is seminal vitality (*yuan ching*) and that semen must not leave the body, but be reabsorbed to nourish the brain (*huan jing*)" (p. 101). Sex is good, just don't ejaculate your semen into another person or animal or onto your chest or into a towel. Hold it in. Furthermore, more un-ejaculations are better, beginning with "one act without emission makes the ch'i strong" to "three acts without emission makes all ailments disappear" to "ten acts without emission and one attains the realm of the immortals" (Wile, 1992, p. 93). This appears to be a partial analogue to the Roman Catholic act of penis withdrawal from the vagina (also known as coitus interruptus) as an acceptable act of birth control. While both practices have physical rewards (the former for the preservation of vital energies, the latter to prevent the creation of a fetus), there appear to be physiological repercussions for the testes of the male (i.e., "blue balls" and exquisite pain). Furthermore, this does not account for the small amount of the seminal liquid that precedes an ejaculation nor for the concept of "wet dreams" whereby the male has a dream of having sex and ejaculating and wakes up the next morning with evidence of an ejaculation in his underwear.

Pre-Christian Indigenous Culture

"Guilt" has a curious history. The kind of guilt we are talking about here is the psychological, not the legal, as in "I feel guilty when I eat too much." For many Indigenous peoples around the world, sexual behavior was simply a part of human life similar to the pre-apple Adam and Eve story. Rarely did most native languages have words for such guilt.

D'Emilio and Freedman (1988) reported on the sexual practices of Native Americans in precolonial times as follows:

> Most native American people did not associate either nudity or sexuality with sin. Although sexuality might be embedded within a spiritual context—as in the case of puberty, menstrual seclusion, or the visionary call to cross-dress—sexual intercourse and reproductive functions rarely evoked shame or guilt for Indian men and women. (p. 7)

Furthermore, D'Emilio and Freedman (1988) commented on what they referred to as the "most striking contrast" between the European Christians and the native people as the

> relative absence of sexual conflict among native Americans due in part to their different cultural attitudes toward both property and sexuality. Indians easily resolved marital discord by simply separating and forming new unions without penalty, stigma, or property settlement. In cultures in which one could not "own" another person's sexuality, prostitution—the sale of sex—did not exist prior to the arrival of European settlers. (p. 8)

And finally, D'Emilio and Freedman (1988) described the Europeans' view of the sexual practices of the native peoples in this way: "In every region (of the colonies) in which Europeans and Indians came into contact, however, the Europeans, applying the standards of the Christian tradition, judged the sexual lives of the native peoples as 'savage'" (p. 6).

It is said that history is written by the conquerors, and this history always reminds me of the Christian biblical morality tale of Adam and Eve, with the Native Americans as the innocent human beings and the Europeans playing, of course, God.

Traditional Indigenous Cultures and Missionaries

In the major religions of the world, not all are required by their creed to take their beliefs and spread them all over the world, but three are, in particular, Buddhism, Islam, and Christianity. They are called the "missionary religions" (Sharma, 2012).

First Missionaries in the Americas

Trexler (1995) wrote of Hernan Cortes and his Spanish explorers who first landed near present-day Veracruz (translated from the Spanish as "True Cross") in Mexico and in 1519 wrote to the Spanish King Charles V urging him to request permission from the pope to punish the natives that they had encountered as

> we have learned and have been informed that they are doubtless all sodomites and engage in that abominable sin. . . . The Iberians (Spanish) . . . claimed the right to conquer native American males once they demonstrated that the latter practiced "sodomy," by which they usually meant homosexual behavior, among themselves. This "nefarious," "unmentionable" and "abominable sin" was, it was said, "against nature." (p. 1)

Informed by their church (Roman Catholic), they believed that the only good, acceptable, and natural sexual behavior was procreative sex—that is, where the possible outcome was a human fetus. All (and I do mean all) other behaviors, whether with oneself or with another person (opposite sex or same sex), were considered bad and unnatural and, therefore, a sin. This would include masturbation, fellatio, cunnilingus, frottage, bondage, or any of these sexual behaviors between two people of the same sex. Such were the beliefs of the "enlightened" Spanish conquistadores about these "uncivilized savages," the Aztecs. By the way, the Aztecs were known for their books (codices), art and architecture (including grand pyramids and massive stone sculptures), an impressive water management system, five-level social hierarchies, artisan guilds, and a well-developed polytheist and animist religion, with a total population of 1 million. Two years after the Cortes "discovery" of this civilization, the Aztecs were destroyed and enslaved to work in the gold and silver mines of the Spanish, as they did not have the guns (first recorded use of gun was in Europe in 1364, whereas first Chinese "fire lances" appeared in China in the 10th century) or the domesticated horses that the Spanish brought with them.

Missionaries in the United States

The year 1801 saw the arrival into Native American lands of the Protestant missionaries—Moravian, Presbyterian, Baptist, Methodist, and Quaker. The Cherokees and other Native American tribes wanted to learn to read and write, and the missionaries were eager to provide such education, using their Bibles as the medium of instruction (Mails, 1996). As Mankiller and Wallis (1993) described it,

> Early on in the 19th century, some of our (Cherokee) people's spiritual needs were ministered to by various white missionaries, starting with a small group of Moravians who established a mission in Georgia in 1801. Other white Christian missionaries—Presbyterians, Baptist, Methodist, and Quaker—all anxious to "save the savages," soon moved into our homeland. They built churches and mission schools where, in most instances, academic lessons were supplemented with an abundance of hymn singing, public prayers, and scripture readings. (pp. 79–80)

Wilma Mankiller was principal chief of the Cherokee Nation of Oklahoma (the largest of the Cherokee tribes and second largest of all tribes in the United States) from 1985 to 1995 (Mankiller & Wallis, 1993). She spoke eloquently in her family biography about the role of the Christian missionaries and federal government in trying to destroy the traditional culture of the Cherokee people:

> Back in the bad old days, the BIA (Bureau of Indian Affairs) representatives who maintained boarding schools such as (the) Sequoyah (School) would go hundreds of miles and return with native children. The philosophy, reflecting an errant missionary zeal, was to get native children away from their families, their elders, their tribes, their language, their heritage. They isolated native children so they would forget their culture. The boarding-school concept was simply another way for the federal government to deal with what its officials always called "the Indian problem." After first trying to wipe all of us off the face of the earth with violence, they attempted to isolate us on reservations or, in the case of many people as the Cherokees, place us in an area that the government called Indian Territory. All the while, they systematically conjured up policies to kill our culture. So the federal government rounded up Indian youngsters and forced them to attend boarding schools whether they wanted to or not. This was true for most tribes, not just the Cherokees. (Mankiller & Wallis, 1993, p. 7)

At Sequoyah School, just south of Tahlequah, the capital of the Cherokee Nation of Oklahoma, Mankiller's father and his younger sister were forbidden to speak their native language (called Cherokee or Tsalagi). According to Mankiller and Wallis (1993), even though they could not speak a word of English when they first entered the school, when they tried to talk to each other in their native language, they were whipped repeatedly. The whole idea behind these boarding schools, whether they were government-operated, like Sequoyah School, or a religious operation, was "to acculturate native people into the mainstream of white society and, at the same time, destroy their sense of self. The boarding school officials hoped to make the 'little Indians' into 'ladies and gentlemen'" (Mankiller & Wallis, 1993, p. 8). So the teachers cut the Cherokee children's hair short and did not allow them to utter one word of their native language. Oftentimes, all visits to family and friends back home were denied. The idea was to civilize the "heathen" children in the boarding schools by forcing them to leave everything behind that related to their native culture, heritage, history, and language. "In short, there was a full-scale attempt at deracination—the uprooting or destruction of a race and its culture (Mankiller & Wallis, 1993, p. 8).

Perdue (1989) reported how the missionaries and federal government worked hand in hand to eliminate the Cherokee culture. In 1881, Quakers opened schools in North Carolina, which were taken over by the U.S. government in 1890. Through these day schools and boarding schools, first the Quakers and then the U.S. government "attempted to eradicate the traditional Cherokee practices and beliefs among their students" (Perdue, 1989, p. 87). Students were forbidden to speak their native language, and the teachers washed the student's mouth out with soap if they were caught speaking Cherokee. Through these and other measures, the U.S. government attempted to destroy the Cherokee culture and force the Cherokee to assimilate. *Hayv* (Cherokee for "I have nothing else to say about this").

The Sin Hierarchy

These European missionaries' sexual beliefs came from somewhere. Beginning in the Middle Ages (476–1453)—the time between the fall of the Roman empire and the beginning of early modern Europe—theologians and Christian philosophers of this time, such as Thomas Aquinas, Roger Bacon, and John Wycliffe, began to draw stark religious lines for sexual behavior. Wycliffe emphasized that the divine law was also a natural law and developed the concept of "perversion" as in "perverting divine law." William Derham (1713), the canon of Windsor in England, wrote that God had created nature and that everything in the universe had a natural order to it. A perversion was then used to denote an aberration or a deviation from a divine norm. Therefore, any act that violated the laws of God was considered a perversion (de Block & Adriaens, 2013). As described by Peakman (2009),

> "Perversion" emerged from a complicated interwoven understanding of nature, theology, the understanding of man's evil and the concept of sin. Within this structure, people's perception of the world at large was based around their comprehension of the social order of things—the nature order of the world was seen to be ordained by God and any act which upset this order was not merely deemed unnatural but seen to be against God's will. Disruption to that social order was regarded with suspicion and dealt with either by the Church, the State, or the Community. In other words, in England during the early modern period, the boundaries of acceptable sexual behavior were set by religion, the law, and tradition, the latter two aspects emanating from the rigid framework of the first. Outside of these boundaries, certain sexual behaviours or acts were deemed to be unnatural, and these acts made for "perversion." (p. 10)

Then, as an adjunct to perversion and in keeping with their "divine law equals natural law" construct, these theologians and philosophers classified sexual vices as either *natural* or *unnatural.* According to this schema, there was a hierarchy of sin where the sexual vices in line with nature (e.g., adultery, rape, incest) were bad and certainly sins, but the unnatural vices (e.g., masturbation [self-sex], sodomy [anal sex], and bestiality [sex between a human and a nonhuman animal]) were the worst sins because they could not result in conception (Oosterhuis, 2000). These sins were then quickly turned into laws because there was no separation between religions and the government at that time with, for example, punishment by death for sodomy. The concept of a separation of church and state was not to be realized until these revolutionary ideas were included in the U.S. Constitution by James Madison and Thomas Jefferson in the 1770s, presaged by the writings of John Locke in the early 1700s.

The Medicalization of Sin

By the mid to late 1700s, there was a consensus by the medical practitioners that "masturbation and other kinds of nonreproductive sexual behavior could cause serious health hazards to both body and mind" (de Block & Adriaens, 2013, p. 277). This conceptualization began to take such behavior out of the religious arena and move it into the medical and more scientific arena. And even though pathological anatomists saw sexual perversions as diseases of the genitals, caused by an anatomical abnormality (as they were of course looking for an organic disease/cause), they were moving society forward historically.

Looking for a scientific schema to understand these phenomena, Franz Joseph Gall (1835), a German neuroanatomist, developed the study of *phrenology*, whereby the physical bumps on the skull of a person were used to predict mental traits. This was just another bump on the road to truly understanding what makes the world work, but someone had to begin the journey and Gall started it all. Influenced by such "organological" (Gall's dive into the brain started with his theory of organology) and "phrenological" theories, the focus moved to a link between sexual desire and sexual instinct (then thought to be a reproductive instinct/drive or an instinct for the propagation of the species). Perversions were thought to be more and more a functional disease of this instinct. The logic goes something like this: Since this unnatural and not reproduction-focused sexual behavior is not specifically directed toward procreation, there must be something wrong with the person. Later on, mental health professionals would recognize a need or drive toward pleasure and play—that is, needs that are more process-oriented than the strictly outcome-oriented need for procreation. We've come a long way, baby.

From Instincts to the *Psychopathia Sexualis*

In the early 1800s, psychiatry as a medical discipline would develop, and French psychiatrists would replace the clergy as authorities in sexual behavior as the French government began to pay them for their work with the mental hygiene of the French people (de Block & Adriaens, 2013). Religion would continue to play a large role in determining what was acceptable sexual behavior, but not as the primary source for determining what was legal and what had to be punished. The idea of instincts in general and of a sexual instinct in particular would be debated and advanced as the foundation of psychology and psychiatry (Ellenberger, 1970; James, 1887), but while this concept of instincts would not survive, the idea of sex playing an important role in human life did.

From this new medicalization came the disease constructs at the foundation of psychiatry and the first classification system for sexual diseases or psychopathologies. Heinrich Kaan, a Russian physician and personal physician to the czar, wrote the first *Psychopathia Sexualis* (1844/2016), a book that provided a framework to reinterpret the Christian sins as neurological/psychiatric diseases. Later in this chapter, there is a discussion on masturbation and the work of the French physician Samuel-Auguste Tissot (1758/1781) about the "maladies produced by masturbation," which laid the groundwork for masturbation as a disease that produces physiological symptoms of ill health. Kaan came from that tradition and believed that masturbation was the root of all sexual diseases and disordered sexual behavior. It's not much different than the religious conceptualizations as it starts with the idea that only sex that has as its goal procreation is good and healthy. All other sexual behavior, especially if it involved fantasies, is bad or diseased.

From Punishment to Cure

Charles Darwin's *Origin of the Species by Means of Natural Selection* (1859) presented a new way of looking at animals and plants on our planet. Influenced by Darwin's more scientific approach, Paul Moreau de Tours (1880), a French psychiatrist, wrote in *Des aberations du sens genesique* (*On the Aberration of the Reproductive Sense*) that the sexual instinct was a sixth sense that could be disturbed, like the other senses, without affecting the functioning of the other (mental) organs. According to Moreau de Tours and many other 19th-century psychiatrists, the "sexual instinct" could be disturbed in different ways, suggesting the categories of too strong (augmentation), too weak (dimunition), or totally absent (abolition). These first three categories were just for "normal" sex—that is, sex only for procreation. Acknowledging that there were cases where sex was not for procreation per se, and as a nod to the power of the religious groups of the time, Moreau de Tours offered a fourth category that included the sexual perversions, a class of pathologies of the sexual instinct, characterized by deviation of this instinct from its natural aim (which was, of course, procreation).

The next *Psychopathia Sexualis* (1886/1930) by Richard von Krafft-Ebing marked a turning point in the understanding and medicalization of sexual deviance. Even though Krafft-Ebing continued to echo "other psychiatrists by emphasizing the role of masturbation in the etiologies of perversion and other forms of insanity" (de Block & Adriaens, 2013, p. 280), his book was the first thoroughly comprehensive medical account of sexual deviance buttressed by a large number of case studies containing extensive quotations of the patients (Oosterhuis, 2000). Most important was his approach to those who were considered perverts by the religions of the time, as such individuals were spoken of as persons who had turned to sin and evil. Krafft-Ebing "spoke of the different perversions as (simply) different ways of being a person" (de Block & Adriaens, 2013, p. 280). He differentiated between "perversities" and "perversions"—for example, sadistic behavior was a perversity (the vice, maybe a mere immorality or a crime), whereas sadism was a perversion (the disease). After all, medical professionals could treat a disease. The theory was that because disease was the underlying cause of the behavior, if the disease was treated, the behavior would diminish or disappear. Conceptualizing the sin or crime (as a behavior) as distinguishable from the disease (in the mind) was another step in this progression from sin to difference.

Sex and the Scientific Method

Science has played a critically important role in this history of sexual behavior from the pseudoscientific writings of Tissot, to the clinical observations of Freud, to the science of Kinsey and Hooker. Another way to look at all this is from the more subjective with greater error processes of Tissot, to the still subjective with increasing reliability of Freud, to the more objective and still greater reliability of Kinsey's and Hooker's social scientific studies. The bottom line is that we have been steadily, if slowly, moving toward greater accuracy in our scientific processes. This was as a direct result of the contribution of the scientific method, as documented by Sir Francis Bacon (1561–1626)—observe the world, ask a question based on your observations, develop hypotheses, collect data, analyze data, draw conclusions, and use your results to make new hypotheses. Such a structured process allows for greater accuracy in findings because it tries to control errors that creep in and that may reduce accuracy.

The inherent difficulties of such studies lie in us. As human beings, we are imperfect—a simple truth. And our methods of gathering data are also imperfect, and our perceptions are refracted through the imperfect lens of our brain and our memory. Such imperfections create error, and error is the limiter of accurate findings.

Here are a couple of examples.

Observation is a data collection technique that requires one person observing others and recording what they see. For example, we look at the Samoa studies by anthropologist Margaret Mead (1928). She visited Samoa, an island in the central South Pacific Ocean, to research the culture and traditions of the inhabitants. She lived with the people there and recorded her personal observations in a journal. Upon returning home, she published books discussing her findings but was criticized for her data collection process, whereby she became a "participant observer" who simply by her presence there could change the dynamics of the people she was observing, even if only a little.

Survey is another type of data collection technique, whereby a written list of questions is prepared for the participants, who record their own responses. Errors can arise from the imperfect recall of participants, from the way that the questions are written, and in the analysis and interpretation of the results through techniques of statistical analysis. Generally, however, the larger the number of people who respond, the more confidence there is in the accuracy of the findings. That counts as truth in this method.

Masturbation, Tissot, and Kellogg's Corn Flakes

Samuel-Auguste Tissot (1758/1781), a French physician, wrote *L'onanisme: Dissertation sur les maladies produites par la masturbation* (*Onanism: A Treatise on the Maladies Produced by Masturbation*). His medical observations on male masturbation set off a crusade against "self-pleasuring" that lasted for over 200 years. Tissot did not study women. He wrote that, since semen was a vital bodily fluid (*liqueur seminale*) and that this manual manipulation of the male sexual organ was the easiest way to lose this precious fluid, then "excessive masturbation, nocturnal emissions (wet dreams), and coitus interruptus (withdrawal without ejaculation) caused the body to simply waste away" (Lister, 2020, p. 107). Physicians accepted Tissot's writing as truth, and in the 1800s, some were warning that masturbation could lead to death.

Such beliefs even carried over to the founder of the great American breakfast cereal, John Harvey Kellogg, a physician who believed that plain cereals (like his cornflakes, no doubt) could deter lust and that to stop "habitual" masturbation in women all you had to do was perform a chemical burn of the clitoris with carbolic acid (Kellogg, 1887). Such mutilation of a woman's sexual organs was certainly excessive (barbaric) by later standards, but when you realize that he was against "race mixing"—promoting eugenics for a better White race by weeding out Blacks and other people whom he considered "inferior"—and in favor of sterilizing "mentally defective persons" (i.e., the developmentally disabled), it makes sense. Must be where the idea of a "nut" originated. Sadly, he was quite dangerous as he served on the Michigan Board of Health for a time where he helped establish a eugenics registry to keep a list of those who were considered less intelligent, less beautiful, and less "white" and should, therefore, not be allowed to procreate (Leung, 2020).

Sexual Energy and Freud

Sigmund Freud was an Austrian physician (neurologist) whose entire theory of psychoanalysis was built around sexual energy. His theories were based on his clinical practice in Austria where women comprised two thirds of his published cases; 90% of his total patient group were in the 20–44 age range, predominantly from the upper socioeconomic classes; and 95% were given some type of "neurotic" diagnosis (hysteria, phobia, anxiety, or obsessional neurosis; Fisher & Greenberg, 1977).

Freud's groundbreaking work in psychiatry was founded on the role of the "sexual instinct" in human beings. He, however, used the word "sexual" in a more general way, representing not so much a specific sexual behavior but more any pleasurable thought or behavior. In this way, he moved sex into a prominent role in his theory of psychosexual development with five ordered stages—oral, anal, phallic, latent, and genital—with each of these stages involving a specific conflict that requires resolution before the individual can move on to the next stage with its own conflicts. Energy, specifically sexual energy, was required to achieve resolution of the conflict of each stage.

As can be seen, Freud spoke frankly and specifically about sex both in his theories and in his discussion of his clinical cases in his lectures. Havelock Ellis (1939), one of the founders of the field of sexology, wrote of Freud's contributions to sexual attitudes that

> Freud cannot be said even to have attacked conventional sexual morality. He pointed out some of the evils which it involves, but he can scarcely be said ever to have advocated definitely any revolutionary moral change. In that respect he preserved the correct attitude of the conventional physician. But in the matter of expression and speech his attitude was completely revolutionary. In this way he shocked alike those who viewed sex as very sacred and those who viewed it as very indecent. In a simple, precise, and detailed manner he described the sex phenomena presented by his patients, without attenuation or apology, but as a matter of course. This had never been done before in medical literature. (p. 310)

Freud facilitated the open discussion of sex in both the medical and psychological professions of the time and moved the discussion of sex away from the medicalization of sin to a pleasure focus, from a discussion of sex on the outskirts of society to a central focus. As Ellis (1939) wrote,

> There is thus really no doubt about Freud's specific contribution to the changed attitude to sex which marks our time. Whatever we may ultimately come to think of psychoanalysis as a technical method, it supplied an immense emphasis to the general recognition and acceptance of the place of sex in life. (p. 317)

Finally, Freud had some valuable if somewhat contradictory historical theories that explicitly involved sex. He stated that civilization came about due to the sublimation of these sexual instincts:

> We believe that civilization has been built up . . . by sacrifices in gratification of the primitive impulses, [that is] the sacrifice of [a person's] instinctive pleasures for the common good. . . . [T]hey are in this way sublimated, that is to say, their energy is turned aside from its sexual goal and diverted toward other ends, no longer sexual and socially more valuable. (Freud, 1917/1943, p. 132)

Yet, Freud also believed that unsuccessful attempts at repression of the sexual instinct were the cause of neurosis. He seemed to be able to live with this contradiction, however, whereas some of his followers were not—especially Wilhelm Reich in *The Sexual Revolution* (1962) and *The Function of the Orgasm* (1961), both of which are good reading if you are a psychodynamic devotee or simply as a critique of Freud's work.

Scientific Method, Sex, and Kinsey

Alfred Charles Kinsey was a biologist and sexologist who founded the Kinsey Institute for Research in Sex, Gender, and Reproduction (now the Institute for Sex Research) at Indiana University in 1947. His greatest contribution to the study of sexual behavior was his application of the principles of science to this research. Gone were the subjective observations and interpretations of previous writers such as Freud, Tissot, and Kellogg in favor of individual research interviews with his sample of 5,300 males and 6,000 females over a 15-year period.

He also developed a scale (commonly referred to as the Kinsey Scale) to measure the sexual behavior of human beings. Kinsey et al. (1948) wrote that

> males do not represent two discrete populations, heterosexual and homosexual. The world is not to be divided into sheep and goats. It is a fundamental of taxonomy that nature rarely deals with discrete categories. . . . An individual may be assigned a position on this scale for each period in his life. (p. 639) . . . A seven-point scale comes nearer to showing the many gradations that actually exist. (p. 656)

This Likert-type scale measured a continuum of sexual behavior ranging from 0 for *exclusively heterosexual* to 6 for *exclusively homosexual.* The midpoint of the scale, 3, represented *equally heterosexual and homosexual.*

Some statisticians criticized Kinsey's sample selection process, but even after sample biases were corrected and statistical analyses rerun, it was found that none of Kinsey's original findings were significantly affected by such a bias (Gebhard & Johnson, 1979). Nevertheless, his two seminal scholarly works on sexual behavior in males and females respectively (Kinsey et al., 1948, 1953) were both immediate best-sellers even though they were quite controversial at that time for their open discussion of subjects that were considered taboo, including homosexuality; the clitoris as location of female sexual orgasm; and the frequency of marital sex, extramarital sex, sadomasochism, fetishism, and much more. According to de Block and Adriaens (2013), Kinsey

> believed his reports indicated that many supposedly deviant sexual practices were actually quite common in the American population. This statistical argument was complemented by a biological argument: Because most of the perversions can also be found in nonhuman animals, it makes no sense to assume that the perversions violate some natural norm. (p. 284)

As to his "it occurs in nature, so it must be natural" argument, this reflected the scientific work of Konrad Lorenz and other zoologists and ethologists.

Kinsey and his associates flung open the doors to the bedrooms of the United States and shined the brightest of bright klieg light into a place where no one knew what really happened and . . . the world would forever be changed.

Gay Men and Hooker

Through her pioneering study in 1957 comparing two nonclinical samples of heterosexual men and gay men, Evelyn Hooker reported that homosexuality was not a mental disorder as there were no detectable differences between gay and heterosexual men in terms of emotional adjustment (Hooker, 1957).

A psychologist, Hooker gathered psychological test profiles on 60 men (30 gay and 30 straight), matching the two groups for age, IQ, and education. The gay men were members of the Los Angeles chapter of the Mattachine Society. The tests used were the Thematic Apperception Test, the Make-a-Picture-Story test, and the Rorschach inkblot test. Hooker had three prominent experts in these instruments examine the randomized profiles and attempt to determine which men were emotionally disturbed and which men were gay and which were not. She found that the experts' ability to accurately predict the sexual orientation of the men was no better than chance and that the two groups did not differ significantly in adjustment ratings (Hooker, 1957; Pope, 2020).

Hooker (1957) found that

> Some homosexuals may be very ordinary individuals, indistinguishable, except in sexual pattern, from ordinary individuals who are heterosexual. Or—and I do not know whether this would be more or less difficult to accept—that some may be quite superior individuals, not only devoid of pathology (unless one insists that homosexuality itself is a sign of pathology) but also functioning at a superior level. (p. 29)

Simply doing a study like this in the 1950s in the United States was groundbreaking, and having such a study funded by the National Institutes of Health was unheard of, but Hooker's findings were a shock to the mythology (and purveyors of that myth) that had permeated popular and psychoanalytic culture for decades. Her work was the evidentiary piece of the puzzle that led to the eventual removal of homosexuality from the *Diagnostic and Statistical Manual of Mental Disorders* (*DSM*), published by the American Psychiatric Association (APA), and to the overturning of all the antigay laws in the United States and beyond. The world is still a work in progress, but the progression is steadily toward that outcome.

Sex With Masters and Johnson

In the late 1950s to the 1990s, William H. Masters and Virginia E. Johnson led a research team that pioneered the diagnosis and treatment of sexual disorders and dysfunctions (Masters & Johnson, 2022). Their work began in 1957 in the Department of Obstetrics and Gynecology at Washington University in St. Louis, Missouri, and continued from 1964 at their Reproductive Biology Research Foundation (renamed the Masters and Johnson Institute in 1978).

Kinsey and colleagues at the Kinsey Institute had taken the great leap into the study of sexual behavior, but their study was based on what individuals told them in a one-on-one interview. The next step in the study of sexual behavior was to observe and to measure the physiological responses of two human beings engaged in actual sexual behavior.

Masters and Johnson (1966) reported on what happens to the male and female body at every phase of sexual intercourse and masturbation. In fact, they even provided the names we now use for these four phases of total body sexual response: excitement, plateau, orgasm, and resolution. Although these sexual stages are fundamentally the same in both females and males, there are some relatively minor differences that are detailed more in Chapters 3 and 4 in that book.

Masters and Johnson also studied sexual dysfunction in couples, but did not use the same methods, as there was no observation of sexual activity between the couples. Instead, they devised a brief (2-week) psychotherapy approach whereby a male/female therapist team worked with the couple using a verbal therapy approach. They also studied the sexual responses of individuals who were aging as well as same-sex male couples and female couples (Masters & Johnson, 1979).

The Rise of European and American Sexology

The study of sexuality should not be left only to psychiatrists and other physicians or even to psychologists, counselors, and other mental health professionals. The medical model with its disease focus has limited the study of sexual behavior to the problems, rarely the joys (Comfort, 1972). At the beginning of the 20th century, historians, biologists, anthropologists, and other scholars began to think seriously about sexuality.

In many ways, it all began in Germany with German physician and sexologist Magnus Hirschfeld, the founder of the first sexology journal (*Jahrbuch fur sexuelle Zwischenstufen*), the Institute for Sexual Science (1919–1933), and the Scientific-Humanitarian Committee in Berlin. He worked tirelessly to promote the "progressive science" of sexology. Henry Havelock Ellis was an English physician, writer, progressive intellectual, and social reformer and a contemporary of Hirschfeld. They were the intellectual founders of the new discipline of sexology in Europe.

They proposed that the new study of sexuality had great potential for good, claiming that "sexology should have a central role in the politics of sex reform" (de Block & Adriaens, 2013, p. 283). Their focus especially was on the causes and history of homosexuality with their political advocacy focused on reforming the laws concerning homosexuality, especially Paragraph 175, which criminalized sexual acts between two men in Germany (Mildenberger, 2007).

Politics of Sexual Deviance to Sexual Difference

As previously discussed, there are examples throughout history of how a sexual behavior that was once judged aberrant societally (many times by some type of religion) and made illegal because of that (by a government) comes to be better understood, tolerated, accepted, and certainly then legal. In these transitions, many people's lives are changed or destroyed whether socially, vocationally, or financially.

Deviation and Normalcy

These academic statistical terms "deviation" and "normalcy" have been used and adopted by popular culture as descriptors for humans at the margins of society, such as "you deviate (or deviant)" and "you're not normal."

In their purely academic statistical form, they are short forms of "standard deviation" and "normal distribution." I'll not go into a protracted treatise on their statistical use, but simply put, both are measures of how far an individual response is from the mathematical mean (or average) of responses for a group of people. You might say that a person's response is one standard deviation above the mean or two standard deviations below the mean when you are trying to describe how far it is from this mean.

A normal distribution (also known popularly as the "bell [or bell-shaped] curve") is an effect that we see with many types of human data—that is, it occurs in nature time and time again. Examples include the heights of adults, blood pressure, shoe sizes, and many more. For a normal distribution, any data point in any data set is "normal"; the only distinction is how far away from the group mean is this data point. People who use "deviate," "deviancy," and "abnormal" as epithets are misusing these terms. Scholars are more circumspect and precise in their uses.

The Sexual Liberation Movements of the 1960s and 1970s

Beginning in the 1960s in the United States, it seemed like "the history of civilization is the history of a long warfare between the dangerous and powerful forces of the id, and the various systems of taboos and inhibitions . . . erected to control them" (Taylor, 1973, p. 23). Eight great social movements, along with some popular nonfiction, rose up and led the way.

These eight great social movements were the civil rights, antiwar, counterculture, women's, gay and lesbian liberation, environmental, migrant workers' rights, and students' rights movements (Taylor, 1973). It was all quite intersectional as one begat the other which begat another and so on, but they all started with the struggle for basic civil rights for African Americans. These uprisings of and their concomitant political changes were intensively linked with an increasing density of American voices speaking and acting together, as one.

Like all changes in the world, it is rarely one single event or issue or person that creates change (although we are told in our history books that this is so). Instead, it is an intersection of events and issues and people that drive these changes. The forces that drove the changes in sexual attitudes and behaviors were (a) the development of the birth control pill that enabled women's control over their own bodies and reproductive cycles; (b) the Stonewall Rebellion where gay people for the first time fought back against police for their right to simply exist in the world; (c) Woodstock where music and youth birthed a counterculture to the dominant consumer-driven culture of the times; (d) LSD and marijuana allowed young people to experience the world in different ways; (e) the military draft and Vietnam War asked young men to fight for a war they did not start and felt was immoral; (f) the rise of consumer boycotts for political aims including grapes, Coors beer, divestiture of South African companies' stocks (with apartheid (social separation of Blacks and Whites) as the driving force for that movement), and many others; and (g) advancements in technology through computers and worldwide communication that made the world a less isolated and much smaller place.

Presaged by the popular success of Kinsey et al.'s scientific books on sexual behavior of men (1948) and women (1953), popular literature began to see an awakening of interest in books openly discussing sexual behavior. Here's a sampling, beginning with Helen Gurley Brown's *Sex and the Single Girl* (1962), Betty Friedan's *The Feminine Mystique* (1963), Germaine Greer's *The Female Eunuch* (1970), Alex Comfort's *The Joy of Sex* (1972), Shere Hite's *The Hite Report* (1976), and Charles Silverstein and Edmund White's *The Joy of Gay Sex* (1977) all the way up to Peggy Orenstein's *Girls & Sex* (2017) and *Boys & Sex* (2020) and Laurie Mintz's *Becoming Cliterate* (2018). Following Kinsey, several of these books made or topped *The New York Times* bestseller list, some remaining on that list for many weeks. It appears that people have an insatiable interest in reading about sexual behaviors and potentially finding out how they compare to other people in what they want to do sexually and how.

Even the writers of advice columns such as *Dear Abby* and *Ann Landers*, which were published regularly in U.S. newspapers, began to artfully and openly address the sexual problems that their readers brought to them. More recently, sex advice columns and radio/TV programs have arisen as a specialized offshoot of the "old school" more general columns of Abby and Ann. Beginning in 1980, Ruth Westheimer on her sex advice radio show "Good Sex! With Dr. Ruth Westheimer" dispensed sexual knowledge in a grandmotherly casual tone that was quite disarming. Anna Radakovich's sex column in the magazine *Details* from 1990 to 1999 set the standard for these modernist columns, and beginning in 1991, the "Savage Love" syndicated column by Dan Savage has met the public's need to know with his witty and provocative take on his readers' sex questions.

In terms of sexual behavior, this was the final attitudinal shift from a purely procreational sexual behavior to a more recreational one, from a focus on sex as acceptable only within a marriage covenant to an acceptance of premarital sex and living together before marriage to see if there was compatibility, from gay people as hidden perverts and sinners to gay people who were next door and living their lives openly. All of this was a shift away from the control of sex by religious organizations and their institutionally enforced morality to a more individual morality informed but not regulated by the ethics and mores of the society, family, and religious institutions. It is important to note that we are talking here about a change in emphasis, not that such positions had never been seen prior to the 1960s. These ways of looking at the world rose to more prominent if not popular majority roles within the American culture during this time.

While much of this section has focused on these social movements in the United States, it is important to note that many of these American social movements had their analogues in European, Asian, Latin American, and other countries around the world.

From Disease to Difference

The historical step from the medical disease model to an *individual differences* model of sexual behavior was taken through a protracted struggle in American society from

1969 to present day to achieve freedom from antigay laws and discrimination in employment, housing, and public transportation. There may be no better example of this struggle than the fight for the removal of "homosexuality" from the *DSM*, the APA's handbook for diagnosing mental illnesses. This process had all the excitement of a Tom Cruise or Bruce Willis movie, and it was even more important because it was real, affecting people's lives, careers, relationships, health care, and more. To quote from Kimmel and Browning (1999),

> In the 1950s and 1960s homosexuality was often seen as an abnormal mental condition, treated by hormones, electroconvulsive shock, psychotherapy, psychoanalysis, and institutionalization. Published scientific articles were based on clinical, institutionalized, or prison samples. Same-sex behavior was illegal in most states, and was actively used as a reason to discharge military personnel and to deny security clearance for government employees. During this period Sen. Joseph McCarthy and J. Edgar Hoover, director of the FBI, persecuted supposed communists and "sexual deviates." Homosexuals were sought out and exposed, resulting in scandal, jeopardizing employment, and blacklisting. Police raids of gay bars were commonplace events, and often the names of those arrested were published in newspapers, leading to loss of employment and reputation. (p. 129)

It sounds bad but it can never sound as bad as it actually was for those who lived during that period. That was the context in which the movement for lesbian, gay, bisexual, and transgender (LGBT) civil rights arose. Out of that darkness, of that individual, familial, community, and social pain, came a new social and political movement in the United States of America; however, it took a riot, a rebellion, an uprising on the streets of New York City to galvanize that movement.

The Stonewall Rebellion of 1969

The Stonewall Inn was a gay bar in Greenwich Village. The Stonewall uprising in 1969 is considered by many to mark the beginning of the modern LGBT civil rights movements. The Stonewall uprising was a protracted struggle in which the LGBT community in New York City fought back against what had become regular, city-sanctioned harassment by the police. The spontaneous 6-night conflict gained national attention and inspired a new movement for full equality and acceptance. It was led by Puerto Rican and African American trans people and gay street youth who stood up to the police who raided the bar in the early morning of June 28, 1969. And for 6 nights LGBT people held the streets. Sylvia Rivera and Marsha Johnson led the stand for these rights. The action would end, but the world would never be the same.

The Three Pillars of Oppression: Sanity, Legality, and Morality

As a result of the Stonewall Rebellion, gay mainstream and left-leaning activists began meeting and organizing (Bronski, 2011; Hirshman, 2012; Kimmel & Browning, 1999). The three pillars of LGBT people's oppression in the United States were mental health policy as represented by psychiatry's *DSM*, antisodomy laws that were being selectively used against LGBT people, and religious institutions that framed their arguments in moral terms (Pope, 2012).

A consensus emerged from these meetings that a foundational element of the problem lay in the definition of "homosexuality" as a mental illness. This was a theme that had been consistently raised by conservatives, moderates, and even liberals as laws were being considered that would prohibit discrimination again LGBT people in employment, housing, and other life areas. Of course, this was a ruse to cover moral qualms, but it was consistently raised in these policy discussions with politicians and others in government.

As a result of such discussions, a strategy was formulated by gay rights activists who were led by Frank Kameny and Barbara Gittings, and carried throughout the mental health professions by LGBT professionals in their respective professions, to remove the term homosexuality from the *DSM* (Bayer, 1981; Drescher & Merlino, 2003; Kimmel & Browning, 1999; Minton, 2002).

Gittings, who began her lesbian and gay activist journey in the American Library Association, said it this way:

> It is difficult to explain to anyone who didn't live through that time how much homosexuality was under the thumb of psychiatry. The sickness label was an albatross around the neck of our early gay rights groups—it infected all our work on other issues. Anything we said on our behalf could be dismissed as "That's just your sickness talking." The sickness label was used to justify discrimination, especially in employment, and especially by our own government. (Drescher & Merlino, 2003, p. xv)

This change was seen as the critical first step on the first rung in a long ladder that would eventually lead to full equality for all LGBT people. This was seen by that far-sighted group of LGBT leaders, as the lynchpin of an entire strategy to change the attitudes and laws regarding LGBT people in the United States. But this first change was critical to the entire strategy (Hirshman, 2012; Minton, 2002; Mondimore, 1996; Pope, 2012).

The Great Strategy Arises

The central strategy that LGBT mental health professionals in their various professions have employed is *facting*—that is, using science to combat inaccurate portrayals of LGBT people.

Why has this strategy been so successful? It has been successful because it flows from the culture of the mental health professions itself. The strategy was not an alien, outside force seeking to annihilate all mental health organizations as the enemy and oppressor. In fact, annihilating these professions would be antithetical to this strategy. The culture of the mental health professions embraces science as a core and primary component of its professional identity. Facting lies at the heart and soul of this identity and that is why it has been successful. It should be noted, however, that it does not work if the data are just plain bad. It only works because the data have been compelling, methodologically sound, and reasonable, and because they stand up to scrutiny. That is the beauty of science.

The Zap as Tactic

Facting tactics include zapping, boycotting, building relationships, developing policy, participating in amicus briefs for the courts, and participating at all levels of the association (i.e., participating so that your voice is heard). *Zapping* is a tactic developed during the great civil rights movements of the 1960s in the United States. It is an active but nonviolent form of confrontation. It can take many different forms, but some of the classic interventions are attending a meeting of your adversaries and taking over the meeting through pointed questioning of the presenters, leading a walk out of the meeting en masse, standing during the meeting with your back turned to the presenters, requesting time from the organizers to present your disagreements with their presentation, seizing the microphone of the meeting and presenting your information, or even using guerilla theatre to disrupt the meeting (Kimmel & Browning, 1999; Minton, 2002; Pope, 2012).

Where did zapping arise as a tactic? It really came from the successes of the struggle for African American civil rights in the 1950s and 1960s. Other marginalized social groups also were empowered, including women, Latinx, Native American, and LGBT people—to name but a few. So very much was learned from the successes and failures of the civil rights movement. Many of our LGBT leaders cut our activist teeth in those struggles as well, such as Bayard Rustin, Harry Hay, and so many others (D'Emilio, 2003; Minton, 2002). We owe much of what we have achieved to the leadership and courage of our African American fellow citizens and their supporters who stood and sat down so defiantly all over our great land in the 1950s and 1960s. This great struggle paved the way for all the many social changes that followed (Minton, 2002).

The Results

On December 15, 1973, the APA announced the decision of their board of directors to remove homosexuality from their list of mental disorders (by a vote of 13 to 0 with two abstentions) in the *DSM* (Bayer, 1981). This action was the culmination of a protracted effort initiated by gay and lesbian activists from both within and outside of the APA in support of this action.

On June 26, 2003, the U.S. Supreme Court in *Lawrence v. Texas* found that sodomy laws were unconstitutional, making same-sex sexual behavior legal in every state and territory. Amicus curiae (or friend of the court) briefs were filed by all of the major mental health professions in the United States supporting the rights of LGBT people.

On June 15, 2020, the U.S. Supreme Court in *Bostock v. Clayton County, Georgia,* found that Title VII of the 1964 Civil Rights Act protects LGBT people from discrimination in employment, making such discrimination illegal in every state and territory. And, once again, amicus curiae briefs were filed by all of the major mental health professions in the United States supporting the rights of LGBT people.

And finally, the *DSM* change was not just a victory over psychiatry, it ignited a prairie fire that would sweep through all the mental health professions, as it inspired a new generation of LGBT people to choose to enter our professions, where it was now safe, at least safer. This victory also laid the groundwork for all of the changes in every other mental health profession that we have seen over the last 50 years. Many other mental health professionals were active in that change; but it had to start with the field of psychiatry, for the *DSM* was their book. As counselors, we owe a great debt to our colleagues in that field, such as Jack Drescher, John Fryer, Judd Marmor, Nanette Gartrell, Martha Kirkpatrick, Robert Spitzer, and so many others who stood tall during that time.

Conclusion

The history of sexual behavior is a history of discovery and progress, from the more naturalistic responses seen in many Indigenous cultures, to the exclusively procreative and morality-based sin responses, to the criminalizing of nonprocreative forms of sexual behavior, to the disease and medical model of sexual behavior, to the recreative sex and differences model in conceptualizing sexual behavior. Such progress, however, only came about through the work of so many human beings who believed that human sexual behavior deserved a full and open discussion and study of the realities of sex. Sexual behavior had to be brought into the light, rather than sit in dark back rooms, to take its place in the important discussions in scientific inquiry. All human behavior is complex, but it can only be understood if we as a species expose it to scientific inquiry rather than hide it.

Nearly all problems human beings have with sexual behavior of their own and of others can be resolved, but they must be approached with scientific and sex positive attitudes that allow for such open discussion at all levels of our society—family, schools, community service agencies, and even governments. These are the lessons of history. As mental health professionals, we must take responsibility for our own attitudes toward human sexuality, so that we can be better helpers for those who seek our counsel. Our students, clients, and patients have the right to expect that from us.

The *New York Times* (1956) in its obituary at the passing of Alfred Kinsey eloquently stated,

> The untimely death of Dr. Alfred C. Kinsey takes from the American scene an important and valuable, as well as controversial, figure. Whatever may have been the reaction to his findings—and to the unscrupulous use of some of them—the fact remains that he was first, last and always a scientist. In the long run it is probable that the values of his contribution to contemporary thought will lie much less in what he found out than in the method he used and his way of applying it. Any sort of scientific approach to the problems of sex is difficult because the field is so deeply overlaid with such things as moral precept, taboo, individual and group training, and long-established behavior patterns. Some of these may be good in themselves, but they are no help to the scientific and empirical method of getting at the truth. Dr. Kinsey cut through this overlay with detachment and precision. His work was conscientious and comprehensive. Naturally, it will receive a serious setback with his death. Let us earnestly hope that the scientific spirit that inspired it will not be similarly impaired. (p. 18)

And let us jealously guard the progress that we have made in this understanding. There is so much more to know.

References

Balter, M. (2012, May 14). Engravings of female genitalia may be the world's oldest cave art. *Science*. https://www.sciencemag.org/news/2012/05/engravings-female-genitalia-may-be-worlds-oldest-cave-art

Bayer, R. (1981). *Homosexuality and American psychiatry: The politics of diagnosis*. Basic Books.

Bostock v. Clayton County, 590 US __ (2020). https://www.supremecourt.gov/opinions/19pdf/17-1618_hfci.pdf

Brindle, M., & Opie, C. (2016). Postcopulatory sexual selection influences baculum evolution in primates and carnivores. *Proceedings of the Royal Society B, 283*(1844), Article 20161736. https://doi.org/10.1098/rspb.2016.1736

Bronski, M. (2011). *A queer history of the United States*. Beacon Press.

Brown, H. G. (1962). *Sex and the single girl*. Pocket Books.

Bullough, V. L. (1971). Attitudes toward deviant sex in ancient Mesopotamia. *Journal of Sex Research, 7*(3), 184–203. https://doi.org/10.1080/00224497109550708

Bullough, V. L. (1972). Sex in history: A virgin field. *Journal of Sex Research, 8*(2), 101–116. https://doi.org/10.1080/00224497209550736

Bullough, V. L. (1985). Problems of research on a delicate topic: A personal view. *Journal of Sex Research, 21*(4), 375–386. https://doi.org/10.1080/00224498509551276

Comfort, A. (1972). *The joy of sex.* Crown.

Cutner, H. (1940). *A short history of sex worship.* Watts & Company.

Darwin, C. (1859). *On the origin of species by means of natural selection.* John Murray Publishers.

de Block, A., & Adriaens, P. R. (2013). Pathologizing sexual deviance: A history. *Journal of Sex Research, 50*(3-4), 276–298. https://doi.org/10.1080/00224499.2012.738259

D'Emilio, J. (2003). *Lost prophet: The life and times of Bayard Rustin.* Free Press.

D'Emilio, J., & Freedman, E. (1988). *Intimate matters: A history of sexuality in America.* Harper & Row.

Derham, W. (1713). *Physico-theology: Or a demonstration of the being and attributes of God, from his works of creation.* W. Innys.

Drescher, J., & Merlino, J. P. (Eds.). (2003). *American psychiatry and homosexuality: An oral history.* Harrington Park Press.

Ellenberger, H. F. (1970). *The discovery of the unconscious: The history and evolution of dynamic psychiatry.* Basic Books.

Ellis, H. (1939). Freud's influence on the changed attitude toward sex. *American Journal of Sociology, 45*(3), 309–317. https://www.jstor.org/stable/2769848

Fisher, S., & Greenberg, R. P. (1977). *The scientific credibility of Freud's theories and therapy.* Harvester Press.

Forsyth, A. (2001). *A natural history of sex: The ecology and evolution of mating behavior.* Firefly Books.

Frandsen, P. (2016, October 27). Revealed: The ancient genetic link between chimpanzees and bonobos. *The Conversation.* https://theconversation.com/revealed-the-ancient-genetic-link-between-chimpanzees-and-bonobos-67760

Frazer, J. G. (1894). *The golden bough: A study in comparative religion.* Macmillan and Co.

Freud, S. (1943). *A general introduction to psychoanalysis* (J. Riviere, Trans.). Garden City Publishing Company. (Original work published 1917)

Friedan, B. (1963). *The feminine mystique.* W. W. Norton.

Gall, F. J. (1835). *On the functions of the brain and of each of its parts: With observations on the possibility of determining the instincts, propensities, and talents, or the moral and intellectual dispositions of men and animals, by the configuration of the brain and head* (W. Lewis, Trans.; Vol. 1). Marsh, Capen & Lyon.

Gebhard, P., & Johnson, A. B. (1979). *The Kinsey data: Marginal tabulations of the 1938–1963 interviews conducted by the Institute for Sex Research.* W. B. Saunders.

Gibbons, A. (2012, June 13). Bonobos join chimps as closest human relatives. *Science.* https://www.sciencemag.org/news/2012/06/bonobos-join-chimps-closest-human-relatives

Greer, G. (1970). *The female eunuch.* Paladin.

Hirshman, L. (2012). *Victory: The triumphant gay revolution.* Harper.

Hite, S. (1976). *The Hite report.* Macmillan.

Hooker, E. (1957). The adjustment of the male overt homosexual. *Journal of Projective Techniques, 21*, 18–31.
James, W. (1887). What is an instinct? *Scribner's Magazine, 1*, 355–365.
Kaan, H. (2016). *Psychopathia sexualis* (B. Kahan, Ed., & M. Haynes, Trans.). Cornell University Press. (Original work published 1844)
Kellogg, J. H. (1887). *Plain facts for the old and young*. Segner.
Kimmel, D. C., & Browning, C. (1999). A history of Division 44 (Society for the Psychological Study of Lesbian, Gay, and Bisexual Issues). In D. A. Dewsbury (Ed.), *Unification through division: Histories of the American Psychological Association* (Vol. IV; pp. 128–150). American Psychological Association.
King, M. L., Jr. (1968, March 31). *Remaining awake through a great revolution* [Speech excerpt]. Smithsonian Institution. https://www.si.edu/spotlight/mlk
Kinsey, A. C., Pomeroy, W. B., & Martin, C. E. (1948). *Sexual behavior in the human male*. W. B. Saunders.
Kinsey, A. C., Pomeroy, W. B., Martin, C. E., & Gebhard, P. H. (1953). *Sexual behavior in the human female*. W. B. Saunders.
Krafft-Ebing, R. v. (1930). *Psychopathia sexualis* (F. J. Rebman, Trans.; 12th ed.). Physicians and Surgeons Book Company. (Original work published 1886)
Lawrence v. Texas, 539 U.S. 558 (2003). https://www.supremecourt.gov/oral_arguments/argument_transcripts/2002/02-102.pdf
Leung, C. (2020). *Kellogg, John Harvey*. Eugenics Archives. Social Sciences and Humanities Research Council of Canada. http://eugenicsarchive.ca/discover/connections/512fa0d334c5399e2c000005
Li, S., Shih, C., Wang, C., Pang, H., & Ren, D. (2013). Forever love: The hitherto earliest record of copulating insects from the Middle Jurassic of China. *PLOS ONE, 9*(1), Article e78188. https://doi.org/10.1371/journal.pone.0078188
Lister, K. (2020). *The curious history of sex*. Unbound Publishers.
Mails, T. E. (1996). *The Cherokee people: The story of the Cherokees from earliest origins to contemporary times*. Council Oak Books.
Mankiewicz, J. L. (1951). *All about Eve*. Twentieth Century Studios.
Mankiller, W., & Wallis, M. (1993). *Mankiller: A chief and her people*. St. Martin's Press.
Masters and Johnson. (2022, May 12). In *Wikipedia*. https://en.wikipedia.org/wiki/Masters_and_Johnson
Masters, W. H., & Johnson, V. E. (1966). *Human sexual response*. Bantam Books.
Masters, W. H., & Johnson, V. E. (1979). *Homosexuality in perspective*. Bantam Books.
Mead, M. (1928). *Coming of age in Samoa*. William Morrow & Company.
Mildenberger, F. (2007). Kraepelin and the "urnings": Male homosexuality in psychiatric discourse. *History of Psychiatry, 18*, 321–325. https://doi.org/10.1177/0957154X07079796
Minton, H. L. (2002). *Departing from deviance: A history of homosexual rights and emancipatory science in America*. University of Chicago Press.
Mintz, L. (2018). *Becoming cliterate: Why orgasm equality matters—and how to get it*. HarperOne.
Mondimore, F. M. (1996). *The natural history of homosexuality*. The Johns Hopkins University Press.

Moreau de Tours, P. (1880). *Des aberations du sens genesique* [On the aberration of the reproductive sense]. Asselin.
The New York Times. (1956, August 27). *Dr. Kinsey*. https://www.nytimes.com/1956/08/27/archives/dr-kinsey.html
Oosterhuis, H. (2000). *Stepchildren of nature: Krafft-Ebing, psychiatry, and the making of sexual identity*. University of Chicago Press.
Orenstein, P. (2017). *Girls & sex: Navigating the complicated new landscape*. Harper.
Orenstein, P. (2020). *Boys & sex: Young men on hookups, love, porn, consent, and navigating the new masculinity*. Harper.
Peakman, J. (2009). Sexual perversion in history: An introduction. In J. Peakman (Ed.), *Sexual perversions, 1670–1890* (pp. 1–49). Palgrave Macmillan.
Perdue, T. (1989). *The Cherokee (Indians of North America)*. Chelsea House Publishers.
Pope, M. (2012, Fall). First we were sane, now we are legal: The historic position of Division 44 in the LGBT civil rights movement. *Division 44 Newsletter, 28*(3), 14–21. https://www.apa.org/pi/lgbt/resources/div-44-newsletter.pdf
Pope, M. (2020). History of LGBTQQIA rising up in the American Counseling Association: In the beginning. *Journal of LGBT Issues in Counseling, 14*(4), 291–306. https://doi.org/10.1080/15538605.2020.1827475
Reich, W. (1961). *The function of the orgasm*. Farrar, Straus & Giroux.
Reich, W. (1962). *The sexual revolution*. Farrar, Straus & Giroux.
Sharma, A. (2012). *Problematizing religious freedom*. Springer.
Silverstein, C., & White, E. (1977). *The joy of gay sex*. Simon & Schuster.
Taylor, G. R. (1973). *Sex in history*. Harper.
Tissot, S. A. D. (1781). *Onanism: Or, a treatise upon the disorders produced by masturbation: Or, the dangerous effects of secret and excessive venery* (A. Hume, Trans.). Richardson and Urquhart. (Original work published 1758)
Trexler, R. C. (1995). *Sex and conquest: Gendered violence, political order, and the European conquest of the Americas*. Cornell University Press.
Wile, D. (1992). *Art of the bedchamber: The Chinese sexual yoga classics*. University of New York Press.

CHAPTER 3

Nonmaleficence: A Terrible Safe Word But a Necessary Component of Counseling Ethics in Sex Positive Practice

Robert J. Zeglin, Hannah Glusenkamp, and Faith Ponti

Sex is integral to human life. It is the cause of both ecstasy and distress for many. Distress surrounding sex and/or sexuality is a common reason for individuals to seek therapy (Heiman, 2002; Simons & Carey, 2001). Moreover, discussing sex within the counseling relationship, or counseling room, can be uncomfortable for both clients and counselors. Clients may fear the judgment of their counselors and therefore avoid the topic, whereas therapists may feel ill prepared to broach it and therefore also avoid the topic (Cruz et al., 2017; Dermer & Bachenberg, 2017; Love & Farber, 2017; Zeglin et al., 2018). The best approach to overcome this stalemate is to rely on the counseling field's prioritization of nonjudgment (American Counseling Association [ACA], 2014) through a framework called "sex positivity." Sex positivity seeks to eliminate the taboo and stigma from conversations about sex by intentionally and consistently avoiding labeling any sexual act as abhorrent, dangerous, or disordered (Burnes et al., 2017; Dermer & Bachenberg, 2017; Downing, 2015; Williams et al., 2013; Wilson, 2017, 2019), congruent with the World Health Organization's (2006) definition of sexuality. It is imperative that counselors be trained to embody sex positivity, embracing it as a core tenet of their conceptualization and treatment of each client. In this chapter, *sexuality* refers not only to one's sexual identity but to all things that make up the client's sense of living as a sexual being (e.g., turn-ons, turnoffs, sexual health practices, desire for affection, enjoyment of physical touch).

Ethics of Sex Positivity

The *ACA Code of Ethics* (ACA, 2014) lends itself to a sex positive counseling approach, which therefore should not require mental, ethical, or moral gymnastics on the part of counselors. The preamble to the code outlines six "fundamental principles of professional ethical behavior" (ACA, 2014, p. 3) that should guide ethical practice and decision-making. Table 3.1 shows how a sex positive approach aligns with the fundamental principles described in the 2014 ethics code.

Even with the knowledge that sex positivity is congruent with the *ACA Code of Ethics* (ACA, 2014), many counseling professionals may wonder if there is a limit to exactly how "positive" one should be toward a client's sexuality. The short answer to this questions is, as with many questions within the counseling field, "it depends." First and worth repeating, counselors are tasked with creating a safe and affirming

Table 3.1

How the American Counseling Association's (ACA, 2014) *ACA Code of Ethics* Relates to Sex Positivity

ACA (2014) Principle	*How It Relates to Counselor Sex Positivity*
"Autonomy, or fostering the right to control the direction of one's life" (ACA, 2014, p. 3)	Counselors should recognize sexual expression as a normal and healthy aspect of clients' cognitive, emotional, and behavioral development. This sexual expression is freely chosen by the client; counselors should not seek to shape, alter, or manipulate the client's choice of sexual expression.
"Nonmaleficence, or avoiding actions that cause harm" (ACA, 2014, p. 3)	Because sexuality is so personal and individual, counselors should take care to understand the client's sexuality and integrate it into their case conceptualization. Counselors should not classify any sexual acts or expressions as inherently disordered, unhealthy, or abhorrent. Counselors must avoid allowing judgment or personal biases/values about sex to affect the therapeutic relationship.
"Beneficence, or working for the good of the individual and society by promoting mental health and well-being" (ACA, 2014, p. 3)	Counselors should approach the therapeutic relationship with a fundamental goal of enhancing their clients' overall well-being, including their sexual wellness. Helping a client to feel more fulfilled by and comfortable with their sexuality should be an intentional component of achieving this goal.
"Justice, or treating individuals equitably and fostering fairness and equality" (ACA, 2014, p. 3)	Counselors should work to give voice to their clients who, for so long, have had their forms of sexual expression labeled as deviant or disordered. Counselors should be prepared with resources for clients requiring more support, as well as advocate for their clients with historically marginalized sexualities. Fundamentally, counselors should receive and work with no client differently because of their choice of sexual expression.
"Fidelity, or honoring commitments and keeping promises, including fulfilling one's responsibilities of trust in professional relationships"(ACA, 2014, p. 3)	Counselors should facilitate forthright conversations about sex and sexuality while displaying empathy and respect, encouraging comfort, honesty, and transparency in their clients. Counselors should seek to create an atmosphere of trust so that clients feel safe discussing sex and sexuality.
"Veracity, or dealing truthfully with individuals with whom counselors come into professional contact" (ACA, 2014, p. 3)	Counselors should seek to provide medically accurate and nonstigmatizing information related to sex and sexual health. Counselors must be honest about their knowledge, or lack thereof, with respect to sexuality. Counselors should avoid relying on personal values or outdated/inaccurate sex education when providing services.

space for clients, regardless of the client's presenting issue, culture, or diagnosis. This is fundamental to the field and there are no exceptions within the code (ACA, 2014). Second, and relatedly, sex positivity does not mean advocating for or promoting a sexual free-for-all. Sexuality is, as discussed above, a deeply personal component of one's identity and is informed by a lifetime of values, morals, messaging, desire, urges, feelings, and experiences. It is not the counselor's job to unduly implant in the client a sense that a liberal sexuality is ideal, normal, or more satisfying; this is merely *sex negativity* wrapped in an ostensibly progressive sheep's clothing. Sex positivity celebrates all sexualities as equally fulfilling so long as the client has freely identified with that sexuality free from coercion by people and/or institutions. Third and finally, of course there will be sex-related situations that require counselors to thoughtfully consider and revisit the ethical decision-making models (e.g., Corey et al., 2019; Forester-Miller & Davis, 1995; Garcia et al., 2003) to guide their work with clients' sex-related presentations and discussions.

One common presentation is a client who has inaccurate information related to sex. One example is that of a cisgender male client who asks whether masturbation will result in a shrinking of his penis. A sex positive counselor must provide medically accurate information (i.e., the penis will not shrink as a result of masturbation) while also seeking to understand the source of anxiety driving the client's question, which could be a cultural expectation to abstain from sexual pleasure of any kind, including self-pleasure. The counselor should neither advocate for masturbation (thus minimizing the client's cultural value) nor reinforce faulty health-related information (thus propagating sexual shame). Another, although perhaps less common presentation, may be that of a client whose sexuality involves illegal components. It is imperative that counselors have an actual understanding of the laws in their jurisdiction related to the suspected illegality. Subsequently, sex positive counselors should not seek to endorse the illegal behavior or reform the client's sexuality. This is a subtle but crucial distinction, for many sexualities with illegal components can be sufficiently satiated through entirely legal means; it is not the sexuality itself that is illegal, but rather specific derivative behaviors (see Chapter 20).

The preceding discussion of sex positivity and boundaries may be best reified by Gayle Rubin's (1980) charmed circle. The *charmed circle* (see Figure 3.1) is a conceptualization to describe how sexualities are labeled as either "good" or "bad." Those sexualities closest to the center, or inside the charmed circle, are considered the good sexualities. Sex that possesses these qualities receives little to no scrutiny from society. In fact, this is probably exactly the type of sex to which many of us were either overtly or tacitly told as children and young adults to aspire. Unfortunately, in schools across the United States, this is the type of sex prioritized in sex education classes, despite evidence that it is ineffective, stigmatizing, often medically inaccurate, and exclusive (Elia & Eliason, 2010; Fox et al., 2019; Santelli et al., 2017).

For counselors, it can be easy to unwittingly reinforce the idea of good sexuality. This can be done in two general ways. First, for clients who do not mention sex or sexuality, a sex negative counselor may fall into the trap of assuming that the client's sexuality is one within the charmed circle, not requiring investigation or inquiry because it is fundamentally good and therefore devoid of conflict, confusion, or counterproductiveness. Second, for clients who report a sexuality that appears to be inside the charmed circle, sex negative counselors may either neglect to include the client's sexuality as part of the case conceptualization or, in an attempt to align with the client, accidentally show bias against sexualities outside of the charmed circle, including those

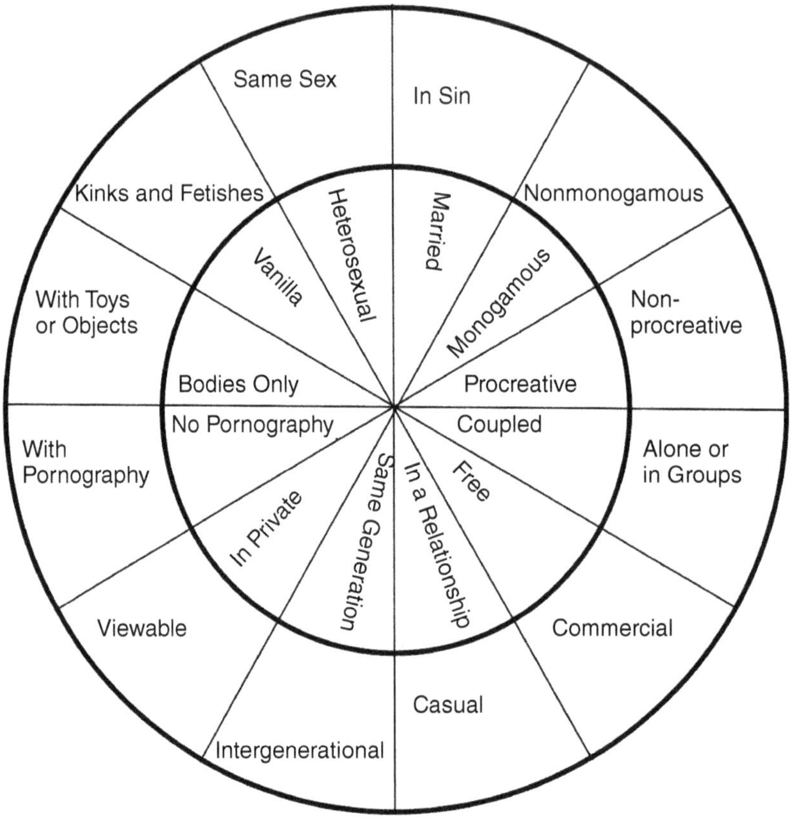

Figure 3.1
Rubin's (1980) Charmed Circle

Note. Adapted from "Thinking Sex: Notes for a Radical Theory of the Politics of Sexuality," by G. Rubin, 1980, in R. Parker & P. Aggleton (Eds.), *Culture, Society and Sexuality: A Reader* (p. 153). © 1980 UCL Press. Reproduced by permission of Taylor & Francis Group through PLSclear.

that the counselor may not yet be aware actually apply to the client. As a result, the client may feel the need to self-censor or decide to terminate counseling prematurely.

Sex outside the charmed circle, or sex that possesses the qualities on the outer ring, is considered bad, abhorrent, and morally corrupt. Society often questions, criticizes, and marginalizes (through revocation of rights) these sexualities (Elia, 2003; Elia & Eliason, 2010). In the counseling room, this can take the form of counselors pathologizing sexualities outside the charmed circle (Downing, 2015; Moors & Schechinger, 2014). There are two general manifestations of this. First, sex negative counselors may erroneously overprioritize the client's uncharmed components of their sexuality within the case conceptualization, possibly even directly attributing the client's distress to those components. Second, and often derivative of the first, sex negative counselors may seek to change the uncharmed component of the client's sexuality solely for moral reasons and guided by their own moral values, rather than those of the client.

One simple way to conceptualize sex positivity is to think of it as broadening Rubin's charmed circle to the outer edge and to eschew the concepts of good and bad in favor of "safe" and "unsafe." All sex is charmed because it can bring pleasure, connection, wholeness, and a sense of self to the client—individually and in relation to others. Furthermore, and perhaps more radically, all sex should be considered safe by default, save for the truly exceptional scenarios. For example, BDSM (e.g., bondage, discipline, domination, submission, sadism, masochism) sex is often considered unsafe and pathological by therapists (Dunkley & Brotto, 2018; Hoff & Sprott, 2009). However, ethical practitioners of BDSM routinely prioritize consent, safety, and communication as essential components of BDSM (or kinky) sex (Kleinplatz & Moser, 2006). Sex negative counselors may seek to reduce or eliminate the kinky sex, while sex positive counselors would instead seek to support and encourage the communication and consent between partners. As a second exemple, sex negative counselors may seek to reduce the number of concurrent sexual partners a client has (since having multiple partners is outside the charmed circle), while a sex positive counselor would possibly instead seek to maintain and increase the safety of the client's sexual encounters with any partner by providing medically accurate sexual health education and resources. Such a shift in conceptualization can cause value-based dissonance for the counselor. The counselor value-based conflict model (Kocet & Herlihy, 2014) can help counselors remain compliant with the *ACA Code of Ethics* (ACA, 2014) with respect to their values regarding the charmed circle.

Boundary and Relationship Considerations

It may seem obvious, but it bears repeating that counselors and other therapists should not have sex with their clients. Although most people may think "of course not," counseling and psychotherapy have both a complex history and current reality with sexual boundary violations (SBVs) between counselors and their clients (Slochower, 2017). Counseling and psychotherapy are not alone in this. Educational, political, and religious institutions all experience similar and pervasive sexual boundary violations between professionals and their clients, students, members, and congregants. This may suggest that, in addition to factors specific to the counseling field, there may be societal factors that contribute to a culture where SBVs occur within many of the helping professions. The power dynamics that exist in each of these fields are a notable similarity among them and may serve as the cornerstone to preventing SBVs. Sex positive counselors are aware of this power dynamic and the way that it influences the relationship in the room.

Sex positive counselors fundamentally prioritize consent within sexual relationships (Burnes et al., 2017). Because of the power imbalance in the client-counselor relationship, it is never truly possible for a client to consent to a sexual relationship, making sexual relationships between counselor and client inherently exploitative. This is why such relationships are expressly prohibited by the major counseling organizations (e.g., ACA, 2014; American Mental Health Counseling Association, 2015; National Board for Certified Counselors, 2016) and state laws governing counseling practice. In addition to valuing and teaching consent, sex positive counselors must be honest about and therefore proactive in dealing professionally and ethically with the dynamics of transference and countertransference (Goren, 2017), especially when addressing sexuality and sexual content within the context of the therapeutic relationship.

Inviting sexual conversations into the counseling room requires counselors to broach such topics while remaining aware of and sensitive to sexual feelings or desires that may arise in the client and/or counselor during the process. A counselor's greatest asset is their humanness. As humans, counselors will, sooner or later, find themselves physically or emotionally attracted to a client. This is natural and common, with nearly 90% of psychotherapists reporting having experienced sexual attraction toward a client (Pope et al., 1986). Denying or suppressing these thoughts and feelings can actually be counterproductive to the counseling process (Barnett, 2014; Bridges, 1994). Barnett (2014) offers helpful practical advice to navigate this potential ethical dilemma and boundary incursion, including practicing self-awareness, assessing motivations, referencing their codes of ethics, and consulting with colleagues and supervisors.

Ostensibly small boundary incursions can give way to larger incursions (Barnett, 2014; Dimen, 2011) and should therefore be given their due consideration. One such incursion is that of physical touch in the counseling room. Because the essential constructs of sexuality remain difficult to define (Zeglin & Mitchell, 2014), it can be even more challenging to understand what is or is not sexual to any individual person, as sexuality is extremely individualized (Van Anders, 2015). Understanding sexuality as extremely individualized is another cornerstone of sex positive counseling. A sex negative counselor may manifest this dialogue by trying to split hairs and find the exact place on the line of what truly constitutes a sexual boundary violation. Conversely, a sex positive counselor has "a framework that integrates the physical, somatic, emotional, intellectual, social and spiritual aspects of sexual practice and sexual being in positive, enriching ways" (Burnes et al., 2017, p. 471) and views everything that is done in the therapeutic relationship within this framework. Therefore, the question of what constitutes a boundary violation shifts from a focus on the question of "Is this specific action crossing a boundary?" to "Is this decision supporting the integration and well-being of the multifaceted aspects of the client in positive ways?" Plainly, this means taking the time to broach, explore, and process the client's and your own motivations as the counselor for or against physical touch. For sex positive counselors, this reflective and collaborative engagement is congruent with the concept of informed consent, modeling self-advocacy and self-awareness.

The Multicultural and Social Justice Counseling Competencies (MSJCC; Ratts et al., 2016) call for counselors to engage in social justice advocacy efforts, including in their local communities. Sex positive counselors may choose to engage in advocacy for populations with traditionally marginalized sexualities (e.g., kink; lesbian, gay, bisexual, transgender, and queer [LGBTQ]; consensually nonmonogamous). If these counselors have a reputation in the community for being sex positive and safe, it is possible that they will encounter clients outside the therapy office while in their advocate role (e.g., task forces, speaking engagements, community advisory committees, trainings). The *ACA Code of Ethics* (ACA, 2014) does not prohibit these interactions. However, the counselor must first and foremost take care to not inadvertently breach confidentiality, burdening the counselor with the task of temporarily compartmentalizing the relationship roles. Second, and more amorphous, the counselor should be mindful of the power dynamics at play while interacting with the client in the advocacy space. The client does not share the counselor's aforementioned burden of compartmentalization and thus may bring into the shared advocacy space the same sense of power and roles that exist in the therapy space. Because of this, counselors who find themselves in this situation should broach such with their clients in the therapy space as soon as feasible and clinically indicated. In other words, the counselor should intentionally and deliberately provide the client an opportunity in the therapy session to explore and process their feelings, thoughts, and reactions to sharing an advocacy space, a space in which the power dynamics are different than they are in therapy, with the counselor.

Larger boundary incursions almost exclusively occur out of a well-intended but ill-informed desire to be helpful. One clear and dramatic example is that of what to do when a client discloses a sexual attraction to children. Rightly, counselors are ethically (ACA, 2014) and legally required to report suspected child abuse; however, there is no such requirement to report the attraction itself. Cantor (2014) noted that breaking client confidentiality merely due to disclosure of attraction dissuades such clients from seeking therapy, therapy that can help prevent the illegal and harmful behaviors the counselor aimed to mitigate in the first place (Cantor & McPhail, 2016). A similar and even cloudier example would be clients who admit to having viewed sexually explicit material involving children. This is an ethical dilemma requiring more nuanced attention than the present chapter can provide, especially considering each state's specific statutory language around this topic. However, counselors should take care to properly employ the ethical decision-making models before making any decision to break confidentiality (e.g., Corey et al., 2019; Forester-Miller & Davis, 1995; Garcia et al., 2003), as easy as it may be to justify in this and other similar situations. Breaking confidentiality should be done thoughtfully, no matter how objectionable the client's behavior may be.

The counseling field often touts as its niche the holistic and developmental lens through which counselors view clients' distress, goals, and concerns. Holistic health models (e.g., Myers & Sweeney, 2004) include all of the physical, mental, environmental, social, and spiritual elements of health; yet, they nearly always exclude sexual health (Mallicoat, 2013; Wilson, 2019). Additionally, as Zeglin et al. (2019) noted, the Council for Accreditation of Counseling and Related Educational Programs (CACREP) does not require sexuality-related material in training programs, except within marriage and family and rehabilitation counseling programs. It is not a surprise, then, that most counselors and counselors-in-training do not include sex and sexual health in conversations with clients (Wilson, 2017). Nonetheless, sex positive counselors of all specialties view sexual health as an integral part of holistic health (Zeglin et al., 2019). Sexual health and wellness intersect with all domains of traditional holistic health models; every person's physical, mental, social, and spiritual health is bidirectionally related to their sexual health. For example, acute erectile difficulties in older clients are often a sign of an underlying cardiovascular issue (Gandaglia et al., 2014).

Sexual health and wellness are also a critical part of human development. All people, regardless of sexual orientation, relationship status, gender expression, or gender identity, experience sexuality as part of their development across the life span. How and whether one and one's caregivers experience these sexual development milestones can influence and shape later sexual values. Examples of early life sexual developmental milestones include first time masturbating, first time orgasming, first crush, first sexual contact with another person, first orgasm with another person, first date, first relationship, first love, and first breakup. The sense of one's body in relation to oneself and in relationship to others is a developmental process that intertwines with the other physical, emotional, and social developmental stages in early life (Zoldbrod, 1998). You (the reader) can probably recall your own experiences with some of those milestones and how your placement in other developmental contexts and timelines influenced those experiences and vice versa. Sex positive counselors understand, appreciate, and, when clinically indicated, work with clients to investigate this relationship.

To this end, counselors should know that asking about sex does not make the session or relationship inherently sexual and therefore is not ipso facto an ethical violation. If, as discussed, sexual health is a critical part of a holistic developmental approach to wellness, then asking about sex is a natural part of a counselor's work. Any potential inappropriateness lies not in the topic, but in the question. For example, it would be equally inappropriate in most therapeutic contexts for a counselor's first question during an intake to be "Tell me about the first time you masturbated" or "Tell me about the first time you considered suicide." Asking probing sexual questions without purpose or therapeutic intent is unlikely to serve the interest of your client, as with any topic. However, making your office or place of work a sanctuary in which all aspects of your client's life are listened to, accepted, and actively explored is paramount in the formation and maintenance of the counseling relationship. Sex positive counselors know that sexuality should not be an exception.

In light of this, counselors who are led to ask a question about a client's sexuality should not flee from the opportunity but instead use the professional stance taken when asking about any other ostensibly sensitive topic. Beginning counselors and counselors-in-training often "ramp up" to questions about suicide (e.g., "This might be awkward to talk about . . . ," "This could be a kind of a difficult question . . ."). This ramping up is nearly always to ease their own anxieties and often only heightens the client's sense of impending awkwardness—a clinical example of the nocebo effect (Tracey, 2010). Counselors, to ease their discomfort with sexual topics, might be tempted to engage in a similar ramping up before asking sexual questions (e.g., "I know this might be personal . . . ," "You may not talk about this a lot . . ."). Doing so reinforces the perceived taboo and awkwardness of discussing sex. Instead, sex positive counselors simply ask their question and include the rationale for doing so. For example, "I am noticing 'x, y, and z' about the way you speak about yourself. I'm wondering if past sexual experiences have affected the way you view your body." By taking this approach, as with any other topic (e.g., drug use, eating behaviors), a sex positive counselor has communicated to the client that sex and sexuality are permitted, appropriate, and welcomed topics to discuss (Dermer & Bachenberg, 2017).

Scope of Practice

One foundational model used by sex therapists, educators, and sexologists is the PLISSIT model (Annon, 1976), which represents a *cascading* clinical intervention strategy of permission, limited information, specific suggestions, and intensive therapy. According to the model, a significant proportion of clients presenting with sexual issues can be supported simply by giving them permission to discuss the issue openly, honestly, and free from judgment. A significant proportion of the remaining clients can be helped by providing limited information related to the issue (i.e., psychosexual education) or by providing specific suggestions to help address and/or practice solutions to the sexual issue (i.e., homework to complete between sessions). Still others will benefit from intensive therapy (i.e., psychotherapy to address and resolve psychological facilitators of the sexual issue). Lindsey Doe, a clinical sexologist, provides a very succinct explanation of the PLISSIT model on her YouTube channel "Sexplanations" at https://www.youtube.com/watch?v=jBleG8SU0NI.

In general, counselors without formal training in sexual health and wellness are ill-equipped to provide specific sexuality-related suggestions (Zeglin et al., 2018, 2019). This is the one level of the PLISSIT cascade that may be, save for few exceptions, reserved for counselors and other professionals who possess the training necessary to provide evidence-based and ethical homework related to sex and sexuality. Counselors should consult and/or seek supervision before providing specific suggestions (i.e., homework) to clients for sexuality-related issues. Conversely, giving permission to clients to openly discuss sexual issues is a hallmark of sex positive clinical practice and should be a foundational skill of all counselors. Congruent with PLISSIT (Annon, 1976), such permission alone will help a significant portion of clients address their sex-related issues. The remaining two levels of the cascade, limited information and intensive therapy, require a more nuanced inspection to determine if a client's issue may be outside the counselor's scope of practice. The relationship between these two levels is best captured within a knowledge-based decision-making matrix (see Figure 3.2). Counselors should be intentionally self-reflective when navigating this matrix, as it is in the best interest of the client that the counselor arrive at the most appropriate clinical decision as early as possible in the clinical relationship.

The knowledge-based decision-making matrix is a simple two-question process. First, a counselor should assess to what extent the sexual concern is a primary or auxiliary issue. If the sexual concern is a primary issue, depending on the counselor's level of medically accurate evidence-based knowledge on the topic, the counselor may ultimately decide either that consultation is necessary or that the client's concern is outside their scope of practice, congruent with the ACA (2014) ethics code. If the counselor has training related to the issue, then the counselor can typically consider the client to be within their scope of practice and should periodically consult with a sexual health expert to help inform their work with the client. On the other hand, if the counselor does not have training on the topic, the counselor should consider supporting the client in finding a sex therapist or other sexual health specialist who can more appropriately provide the necessary services. If the sexual concern is an auxiliary issue, depending on the counselor's level of medically accurate evidence-based knowledge on the topic, the counselor may ultimately decide either that some training or education is necessary or that the client is inside their scope of practice, congruent with ACA ethics. If the counselor has training related to the issue, then the counselor can safely consider the client to be within their scope of practice and should consult

Intensive Therapy

Is the client's presenting issue related to sex and/or sexual health and wellness?

OR

Is a significant portion of the client's distress related to sex and/or sexual health and wellness?

Limited Information

Does the counselor possess sufficient knowledge on the specific sexual topic, informed by formal training and/or study rather than personal values and layperson sex education?

	Yes Sex is focus	**No** Sex is auxiliary
Yes Has knowledge	*Consultation*: Counselor should periodically consult with sex therapist or specialist	*Within scope*: Counselor should refer to and/or consult with adjunctive services only as necessary
No Does not have knowledge	*Outside scope*: Counselor should consider referring the client to a sex therapist or specialist for services	*Educate*: Counselor should seek out training, supervision, and/or consultation to address the sexuality-related components of the client's case

Figure 3.2

Knowledge-Based Decision-Making Matrix

with a sexual health expert when specific issues arise for which the counselor feels ill-equipped to handle alone.

On the other hand, if the counselor does not have training on the topic, the counselor can continue to work with the client on the primary issue and should dedicate time to educating themselves on the auxiliary sexual issues (e.g., seeking out supervision or consultation, reading journal articles, watching webinars, earning continuing education credits). In all, 75% of the resulting dispositions in the knowledge-based decision-making matrix recommend consulting with a sexual health expert to varying degrees. This is because, as mentioned previously, sexual issues are inherently intertwined with values and personal biases. It is important for sex positive counselors working with clients with sexual issues to consult with sexual health experts at least occasionally as a means by which to keep these values and biases in check.

Part of practicing from a sex positive perspective includes seeing a client's sexuality as dynamic, evolving, and multifaceted. Client sexuality is not to be shamed or ignored but rather respected and supported. As such, there may be periods, topics, and components of clients' sexuality that a counselor is not best suited to help them address in a competent way. This is not a foreign idea for counselors, as we have consistently considered ourselves to be one part of a much larger health menagerie, referring clients to primary care providers, psychiatrists, psychologists, and other health professionals (e.g., nutritionists) when warranted. Typically, we do so intending for the other professional(s) to offer adjunctive services to our counseling service. Sexual health need not be the exception.

The earlier discussion of the PLISSIT model (Annon, 1976) highlighted our scope of practice related to sexuality as counselors. When some aspects of a client's sexuality-related issues fall outside of our scope of practice, we can refer them to adjunctive services that are best suited to address those issues. In fact, sex positive counselors see this as a way to honor a client's sexuality, as long as the counselor takes the time to process this with the client. Examples of adjunctive services specific to sexuality-related issues are sex educators, sex surrogates, sexual medicine professionals, and sex therapists.

Sex educators (and clinical sexologists) receive advanced training in human sexuality. They typically are not mental health clinicians and therefore cannot provide the mental health services that we can as counselors. What they can offer, however, is a wealth of knowledge about nearly all topics related to sexuality (Schroeder, 2009). Clients may benefit from even one appointment with a sex educator to provide foundational knowledge related to the sexual topic(s) pertinent to the therapeutic process (e.g., common mistakes in exploring consensual nonmonogamy, the proper lubrication to use for various sex acts, physiological information related to aging and sex). For clients with sexuality-related issues requiring more direct intervention or assistance (e.g., for clients who do not have a sexual partner to aid in completing therapeutic homework tasks), counselors may consider the use of surrogate partner therapy. Surrogate partners receive training in how to intimately address sexual health issues with clients under the clinical supervision of a clinician. Before considering the use of surrogates, counselors should be mindful of the ethical and legal considerations at play (Emelianchik-Key & Stickney, 2019; Rosenbaum et al., 2014).

Occasionally, it may be necessary to receive a medical consult to rule out physiological etiologies or contributors to a client's sexuality-related issues. This can be particularly true if the client describes experiencing any unwanted pain during sexual activity or in any sexual scenario. Urologists, gynecologists, proctologists, pelvic floor specialists, and obstetricians are helpful resources in these circumstances. For example, a young adult male with autism spectrum disorder who mentions experiencing pain with his erections could benefit from a referral to a urologist to first rule out any "plumbing" issues. If none, then the counselor can consider other psychosocial developmental explanations (e.g., normal discomfort from extreme penile tumescence exacerbated by sensory integration dysfunction not uncommon for people with autism disorders). Finally, if the sexual and mental health concerns are strongly intertwined, a counselor may seek to enlist the assistance of a sex therapist.

Although there are several certifying bodies for sex therapists, among the states only Florida statutorily protects this title (i.e., there are little to no legal restrictions on calling oneself a sex therapist in other states). Sex therapists are trained clinicians who generally do not have the same depth of knowledge of human sexuality as sex educators but do have substantially more human sexuality knowledge than general practice counselors. They can be a wonderful resource as either a consult or a referral, and they can help counselors ethically stay within their scope of practice. The Society for Sex Therapy and Research offers a "Find a Therapist" feature on its website at https://sstarnet.org/find-a-therapist.

Despite all of this, counselors must also be sure that they are not prematurely referring clients to adjunctive or altogether alternative services just because they mention sexuality-related issues. The decision to prematurely terminate and refer clients elsewhere carries with it various clinical, ethical, and legal considerations (Martz & Kaplan, 2014; Natwick, 2017). The sexual values and behaviors discrepancy model (Bloom et al., 2019) can aid counselors in determining when it may be appropriate to consider such a move. Counselors should take care to first assess whether the topic(s) outside their scope are only part of the client's presentation or the specific presenting issue (see Table 3.1). The answer to this question could greatly inform how they select their path within the model.

Research Ethics

Effective research begins with a clear research question (Wright, 2013). Section G of the *ACA Code of Ethics* (2014) stipulates that "counselors minimize bias and respect diversity in designing and implementing research" (p. 15). Sex positive counseling researchers reify this by ensuring that their research questions are sufficiently based on current best evidence on the topic. Conducting sexuality-related research with the intent to *prove* anything about the human sexual experience is misguided and unethical, especially when one's motivation is personal sexual values, beliefs, and identities. A researcher trying to prove that people in monogamous relationships are happier than their nonmonogamous peers is operating out of a sex negative space shared in equal parts by their colleague who seeks to prove the opposite. Even researchers desiring to conduct their research through a social justice lens (Ratts et al., 2016) may inadvertently perpetuate the "othering" of sexualities by designing research protocols seeking to understand the sexuality without considering the lived experience of those with the sexuality (Carroll, 2016); these are sexual safari studies (see Tanzer, 2005). One way to avoid this trap is to intentionally diversify the research team as much as possible. This can include adapting a community-based participatory research (CBPR) model. A CBPR team is composed of academics, community organizational representatives, and community stakeholders (Hacker, 2013; Hergenrather et al., 2010). This latter constituency is the most beneficial when it includes individuals who would otherwise qualify to participate in the study.

Sex positive counselors who conduct research are also aware of the unique ethical considerations within a sexuality-related research protocol. The primary areas in which this may be particularly salient are recruitment, informed consent, and incentives. Recruiting for a sexuality-related study can be challenging. This is mostly due to the overlap between sex and personal values, which are often informed by salient cultural identities. Very few other research topics have quite as strong of a relationship with value systems. For example, a research study marketed as investigated masturbatory motivation toward same-sex sexually explicit material contains several latent value assumptions: values toward masturbation, values toward sexually explicit material, and values toward same-sex sex acts. Sex positive counseling researchers should be aware of the potential for sampling bias because of personal values. A second recruitment consideration is that of recruiting from marginalized communities (e.g., LGBTQ community, kink community, poly community). Sex positive counseling researchers seeking to specifically recruit participants from communities outside Rubin's (1980) charmed circle should consider the self-disclosure inherent within the process of volunteering for a study on a specific community and the history these communities have with disclosure of their marginalized sexualities (particularly to researchers and mental health professionals). Alternatively, sex positive counseling researchers conducting studies for which identification with a marginalized community is not an eligibility requirement should use sex positive, nonstigmatizing, and medically accurate language in all recruitment material in order to capture as wide a variety of sexualities as possible.

The necessity for sex positive, nonstigmatizing, and medically accurate language extends to the study's informed consent document. Sex positive researchers strive to be as transparent as possible in the informed consent document, realizing the historical relationship that sexual minority communities have had with researchers and mental health professionals. Sex positive counseling researchers also prioritize the participants' experience. First, if the study includes any emotional or affective variables, particularly those related to trauma, depression, suicidality, and stigma, sex positive counseling researchers should include some measure of adverse reactions to research participation (e.g., the Reactions to Research Participation Questionnaire [Newman et al., 2001]). If said assessment indicates adverse reactions, the participant should be connected to mental health services, perhaps even directly to the principal investigator who is a professional counselor. Second, sexuality-related research typically addresses misinformation, stigma, false beliefs, risky behavior, or inadequate sex education. In light of this, sex positive counseling researchers conducting sexuality-related research should consider providing resources at the end of the study. For example, the final page of a Qualtrics survey could provide links to any of the many sex positive, nonstigmatizing, and medically accurate resources available across the country and locally. (For examples of such resources, see the Community Sexual Health Education and Research Initiative website at www.csheri.com/resources.)

Finally, researchers must always be mindful of the role of incentives in their research protocols. Incentives in any research protocol must not be so high that it makes it too costly for participants not to participate, as this is coercive and unethical. Many sexual minority communities experience poor social determinants of health (Emlet, 2016; Hatzenbuehler & Pachankis, 2016). In fact, 40% of homeless teens are LGBTQ (Human Rights Campaign, 2017). As such, sex positive counseling researchers understand that determining how to incentivize participants should be a well-considered decision. Financial incentives should not be coercively high. In fact, sex positive counseling researchers should consider supplementing their financial incentives with nonfinancial benefits of participation. For example, local departments of health could offer free testing for sexually transmitted infections (STIs) at the study site, local sexual health agencies can offer free sexual health screenings and referrals, local food pantries could bring some of their stores to the study site, or local public transportation may provide reduced or free transportation vouchers. With these and other similarly creative incentives, participants are treated as human being rather than as research subjects.

The final stage of research, research dissemination, includes both procedural and ethical considerations (ACA, 2014; Wright, 2013). Disseminating research via traditional means (i.e., peer-reviewed journals and professional conferences) is still prioritized by academia in considerations of tenure and promotion. However, research disseminated purely by these means is often delayed or prevented from reaching the sexual health and wellness professionals serving communities and individuals. This perpetuates the very health disparities and inequities that many sex researchers are seeking to dismantle. Sex positive counselors understand this barrier and, aligning with the spirit of advocacy outlined by the MSJCC (Ratts et al., 2016), seek out additional dissemination avenues. Examples include providing trainings/seminars for local service organizations, posting a link to the article (with a plain language summary) on social media, sending a link to the article with a brief summary to relevant policymakers (e.g., study on effectiveness of condom distribution in schools at reducing intended pregnancies sent to local school board and/or state Department of Education), and/or presenting the study's results to the CBPR team.

Case Example

Angel is a 26-year-old nonbinary person who presents to counseling because of recent symptoms of depression. Angel has felt unmotivated to complete their schoolwork (they are a master's-level student in a marketing program), has difficulty getting out of bed in the morning, has several "crying spells" per week lasting about 10 minutes each, and has passive suicidal ideation. These symptoms have been present for about 6 months and have "gotten way worse" in the last several weeks. The client cannot identify any specific event that may have triggered the symptoms. Angel is married to a cisgender man for the past 6 years, they have one child, and they are consensually nonmonogamous. Angel reported during the initial intake that they have approximately five concurrent sexual partners of multiple genders and practice safer sex, often using two condoms at once "for double protection." The client's therapy goal is to "get back to normal." Their primary concern is their schoolwork, as they are close to graduating.

Reflections About the Case Example

In the context of Angel's case example, consider the following questions:

1. What are clear opportunities for a sex negative response from the counselor?
2. In what ways can a sex positive counselor leverage the sexuality-related information gathered about the client's life to help the client achieve their goal?
3. Is this client within the scope of practice for you as a counselor? Why or why not?

4. Sometimes counselors don't know what they don't know. For example, using two condoms at once actually increases the risk of STIs and unintended pregnancy because the friction between the condoms can cause the condoms to tear. Is the client still within the scope of practice for a counselor who did not know this information and did not catch this transient reporting of risk? Why or why not? How would you provide this sexual psychoeducation to your client while also staying focused on their goal?

Conclusion

A sex positive approach aligns perfectly with the counseling ethical virtues of autonomy, nonmaleficence, beneficence, justice, fidelity, and veracity. Sex positivity does not mean promoting liberal or progressive sexuality as inherently better, healthier, or more satisfying, but rather promoting a medically accurate nonstigmatizing exploration of clients' sexualities. Discussing sexual issues, topics, and concerns with clients is not inherently unethical or inappropriate. Because of the role of advocacy work in counseling, counselors may find themselves in dual relationships with clients; counselors should intentionally and deliberately broach and process these relationships with clients in session. The PLISSIT model (Annon, 1976) can be used to help determine whether a client's sexual concerns are within a counselor's scope of practice, particularly by using the knowledge-based decision-making matrix. Counseling sexology research should be hypothesis- or literature-based and should never seek to prove that one sexuality is healthier than another. Counseling sexology researchers can use their research to support social justice and advocacy causes for sexual minority communities.

References

American Counseling Association. (2014). *ACA code of ethics.* https://www.counseling.org/resources/aca-code-of-ethics.pdf

American Mental Health Counseling Association. (2015). *AMHCA code of ethics.*

Annon, J. S. (1976). The PLISSIT model: A proposed conceptual scheme for the behavioral treatment of sexual problems. *Journal of Sex Education and Therapy, 2*(1), 1–15.

Barnett, J. E. (2014). Sexual feelings and behaviors in the psychotherapy relationship: An ethics perspective. *Journal of Clinical Psychology, 70*(2), 170–181.

Bloom, Z. D., Blount, A. J., Taylor, D., Dalena, L., & Lipkin, G. (2019). The sexual values and behaviors discrepancy model. *Journal of Counseling Sexology & Sexual Wellness, 1*(2), 69–79. https://doi.org/10.34296/01021025

Bridges, N. (1994). Meaning and management of attraction: Neglected areas of psychotherapy training and practice. *Psychotherapy, 31*(3), 424–433. https://doi.org/10.1037/0033-3204.31.3.424

Burnes, T. R., Singh, A. A., & Witherspoon, R. G. (2017). Sex positivity and counseling psychology: An introduction to the major contribution. *The Counseling Psychologist, 45*, 470–486.

Cantor, J. M. (2014). "Gold-star" pedophiles in general sex therapy practice. In Y. M. Binik & K. S. K. Hall (Eds.), *Principles and practice of sex therapy* (5th ed., pp. 219–234). Guilford Press.

Cantor, J. M., & McPhail, I. V. (2016). Non-offending pedophiles. *Current Sexual Health Reports, 8*(3), 121–128.
Carroll, M. (2016). Othering and its guises. *Philosophy, Psychiatry, & Psychology, 23*(3), 253–256.
Corey, G., Corey, M. S., Corey, C., & Callanan, P. (2019). *Issues and ethics in the helping professions* (10th ed.). Brooks/Cole.
Cruz, C., Greenwald, E., & Sandil, R. (2017). Let's talk about sex: Integrating sex positivity in counseling psychology practice. *The Counseling Psychologist, 45*(4), 547–569.
Dermer, S., & Bachenberg, M. (2017, October 4–8). *Teaching sexuality and assessing trainee competence* [Conference session]. Association for Counselor Education and Supervision Biannual Conference, Chicago, IL, United States. https://acesonline.net/wp-content/uploads/2020/01/ACES-2017-Conference-Program.pdf
Dimen, M. (2011). *Lapsus linguae*, or a slip of the tongue? A sexual violation in an analytic treatment and it's personal and theoretical aftermath. *Contemporary Psychoanalysis, 47*(1), 35–79. https://doi.org/10.1080/00107530.2011.10746441
Downing, L. (2015). Heteronormativity and repronormativity in sexological "perversion theory" and the *DSM-5*'s "paraphilic disorder" diagnoses. *Archives of Sexual Behavior, 44*(5), 1139–1145.
Dunkley, C. R., & Brotto, L. A. (2018). Clinical considerations in treating BDSM practitioners: A review. *Journal of Sex & Marital Therapy, 44*(7), 701–712.
Elia, J. P. (2003). Queering relationships: Toward a paradigmatic shift. *Journal of Homosexuality, 45*(2–4), 61–86.
Elia, J. P., & Eliason, M. J. (2010). Dangerous omissions: Abstinence-only-until-marriage school-based sexuality education and the betrayal of LGBTQ youth. *American Journal of Sexuality Education, 5*(1), 17–35.
Emelianchik-Key, K., & Stickney, K. (2019). Using surrogate partner therapy in counseling: Treatment considerations. *Journal of Counseling Sexology & Sexual Wellness, 1*(2), 105–113. https://doi.org/10.34296/01021020
Emlet, C. A. (2016). Social, economic, and health disparities among LGBT older adults. *Generations, 40*(2), 16–22.
Forester-Miller, H., & Davis, T. E. (1995). *A practitioner's guide to ethical decision making*. American Counseling Association.
Fox, A. M., Himmelstein, G., Khalid, H., & Howell, E. A. (2019). Funding for abstinence-only education and adolescent pregnancy prevention: Does state ideology affect outcomes? *American Journal of Public Health, 109*(3), 497–504.
Gandaglia, G., Briganti, A., Jackson, G., Kloner, R. A., Montorsi, F., Montorsi, P., & Vlachopoulos, C. (2014). A systematic review of the association between erectile dysfunction and cardiovascular disease. *European Urology, 65*(5), 968–978.
Garcia, J. G., Cartwright, B., Winston, S. M., & Borzuchowska, B. (2003). A transcultural integrative model for ethical decision making in counseling. *Journal of Counseling & Development, 81*(3), 268–277. https://doi.org/10.1002/j.1556-6678.2003.tb00253.x
Goren, E. R. (2017). A call for more talk and less abuse in the consulting room: One psychoanalyst–sex therapist's perspective. *Psychoanalytic Psychology, 34*, 215–220. https://doi.apa.org/doi/10.1037/pap0000092
Hacker, K. (2013). *Community-based participatory research*. Sage Publications.

Hatzenbuehler, M. L., & Pachankis, J. E. (2016). Stigma and minority stress as social determinants of health among lesbian, gay, bisexual, and transgender youth: Research evidence and clinical implications. *Pediatric Clinics*, *63*(6), 985–997.

Heiman, J. R. (2002). Sexual dysfunction: Overview of prevalence, etiological factors, and treatments. *Journal of Sex Research*, *39*(1), 73–78.

Hergenrather, K. C., Geishecker, S., McGuire-Kuletz, M., Gitlin, D. J., & Rhodes, S. D. (2010). An introduction to community-based participatory research. *Rehabilitation Research, Policy, and Education*, *24*(3–4), 225–238.

Hoff, G., & Sprott, R. A. (2009). Therapy experiences of clients with BDSM sexualities: Listening to a stigmatized sexuality. *Electronic Journal of Human Sexuality, 12*(9). http://www.ejhs.org/Volume12/bdsm.htm

Human Rights Campaign. (2017, November 15). *New report on youth homeless affirms that LGBTQ youth disproportionately experience homelessness.* https://www.hrc.org/blog/new-report-on-youth-homeless-affirms-that-lgbtq-youth-disproportionately-ex

Kleinplatz, P. J., & Moser, C. (2006). *Sadomasochism: Powerful pleasures.* Harrington Park Press.

Kocet, M. M., & Herlihy, B. J. (2014). Addressing value-based conflicts within the counseling relationship: A decision-making model. *Journal of Counseling & Development, 92*(2), 180–186. https://doi.org/10.1002/j.1556-6676.2014.00146.x

Love, M., & Farber, B. A. (2017). Let's not talk about sex. *Journal of Clinical Psychology*, *73*(11), 1489–1498.

Mallicoat, W. D. (2013). *A constructivist examination of counselors' conceptualization of "sexuality": Implications for counselor education* [Doctoral dissertation, University of South Carolina]. University of South Carolina Theses and Dissertations. https://scholarcommons.sc.edu/etd/829/

Martz, E., & Kaplan, D. (2014, October). New responsibilities when making referrals. *Counseling Today.* https://www.counseling.org/docs/default-source/ethics/ethics-columns/ethics_october-2014_making-referrals.pdf?sfvrsn=8924522c_4

Moors, A. C., & Schechinger, H. (2014). Understanding sexuality: Implications of Rubin for relationship research and clinical practice. *Sexual and Relationship Therapy, 29*(4), 476–482.

Myers, J. E., & Sweeney, T. J. (2004). The indivisible self: An evidence-based model of wellness. *Journal of Individual Psychology, 60*, 234–244.

National Board for Certified Counselors. (2016). *NBCC code of ethics.* https://www.nbcc.org/Assets/Ethics/NBCCCodeofEthics.pdf

Natwick, J. (2017, May). On the ethics of ending: Terminations and referrals. *Counseling Today.* https://www.counseling.org/docs/default-source/ethics/ethics-columns/ethics_may_2017_terminations-and-referrals.pdf?sfvrsn=ea25522c_6

Newman, E., Willard, T., Sinclair, R., & Kaloupek, D. (2001). Empirically supported ethical research practice: The costs and benefits of research from the participants' view. *Accountability in Research*, *8*(4), 309–329.

Pope, K. S., Keith-Spiegel, P., & Tabachnick, B. G. (1986). Sexual attraction to clients: The human therapist and the (sometimes) inhuman training system. *American Psychologist*, *41*(2), 147–158.

Ratts, M. J., Singh, A. A., Nassar-McMillan, S., Butler, S. K., & McCullough, J. R. (2016). Multicultural and social justice counseling competencies: Guidelines for the counseling profession. *Journal of Multicultural Counseling and Development, 44*(1), 28–48. https://doi.org/10.1002/jmcd.12035

Rosenbaum, T., Aloni, R., & Heruti, R. (2014). Surrogate partner therapy: Ethical considerations in sexual medicine. *The Journal of Sexual Medicine, 11*(2), 321–329.

Rubin, G. (1980). Thinking sex: Notes for a radical theory of the politics of sexuality. In R. Parker & P. Aggleton (Eds.), *Culture, society and sexuality: A reader* (pp. 143–178). UCL Press.

Santelli, J. S., Kantor, L. M., Grilo, S. A., Speizer, I. S., Lindberg, L. D., Heitel, J., Schalet, A. T., Lyon, M. E., Mason-Jones, A. J., McGovern, T., Heck, C. J., Rogers, J., & Ott, M. A. (2017). Abstinence-only-until-marriage: An updated review of U.S. policies and programs and their impact. *Journal of Adolescent Health, 61*(3), 273–280. https://doi.org/10.1016/j.jadohealth.2017.05.031

Schroeder, E. (2009). What is sexuality education? Definitions and models. In E. Schroeder & J. Kuriansky (Eds.), *Sexuality education: Past, present, and future, Vol 1. History and foundations* (pp. 3–7). Praeger Publishers/ Greenwood Publishing Group.

Simons, J. S., & Carey, M. P. (2001). Prevalence of sexual dysfunctions: Results from a decade of research. *Archives of Sexual Behavior, 30*(2), 177–219.

Slochower, J. (2017). Don't tell anyone. *Psychoanalytic Psychology, 34*, 195–200. https://doi.apa.org/doi/10.1037/pap0000082

Tanzer, N. K. (2005). Developing tests for use in multiple languages and cultures: A plea for simultaneous development. In R. K. Hambleton, P. F. Merenda, & C. D. Spielberger (Eds.), *Adapting educational and psychological tests for cross-cultural assessment* (pp. 235–263). Lawrence Erlbaum Associates.

Tracey, I. (2010). Getting the pain you expect: Mechanisms of placebo, nocebo and reappraisal effects in humans. *Nature Medicine, 16*(11), 1277–1283.

Van Anders, S. M. (2015). Beyond sexual orientation: Integrating gender/sex and diverse sexualities via sexual configurations theory. *Archives of Sexual Behavior, 44*(5), 1177–1213.

Williams, D. J., Prior, E., & Wegner, J. (2013). Resolving social problems associated with sexuality: Can a "sex-positive" approach help? *Social Work, 58*(3), 273–276.

Wilson, M. R. (2017). *"That's a big thing to miss": A narrative inquiry of how counselors experience client sexuality* (Publication No. AAI10272144) [Doctoral dissertation, University of Wyoming]. ProQuest Dissertations & Theses Global.

Wilson, M. R. (2019). Too taboo?: Preliminary explorations of counselor experiences of client sexuality. *Journal of Counseling Sexology & Sexual Wellness, 1*(1) 60–68. https://doi.org/10.34296/01011010

Wright, R. J. (2013). *Research methods for counseling: An introduction.* SAGE Publications.

World Health Organization. (2006). *Defining sexual health: Report of a technical consultation on sexual health 28–31 January 2002, Geneva.* https://www.who.int/reproductivehealth/publications/sexual_health/defining_sexual_health.pdf

Zeglin, R. J., Van Dam, D., & Hergenrather, K. C. (2018). An introduction to proposed human sexuality counseling competencies. *International Journal for the Advancement of Counselling, 40*(2), 105–121.

Zeglin, R. J., & Mitchell, J. (2014). Using social media to assess conceptualizations of sexuality. *American Journal of Sexuality Education, 9*(3), 276–291. https://doi.org/10.1080/15546128.2014.933994

Zeglin, R. J., Niemela, D. R. M., & Vandenberg, M. (2019). What does the counseling field say about sexuality? A content analysis. *American Journal of Sexuality Education, 14*(1), 55–73. https://doi.org/10.1080/15546128.2018.1518175

Zoldbrod, A. P. (1998). *Sex smart: How your childhood shaped your sexual life and what to do about it.* New Harbinger Publications.

PART 2

Physiological and Psychological

The Physiology of Sex

Barbara M. Chuback, James A. Young, and Ilene Wong

The most important thing for counselors to recognize about the physiology of sex is that the functional anatomy and biochemistry of sex are inseparable from its psychology. Sex engages both mind and body, which interact in a mutually supportive feedback loop encouraging or discouraging eroticism, depending on the condition of one's body and the context in which it is operating. Professional counseling can play an essential role in promoting healthy, pleasurable sexual function and correcting sexual dysfunction throughout the life span—a role that the rest of this book is dedicated to elaborating. However, this chapter describes the ways that a patient's physical body interacts with their psyche to promote or inhibit sexual health and response to therapeutic psychological interventions.

Biology 101, or Some Caveats Regarding Oversimplification

Standard sexual education curricula teach a binary understanding of sexual biology—that is, males have penises and testicles, whereas females have vaginas, uteruses, and ovaries; males have XY chromosomes, whereas females have XX; testosterone is the male sex hormone, whereas estrogen is the female. There are various ways in which this binary is an inaccurate representation of a more complex reality. Transgender individuals may have stereotypically male anatomy and physiology but identify as female, or vice versa. Intersex individuals, also known as people with differences of sex development, may have anatomy, genetics, and hormone levels that are both stereotypically male and female (e.g., XY genes and a vagina or XX genes with elevated testosterone and a prominent phallus—to name just two of many potential variations)—and thus do not conform to the typical definition of either.

Cases of conflict between gender identity or assignment and biological characteristics can cause great distress to the affected individuals and their families. Human society and culture, including language and health care practices, are generally structured around the notion of binary sex gender, with few safe spaces for those whose embodied existence violates those norms. Transgender persons sometimes seek medical and/or surgical therapies to align their anatomy and physiology with their gendered selves; often they meet resistance from people and systems that would prefer they alter their identity to fit their stereotypically male or female bodies. In contrast, intersex children have often had treatments thrust upon them without their choosing, including masculinizing or feminizing surgeries to alter genital appearance or remove gonads, and medications to manipulate sex hormone levels. While some of these interventions are lifesaving and necessary, others could potentially be deferred or avoided altogether (see Box 4.1.)

Although sexual surgery and pharmacotherapy treatments are often debated in the context of transgender and intersex cases, they are most common among cisgender males and females. Surgery is frequently the treatment of choice for diseases of the genitalia and other erogenous zones, from the benign (e.g., phimosis of the foreskin [in which the skin is too tight] or uterine fibroids [benign tumors] to the malignant [e.g., prostate cancer, breast cancer]). The aforementioned disease conditions are all extremely common; some are also treated with pharmacotherapy manipulating sex hormone levels (e.g., androgen deprivation therapy for prostate cancer, estrogen blockade for hormone-sensitive breast cancers). Thus, when talking to patients about their bodies and sexual activity, it is essential to avoid making assumptions about which parts are present and/or relevant. When discussing sex organs, sensitivity is essential because people who have experienced repeated, unwanted genital manipulation in a medical context (whether for examination or surgery), especially in childhood, may have associated trauma and posttraumatic stress disorder that are triggered by that discourse.

Talking About Sexual Dysfunction: Nomenclature

Talking about sexual problems is complicated by the abundance of diagnostic terms available to characterize sexual problems. Different medical specialties preferentially use

BOX 4.1

Impact of Childhood Surgeries on the Sex Lives of Intersex People

Occurring once in about every 20,000 births, congenital adrenal hyperplasia (CAH) is one of the most common intersex variations or differences in sex differentiation. Children with classic virilizing CAH have XX chromosomes but abnormally high prenatal exposure to testosterone because of the lack of an enzyme in the hormone metabolism pathway. This results in a spectrum of changes in the external genitalia that most commonly include clitoral enlargement but can also include a common urogenital sinus, whereby the vagina and bladder have a common opening. Virilization can also be extragenital and manifested by vocal changes, hair growth, and discordant gender identity. Anywhere from 5% to 17% of children with XX-CAH do not identify as female.

In the past, intersex children with CAH were subject to childhood surgeries to "feminize" their bodies, with the assumption that they would grow up with a female gender identity and desire penetrative vaginal intercourse. As these children grew into adulthood, though, it became apparent that the surgeries imposed upon them before they were too young to consent had severe consequences, including scarring, anorgasmia, and pain with intercourse.

More recently, intersex adults and advocates have raised alarms about the irreversible harms that can result from infant surgery, suggesting that elective procedures should be delayed until children are old enough to declare their gender identity and assent to surgery. For more information on initiatives to celebrate and protect the bodies of intersex youth, visit interACT: Advocates for Intersex Youth at https://interactadvocates.org.

different nomenclatures. Counselors, psychologists, and psychiatrists generally privilege the American Psychiatric Association (APA) *Diagnostic and Statistical Manual of Mental Disorders* (*DSM*) diagnoses, whereas urologists and gynecologists typically use the World Health Organization (WHO) *International Classification of Diseases* (*ICD*) and/or the International Consultation on Sexual Medicine (ICSM)/International Society for the Study of Women's Sexual Health (ISSWSH) terminology (Derogatis et al., 2016; McCabe et al., 2016). It is important to have at least passing familiarity with all of these systems of nomenclature to be able to communicate effectively with health care providers of all kinds and to take advantage of the full array of educational and research literature on human sexuality. Tables 4.1 and 4.2 compare the most recent iterations of *DSM*, *ICD*, and ICSM/ISSWSH diagnostic terminology.

The complexity of Tables 4.1 and 4.2 reflects how far sexual science has evolved since the first edition of the *DSM* (APA, 1952), which listed two diagnoses, "impotence" and "frigidity," in a chapter on "psychological autonomic and visceral disorders." The fifth edition of the manual (*DSM-5*; APA, 2013) is the current state of the art in terms of psychiatric diagnosis of sexual disorders; however, most recent therapeutic research and guidelines are based on the preceding *DSM IV-TR* (APA, 2000) diagnoses or on the ICSM/ISSWSH terminology, which offers a more granular description of sexual pathophysiology. The terminology in the 11th revision of the *ICD* (WHO, 2019) was based primarily on the latter system (Reed et al., 2016).

Table 4.1

Evolution of Sexual Diagnoses Since 1994—Female

DSM-IV (1994)	*ICD-10 (1999)*	*DSM-5 (2013)*	*ICSM-5 (2015)/ ISSWSH (2016)*
Female hypoactive desire disorder	Lack or loss of sexual desire	Female sexual interest/arousal disorder	Hypoactive sexual desire disorder
Female arousal disorder	Female sexual arousal disorder	Female orgasmic disorder	Female genital arousal disorder
		Genital-pelvic pain/penetration disorder	
Female orgasmic disorder	Female orgasmic dysfunction: failure to reach orgasm		Female orgasm disorders Anorgasmia Decreased frequency Muted intensity Premature or delayed anhedonic
Dyspareunia	Nonorganic dyspareunia		Female genital-pelvic pain dysfunction
Vaginismus	Nonorganic vaginismus		
Sexual aversion disorder	Sexual aversion		
Sexual dysfunction due to a general medical condition			
Substance/medication-induced sexual dysfunction		Substance/medication-induced sexual dysfunction	
Sexual dysfunction not otherwise specified		Other specified sexual dysfunctions	Female orgasmic illness syndrome
		Unspecified sexual dysfunction	Persistent genital arousal disorder

Note. DSM-IV = Diagnostic and Statistical Manual of Mental Disorders, Fourth Edition; ICD-10 = International Classification of Diseases, 10th Revision; DSM-5 = Diagnostic and Statistical Manual of Mental Disorders, Fifth Edition; ICSM-5 = International Consultation of Sexual Medicine, Fifth Edition; ISSWSH = International Society for the Study of Women's Sexual Health.

Table 4.2
Evolution of Sexual Diagnoses Since 1994—Male

DSM-IV (1994)	*ICD-10 (1999)*	*DSM-5 (2013)*	*ICSM-5 (2015)*
Male erectile disorder	Erectile dysfunction	Erectile disorder	Erectile dysfunction
Hypoactive sexual desire disorder	Lack of sexual desire	Male hypoactive sexual desire disorder	Male hypoactive sexual desire disorder
Premature (early) ejaculation	Premature ejaculation	Premature (early) ejaculation	Premature ejaculation
Male orgasmic disorder	Orgasmic dysfunction	Delayed ejaculation	Delayed ejaculation: primary or acquired Retrograde ejaculation Anejaculation Anhedonic ejaculation Anorgasmia Hypohedonic orgasm
Male dyspareunia			
Male sexual pain			Painful ejaculation or orgasm
Sexual aversion disorder	Sexual aversion		
Sexual dysfunction due to a general medical condition			
Substance/medication-induced sexual dysfunction		Substance/medication-induced sexual dysfunction	
Sexual dysfunction not otherwise specified		Other specified sexual dysfunctions Unspecified sexual dysfunction	Postorgasmic illness syndrome (provisional diagnoses of restless genital syndromes)

Note. DSM-IV = Diagnostic and Statistical Manual of Mental Disorders, Fourth Edition; ICD-10 = International Classification of Diseases, 10th Revision; DSM-5 = Diagnostic and Statistical Manual of Mental Disorders, Fifth Edition; ICSM-5 = International Consultation of Sexual Medicine, Fifth Edition.

Of note, the various nomenclatures all have different diagnostic terms for male and female dysfunctions, even when the pathology is identical, as with "hypoactive sexual desire disorder," to which the *DSM-5* (APA, 2013) and ICSM-5 (McCabe et al., 2016) append "male" or "female." That this is more a reflection of sociocultural commitment to maintenance of a normative sex or gender binary than of biological reality will be explained in the relevant section on desire later in this chapter. In the remainder of this chapter, we will continue to use male and female with reference to various stereotypical sex binary characteristics. Please recognize that this is a linguistic shorthand and not intended to deny the true complexity of sex gender previously acknowledged.

Lines and Circles: Diagramming Sexual Response

All diagnostic nomenclatures rely on a specific, diagrammatic concept of sexual response. The *DSM-IV-TR* (APA, 2000) reflects a linear understanding of sexual function first formulated by Masters and Johnson (1966) as a trajectory from arousal → plateau → climax → orgasm and later refined by Helen Singer Kaplan (1974) to include sexual desire as an important starting point. This step-by-step progression, based on research study of both male and female subjects, was later criticized by Rosemary Basson, who proposed a cyclic model to better reflect the reactive quality of sexual interest and desire, particularly for women (Basson, 2001; see Figure 4.1.) The combination of female sexual interest/arousal disorder in the *DSM-5* is in part an effort to accommodate the feedback-loop interplay of arousing stimulus and reactive desire that Basson described. Some women report, however, that a linear trajectory better describes their lived sexual experiences (Ferenidou et al., 2016), and the ICSM and ISSWSH argue (McCabe et al., 2016) that there is scientific and therapeutic value in separating desire from arousal response when analyzing sexual (dys)function. In practice, these sexual response models are best considered as a tool with which to think and talk about the experience of sex, rather than as a universal erotic map that must be followed: Not all people experience all stages, nor will they necessarily occur in isolation or in the same sequence each time.

But these tools have utility, and so the remainder of this chapter is structured according to the points of agreement among sexual response models and organized into separate sections addressing the physiologic changes associated with sexual desire, arousal, climax, and resolution.

Desire

Sexual desire is a biopsychosocial motivational state consisting of the sum of various forces that lean toward or away from sexual interest and engagement. It can be discussed in terms of biological drive or response, individual or relational psychology, and sociocultural ideals; desire becomes problematic and may be pathologized when these terms of desire are in conflict (Levine, 2003). For example, *hypoactive sexual desire disorder* is a condition of persistent low sexual interest that is bothersome to the person experiencing it, whether that bother is due to its effects on self-image and/

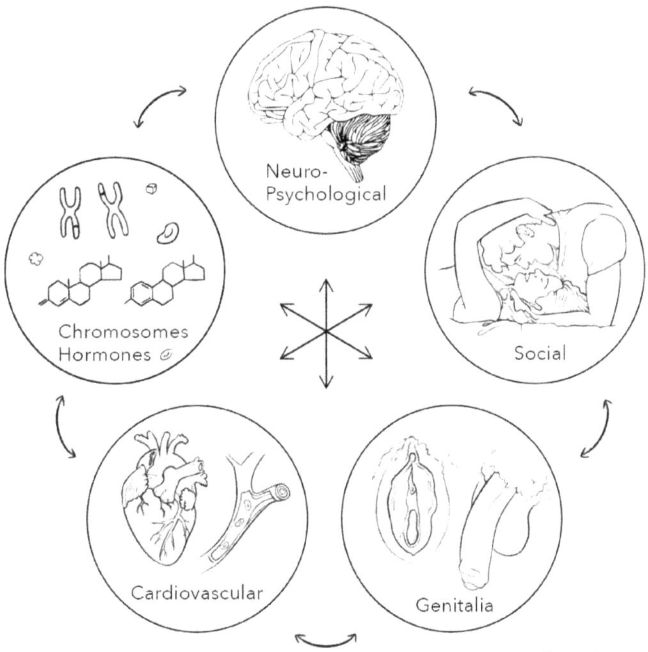

Figure 4.1

Cyclic Model of Sexual Physiology

or intimate relationships. Hypoactive sexual desire disorder is the most commonly reported and studied female sexual dysfunction (Goldstein et al., 2017). At the same time, there is a paucity of research studying and report of low sexual desire in men (Nimbi et al., 2018). This may be a consequence of gendered sociocultural norms, which valorize male libido and female chastity.

Despite this epidemiological difference between the sexes, the biology of sexual desire is similar in both genders, involving identical neurologic pathways that are jumpstarted by any of a number of erotic stimuli, including audible (erotic speech or sound), physical (touch), visual (images), and psychological (fantasies and memories). Portions of the brain that are preferentially activated in response to these stimuli include the orbital frontal region, which controls appraisal and reward systems, and the limbic system, which regulates autonomic function and reinforces behavior through assignation of positive or negative valence to appetitive stimuli (see Figure 4.2.) In contrast, portions of the temporal lobes that are associated with guilt and moral judgment show decreased functional magnetic resonance imaging (fMRI) activity in studies assessing response to erotic stimuli (Maravilla & Yang, 2008). This provides neuroanatomical support for the sexual tipping point model (see Figure 4.3), which describes sexual function as a balance of biopsychosocial excitatory and inhibitory factors (Perelman, 2009).

Support for this model is also found in neurochemical research, which has identified various hormones and neurotransmitters with activity that promotes or inhibits sexual interest (Pfaus, 2009; see Figure 4.4). The neuroactive sex hormones testosterone and estrogen are both present in all people to varying degrees and encourage libido. Decreased sexual interest is a symptom of low sex hormone levels (hypogonadism), whether due to medications, illness, or normal aging in both sexes, and it can be corrected with hormone replacement therapy, including testosterone administration

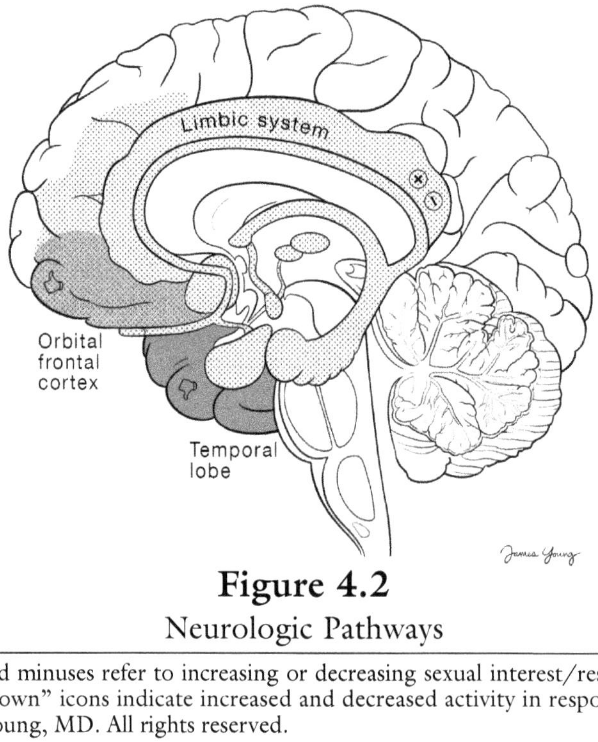

Figure 4.2

Neurologic Pathways

Note. The pluses and minuses refer to increasing or decreasing sexual interest/response. The "thumbs up" and "thumbs down" icons indicate increased and decreased activity in response to erotic stimuli.

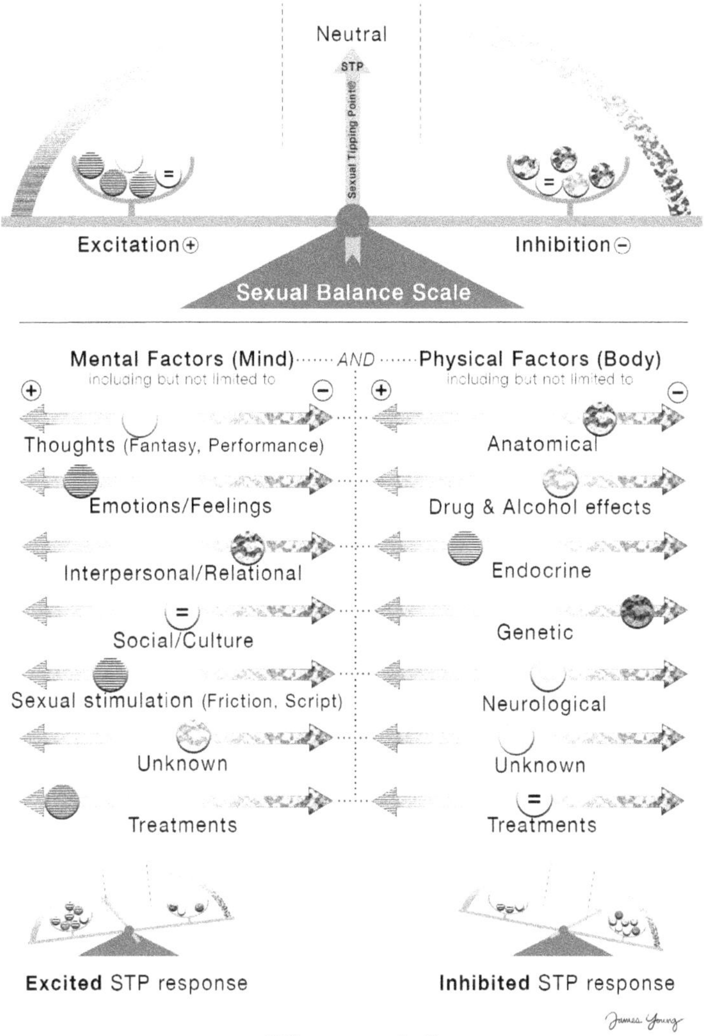

Figure 4.3

Sexual Tipping Point®: A Biomedical-Psychosocial and Cultural Model

Note. Adapted from the Sexual Tipping Point® model by Perelman (2009), describing sexuality as a balance of biopsychosocial excitatory and inhibitory factors. The pluses and minuses refer to increasing or decreasing sexual interest/response. STP = sexual tipping point.

to postmenopausal women with hypoactive sexual desire disorder and maintenance of normal estrogen levels in men. Dopamine and melanocortin are neurotransmitters that stimulate attention and appetite in response to sexual cues, whereas most serotonin activity inhibits sexual interest and responsiveness by inducing a physiologic state similar to that of postorgasmic sexual satiety.

These neurochemical effects have important implications for the pharmacotherapy of neuropsychiatric disease (see Figure 4.4). Diminished sexual response is a common adverse effect of antipsychotic medications, such as olanzapine (brand name Zyprexa) and risperidone, that block dopamine receptors, and of SSRIs, such as fluoxetine (brand name Prozac) and citalopram (brand name Celexa), used to treat depression and anxiety. In contrast, medications that increase dopamine activity, such as levodopa

Neurotransmitter	Role in Sexual Response
⊕ Dopamine	stimulates attention and appetite in response to sexual cues
⊕ Estrogen	stimulates libido
⊕ Melanocortin	stimulates attention and appetite in response to sexual cues
⊕ Norepinephrine	stimulates smooth muscle in corpora cavernosa to relax and dilate
⊕ Nitric Oxide	stimulates smooth muscle in corpora cavernosa to relax and dilate
⊕ Oxytocin	stimulates analgesia and positive feelings
⊕ Prostaglandin	stimulates smooth muscle in corpora cavernosa to relax and dilate
⊖ Serotonin	inhibits sexual interest and responsiveness
⊕ Testosterone	stimulates libido

Figure 4.4

Neurotransmitters in Sexual Response

Note. The pluses and minuses refer to increasing or decreasing sexual interest/response.

and carbidopa, that are used to treat Parkinson's disease and hyperprolactinemia can enhance libido, as can bupropion, which works as a norepinephrine and dopamine reuptake inhibitor. Flibanserin and bremelanotide—two medications that are currently approved by the U.S. Food and Drug Administration (FDA) for the treatment of hypoactive sexual desire disorder in premenopausal women—have similar mechanisms of action, promoting norepinephrine/dopamine and melanocortin activity, respectively.

When considering norepinephrine-like drugs, it is important to note that they can affect both the sympathetic ("fight or flight") and parasympathetic ("rest and digest") arms of the peripheral nervous system. Thus, sexual stimuli increase blood flow from the heart (via the sympathetic nerves) and increase blood flow to the genitals (via the parasympathetic). Some perception of threat, anger, or fear can promote sexual response through this autonomic excitation transfer process. However, the type and degree of stimuli that evoke sexual excitation or inhibition vary among individuals and may be augmented or attenuated by the relational or cultural context in which the stimuli are processed.

Arousal

Sexual arousal typically follows from neuropsychological interest but can also result reflexively from certain kinds of physical stimuli. Arousal responses include increased heart rate, blood pressure, and respiration, with increased genital blood flow. This further enhances the sensitivity of the penis and clitoris, both of which have some of the most dense collections of nerves in the human body (see Figure 4.5).

Male erection occurs when the arteries in the corpora cavernosa (the two tubes of spongy erectile tissue in the penis) become engorged with blood when nerves are stimulated either by touch (via parasympathetic nerves in the lower spine) or by arousing thoughts (through the so-called "erection center" in the mid spine; Dean & Lue, 2005; see Figure 4.5). These stimuli cause the release of nitric oxide, norepinephrine, and prostaglandin chemicals, which cause the smooth muscle in the corpora cavernosa to relax and dilate. The expanding of the arterial sinuses actually compresses the venous outflow of the penis, allowing blood to build up against the *tunica albuginea* (the sheath of tissue surrounding the corpora cavernosa), creating an erection. Medications and diseases that reduce genital blood flow (e.g., medications for blood pressure and heart disease) can cause erectile dysfunction (see Box 4.2). Conversely, medications that increase arterial dilation, such as sildenafil (brand name Viagra) and tadalafil (brand name Cialis), can improve erectile function.

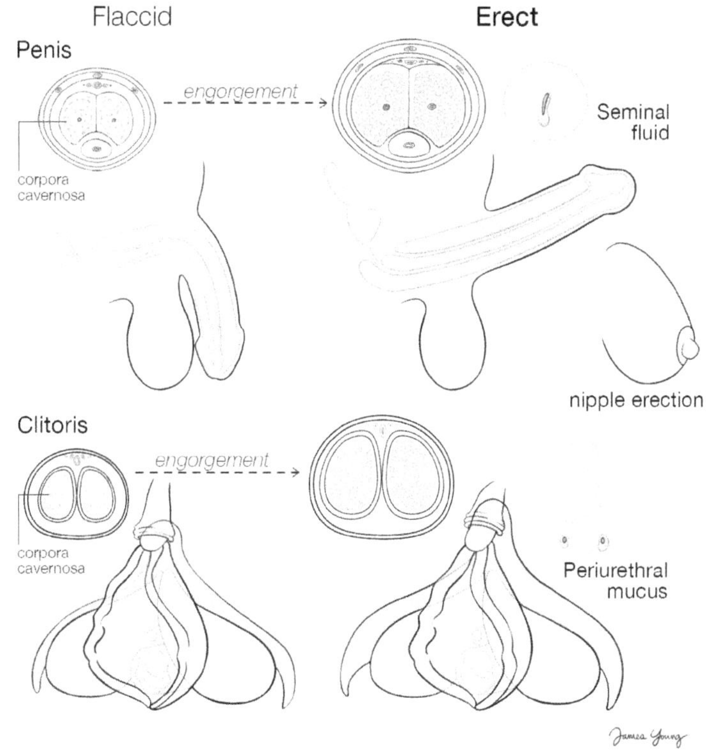

Figure 4.5

Comparison of Arousal Physiology

Note.

BOX 4.2

Erectile Dysfunction: An Overview

The large host of factors that may result in erectile dysfunction can be loosely categorized into cardiovascular, neurological, hormonal, psychological, local, and drug-induced etiologies (Hatzimouratidis et al., 2010) as follows:

Cardiovascular
- High blood pressure
- Diabetes
- Coronary artery disease
- High cholesterol/lipids
- Smoking
- Surgery (prostatectomy)
- Radiation

Neurological
- Spinal cord and brain injuries
- Parkinson's disease and Alzheimer's disease
- Multiple sclerosis
- Stroke
- Surgery (prostatectomy, rectal resection)
- Radiation

Hormonal
- Low testosterone
- Abnormal thyroid
- Abnormal cortisol
- Elevated prolactin

Psychological
- Anxiety/depression
- Posttraumatic stress disorder
- Performance-related anxiety
- Interpersonal issues with partner

Local (due to penile factors)
- Peyronie's disease (penile curvature due to plaques)
- Phimosis (scarring that prevents retraction of foreskin)
- Penile fracture

Drug-induced
- Beta-blockers (e.g., Lopressor)
- Antidepressants (e.g., Prozac)
- Antipsychotics (e.g., Risperidol)
- Antiandrogens (e.g., Lupron)
- Drugs used recreationally, including alcohol, cannabis, and heroin

Females have similar physiology, despite differences in anatomy (see Figure 4.5). Similar to the penis, the female clitoris also has *corpora cavernosa*, which dilate and engorge in response to sexual stimuli. Unlike the male corpora, the female corpora are mostly internal to the pelvis, with the glans (or head) of the clitoris being the only external portion. The head of the clitoris, like the head of the penis, does not have a tunica albuginea surrounding it; thus, although blood flow produces swelling, the clitoris doesn't become quite as rigid as the male erection, with its external corpora cavernosa. Similarly, much has been made of the *G spot*, which refers to tissue between the vagina and urethra (urinary tube) that is packed with nerves and blood vessels. This tissue is analogous to the corpus spongiosum at the bottom of the penile shaft and the prostate in males, so it is no surprise that stimulation of that area would feel good. During arousal, the other labial and vaginal tissues engorge with blood as well, further increasing their sensitivity to stimuli.

Women also experience relaxation of the muscles in the pelvis and vagina, which lengthen and widen the vagina. Additionally, increased blood flow to the vaginal mucosa induces vaginal lubrication, which is fluid secreted by the cells of the vaginal lining (Pastor & Chmel, 2018). In addition to easing vaginal penetration, lubrication is also thought to neutralize acids, making the vaginal milieu more favorable to sperm in a way that is similar to the pre-ejaculate fluid that is secreted from male *Cowper's glands* (small glands located at the base of the penis near the urinary tube). Suboptimal lubrication in women can be associated with painful intercourse, particularly in postmenopausal women, whose deficit of estrogen and testosterone causes atrophy and dryness of the vaginal tissues.

Male erection and female lubrication are the most obvious examples of genital arousal; however, the concept of subjective or cognitive arousal—namely, one's awareness of the aforementioned physical changes in the body and their interpretation as signifiers of arousal—is also important. Particularly among women, for whom arousal disorders are more common, there can be a disconnect between physiological response to sexual stimuli and mental arousal. Not all women experience genital engorgement and lubrication as signs of sexual arousal or are aroused by genital cues; conversely, some women who do not experience the classic symptoms of genital arousal can feel subjective arousal (Meston & Stanton, 2019). This is why the medications that are most commonly used to treat male erectile dysfunction (e.g., sildenafil, tadalafil) are not FDA approved to treat sexual dysfunction in women: Studies showed that while the medications do increase blood flow to the female genitalia as well as the male, women did not experience this as an erotic benefit.

Almost any area of the body can be considered an erogenous zone, and extragenital areas of the body can be as important as the genitals during the arousal phase. The obvious example is that of breast stimulation leading to the release of oxytocin, which causes nipple erection via the contraction of smooth muscle under the skin (see Figure 4.5). For women, in particular, fMRI studies have shown that nipple stimulation produces increased activity in the same paracentral lobule of the brain that registers vaginal, clitoral, and cervical sensation (Misery & Talagas, 2017). But in addition to the classic "hot spots" of the genitals, anus, and breasts, the erogenous zone maps generated by one Finnish study included the mouth, buttocks, thigh, and neck, with the researchers acknowledging that "practically, the whole body was capable of triggering sexually arousing sensations when touched by a partner" (Nummenmaa et al., 2016, p. 1215).

Climax

Orgasm, or sexual climax, is an intense, transient sensation of pleasure that is associated with a state of altered consciousness and spastic pelvic muscle contractions. It is generally achieved through rhythmic stimulation of the genitalia, although it can result from stimulation of any highly sensate body part and even through imagined rhythmic sexual activities with embodied fantasy. The historical debate over whether female orgasm is or ought to be of clitoral or vaginal origin is in part a false dichotomy, as both external vulvar and intravaginal contact stimulate the clitoris along different portions of its length (Dean & Lue, 2005). Vibratory mechanical devices can help to meet the necessary sensory threshold when nerve function is compromised and/or a sufficiently rhythmic stimulus cannot be achieved by bodily contact or other means. Orgasm may be a function of synchronized sensory and somatic signals mutually reinforcing each other, both within an individual nervous system and interpersonally in the setting of partnered intercourse. This feedback loop of mind-body stimulation leads to a trance state (Pastor & Chmel, 2018).

In males, this experience is typically simultaneous with the ejaculation of semen, and premature, delayed, and absent orgasm in males are described by the diagnostic terms "premature ejaculation," "delayed ejaculation," and "anejaculation." Although expulsion of semen from the posterior urethra is aided by the forceful pelvic muscle contractions that are characteristic of orgasm, these terms are often misnomers, as various medical and surgical conditions (e.g., those affecting the prostate) can interfere with ejaculation without compromising the capacity for orgasm (Meston & Stanton, 2019). Contrarily, some women produce a sufficient volume of periurethral mucous with arousal that their powerful pelvic muscle contractions manifest in "squirting" as part of their normal orgasm experience. This is sometimes confused with *climacturia*, or urinary incontinence during orgasm, which can occur in both sexes.

Such muscle spasms can be experienced as a painful "charley horse" and can cause pain both during and after sexual activity. But the neurochemistry of orgasm offers protection against this, as during the start of orgasm dopamine and norepinephrine levels are elevated, and during peak trance state, natural opioids are released within the brain, along with oxytocin and vasopressin, which also reduce pain and produce pleasure (Pastor & Chmel, 2018; see Figure 4.4). This brain signaling also promotes feelings of reward and affection for one's partner. Brain imaging during orgasm reveals decreased blood flow across the prefrontal cortex, which is the portion of the brain that controls executive function (Misery & Talagas, 2017; see Figure 4.2). Some theorize that this may explain why *excessive cognition*, or "thinking too hard," inhibits orgasm, as an otherwise engaged prefrontal cortex will not shut down in the manner required. In contrast, mindfulness meditation and other attentive, interoceptive practices promote orgasmic response (Pastor & Chmel, 2018).

Because orgasm integrates cognitive, neurochemical, and pelvic muscular processes, its associated disorders may respond to treatments targeting any of these mechanisms. Muted or weak orgasms might be strengthened through pelvic muscle exercise, particularly regular Kegel contractions (Meston & Stanton, 2019). Delayed or difficult-to-achieve orgasm can respond to increased force and rhythm of the provocative erotic stimulus, administration of medications such as oxytocin (the "feel good" hormone secreted during arousal and breastfeeding, among other activities), and/or meditation (Misery & Talagas, 2017). Premature ejaculation or orgasm is treated with the reverse of these strategies, including application of topical anesthetics to blunt sensation, administration of SSRIs that inhibit orgasm (the mechanism for which is unknown), and stop-start and squeeze behaviors that interfere with entry into a trance state. These are the most common physiologic orgasmic dysfunctions; diagnoses such as *persistent genital arousal disorder*, whereby there is persistent, unwanted genital arousal that is not relieved by orgasm, and *postorgasmic illness syndrome*, whereby one experiences a varied syndrome of flulike symptoms and malaise after orgasm, are more controversial and as yet poorly understood.

Resolution

In the linear Masters and Johnson (1966) model, sexual climax is followed by resolution, in which the body returns to its physiologic baseline. Resolution is characterized by feelings of well-being and fatigue and a sense of satiety that is associated with a rise in serotonin levels. In men, there is a "refractory" period following loss of erection in which the penis is resistant to a subsequent erection, the duration of which is variable and the biological cause not yet understood. In contrast, women may cycle back through states of desire, arousal, and even climax, which is why some consider the resolution phase of questionable clinical significance and prefer the cyclical Basson (2002) model over the Masters and Johnson model.

Conclusion

This chapter, by its nature, presents a brief overview. However, by highlighting the complexity and diversity of sexual physiology, as well as how much medical science still cannot explain, we hope to have shown that the one truism when it comes to human sexuality is that one size does not fit all. The counselor's role, then, is to appreciate the myriad of medical, psychological, and social factors that can contribute to a client's happiness or dissatisfaction with their sex life. We conclude this chapter with some commonly questions asked about the physiology of sex.

Questions You Always Wanted to Ask

1. **I typically have only one orgasm at a time, if I'm able to have one at all. Is there something wrong with me? Also, what's a refractory period?**
   There are very few concepts in the popular perception of sex that generate more interest than the idea of multiple orgasms, which can be the subject of humor, aspiration, and even unhealthy obsession. It goes without saying that having "only" one orgasm is perfectly healthy; indeed, it is likely the norm, particularly for men, due to the refractory period after ejaculation whereby neurochemicals released during ejaculation inhibit the formation of a second erection. The male refractory period—characterized by flaccid penis, reduced interest in sexual activity, and hypersensitivity to stimulation—can last anywhere from minutes to days, with the duration of the refractory period increasing with age.

   In contrast, females do not have a true refractory period and have the potential to achieve multiple orgasms, if there is appropriate desire and sexual stimulation. However, fatigue and/or the peaceful satisfaction during the resolution phase may make women less likely to pursue additional orgasms.
2. **My erection/ability to climax/vaginal lubrication isn't what it used to be when I was younger. Is that normal?**
   Absolutely! Studies on aging show that sexual function begins to change most noticeably when a person enters their 40s (Laumann et al., 2004). Older people are more likely to develop the kind of medical conditions that can impact genital blood supply and innervation, which can affect rigidity of erection, increase the amount of stimulation necessary to achieve orgasm, and even decrease the intensity of orgasm.

   Hormonal levels can also fluctuate during the aging process, with estimates of hypogonadism (low testosterone) being approximately 38% in men over the age of 45 (Mulligan et al., 2006). Hypogonadism can cause decreased libido in both genders. Additionally, women who have gone through menopause have lower estrogen levels and develop vaginal atrophy, a thinning of the genital tissues and decreased lubrication that can cause pain and even bleeding during sex.

3. **How can I make my sex life better? When is the right time to seek medical help?**

Across the board, the best things that a person can do to make their sex life better are the same habits recommended for a heart-healthy lifestyle, such as the following:

Exercise regularly. Studies have shown that moderate-to-vigorous aerobic exercise can improve erectile function (Silva et al., 2017). There is also some evidence to suggest that physical activity—specifically Kegel exercises in postmenopausal women—may positively affect arousal and orgasm (Carcelén-Fraile et al., 2020).

Cultivate healthy eating habits. Diet-based weight loss has been linked to improved sexual function in obese men, and a Mediterranean diet has been shown to slow down the development of sexual dysfunction in diabetics.

Use common sense when drinking alcohol. While some data show that moderate alcohol consumption can actually improve sexual function for both men and women by potentially increasing both arousal and genital blood flow, heavy drinking and alcohol abuse (which can be associated with liver disease) are strongly associated with erectile dysfunction.

Avoid tobacco use. Smoking causes damage to the blood vessels that are essential to genital blood flow during arousal and is thus strongly associated with both erectile dysfunction and female sexual dysfunction (Allen & Walter, 2018).

Stay mentally healthy. Numerous studies have linked anxiety and depression to sexual dysfunction, both in terms of decreased desire and impaired arousal. Therapy and other coping mechanisms including mindfulness and yoga (which was shown in a randomized controlled trial to improve arousal in women with metabolic syndrome) can be crucially important to sexual health.

Regular visits to a doctor can help to identify the medical conditions that adversely affect sexual function, opening up a conversation to determine whether you would benefit from medical help. As a rule of thumb, clinicians are more likely to suggest interventions in people who have significant bother from their symptoms, or whose symptoms have been either persistent (in the range of 6 months in duration) or pervasive (occuring during more than 75% of sexual encounters).

Therapies exist for a number of different conditions that can cause distress, including erectile dysfunction (sildenafil and tadalafil), vaginal dryness (vaginal creams), premature ejaculation (SSRIs and topical lidocaine), and female sexual arousal disorder (flibanserin and bremelanotide). All treatments, of course, have risks and benefits, and only you, in consultation with a medical professional, can determine when it's the right time to try a medication.

References

Allen, M. S., & Walter, E. E. (2018). Health-related lifestyle factors and sexual dysfunction: A meta-analysis of population-based research. *The Journal of Sexual Medicine, 15*(4), 458–475. https://doi.org/10.1016/j.jsxm.2018.02.008

American Psychiatric Association. (1952). *Diagnostic and statistical manual of mental disorders.*

American Psychiatric Association. (1994). *Diagnostic and statistical manual of mental disorders* (4th ed.).

American Psychiatric Association. (2000). *Diagnostic and statistical manual of mental disorders* (4th ed., text rev.).

American Psychiatric Association. (2013). *Diagnostic and statistical manual of mental disorders* (5th ed.). https://doi.org/10.1176/appi.books.9780890425596

Basson, R. (2001). Female sexual response: The role of drugs in the management of sexual dysfunction. *Obstetrics & Gynecology, 98*(2), 350–353. https://doi.org/10.1016/S0029-7844(01)01452-1

Basson, R. (2002). Rethinking low sexual desire in women. *BJOG: An International Journal of Obstetrics and Gynaecology, 109*(4), 357–363. https://doi.org/10.1111/j.1471-0528.2002.01002.x

Carcelén-Fraile, M., Aibar-Almazán, A., Martínez-Amat, A., Cruz-Díaz, D., Díaz-Mohedo, E., Redecillas-Peiró, M., & Hita-Contreras, F. (2020). Effects of physical exercise on sexual function and quality of sexual life related to menopausal symptoms in peri- and postmenopausal women: A systematic review. *International Journal of Environmental Research and Public Health, 17*(8), 2680–2696. https://doi.org/10.3390/ijerph17082680

Dean, R. C., & Lue, T. F. (2005). Physiology of penile erection and pathophysiology of erectile dysfunction. *Urologic Clinics of North America, 32*(4), 379–395. https://doi.org/10.1016/j.ucl.2005.08.007

Derogatis, L., Sand, M., Balon, R., Rosen, R., & Parish, S. (2016). Toward a more evidence-based nosology and nomenclature for female sexual dysfunctions—Part I. *The Journal of Sexual Medicine, 13*(12), 1881–1887. https://doi.org/10.1016/j.jsxm.2016.09.014

Ferenidou, F., Kirana, P. S., Fokas, K., Hatzichristou, D., & Athanasiadis, L. (2016). Sexual response models: Toward a more flexible pattern of women's sexuality. *The Journal of Sexual Medicine, 13*(9), 1369–1376. https://doi.org/10.1016/j.jsxm.2016.07.008

Goldstein, I., Kim, N. N., Clayton, A. H., DeRogatis, L. R., Giraldi, A., Parish, S. J., Pfaus, J., Simon, J. A., Kingsberg, S. A., Meston, C., Stahl, S. M., Wallen, K., & Worsley, R. (2017). Hypoactive sexual desire disorder: International Society for the Study of Women's Sexual Health (ISSWSH) expert consensus panel review. *Mayo Clinic Proceedings, 92*(1), 114–128. https://doi.org/10.1016/j.mayocp.2016.09.018

Hatzimouratidis, K., Amar, E., Eardley, I., Giuliano, F., Hatzichristou, D., Montorsi, F., Vardi, Y., & Wespes, E. (2010). Guidelines on male sexual dysfunction: Erectile dysfunction and premature ejaculation. *European Urology, 57*(5), 804–814. https://doi.org/10.1016/j.eururo.2010.02.020

Kaplan, H. S. (1974). *The new sex therapy: Active treatment of sexual dysfunctions.* Brunner/Mazel.

Laumann, E., Nicolosi, A., Glasser, D., Paik, A., Gingell, C., Moreira, E., & Wang, T. (2004). Sexual problems among women and men aged 40–80 y: Prevalence and correlates identified in the Global Study of Sexual Attitudes and Behaviors. *International Journal of Impotence Research, 17*(1), 39–57. https://doi.org/10.1038/sj.ijir.3901250

Levine, S. B. (2003). The nature of sexual desire: A clinician's perspective. *Archives of Sexual Behavior, 32*(3), 279–285. https://doi.org/10.1023/a:1023421819465

Maravilla, K. R., & Yang, C. C. (2008). Magnetic resonance imaging and the female sexual response: Overview of techniques, results, and future directions. *The Journal of Sexual Medicine*, *5*(7), 1559–1571. https://doi.org/10.1111/j.1743-6109.2008.00839.x
Masters, W. H., & Johnson, V. E. (1966). *Human sexual response.* Little, Brown Co.
McCabe, M. P., Sharlip, I. D., Atalla, E., Balon, R., Fisher, A. D., Laumann, E., Lee, S. W., Lewis, R., & Segraves, R. T. (2016). Definitions of sexual dysfunctions in women and men: A consensus statement from the Fourth International Consultation on Sexual Medicine 2015. *The Journal of Sexual Medicine*, *13*(2), 135–143. https://doi.org/10.1016/j.jsxm.2015.12.019
Meston, C. M., & Stanton, A. M. (2019). Understanding sexual arousal and subjective-genital arousal desynchrony in women. *Nature Reviews Urology*, *16*(2), 107–120. https://doi.org/10.1038/s41585-018-0142-6
Misery, L., & Talagas, M. (2017). Innervation of the male breast: Psychological and physiological consequences. *Journal of Mammary Gland Biology and Neoplasia*, *22*(2), 109–115. https://doi.org/10.1007/s10911-017-9380-0
Mulligan, T., Frick, M. F., Zuraw, Q. C., Stemhagen, A., & McWhirter, C. (2006). Prevalence of hypogonadism in males aged at least 45 years: The HIM study. *International Journal of Clinical Practice*, *60*(7), 762–769. https://doi.org/10.1111/j.1742-1241.2006.00992.x
Nimbi, F. M., Tripodi, F., Rossi, R., & Simonelli, C. (2018). Expanding the analysis of psychosocial factors of sexual desire in men. *The Journal of Sexual Medicine*, *15*(2), 230–244. https://doi.org/10.1016/j.jsxm.2017.11.227
Nummenmaa, L., Suvilehto, J. T., Glerean, E., Santtila, P., & Hietanen, J. K. (2016). Topography of human erogenous zones. *Archives of Sexual Behavior*, *45*(5), 1207–1216. https://doi.org/10.1007/s10508-016-0745-z
Pastor, Z., & Chmel, R. (2018). Differential diagnostics of female "sexual" fluids: A narrative review. *International Urogynecology Journal*, *29*(5), 621–629. https://doi.org/10.1007/s00192-017-3527-9
Perelman, M. A. (2009). The sexual tipping point: A mind/body model for sexual medicine. *The Journal of Sexual Medicine*, *6*(3), 629–632. https://doi.org/10.1111/j.1743-6109.2008.01177.x
Pfaus, J. G. (2009). Pathways of sexual desire. *The Journal of Sexual Medicine*, *6*(6), 1506–1533. https://doi.org/10.1111/j.1743-6109.2009.01309.x
Reed, G. M., Drescher, J., Krueger, R. B., Atalla, E., Cochran, S. D., First, M. B., Cohen-Kettenis, P. T., Arango-de Montis, I., Parish, S. J., Cottler, S., Briken, P., & Saxena, S. (2016). Disorders related to sexuality and gender identity in the ICD-11: Revising the ICD-10 classification based on current scientific evidence, best clinical practices, and human rights considerations. *World Psychiatry*, *15*(3), 205–221. https://doi.org/10.1002/wps.20354
Silva, A. B., Sousa, N., Azevedo, L. F., & Martins, C. (2017). Physical activity and exercise for erectile dysfunction: Systematic review and meta-analysis. *British Journal of Sports Medicine*, *51*(19), 1419–1424. https://doi.org/10.1136/bjsports-2016-096418
World Health Organization. (1999). *International classification of diseases, 10th revision.*
World Health Organization. (2019). *International classification of diseases, 11th revision.* https://icd.who.int/

The Role of the Brain in Sex and Desire

Cheryl A. Faber and Aninda B. Acharya

We have evolved a nervous system that acts in the interest of our gonads, and one attuned to the demands of reproductive competition.
— M. T. Ghiselin,
The Economy of Nature and the Evolution of Sex

Sex is fun. Sex is exciting. Sex can be pleasurable, painful, exhilarating, frightening, naughty, and a little bit nice. It can sometimes be all those things at once. It can be like getting hit by a ton of bricks and liking it. To what do we owe this avalanche of sensations? Why, to the most important sex organ, of course: the brain.

This does not mean that other sex organs of the body are less important, but without our brains we would not be able to experience or physically perform most of the activities required to make sex happen. The exception to this is penile erection and ejaculation, which can occur from a spinal cord reflex, without the brain's input, which certainly gives one food for thought (Giuliano & Rampin, 2000; Truitt & Coolen, 2002). It is also true that, even in the absence of direct involvement of any of our other traditional sex organs, our brain can take us all the way to sexual fulfillment.

Sex is fundamental. Sex is instrumental to individual procreation and the survival of the species. It is one of our most basic drives. Moreover, sexual health and the pleasure derived from it positively predict general health outcomes (Jannini et al., 2016). Other studies have shown that older individuals maintain greater cognitive abilities if they remain sexually active (Wright & Jenks, 2016). Despite its crucial role in our lives and livelihood, a scientific understanding of human sexual behavior has remained elusive.

Across species, there is a great diversity of behavior associated with reproduction. Much of what we have learned about sexual behavior has been derived from studies of animals. In fact, the vast majority of neuroscientific research on the subject of sex has been on the rat (Georgiadis et al., 2012; Pfaus, 2009). It remains to be seen whether research on animals can be translated to humans (Pfaus et al., 2003). See Box 5.1.

BOX 5.1

What Makes Us Human?

All mammals have sex. In fact, there is considerable evidence that mammals other than humans have sex for pleasure, not just for procreation (De la Garza-Mercer, 2007). There are many instances of same-sex copulation among other species. Self-stimulatory behavior has also been well described in other mammals. As humans, we do like to think, however, that we are something special compared with other creatures. Anders Ågmo (2007) argued in his book on comparative sexual behavior that humans benefit from social learning (learning from observation) and language (enabling vivid mental representation). Introspection and moral thinking might also be additional factors (Ågmo, 2007). The full extent of sexual divergence between species is yet unknown.

Humans exhibit a much wider diversity of sexual preferences and behaviors than other animals. This could support the hypothesis that sexual learning plays a greater role in the sexual lives of humans than in other species. Furthermore, societal and cultural norms heavily influence our views on sex and its application. There is even speculation that the major anatomical changes that occurred when we became upright bipeds, allowing improved vaginal access from the face-to-face position, may have transformed sex into an even more socially engaging and emotionally bonding activity (Gallup, 2015). Combined with the virtues of human intelligence, creativity, and precise motor control, human sex is full of practices not aimed at reproduction, while such behavior is comparatively rare in other species.

Fortunately, in recent years new advances in brain imaging have allowed us to explore the human brain in ways impossible even a decade ago. With the advent of functional magnetic resonance imaging (fMRI) and improvements in positron-emission tomography (PET) scanning technology, we can see the brain in action. This has allowed us to explore which areas of the brain are turned on and off during sexual activity. Trying to reproduce the act of sex in a medical scanner, however, poses its own set of challenges. See Box 5.2.

Because sex is such an intrinsic part of reproductive life, it should not come as a surprise that many of the structures in our brain that are most fundamental to sexual pleasure are also the most primitive from an evolutionary standpoint. The limbic system is a group of structures deep in the brain that includes the olfactory bulb, amygdala, thalamus, hypothalamus, hippocampus, corpus callosum, and several other brain areas (see Figure 5.1). The limbic system was introduced as a concept by Paul MacLean in 1952 and was long considered the seat of emotions (MacLean, 1998). The limbic lobe, as a unified system, mediates psychological responses to emotional stimuli. It is associated with memory, attention, and emotional response and thereby has a substantial impact on behavior. It is this area of the brain that is fundamental to learned responses associated with fear, pleasure, and reward (Roxo et al., 2011). The limbic system also has an important olfactory function. The olfactory bulb, a component of the limbic system, processes odor stimuli and is responsible for smell perception. Its close ties with its other neighbors in the limbic system explain why a smell can trigger a complex jumble of emotions and memories (Salloway, 1997).

Not surprisingly, damage to the limbic areas can substantially impact an individual's behavior and response to their environment. This includes dysregulation of impulses such as eating, drinking, and sexual behavior. For example, Klüver-Bucy syndrome results from bilateral lesions of the temporal lobe, including the amygdala (see Figures 5.1 and 5.2). This condition presents with compulsive eating, hypersexuality, insertion of inappropriate objects in the mouth (hyperorality), trouble recognizing objects

BOX 5.2

The Challenges of Sex in the Scanner

Positron-emission tomography (PET) and functional MRI (fMRI) are two widely used technologies for studying brain function during sexual activity. Functional neuroimaging works on the principle that areas of the brain that are more active will demonstrate increased blood flow and oxygen. PET involves the injection of a radioactive tracer, which means this method can only be used sparingly to avoid radiation-related complications. While fMRI is not associated with significant side effects, it has other limitations on account of it being performed in a noisy and cramped environment. Neither technique tolerates movement of the subject, which is a problem when studying sex, a dynamic activity. Also, while changes in the brain can occur over microseconds, these scanners only capture changes over seconds (fMRI) to minutes (PET). Unfortunately, these technologies are not conducive to capturing the act of sex in a natural environment.

The most common technique for studying sexual activity by neuroimaging involves showing visual erotica while a person is being scanned. In addition to scanning the brain, the subject is often asked subjective questions (e.g., Do you find this picture arousing?). There are also other more objective measures of sexual arousal, such as devices that measure penile tumescence (erection) or vaginal vasocongestion (increased blood flow). There are studies that have looked at other forms of sexual stimulation, such as mental imagery, in which case the subject is asked to imagine a sexually charged scenario. Tactile genital stimulation studies have also been done. These generally involve self-stimulation or use of a sexual aid (e.g., vibrator). There have been partnered studies, but these are few and far between. These generally involve a jointly participating couple, because of the ethical ramifications of a participant having sex with a stranger (Georgiadis & Kringelbach, 2012).

visually (visual agnosia), and docility (Glick & Roose, 1993). Other damage to the limbic system can lead to sleep disorders, psychosensory disorders in the form of illusions and hallucinations, changes in the level of consciousness, and even seizures (Wen et al., 2017).

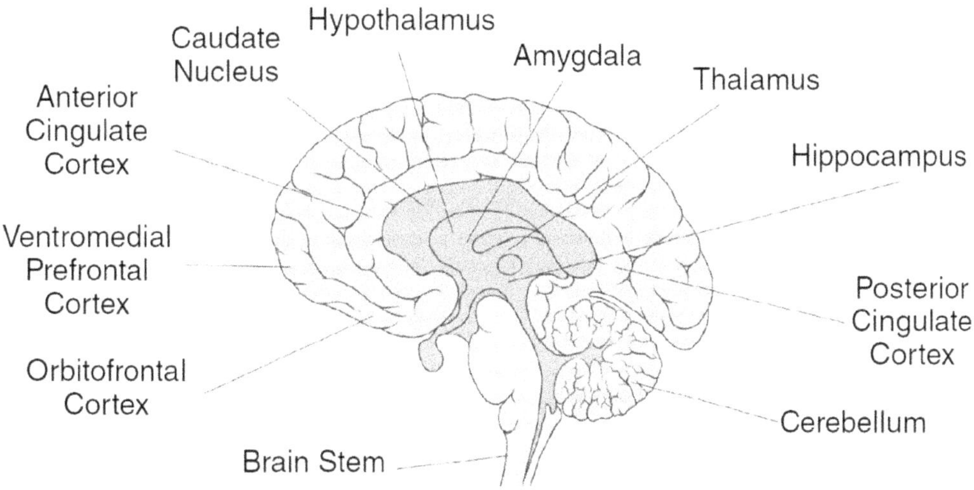

Figure 5.1

Medial View of the Brain Showing Location of Brain Structures

Note. From Patrick J. Lynch, medical illustrator and C. Carl Jaffe, MD, cardiologist. Used under Creative Commons Attribution 2.5 License, 2006. Components of the limbic system include the amygdala, cingulate gyrus, hypothalamus, and hippocampus. The olfactory bulb is not shown.

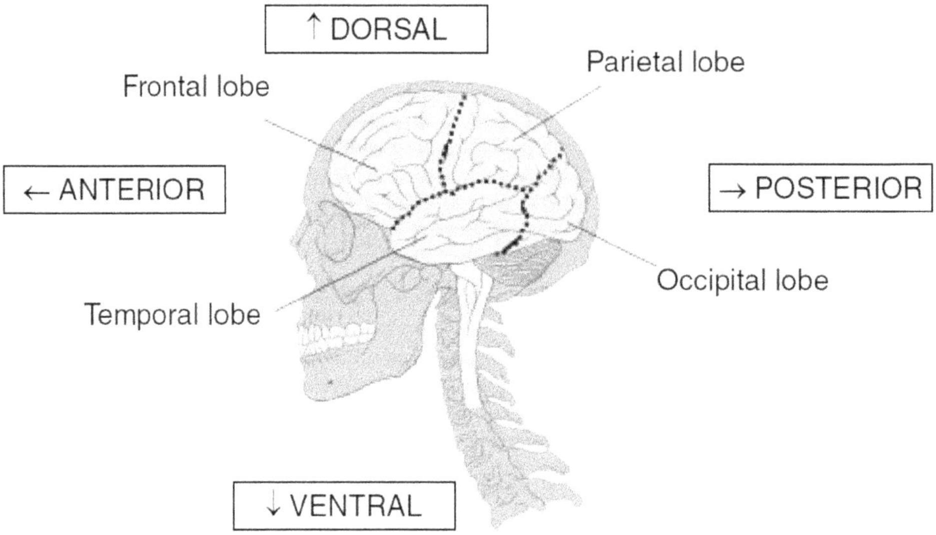

Figure 5.2

Topographical View of the Brain Showing the Lobes of the Cerebrum

Note. From Patrick J. Lynch, medical illustrator and C. Carl Jaffe, MD, cardiologist. Used under Creative Commons Attribution 2.5 License, 2006. The brain is composed of two hemispheres. This figure shows the left hemisphere.

Sexual experiences are not, however, simply a jumble of primal emotions, urges, and associations. Recent research using advanced brain imaging such as fMRI and PET scans have revealed that during sexual activity many of the areas of the brain that "light up" are those same areas that are important to our most sophisticated forms of thought. The activity of the subcortical structures of the brain (including the limbic system) is intrinsically linked to the prefrontal cortex (see Figure 5.1), which is the seat of planning, analysis, and decision-making—that is, the *executive functions* (Petrides & Pandya, 2012).

Although you might think that the emotional part of your brain fires up first and then the executive part takes over to guide you to the final outcome of a sexual encounter, you would be in error. In actuality, there is an intensely complex interplay between these regions that ultimately leads to an outcome (Georgiadis & Kringelbach, 2012). This outcome may not always be the most prudent one, but it is ultimately always a teaching point. We learn from each encounter and build on it with subsequent encounters, a concept that is known as *sexual learning*. This is deeply important to the ultimate development of our sexual lives, as we form memories, opinions, preferences, biases, fears, and even fetishes that will guide us—for better or worse—through the remainder of our lives (Golden et al., 2016; Pfaus et al., 2012).

The Brain in a Nutshell

Before we get into the nitty-gritty about how precisely sex "happens" in the brain, it would be prudent to give an overview of how the brain is structured. This 3-pound grayish-pink gelatinous organ is composed of two halves, the right and left cerebral hemispheres, that communicate with each other through a midline structure called the *corpus callosum*. The right side of the brain controls the left side of the body, and the left brain the right body. The outermost layer of the brain, the part you see when you look at its surface, is the cerebral cortex (see Figure 5.2).

Cortex means "bark" in Latin, and appropriately, the cerebral cortex can be considered the bark of the brain. It is made up primarily of gray matter that consists of densely packed neurons (brain cells). Although the cortex is only a few millimeters thick, it comprises about half of the weight of the brain. The surface of the cerebral cortex is extensively folded, forming ridges called *gyri* and valleys called *sulci*. The folding allows for the surface area of the cerebral cortex to be increased significantly, making room for more neurons. The brain is larger in humans than in other primates mainly because of the evolutionary expansion of the cerebral cortex. From an evolutionary standpoint, the cerebral cortex is more "advanced." It is largely responsible for much of our cognition and behavior. It interacts with deeper, subcortical structures to integrate and modulate sensory inputs and to direct motor activity (movement). Association areas are spread throughout the cortex and are involved in the integration of information from multiple brain regions. This integration can add complexity to the perception attained with one sensory modality, or it can facilitate complex cognitive processes such as language, artistic creation, and decision-making.

In each hemisphere, the cerebral cortex can be broadly divided into the frontal lobe, temporal lobe, parietal lobe, and occipital lobe (see Figure 5.2). The frontal lobe includes the prefrontal cortex, which is instrumental in planning and motivation; the premotor area, which directs skilled actions; Broca's area, which is involved in speech production; and the motor cortex, which controls movement. The parietal lobe is involved in processing sensory information. The visuospatial map of our body and our environment is stored in the right parietal lobe. A stroke in this area can lead to a phenomenon called *neglect*, in which the person does not recognize the left side of the body as their own. The interpretation of touch sensation also is mediated by this region. The temporal lobe is involved in hearing (auditory cortex), smell (olfactory cortex), understanding language (Wernicke's area), and forming memory (hippocampus). The occipital lobe is involved in the processing of visual information.

Beneath the cortex are structures that are referred to as "subcortical." Just beneath the thin layer of gray matter is a thicker layer of white matter. The cortical regions send signals through *axons* (brain cell projections) to the rest of the central nervous system (see Figure 5.3). Sheets of axons compose the white matter. These axons are covered by the insulation (myelin) that gives this region its white color.

In addition to the cortex and white matter, there are deeper structures in the brain that also connect to the cortical regions (see Figure 5.1). Tucked into the central portion of both hemispheres is the *limbic system*, which mediates emotional responses. Deep in the brain are the *basal ganglia*, which regulate movement; the *thalamus*, which is a relay center for signals from the brain and body; and the *hypothalamus*, which regulates appetite, temperature, and hormone production.

The cerebral hemispheres sit upon the brain stem, which has centers vital for control of respiratory and cardiovascular function. Adjacent to the brainstem is the *cerebellum*, which is involved in the coordination of movement (see Figure 5.1)

What Happens in the Brain During Sex?

Now that we have laid out the groundwork of brain basics and how activity in the brain is studied, let's move on to the specifics of what happens in the brain during a sexual encounter. Sexual experience is orchestrated by the brain through the integration of incoming sensory information with the physiological brain state that has been influenced by a lifetime of experiences. The senses act as the doorway into our sexual

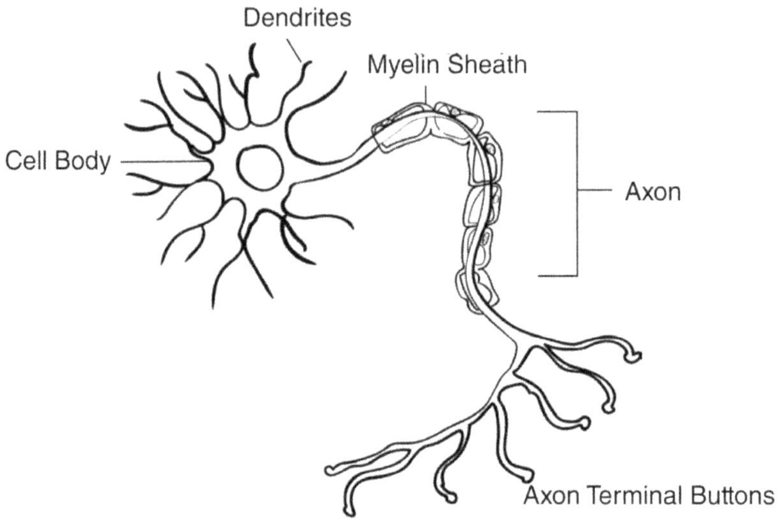

Figure 5.3
The Nerve Cell

Note. From National Institute on Drug Abuse (2005) in Wikimedia Commons. Neuronal cell bodies (gray matter) send out axons which are covered with myelin (white matter).

response cycle. Each of us experiences a host of cognitive, motivational, emotional, and autonomic responses when something enters our world and attracts our attention. All of the sensory systems—touch, vision, smell, hearing, taste, and even mental imagery—offer potential routes to sexual responsiveness.

The olfactory (smell) route to sexual responsiveness is especially intriguing. The olfactory bulb, triggered by odors, is a part of the limbic system. A smell can robustly evoke emotions, memories, and other less conscious processes in the brain. Olfactory signals have been shown to induce emotional responses even if an olfactory stimulus is not consciously perceived, presumably because olfactory receptors send projections not only to the cortex for conscious processing but also to the limbic system for emotional processing (Grammer et al., 2005). In other species, sex-specific odors called *pheromones* are known to play an important role in mate selection and sexual responsiveness. Their role in humans, however, is not as clear. The male pheromone that putatively triggers sexual attraction is androstenone, which exerts a positive effect on mood, cognition, and heightening sympathetic nervous system arousal in a receptive partner. The equivalent in females is androstenol (Jacob & McClintock, 2000). These are secreted in human sweat. There is evidence that pheromones do influence sexual selection and receptivity in humans. In one study, women were shown photographs of male faces and asked to rate them on attractiveness. Women who had been exposed to male pheromones prior to viewing the photos rated the faces as significantly more attractive (Thorne et al., 2002). In another study, women and men with heightened sensitivity to smell reported more frequent and more satisfying sexual encounters. Women with a more sensitive sense of smell experienced orgasms more frequently during sex (Bendas et al., 2017).

Touch is also important in triggering sexual responsiveness. Stimulation of the skin can be a potent stimulant for sexual desire. The term *erogenous zone* (from Greek *érōs* for love and *genēs* for born) refers to an area of the human body that, when stimulated, may generate a sexual response. This of course includes the genitals, breasts, and lips. In truth, any part of the body, however, can be an erogenous zone. A touch at the right time, in the right place, by the right person can make all the difference. Research has shown that touch might heighten erotic perception by creating a sort of emotional backdrop to sexual feelings. Therefore, other factors should be taken into account when considering erotic touch perception. For example, tactile interactions in a newly established romantic relationship may be perceived as more erotic than the same touch in longer term couples. The expectations of the giver of the touch and the recipient are important as well. Studies have shown that when either the one touching or the recipient of the touch is thinking erotic thoughts, the perceived sexual excitement of the touch is heightened. Furthermore, touch that was sexually arousing for the receiver was rated as more sexually arousing for the giver as well, pointing to a top-down, learned expectation of sensory pleasure and erogeneity (Panagiotopoulou et al., 2018).

There has been little to no research in the areas of auditory (hearing) or gustatory (taste) stimuli in regard to sexual stimulation. It is well known, however, that hearing a voice that the perceiver considers erotic can lead to sexual arousal. This is evidenced by the multimillion-dollar market for phone sex and sexually explicit audio material, which remain popular despite the wide availability of sexually explicit visual material. Regarding tastes that make us sexually titillated, there is virtually no research available, making this topic wide open to speculation. There are many foods, however, that are anecdotally said to trigger sexual desire or heighten erotic pleasure. These so-called aphrodisiacs include oysters, hot peppers, varieties of nuts, and dark chocolate, among other things. One study (Salonia et al., 2006) correlated a higher degree of sexual satisfaction in women who consumed more chocolate. It is alluring to hypothesize that chocolate can have either a psychological or biological impact on women's sexual response.

This brings us to vision. There is a strong visual bias in human sexual behavior. Robust recognition of visual sexual cues is a quality shared by all primates, driving mate selection in many monkey species (Ghazanfar et al., 2005). Visual erotic stimuli have been shown to readily tap into the brain's motivational circuits, a biological necessity in the face of sexual opportunity (Georgiadis & Kringelbach, 2012). Visual stimulation is also by far the modality of sexual stimulation that has been most often studied in humans. The vast majority of research on brain activation during sexual excitation has been done using still pictures or videos showcasing erotic content (i.e., sexually explicit material). Most of this research studied heterosexual men—a point that deserves further discussion but is beyond the scope of this chapter. Another problematic issue is that the actual visual stimuli used vary enormously across studies, making it difficult to compare findings. There is also growing evidence of variability between how women and men respond to visual stimuli. See Box 5.3.

No single sensory modality can trigger sexual responsiveness on its own. In all cases, multiple types of sensory stimuli in concert are important for full sexual arousal (Ågmo & Snoeren, 2017). Unfortunately, multisensory sexual stimulation in humans has not been well studied. It has been theorized that individuals suffering from difficulties with sexual arousal could benefit from multimodal sensory stimulation techniques. For example, a person suffering from poor sensory perception in the genitals due to a spinal cord injury might benefit from heightened auditory and/or visual stimuli during sexual intercourse. See Box 5.4.

BOX 5.3

Do Women and Men Process Sexual Pleasure Differently?

Does brain function during the act of sex differ based on gender? The answer to that question like many others in the arena of sex, is . . . it's complicated. Much attention has been given to gender differences in the brain, on a variety of fronts. Sexual pleasure is no different. The assumption has been that because women and men differ in regard to sexual organs and sexual expression, brain function most likely mirrors those differences in some tangible way. However, studies intended to examine this very issue have yielded varied and often contradictory results (Hamann et al., 2004; Marwha et al., 2017; Mitricheva et al., 2019; Poeppl et al., 2016; Ruigrok et al., 2014; Rupp & Wallen, 2008).

There is a common presumption that men respond to visual sexual stimuli more strongly than do women. Indeed, the sexually explicit film industry has for the most part targeted men. Superficially, a number of studies have suggested that women react less intensely to viewing such sexually explicit films. With closer scrutiny, however, the case is not so clear. For one, most such films are made by men, for men. Women who viewed clips from erotic films reported higher levels of sexual arousal to films made by women than films made by men. Also, when viewing erotica, women often show a greater discordance between self-reported subjective sexual arousal and their measured physiological response. Specifically, they would report a lower subjective level of arousal than their physiological measures would suggest (Laan et al., 1994). It is possible that societal perception that women should not enjoy sexually explicit films is contributing to this effect. In the case of visual erotica, there is evidence that women, relative to men, are more interested in context (Rupp & Wallen, 2008) and also show less specific preference for opposite-sex stimuli (Chivers et al., 2004).

In his elaboration of psychoanalytic theory, Sigmund Freud understood that the nervous system played an important role in sexual drive. The key to his theory was that sexual inhibition can have profound psychological consequences. Although we often think of Freud's theories as being rooted in psychoanalytic principles of childhood experience and emotional trauma, the reality is that he was very open to the idea that there was a biological basis for sexual dysfunction. His research was limited by his ability to image and measure brain activity. He hypothesized that the brain played an important role in sexual excitement, desire, and inhibition. Freud (1989) stated that

> the deficiencies in our description would probably vanish if we were already in a position to replace the psychological terms by physiological or chemical ones. . . . Biology is truly a land of unlimited possibilities. We may expect it to give us the most surprising information and we cannot guess what answers it will return in a few dozen years to the questions we have put to it. (p. 624)

The concept of the sexual pleasure cycle was popularized in the 1960s by Masters and Johnson, who were pioneers in the study of human sexuality. They described a four-part cycle consisting of excitement, plateau, orgasm, and refraction (Masters & Johnson, 1966), each with a neurological correlate. This cycle is similar to those described for other reward-based pleasures (such as food) and is thus now often described in terms of wanting, liking, and satiety (Georgiadis & Kringelbach, 2012; Kringelbach & Berridge, 2009). This model has been useful for the purpose of organizing concepts of brain function during a sexual experience.

BOX 5.4

The Impact of Neurological Disease on Sexual Wellness

Physical disease can seriously impact sexual health. The focus here will be on how neurological conditions impact brain function and thereby interfere with sexual wellness. Common conditions that fall into this category include stroke, epilepsy, multiple sclerosis, and head injury. Delving into the specifics of these conditions is beyond the scope of this chapter. Instead, we will discuss this in more general terms.

A direct impact on a brain pathway that mediates sexual function can have devastating effects. For example, injury to the prefrontal cortex that plays a key role in generating sexual arousal can lead to either apathy with hyposexuality or, less commonly, disinhibition with resultant hypersexuality (Rees et al., 2007). There are rare reports of patients with temporal lobe epilepsy who experience spontaneous orgasm as part of their seizure (Rémillard et al., 1983).

Furthermore, neurological disease can lead to physical disabilities that interfere with the act of sex. It can be difficult to participate in sexual intercourse if pain, weakness, numbness, incontinence, and other issues make sex difficult or awkward. There is a growing industry aimed at making sex more accessible through the use of sex aids such as harnesses, wedge pillows, and other devices.

We should also not discount the emotional impact of neurological disease. Many individuals with neurological disease report depression, anxiety, and negative self-image as among the reasons that they lose interest in sex. A review of the literature concerning sex after stroke confirms the correlation between poststroke depression, anxiety, and sexual dysfunction (Rosenbaum et al., 2014). Misinformation and inadequate patient education also play a role. Fear of a new stroke was reported as a cause for ceasing sexual activity in nearly a quarter of patients following stroke (Korpelainen, 1998). Clearly, as health care providers, we can do better.

Even our treatment of patients can contribute to this problem. Up to a quarter of cases of ejaculatory dysfunction are attributed to medications, often those given to treat seizures or mood disorders (Glass & Soni, 1999). Medications that block dopamine pathways (antipsychotics) can dampen sexual desire, whereas those that stimulate dopamine pathways (Parkinson's disease medication) can cause sexually exuberant behavior.

A Step-by-Step Guide

Let's say you see someone who is sexy or you smell a scent that reminds you of someone you love. What exactly is happening in your brain? Visual, tactile, auditory, and olfactory stimulation, each or in combination, can arouse sexual desire. These sensory modalities have regions in the brain that process the information. Visual information is processed in the occipital lobe, hearing and olfaction in the temporal lobe, and touch sensation in the parietal lobe (see Figure 5.2). The combined sensory experience is integrated in "association areas" to create a coherent picture of the world.

Wanting involves both a cognitive and emotional component. The cognitive component of wanting involves appraising the stimuli and categorizing it as sexual or nonsexual in nature. The prefrontal cortex and the fusiform gyri in the temporal lobes are activated during this process. The prefrontal cortex makes a judgment about the nature of the stimuli. It also weighs the consequences of different actions and choices and determines the most appropriate action under a given set of circumstances. This area is also involved in both initiating and inhibiting sexual behavior. The parietal lobe, premotor area, and brainstem nuclei are also activated as the brain increases attention to the sexual object. Wanting is driven by the release of the neurotransmitter dopamine from brainstem nuclei, which focuses attention and behavior toward acquiring the object of sexual desire (Pfaus, 2009).

The emotional component of wanting encompasses a sense of tension, hope, and fear in reaction to an object of sexual desire, mediated by the amygdala, a part of the limbic system instrumental to emotional output. The amygdala interprets the incoming erotic stimulation and coordinates the emotional response. It is largely responsible for giving emotional significance to erotic stimuli. There is evidence that changes in the amygdala are critical to the development of emotional attachment and pair bonding (Kringelbach & Berridge, 2009).

The motivational component, *liking*, specifically directs behavior toward the sexual goal. During this phase, the anterior cingulate cortex, hypothalamus, and brainstem nuclei become activated (see Figure 5.1). While wanting is driven by dopamine, liking is synonymous with reward or pleasure. This is driven by opioid and other reward systems. This links the erotic stimulation to a feeling of well-being. These are the same areas stimulated by other reward-based activities, such as gambling (Georgiadis et al., 2012). That is why having sex can feel like hitting the jackpot. As one approaches orgasm and sexual consummation, the pathways stimulated in the brain overlap with arousal states induced by music, cocaine, and pain (Georgiadis & Kringelbach, 2012). Whereas high arousal states are seen in the brain in certain areas as one moves toward climax, certain other areas are turned down. Decreased activity occurs in the temporal lobes and prefrontal cortex. These are areas associated with interpersonal judgment and self-referential thought. This might explain why "losing oneself" is a feeling often associated with attaining sexual climax. It would also explain why individuals with anorgasmia (an inability to achieve orgasm) are found to have unusually high activity in the prefrontal cortex. It seems that the ability to shut down self-monitoring and judgmental thoughts may be essential to good sex (Georgiadis & Kringelbach, 2012).

The last phase of the sexual response, *satiety*, has been the least studied. This is also referred to as the postejaculatory refractory period, which is a period of decreased sexual responsiveness that occurs following sexual consummation. This occurs in all animals that employ sexual reproduction. It is a much more well-defined phenomenon in men, who generally have an inability to achieve an erection or orgasm for a period of minutes or hours following sexual climax. In women this is not as clear cut. In fact, some women are capable of having multiple orgasms in one session (Levin, 2009). The postejaculatory refractory period is remarkable for a rather dramatic shift in mental state. Discovering the responsible brain mechanisms would be important to furthering our understanding of human neuro-sexology. Much remains to be done, however, in this area of study.

Brain Plasticity and Sexual Learning

Now that we have discussed the neuroanatomical and neurochemical principles behind the act of sex, let's move away from these more mechanistic concepts. Sex is clearly much more than a series of acts geared toward reproduction. Although our brains are wired for sex, what each individual believes to be true about sex—and the act of getting there—is based on a lifetime of observation, personal experience, societal norms, spiritual belief, and a host of other factors. It is evident that experiences, even non-sexual ones, early in life can shape our concept of the perfect partner, the "right" time to have sex, or what outfit to wear on that first date. This is the concept of sexual learning.

The idea of sexual learning is not, however, unique to humans. It has, in fact, been best studied in rats, which are much easier to control with regard to their sexual behavior. Studies have confirmed that experience with sexual reward strengthens the development of sexual behavior and can affect partner preference in rats. In both female and male rats, early sexual experiences with a partner scented with a neutral or even a noxious odor will lead to a preference for a similarly scented partner later in life. Rats who were trained to wear jackets during sex later demonstrated marked difficulty copulating without the jacket (Pfaus et al., 2012). This can give us valuable insight into the development of psychologically mediated sexual dysfunction in humans.

We know that the brain is changeable. The principle of plasticity means that the brain is ever changing. In response to our environment and experience, our brains are constantly rewiring and forming new connections. This is especially true during childhood when our brains are rapidly developing, but it continues throughout adulthood. This is what allows a person with a stroke or head injury to be rehabilitated. What this means is that, although some of our brain pathways might be created earlier in life, they are subject to rewiring (Rosenzweig, 2003). This is encouraging for those who might experience sexual trauma early in life. Their frightening or painful associations with sex can, in a sense, be rewritten with the right future experiences and proper emotional support.

Conclusion

Understanding what is going on inside our brains when we experience sex is much more than a novelty. Sex is one of the most basic and important acts that we participate in during our lifetime. This is an act that we as biological beings have evolved to approach with all seriousness, as our own mortality and the perpetuity of the species are on the line. It is at once intensely personal and profoundly communal in its implications. To understand sex is to understand who we are.

It would seem an act so fundamental to survival would be, to some extent, "hardwired" to meet our biological imperative. The more we learn about sex, however, the more we are surprised. This biological imperative, with all of its grave implications, is a source of joy, physical fitness, and emotional fulfillment. It is expressed in a multitude of ways, many of which have little or nothing to do with procreation. We pursue love not because we want to procreate, but because it makes us better, more complete human beings. That is why it is tragic when this vital aspect of human engagement is marred by sexual trauma, physical disease, or other impediments to a gratifying sex life. By understanding how the brain operates, we can better devise treatment strategies to aid individuals in overcoming barriers to sexual wellness. We know that the "hardware" of the brain can be redirected by the "software" of human experience, education, and emotional support. That is the very role of human sexuality counseling.

References

Ågmo, A. (2007). *Functional and dysfunctional sexual behaviour: A synthesis of neuroscience and comparative psychology*. Academic Press.

Ågmo, A., & Snoeren, E. M. S. (2017). A cooperative function for multisensory stimuli in the induction of approach behavior of a potential mate. *PLOS ONE, 12*(3), Article e0174339. https://doi.org/10.1371/journal.pone.0174339

Bendas, J., Georgiadis, J., Olausson, H., Weidner, K., & Croy, I. (2017). P-02-006 The roles of tactile and olfactory sensory inputs on sexual desire and performance. *Journal of Sexual Medicine, 14*(4, Suppl.), Article e184. https://doi.org/10.1016/J.JSXM.2017.03.207

Chivers, M. L., Rieger, G., Latty, E., & Bailey, J. M. (2004). A sex difference in the specificity of sexual arousal. *Psychological Science, 15*(11), 736–744. https://doi.org/10.1111/j.0956-7976.2004.00750.x

De la Garza-Mercer, F. (2007). The evolution of sexual pleasure. *Journal of Psychology & Human Sexuality, 18*(2–3), 107–124. https://doi.org/10.1300/J056v18n02_04

Freud, S. (1989). *The Freud reader* (P. Gay, Ed.). W. W. Norton & Co.

Gallup, G. G., Jr. (2015). Bipedalism and sex. *The international encyclopedia of human sexuality*. John Wiley & Sons.

Georgiadis, J. R., & Kringelbach, M. L. (2012). The human sexual response cycle: Brain imaging evidence linking sex to other pleasures. *Progress in Neurobiology, 98*(1), 49–81. https://doi.org/10.1016/j.pneurobio.2012.05.004

Georgiadis, J. R., Kringelbach, M. L., & Pfaus, J. G. (2012). Sex for fun: A synthesis of human and animal neurobiology. *Nature Reviews Urology, 9*(9), 486–498. https://doi.org/10.1038/nrurol.2012.151

Ghazanfar, A. A., Maier, J. X., Hoffman, K. L., & Logothetis, N. K. (2005). Multisensory integration of dynamic faces and voices in rhesus monkey auditory cortex. *Journal of Neuroscience, 25*(20), 5004–5012. https://doi.org/10.1523/jneurosci.0799-05.2005

Giuliano, F., & Rampin, O. (2000). Central noradrenergic control of penile erection. *International Journal of Impotence Research, 12*(Suppl. 1), S13–S19.

Glass, C., & Soni, B. (1999). Sexual problems of disabled patients. *BMJ, 318*(7182), 518–521. https://doi.org/10.1136/bmj.318.7182.518

Glick, R. A., & Roose, S. P. (1993). *Rage, power, and aggression*. Yale University Press.

Golden, R. L., Furman, W., & Collibee, C. (2016). The risks and rewards of sexual debut. *Developmental Psychology, 52*(11), 1913–1925. https://doi.org/10.1037/dev0000206

Grammer, K., Fink, B., & Neave, N. (2005). Human pheromones and sexual attraction. *European Journal of Obstetrics, Gynecology, and Reproductive Biology, 118*(2), 135–142. https://doi.org/10.1016/j.ejogrb.2004.08.010

Hamann, S., Herman, R. A., Nolan, C. L., & Wallen, K. (2004). Men and women differ in amygdala response to visual sexual stimuli. *Nature Neuroscience, 7*(4), 411–416. https://doi.org/10.1038/nn1208

Jacob, S., & McClintock, M. K. (2000). Psychological state and mood effects of steroidal chemosignals in women and men. *Hormones and Behavior, 37*(1), 57–78. https://doi.org/10.1006/hbeh.1999.1559

Jannini, E. A., Fisher W. A., Bitzer, J., & McMahon, C. G. (2016). Is sex just fun? How sexual activity improves health. *Journal of Sexual Medicine, 6*(10), 2640–2648. https://doi.org/10.1111/j.1743-6109.2009.01477.x

Korpelainen, J. T., Kauhanen, M. L., Kemola, H., Malinen, U., & Myllylä, V. V. (1998). Sexual dysfunction in stroke patients. *Acta Neurologica Scandinavica, 98*(6), 400–405. https://doi.org/10.1111/j.1600-0404.1998.tb07321.x

Kringelbach, M. L., & Berridge, K. C. (2009). Towards a functional neuroanatomy of pleasure and happiness. *Trends in Cognitive Sciences, 13*(11), 479–487. https://doi.org/10.1016/j.tics.2009.08.006

Laan, E., Everaerd, W., van Bellen, G., & Hanewald, G. (1994). Women's sexual and emotional responses to male- and female-produced erotica. *Archives of Sexual Behavior, 23*(2), 153–169. https://doi.org/10.1007/BF01542096

Levin, R. J. (2009). Revisiting post-ejaculation refractory time—What we know and what we do not know in males and in females. *Journal of Sexual Medicine, 6*(9), 2376–2389. https://doi.org/10.1111/j.1743-6109.2009.01350.x

MacLean, P. D. (1998). Introduction. In L. R. Squire (Ed.), *The history of neuroscience in autobiography* (Vol. 2, pp. 244–275). Academic Press.

Marwha, D., Halari, M., & Eliot, L. (2017). Meta-analysis reveals a lack of sexual dimorphism in human amygdala volume. *NeuroImage, 147*, 282–294. https://doi.org/10.1016/j.neuroimage.2016.12.021

Masters, W. H., & Johnson, V. E. (1966). *Human sexual response.* Brown & Company.

Mitricheva, E., Kimura, R., Logothetis, N. K., & Noori, H. R. (2019). Neural substrates of sexual arousal are not sex dependent. *PNAS, 116*(31), 15671–15676. https://doi.org/10.1073/pnas.1904975116

Panagiotopoulou, E., Filippetti, M. L., Gentsch, A., & Fotopoulou, A. (2018). Dissociable sources of erogeneity in social touch: Imagining and perceiving C-tactile optimal touch in erogenous zones. *PLOS ONE, 13*(8), Article e0203039. https://doi.org/10.1371/journal.pone.0203039

Petrides, M., & Pandya, D. N. (2012). The frontal cortex. In J. K. Mai & G. Paxinos (Eds.), *The human nervous system* (3rd ed., pp. 618–677). Elsevier.

Pfaus, J. G. (2009). Pathways of sexual desire. *The Journal of Sexual Medicine, 6*(6), 1506–1533. https://doi.org/10.1111/j.1743-6109.2009.01309.x

Pfaus, J. G., Kippin, T. E., & Coria-Avila, G. (2003). What can animal models tell us about human sexual response? *Annual Review of Sex Research, 14*, 1–63.

Pfaus, J. G., Kippin, T. E., Coria-Avila, G. A., Gelez, H., Afonso, V. M., Ismail, N., & Parada, M. (2012). Who, what, where, when (and maybe even why)? How the experience of sexual reward connects sexual desire, preference, and performance. *Archives of Sexual Behavior, 41*(1), 31–62. https://doi.org/10.1007/s10508-012-9935-5

Poeppl, T. B., Langguth, B., Rupprecht, R., Safron, A., Bzdok, D., Laird, A. R., & Eickhoff, S. B. (2016). The neural basis of sex differences in sexual behavior: A quantitative meta-analysis. *Frontiers in Neuroendocrinology, 43*, 28–43. https://doi.org/10.1016/j.yfrne.2016.10.001

Rees, P. M., Fowler, C. J., & Maas, C. P. (2007). Sexual function in men and women with neurological disorders. *Lancet, 369*(9560), 512–525. https://doi.org/10.1016/S0140-6736(07)60238-4

Rémillard, G. M., Andermann, F., Testa, G. F., Gloor, P., Aubé, M., Martin, J. B., Feindel, W., Guberman, A., & Simpson, C. (1983). Sexual ictal manifestations predominate in women with temporal lobe epilepsy: A finding suggesting sexual dimorphism in the human brain. *Neurology, 33*(3), 323–330. https://doi.org/10.1212/wnl.33.3.323

Rosenbaum, T., Vadas, D., & Kalichman, L. (2014). Sexual function in post-stroke patients: Considerations for rehabilitation. *The Journal of Sexual Medicine, 11*(1), 15–21.

Rosenzweig, M. R. (2003). Effects of differential experience on the brain and behavior. *Developmental Neuropsychology, 24*(2–3), 523–540. https://doi.org/10.1080/87565641.2003.9651909

Roxo, M. R., Franceschini, P. R., Zubaran, C., Kleber, F. D., & Sander, J. W. (2011). The limbic system conception and its historical evolution. *Scientific World Journal, 11*, Article 157150. https://doi.org/10.1100/2011/157150

Ruigrok, A. N., Salimi-Khorshidi, G., Lai, M., Baron-Cohen, S., Lombardo, M. V., Tait, R. J., & Suckling, J. (2014). Meta-analysis of sex differences in human brain structure. *Neuroscience and Biobehavioral Reviews, 39*(100), 34–50. https://doi.org/10.1016/j.neubiorev.2013.12.004

Rupp, H. A., & Wallen, K. (2008). Sex differences in response to visual sexual stimuli: A review. *Archives of Sexual Behavior, 37*(2), 206–218. https://doi.org/10.1007/s10508-007-9217-9

Salloway, S., Malloy, P., & Cummings, J. L. (1997). *The neuropsychiatry of limbic and subcortical disorders*. American Psychiatric Publishing.

Salonia, A., Fabbri, F., & Zanni, G. (2006). Chocolate and women's sexual health: An intriguing correlation. *Journal of Sexual Medicine, 3*(3), 476–482. https://doi.org/10.1111/j.1743-6109.2006.00236.x

Thorne, F., Neave, N., Scholey, A., Moss, M., & Fink, B. (2002). Effects of putative male pheromones on female ratings of male attractiveness: Influence of oral contraception and the menstrual cycle. *Neuroendocrinology Letters, 23*(4), 291–297.

Truitt, W. A., & Coolen, L. M. (2002). Identification of a potential ejaculation generator in the spinal cord. *Science, 297*(5586), 1566–1569. https://doi.org/10.1126/science.1073885

Wen, J., Yablonskiy, D. A., Salter, A., & Cross, A. H. (2017). Limbic system damage in MS: MRI assessment and correlations with clinical testing. *PLOS ONE, 12*(11), Article e0187915. https://doi.org/10.1371/journal.pone.0187915

Wright, H., & Jenks, R. A. (2016). Sex on the brain! Associations between sexual activity and cognitive function in older age. *Age and Ageing, 45*(2), 313–317. https://doi.org/10.1093/ageing/afv197

The Big Bang? The Role of Orgasm

Christian D. Chan, Tanisha N. Sapp, and Laurie Bonjo

The field of human sexuality has developed through an explosion of conceptual and empirical research devoted to augmenting its practice in counseling (Zeglin et al., 2018, 2019). Because human sexuality is typically viewed as a phenomenon outside of counseling or as requiring specialized training, professional counselors have used recent research to illustrate its importance across all counseling specialties (e.g., clinical mental health counseling, couple and family counseling, school counseling, college counseling) and to challenge cultural norms about sexuality (Speciale, 2020; Zeglin et al., 2019). The missing gaps surrounding sexuality research in counseling are likely related to apprehension about discussing sexuality in counseling and responding to internalized, social, and cultural biases around its relevant topics (Murray et al., 2016). The absence of human sexuality as a core area in the 2016 Council for Accreditation of Counseling and Related Educational Programs (CACREP) Standards forecloses any discussion of these practices within a multitude of counseling courses (CACREP, 2016). Even more alarmingly, the field of counselor education has excluded this information in crucial courses, such as family counseling and couples counseling, without clear and explicit language for sexuality within accreditation standards (Sanabria & Murray, 2018; Zeglin et al., 2019).

Unfortunately, the CACREP (2016) accreditation standards are not alone in this disconnect between standards and practice, given that the *ACA Code of Ethics* (American Counseling Association [ACA], 2014) fails to explicitly include sexuality in its language (Zeglin et al., 2018). With this apparent discrepancy, professional counselors and counselor educators alike will face a variety of professional and ethical dilemmas. For professional counselors, the lack of information on applying sexuality in counseling practice gives permission to perpetuate stereotypes, mismanage conversations surrounding sexuality, or avoid the topic entirely. Within counselor education, counselor educators face substantial pressure to find ways to fit the content into preexisting counseling courses or transform these priorities into specialized trainings, continuing education, or electives rather than a foundational base of training. Researchers have also pointed to this major concern as an implicit message that attention to human sexuality in counseling is obscure, undefined, and relevant exclusively for researchers outside the counseling profession (see Zeglin et al., 2018, 2019).

By categorizing a taxonomy of human sexuality in counseling, professional counselors have built a substantial basis of human sexuality topics surrounding intimacy and communication. Within this amalgamation of topics, the conceptualization of orgasm has a complicated connotation. On one hand, professional counselors mismanage their communication about intimacy, sexuality, and relationships and pervasively conflate these topics with the ultimate goal of reaching orgasm (Buehler, 2017). Many societal norms may also identify orgasm as a binary goal that exists as a monolithic experience (McCarthy & McCarthy, 2019). At worst, a plethora of biases further nuances these issues for individuals and couples at the intersection of racial, ethnic, gender, sexual, disability, and affectional diversity (see Buehler, 2017; Pope et al., 2007; Zeglin et al., 2019). On the other hand, professional counselors fail to broach the topic at all due to their own discomfort with sexuality, sexology, and intimacy issues (see Murray et al., 2016). Zeglin et al. (2019) distinctly identified that orgasm, desire, and pleasure generally coincide with developmental and psychosocial issues pertinent to professional counselors (e.g., traumatic experiences, physical development, partner communication). Thus, contemporary discussions on orgasm and other related sexual phenomena (e.g., desire, pleasure, intimacy) draw from a myriad of sources for assessment, including sexual partners' understanding of trauma, positive relationships with family of origin and social networks, disclosure of sexual problems, foreplay, and afterplay (see Guo et al., 2004; Merwin et al., 2017; Rosen et al., 2017; Rottmann et al., 2017; Strait et al., 2015). Dovetailing with the Zeglin et al. (2019) study, works by several other researchers (e.g., Behnia et al., 2014; Jones et al., 2018; McCarthy & McCarthy, 2019; Wallen & Lloyd, 2011) have demystified the psychosocial experience of orgasm as a phenomenon that is not solely limited to sexual intercourse. In fact, Behnia et al. (2014) showed that other biological factors, such as oxytocin, play a role in heightening levels of orgasm. Indeed, this combination of research studies alludes to a clear distinction that orgasm is a multifaceted experience and relies on several psychological, social, and biological factors.

It behooves professional counselors to specifically dispel myths surrounding orgasm and its relationship to the continuum of pleasure-inclusive practices. To this end, professional counselors have a responsibility to openly address their biases through education and increase their knowledge on the implications of orgasm in several counseling modalities (Mercer & Dermer, 2020; Speciale, 2020). Professional counselors also face an important task of gaining appropriate skill sets for broaching the topic of orgasm and effectively incorporating these practices into their counseling discussions (Wilson, 2019). Additionally, pervading beliefs on orgasm surface as an important topic in counseling discussions, as counselors can use these opportunities to dispel myths and provide effective education on psychological, biological, and social tensions affecting pleasure and orgasm (Schubert & Pope, 2020). Merwin et al. (2017) elaborated on the importance of these discussions, given that the nondisclosure of sexual issues can exacerbate psychological symptoms, arousal, and relational satisfaction. In this chapter, we will explain (a) foundational definitions and concepts illustrating the pleasure-inclusive practices for orgasm, (b) nuances around the conceptualization and broaching of orgasm in counseling, and (c) discussion points to further the inclusion of orgasm in professional counseling practice.

Addressing Orgasm in Counseling

A review of the literature on orgasm within the fields of counseling and counselor education shows that very little scholarly discourse is generated on orgasm (Farago, 2021). Much of the extant research published in *Archives of Sexual Behavior, Sex Education, The Journal of Sex Research, American Journal of Sexuality Education, Journal of Sex & Marital Therapy,* and *International Journal of Sexual Health* has been generated outside of counseling and counselor education. With the 2019 launch of the new *Journal of Counseling Sexology & Sexual Wellness*, scholars have an additional forum for generating discourse on sex to include discussions of orgasm that can inform clinical practice as well as preservice counselor training.

The absence of scholarly discourse on orgasm in the counseling literature highlights a gap both in research and in the training of preservice counselors (Speciale, 2020). Given the paramount role of orgasm in scenarios from entertainment media to sexual how-to manuals, as well as the focus on orgasm from the medical and pharmaceutical industries (see Towne, 2019; Wongsomboon et al., 2020), it is surprising that so little attention has been given to this component of human sexual experience in the field of counseling. Although orgasm is rarely addressed in counseling literature or in counselor education programs, clients can certainly benefit from working with a counselor who is prepared to engage in conversations about orgasm. Many clients want counselors to initiate talk about orgasm (Buehler, 2017; Farago, 2021), which necessitates a responsibility for counselors to initiate these conversations. When counselors incorporate sexology and orgasm into their counseling discussions and practices, they normalize the fact that orgasms are developmentally a part of life and that sometimes people need to talk about orgasms in counseling.

Cultural messages about orgasm can be confusing and can lead to misconceptions that have the potential to damage people of all genders (Rowland et al., 2018; Towne, 2019). Entertainment media are rife with inaccurate, culturally embedded messages about the role that orgasm plays in sex. Some common messages include the following:

- Orgasm is the expected outcome of successful sex.
- Orgasm is like punctuation for sex.
- Men orgasm easily, while women struggle to have orgasms.
- All men want out of sex is to orgasm.
- When men have sex, the focus is always on reaching orgasm.
- Women only want romance and intimacy, not orgasm.
- Everyone needs to have an orgasm to enjoy sex.
- Orgasm with a partner is more meaningful than orgasm through masturbation.
- "Good people" don't orgasm.
- If you haven't had an orgasm by the time you are ________, you will never have one.
- Women who have orgasms are whores and are dirty and/or salacious, while women who never have orgasms are virgins and are pure and/or pious.
- If only one person in a couple orgasms during sex, the relationship is dysfunctional.
- Orgasm is easy and effortless for everyone.
- Orgasm should not be discussed openly but should be sought after by everyone.
- Orgasm always happens along with sex, with no discussion needed.

This list could continue indefinitely. More importantly, orgasm shows up in the broader systems of culture, and populations of clients and students constantly receive culturally endorsed messages that include misconceptions, myths, and prescriptions around orgasm (Hall & Graham, 2014). Individuals absorb those messages to varying degrees, which can influence how they feel about orgasm, behaviors around orgasm, and cognitions about orgasm (Graham, 2014; Graham & Hall, 2013). Counselors should be prepared to partner with their clients to challenge these messages and redirect the client to develop a relationship with orgasm that is not controlled by cultural paradigms and satisfies the client's needs (Rowland et al., 2018; Séguin & Blais, 2019). Orgasm, sexuality, vulnerability, shame, and religion are inextricably connected for many clients, and exploring the intersection of these constructs can lead to deep veins of rich material for counseling. Most counselors enter the field prepared to talk to clients about values and belief systems, but if sex and the social prescriptions associated with orgasm are not explored, there is the risk of unfinished business leading to a less fulfilling life (Adam et al., 2020; Chadwick et al., 2019; Hall & Graham, 2014).

Examples of how orgasm, sexuality, vulnerability, and shame may intersect with religion include (a) a cisgender female client who, for religious reasons, did not engage in sex before marriage finds that sex with her husband is not enjoyable and worries that she is not a "real woman" or a "good wife," or that maybe her inability to experience the pleasure of orgasm with her husband was punishment for something; (b) a cisgender male client who was raised a devout Catholic reports only rarely having had sex with women, refers to his orgasms as historically "unremarkable," begins to realize he is attracted to men, and experiences great shame after having "explosive and earth-shattering" orgasms with his first male partner; and (c) a transfeminine client who was raised in a religious system that deprecates women's sexual pleasure had no difficulty enjoying orgasm prior to transitioning, but since transitioning has not been able to reach orgasm. Each of these examples demonstrates how a client's intersection of identities has the potential to reinforce prescriptions about orgasm (Hall & Graham, 2014). Counselors can support clients as they explore how their intersectional identities impact their feelings about orgasm and the meaning that orgasm has in their lives and in their intimate relationships (Speciale, 2020; Taylor et al., 2019).

Everyone deserves to know how orgasm works, and clients need professional counselors to know how to normalize talk about orgasm and how to be present with clients as they learn to maximize pleasure for themselves and for those with whom they choose to be consensually intimate (McCarthy & McCarthy, 2019; Mercer & Dermer, 2019; Zeglin et al., 2019). When counselors meet clients with knowledge about orgasmic functioning, counselors are a resource that supports clients' efforts to maximize their sexual relationships and intimate connections in the context of changing abilities, bodies, and life circumstances (Schubert & Pope, 2020; Taylor et al., 2019). We envision a world where counselors enter the field prepared to support clients as they learn about the role that orgasm plays in their intimacy with themselves and with others, learn the ways that orgasm functions physiologically, and begin to build a relationship with orgasm that is congruent with and satisfies their sexual needs.

Defining Orgasm

In males or persons with a penis, orgasm is defined by ejaculation (Graham, 2014; Levin, 2011). While most definitions for women, or persons with vaginas, incorporate a person's subjective experiences and physiological changes, there is no single accepted definition of orgasm for women (Graham, 2014; King et al., 2011; Mah & Binik, 2001). However, an orgasm is generally described as waves of pleasure followed by a release of tension (Buehler, 2017; Sayin, 2012). Additionally, the orgasm, and meaning attached to orgasm, will vary across age, gender, and experience (McCarthy & McCarthy, 2019).

For women, orgasms can be induced by genital stimulation (most common method) or imagery (Graham, 2014; Komisaruk & Whipple, 2011). Komisaruk and Whipple (2011) identified over 10 different ways that women may experience orgasms through nongenital stimulation. According to Meston et al. (2004), the female orgasmic response is a reflexive response that lasts for approximately 13 to 50 seconds, which is longer than the average male climax. It begins with an intensity that is built up in the body. Upon release, the uterus and rectal sphincter contract, the cervix opens, and a wave of pleasure ensues (Meston et al., 2004). The body responds through facial expressions, muscle tensions, and heavy breathing, along with moaning. However, some women may not experience all these symptoms or feelings due to fear of gendered norms (Buehler, 2017; McCarthy & McCarthy, 2019). Because the female orgasm is a physiological and psychological experience, women can achieve multiple orgasms (Komisaruk & Whipple, 2011; Meston & Stanton, 2019). The only limitation is stamina and desire; however, the female orgasm may be interrupted at any point in time due to a change in thought or feeling (Meston et al., 2004).

For men, orgasms may be induced by genital stimulation as well as thoughts and somatic experiences (Buehler, 2017). Meston and Stanton (2019) indicated that the male orgasmic response occurs in two stages. In the first stage, the internal genitalia respond slightly before ejaculation with contractions in the seminal duct, rectal sphincter, and urinary bladder. In the second stage, the ejaculate (seminal fluid and sperm) is released. Unlike in women, the expression of the male orgasm cannot be interrupted. When men enter the second stage, they are at the point of ejaculatory inevitability whereby there is no other recourse except through release of the ejaculate. Like the female body, the male body response demonstrates reactions, including gasping, changes in blood pressure, rhythmic pelvic contractions, and foot spasms (Courtois & Dubray, 2014). Although many clients may enjoy these experiences, counselors may encounter clients who have barriers that prohibit the orgasmic function and cause distress.

Sex Positive Approach to Barriers to Orgasm

According to several researchers, most women find it easier to have an orgasm through self-stimulation than through partnered stimulation, with younger women reporting the most frequent difficulty achieving or experiencing orgasm (Hall & Graham, 2014; Laumann et al., 1999; Zietsch et al., 2011). Thus, it might be helpful for counselors to consider psychological experiences, barriers, and generational differences to maximize the expression of orgasm (Courtois & Dubray, 2014; Levin, 2001; Meston & Stanton, 2019). Women who can achieve orgasm through clitoral stimulation but not through vaginal penetration do not meet diagnostic criteria for female orgasmic disorder (American Psychiatric Association [APA], 2022). For men, barriers to orgasm may include premature ejaculation or delayed ejaculation. For someone to be diagnosed with premature ejaculation, ejaculation must occur within 1 minute of penetration and cause distress. To create a more sex positive approach to orgasm, we would like to rethink use of the term *orgasmic disorder* and consider instead use of the term *barriers to orgasm.*

For women, the orgasm tends to be what is considered a psychological and pleasurable event that may also encompass a bonding experience similar to attachment (Buehler, 2017; Sayin, 2012). When there are barriers to this experience, frustration, insecurity, and even feelings of inadequacy may ensue. Although there are psychological barriers to orgasm, there are also medical barriers to achieving orgasm, such as chronic kidney disease, diabetes, and hypertension—to name a few (Buehler, 2017). Women are often faced with inaccurate information about sexual pleasure and sexual education, including information about vaginal cleanliness, vaginal odors, vaginal rejuvenation, and, most commonly, that orgasm is achieved only through vaginal intercourse (Buehler, 2017). This inaccurate information maintains the barriers to orgasmic achievement by lending faulty beliefs that women must maintain control over their bodies. However, it is important that women understand that orgasm requires the woman to release control and allow the body to relax while giving permission to feel and experience pleasure (Buehler, 2017).

For men, barriers to orgasm can cause psychological distress leading to performance anxiety, which may lead to other sexual health problems such as erectile disorder. There are two main disorders associated with orgasm in the *Diagnostic and Statistical Manual of Mental Disorders, Text Revision* (5th ed.; APA, 2022): premature ejaculation and delayed ejaculation. Premature ejaculation is the orgasm and emission of semen with minimal stimulation before, on, or shortly after penetration (McMahon, 2007), and delayed ejaculation is the condition in which a person with a penis takes a prolonged period of sexual stimulation to ejaculate.

Barriers due to premature ejaculation may be contributed to by one or more biological, psychological, or medical factors, such as genetics, thyroid imbalance, anxiety, prostatitis, chronic pelvic pain, and some medications (Althof et al., 2014; Buehler, 2017; Ralph & Wylie, 2005). As with premature ejaculation, barriers due to delayed ejaculation may be caused by low testosterone, thyroid problems, diabetes, as well as medications (Buehler, 2017; Richardson et al., 2006). Emotional factors, including fear of pregnancy, fear of contracting a sexually transmitted infection, excessive masturbation, worry of sexual performance norms, or prolonged viewing of sexually explicit material, may also contribute to delayed ejaculation (Perelman & Rowland, 2006).

Treatment Approach and Practice With Barriers to Orgasm

Problems with orgasm present as either premature orgasm or delay or absence of orgasm (Graham, 2014; Laumann et al., 1999; Metz & McCarthy, 2004), which may be situational or occur over time. Additionally, problems may be influenced by situation, partners, medications, and other factors. Therefore, it is important to complete a thorough assessment before beginning any treatment. In most cases, as a counselor you will not treat orgasmic disorders. You will likely refer the client back to their gynecologist, urologist, neurologist, urogynecologist, or pelvic floor specialist. Such referrals should be made to rule out any medical conditions before beginning treatment.

Beginning with the assessment of the client in early sessions, it is important to determine if arousal has occurred. If arousal is not present, then orgasm cannot be achieved. Counselors should ask specific questions that address the frequency and situations in which the problems may occur. Counselors may also notice that clients have a general lack of knowledge of the female and male genitalia. Having a simple drawing on hand of the female and male external genitals may be helpful for education of these areas. Many prospective clients will self-report problems that do not meet diagnostic criteria. For example, men may report experiencing symptoms of premature ejaculation because of stigma about how long one should last between penetration and ejaculation. Therefore, it is important that counselors can educate clients and inform them that the average time for ejaculation is approximately 5 minutes (Buehler, 2017). Lastly, questions surrounding the history of masturbation and feelings toward masturbation should be included in the assessment. It is also important to consider cultural factors, religious practices, and implications to ensure a person's ability to comply with treatment recommendations (McCarthy & McCarthy, 2019; Meston & Stanton, 2019).

Once the assessment is complete and referral and treatment recommendations have been received, counselors with more advanced training may begin working with clients using a cognitive behavioral approach (Buehler, 2017). Counselors may begin by teaching the client techniques such as relaxation, mindfulness skills, and breath work. If the barriers are too complex, the counselor may refer the client to a sex therapist, who may utilize more skilled techniques such as sensate focus or directed masturbation.

For women who may experience barriers to orgasm, Graham (2014) stated that directed masturbation is the most successful treatment approach, along with medication and mindfulness. For clients who have little knowledge of the female genitalia, counselors can use a drawing of the female external genitals or a vulva puppet to help describe the genitalia and to demonstrate some of the techniques used in directed masturbation. As well, educating women about their sexual response cycle can be beneficial in helping women achieve optimal sexual health and pleasure through orgasm (Basson, 2001; Buehler, 2017). Along with these methods, cognitive techniques such as refocusing on pleasure rather than setting a goal of orgasm are also key to successful treatment. Starting with the end in mind, counselors can begin providing treatment and help women work through these barriers.

For men who may have barriers to ejaculatory control, Buehler (2017) recommended that counselors begin with educating their partner. The focus is on reducing the pressure to perform and ensuring that sexual partners are not demanding that other sexual partners "give" them an orgasm. Establishing realistic expectations and goals is key to successful treatment. Teaching clients relaxation techniques to reduce anxiety by learning how to quiet the noise is also instrumental. This may include deep breathing, progressive muscle relaxation, and mindfulness. Other techniques that focus on ejaculatory control include (a) the *squeeze* technique, whereby the intercourse is stopped, and the partner squeezes the glans of the penis until the urge to ejaculate stops; and (b) the *stop/start* technique, whereby intercourse is stopped until the man is able to continue. Such techniques can help clients strengthen their pelvic floor muscles and make their responses less sensitive (Buehler, 2017; Metz & McCarthy, 2004). The squeeze and start/stop techniques can also be used as directed masturbation techniques, along with waiting for full arousal and erection as a means for masturbation retraining (Metz & McCarthy, 2004; Perelman & Rowland, 2006). Although these techniques are not a one-size-fits-all solution to these barriers, they can serve as a launching point to address concerns about orgasm.

Case Example: J and Lewis

This hypothetical case example discusses J and Lewis, a couple understanding their own cultural definitions of intimacy and sexuality, seeking couples counseling for the first time in their relationship. J is a genderfluid, queer individual with Asian American heritages attached to Indonesian and Chinese culture and uses the pronouns he, him, his, they, them, and theirs. J grew up as a child of two immigrants in the United States with access to a master's degree in education, additional career opportunities, and resources from immediate and extended family members. J grew up in Southern California and has strong ties to family members there. Lewis is a White, queer cisgender male who grew up in a middle-class family in the Deep South. Lewis uses the pronouns he, him, and his and is estranged from many of his family members. J and Lewis both live near Washington, DC, and work primarily in the nonprofit sector with community organizations.

J and Lewis have been together in their relationship for a year and are still learning about their needs and wants in relationships. They met upon moving to Washington, DC, and have since been reflecting on challenges in their intimate partner relationship. They sought couples counseling to improve their relationship and, most importantly, communication, because they love each other and have encountered a series of verbal disagreements recently. As Lewis initiated the contact for screening of services, J was initially reluctant to join for couples counseling, but eventually agreed on account of love and the importance of their intimate partner relationship.

As the counselor, you begin to elicit more information through couples assessments, relational satisfaction inquiries, and questions about intimacy. Both J and Lewis share that they are not necessarily arguing in any capacity at home, but they are concerned with gaps in their sexual communication, which have led to some relational dissatisfaction. Lewis has become more self-conscious about his sexual interactions and performance but does not know how to communicate with J during sexual interactions. To that end, they both relate challenges in achieving orgasm and find that sex has been minimally pleasurable. Within recent sexual interactions, J and Lewis have been experiencing difficulty achieving orgasm, despite engaging in significant foreplay and afterplay. As the counselor, you discover that they both have a number of perceptions about orgasm, including one-sided perspectives on orgasm through experiences with previous intimate relationships and sexual partners. You also discover that Lewis has not talked to J about past hurts with previous intimate partners, particularly as Lewis disclosed that a recent former intimate partner would make negative comments about Lewis during sex. Similarly, Lewis has been fearful of discussing this information with J and has identified that he has never asked J about what they find pleasurable. The couple has attended primarily to their emotional attraction and intimacy, but in the process, Lewis has not asked J about experiences with orgasm—although J has disclosed that orgasm is not the sole driver of their sexual intimacy.

Broaching Orgasm

J and Lewis have been responding to several facets surrounding orgasm in this case example, including social factors influencing perceptions of orgasm within sexual wellness practices. Notably, J and Lewis have been struggling to communicate with each other about sexual intimacy and some of these concerns may be placing pressure on their emotional intimacy. Aside from communication issues, it seems that J and Lewis may be responding to societal norms and biases, albeit negative beliefs, about orgasm. They may be deriving many beliefs from binary ideas and unilateral perspectives that orgasm is essentially an apex rather than a continuum. This aspect also combines with the continuum of pleasure that promotes pleasure-inclusive practices across different cultural factors and sexual, affectional, and gender identities. Professional counselors can begin to broach these factors in a multitude of ways. For instance, professional counselors can first identify current assumptions around sexual practices and their relation to orgasm. Assessing these initial assumptions by explicitly naming them in counseling may allow professional counselors to understand the origin of the assumptions (e.g., family, cultural background, broader society) surrounding sexuality. Following are suggestions for ways to begin broaching these assumptions:

- You named a few ideas about your sexual practices in your relationship. Where did some of these ideas start for you? How did you learn about sexual intimacy or sex growing up? How do you think sex might be influenced by the way you grew up?
- How have you communicated about sexuality and sexual intimacy with previous partners? If at all, how might the social identities of those partners, such as race, ethnicity, gender identity, and sexuality, have influenced your views on sex?
- How would you like to communicate about sexuality and sexual intimacy as you move forward in your relationship? How do you see your views on sex influenced by cultural values connected to your ethnic heritages?

Related to orgasm, professional counselors can begin to ascertain how perceptions of orgasm fit into these belief systems for J and Lewis. Each partner will likely have their own beliefs on what constitutes a successful orgasm, but more importantly, the counselor can further engage this content by explicitly addressing how each partner can communicate about their sexual practices. Additionally, the counselor can identify stereotypes often associated with gender identity and gender expression while offering external examples. For instance, the counselor can explain that society frequently creates assumptions about sex, including stereotypes about one partner performing to achieve orgasm for both sexual partners.

It also seems that J and Lewis may not have communicated about previous sexual histories in their own relationship, which can serve as an essential factor driving emotional and sexual intimacy. Lewis may be responding to assumptions from previous partners that may incite further instances of internalized heterosexism and hegemonic masculinity. These forces may instigate numerous beliefs that Lewis is responsible for the orgasm and that they both need to reach an orgasm for successful sex. Additionally, internalized heterosexism and genderism can play a part in the silence for J and Lewis with their sexual communication, particularly about pleasure-inclusive sexual activities aside from orgasm. It would be important to highlight these forces and their effects on sexual communication, especially if multiple instances of heterosexism and genderism may predispose J and Lewis to further assumptions. These oppressive forces can play a part in silencing and censorship around sexual communication if inclusive conversations around gender, sexual, and affectional diversity in sex and sexuality education were nonexistent growing up.

It is also crucial to emphasize strengths as J and Lewis bring several assets to their relationship. They have primarily focused on maintaining strong communication and explored more emotional intimacy, which have created some success within their relationship. Additionally, the emotional intimacy could lead to pleasurable activities for both intimate partners as they continue exploring these connections with sexual intimacy. J and Lewis also sought counseling earlier in their relationship as a preventive means, which will likely guide their sexual communication and intimacy moving forward. They also participate in significant amounts of foreplay and afterplay, which expand the continuum of their pleasure-inclusive activities and allow for further forms of sexual expression. The goal is to continue creating an affirmative and sex positive approach through these discussions, which entail broaching of cultural factors in tandem with sexuality education.

Conclusion

From the time we are born (albeit, there are pictures of touching in utero), we are inclined to touch ourselves. Everyone deserves access to accurate information about orgasm, including a clear understanding of what and where the body parts that contribute to orgasm are, how they work, and how orgasm happens in the body and brain (McCarthy & McCarthy, 2019; Strait et al., 2015). Thus, counselor educators need to provide opportunities for counselors to develop skills in broaching the topic of orgasm with their clients (Speciale, 2020). In our experience, when we as counselor educators bring these topics up with students, we frequently hear comments such as "I should have had this information a long time ago!" and "Why did I have to graduate school to learn how my body works?" Clinicians who engage in a gentle, open conversation about masturbation and sexuality are far more likely to witness a parallel process wherein a client begins to open up about their own desires and needs.

Questions You Always Wanted to Ask

1. **Would you share some ways to help clients develop comfort in discussing orgasm in counseling?**
   It is important for clinicians to be aware of their own reactions to discussing orgasm. If the clinician is not comfortable with the topic, this can be communicated through microexpressions. When clinicians develop a sense of comfort and confidence in their ability to receive questions and assist in processing challenges related to orgasm, this filters through in their mannerisms. To desensitize and develop comfort with this topic among counselors, counselor educators need to bring orgasm into the classrooms so that students enter practicum and internship already prepared to support clients who need to work on this in counseling.
2. **Would you share some ways to inquire about whether a client is able to reach orgasm when masturbating?**
   In most situations, it is best to approach these situations directly. Asking directly about a client's ability to reach orgasm when masturbating will effectively bring both orgasm and masturbation into the discussion, thus reducing the potential for these topics to be avoided and unaddressed.
3. **Would you share some ways to talk about orgasm with a couple where one partner is not reaching orgasm?**
   When one partner is not achieving orgasm, it can be helpful to begin with a sexual history for each of the partners. This helps the clinician understand whether the difficulty reaching orgasm is something that happens specifically when engaging sexually with a partner or if the problem occurs when the individual tries to reach orgasm through masturbation as well. If the sexual history reveals that the individual struggles to reach orgasm whether with a partner or not, the work must begin by exploring what factors may be impeding the individual's

ability to reach orgasm independently. Once the individual has established the capacity for orgasm through masturbation, the couple can begin to incorporate the techniques that work for masturbation into their sexual play.

4. **Would you share some things about how to reach orgasm with a partner who is transfeminine and has had gender-confirming surgery?**
   For transfeminine individuals, gender-confirming surgery involves the creation of female genitalia. The surgeon removes the penis and testicles and creates a vagina from penile skin (vaginoplasty). Labia are constructed from scrotal skin. The clitoris is usually created using the highly sensitive glans found at the tip of the penis (clitoroplasty). One of the goals of gender-confirming surgery is the ability to enjoy intimacy and reach orgasm.

   Counselors can reassure clients that it often takes time for trans women to begin having orgasms after gender-confirming surgery (see Sigurjónsson et al., 2017). Time is needed for the body to heal, and the client needs to become familiar with her new genitalia. Counselors can encourage clients to explore different varieties of stimulation and to experiment to find the areas that bring her the most pleasure. Some clients prefer to navigate the discovery process alone and then invite their partner to share experiences with them, and other partners enjoy experiencing the discovery process together.

5. **Would you share some things about talking about orgasm with clients who identify as asexual?**
   It is true that even people who have little or no interest in sex and orgasm, including those who identify as asexual, can find it helpful to discuss that aspect of their life in counseling, particularly when they encounter people who question their relationship to orgasm. A person does not have to be interested in orgasm for orgasm to be something that comes up, and this is something that clients want to discuss with a counselor who will keep the information private and provide them with a safe place to explore their experiences and reactions to their experiences.

6. **Would you share some things about orgasm with a partner who is transmasculine? What if the male partner has a vagina? What differences should I be aware of with a transmasculine partner who has had bottom surgery (phalloplasty)?**
   Many individuals who are transmasculine do not opt for phalloplasty. For some of these individuals, it can take time to come to terms with being a man with a vagina and some will need time to “make friends with” this part of their bodies as men. This said, due to the impact of testosterone through hormone replacement therapy (HRT), many transmasculine men report a newly heightened sexual awareness and desire for sex. Testosterone causes trans male vaginas and vulvas to enlarge, particularly the clitoris, and along with that, transmasculine individuals experience an increase in sensitivity.

   A study conducted in 2005 reported that transfeminine participants had more intense, smoother, and longer orgasms after HRT gender-confirming surgery (vaginoplasty), whereas trans men said their orgasms were more powerful and shorter after phalloplasty (see De Cuypere et al., 2005).

   More recently, Wierckx et al. (2011) conducted a study with 49 transmasculine participants who had been on long-term testosterone therapy and who were on average 8 years post gender-confirming surgery, with 94% of the participants having had phalloplasty. Nearly all were able to reach orgasm through masturbation and through sexual intercourse, and the majority reported a change whereby orgasm was experienced as more powerful but briefer. Satisfaction rates with the phalloplasty were high, despite a fairly high complication rate. Most importantly, the myth that transmasculine/transfeminine individuals do not orgasm needs to be addressed in the counseling literature.

References

Adam, F., De Sutter, P., Day, J., & Grimm, E. (2020). A randomized study comparing video-based mindfulness-based cognitive therapy with video-based traditional cognitive behavioral therapy in a sample of women struggling to achieve orgasm. *The Journal of Sexual Medicine*, *17*(2), 312–324. https://doi.org/10.1016/j.jsxm.2019.10.022

Althof, S. E., McMahon, C. G., Waldinger, M. D., Serefoglu, E. C., Shindel, A. W., Adaikan, P. G., Becher, E., Dean, J., Giuliano, F., Hellstrom, W. J. G., Giraldi, A., Glina, S., Incrocci, L., Jannini, E., McCabe, M., Parish, S., Rowland, D., Segraves, R. T., Sharlip, I., & Torres, L. O. (2014). An update of the International Society of Sexual Medicine's guidelines for the diagnosis and treatment of premature ejaculation (PE). *The Journal of Sexual Medicine*, *11*(6), 1392–1422. https://doi.org/10.1111/jsm.12504

American Counseling Association. (2014). *ACA code of ethics.* https://www.counseling.org/resources/aca-code-of-ethics.pdf

American Psychiatric Association. (2022). *Diagnostic and statistical manual of mental disorders* (5th ed., text rev).

Basson, R. (2001). Using a different model for female sexual response to address women's problematic low sexual desire. *Journal of Sex & Marital Therapy*, *27*(5), 395–403. https://doi.org/10.1080/713846827

Behnia, B., Heinrichs, M., Bergmann, W., Jung, S., Germann, J., Schedlowski, M., Hartmann, U., & Kruger, T. H. C. (2014). Differential effects of intranasal oxytocin on sexual experiences and partner interactions in couples. *Hormones and Behavior*, *65*(3), 308–318. https://doi.org/10.1016/j.yhbeh.2014.01.009

Buehler, S. (2017). *What every mental health professional needs to know about sex* (2nd ed.). Springer Publishing.

Chadwick, S. B., Francisco, M., & van Anders, S. M. (2019). When orgasms do not equal pleasure: Accounts of "bad" orgasm experiences during consensual sexual encounters. *Archives of Sexual Behavior*, *48*(8), 2435–2459. https://doi.org/10.1007/s10508-019-01527-7

Council for Accreditation of Counseling and Related Educational Programs. (2016). *2016 CACREP standards.* http://www.cacrep.org/for-programs/2016-cacrep-standards/

Courtois, F., & Dubray, S. (2014). The neurophysiology of orgasm. *Current Sexual Health Reports*, *6*(3), 201–210. https://doi.org/10.1007/s11930-014-0026-6

De Cuypere, G., T'Sjoen, G., Beerten, R., Selvaggi, G., De Sutter, P., Hoebeke, P., Monstrey, S., Vansteenwegen, A., & Rubens, R. (2005). Sexual and physical health after sex reassignment surgery. *Archives of Sexual Behavior*, *34*(6), 679–690. https://doi.org/10.1007/s10508-005-7926-5

Farago, R. K. (2021). Implications for supervisors and counselor educators in human sexuality. *Journal of Counseling Sexology & Sexual Wellness*, *2*(2), 117–129. https://doi.org/10.34296/02021034

Graham, C. A. (2014). Orgasm disorders in women. In Y. M. Binik & K. S. K. Hall (Eds.), *Principles and practice of sex therapy* (5th ed., pp. 89–111). The Guilford Press.
Graham, C. A., & Hall, K. S. K. (2013). *The cultural context of sexual pleasure and problems: Psychotherapy with diverse clients.* Routledge.
Guo, Y. N., Ng, E. M. L., & Chan, K. (2004). Foreplay, orgasm and after-play among Shanghai couples and its integrative relation with their marital satisfaction. *Sexual and Relationship Therapy, 19*(1), 65–78. https://doi.org/10.1080/14681990410001640844
Hall, K. S. K., & Graham, C. A. (2014). Culturally sensitive sex therapy: The need for shared meanings in the treatment of sexual problems. In Y. M. Binik & K. S. K. Hall (Eds.), *Principles and practice of sex therapy* (5th ed., pp. 334–358). The Guilford Press.
Jones, A. C., Robinson, W. D., & Seedall, R. B. (2018). The role of sexual communication in couples' sexual outcomes: A dyadic path analysis. *Journal of Marital and Family Therapy, 44*(4), 606–623. https://doi.org/10.1111/jmft.12282
King, M., Belsky, J., Mah, K., & Binik, Y. M. (2011). Are there different types of female orgasm? *Archives of Sexual Behavior, 40*(5), 865–875. https://doi.org/10.1007/s10508-010-9639-7
Komisaruk, B. R., & Whipple, B. (2011). Non-genital orgasms. *Sexual and Relationship Therapy, 26*(4), 356–372. https://doi.org/10.1080/14681994.2011.649252
Laumann, E. O., Paik, A., & Rosen, R. C. (1999). SSI Grand Master Lecture 6 "The epidemiology of erectile dysfunction: Results from the National Health and Social Life Survey." *International Journal of Impotence Research, 11*, S60–S64. https://doi.org/10.1038/sj.ijir.3900487
Levin, R. J. (2001). Sexual desire and the deconstruction and reconstruction of the human female sexual response model of Masters and Johnson. In W. Everaerd, E. Laan, & S. Both (Eds.), *Sexual appetite, desire and motivation: Energetics of the sexual system* (pp. 63–93). Royal Netherlands Academy of Arts and Sciences.
Levin, R. J. (2011). The human female orgasm: A critical evaluation of its proposed reproductive functions. *Sexual and Relationship Therapy, 26*(4), 301–314. https://doi.org/10.1080/14681994.2011.649692
Mah, K., & Binik, Y. M. (2001). The nature of human orgasm: A critical review of major trends. *Clinical Psychology Review, 21*(6), 823–856. https://doi.org/10.1016/S0272-7358(00)00069-6
McCarthy, B., & McCarthy, E. J. (2019). *Finding your sexual voice: Celebrating female sexuality.* Routledge.
McMahon, C. G. (2007). Premature ejaculation. *Indian Journal of Urology, 23*(2), 97–108. https://doi.org/10.4103/0970-1591.32056
Mercer, M. E., & Dermer, S. B. (2020). Development of the Comfort With Sexual Behaviors Scale. *Journal of Counseling Sexology & Sexual Wellness, 2*(1), 58–68. https://doi.org/10.34296/02011023
Merwin, K. E., O'Sullivan, L. F., & Rosen, N. O. (2017). We need to talk: Disclosure of sexual problems is associated with depression, sexual functioning, and relationship satisfaction in women. *Journal of Sex and Marital Therapy, 43*(8), 786–800. https://doi.org/10.1080/0092623X.2017.1283378
Meston, C. M., Levin, R. J., Sipski, M. L., Hull, E. M., & Heiman, J. R. (2004). Women's orgasm. *Annual Review of Sex Research, 15*(1), 173–257.
Meston, C. M., & Stanton, A. M. (2019). Understanding sexual arousal and subjective–genital arousal desynchrony in women. *Nature Reviews Urology, 16*(2), 107–120. https://doi.org/10.1038/s41585-018-0142-6

Metz, M. E., & McCarthy, B. W. (2004). *Coping with erectile dysfunction: How to regain confidence and enjoy great sex.* New Harbinger.

Murray, C. E., Pope, A. L., & Willis, B. T. (2016). *Sexuality counseling: Theory, research, and practice.* SAGE Publications.

Perelman, M. A., & Rowland, D. L. (2006). Retarded ejaculation. *World Journal of Urology, 24*(6), 645–652. https://doi.org/10.1007/s00345-006-0127-6

Pope, M., Wierzalis, E. A., Barret, B., & Rankins, M. (2007). Sexual and intimacy issues for aging gay men. *Adultspan Journal, 6*(2), 68–82. https://doi.org/10.1002/j.2161-0029.2007.tb00033.x

Ralph, D. J., & Wylie, K. R. (2005). Ejaculatory disorders and sexual function. *BJU International, 95*(9), 1181–1186. https://doi.org/10.1111/j.1464-410X.2005.05536.x

Richardson, D., Nalabanda, A., & Goldmeier, D. (2006). Retarded ejaculation: A review. *International Journal of STD & AIDS, 17*(3), 143–150.

Rosen, N. O., Mooney, K., & Muise, A. (2017). Dyadic empathy predicts sexual and relationship well-being in couples transitioning to parenthood. *Journal of Sex & Marital Therapy, 43*(6), 543–559. https://doi.org/10.1080/0092623X.2016.1208698

Rottmann, N., Hansen, D. G., Christensen, R. d., Hagedoorn, M., Frisch, M., Nicolaisen, A., Kroman, N., Flyger, H., & Johansen, C. (2017). Satisfaction with sex life in sexually active heterosexual couples dealing with breast cancer: A nationwide longitudinal study. *Acta Oncologica, 56*(2), 212–219. https://doi.org/10.1080/0284186X.2016.1266086

Rowland, D. L., Cempel, L. M., & Tempel, A. R. (2018). Women's attributions regarding why they have difficulty reaching orgasm. *Journal of Sex & Marital Therapy, 44*(5), 475–484. https://doi.org/10.1080/0092623X.2017.1408046

Sanabria, S., & Murray, T. L., Jr. (2018). Infusing human sexuality content and counseling in counselor education curriculum. *American Journal of Sexuality Education, 13*(2), 190–204. https://doi.org/10.1080/15546128.2018.1457461

Sayin, H. Ü. (2012). Doors of female orgasmic consciousness: New theories on the peak experience and mechanisms of female orgasm and expanded sexual response. *NeuroQuantology, 10*(4), 692–714. https://doi.org/10.14704/nq.2012.10.4.627

Schubert, A., & Pope, M. (2020). Sexuality beyond young adulthood: Affordances and barriers to sexual expression in the nursing home. *Journal of Counseling Sexology & Sexual Wellness, 2*(1), 35–47. https://doi.org/10.34296/02011022

Séguin, L. J., & Blais, M. (2019). Pleasure is just the tip of the iceberg: Social representations, personal beliefs, and attributed meanings to partnered orgasm. *Canadian Journal of Human Sexuality, 28*(3), 328–342. https://doi.org/10.3138/cjhs.2019-0027

Sigurjónsson, H., Möllermark, C., Rinder, J., Farnebo, F., & Lundgren, T. K. (2017). Long-term sensitivity and patient-reported functionality of the neoclitoris after gender reassignment surgery. *The Journal of Sexual Medicine, 14*(2), 269–273. https://doi.org/10.1016/j.jsxm.2016.12.003

Speciale, M. (2020). Negotiating sexual values in counselor education: A qualitative case exploration. *Journal of Counseling Sexology & Sexual Wellness, 2*(1), 10–21. https://doi.org/10.34296/02011032

Strait, J. G., Sandberg, J. G., Larson, J. H., & Harper, J. M. (2015). The relationship between family-of-origin experiences and sexual satisfaction in married couples. *Journal of Family Therapy, 37*(3), 361–385. https://doi.org/10.1111/1467-6427.12007

Taylor, J. Z., Lewis, C. L., & Davis, L. E. (2019). Sexual wellness and rare disease considerations: A behavioral case conceptualization and approach to counseling treatment. *Journal of Counseling Sexology & Sexual Wellness, 1*(2), 96–104. https://doi.org/10.34296/01021018

Towne, A. (2019). Clitoral stimulation during penile-vaginal intercourse: A phenomenological study exploring sexual experiences in support of female orgasm. *Canadian Journal of Human Sexuality*, *28*(1), 68–80. https://doi.org/10.3138/cjhs.2018-0022

Wallen, K., & Lloyd, E. A. (2011). Female sexual arousal: Genital anatomy and orgasm in intercourse. *Hormones and Behavior*, *59*(5), 780–792. https://doi.org/10.1016/j.yhbeh.2010.12.004

Wierckx, K., Van Caenegem, E., Elaut, E., Dedecker, D., Van de Peer, F., Toye, K., Weyers, S., Hoebeke, P., Monstrey, S., De Cuypere, G., & T'Sjoen, G. (2011). Quality of life and sexual health after sex reassignment surgery in transsexual men. *The Journal of Sexual Medicine, 8*(12), 3379–3388. https://doi.org/10.1111/j.1743-6109.2011.02348.x

Wilson, M. R. (2019). Too taboo? Preliminary explorations of counselor experiences of client sexuality. *Journal of Counseling Sexology & Sexual Wellness, 1*(1), 60–68. https://doi.org/10.34296/01011010

Wongsomboon, V., Burleson, M. H., & Webster, G. D. (2020). Women's orgasm and sexual satisfaction in committed sex and casual sex: Relationship between sociosexuality and sexual outcomes in different sexual contexts. *Journal of Sex Research*, *57*(3), 285–295. https://doi.org/10.1080/00224499.2019.1672036

Zeglin, R. J., Niemela, D. R. M., & Vandenberg, M. (2019). What does the counseling field say about sexuality? A content analysis. *American Journal of Sexuality Education*, *14*(1), 55–73. https://doi.org/10.1080/15546128.2018.1518175

Zeglin, R. J., Van Dam, D., & Hergenrather, K. C. (2018). An introduction to proposed human sexuality counseling competencies. *International Journal for the Advancement of Counselling*, *40*(2), 105–121. https://doi.org/10.1007/s10447-017-9314-y

Zietsch, B. P., Miller, G. F., Bailey, M., & Martin, N. G. (2011). Female orgasm rates are largely independent of other traits: Implications for "female orgasmic disorder" and evolutionary theories of orgasm. *Journal of Sexual Medicine, 8*(8), 2305–2316. https://doi.org/10.1111/j.1743-6109.2011.02300.x

It's Not All in Your Head, But It's Pretty Close: Those Damn Societal Messages

Samuel Sanabria and Caitlyn McKinzie Bennett

Sexuality is more than a behavioral or physical function or biological disposition; it is linked to one's identity, relationship with sex, and how these encounters are experienced. It is important to conceptualize sexuality within a holistic framework that encompasses biology, psychology, and sociology. Unfortunately, research in sexuality studies has a long history of emphasizing evolutionary and biological influences that linger today. For example, before publication of the *Diagnostic and Statistical Manual of Mental Disorders, Fifth Edition* (American Psychiatric Association, 2013), contemporary sex therapy scholars and clinicians advocated against the proposed revisions of sexual dysfunctions that strengthened a medical model approach, claiming that it was inadequate and focused too much on genital-centered sexual satisfaction as opposed to more person-centered sexual satisfaction (Clayton et al., 2012; Tobia & IsHak, 2013). Ultimately and regrettably, their criticisms were dismissed, thus disadvantaging valid and more holistic treatment methods. These advancements in the medical model approach to diagnosing sexual dissatisfaction influence mainstream treatment options, controlling the direction in how sexuality is and "should be" understood. This approach provides only a partial and reductionist understanding based on a standardized definition of sexual satisfaction, which is heteronormative, influenced by cisgender male desire and needs. Moreover, the medical model approach, which views sexual difficulties as a physiological problem, assumes a universal human sexuality response cycle that is "hardwired" and needs to be completed for one to feel sexually "fulfilled."

One of the central criticisms of a medical model approach is the tendency to reduce or eliminate psychological, developmental, and social structures that affect individuals' sexual development, identity, and ability to form sexual health. The World Health

Organization (WHO) provides a broader definition of *sexual health* as "a state of physical, emotional, mental and social well-being in relation to sexuality" (WHO, n.d., para. 4). WHO also recognizes that sexuality includes a broad range of identities, which encompass gender (e.g., cisgender, transgender, gender expansive), affectional orientation (e.g., lesbian, gay, or bisexual; asexual), erotic expressions (e.g., polyamory, monogamy, kink), and biological functioning (e.g., reproduction, disabilities). An essential aspect of this approach to sexuality is the understanding that biological, political, social, religious, cultural, and economic factors influence these identities. For this chapter, this holistic approach to sexual health and sexuality will serve as a conceptual framework for understanding the complexities of our clients' experiences.

Socially Constructed Sexuality

Sexologists commonly understand sexuality as socially constructed, informed by culture, race, gender, politics, history, and religion. One way to conceptualize sexuality is through social construction theory. Social construction theory (Berger & Luckmann, 1967) posits that an individual's sense of reality forms through collective meanings reinforced by sociopolitical and institutional norms. This sense of reality influences social roles (behaviors) and social norms (cognitions) and how individuals experience reality. The combination of these influences becomes internalized and forms metaphorical blueprints called *social scripts*, which influence presuppositions.

Using script theory from social constructivism, Gagnon and Simon (1973) conceptualized the development of gendered *sexual scripts*, the internalized formation of "right" or "wrong" values, behaviors, and meanings for sexuality and gender. Sexual scripts are cognitive and social and provide guidelines for sexual behavior that affect to whom we are attracted, how we will or will not sexually engage with others, and how we feel about those encounters. Sexual scripts interconnect with various sexuality theories but reject the idea of viewing sexual desire from a purely biological approach.

Sexual Scripts

Sexual scripting occurs on societal, relational, and personal levels, each simultaneously influencing the other. Societal (sexual) scripts are broader and reflect societal norms and definitions of acceptable or unacceptable gendered behaviors. Although cultural norms vary globally, there are identifiable sexual norms that are common. For example, for most cultures, sexual norms are highly gendered, heterosexual, and between two married adults. One of the most influential socializing institutions in the development of sexual norms is religion. The major world religions each have doctrines regarding what is sexually permissible or prohibited, whether that relates to chastity, premarital sexual relations, masturbation, or diverse sexual identities (i.e., lesbian; gay; bisexual; transgender and Two-Spirit; gender-expansive; queer and questioning; intersex; agender, asexual, and aromantic; pansexual, pan/polygender, and poly relationship systems and other related identities, known as LGBTGEQIAP+). These sets of religious beliefs are communicated either explicitly or implicitly to believers, who then internalize them, influencing their sexual attitudes, beliefs, and behaviors (S. S. Hall et al., 2020; Yarhouse et al., 2017). These internalized messages could have a profound effect on clients' sexual health, mainly when conflicts occur between religious and sexual identities (Turner et al., 2004; Yarhouse et al., 2017). A client who has difficulty reconciling their sexual identity with their religious beliefs is more likely to experience guilt, shame (Levy, 2012; Sherry et al., 2010), and depression (Eleuteri & Farulla, 2016; Page et al., 2013). Although religious beliefs can significantly affect one's relationship to sex, they are certainly not the only influence. Consider the abstinence-only educational programs found in individual states, which emphasize heteronormative sexual practices as the only acceptable approach to sex and reinforce the idea that any sexual encounters outside of this are wrong and dangerous.

Although sexual scripts start with societal norm reinforcements, they certainly do not end there. Sexual scripts become internalized with each relational encounter. While sexual relationships are unique and come with specific transactions, they are experienced through the lens of societal norms, making each sexual script distinctly personal. For example, one of the societally reinforced messages on gender and sexual desire is that "men desire sex while women desire love." Likewise, men are the ones to desire, and women are the ones to be desired. These social messages influence how men and women should behave, appear, and feel when it comes to sexual experiences. A man who is sexually propositioned by a woman may find himself cognitively and emotionally at odds with himself, struggling with how to respond. Depending on whether this encounter was pleasant, he may either modify his sexual script to allow for being the object of sexual desire or reinforce his sexual script by rejecting her advances and aggressively pursuing another woman.

The challenge of understanding personal sexuality through sexual script theory increases when considering society's diverse nature, especially when viewed from macro- and mesolevels. The perspective of society on a macrolevel can be global, which limits norms to universal experiences, or geographical, which expands norms to distinct nations. At the mesolevel, society is divided into the influences of cultural groups and is further divided into subcultural groups. When the influence of each interpersonal relationship—especially when the relationship involves someone from a different cultural or social group—is added to the ongoing evolution of sexual scripts, it becomes clear how impossible it is to fully understand personal sexuality. Regardless, the journey toward sexual health needs to include exploring the influence that our sexual scripts have on our sexual identity, behaviors, beliefs, affect, and ability to enjoy sex.

Culturally Informed Sex Positive Approach

Personal insights are vital to establishing and maintaining sexual health. These insights are developed by unpacking the social and cultural messages that helped shape and inform our client's sexuality. For these insights to have therapeutic value, however, clinicians need to cultivate a culturally informed sex positive approach that challenges long-held heteronormative views on sexuality while understanding and embracing diverse sexual expressions that are developmentally affirming and consensual. Likewise, a culturally informed sex positive approach does not rely on a medicalized view of sexual health and rejects the need to diagnose sexual behavior or experiences. There are three areas of focus when practicing from a culturally informed sex positive approach. The first focus is *conceptualizing* sexual problems either *unidimensionally*, caused by a specific psychological or physical factor, or *multidimensionally*, caused by a variety of factors (e.g., biopsychosocial). The second focus is *approaching* sexual problems from a critical or constructive disposition (e.g., dysfunction vs. relational distress). The final focus includes *treating* sexual problems from a performance-based outcome or a meaning-making outcome. In this section, we will present three conceptual and therapeutic models to help clinicians cultivate a more culturally informed sex positive approach to therapy.

The first model, known as the *new view* (Teifer, 2012), offers a multidimensional conceptual understanding of, and a constructive approach to, sexual problems through the critical analysis of professional standards and practices. A second model, *good enough sex* (GES; Metz & McCarthy, 2012), promotes a similar conceptual understanding and constructive approach through the critical analysis of public discourse and media representations, as well as a treatment approach based on meaning making. The final model, *culturally sensitive sex therapy* (CSST; K. S. K. Hall & Graham, 2014), provides the foundation for incorporating cultural sensitivity in understanding clients' sexual problems in order to tailor treatment to the unique cultural needs of clients.

The New View

In response to the expanding process of medicalizing sexual experiences, Teifer (2012), founder of the New View Campaign (see the archived website at http://www.newviewcampaign.org/history.asp), recommended revising and expanding traditional sex therapy approaches to include a different understanding of sexual problems. The new view took a feminist approach to sexual satisfaction by focusing on sociocultural contexts to understand causation, rather than blaming individual failings. Likewise, a "client as an expert" replaced "clinician as an expert," creating a collaborative and egalitarian therapeutic relationship. By changing the perspective on sexual problems from the profession-based definition of "sexual dysfunction" to a client-based definition of "sexual stress dissatisfaction," clinicians can broaden assumptions to accommodate social and cultural influences without excluding possible biological causes. Clinicians can increase therapeutic outcomes by taking a more meaning-centered approach than the traditional genital-centered approach to therapy.

Good Enough Sex

One of the central tenets of the GES model is the understanding of how normative notions of sex negatively affect sexual satisfaction. Much like traditional sex therapy approaches, the emphasis on performance within a limited relationship construct inhibits sexual growth and fulfillment; however, this model concentrates more on the influence of public discourse and media. Public discourse and media create and reinforce unrealistic and idyllic expectations that sex is specific, dynamic, and perfect (McCabe, 2005). These ideals seep into physical attributes by reinforcing social standards of beauty and attractiveness. As a result, people get absorbed into these concepts of "good sex," dedicating significant time and energy into achieving it. The pursuit of ideally good sex leads to performance anxiety, fears, and other relational problems (McCabe, 2005). These experiences may be prevalent in males who are socialized to assume the role of expert and leader in sexual encounters. GES works from two positions: (a) to relieve distress by challenging self-defeating beliefs caused by these ideals, and (b) promoting sexual satisfaction through more realistic and similarly stimulating beliefs. The latter position encourages partners to be responsible for their sexuality and collaborate to create a new, mutually satisfying sexual style. This new sex style may include transitioning to nonpenetrative sensual forms of sex while emphasizing emotional meaning and connectivity. Again, this direction may be challenging for males who are used to finding pleasure in penetrative sex and being "in control."

Culturally Sensitive Sex Therapy

CSST approaches sexuality with the understanding that although people experience sexual problems globally, they do not always reflect Western society's experiences. This understanding applies not only to the type of sexual problem, but also to its prevalence, causation, impact on distress, and significance. This distinction is important because ethnic and cultural minorities are less likely to seek therapy and are more likely to end their treatment prematurely (Owen et al., 2012; Sue & Chu, 2003). The reluctance to seek therapy increases when the area of concern is sexual in nature. Therefore, CSST requires clinicians to comprehend sexuality from a community context, incorporating the client's ethnic, cultural, religious, and social background. CSST applies cultural sensitivity to the process of assessing, diagnosing, setting goals, and selecting interventions. CSST encourages clinicians to use their client's culture as part of the solution-making process. By operating from a client-shared meaning of sexual problems, including its meaning and impact on distress, clinicians can modify their approach to sex therapy to meet clients' unique needs. For example, a client's cultural background may require more directive interventions. Counselors should know, however, the dangers of overgeneralizing or stereotyping clients. CSST emphasizes the importance of shared meaning of sexual problems between the counselor and client to develop a flexible approach as opposed to a fixed approach.

Throughout the following case illustration, the applied and recommended approach incorporates all three models and is largely rooted within a CSST approach. CSST is infused throughout the entire therapeutic process, beginning with establishing trust and ending with outcome. The new view and GES models are then incorporated throughout identifying sexual scripts and addressing sexual scripts, specifically in the intentional practice of (a) exploring the sociocultural context of sexual satisfaction; (b) creating new, adaptable meanings of sexual scripts; and (c) inviting the couple to share about their relationship, sexual scripts, and sexual satisfaction as personal experts of their experience

Case Example: Seth and Magaly

Magaly and Seth scheduled an appointment with a sex therapist regarding difficulties with intimacy after 7 months of working closely with their church pastor. Magaly is a 28-year-old cisgender, biracial, nonlesbian female. She was born and raised in a city in Puerto Rico and moved to a state in the northeastern United States when she was 18 years old to attend a private, Catholic college in New England. Seth is 27 years old and identifies as a White, cisgender, nongay male. He was born and raised in the northeastern United States and attended the same private, Catholic college as Magaly. The couple met in one of their theology courses and instantly felt a romantic connection. They started dating after the course ended and married soon after graduation; they are now celebrating 3 years of marriage. They describe their overall relationship as good; however, both report feeling unfulfilled with their level of sexual intimacy.

During the assessment process, the counselor learns that both Seth and Magaly identify as evangelical Christians, and during their dating period, they consciously decided not to engage in sexual intercourse until their marriage. They expressed, however, physical intimacy with each other through kissing and heavy petting and, on occasion, while sexually aroused, would mutually masturbate. They often felt guilty for "pushing the boundaries" of what their faith allows and would often pray for forgiveness. Neither Magaly nor Seth had any sexual experiences with other partners before meeting each other.

Magaly and Seth admitted to being excited about their wedding night and had anticipated that, after so many years of dating without having sexual intercourse, they would have an unforgettable experience. This message was reinforced while attending a weekend religious retreat on marriage. One of the central messages in the retreat was the importance of sexual abstinence, and that, if they remained abstinent, "God would bless them on their wedding night." Unfortunately, this was not the case. On their wedding night, after engaging in some foreplay, Seth attempted to penetrate Magaly, which resulted in excruciating pain for her. After several failed attempts, they decided to stop and try another time. For months after their wedding, Magaly was unable to receive Seth. Her doctor suggested using dilators and Botox treatment to help with the pain. She decided to try this treatment approach and had Seth help her with the process. Seth was supportive of Magaly's treatment but kept his discomfort and concerns about this process to himself.

After a period of time with Botox treatments and using the dilator, Magaly's pain started to decrease. Seeing this reduced pain as a sign, Magaly wanted to try intercourse again. When she approached Seth, he refused and asked if they could try another time. This exchange continued for days, and after 2 weeks, Magaly, concerned about pressuring Seth, stopped initiating. Seth was relieved because he did not want to "deal with it" anymore. Magaly, feeling rejected, decided to confide in her mother, who told her that she was not doing enough to take care of her appearance and that it was the wife's job to "entice" her husband. This message caused Magaly to feel that she was not attractive enough.

Because of Magaly's pain, they have not had sexual intercourse. Seth stated that he could not get aroused enough to penetrate her. They have engaged in other sexual activities, including heavy petting, oral sex, and mutual masturbation. They have experienced, however, a gradual decline in these sexual activities since her treatment, further exacerbating their sexual dissatisfaction. Seth admits he is embarrassed and significantly distressed. To complicate their experiences further, Magaly discovered that, approximately 6 months ago, Seth had been purchasing adult videos online. She felt shocked and confused. When she confronted him, he said that it was "not a big deal" and that he just prefers to masturbate late at night while she is asleep.

They decided to seek spiritual counseling with their church pastor. Although the pastor was empathetic, he said that masturbating to "pornography" was a sin and that the pain she was experiencing was a form of retribution for their premarital sexual behaviors. His advice was for Seth to refrain immediately from masturbation and for the couple to ask for forgiveness through prayer. They felt overwhelmed by their pastor's approach, which became the catalyst for them to seek counseling.

Conceptualizing Magaly and Seth: Sexual Scripts

It is important to understand that, given the taboo nature of sex, most people are hesitant to seek help for sexual dissatisfaction. This is especially true for ethnic and racial minorities who may be skeptical of a system that may be insensitive to cultural differences. Experiences with anxiety, microaggressions, discrimination, and rejection inhibit feeling comfortable to seek out and enter sex therapy. Sexual scripts that include the belief that sex is sacred and should only be discussed between two individuals in a traditional marriage can add to the hesitancy in seeking out sex therapy.

Magaly

In the case of Magaly, she grew up in Puerto Rico with a strong family value system. Magaly also grew up in the Catholic faith and attended the local church regularly. When it came to addressing personal problems, she received explicit cultural messages about not divulging anything to people outside the family, especially when it came to family affairs, and if there was a serious issue, their Catholic priest would be able to provide the best counsel.

When Magaly experienced physiological changes due to puberty around age 11, she began feeling increased discomfort about her body and how others perceived her body; she recalls it being a confusing time and feeling uncomfortable about asking others about her new physiological changes. When she experienced her first menstrual cycle, Magaly attempted to seek advice from her mother and was merely told that she was becoming a woman. Upon Magaly's *quinceañera* (her 15th birthday), her family formally celebrated her passage to womanhood and conveyed the importance of being a Godly woman who is committed to prayer and faith.

Throughout high school, Magaly was social, well liked, and had a supportive group of friends. She excelled in her academics and felt proud of her achievements. Magaly found herself attracted to and interested in some of her male peers; however, she expressed feeling uncertain of how to navigate relationships with males her age, as she feared going against her faith.

Seth

Seth, on the other hand, grew up in a predominantly White, middle-class community in central Massachusetts. Seth was raised in the Protestant faith with a father who was the pastor of their church. They attended church services up to three times a week. Seth's family was more reserved about expressing personal problems and did not encourage Seth to be open about any personal issues he was experiencing. Although Seth felt like he could not talk about any sexual issues, he felt comfortable with his sexuality. As a young man, he had a healthy sex drive and would often view and masturbate to adult videos on the internet to satisfy his sexual desires.

When Seth was 16, and in the 11th grade, he joined the Junior Christian Student Group at his high school. He joined after dating his first girlfriend, who was also a member. It was during this time that Seth also joined a Pentecostal church and began identifying with their evangelical teachings. He attended a weekend retreat on relationships and sex for young men. During this retreat, certain sex doctrines were reinforced, including refraining from premarital sex and masturbation. One of the messages shared, which was the importance of finding a spouse who is "pure" and devoted to the teachings of Christ, had an impact on Seth.

Treatment Approach and Outcomes

When Magaly and Seth arrived for their first session, they were noticeably anxious. They have never sought counseling outside of their church and felt unsure of what to expect. They were uncertain whether their counselor would support their religious beliefs or understand their unique cultural experiences. They sat together while quietly scanning the room for any items that would reveal anything about their counselor. Magaly noticed that the waiting area was organized and free of any religious or Spanish reading materials, and the art on the wall consisted of pleasing watercolors of various landscapes. Seth was not as observant regarding any religious or Spanish representation; however, he did notice that the interior decor was more feminine in style, which made him feel more alert to his situation. After a few minutes, the counselor met and invited them to her office. Magaly immediately noticed the counselor's White identity while Seth noticed her represented gender. As a result, and for different reasons, the couple automatically felt distrustful of the counselor and doubtful that counseling would help. Fortunately, the counselor had an increased level of social consciousness and noticed the couple's discomfort. The counselor also knew that, based on their intake form and shared identities, there might be some cross-cultural transference experiences. The counselor invited the couple to be aware of how her cultural and social identities may hinder the development of trust and safety within the therapeutic relationship.

Establishing Trust

As part of the counselors' development and personal work, it is vital to consider one's multicultural orientation (MCO) and subsequent practices of cultural humility. In particular, women of color have reported recurrent racial and ethnic microaggressions from White counselors, including decreased perceptions of the counselors' ability to engage in cultural humility practices (Davis et al., 2018). In implementing an MCO framework, counselors integrate three constructs in clinical practice: cultural humility, cultural comfort, and cultural opportunities (Owen, 2013; Owen et al., 2011). Cultural humility is the underlying value guiding the MCO framework that includes being open to clients' needs as it relates to their cultural identities and being aware of personal concerns that may interfere with being other-oriented. Cultural opportunities involve being attentive to markers that clients reveal in therapy that connect to their cultural identities that can be explored in more depth. These markers may include beliefs, values, or any other aspects that relate to their cultural identities. Lastly, cultural comfort is the process of being aware of any thoughts and feelings that occur that prevent the counselor from engaging in the opportunities to explore further clients' identities for deeper understanding. MCO scholars have referred to this framework for counselors as a "way of being with clients" (Davis et al., 2018) that enhances thoughtfulness and responsiveness. Davis et al. (2018) recommend that counselors integrate an MCO framework within logistical practices (i.e., intake, conceptualizing clients' presenting concerns, and treatment planning) and relational practices (i.e., developing a working alliance, working through conflicting values, and owning limitations of cultural knowledge).

In the case of Magaly and Seth, the counselor implemented an MCO framework throughout the therapeutic process. The counselor approached the counseling relationship with cultural humility by reflecting on any thoughts and feelings about the couple that may interfere with the intercultural therapeutic relationship. This reflection allows the counselor to move into necessary interpersonal awareness and practice. The shift to interpersonal awareness and practice allows the counselor to focus on the clients' worldviews and experiences, creating a movement from self (i.e., focus on self-perspectives) to others (i.e., awareness of how privileged identities and positionality can affect clients' sense of safety and comfort). Through intrapersonal reflection, the counselor has engaged in personal work to provide competent practices. For example, the counselor recognizes the privilege and power in her White identity, which can create valid feelings of anxiety, fear, and distrust for clients of color who may have lived experiences of discrimination, microaggressions, and racism.

The counselor does not wait to meet with clients before taking advantage of opportunities for cultural engagement. The counselor incorporates specific questions in her intake form that aim to gather information about clients' essential identities and experiences. Collecting initial information related to Magaly's and Seth's individual and couple identities allowed the counselor to recognize the need to focus on the intrapersonal and interpersonal processes that ground cultural humility practices within the counseling process.

The counselor used the cultural markers on the intake form as a starting point to normalize and validate Magaly and Seth's experiences. The counselor shared about the discomfort that couples may feel in sharing about personal experiences and that this discomfort can feel especially heightened when racial and ethnic identities between counselor and client are different. For example, this counselor shared, "Couples counseling can be a time of increased vulnerability and anxiety, especially as you may want to share personal experiences within your relationship. Within your intake paperwork, you also shared cultural identities and experiences that are important to you. I wanted to see how you two feel about potentially engaging in couples counseling with a White counselor." Opening the door to this intentional and needed discussion about nonshared counselor-client identities can demonstrate to the client that the counselor is aware of cultural differences and wants to create a space where they feel heard, validated, and important.

Assessment

A culturally competent counselor knows the importance of listening and understanding the history and context of the couple's relationship during the assessment process. The first step of the assessment process involved exploring how the couple viewed their sexual problems. The counselor engaged in cultural humility by being careful not to interject any evaluative content, allowing the couple to define their problems. The counselor then conducted individual sexual histories to understand each client's social and cultural influences, as well as what each client identifies as the strengths and weaknesses in their relationship. During this part of the assessment process, the counselor began to identify notable messaging themes arising from the clients' religious, ethnic, and gender identities. The last part of the assessment process included preparing the couple for therapy by obtaining commitment and establishing norms. The counselor explained that she works from an integrative biopsychosocial perspective that requires couples to form a collaborative relationship. Magaly and Seth not only verbalized their commitment but also expressed how hopeful they felt. They left the first session feeling a new sense of hope and were eager to return.

In the second session, the counselor decided to look for cultural opportunities for broader understanding by introducing the theory of sexual scripts to explore the couple's belief systems. This exploration allowed the counselor to have a deeper appreciation for the couple, which cultivated the cultural comfort to engage in conversations that are more meaningful. She explained how people unconsciously and consciously develop guidelines of what is appropriate regarding various gender and sexual expressions, and that their social and cultural environment will influence these moral guidelines. The counselor also explained that internalizing these social and cultural messages through personalized filters affects our sexual self and our ability to experience sexual satisfaction. The notion of understanding our sexual scripts from a social and cultural perspective connected with Magaly, and she instantly conjured some of the specific messages she received from her mother and church. Given her experiences as a Puerto Rican woman of color, she was aware of how the values, beliefs, and practices she learned in Puerto Rico differed from those found in the mainland United

States. On the other hand, Seth was uncertain about what he would learn from the messaging he received. The counselor reassured Seth by explaining how she would help facilitate the process of exploring their sexual scripts.

After the second session, Magaly felt considerably more comfortable with their decision to seek counseling, especially since she felt that the counselor was affirming and genuine in her interest in their religious and cultural backgrounds. Although Seth had difficulty understanding the concept of sexual scripts, he also felt comfortable with the counselor. He realized that he had been concerned about having a female counselor, believing that she would criticize his recent viewing of adult videos and side with Magaly. Seth felt the counselor had a value-free approach and validated his experiences. They agreed to go back to therapy.

Identifying Sexual Scripts

In the third session, the counselor began inviting the couple to further share about their religious and cultural upbringing (cultural comfort), listening closely for any opportunities to encourage additional exploration and meaning making. She was also careful not to approach inquiries that would reinforce value judgments (cultural humility). Magaly began by sharing how, as a young girl, she would sit quietly on the bathroom floor as her mother got ready in the morning. She remembers how her mother would carefully apply her makeup and style her hair. Magaly also recalls her mother's joy when her father would embrace her saying, "Soy el hombre más afortunado del mundo en tener una esposa tan bella" (I am the luckiest man in the world to have such a beautiful wife). Magaly enjoyed seeing her parents express affection with each other and looked forward to having the same relationship. After hearing Magaly's memory, Seth acknowledged how he did not grow up in a family where physical expression of love was common. Although his parents were married, they did not interact much with each other and only showed physical affection to each other during church social gatherings or after service. Even then, the displays of affection consisted of handholding or his mother clutching to his father's arm. Seth also recognized that, as a result, he does not express his love through affection.

Magaly's recounting of her memory provided an example of what the counselor meant by exploring social messaging. Seth remembers receiving clear messages about what it means to be a man from his father, who was the pastor of their church. Seth described his father as being stern and often preoccupied with studying and planning for his sermons. His father often shared his sermons with Seth to prepare him for his role as a church leader. One of the sermons that stood out for Seth was the virtues of a "good wife," which consisted of a woman dedicated to God and who was "pure," untouched by another man. His father went on to use his mother as an example of a virtuous woman, further saying that she is a gift from God. This message was particularly meaningful since, at an early age, Seth wanted to assume his father's role as a pastor. He admired his father and saw him as a model for being a leader. Seth also had a strong connection with his mother, further reinforcing his idealization of women.

Given the counselor's cultural competence level, she was aware of the tendency to identify dogmatic belief systems as the cause of the problem instead of understanding these beliefs from a broader context. Therefore, the counselor encouraged (cultural comfort) Magaly and Seth to expose their sexual scripts by sharing their social messages. During the next couple of sessions, Magaly and Seth were able to identify several of their sexual scripts and connect to how they contribute to their sexual problems. They were ready to move to the next step of counseling, addressing these sexual scripts.

Addressing Sexual Scripts

Before addressing clients' sexual scripts, it is essential to recognize the significant influence that religious and cultural beliefs have on the formation of sexual scripts. These beliefs have deep meaning for clients and are a source of motivation. Counselors who work with this understanding and are open to using clients' religious and cultural belief systems as a foundation for problem-solving will experience less client resistance and better therapeutic outcomes. Given this recognition, it would be more beneficial to encourage the client to address the impact their religious and cultural upbringing have on their sexual scripts and explore different interpretations of their beliefs rather than to discard them. This method requires the counselor to develop spiritual and religious competencies in addition to their cultural competence. This may also require a partnership with someone who is knowledgeable about the clients' faith, such as a religious leader or pastoral counselor, and who is comfortable with sexuality and can approach this subject from an affirming position. In this case, the counselor was familiar with the basic tenets of the major world religions and was comfortable broaching the topic.

The counselor uses elements of narrative therapy as a way of addressing sexual scripts. *Narrative therapy*, much like script theory, is a social constructionist approach, which postulates that individuals coconstruct stories throughout their lives to make meaning of their experiences. This process of meaning making applies when clients add their unique interpretations to their received religious and cultural messages. Narrative therapy works well given its collaborative and nonblaming approach that views the client as the expert to their problems. The counselor started with Magaly, who had already demonstrated a working understanding of religious and cultural messaging. The added benefit of starting with Magaly helped to provide Seth with an example of how to explore his religious and cultural messaging in order to understand better his sexual scripts. The first step in using narrative therapy to address sexual scripts was to assist the couple in externalizing their interpersonal sexual scripts. Through Socratic questioning, Magaly was able to connect her feelings of unattractiveness with the messages she received from her mother about the importance of being beautiful. She also recognized how she assumed that, since Seth was not physically expressive and using adult videos, he was not attracted to her. These connections not only raised Magaly's insights, which allowed her to restructure her scripts, but also raised Seth's insights into how Magaly was experiencing their relationship.

Seth then felt more confident in addressing his sexual scripts. He was able to connect the messages he received from his father about what it means to be a man with his discomfort with giving and receiving affection. Upon further reflection, Seth realized that he equated stoicism with masculinity. When the counselor asked him to extend this awareness to how he viewed physical affection behaviors, Seth stated that he saw them as weak. These feelings amplified when Magaly and Seth attempted to have intercourse on their wedding night. Seth felt that they were being punished for their premarital sexual play and that, as the man in the relationship, he needed more restraint. He became more rigid with his restraint when Magaly began seeking medical treatment for her pain, especially from a male doctor. The counselor took this (cultural) opportunity to encourage Seth to go deeper into uncovering his sexual scripts. Seth felt guilty that his perceived punishment caused Magaly pain, and he also felt shame for her having to expose herself to another male. He felt that he let her down and that she no longer valued him as a husband. This was a pivotal moment in therapy, which led to other insights and opportunities to retell their sexual script stories.

Outcome

Throughout a few more sessions, Seth and Magaly uncovered their sexual scripts further and worked on retelling the stories they created. The counselor moved through the narrative therapy stages, helping the couple reauthor their story to provide new meaning to their unique experiences while also strengthening intimacy. Seth realized that instead of turning to Magaly for support, his script on masculinity caused him to be more rigid in his show of affection. He identified his internalized messages ("I am not a good husband" and "She lost respect for me") and understood how these messages interfered with his ability to be intimate with Magaly. Seth was pleased to learn that Magaly did respect him and was struggling with her feelings of insecurities as she was trying to make sense of his stoicism. The counselor decided to bring in the idea of forgiveness from a Christian perspective, and Seth was able to make peace with his involvement in premarital sexual behaviors. Magaly also made important discoveries, including how her internalized messages ("I am unattractive" and "He does not desire me") were affecting her and their relationship. She was relieved to learn that Seth was attracted to her.

Because of their counseling, Magaly and Seth were able to increase their sexual intimacy, which consisted of a gradual reintroduction to intimate behaviors like touching each other, kissing, and sharing sexual fantasies. They eventually were able to increase sexual intimacy through mutual masturbation and oral sex. After 6 months, Magaly and Seth continued to struggle with penetrative sex; however, they were committed to keep trying without any external pressures. Despite this limitation, the couple reported an increase in sexual satisfaction and their overall relationship.

Suggested Practices

In addition to using a culturally informed sex positive approach, counselors should consider additional practices to help inform intentional therapeutic work to better meet clients where they are in exploring their sexual experiences. These may include the following:

Develop religious competencies. Sexuality counselors and therapists working with such individuals must not only engage with the individual, relational, and cultural factors that are causing difficulties in a person's sexual relationships or function, they must interact with the spiritual. Part of this practice can include counselors becoming familiar with bodies of research that demonstrate the protective and healing factors associated with spirituality and mental wellness. Sexuality counselors could also benefit from becoming familiar with the Association for Spiritual, Ethical, and Religious Values in Counseling (2019) competencies.

Assess your own biases. It is crucial that sexuality counselors understand that differences are not disorders. Counselors must be intentional in engaging in cultural humility work to further assess self- and other-awareness, biases, and beliefs. Within this practice, it is important for counselors to consider how their own cultural and societal beliefs (and corresponding internalized messages) create their personal worldview and how this personal worldview can move counselors away from being intentional in better understanding their clients' lived experiences.

Use a sexual history/genogram. Sexuality counselors should include a spirituality assessment as part of the sexual history assessment and genogram process. In addition to asking about their religious beliefs and practices, counselors also need to assess clients' levels of religiosity (i.e., how often they engage in preferred religious practices), what ways they engage with their faith, who (if anyone) they turn to for religious guidance, and what (if any) spiritual or religious education they received during childhood.

Identify and clarify values. A values identification and clarification exercise can help couples increase awareness to both individual values and shared values within the relationship dyad. Increasing awareness of shared values may allow for a greater sense of connection, direction, and fulfillment. Exploring values in this way can also provide an opportunity for discussion about how cultural and societal messages play a role in what the couple may deem as valuable within their relationship.

Provide safe space. Sexuality counselors normalize their clients' lived experiences, use inclusive language, and ask permission to explore difficult emotions and experiences related to sexual concerns. In creating safety, counselors can also ask clients about their preference of terms to use in session to describe areas such as intimacy, anatomy, and sexual play/practice (i.e., do they prefer using the phrase "making love" versus "having sex"?).

Externalize presenting concerns. Aligning with narrative therapy, sexuality counselors can assist the couple in identifying the presenting concern as an external factor that creates disconnection within the relationship. This process could include asking clients, "If the presenting concern were here in this room, next to you, what would it look like? What shape would it be? What color? Would it have any other defining features? What sounds might it make? Would it have any odor/scent?"

Integrate religious scripture and/or metaphors. If clients express finding a sense of peace and safety in religious scripture, counselors can use mediums such as a whiteboard or other writing surface to create a chart where clients can write out preferred/favorite scripture that helps during times of anxiety, uncertainty, or other difficult emotional processes. This can serve as a secure base or foundation that clients can refer to (inside or outside of session) when they may be in need.

Conclusion

This proposed model of sex therapy presents an integrative, inclusive, and sex positive approach to working with clients' sexual scripts. The primary motivation is to replace existing traditional approaches to sex therapy that centers on a heteronormative genital-centered sex with an approach that is flexible, adjustable, and pleasure centered. Individuals' sexual scripts that develop from mainstream views and values of what is good sex contribute to sexual dissatisfaction. This approach also emphasizes the importance of culturally bound meaning making in increasing sexual satisfaction. This model features using narrative therapy to help clients to deconstruct and reauthor their sexual scripts. Counselors play an important part in discussing issues of sexuality and sexual intimacy with dissatisfied couples. Counselors must recognize the numerous social influences that affect individual and lived couples' experiences and desires. Understanding the social construct of sexuality will assist counselors as they work with individuals and couples who present with sexual dissatisfaction.

References

American Psychiatric Association. (2013). *Diagnostic and statistical manual of mental disorders* (5th ed.). https://doi.org/10.1176/appi.books.9780890425596

Association for Spiritual, Ethical, and Religious Values in Counseling. (2009). *Competencies for addressing spiritual and religious issues in counseling*. https://aservic.org/spiritual-and-religious-competencies/

Berger, P. L., & Luckmann, T. (1967). *The social construction of reality: A treatise in the sociology of knowledge*. Anchor Books.

Clayton, A. H., DeRogatis, L. R., Rosen, R. C., & Pyke, R. (2012). Intended or unintended consequences? The likely implications of raising the bar for sexual dysfunction diagnosis in the proposed *DSM-V* revisions: 2. For women with loss of subjective sexual arousal. *The Journal of Sexual Medicine, 9*(8), 2040–2046. https://doi.org/10.1111/j.1743-6109.2012.02859.x

Davis, D. E., DeBlaere, C., Owen, J., Hook, J. N., Rivera, D. P., Choe, E., Van Tongeren, D. R., Worthington, E. L., Jr., & Placeres, V. (2018). The multicultural orientation framework: A narrative review. *Psychotherapy, 55*(1), 89–100. https://doi.org/10.1037/pst0000160

Eleuteri, S., & Farulla, C. (2016). Sexual counselling with Catholics: How to cope with sexual issues with Catholic clients? *Sexual and Relationship Therapy, 31*(3), 289–300.

Gagnon, J. H., & Simon, W. (1973). *Sexual conduct: The social sources of human sexuality*. Aldine Press.

Hall, K. S. K., & Graham, C. A. (2014). Culturally sensitive sex therapy: The need for shared meanings in the treatment of sexual problems. In Y. M. Binik & K. S. K. Hall (Eds.), *Principles and practice of sex therapy* (pp. 334–358). The Guilford Press.

Hall, S. S., Fox, K. M., Knox, D., & Kuck, D. (2020). Young adults' relationship beliefs and sexual behavior: The intersection of religion, race, and sexual identity. *Sexuality & Culture, 24*, 1443–1456. https://doi.org/10.1007/s12119-019-09700-9

Levy, D. L. (2012). The importance of personal and contextual factors in resolving conflict between sexual identity and Christian upbringing. *Journal of Social Service Research, 38*(1), 56–73. https://doi.org/10.1080/01488376.2011.586308

McCabe, M. P. (2005). The role of performance anxiety in the development and maintenance of sexual dysfunction in men and women. *International Journal of Stress Management, 12*(4), 379–388.

Metz, M. E., & McCarthy, B. W. (2012). The good enough sex (GES) model: Perspectives and clinical applications. In P. J. Kleinplatz (Ed.), *New directions in sex therapy: Innovations and alternatives* (pp. 213–229). Routledge/Taylor & Francis Group.

Owen, J. (2013). Early career perspectives on psychotherapy research and practice: Psychotherapist effects, multicultural orientation, and couple interventions. *Psychotherapy, 50*(4), 496–502. https://doi.org/10.1037/a0034617

Owen, J., Imel, Z., Adelson, J., & Rodolfa, E. (2012). "No-show": Therapist racial/ethnic disparities in client unilateral termination. *Journal of Counseling Psychology, 59*, 314–320. https://www.doi.org/10.1037/a0027091

Owen, J. J., Tao, K., Leach, M. M., & Rodolfa, E. (2011). Clients' perceptions of their psychotherapists' multicultural orientation. *Psychotherapy, 48*(3), 274–282. https://www.doi.org/10.1037/a0022065

Page, M. J. L., Lindahl, K. M., & Malik, N. M. (2013). The role of religion and stress in sexual identity and mental health among lesbian, gay, and bisexual youth. *Journal of Research on Adolescence, 23*(4), 665–677. https://doi.org/10.1111/jora.12025

Sherry, A., Adelman, A., Whilde, M. R., & Quick, D. (2010). Competing selves: Negotiating the intersection of spiritual and sexual identities. *Professional Psychology: Research and Practice, 41*(2), 112–119. https://doi.org/10.1037/a0017471

Sue, S., & Chu, J. Y. (2003). The mental health of ethnic minority groups: Challenges posed by the supplement to the Surgeon General's report on mental health. *Culture, Medicine and Psychiatry, 27*, 447–465. https://doi.org/10.1023/B:MEDI.0000005483.80655.15

Teifer, L. (2012). The "new view" campaign: A feminist critique of sex therapy and an alternative vision. In P. J. Kleinplatz (Ed.), *New directions in sex therapy* (pp. 21–36). Routledge.

Tobia, G., & IsHak, W. W. (2013). *DSM-5* changes in diagnostic criteria of sexual dysfunctions. *Reproductive System and Sexual Disorders: Current Research, 2*(2), 1–3. https://doi.org/10.4172/2161-038X.1000122

Turner, T. E., Center, H., & Kiser, J. D. (2004). Uniting spirituality and sexual counseling. *The Family Journal, 12*(4), 419–422. https://doi.org/10.1177/1066480704267052

World Health Organization. (n.d.) *Sexual health: Definitions.* https://www.who.int/health-topics/sexual-health#tab=tab_2

Yarhouse, M. A., Morgan, T., Anthony, K., & Sadusky, J. (2017). Celibate gay Christians: Sexual identity and religious beliefs and practices. *Journal of Pastoral Care & Counseling, 71*(1) 52–59. https://doi.org/10.1177/1542305017693245

PART 3

Attraction, Orientation, and Gender

The Multidimensional Nature of Attraction

Stacey Diane Arañez Litam and Megan Speciale

We tend to think of the erotic as an easy, tantalizing sexual arousal. I speak of the erotic as the deepest life force, a force which moves us toward living in a fundamental way.

—Audre Lorde, *Sister Outsider: Essays and Speeches*

Few experiences have captured the eyes and minds of the world's artists, musicians, poets, and writers quite like sexual attraction. Throughout history and across civilizations, attraction has been a subject of intense exploration and speculation: What are the forces that compel living creatures toward and away from one another? As humans, our need for love, connectedness, and belonging lies at the heart of our existential journey; therefore, it is unsurprising that our preoccupation with the bonds of interest and pleasure sparks such passion-filled quests to comprehend this complex phenomenon. In this chapter, we explore the dynamic and multifaceted experience of attraction across the life span and provide strategies for understanding the role of attraction in emotional, relational, and sexual satisfaction.

What Is Attraction? Unpacking Common Myths

In today's society, we tend to view attraction as a compelling urge of desire, longing, or passion toward another person. Media depictions often frame attraction as an inescapable and even chemical impulse that persuades and beguiles, rendering helpless those who succumb to its grasp. Through subtle and overt messaging, there is often a broad assumption that sex is the intended outcome of attraction. This notion, however, is a vastly limiting view of attraction, one that omits the nuances of the holistic experience of attraction and that can reinforce a narrative of predation (that sexual urges are uncontainable and beyond our control). Thus, endorsing a multidimensional definition of attraction empowers us to explore the nuances of our attraction and affectional identities with deep reflection, self-agency, and regard for the agency of others. Let's explore other common myths of attraction.

Myth 1: All Attraction Leads to Sexual Attraction

In a 2018 essay "Beyond Sex: The Multilayered Model of Attraction," Michael Paramo provided a comprehensive framework of attraction that expands and critiques the historical definition of attraction. In this model, sexual attraction is deprioritized and viewed as simply one type of attraction. Other equally significant forms of attraction include aesthetic, emotional, intellectual, romantic, and sensual attraction. Each form of attraction may be parallel to or disconnected from other forms of attraction. Because many of us grow up with the assumption that all forms of attraction are parallel to one another (which are all ultimately associated with sexual attraction), many individuals have limited understanding of the distinctions they may experience with respect to each form of attraction. The classic view of attraction is especially limiting for people who do not experience parallels across all forms of attraction, such as people who have asexual, aromantic, demisexual, and sapiosexual identities.

Paramo (2018) defined *aesthetic attraction* as a form of attraction that is based on the visual appeal or an appreciation of the beauty of another person(s). This may be parallel to or separate from sexual or romantic attraction; however, it is often meaningfully connected to how a person experiences relationships and/or admiration of others. Maybe you've thought to yourself, "Wow, that person is striking. We should definitely be friends." That's aesthetic attraction! *Emotional attraction* goes a little deeper, involving "the desire to be in non-tactile contact with another person for the purposes of forming, fostering, or maintaining an emotional and personal bond with them" (Paramo, 2018, p. 54). Emotional attraction often develops through an appreciation of another's personality or vibe and may lead to seeking closeness and deepened intimacy with the person(s). *Intellectual attraction* involves an appeal to develop or maintain an intellectual or cerebral bond with others, which may be separate from their body or physical characteristics. *Romantic attraction* is a longing to be in "romantic contact" with others, however that is defined. Romantic attraction may be separate from sexual attraction and can include many forms of nonsexual intimacy, such as engaging in intimate conversations, sharing meals, sleeping next to one another, and having formal partnership agreements. *Sensual attraction* involves the desire to be in physical or sensory contact with another person(s), such as holding hands, cuddling, kissing, or body massage. Finally, *sexual attraction* involves an attraction to others that sparks arousal and/or the desire to engage in a sexual activity, which may or may not lead to sexual intercourse. Considering the multidimensional nature of attraction, it is best to hold off on making assumptions about others until they have consented.

Myth 2: Everyone Experiences Sexual Attraction

Current research suggests that about 1% (or likely more) of the population is *asexual*, an affectional orientation that is defined as an enduring, often lifelong, lack of sexual attraction (Bogaert, 2006). Individuals who do not experience sexual attraction may experience other forms of attraction, such as romantic or sensual attraction, and may engage in sexual intimacy with self and others. Like other sexual/affectional identities, asexuality exists on a spectrum and is unique to each person. For example, some individuals who identify as asexual may engage in masturbation, enjoy watching sexually explicit material (i.e., pornography), and enjoy sexual activities with their partner(s). Ultimately, asexuality represents a normal variation in the experience of human sexuality and attraction (Yule et al., 2017). It is important to note that asexuality is distinct from celibacy, sexual desire disorders (e.g., hypoactive sexual desire disorder), and hyposexuality related to physiological conditions, sexual trauma, and hormonal imbalances.

Myth 3: Sexual Attraction Should Be Easy

As with most things related to sex, society has formed a rather oversimplified view of how humans experience sexual longing. If you were to form an opinion on desire and arousal based on what is depicted in movies and romance novels, you might assume that they happen simultaneously and that, in the moment of attraction, your body immediately responds with sexual arousal and pleasurable longing. But for most of us, it's clear that such feelings often take time to develop, occurring only within the right set of circumstances (i.e., not while sitting in your child's parent-teacher meeting or in the pews of your church service) and when the other elements of attraction are responding somewhat in tandem with one another.

McCall and Meston (2006) explored the factors involved in women's experiences of sexual desire and found that desire is often prompted by four broad cues: love/emotional bonding cues, explicit/erotic cues, visual/proximity cues, and romantic/implicit cues. These cues often work together to create situations where desire is established, fostered, and safe to explore. With respect to love and belonging, desire can emerge from feelings of love, emotional securing, connectedness, and intimacy. Desire can also be a response to explicit cues, such as watching a sexy film, witnessing a partner's desire for you, or noticing your own arousal. Visual cues such as seeing an attractive or intelligent person can also spark sexual desire, as can romantic cues, which tend to involve sensual touching or situations. Sounds similar to Paramo's (2018) model of attraction, right? It turns out that for people who experience sexual desire, desire is strongest when prompted by multiple cues. In other words, when it comes to cues for sexual desire, the more the merrier!

However, for many people these cues don't always lead to sexual desire. For asexual folx, these cues may cultivate deepened desire in other nonsexual areas, such as emotional or sensual closeness. For folx with a capacity for sexual desire (i.e., *allosexual* folx), these cues may be hampered by other contextual elements that can impede desire and arousal. Oftentimes we can be completely unaware of these inhibiting cues, which can lead to an entirely frustrating and disempowering experience for all those involved. You may be wondering whether, if desire can be impacted by cues that are outside of our awareness, we can ever know what will turn us on. Enter the dual control model of sexual response (Janssen & Bancroft, 2006).

Myth 4: Everyone Is Turned On and Turned Off by the Same Things

The dual control model of sexual response gives us a method for understanding the dynamic nature of sexual arousal by exploring the ways our bodies respond to sexual excitation cues (turn-ons) and sexual inhibition cues (turnoffs). Emily Nagoski, author of *Come as You Are: The Surprising New Science That Will Transform Your Sex Life*, referred to these systems as the "accelerator" and "brakes" of sexual response (Nagoski, 2015, p. 48). Our accelerator (or gas pedal, the sexual excitation system) comprises all the relevant internal and external stimuli that a person finds sexually relevant, such as McCall and Meston's (2006) cues of sexual desire. These cues vary in salience from person to person and may change throughout the life span. The brakes (sexual inhibition system) are enacted through internal and external stimuli that threaten desire, such as feelings of body insecurity, fear of sexual consequences like pregnancy or shame, lack of safety with one's partner, negative affect or conflict, or desire discrepancies. In this model, sexual desire is attained not only by the pushing of one's gas pedal but also by being able to step off the brakes. This may not be easy for people given their immediate circumstances or sexual socialization histories. Sexual problems arise when a person has trouble accessing excitatory cues, has overwhelming inhibitory cues, or has some combination of both.

Myth 5: Sexual Attraction Is Static and Unchanging Across the Life Span

Historically, sexual attraction has been viewed categorically—that is, there are distinct types of sexual attraction: same-sex *versus* other-sex attraction and same-sex *and* other-sex attraction (bisexuality). Recently, however, evidence has emerged to suggest that attraction is much more fluid throughout the life span than originally envisioned. Diamond (2016) conducted a review of several studies measuring sexual attraction and found that researchers have observed three phenomena: (a) nonexclusive (bisexual) attractions are experienced commonly in bisexual and monosexual populations of all genders; (b) change in sexual attraction across the life span is common across all genders and sexual orientations; and (c) there are widespread discrepancies among attraction, behavior, and identity. This means that, although a person's sexual or affectional identity may be relatively stable throughout the life span, it is not uncommon for people to experience spontaneous change in erotic responsiveness and/or changes in the genders of partners throughout the life span.

Context in Attraction

Now that you've begun to explore and understand the many forms of attraction, what do you notice? Encountering and rediscovering language that captures the diverse ways that we relate to others can be deeply validating. How wonderful it is to have words that describe the delicious gravitational pull we may feel toward others who stimulate our need for intellectual conversation, sensual connection, or internal wholeness. As evidenced by its many forms, the nature of attraction is both complex and multifaceted. Although experiences of sexual attraction are most often highlighted, the cravings we may feel for affectional, romantic, and intellectual forms of attraction are not to be diminished. Understanding elements of attraction emboldens us to better understand ourselves, and understanding ourselves positions us to better empathize with our clients. This section encourages counselors to expand their gaze toward the many ways in which attraction may be influenced by context. Understanding the developmental and sociocultural factors that influence aspects of attraction is important to establishing a foundational understanding of how experiences of attraction relate to wellness and health.

Developmental Influences

Various developmental influences have been identified as contributing to aspects of sexual attraction and sexual identity, including hormonal, genetic, and in utero factors. For instance, infants exposed to high levels of prenatal androgens are more likely to report lesbian, gay, bisexual, transgender, or nonbinary identities (Hines, 2010, 2011). In addition to environmental influences in utero, the presence of genetic factors on sexual attraction and sexual identity has also been established. Across several studies, identical twins were more likely to engage in same-sex sexual behavior than are fraternal twins or other siblings (Långström et al., 2010). Queer parents were also more likely to give birth to children with diverse sexual identities, possibly as a result of shared genetics (Goldberg, 2010). Of note, one must consider how children with parents who are lesbian, gay, bisexual, transgender, queer, or other identities (LGBTQ+) may have reported more diverse sexual identities because they were socialized in more open and accepting environments compared to children raised by heterosexual parents. Further evidence supporting the role of in utero environment on sexual attraction and sexual identity is the influence of birth order. Gay men tend to have more biological older brothers than do their heterosexual or lesbian counterparts (Blanchard & VanderLaan, 2015; Bogaert et al., 2018).

Neurological Influences

Upon experiencing moments of attraction and arousal, it's a good thing we aren't swept up in a frenzied state of behavioral activation. Instead, once our brain interprets stimuli as attractive, signals in our brain move through a series of arbitration mechanisms that consider the motivational significance and cost of obtaining sexual rewards (Fonteille & Stoléru, 2011). In other words, there are quite a few neurological steps between experiencing attraction and acting on our sexual impulses and drives! When we see something that tickles our fancy, our orbitofrontal cortex kicks in to determine the motivational significance and sexual relevance of pleasant smells or touch (Rolls, 2000). If we like what we see, you can bet that our parietal cortex has responded to visually sexual stimuli. Specifically, activation of the left inferior parietal lobule is linked to sexual indicators of arousal (e.g., degree of sexual arousal and penile tumescence; Moulier et al., 2006; Redouté et al., 2000). Those powerful moments where you can't help but stare at the object of your desire occur because of the activation of your superior parietal cortex, which controls your attentional process to visual stimuli. Next, the caudal anterior cingulate cortex (ACC) is responsible for initiating and motivating behavior toward a goal (e.g., striking up a conversation with the person[s] piquing your interest; Devinsky et al., 1995). Regions in the ACC are also responsible for autonomic responses such as erection and self-lubrication. Once we have determined that the stimulus is attractive enough to pursue and that the benefits outweigh the costs, the basal ganglia have done their part (Fonteille & Stoléru, 2011).

When preparing for sexual activities, the left rostral ACC and hypothalamus work in tandem to trigger sensations of physiological readiness for sexual desire (e.g., cardiovascular, respiratory, genital, and endocrine responses; Fonteille & Stoléru, 2011). These pleasurable emotional experiences are associated with the delicious sensation of rising excitement and feelings of arousal are triggered by the insula. Finally, the amygdala is another part of our brain implicated in the attraction process and is responsible for evaluating the emotional significance and intensity of various stimuli (Bonnet et al., 2015). Taken together, the various neurological interplays, from initial attraction to sexual behavior, evidence the ways in which costs, benefits, and motivation influence the ultimate pursuit of one's sexual desires and impulses.

Sociocultural Influences

The presence of social and cultural factors also influences sexual attraction. Experiences of sexual attraction often begin to emerge in early adolescence. Although puberty has historically been implicated as the time upon which sexual attraction begins, studies suggest experiences of first sexual attraction occur even earlier. For heterosexual and queer adolescents, the first reported experiences of sexual attraction emerged around the age of 10 (Hamer et al., 1993; Herdt & Boxer, 1993; McClintock & Herdt, 1996; Pattatuci & Hamer, 1995). These findings are important as individuals have not yet achieved full sexual development. Thus, experiences of sexual attraction arise before puberty has been achieved.

When experiences of attraction are portrayed in the media, the saucy aspects of sensual and sexual attraction seem to take precedence. These render other healthy variations of attraction, or lack thereof, invisible. Because society fails to describe the experiences of asexual individuals, we must challenge the assumptions that exist around asexuality. Our sociocultural influences may also contribute to preconceived notions about gender roles. Men may be expected to experience attraction to men and/or women, but what about instances when little or no attraction occurs? Even the most affirming and open-minded professional counselors are not immune to the effects of socialization through parents, peers, and media. Luckily, learning about human sexuality and aspects of attraction is a lifelong process.

Exploring Attraction in Clinical Practice

Considering the low prevalence of comprehensive sex education and the predominance of sex negative sociocultural messaging in the United States, it is no surprise that issues related to sex and intimacy are extremely common throughout the life span. Recent reports indicate that 40%–45% of women and 20%–30% of men have at least one ongoing sexual concern or problem (Lewis et al., 2010) and the experience of sexual shame, guilt, and confusion is near universal (Clark, 2017). Regardless of clinical setting, the chance of encountering clients' sexual challenges is high for all professional counselors. Thus, it is imperative that counselors regularly incorporate opportunities for clients to share and explore their sexual wellness in session through formal and informal assessment both during intake and throughout the duration of counseling.

Issues related to sexual attraction and desire can manifest in a variety of ways. Clients may experience concerns related to low desire, high desire, and desire discrepancies with partners. Clients may feel shame related to their sexual identities, sexual desires, and body image that leads to unfulfilling sexual encounters. Sexual wellness may also be impacted by internalized misinformation about what is considered "normal" or "healthy" sexual desire, which can be especially prevalent for clients from conservative or religious backgrounds, as well as clients who come from cultural backgrounds that contain restrictive beliefs about sexuality and sexual pleasure. Rigid gender-role adherence may also contribute to decreased flexibility and understanding of sexual attraction, which may have significant impacts for clients in heterosexual partnerships. Although sexual attraction and desire are natural and common occurrences from youth to old age, many clients may experience discomfort when acknowledging issues related to sexuality and therefore benefit greatly from counseling that is sex affirming, normalizing, and comfortable regarding the discussion of sex.

Useful Interventions

Counselors can enact a sex-affirming stance with clients throughout the counseling process using the PLISSIT model (Permission, Limited Information, Specific Suggestions, and Intensive Therapy; Annon, 1976). In the PLISSIT model, counselors are encouraged to give all clients, regardless of presenting issue, permission to incorporate their sexual wellness into the therapeutic space. This can be achieved by simply welcoming clients to share sexuality-related concerns by stating during the informed consent process that sexuality is an important and natural aspect of human life. It is important to note that counselors should not assume that sexual attraction is the ultimate form of attraction for the client and should remain open to clients' unique ways of connecting with others.

Psychoeducation, or limited information, may also be helpful for clients experiencing sexual challenges. Outside information, such as books, websites, and films, can be essential for normalizing issues related to sexual desire (Nagoski, 2015) and sexual shame (Sellers, 2017). Clients may also benefit from learning the multidimensional model of attraction to expand their understanding of intimacy and explore how nonsexual forms of attraction can enhance sexual satisfaction. For clients facing specific issues related to sex, treatment may require the use of specific interventions aimed at exploring sexuality. An example of this may include the use of creative art techniques to explore sexual desires, body image issues, and internalized shame. The use of mindfulness and guided meditation may also be a useful strategy to strengthen clients' mind-body connection and to help them better tune into their unique sexual cues and the impact of those cues on their body. Finally, intensive therapy is helpful for clients who need sex therapy and/or biomedical approaches. Counselors are encouraged to recognize when clients' treatment goals are beyond the scope of their practice and must refer clients to other professionals who have developed relevant specializations (i.e., certified sex therapists, endocrinologists, and pelvic physical therapists) to avoid inadvertently doing harm.

Transference and Countertransference

Professional counselors working with clients who present with issues related to sexual attraction are called to identify and challenge any internalized and preconceived notions they may hold about the experiences, processes, or etiologies of sexual attraction. Professional counselors must also bracket off any internal experiences that may arise when clients disclose paraphilias, fetishes, and practices related to consensual nonmonogamy, kink, and BDSM (Litam & Speciale, 2020). As when other value conflicts arise within the therapeutic setting, professional counselors should avoid conflating their values and behaviors with the values and behaviors of their clients. Doing so can be damaging to the therapeutic relationship and decrease the likelihood of clients to disclose sexuality-related topics in the future.

Counselors must also be prepared to ethically navigate experiences of sexual attraction they may experience toward clients. In a foundational study with 575 psychotherapists, 87% of participants (95% of men and 76% of women) reported experiencing feelings of sexual attraction to their clients on occasion (Pope et al., 1986). Other studies suggest that between 78% (Giavazolias & Davis, 2001) and 90% of mental health professionals have experienced erotic countertransference (Hayes et al., 2011). Furthermore, about half of the participants in the earlier study had not received training on how to navigate feelings of sexual attraction within the therapeutic setting and most reported their training on the topic was inadequate (Pope et al., 1986). Counselors must work to overcome any feeling of shame, embarrassment, or anxiety they may experience when feelings of sexual attraction toward clients emerge. Professional counselors are encouraged to seek supervision, engage in self-care practices, and pursue their own individual counseling when erotic countertransference occurs to obtain a deeper understanding of the meaning of these feelings. Legal and ethical requirements must also be considered prior to pursuing sexual relationships with clients following termination. Ultimately, documentation, supervision or peer supervision, and engaging in an ethical decision-making model may be helpful to determine the appropriateness of pursuing sexual relationships with clients following treatment.

Sexual attraction is a dynamic, complex construct that is experienced differently by each person. When considering the role of sexual attraction across the life span, professional counselors are called to reflect on whether they hold any preconceived notions related to the ways in which sexual attraction is supposed to be experienced. For one or more reasons, sexual attraction and sexual behaviors may not occur at all, or they may exist independent of one another. Contrary to how they are portrayed, experiences of sexual attraction do not represent a quintessential component in the daily lives of many individuals. Similarly, incongruences may exist between the gender(s) of those to whom someone experiences sexual attraction and the gender(s) with whom they engage in sexual behaviors. Although overlaps may occur, it is important to note that sexual attraction, sexual behavior, sexual identity, and romantic affiliation each represent distinct factors.

Multicultural Considerations

Professional counselors should consider a variety of cultural influences that may contribute to experiences of sexual attraction in clients. The roles of gender identity, sexual identity, religious identity, ethnic and racial identities, age, ability status, trauma history, and other endless identities each uniquely contribute to the ways in which individuals experience sexual attraction and engage in sexual behaviors.

Professional counselors and other helping professionals are called to consider the ways in which religious institutions have historically been unsupportive of queer identities. For instance, the term *clobber passages* refers to traditionally marginalizing scriptures often used to condemn same-sex activity (Miner & Connoley, 2002). Clobber passages are often taken out of context and may be used by members of religious communities to denigrate individuals with diverse sexual identities and discriminate others based on sexuality, same-sex attraction, and same-sex behavior (Altman et al., 2012). As many queer folx value the role of religion in their lives, individuals who find themselves in unsupportive religious communities may be faced with unique challenges that compromise their mental health and wellness. Queer folx who struggle to reconcile their religious and sexual identities report higher levels of mental health concerns, including feelings of shame, guilt, isolation, trauma, low self-esteem, and suicidality (Dahl & Galliher, 2012; Hattie & Beagan, 2013; Murr, 2013; Sherry et al., 2010). Queer individuals may also lose their families of origin and religious communities upon coming out, which may further lead to experiences of sexual trauma and human trafficking (Browne-James et al., 2021; Litam, 2017), rejection, isolation, and compounding mental health concerns (Barrow & Kuvlanka, 2011; Hattie & Beagan, 2013; Sherry et al., 2010).

Challenges associated with resolving sexual and religious identities may be especially detrimental and salient for Black members of the LGBTQ+ community for whom religion plays an important role in life. Indeed, in a study of 175 Black lesbian, gay, and bisexual individuals, the presence of religious faith was strongly associated with higher levels of resilience (Walker & Longmire-Avital, 2013). Professional counselors and other helping professionals are called to empower religious LGBTQ+ folx to consider the historical influences of when traditionally marginalizing clobber passages were written (Litam et al., 2020). Notably, historical translations did not consider the ways in which language has changed over time. For example, when the Bible was written, gender identity was not understood or conceptualized as one's adherence to gender roles or sexual identity, but by one's ability to bear children (Roscoe, 1996). Therefore, counselors are encouraged to help clients reinterpret traditional clobber passages to consider the contextual and historical influences of when these passages were written to deconstruct condemning messages and successfully integrate religious and sexual identities (see Litam et al., 2020).

Case Example: Jack

Jack is a 32-year-old cisgender, heterosexual man who presents to individual counseling for the first time. The client reports he has been in a relationship with his partner, Jennifer, for approximately 7 months. Jack reports feelings of frustration regarding the relationship. Specifically, he explains ongoing arguments that continue to occur surrounding differences in sexual desire.

Jack describes Jennifer as a highly energized woman who enjoys engaging in sexual activities. Conversely, he reports he does not feel the urge to engage in sexual experiences and feels intimately connected with his partner despite his lack of desire to pursue a sexual relationship with her. Jack reports no previous history of trauma, substance use, or other medical concerns. He says that aside from the ongoing challenges of his relationship, he leads a happy and fulfilling life. Jack comes to you now to help him address the experiences of discouragement he feels within his relationship. He reports that although he has tried to increase his feelings of sexual attraction to Jennifer by watching ethically produced sexually explicit material online, he has been unsuccessful in cultivating feelings of sexual desire toward his partner. Although Jack engages in other forms of sexual activity to please Jennifer, such as the use of toys, sensual massage, and performing oral sex, he worries that these activities are insufficient for maintaining a deep, intimate connection and relationship with her and fears that she will leave him.

Treatment Approaches and Practice Issues

When reading about Jack's case scenario, which types of biases, thoughts, or reactions did you notice? It is important to remember that Jack's experience represents a normal variation in the experience of human sexuality. Professional counselors working with Jack are encouraged to collect an attraction history. Obtaining information regarding the age, gender, and experiences of attraction Jack may or may not have experienced throughout his development would be helpful to identify the presence of any clinically significant changes that may have occurred. Jack reports no instances of sexual, emotional, or physical trauma, which additionally represents important information because traumatic experiences can affect the ways that we relate, connect, and engage with one another. Next, it may benefit Jack to develop communication skills that empower him to engage in a meaningful dialogue with his partner. How does she feel about the sexual experiences shared within the relationship? To what extent does Jennifer feel intimately connected with her partner? Learning empathic communication skills, restatements, and reflections are important tools for any healthy relationship. Jack may additionally benefit from psychoeducation about the various forms of attraction. This information may also be helpful to share with his partner to facilitate a dialogue about how their forms of attraction align and to validate the various experiences of attraction and connection that exist. Finally, Jack may benefit from counseling interventions that focus on self-acceptance and on developing skills to help him navigate his relationship with Jennifer.

Conclusion

In summary, professional counselors are well positioned to assist clients in exploring the myriad of ways that attraction presents and evolves throughout the life span. Using a multiculturally responsive framework, counselors can support clients to explore shame and biases surrounding sexuality and attraction, provide psychoeducation to normalize and expand clients' awareness of sexual diversity, and challenge internalized sex negativity and other discriminatory beliefs related to sexuality and attraction. Counselors must also be aware that client attraction and erotic countertransference are frequently occurring experiences within the therapeutic relationship and should be addressed in session with clients, outside of session with supervisors, and in counselors' own self-reflection processes.

Questions You Always Wanted to Ask

1. **Do my asexual clients really avoid all types of sexual behavior?**
   Each of us experiences varying levels of interest in sexual behavior and asexual clients are no different! It is not true that asexual clients avoid all types of sexual behavior, although the frequency and forms of sexual behaviors may vary. Whereas some folx may perform sexual acts with their partners or engage in masturbation, others may not engage in any sexual behavior at all. The reasons associated with why asexual individuals engage in sexual behaviors vary and may include the desire to cultivate romantic connections or to please their partners. Professional counselors must work with all clients, including those with asexual identities, on an individual basis to obtain an understanding of their unique experiences.
2. **What if my clients do not experience any sexual attraction?**
   Congratulations, your client is a normal human being! Remember, asexuality represents a normal variation of the human experience and can look different for each client (and person!). For example, clients who identify as demisexual need to cultivate a deep emotional connection before experiences of sexual attraction may occur. Regardless of your clients' experiences, it is OK if they do not experience any sexual attraction, so long as their quality of life and relationships are not negatively affected. In the end, the client knows what is attractive or not, what is kink or not, what is desirable and what is not—counselors are here to help clients explore their concerns around attraction, not to judge whether their attraction is good or bad.
3. **What if clients don't feel comfortable with whom they experience sexual attraction?**
   Feelings of discomfort regarding the person(s) to whom clients experience sexual attraction is normal. If and when this occurs, we encourage clients to engage in deep, critical reflection. In other words, chase the feeling. Understanding

the origin of our clients' discomfort is important to identify the best ways to challenge any preconceived notions they may have about to whom they are supposed to experience attraction. Professional counselors working with clients who present with this specific presenting concern are encouraged to identify and challenge the maladaptive thoughts, preconceived notions, or unhelpful beliefs clients may hold about to whom they should experience sexual attraction. This process can be especially confusing for clients who experience sexual desires that are illegal and/or taboo, such as minor attraction, animal or object attraction, or incest fantasies. Clients with illegal or taboo desires often experience considerable shame about these fantasies, so while it is important to assess whether the client is putting themselves or others at harm, counselors should also prioritize building trust through nonjudgmental and compassionate assessment and exploration of these fantasies.

4. **Are clients ever too old to experience sexual attraction?**
   Experiences of sexual attraction are normal and healthy across the life span. Although the frequency and intensity of sexual attraction may change as clients age, if their baseline includes the propensity for sexual attraction and healthy sexual behaviors, we hope this is an experience they can continue to enjoy with consenting partners, or with themselves! Clients are never too old to experience sexual attraction, although it is important to continue using safer sex practices no matter our age to minimize the risk of contracting sexually transmitted infections and unplanned pregnancy. Clients who reside in assisted-living facilities may benefit from direct conversations about the importance of safer sex practices because many are no longer worried about pregnancy and may consider skipping protection altogether.
5. **Are my clients' sexual attractions normal?**
   Alternative sexual desires such as kink, BDSM, paraphilias, fetishes, and nonmonogamy/polyamory are incredibly common within the spectrum of healthy sexual desire (Pascoal et al., 2015; Yates & Neuer-Colburn, 2019). Given the high rates of these desires, it may in fact be time to remove the word "alternative" from their descriptions. If a client is concerned about their sexual desires, a standard rule of thumb exists—if the behavior is consensual and enjoyed by all partners, then it likely falls in the spectrum of healthy sexual desire. Remember that minors cannot legally consent to sexual behaviors with adults, so special consideration and support must be given to clients who describe sexual attraction to minors. Ultimately, experiences of sexual attraction are only problematic when they cause extreme distress or result in nonconsensual harm or risk of nonconsensual harm to self or others. If clients are experiencing distress related to their desires, it is important to explore from where the distress originates and determine if the distress is related to internalized shame or discrimination related to sexual variation. Normalization, psychoeducation, and affirming counseling approaches are helpful ways to explore and counter shame. Learn more about alternative sexual desire in Chapter 20.

References

Altman, D., Aggleton, P., Williams, M., Kong, T., Reddy, V., Harrad, D., Reis, T., & Parker, R. (2012). Men who have sex with men: Stigma and discrimination. *Lancet, 380*, 439–445.

Annon, J. S. (1976). The PLISSIT model: A proposed conceptual scheme for the behavioral treatment of sexual problems. *Journal of Sex Education and Therapy, 2*(1), 1–15.

Barrow, K. M., & Kuvlanka, K. A. (2011). To be Jewish and lesbian: An exploration of religion, sexual identity, and familial relationships. *Journal of LGBT Family Studies, 7*(5), 470–492. https://doi.org/10.1080/1550428X.2011.623980

Blanchard, R., & VanderLaan, D. P. (2015). Commentary on Kishida and Rahman (2015), including a meta-analysis of relevant studies on fraternal birth order and sexual orientation in men. *Archives of Sexual Behavior, 44,* 1503–1509. https://doi.org/10.1007/ s10508-015-0555-8

Bogaert, A. F. (2006). Toward a conceptual understanding of asexuality. *Review of General Psychology, 10*(3), 241–250. https://doi.org/10.1037/1089-2680.10.3.241

Bogaert, A. F., Skorska, M. N., Wang, C., Gabrie, J., MacNeil, A. J., Hoffarth, M. R., & Blanchard, R. (2018). Male homosexuality and maternal immune responsivity to the Y-linked protein NLGN4Y. *Proceedings of the National Academy of Sciences, 115,* 302–306. https://doi.org/10.1073/pnas.1705895114

Bonnet, L., Comte, A., Tatu, L., Millot, J.-L., Moulin, T., & de Bustos, E. M. (2015). The role of the amygdala in the perception of positive emotions: An "intensity detector." *Frontiers in Behavioral Neuroscience, 9,* Article 178. https://doi.org/10.3389/fnbeh.2015.00178

Browne-James, L., Litam, S. D. A., & McRae, L. (2021). Child sex trafficking: Strategies for identification, counseling, and advocacy. *International Journal for the Advancement of Counselling, 43,* 113–125. https://doi.org/10.1007/s10447-020-09420-y

Clark, N. (2017). *The etiology and phenomenology of sexual shame: A grounded theory study* [Doctoral dissertation, Seattle Pacific University]. Digital Commons @ SPU. https://digitalcommons.spu.edu/cpy_etd/25/

Dahl, A., & Galliher, R. V. (2012). The interplay of sexual and religious identity development in LGBTQ adolescents and young adults: A qualitative inquiry. *Identity an International Journal of Theory and Research, 12*(3), 217–246. https://doi.org/10.1080/15283488.2012.691255

Devinsky, O., Morrell, M. J., & Vogt, B. A. (1995). Contributions of anterior cingulate cortex to behavior. *Brain, 118,* 279–306. https://doi.org/10.1093/brain/118.1.279

Diamond, L. M. (2016). Sexual fluidity in males and females. *Current Sexual Health Reports, 8*(4), 249–256. https://doi.org/10.1007/s11930-016-0092-z

Fonteille, V., & Stoléru, S. (2011). The cerebral correlates of sexual desire: Functional neuroimaging approach. *Sexologies, 20*(3), 142–148. https://doi.org/10.1016/j.sexol.2010.03.011

Giavazolias, T., & Davis, P. (2001). How common is sexual attraction toward clients? The experiences of sexual attraction of counseling psychologists toward their clients and its impact on the therapeutic process. *Counseling Psychology Quarterly, 14,* 281–286. https://doi.org/10.1080/09515070110100974

Goldberg, A. E. (2010). *Lesbian and gay parents and their children: Research on the family life cycle.* American Psychological Association.

Hamer, D. H., Hu, S., Magnuson, V. L., Hu, N., & Pattatuchu, A. M. L. (1993). A linkage between DNA markers on the X chromosome and male sexual orientation. *Science, 261,* 321–327.

Hattie, B., & Beagan, B. L. (2013). Reconfiguring spirituality and sexual/gender identity: "It's a feeling of connection to something bigger, it's part of a wholeness." *Journal of Religion and Spirituality in Social Work: Social Thought, 32*(3), 244–268. http://doi.org/10.1080/15426432.2013.801733

Hayes, J. A., Gelso, C. J., & Hummel, A. M. (2011). Managing countertransference. *Psychotherapy, 48*, 88–97. https://doi.org/97.10.1037/a0022182

Herdt, G., & Boxer, A. (1993). *Children of horizons.* Beacon Press.

Hines, M. (2010). Sex-related variation in human behavior and the brain. *Trends in Cognitive Sciences, 14*, 448–456. https://doi.org/10.1016/j.tics.2010.07.005

Hines, M. (2011). Prenatal endocrine influences on sexual orientation and on sexually differentiated childhood behavior. *Frontiers in Neuroendocrinology, 32*, 170–182. https://doi.org/10.1016/j.yfrne.2011.02.006

Janssen, E., & Bancroft, J. (2006). The dual control model: The role of sexual inhibition and excitation in sexual arousal and behavior. In E. Janssen (Ed.), *The psychophysiology of sex* (pp. 197–222). Indiana University Press.

Långström, N., Rahman, Q., Carlström, E., & Lichtenstein, P. (2010). Genetic and environmental effects on same-sex sexual behavior: A population study of twins in Sweden. *Archives of Sexual Behavior, 39*, 75–80. https://doi.org/10.1007/s10508-008-9386-1

Lewis, R. W., Fugl-Meyer, K. S., Corona, G., Hayes, R. D., Laumann, E. O., Moreira, E. D., Jr., Rellini, A. H., & Segraves, T. (2010). Definitions/epidemiology/risk factors for sexual dysfunction. *The Journal of Sexual Medicine*, *7*(4), P1598–1607. https://doi.org/10.1111/j.1743-6109.2010.01778.x

Litam, S. (2017). Sex trafficking in America: What counselors need to know. *The Professional Counselor, 7*(1), 45–61. https://doi.org/10.15241/sdal.7.1.45

Litam, S., Ford, D. J., Friday, A. R., Walker, B., Sutherlin, T. D., & Band, M. (2020). Understanding the historical context of traditionally marginalizing biblical passages: Helping LGBTQ clients navigate the intersection of religion and sexual identity. In *Queering the Deep South: Research on queer studies and LGBTQ lives in the Southeast* (pp. 73–91). Information Age Publishing.

Litam, S., & Speciale, M. (2020, Fall). Kink culture: What counselors need to know. *ACA Practice Briefs.* American Counseling Association. https://www.counseling.org/docs/default-source/practice-briefs/acapb-kink-culture-2020.pdf

McCall, K., & Meston, C. (2006). Cues resulting in desire for sexual activity in women. *The Journal of Sexual Medicine, 3*(5), 838–852. https://doi.org/10.1111/j.1743-6109.2006.00301.x

McClintock, M. K., & Herdt, G. (1996). Rethinking puberty: The development of sexual attraction. *Current Directions in Psychological Science, 5*(6), 178–183.

Miner, J., & Connoley, J. T. (2002). *The children are free: Reexamining the biblical evidence on same-sex relationships.* Jesus Metropolitan Community Church.

Moulier, V., Mouras, H., Pélégrini-Issac, M., Glutron, D., Rouxel, R., Grandjean, B., Bittoun, J., & Stoléru, S. (2006). Neuroanatomical correlates of penile erection evoked by photographic stimuli in human males. *NeuroImage, 33*(2), 689–699. https://doi.org/10.1016/j.neuroimage.2006.06.037

Murr, R. (2013). "I became proud of being gay and proud of being Christian": The spiritual journeys of queer Christian women. *Journal of Religion & Spirituality in Social Work: Social Thought, 32*, 349–372. https://doi.org/10.1080/15426432.2013.839241

Nagoski, E. (2015). *Come as you are: The surprising new science that will transform your sex life.* Simon & Schuster.

Paramo, M. (2018). Beyond sex: The multi-layered model of attraction. *AZE, 2*(1), 52–58. https://azejournal.com/article/2018/2/1/the-asexual-vol-2-issue-1

Pascoal, P. M., Cardoso, D., & Henriques, R. (2015). Sexual satisfaction and distress in sexual functioning in a sample of the BDSM community: A comparison study between BDSM and non-BDSM contexts. *The Journal of Sexual Medicine, 12*(4), P1052–1061. https://doi.org/10.1111/jsm.12835

Pattatuchi, A. M. L., & Hamer, D. H. (1995). Development and familiarity of sexual orientation in females. *Behavior Genetics, 25*, 407–420.

Pope, K. S., Keith-Spiegel, P., & Tabachnick, B. G. (1986). Sexual attraction to clients: The human therapist and (sometimes) inhuman training system. *American Psychologist, 41*(2), 147–158

Redouté, J., Stoléru, S., Grégoire, M. C., Costes, N., Cinotti, L., Lavenne F., Le Bars, D., Forest, M. G., & Pujol, J. F. (2000). Brain processing of visual sexual stimuli in human males. *Human Brain Mapping, 11*(3), 162–177. https://doi.org/10.1002/1097-0193(200011)11:3%3C162::aid-hbm30%3E3.0.co;2-a

Rolls, E. T. (2000). The orbitofrontal cortex and reward. *Cerebral Cortex, 10*(3), 284–294. https://doi.org/10.1093/cercor/10.3.284

Roscoe, W. (1996). Priests of the goddess: Gender transgression in ancient religion. *History of Religions, 35*(3), 195–230. https://www.jstor.org/stable/1062813

Sellers, T. S. (2017). *Sex, God, and the conservative church: Erasing shame from sexual intimacy.* Taylor & Francis.

Sherry, A., Adelman, A., Whilde, M. R., & Quick, D. (2010). Competing selves: Negotiating the intersection of spiritual and sexual identities. *Professional Psychology: Research and Practice, 41*, 112–119. https://doi.org/10.1037/a0017471

Walker, J. J., & Longmire-Avital, B. (2013). The impact of religious faith and internalized homonegativity on resiliency for Black lesbian, gay, and bisexual emerging adults. *Developmental Psychology, 49*(9), 1723–1731. https://doi.org/10.1037/a0031059

Yates, S. M., & Neuer-Colburn, A. A. (2019). Counseling the kink community: What clinicians need to know. *Journal of Counseling Sexology & Sexual Wellness, 1*(1), Article 4. https://doi.org/10.34296/01011007

Yule, M. A., Brotto, L. A., & Gorzalka, B. B. (2017). Human asexuality: What do we know about a lack of sexual attraction? *Current Sexual Health and Reproduction, 9*, 50–56. https://doi.org/10.1007/s11930-017-0100-y

Sexual Orientation and Identity: Let Me Be Perfectly Queer

Joy S. Whitman, Michael P. Chaney, and Jun Park

Sexuality has been conceptualized as an amalgamation of behaviors or acts and desires that influence sexual identity and is considered to be an essential facet of an individual (Kunzel, 2008). However, sexuality is much more complex than mere sex acts, involving physical and emotional attractions, beliefs, fantasies, and sexual roles (Ventriglio & Bhugra, 2019). Behavioral expressions of our sexuality are impacted by individual attractions, availability of partners, personal fantasies, and the behavior itself. In addition, our sexuality is influenced by our gender and cultural identities along with the intersection of those identities. Expressions of sexuality, therefore, are diverse and varied, and, as a result, require a sex positive approach. Williams et al. (2013) stated, "a sex-positive approach is about allowing for a wide range of sexual expression that takes into account sexual identities, orientations, and behaviors; gender presentation; accessible health care and education; and multiple important dimensions of human diversity" (p. 273). Consequently, a sex positive approach, as it relates to sexual orientation and identity, is one where all sexualities and sexual expressions are validated and normalized for clients. This is especially significant for clients whose identities have historically been stigmatized and treated as mental illnesses, such as individuals who are attracted to their same gender, identify as asexual, or who are attracted to others who embody a variety of gender expressions.

This chapter, therefore, focuses on the sexual orientation and identity spectrum, including sexual and romantic attraction and various sexual identities that have been marginalized (gay, lesbian, bisexual, pansexual, and asexual). This chapter also addresses constructs of sexual attraction that fall outside of the aforementioned labels including men who have sex with men (MSM). To do so, we define and discuss sexual orientation and identity, provide current information to debunk stereotypes about what sexual orientation and identity is, and present a case that uses a sex positive approach.

What Is Sexual Orientation?

Given the complexity of sexual orientation, it is no surprise that there are varying definitions of the construct; however, there are commonalities as to how it has been operationalized. Worthington and Reynolds (2009) described *sexual orientation* as referring to sexual predispositions, including arousal and attraction, and how individuals identify themselves related to those predispositions. Other researchers have referred to sexual orientation as the attractions (physical, emotional, and sexual), fantasies, arousals, and behaviors that individuals have for one gender, the other gender, or all genders (LeVay & Baldwin, 2012; Savin-Williams, 2016).

Increasingly, greater attention is being given to understand the complicated makeup of sexual orientation in the social-behavioral sciences. For example, Mustanski et al. (2002) purported that sexual orientation consists of four primary facets. The first component includes self-identified labels that individuals choose to use (e.g., lesbian, pansexual). Mustanski and colleagues suggested that for some individuals, these labels may change over time due to sexual fluidity. The second component of sexual orientation is the actual sexual behavior in which individuals choose to participate. These sexual acts and behaviors are dependent on availability of partners and opportunity. The third facet of sexual orientation are the sexual feelings and desires that people possess. These are typically personal and not always shared publicly. The final component of sexual orientation are the physiological arousal reactions (e.g., genital and brain responses) that we experience when we see and interact with other people. In sum, sexual orientation, like a puzzle, is made up of many pieces that, when put together, form a unique image. How individuals self-label that image adds another layer of complexity.

How sexual orientation has been categorized historically reflects a pattern of expanding the number of self-identifiers. This is partly due to increased awareness and understanding of the physiological, social, psychological, emotional, and political aspects of sexual orientation. Over the past few decades, only three primary sexual orientation categories have been highlighted: heterosexual, gay, and bisexual. These three orientation categories are commonly used because they are theorized to be natural variations of sexual expression, rather than socially constructed identities (Vrangalova & Savin-Williams, 2012). A major critique of only three categories is that they compartmentalize people into only these three orientations, which not only is limiting but also excludes large numbers of people who may not identify as heterosexual, gay, or bisexual.

In recent years, researchers attempting to measure sexual orientation have found that more than three categories is a better reflection of the numerous variables associated with sexual orientation. Vrangalova and Savin-Williams (2012) found that five groups provided a more accurate depiction of the components of sexual orientation. The five categories included heterosexual, mostly heterosexual, bisexual, mostly gay/lesbian, and gay/lesbian. When individuals' sexual attractions were measured using five categories rather than three, the percentage of nonheterosexuals doubled among women (from 10% to 20%) and men (from 5% to 10%; Savin-Williams, 2016). Worthington and Reynolds (2009) identified 12 different sexual orientations: three types of bisexual women, three types of bisexual men, two types of heterosexual women, two types of lesbians, gay men, and heterosexual men.

Even with an increased number of categories, there are a couple of criticisms associated with attempting to quantify the number of sexual orientations. First, socially constructed categories risk disenfranchising and excluding individuals who self-identify between and beyond those categories. Second, some individuals do not view their sexual orientations as a combination of two monosexual (heterosexual/gay) ends of a spectrum. This idea is supported by recent interview research that found bisexual, pansexual, and queer participants rebuffed the idea that their plurisexual orientations were a hybrid identity between a gay-heterosexual continuum (Galupo et al., 2014).

To eliminate these categorical pitfalls, sexual orientation is more accurately understood as a continuous variable or continuum. A continuum model of sexual orientation is supported by recent empirical research. One such study, which included 17,785 people from the United States and 47 other countries (ages 11–98 years), found support for a fluid-continuum model of sexual orientation, on which people differed in sexual orientation range (Epstein et al., 2012). The authors of this study summarized their findings with a thought-provoking analogy. They posed the rhetorical question, considering sexual orientation is more like height than eye color, why push it into just a few categories? In sum, a sex positive approach necessitates the need for viewing sexual orientation as a fluid continuum that is inclusive and affirming.

What Is Sexual Identity?

Although related to sexual orientation, sexual identity is a qualitatively different construct. *Sexual identity* refers to a person's sense of self as it relates to their self-labeled sexuality. According to Ventriglio and Bhugra (2019), not only is there a personal component to sexual identity, but it also is influenced by the social and cultural contexts in which we live. Counselors working from a sex positive perspective understand that sexual identity is influenced by gender identity and cultural identities, and with culture understood in a variety of ways (e.g., ethnicity, age, ability, socioeconomic status).

Additionally, sexual identities vary between and within cultures and are influenced by different time periods (Silva & Whaley, 2018). For example, many Latinx MSM are considered heterosexual if they take on the role of top (insertive partner during anal sex), whereas the bottom (penetrated partner during anal sex) is perceived to be gay (Jeffries, 2009). To better understand what this means, for MSM, sexual and affectional orientations, identities, and behaviors may seem contrary, and their sexual behavior may be distinct from their various identities. The term MSM was originally coined within the public health arena to refer to a diverse range of men who identify as gay, bisexual, or heterosexual, and engage in sexual activities with other men. Although there are some MSM who may be gay or bisexual yet identify as heterosexual due to stigma and fear associated with being gay or bisexual, there are many heterosexual MSM who are not gay or bisexual.

There are a couple of reasons why heterosexually identified MSM engage in sex with other men. One explanation is that for many MSM, sex with another man is viewed as a task or act of pleasure or convenience (Hudson, 2013). The sex act does not necessitate the need to define one's identity nor is there any psychological or emotional connections involved. It is simply a sexual act. The findings of a recent interview study of the sexual behavior of Canadian men who had sex with other men while incarcerated in federal prison support that sexual behavior for many MSM is separate from their identities (Ricciardelli et al., 2016). Results suggested that having sex with other men did not equate to identifying as gay or bisexual. Ricciardelli et al. (2016) summarized that how the MSM negotiated their identities was much more complex than situational homosexuality. The men created space within their heterosexuality to have sex with other men.

Sexual identity is made up of four dimensions. The first facet of sexual identity is *identity prominence*, which refers to what extent an individual prioritizes their sexual identity in relation to all of their other identities (Ashmore et al., 2004). This is also known as identity importance. The second dimension is *identity valence*, which refers to how positively or negatively someone evaluates their sexual identity (Ashmore et al., 2004). *Identity integration* is the third component and pertains to how closely an individual's sexual identity is related to or shares similar characteristics with the other identities in their identity hierarchy. Lastly, *identity complexity* refers to how cohesive or differentiated one's sexual identity is to their own self-concept (Roccas & Brewer, 2002).

Sexual orientation and sexual identity combine to inform our sexual orientation identity. Sexual orientation identity pertains to our conscious recognition and self-identification as it relates to where we fall on the continuum of sexual identities (Worthington & Reynolds, 2009). For example, self-labels may include queer, pansexual, lesbian, androphilic, asexual, heterosexual, and demiromantic, to name a few. It is important to remember that sexual orientation identity is not solely based on one variable (e.g., sexual behavior). In fact, recent interview research revealed that to truly understand the relevance of a person's sexual orientation identity, it must be considered from all of the multiple dimensions that comprise it to have a clear picture of an individual's overall identity (Galupo et al., 2014). Moreover, the same study found that there are social aspects to sexual orientation identity. Specifically, sexual orientation identity is experienced within four different social contexts: (a) societal impact on identity, (b) self-identification versus the perception of others, (c) the interpersonal nature of sexual orientation identity, and (d) the exclusion or invisibility of certain sexual orientation identities (e.g., identities between and beyond lesbian, gay, and bisexual). Indeed, sex positive counselors take into consideration the multiple social dimensions associated with clients' sexual identities. Some common identities and their terminology include the following:

androphile: someone who is attracted to men and masculinity.

asexual: the lack of spontaneous sexual attraction.

demiromantic: someone who experiences attractions only after an emotional connection is established.

fluid: someone whose attractions vary depending on situations, environments, individuals, or relationships.

gynephile: someone who is attracted to women and femininity.

heteroflexible: someone who is "mostly heterosexual" and occasionally experiences attractions to others of the same gender.

omnisexual: someone who is attracted to people regardless of gender or orientation.

pansexual: someone who is aware of gender and orientation but is not attracted to particular gender or orientation.

polyamorous: someone whose identity involves the practice of participating in consensual multiple sexual relationships (i.e., consensual nonmonogamy).

pomosexual: someone whose sexual/affectional identities cannot be put into any conventional category as currently considered in social/behavioral sciences—grew out of postmodernism.

It is important to note that this list does not include all identities with which clients may identify. Also, clients may have their own meanings and definitions for the above-mentioned terms. It is important to ask the clients how they identify their orientations and relationship structure.

It is beyond the scope of this chapter to discuss every sexual identity and attraction in detail with clinical examples and discussion. Therefore, we chose to discuss one case that offers clinicians sex positive treatment perspectives. The basis of our work will be addressing the case from a lesbian, gay, bisexual, transgender, queer, and intersex plus (LGBTQI+) affirmative perspective, with attention to the intersection of this client's identities.

Case Example: Ryu

Ryu is a 22-year-old cisgender male who identifies as Japanese and American. His parents immigrated to the United States before Ryu and his siblings were born. Ryu is the oldest of four children and the only cisgender male (his siblings all identify as cisgender females). He is in his last year of college majoring in secondary education.

Ryu has had feelings toward cisgender males and females (both genders) since he was young, although he primarily dates women and finds great satisfaction sexually and emotionally with them. He has had no sexual encounters with men; however, most recently, Ryu noticed a strong emotional and sexual attraction to his friend Adam, a cisgender male. He is interested in pursuing a relationship with him, leading him to consider his sexual identity as more fluid and possibly as bisexual. This brought him to counseling, where he wants to explore his sexuality and develop strategies to build a social support system that affirms his sexual and cultural identities.

Treatment and Intervention

We developed this case to illustrate ways we might work with a client like Ryu using an affirming and sex positive perspective. To do so, we use an integrative approach to support our conceptualization and interventions—namely, both relational-cultural theory (RCT) and LGBTQI+ affirmative counseling.

RCT

To start, the theoretical lens through which we can understand Ryu's presenting concerns is RCT. RCT is a feminist approach to counseling that encourages empowerment of individuals and explores the cultural context of clients' lives (Jordan, 2010; J. B. Miller & Stiver, 1997). Central to this theory is the importance and impact of culture and social systems on emotional and psychological development (Jordan, 2010; Walker, 2008). Development and relationships with others cannot be understood separately from how those connections have been "raced, engendered, sexualized, and situated along dimensions of class, physical ability, religion or whatever constructions carry ontological significance in the culture" (Walker, 2008, p. 90). Attention to oppression and marginalization in all their forms are integrated into the counseling process as counselors and clients explore how those forces impact clients' self-worth and the counseling relationship.

RCT views social connections and mutually empowering relationships as paramount to growth (Jordan, 2010). Wellness and health are achieved by developing and maintaining genuine and authentic relationships that are characterized by mutuality and vulnerability (Walker, 2008). It is through relationships that encourage empathy, authenticity, and empowerment that individuals can realize their relational competence and create relationships that can sustain disruption and relational injury (Jordan, 2010). Relational injury, isolation, microaggression, trauma, and shame are some of the by-products of societal oppression, injustice, and marginalization, and sifting through the many ways individuals created their self-image through their life span as a result of these experiences is key to RCT (Birrell & Freyd, 2006; Jordan, 2010).

LGBTQI+ Affirmative Counseling

In addition to RCT, we take an LGBTQI+ affirmative counseling approach with Ryu. This approach includes counselors creating psychologically safe spaces in which clients are supported and affirmed in a culturally responsive manner so that they can explore, grow, heal, and thrive throughout the life span (Chaney & Whitman, 2020). This perspective is founded on the Association for Lesbian, Gay, Bisexual, and Transgender Issues in Counseling (ALGBTIC) Competencies for Counseling With LGBQQIA Individuals (Harper et al., 2013) and the Multicultural and Social Justice Counseling Competencies (MSJCC; Ratts et al., 2015). The ALGBTIC Competencies prepare counselors to create affirming relationships with LGBTQI+ people to support their development and to foster self-acceptance, whereas the purpose of the MSJCC is to address how culture, privilege, and marginalization impact clients and counselors and to bring awareness of these experiences into the counseling relationship. Together, these competencies attend to the intersectionality of identities and seek to support clients in an affirming way as they explore their experiences with marginalization, privilege, and oppression.

Additionally, counselors using this approach search for client resilience and assets (Ginicola et al., 2017). Resilience is framed within the context of successful management of oppression experienced by LGBTQI+ individuals. One must first understand the unique stressors LGBTQI+ individuals experience. The minority stress model (Myer, 2015) identifies how stigma and prejudice impact their health. The model also suggests how coping and social support help buffer against those stressors and result in greater resilience. Both individual and community resilience are significant in mitigating the impact of oppression and marginalization, and in the following section, we describe how this may be accomplished.

Sex Positive Interventions With Ryu

Using these approaches, we first orient ourselves toward using RCT to create a therapeutic environment with Ryu that emphasizes a mutually empathic and empowering relationship. We must be our authentic selves with Ryu, demonstrating how relationships are built on mutuality and empathy, and as Walker (2008) stated, we must be vulnerable with others in order to reveal our authentic selves. To be fully present with another means to sit with our vulnerabilities to create a deeper connection and to share them as they shift. We situate our identities within the counseling context, self-disclosing to Ryu who we are (our own gender, racial, and sexual identities) so that we may start our therapeutic relationship openly and honestly. By engaging in a mutually empowering approach, we communicate to Ryu that relationships are based on mutual understanding with power shared. This opens the door for Ryu to be vulnerable with us and for us to discuss how our differences can be resolved by maintaining a mutually empathic stance.

Taking an LGBTQI+ affirmative approach, we discuss Ryu's relational experiences and support his self-understanding while affirming his history. How he defines himself as bisexual guides our work. In a study of young bisexual and pansexual individuals, Flanders et al. (2017) reported what was meaningful to these participants were attractions to someone's personality, attractions that are both romantic and sexual, attractions as fluid and that fluctuate over time, and attractions that are recognized but not necessarily acted on. Using this information, we ask Ryu how he understands his sexuality through his life span. Interest in any sex does not occur in equal measure or at the same period of time, and although Ryu has dated women and been sexually attracted to men, it is possible that his romantic desire for Adam is primary for him at this point in his relational history. Using RCT, we help Ryu to feel empowered to name himself as bisexual in ways that represent himself accurately and personally, only if he is ready to adopt a label for his feelings. Ryu may begin to understand for himself how being bisexual means something different from how others define bisexuality and how his self-understanding may be fluid and organic over time.

As we explore how Ryu understands himself as bisexual, we concurrently explore how his intersecting identities as Japanese and American impact the development of his bisexual identity. Using the bisexual youth of color identity development model (Chun & Singh, 2010), we can explore with Ryu the sociopolitical contexts within which he developed and the oppression and stigma he may have experienced. These contexts include but are not limited to religious and spiritual systems, socioeconomic institutions, and educational settings as well as family and geographic location. For example, in Ryu's family, sexuality is not discussed, and modesty and sexual propriety are upheld. In his family, as is typical for Japanese families, sexuality is understood within a heterosexual marriage, a heterosexual orientation is expected, and same-sex attractions are seen as abnormal (Kazama, 2020; Okazaki, 2002). Although these perspectives contrast with how Ryu feels about his sexuality, we may want to explore whether Ryu has integrated any of those familial and cultural messages and therefore experiences any internalized shame about his sexual identity.

Ryu also was raised in a predominantly White community. This left Ryu feeling like an outsider in school because of his Japanese heritage and an outsider at home because of his same-sex attractions. As we discuss these experiences with Ryu, we keep in mind which identities for him were most salient at various points in his development and in which contexts, noting identity prominence changes with contexts (Ashmore et al., 2004). Using an LGBTQI+ affirmative lens, we are aware of messages Ryu heard about his culture and sexuality, and how marginalized he felt at times. This left him feeling isolated and alone, and operating from a RCT stance, we work with him to feel heard, to empathically explore how alone and marginalized he felt, and to help him find ways to connect to others who can also support his racial, cultural, and bisexual identities without privileging one over the other. By affirming his identities, Ryu can experience what it is like to not hide different parts of himself to accommodate others and to more fully experience himself openly.

Using RCT as a guide, we help Ryu create and sustain relational resilience so that he can engage in mutually empathic and empowering relationships with others who affirm his intersecting identities (Jordan, 2017). In the study focused on positive identity experiences of bisexual and nonmonosexual youth, Flanders et al. (2016) found that interpersonal activities had the greatest impact on resilience and on maintaining a positive identity. These included obtaining social support and a sense of belonging from peers who can normalize their identities and with whom they can discuss their bisexual identity; engaging in affirming, dating, relational, and sexual behavior; and finding social media interactions that are affirming. This is similar to what Myer (2015) discussed as *community resilience* or how the community supports and provides resources to combat minority stress and to enhance coping. Using this research and an LGTBQI+ affirming approach, we help Ryu connect to others who identify as bisexual and especially those individuals whose cultural values and ethnicity are similar to Ryu's. This may allow him to feel safe to discuss his sexuality with others and perhaps eventually with his parents. We work with Ryu to explore the campus resources and social groups that meet his needs. This may mean that we support Ryu when confronting racism and biphobia that he may experience in the LGBTQI+ student group, and to confront biphobia in social groups that support his Japanese American identity.

Using an LGBTQI+ affirmative approach, we pay attention to Ryu's coping strategies and assets and highlight his individual resilience. We begin by exploring how Ryu has managed racial, cultural, and sexual identity oppression and marginalization thus far and affirm the methods that have been effective. Identifying specific skills and strategies Ryu has successfully used in the past may help to underscore points of resilience. We can then offer interventions that may enhance and expand these strategies, such as encouraging him to keep a daily journal in which he records three things that went well for him, or successes he has experienced in a given day, and how he contributed to these positive experiences. For example, did he make any connections with others who affirmed his identity or did he decide to come out to others? Additionally, we may teach Ryu to identify societal messages he may have internalized and any shame he experiences because of these messages. We then provide tools for him to counter the messages and rename any shame with affirming names, which may increase Ryu's sense of resilience and empowerment.

We are also attentive to Ryu's desire to begin a relationship with Adam. He has questions about sexual health and how to discuss his bisexuality with potential partners. He has not come out as bisexual to any of his prior partners and wants to be honest with Adam. We can help Ryu come out as bisexual to Adam through practicing and role-playing in session, with Ryu first being himself and then reversing roles so he can empathically embody Adam's position. Mutual empathy is significant within RCT, and we want to use that approach here so Ryu can communicate clearly and be authentically himself.

He may also have questions about sex with men, and we consider any misconceptions he may have as a result of his cultural background and societal messages. When counseling from a sex positive perspective, it is imperative that we have the knowledge base to be able to accurately discuss man-for-man sex with Ryu in a nonjudgmental way. Furthermore, as sex positive counselors, we work with Ryu so that he may have pleasurable and safe sexual experiences. Given that adult and adolescent gay and bisexual men accounted for 69% of new HIV diagnoses in the United States in 2019 (Centers for Disease Control and Prevention [CDC], n.d.-b) and are overrepresented in new infections of other sexually transmitted infections (e.g., syphillis, chlamydia, gonorrhea; CDC, n.d.-a), we explore his knowledge level of safer sex and to what extent he engaged in safer sex practices in the past with female partners. To do this, we integrate an RCT approach with a strategy from motivational interviewing called the *elicit-provide-elicit* approach (W. R. Miller & Rollnick, 2013). First, we either ask Ryu's permission to provide safer sex information or we elicit by asking him what he already knows about safe sex. Once we hear what Ryu already knows, we provide him information that he needs to have safe, pleasurable sexual experiences or that fills in a gap in what he already knows. As sex positive counselors, we should be prepared to provide Ryu with psychoeducational information regarding how to navigate condom use with Adam and other partners, as well as preexposure prophylaxis options, exploring his sexual fantasies and desires and his values related to sex and intimacy. Once we provide the additional information, we again invite Ryu to share his views on the information we offered. Because we have developed a therapeutic relationship with Ryu built on RCT principles, we can help Ryu practice how to communicate his desires to Adam.

Possible Transference and Countertransference

Throughout our work with Ryu, he may have his own transference reactions to us. Author Joy is a cisgender, White, middle-aged lesbian, whereas author Mike is a cisgender, White, middle-aged gay male. We both represent the White community in which Ryu was raised, and as such, he may have reactions to our Whiteness as representations of the oppression he experiences as a Japanese cisgender male. Maintaining true to our theoretical perspectives, we will discuss this at the onset and throughout our work with him, noting at times when he is holding back any reactions to feeling marginalized. Additionally, we will listen for any concerns Ryu might have about our sexual identities, especially as he may encounter biphobia from the LGBTQI+ communities.

As a cisgender, East Asian male in his mid-20s, author Jun is more similar to Ryu culturally. Ryu may have transference reactions that enhance the counseling relationship, feeling empathically connected because of assumed similar cultural values. He may project onto Jun internalized cultural values that bring up shame about same-sex attractions, and therefore, react negatively to Jun. Jun will be attentive to assumptions Ryu makes about him because of shared cultural values and work to establish a healthy therapeutic relationship that affirms and empowers his exploration.

Finally, as clinicians who have worked with the LGBTQI+ communities for many years, we—specifically, Joy and Mike—may have our own countertransference reactions to Ryu. There may be times when we want to shelter him from oppression or move to empowerment too quickly because of our desire for him to feel affirmed. Neither of us is bisexual and both of us are White, and we will need to be mindful of our own positions of privilege and power in our relationship with Ryu. Additionally, we both have navigated the coming out process and feel comfortable and safe in our current stages of identity development, which may influence how we approach Ryu and the interventions we choose to use. Thus, we must remain mindful and meet Ryu where he is in his identity development. With Jun, there are significant differences in countertransference as he is also East Asian and currently formulating his own sexual orientation identity. As Jun's sexual identity is currently being explored in the context of similar cultural values and experiences, it is vital he bolster professional boundaries through supervision and gain insight into how this can affect working with Ryu.

Potential Outcomes

Although we cannot predict how our interventions will be received by Ryu, from our experience with clients like him, we do know that exploration of sexuality through a sex positive lens using RCT and LGBTQI+ affirmative perspectives often leads to clients feeling less shame, empowered, and more connected to themselves and others. Ryu is at the beginning stages of exploring what being bisexual means to him. For now, knowing he can adopt any label he chooses, or no label at all, can be liberating.

We may at times need to help Ryu navigate reactions from others, such as his parents, who may not be affirming. This may require a session with his parents so that Ryu can be supported, or we may need to role play with him about how to come out to them when and if he chooses. Coming out to them may cause additional distress that may impact his relationship with Adam, and we will remind Ryu that being in conflict with others requires him to remain vulnerable through connection. Again, using RCT as our guide, we model for Ryu how creating and sustaining mutually empathic relationships leads to deeper relationships.

Conclusion

Working with clients who identify as LGBTQ+ offers counselors opportunities to explore sexuality using methods that validate and support the various ways people express their sexual and romantic experiences. In this chapter, we explained how you, as a counselor, can use affirmative counseling theories and techniques when working with LGBTQ+ clients within their cultural contexts. We used a case example to illustrate how this can be accomplished but limited our discussion to working with someone who identifies as bisexual and Japanese American. However, the principles used within RCT and an LGBTQ+ affirmative counseling approach can be used with any LGBTQ+ client to intervene in a sex positive manner.

There are a few points we want to highlight when assuming a sex positive clinical stance. Although we presented a clinical approach that integrates RCT and LGBTQI+ affirmative counseling, these approaches can be integrated with other theoretical perspectives. Whenever working with clients whose sexual orientation and identities have historically been marginalized, maintaining an affirming and culturally integrative perspective that highlights resilience is key to providing counseling that is sex positive.

After reading this chapter, one question you might have is how to develop an orientation using RCT. There are plenty of resources available, and the references we offer provide a starting point. The Jean Baker Miller Training Institute (JBMTI, n.d.) is the home of RCT, and there you will find trainings and resources. However, the major tenets of mutuality, authenticity, social justice, and human development through connections can be developed by reviewing your own stance on each concept. Questions to ask yourself might include, but are not limited to, the following:

- Do I see human development through the lens of relational connection?
- How do I understand relationships?
- What does mutuality in relationships mean to me, and do I strive toward maintaining that stance in my relationships with others?
- How authentic am I in my relationships with others and how do I allow myself to be vulnerable with them?
- How do I experience oppression and social justice in my own life, and what actions do I take to reduce oppression?

Additionally, we must understand the fluidity of sexuality and sexual expression and the power clients claim in naming their sexual orientation and identities. To do so, we must also assess our own biases and potential countertransference reactions. Consider asking yourself the following:

- How comfortable am I talking about same-sex sexual behavior with clients?
- What are some ways I can increase my knowledge about LGBTQ+ sexual practices to better meet the needs of clients?
- How have I explored my own sexual orientation and identity?

We suggest seeking out consultation, supervision, and education to help you navigate your answers.

Finally, we invite you to consider how you can affirm sexual desire and behavior while addressing cultural contexts. There are subgroups and identities within and between LGBTQI+ communities that are often invisible or do not often have "a seat at the table." We must consider how this might contribute to feelings of isolation and not mattering. In addressing these last considerations, we invite you to use the resources included in the chapter as you develop a sex positive approach toward working with clients of fluid and varying sexual expressions.

References

Ashmore, R. D., Deaux, K., & McLaughlin-Volpe, T. (2004). An organizing framework for collective identity: Articulation and significance of multidimensionality. *Psychological Bulletin, 130*, 80–114. https://doi.org/10.1037/0033-2909.130.1.80

Birrell, P. J., & Freyd, J. J. (2006). Betrayal and trauma: Relational models of harm and healing. *Journal of Trauma Practice, 5*, 49–63. https://doi.org/turing.library.northwestern.edu/10.1300/J189v05n01_04

Centers for Disease Control and Prevention. (n.d.-a). *Gay and bisexual men's health. Sexually transmitted diseases.* https://www.cdc.gov/msmhealth/STD.htm

Centers for Disease Control and Prevention. (n.d.-b). *HIV and specific populations: HIV and gay and bisexual men.* https://aidsinfo.nih.gov/understanding-hiv-aids/fact-sheets/25/81/hiv-and-gay-and-bisexual-men

Chaney, M. P., & Whitman, J. S. (2020). Affirmative wellness counseling with older LGBTQ+ adults. *Journal of Mental Health Counseling, 42*(4), 303–322. https://doi.org/10.17744/mehc.42.4.02

Chun, K. Y. S., & Singh, A. A. (2010). The bisexual youth of color intersecting identities development model: A contextual approach to understanding multiple marginalization experiences. *Journal of Bisexuality, 10*(4), 429–451. https://doi.org/10.1080/15299716.2010.521059

Epstein, R., McKinney, P., Fox, S., & Garcia, C. (2012). Support for a fluid-continuum model of sexual orientation: A large-scale internet study. *Journal of Homosexuality, 59*(10), 1356–1381. https://doi.org/10.1080/00918369.2012.724634

Flanders, C. E., LeBreton, M. E., Robinson, M., Bian, J., & Caravaca-Morera, J. A. (2016). Defining bisexuality: Young bisexual and pansexual people's voices. *Journal of Bisexuality, 17*(1), 39–57. https://doi.org/10.1080/15299716.2016.1227016

Flanders, C. E., Tarasoff, L. A., Legge, M. M., Robinson, M., & Gos, G. (2017). Positive identity experiences of young bisexual and other nonmonosexual people: A qualitative inquiry. *Journal of Homosexuality, 64*(8), 1014–1032. https://doi.org/10.1080/00918369.2016.1236592

Galupo, M. P., Davis, K. S., Grynkiewicz, A. L., & Mitchell, R. C. (2014). Conceptualization of sexual orientation identity among sexual minorities: Patterns across sexual and gender identity. *Journal of Bisexuality, 14*(3-4), 433–456. https://doi.org/10.1080/15299716.2014.933466

Ginicola, M. M., Smith, C., & Fillmore, J. M. (Eds.). (2017) *Affirmative counseling with LGBTQI+ people.* American Counseling Association.

Harper, A., Finnerty, P., Martinez, M., Brace, A., Crethar, H. C., Loos, B., Harper, B., Graham, S., Singh, A., Kocet, M., Travis, L., & Lambert, S. (2013). Association for Lesbian, Gay, Bisexual, and Transgender Issues in Counseling competencies for counseling with lesbian, gay, bisexual, queer, questioning, intersex, and ally individuals. *Journal of LGBT Issues in Counseling*, *7*(1), 2–43. https://doi.org/10.1080/15538605.2013.755444

Hudson, J. H. (2013). Comprehensive literature review pertaining to married men who have sex with men (MMSM). *Journal of Bisexuality, 13*(4), 417–601. https://doi.org/10.1080/15299716.2013.842356

Jean Baker-Miller Training Institute (n.d.). *Relational-cultural theory.* https://www.wcwonline.org/JBMTI-Site/relational-cultural-theory

Jeffries, W. L., IV. (2009). A comparative analysis of homosexual behaviors, sex role preferences, and anal sex proclivities in Latino and non-Latino men. *Archives of Sexual Behavior, 38*(5), 765–778. http://doi.org/10.1007/s10508-007-9254-4

Jordan, J. V. (2010). *Relational-cultural therapy.* American Psychological Association.

Jordan, J. V. (2017). Relational-cultural therapy. In M. Kopala & M. Keitel (Eds.), *Handbook of counseling women* (2nd ed., pp. 63–73). SAGE.

Kazama, T. (2020). Conditional inclusion: Sexual minorities, tolerance, and nationalism. *International Journal of Japanese Sociology, 29*(1), 39–51. https://doi.org/10.1111/ijjs.12110

Kunzel, R. G. (2008). *Criminal intimacy: Prison and the uneven history of modern American sexuality.* University of Chicago Press.

LeVay, S., & Baldwin, J. (2012). *Human sexuality* (4th ed.). Siauer Associates.

Miller, J. B., & Stiver, I. P. (1997) *The healing connection: How women form relationships in therapy and in life.* Beacon Books.

Miller, W. R., & Rollnick, S. (2013). *Motivational interviewing: Helping people change* (3rd ed.). Guilford Press.

Mustanski, B. S., Chivers, M. L., & Bailey, J. M. (2002). A critical review of recent biological research on human sexual orientation. *Annual Review of Sexual Research, 13*, 89–140. https://doi.org/10.1080/10532528.2002.10559803

Myer, I. H. (2015). Resilience in the study of minority stress and health of sexual and gender minorities. *Psychology of Sexual Orientation and Gender Diversity, 2*(3), 209–213. https://doi.org/10.1037/sgd0000132

Okazaki, S. (2002). Influences of culture on Asian Americans' sexuality. *Journal of Sex Research, 39*(1), 34–41. https://doi.org/10.1080/00224490209552117

Ratts, M. J., Singh, A. A., Nassar-McMillan, S., Butler, S. K., & McCullough, J. R. (2015). *Multicultural and social justice counseling competencies.* Association for Multicultural Counseling and Development. http://www.counseling.org/docs/default-source/competencies/multicultural-and-social-justice-counseling-competencies.pdf?sfvrsn=20

Ricciardelli, R., Grills, S., & Craig, A. (2016). Constructions and negotiations of sexuality in Canadian federal men's prisons. *Journal of Homosexuality, 63*(12), 1660–1684. https://doi.org/10.1080/00918369.2016.1158010

Roccas, S., & Brewer, M. B. (2002). Social identity complexity. *Personality and Social Psychology Review, 6*, 88–106. https://doi.org/10.1207/S15327957PSPR0602_01

Savin-Williams, R. C. (2016). Sexual orientation: Categories or continuum? Commentary on Bailey et al. (2016). *Psychological Science in the Public Interest, 17*(2), 37–44. https://doi.org/10.1177/1529100616637618
Silva, T. J., & Whaley, R. B. (2018). Bud-sex, dude-sex, and heteroflexible men: The relationship between straight identification and social attitudes in a nationally representative sample of men with same-sex attractions or sexual practices. *Sociological Perspectives, 61*(3), 426–443. https://doi.org/10.1177/0731121417745024
Ventriglio, A., & Bhugra, D. (2019). Sexuality in the 21st century: Sexual fluidity. *East Asian Archives of Psychiatry, 29*, 30–34. https://doi.org/10.12809/eaap1736
Vrangalova, Z., & Savin-Williams, R. C. (2012). Mostly heterosexual and mostly gay/lesbian: Evidence for new sexual orientation identities. *Archives of Sexual Behavior, 41*, 85–101. https://link.springer.com/article/10.1007/s10508-012-9921-y
Walker, M. (2008). How therapy helps when the culture hurts. *Women & Therapy, 31*(2), 87–105. https://doi.org/10.1080/02703140802145979
Williams, D. J., Prior, E., & Wegner, J. (2013). Resolving social problems associated with sexuality: Can a "sex-positive" approach help? *Social Work, 58*(3), 273–276. https://doi.org/10.1093/sw/swt024
Worthington, R. L., & Reynolds, A. L. (2009). Within-group differences in sexual orientation and identity. *Journal of Counseling Psychology, 56*, 44–55. https://doi.org/10.1037/a0013498

Exploring Sex and Gender Diversity

lore m. dickey

Gennyfir is a 33-year-old African American woman with a trans experience. She transitioned about 7 years ago. Gennyfir has completed her medical transition, which included hormone treatment, breast augmentation, and facial feminization surgery. Gennyfir works as a dancer in a men's club in a large, southern city in the United States. Gennyfir began work as a dancer after having lost her job as a dental assistant when she made her transition. She was encouraged by a friend she met at a homeless shelter to try out for a position at one of the men's clubs near the shelter. Gennyfir has been enjoying this work and reports that she is able to support herself and is reluctant to give up the work as she cannot think of another job that would pay as well this one does. She knows that she is working in a field that has the potential to be risky for her.

This chapter is devoted to understanding human sexuality as it relates to people of diverse gender identities, intersex people, and the ways in which sex-role stereotyping impacts sexuality. We will follow Gennyfir's story throughout this chapter as we discuss sexuality and gender identity.

Historical Perspectives

Gender diversity has existed throughout human history and is a normal human experience (dickey, 2020). There are many identity labels used for people whose gender identity is different than the sex they were assigned at birth. Table 10.1 lists some of the terms that are used across cultures and in various places throughout the world. One of the major challenges faced by Indigenous trans people around the world is the way that their community or culture has been colonized. This colonization was primarily by White Christians. Although this is characterized as a historical event, missionaries still continue to visit Indigenous cultures with much the same message as years ago.

As missionaries arrive in a community, they are there to help others find salvation. This means that the missionary assumes that the religious beliefs of the local

Table 10.1
Terms for Transgender People Among Cultures

Trans People	*Culture*
Acaults	Myanmar
Akava'ine	Cook Islands
Alyha, Hwame	Mohave tribe
Ankole[a]	Uganda
Arvani, Aruvani[b], Dhurani, Hijra, Jagappa[b], Kojja, Ombodhu, Rupantarkami	India
Ashtime[b]	Maale, Ethiopia
Bakla, Tom	Philippines
Bangala[a]	Democratic Republic of Congo
Biza'ah, Muxe	Mexico
Burrneesha	Albania
Calabai/Calalai/Bissu	Sulawesi, Indonesia
Chuckchi	Siberia
Dilbaa, Nádleehí	Navajo tribe
Fa'afafine	Samoa
Fakaleiti	Tonga
Femminiello[a]	Italy
Guevedoche	Dominican Republic
Hijra, Khawaja sira[b], Khusra[b], Zenana/Zenani	India and Pakistan
Katohey, Tom	Thailand
Köçek[a]	Ottoman Empire
Kothi, Sak veng/Srey sros	West Bengal and India
Kteuy	Cambodia
Lhamana	Zuni tribe
Mahu	Hawai'i and Polynesia
Mak nyah	Malaysia
Mamluk[a]	Egypt
Mashoga	Kenya and Tanzania
Metis	Nepal
Mino	Benin
Mukhannthun[a]	Early Islamic Arabia
Narnban[b]	Pakistan
Ninauposkitzipxpe	Blackfoot tribe
Quariwarmi[a]	Inca, Peru
Sekrata	Madagascar
Sistergirl/Brotherboy	Australia
Skoptsy[a]	Russia
Third gender	South Asia
Tida wena	Venezuela
Tom, Waria	Indonesia
Travesti	Brazil
Two-Spirit	Native American
Wakatane, Whakawahine	Maori in New Zealand
Winkte	Lakota tribe
Xanith	Oman
X-jenda	Japan

[a]Term is either no longer used, or people with this identity were directly impacted by colonization.
[b]Typically translated as eunuch.

Indigenous people are going to lead them to hell and damnation (Namaste, 2000). If this were not enough, the missionaries also make it clear that there are two, and only two, immutable genders. These genders must conform with the expectations consistent with the sex assigned at birth. Expectations based on the gender binary include feminine (female), such as dependent, easily influenced, emotionally weak, feeler, gentle, indecisive, nurturing, passive, sensitive, submissive, tactful, talkative, and verbal, and masculine (male), such as independent, not easily influenced, emotionally strong, thinker, tough, decisive, not nurturing, aggressive, active, insensitive, dominant, blunt, quiet, and analytical.

As a result of these expectations, if a person was assigned male at birth but had a tendency to behave in ways that are more similar for a woman, there would be sanctions for this type of behavior (Namaste, 2000). The same was true of people who were assigned female at birth and acted in ways that were more consistent with the expectations for males. As if this wasn't enough, people who were recognized by the Indigenous culture to live in a third, fourth, or fifth gender were also sanctioned for their behavior. In many of the Indigenous cultures, people with identities other than masculine or feminine were all but erased. We are beginning to see a resurgence of people from Indigenous cultures in addition to those with a nonbinary identity.

Waves of Gender Identity

In dickey (2017), it has been suggested that there have been four waves of trans identities. The first wave was trans people from Indigenous cultures as described above. The second wave was the medical model. The medical model began early in the 20th century but had its greatest influence beginning in the 1960s. In part, due to the work of Harry Benjamin (1966), more people were then making a medical transition, which at the time included first hormones and then surgery. Also expected during this time was that a trans person would deny the history of their life leading up to their transition. They would also need to be heterosexual posttransition. Providers (mental health and medical) became surprised that their trans patients were telling the same story (Benjamin, 1966; dickey, 2017). What had happened (unbeknown to the providers) is that trans people learned the story that would allow them access to care.

The third wave was the transgender wave (dickey, 2017). Virginia Prince is credited (King & Ekins, 2007) with having coined the term *transgender* and having used the term to describe herself. Prince wanted to be respected as a woman without having to make a medical transition. Thus, transgender began to be used as an individual identity term in the 1990s, but it has since become a term that is inclusive of all people who have a gender identity that is different than the sex they were assigned at birth. This includes transgender, transsexual, cross-dresser, and more.

The fourth wave was the nonbinary wave. Although nonbinary people have existed as long as humans have walked the earth, it wasn't until the 2000s that we began to see more nonbinary people in mainstream culture. In some ways, we can think of trans people as having come full circle from Indigenous identities to mainstream nonbinary identities. There are still people who desire medical treatment in addition to people who do not want to have any medical interventions even though they are on the gender binary. The gender binary holds the belief that there are two, and only two, immutable genders (American Psychological Association, 2015). Given that gender is a social construct (e.g., the definitions and roles that are expected were created by one's society, and usually by those with the greatest power), it makes sense that there are more than two places for a trans person to identify.

Gennyfir may refer to herself as a trans woman, a woman, a transgender person with a masculine history, or something else. Identity labels are very personal. When working with transgender people, it is important to ask them which terms they use to identify themselves. This shows a measure of respect for the trans person and is an indication that you have a good understanding of how to affirmatively interact.

Gender Markers and Pronouns

In recent years, we have seen states acknowledge more than two sexes (Movement Advancement Project [MAP], 2020b). According to MAP, 19 states and Washington, DC, allow people to use a marker other than male or female on their driver's license. Additionally, 13 states allow people to make such a change to their birth certificate. The marker that is used in these situations is an "X." Although this is an important change for trans people, it runs the risk of putting trans people in a dangerous place. For example, if a trans person with X on their driver's license is preparing to fly to another location and is going through a Transportation Security Administration checkpoint in an airport in a state that does not use X as a gender marker, it is possible that they will be subjected to mistreatment. The same could be said if the person was pulled over by the police. It is unfortunate that as we advance in acknowledging the various identities that a trans person might have that those same people can find themselves in a dangerous situation.

Another aspect of a trans person's identity are the pronouns that they use. People who have a binary identity male/female or masculine/feminine are likely to use he/him/his or she/her/hers, respectively. People with nonbinary identities may use they/them/their, which have been accepted as pronouns for individuals. Such usage is accepted in the *Publication Manual of the American Psychological Association, Seventh Edition* (American Psychological Association, 2020) and such dictionaries as the *New Oxford American Dictionary* (n.d.) and the *Merriam-Webster* dictionary (n.d.-a, n.d.-b). Nonbinary people may also use other pronouns. See Table 10.2 for examples of other pronoun options, including the way they would be used in conversation. It used to be the case that pronoun options would be referred to as being "preferred." Pronouns are critically important aspects of a trans person's identity and one that cisgender people rarely contemplate. By suggesting that a person prefers a pronoun, a trans person may feel as though another person will use the pronouns when it is convenient. Another way of thinking about this is the use of personal gender pronoun (PGP). A PGP is the pronoun or pronoun set that a person uses. For instance, the author of this chapter uses the pronoun set he/him/his. Although he rarely experiences people using the wrong pronoun, because he

Table 10.2

Pronoun Usage

Subjective	*Objective*	*Possessive*	*Reflective*
She	Her	Hers	Herself
He	Him	His	Himself
They	Them	Theirs	Themselves
Ze	Hir/zir	Hirs/zirs	Hirself/zirself

was assigned female at birth, there was a period of time when people in his life needed to learn to use the correct pronouns. When a person fails to use the correct pronouns for a trans person, the effect can be demoralizing.

Gennyfir uses the pronouns she/her/hers. This can be a challenge for her when people only hear her voice. Gennyfir has a deep voice, which was the result of completing an endogenous puberty (e.g., puberty that is consistent with the sex a person was assigned at birth). Testosterone thickens a person's vocal cords. If you think about a piano, the thick wires are the low notes, and the thin wires are the high notes. Trans women often need to complete voice training to raise the pitch of their voice. The training is needed because a person can easily damage their vocal cords if they do not use their voice correctly. Although Gennyfir has a female identity and a female name and uses female pronouns, until she learns how to speak in a higher pitch, she may be misgendered by others who only hear her voice.

Misgendering a person can be demoralizing for a trans person. Misgendering happens when a person uses the wrong name (sometimes called a "dead name") or pronoun for a person. If this happens in a private setting, the trans person may feel safe correcting the other person. The person who misgenders the trans person should make an apology that is quick and brief, so as to avoid the possibility of making the interaction more awkward.

Why Is the T With LGB?

Whether you are cisgender, transgender, or a sexual minority (lesbian, gay, bisexual, pansexual, or asexual), you may wonder why transgender (a gender identity label) is included with sexual minority labels. The connection between gender and sexual minorities is that both have a history of transgressing gender. The ways that trans people do this are pretty obvious. For example, someone who is assigned female at birth wants to be recognized as a male-identified person (or vice versa). Sexual minority people do not necessarily seek a different gender identity, rather they may act in ways that push the comfort of cisgender heterosexual people. For example, a lesbian may dress androgynously and wear short hair. A gay man may have an effeminate personality. In both of these ways, sexual minorities are expressing their gender. Laws that protect gender minorities do so based on gender identity or gender expression. When you think then about what brings lesbian, gay, and bisexual (LGB) together with transgender (LGBT), gender expression is the most likely answer.

Just like cisgender people, trans people also have a sexual orientation. Many, although not all, transmasculine people have a lesbian history. Transfeminine people do not usually have a gay male history; rather, they are more likely to have a heterosexual male history. Post transition, assuming a trans man remains attracted to women, his relationships may look like a heterosexual relationship. For trans women, again assuming they remain attracted to women, their relationship will look like a lesbian couple. It can be especially challenging for trans people who came from a heterosexual relationship to be included in the LGBTQ+ (lesbian, gay, bisexual, transgender, queer, plus other identities) group.

Sexuality in Trans People

For some trans people, sexuality may be a fluid experience. Diamond (2009) has noted through her research that people assigned female at birth are likely to experience sexual fluidity. Her work focuses on sexuality in cisgender people. There is no empirical evidence for why some trans people, especially trans men, experience shifts in their sexual orientation. It could be that, like some cisgender people, trans people choose to have sexual encounters as a means of exploring their sexual identity or enjoy sex with a person without letting that encounter define their sexuality. Alternatively, a trans person might identify as pansexual. Pansexual people are attracted to other people based not on their gender or gender identity but rather because they are attracted to the person. This might include the way the person thinks, their looks, or their personality. Being pansexual is not about either person's gender.

Another term that may be used by a trans person to identify their sexuality is the word "queer." Some LGBTQ+ people have reclaimed the word queer, which historically has been an epithet used to harm gay and lesbian people. Although queer is not the same as pansexual, the two terms have commonalities. In the Merriam-Webster.com dictionary, they have the same alternative definition: "Characterized by sexual or romantic attraction that is not limited to people of a particular gender identity or sexual orientation" (Merriam-Webster, n.d.-a). A pansexual person may not identify as queer and vice versa. For trans people, these terms allow a person to define their identity without having to anchor it in their gender. If a gay or lesbian is a person who is in a same-sex relationship, how does that work for a trans person? If a person was assigned female at birth, they transitioned to male, and are still in what started as a lesbian relationship, how would the relationship be characterized posttransition? The simple answer is to ask the person how they identify. Making assumptions about a person's identity can lead to a rupture of the clinical relationship.

Sex Work in the Trans Community

Trans people, especially trans women of color, are overrepresented among those who engage in sex work in what is known as the "street economy." *Sex work* has been defined by Nuttbrock (2018) as

> direct physical contact between a buyer and seller as well as indirect sexual stimulation and may include emotional intimacy and companionship. Sex work may be negotiated and occur in different venues and social contexts, including streets and public spaces, parlors and residences known as places where sex may be purchased, hookups through message boards and the Internet, and various informal arrangements. (p. xv)

Hwahng (2018) suggested that three cultural experiences contribute to trans women engaging in sex work. These are African American and Latinx people involved in the House Ball Community, Asian sex workers, and White cross-dressers. The House Ball Community is a subset of the LGBTQ+ community. Individuals are placed in houses that resemble a family structure. Houses then compete against one another in events known as balls (Alio et al., 2020). Trans women who participate in the House Ball Community tend to be young (in their teens and 20s) and living in poverty. This community primarily exists in the greater New York City area. It is important to note that the House Ball setting is not where sex work happens; rather, people who participate in the House Ball Community become engaged in sex work as a means of economic survival. Hwahng (2018) also noted that drug addiction and a lack of education also contributed to House Ball Community members becoming engaged in sex work. For some, engaging in sex work and drug use became a rite of passage. Unfortunately, being engaged in sex work puts trans women at risk of sexually transmitted infections (STIs), including HIV, and of experiencing violence on a spectrum of physical abuse to murder.

In a qualitative study of trans sex workers, Hwahng (2018) found that Asian sex workers who were trans women had more privilege than two other groups, stating,

> Many Asian sex workers transition sometime between their teenage and early adult years solely through clothing and behavior. Some Asian "girls" may also start taking hormones at puberty, but this practice has a fairly low cost compared with other body modifications. According to the outreach worker, Asian "girls" pass as au naturel females without costly or uncomfortable body modifications such as surgery or silicone injections. . . . [One community member] maintained that because Asians possessed au naturel femininity and had not undergone major surgical or other body modification enhancements, they appeared more feminine—and thus more desirable—to customers. (pp. 11–12)

Asian sex workers tend to work in apartments or hotels, but Asian trans women are exoticized in problematic ways. Although they experience less risks than Black trans women, they are still at risk of violence and of contracting an STI. Asian sex workers also tend to be young and to be living in poverty. In not having had surgical interventions, Asian sex workers are able to offer additional types of sexual encounters (e.g., the inserter in penetrative sex).

White cross-dressers, the last group of sex workers defined by Hwahng (2018), are primarily White middle-class men. Cross-dressers typically live most of their days as heterosexual men. Cross-dressers may keep their identity a secret from their family, friends, and coworkers. Because cross-dressers live primarily as male, they are able to keep their jobs, both blue collar (e.g., trade worker) and white collar (e.g., accountants, bankers, health care workers). A clear advantage that White cross-dressers have is that they are able to work legally. They do not have to worry about being arrested for engaging in the work that is their primary income source (Hwahng, 2018). A term that has been used for cross-dressers is *transvestite.* This term is still in use as there is a mental health disorder in the *Diagnostic and Statistical Manual of Mental Disorders, Fifth Edition* (American Psychiatric Association, 2013) called *transvestic disorder.* Some cross-dressers experience no distress around their cross-dressing behavior. For those that do, diagnosis of transvestic disorder may be appropriate.

Nuttbrock (2018) provided a quantitative view of sex work among trans women in the New York City area, first breaking down the activity level of sex workers by the number of encounters. Sex workers were identified as low (fewer than five sex partners in a month), moderate (five to 49 partners a month), or high (50 to 400 partners monthly) activity. Like Hwahng (2018), Nuttbrock noted that trans women of color are overrepresented in the numbers of people who engage in sex work. Additionally, they are more likely to have engaged in sex work during adolescence, have not graduated from high school, be an immigrant, and be unemployed.

It is important to differentiate between sex work and survival sex, also known as transactional sex. *Sex work* involves the exchange of money for a sexual encounter. *Survival sex*, on the other hand, involves engaging in sex for food, shelter, drugs, money, or some other commodity (Barton, 2018). For adolescents, survival sex may very well be their first entry into sex work. Trans people have a difficult road even as rules and laws begin to be more favorable toward LGBTQ+ people. When the options for income become limited to engaging in street economies, their road becomes that much more difficult.

Considering Gennyfir's life, she is working as a dancer in a men's club. Although this work does not involve sexual interactions, it might be considered to be a type of sex work (Harcourt & Donovan, 2005). If Gennyfir lives in a large city, she may be able to get affirmative health care in a nonjudgmental setting. This would include regular testing for STIs and the use of a harm-reduction approach to hormone treatment. Providers who use a harm-reduction approach to hormone treatment ensure that their trans patients can access hormones without undue expectations (e.g., the need for a letter of referral, an expected number of counseling sessions; Dietz & Halem, 2016). Some sex workers may access their hormones from black market sources, including the internet. Black market hormones are likely to come from an unknown source. As such, there is no guarantee that the drugs are safe. In using a harm-reduction approach, the provider ensures that the trans patient has access to a safe source of hormones and that they are being medically supervised.

Intersex People

There are a number of medical conditions that fall into the label of intersex. A list of intersex conditions can be found in Table 10.3. In the past, the practice has been to put a child through emergency surgery (e.g., a child born with a micropenis has an emergency surgery to correct the phallus) that may or may not have been fully explained to the child's parents. Some intersex conditions require emergency surgery (e.g., if a child is born without an anal opening); however, most do not. This is due in part to the fact that some intersex conditions do not become obvious until a child reaches puberty. The American Counseling Association (2004) approved the Resolution to Protect Intersex Children from Unwanted Surgery, Secrecy, and Shame. This may be the only such resolution by a mental health association.

Although some people may include intersex people in the LGBTQ+ community, and it doesn't hurt to be as inclusive as possible, being intersex is a medical condition. Like trans people, some intersex people may choose to have surgery or need to take hormones. The difference is that the surgeries for an intersex condition are typically considered to be medically necessary. Only in the past decade or so have people been fighting, and winning the fight, to have surgery and hormone treatment considered medically necessary for trans people.

Intersex is sometimes referred to as a disorder or difference in sex development (DSD). DSD is less pathological than disorder in sex development. For some people, DSD is fine. For others it is not. DSD is a more respectful term than any of the versions of "hermaphroditism." The Accord Alliance (n.d.) states that DSD is a better option as it relates to the disorder, not to the person. This is similar to how person-first language is used in disability communities. According to interACT (n.d.), an advocacy organization that works to reduce the stigma and shame associated with intersex conditions, DSD overly pathologizes intersex people. Regardless of what feels comfortable or relevant to you as a counselor, it is most important to use the language of your client.

Thinking of Gennyfir's experience, to this point she has identified as a trans woman. It is possible, however, that she could have had an intersex history. Her parents may not have told her about the reason for medical treatments that occurred during

Table 10.3
Intersex Conditions

Intersex Condition	*Definition*[a]
17-beta reductase deficiency	A person with this condition has a female appearance but cannot make sex hormones. As a result, they will not experience puberty.
3-beta-hydroxysteroid dehydrogenase deficiency	This condition is usually lethal. Endocrine management must be maintained.
5-alpha reductase deficiency	The gender identity of a person with 5-alpha reductase deficiency may be variable. There will likely be masculinizing effects during puberty that may be a concern for a child who was raised as a girl.
Androgen insensitivity syndrome	It is recommended that individuals with androgen insensitivity syndrome be raised as girls. These girls should be allowed to complete puberty before considering an orchiectomy. The need for an orchiectomy is due to the risk of malignancy when a person has undescended testicles.
Aphallia	If a person with aphallia has normal tests, it can be assumed that their brain has been masculinized. If this person has been raised as a female, they may choose to complete a gender transition similar to a trans person.
Clitoromegaly	People with clitoromegaly, or an enlarged clitoris, should be tested for congenital adrenal hyperplasia and PAIS.
Cloacal exstrophy (46, XY)[b]	This chromosomal disorder can be complex and may lead to death. In the past, these children have been forced to complete surgery to remove testicular tissue without personal or parental consent. One of the problems with this is that the child will not be fertile.
Congenital adrenal hyperplasia (46, XX)[b]	This condition is potentially life threatening. A child with "genital ambiguity" should be tested for congenital adrenal hyperplasia.
Gonadal dysgenesis	This condition may be partial or complete. The person is likely to be infertile.
Hypospadias	In this condition, the urethral opening is on the underside of the penis. These children should be tested for congenital adrenal hyperplasia and PAIS. There is increased risk of urinary tract infections and there may be pain with erections. This condition may be surgically corrected.
Kallman syndrome	Males with this condition may be infertile. People may also have an absence of smell.
Klinefelter syndrome (47, XXY)[b]	In this chromosomal condition, a person may have unambiguous male genitalia with small testicles. There may be learning disabilities.
Micropenis (46, XY)[b]	Children born with a micropenis have often been raised as girls. If raised as a girl, the child may choose to make a gender transition later in life. Depending on the cause of this condition, the person may develop lethal hypoglycemia.
Mayer, Rokitanksy, Kuster, Hauser syndrome	In Mayer, Rokitanksy, Kuster, Hauser syndrome, a person has ovaries but does not have a uterus or the uterus is not a normal size or shape. There can also be kidney and spine anomalies.
Ovary and testes (ovotestes)	There is a presence of testicular tissues that may develop malignancies.
Persistent mullerian duct syndrome	There is a risk that the child has undescended testicles. There may be an issue of infertility.
Progestin-induced virilization	This condition arises when there is a history of virilizing exposure in prenatal life. As a result, the child will not virize later in life.
Sex-chromosome mosaicism (45, X; 46, XY)[b]	For children with these chromosomal anomalies, the genotypes and phenotypes will vary. It is important to monitor for genital malignancies.
Swyer syndrome (46, XY)[b]	This is another name for gonadal dysgenesis.
Turner syndrome (45, X)[b]	There is great phenotypic variability in people with Turner syndrome. Usually infertile and may have cardiac or renal issues. There is a risk of learning disabilities.

Note. PAIS = partial androgen insensitivity syndrome.
[a]From Consortium on the Management of Disorders of Sex Development (2006). [b]Chromosomal configurations are in parentheses. Many intersex conditions are caused by chromosomal abnormalities.

childhood. Often the emergency surgeries are or were completed because of so-called "ambiguous genitalia." Intersex conditions are much more than having genitalia that is not consistent with what would be expected "normally." There are five overall classifications of intersex conditions: (a) congenital development of ambiguous genitalia, (b) congenital disjunction of internal and external sex anatomy, (c) incomplete development of sex anatomy, (d) sex chromosome anomalies, and (e) disorders of gonadal development (Accord Alliance, n.d.). Generally, an intersex condition is discovered either at birth or at puberty. As an adult, if Gennyfir has not learned of being intersex at this point in her life, it is unlikely that she is.

Trans People of Color

Flores et al. (2016) reported that trans Black, Indigenous, and people of color (BIPOC) are overrepresented in the U.S. trans population. Flores et al. relied on the Centers for Disease Control and Prevention's Brief Risk Factor Surveillance System (BRFSS) for their report about race and ethnicity in the trans community. The BRFSS is one of few national data collection efforts that include a question on gender identity. Flores et al. (2016) estimated that the number of people who identified as transgender in the United States was 1.4 million or 0.6% of U.S. adults. Table 10.4 compares the racial breakdown of trans people to that of the general population, based on U.S. census data.

Trans BIPOC face discrimination in all aspects of their life. Trans BIPOC also experience inequities or disparities related to social determinants of health, including access to health care, education, and safe and affordable housing; socioeconomic status; and disability. In addition, researchers who have studied suicide risk, cervical cancer, quality of life, HIV, approaches to quantifying the number of trans people, health disparities, bullying, gender-affirming care, reproductive health, and posttraumatic stress disorder in the trans community have consistently pointed to disparities for trans people of color (Bradford et al., 2013; Gamarel et al., 2014; Garthe et al., 2020; Lampe et al., 2020; Reisner et al., 2015, 2020; Reisner, Gamarel, et al., 2014; Reisner, Poteat, et al., 2016; Reisner, White, et al., 2014; Reisner, White Hughto, et al., 2016; Rood et al., 2017; Thompson et al., 2015; White Hughto et al., 2017, 2018). Absent from the literature is the study of the number of trans people who are murdered on an annual basis. On the basis of anecdotal evidence, we believe that trans women of color are the most likely group to be murdered. Especially concerning is the brutal manner in which they are often killed. In most states (MAP, 2020a), the murderer is able to claim the "trans panic defense," which can be used to exonerate the murderer. You might be thinking, "What is the trans panic defense?" This is a defense position that a person can take in which they are saying, "When I learned the

Table 10.4

Proportion of U.S. Transgender Population (2014–2015) by Race or Ethnicity

Race	*BRFSS %*	*GP %*
White	55	66
African American	16	12
Latinx	12	15
Other race	8	8

Note. BRFSS = Brief Risk Factor Surveillance System; GP = general population.

person was trans, I panicked, and this caused me to kill them." A total of 10 states have outlawed the use of a gay/trans panic defense (MAP, 2020a). It is disturbing that a defendant could use this type of defense to avoid incarceration.

Another area where trans BIPOC are overrepresented is HIV infection. James et al. (2016) noted that Black trans women have the highest rates of HIV. The general population averages 0.3% of people are HIV positive. Black trans women average 19%. Some of this is the result of the rates at which Black trans women are engaged in sex work. James et al. (2016) reported that 21% of Black trans women are engaged in sex work, compared with 12% for the full sample in the study.

There are many reasons why trans BIPOC will end up living on the street, lacking access to health care, or with complicated health histories. Trans people of color face disparately greater risks and challenges every day.

Standards and Guidelines

Mental health providers should be aware of the various standards and guidelines that have been published that address work with trans people. Although there is not room to address each of the documents, it is important to be aware of the approaches to work with trans people. See some specific resources:

American Counseling Association
Competencies for counseling with transgender clients can be found at
https://www.counseling.org/resources/competencies/algbtic_competencies.pdf

American Psychological Association
Guidelines for psychological practice with transgender and gender nonconforming people can be found at
https://www.apa.org/practice/guidelines/transgender.pdf

Informed Consent for Access to Health Care
Informed consent for access to trans health care can be found at
https://icath.info/how-does-it-work/

World Professional Association for Transgender Health
Standards of care for the health of transsexual, transgender, and gender nonconforming people can be found at
https://www.wpath.org/publications/soc

Conclusion

Trans people make up a small proportion of the population of the United States. Nevertheless, it is possible that you, as a counselor, will have a trans client at some point in your career. Working successfully with that client requires more than a cursory understanding of gender dysphoria (e.g., the diagnostic label used to identify people whose gender identity is different than the sex they were assigned at birth). It requires knowledge of the types of challenges faced by trans people and an understanding of the identity process a trans person may need to work through. Most important, all trans people deserve to be treated with dignity and respect, which is an ethical mandate for all mental health providers.

This chapter began with a description of Gennyfir, a trans person who works as a dancer in a men's club. Gennyfir has been referred to you for counseling because she is interested in surgery. When you meet Gennyfir, you observe that she has a substantial chest (e.g., significant breast development), and you mistakenly assume that she is interested in genital surgery when, in reality, she is seeking breast augmentation surgery. This is an example of the kind of assumption that can lead to an unrecoverable rupture in the therapeutic alliance. This chapter is intended to help you better understand the needs of trans clients.

References

Accord Alliance. (n.d.). *FAQs*. https://www.accordalliance.org/learn-about-dsd/faqs/

Alio, A. P., Sibley, C., Ouedraogo, H. S., Wallace, S. E., Wakefield, S., Humes, D. L., Fields, S., D., & Keefer, M. C. (2020). House Ball Community leaders' perceptions of HIV and HIV vaccine research. *International Journal of Maternal and Child Health and AIDS, 9*(1), 136–145. https://doi.org/10.21106/ijma.331

American Counseling Association. (2004). *ACA Governing Council meeting minutes: March 30–April 1, 2004*. https://www.counseling.org/docs/default-source/governing-council-minutes/2004-march-30-april-1.pdf?sfvrsn=2ba85914_6

American Psychiatric Association. (2013). *Diagnostic and statistical manual of mental disorders* (5th ed.). https://doi.org/10.1176/appi.books.9780890425596

American Psychological Association. (2015). Guidelines for psychological practice with transgender and gender nonconforming people. *American Psychologist, 70*, 832–864. https://doi.org/10.1037/a0039906

American Psychological Association. (2020). *Publication manual of the American Psychological Association* (7th ed.). https://doi.org/10.1037/0000165-000

Barton, L. C. (2018). What the literature says about survival sex among young trans people in the United Kingdom and the United States. In L. Nuttbrock (Ed.), *Transgender sex work and society* (pp. 48–62). Harrington Park Press.

Benjamin, H. (1966). *The transsexual phenomenon: All the facts about the changing of sex through hormones and surgery*. Warner Books.

Bradford, J., Reisner, S. L., Honnold, J. A., & Xavier, J. (2013). Experiences of transgender-related discrimination and implications for health: Results from the Virginia Transgender Health Initiative Study. *American Journal of Public Health, 103*(10), 1820–1829. https://doi.org/10.2105/ajph.2012.300796

Consortium on the Management of Disorders of Sex Development. (2006). *Clinical guidelines for the management of disorders of sex development*. http://www.accordalliance.org/dsd-guidelines/

Diamond, L. M. (2009). *Sexual fluidity: Understanding women's love and desire*. Harvard University Press.

dickey, l. m. (2017). Gender nonconformity and transgender issues: Overview. In K. L. Nadal (Ed.), *The SAGE encyclopedia of psychology and gender* (pp. 692–697). Sage.

dickey, l. m. (2020). History of gender identity and mental health. In E. Rothblum (Ed.), *The Oxford handbook of sexual and gender minority mental health* (pp. 24–34) Oxford University Press.

Dietz, E., & Halem, J. (2016). How should physicians refer when referral options are limited for transgender patients? [Case and commentary] *AMA Journal of Ethics, 18*(11), 1070–1080. https://doi.org/10.1001/journalofethics.2016.18.11.ecas1-1611

Flores, A. R., Brown, T. N. T., & Heman, J. L. (2016). *Race and ethnicity of adults who identify as transgender in the United States*. The Williams Institute. https://williamsinstitute.law.ucla.edu/wp-content/uploads/Race-Ethnicity-Trans-Adults-US-Oct-2016.pdf

Gamarel, K. E., Reisner, S. L., Laurenceau, J.-P., Nemoto, T., & Operario, D. (2014). Gender minority stress, mental health, and relationship quality: A dyadic investigation of transgender women and their cisgender male partners. *Journal of Family Psychology, 28*(4), 437–447. https://doi.org/10.1037/a0037171

Garthe, R. C., Hidalgo, M. A., Goffnett, J., Hereth, J., Garofalo, R., Reisner, S. L., Mimiaga, M. J., & Kuhns, L. M. (2020). Young transgender women survivors of intimate partner violence: A latent class analysis of protective processes. *Psychology of Sexual Orientation and Gender Diversity*, *7*(4), 386–395. https://doi.org/10.1037/sgd0000379

Harcourt, C., & Donovan, B. (2005). The many faces of sex work. *Sexually Transmitted Infections, 81*(3), 201–206. https://doi.org/10.1136/sti.2004.012468

Hwahng, S. (2018). Qualitative description of sex work among transwomen in New York City. In L. Nuttbrock (Ed.), *Transgender sex work and society* (pp. 2–16). Harrington Park Press.

interACT. (n.d.). *interACT statement on intersex terminology*. https://interactadvocates.org/interact-statement-on-intersex-terminology/

James, S. E., Herman, J. L., Rankin, S., Keisling, M., Mottet, L., & Anafi, M. (2016). *The report of the 2015 U.S. Transgender Survey*. National Center for Transgender Equality.

King, D., & Ekins, R. (2007). Transgender, transvestism, and transsexualism. In G. Ritzer (Ed.), *The Blackwell encyclopedia of sociology* (pp. 1–6). John Wiley & Sons.

Lampe, T. M., Reisner, S. L., Schrimshaw, E. W., Radix, A., Mallick, R., Harry-Hernandez, S., Dubin, S., Khan, A., & Duncan, D. T. (2020). Navigating stigma in neighborhoods and public spaces among transgender and nonbinary adults in New York City. *Stigma and Health*, *5*(4), 477–487. https://doi.org/10.1037/sah0000219

Merriam-Webster. (n.d.-a). Queer. *In Merriam-Webster.com dictionary*. Retrieved May 16, 2022, from https://www.merriam-webster.com/dictionary/queer

Merriam-Webster. (n.d.-b). They. *In Merriam-Webster.com dictionary*. Retrieved May 16, 2022, from https://www.merriam-webster.com/dictionary/they

Movement Advancement Project. (2020a). *Gay/trans panic defense bans*. https://www.lgbtmap.org/equality-maps/panic_defense_bans

Movement Advancement Project. (2020b). *Identity document laws and policies*. https://www.lgbtmap.org/equality-maps/identity_document_laws/

Namaste, V. K. (2000). *Invisible lives: The erasure of transsexual and transgender people*. University of Chicago Press.

New Oxford American Dictionary. (n.d.). They. Retrieved May 16, 2022, from https://www.oxfordreference.com/view/10.1093/acref/9780195392883.001.0001/m_en_us1298318?rskey=IUOEjn&result=1

Nuttbrock, L. A. (2018). Quantitative description of sex work among transwomen in New York City. In L. Nuttbrock (Ed.), *Transgender sex work and society* (pp. 18–32). Harrington Park Press.

Nuttbrock, L. A., & Hwahng, S. J. (2017). Ethnicity, sex work, and incident HIV/STI among transgender women in New York City: A three year prospective study. *AIDS and Behavior*, *21*(12), 3328–3335. https://doi.org/10.1007/s10461-016-1509-4

Reisner, S. L., Conron, K. J., Scout, Baker, K., Herman, J. L., Lombardi, A., Greytak, E. A., Gill, A. M., & Matthews, A. K. (2015). “Counting” transgender and gender-nonconforming adults in health research: Recommendations from the Gender Identity in US Surveillance Group. *Transgender Studies Quarterly, 2*(1), 34–57. https://doi.org/10.1215/23289252-2848877

Reisner, S. L., Gamarel, K. E., Nemoto, T., & Operario, D. (2014). Dyadic effects of gender minority stress in substance use behaviors among transgender women and their non-transgender male partners. *Psychology of Sexual Orientation and Gender Diversity, 1*(1), 3–71. https://doi.org/10.1037/0000013

Reisner, S. L., Pletta, D. R., Potter, J., & Deustch, M. B. (2020). Initial psychometric evaluation of a brief sexual functioning screening tool for transmasculine adults: Transmasculine Sexual Functioning Index. *Journal of Sexual Medicine, 8*(3), 350–360. https://doi.org/10.1016/j.esxm.2020.05.006

Reisner, S. L., Poteat, T., Keatley, J., Cabral, M., Mothopeng, T., Dunham, E., Holland, C. E., Max, R., & Baral, S. D. (2016). Global health burden and needs of transgender populations: A review. *Lancet, 388*(10042), 412–436. https://doi.org/10.1016/S0140-67336(16)00648-X

Reisner, S. L., White, J. M., Bradford, J., B., & Mimiaga, M. J. (2014). Transgender health disparities: Comparing full cohort and nested matched-pair study designs in a community health center. *LGBT Health, 1*(3), 177–184. https://doi.org/10.1089/lgbt.2014.0009

Reisner, S. L., White Hughto, J. M., Gamarel, K. E., Keuroghlian, A. S., Mizock, L., & Pachankis, J. E. (2016). Discriminatory experiences associated with posttraumatic stress disorder symptoms among transgender adults. *Journal of Counseling Psychology, 63*(5), 509–519. https://doi.org/10.1037/cou0000143

Rood, B. A., Maroney, M. R., Puckett, J. A., Berman, A. K., Reisner, S. L., & Pantalone, D. W. (2017). Identity concealment in transgender adults: A qualitative assessment of minority stress and gender affirmation. *American Journal of Orthopsychiatry, 87*(6), 704–713. https://doi.org/ort0000303

Thompson, H. M., Reisner, S. L., VanKim, N., & Raymond, H. F. (2015). Quality-of-life measurement: Assessing the WHOQOL-BREF Scale in a sample of high-HIV-risk transgender women in San Francisco, California. *International Journal of Transgenderism, 16*(1), 36–48. https://doi.org/10.1080/15532739.2015.1039176

White Hughto, J. M., Pachankis, J. E., & Reisner, S. L. (2018). Healthcare mistreatment and avoidance in trans masculine adults: The mediating role of rejection sensitivity. *Psychology of Sexual Orientation and Gender Diversity, 5*(4), 471–481. https://doi.org/10.1037/sgd0000296

White Hughto, J. M., Pachankis, J. E., Willie, T. C., & Reisner, S. L., (2017). Victimization and depressive symptomology in transgender adults: The mediating role of avoidant coping. *Journal of Counseling Psychology, 64*(1), 41–51. https://doi.org/10.1037/cou0000184

PART 4
Sexual Wellness

Masturbation, Vibration, and Lube—Oh My!

Lexx Brown-James and Tanisha N. Sapp

Although sexual desire may ebb and flow, people remain sexual beings from birth until death. Of all forms of sexual expression, masturbation is arguably one of the most intimately human forms. To truly study and explore one's body—one's personalized "O"—requires a great deal of vulnerability and ability to experience oneself. And yet, masturbation is a topic most commonly taboo in the United States and often avoided in discussion. Although commonly defined as a sexual expression linked to adolescence, masturbation is also common in early childhood through later adulthood (McCarthy & McCarthy, 2012; Penner & Penner, 2005). Although the teaching of masturbation may shape one's thoughts, beliefs, and attitudes, it is the negative messages that influence individual shame surrounding masturbation. This chapter explores a brief history of masturbation, along with myths and facts that counselors may experience while working with various clients. We also provide a case example; review the PLISSIT model, which follows the principles of Permission, Limited Information, Specific Suggestions, and Intensive Therapy (Annon, 1976); and encourage counselors to examine their own thoughts, beliefs, and experiences before working with others around this topic.

Brief History of Masturbation

The history of masturbation is long and vast, and the societal attitudes toward masturbation have waxed and waned from the time of recorded history from abhorrent disdain to perceived health and enlightenment. Historian Thomas Lacquer (2003) claimed masturbation was first recorded in the Christian script *Onania* in 1712. He argued that the first writings on the topic condemned masturbation as a moral sickness. Philosophers Thomas Aquinas and Immanuel Kant both claimed masturbation to be an act against natural law of humanity and proclaimed the act of masturbation to be worse than suicide (Soble, 2003). When it comes to the counseling and sexological profession, we see challenges faced by various pioneers in the field, from pathologizing healthy masturbatory acts to viewing health benefits associated with masturbation. Freud was one of the first to view masturbation through the lens of shame and ridicule in the case of Dora (Cornog, 2004). Kinsey (1953) was one of the first to study the prevalence of female masturbatory practices. Masters and Johnson (1966) were among the first to examine the physiological process of orgasm. Carnes (2001) identified masturbatory practices as an aspect of sexual impulsivity and addiction.

Despite these theoretical challenges, many experts argue in favor of masturbation. There is a growing body of research validating the importance of embracing masturbation as a means of positive sexual health (Bancroft et al., 2002; Kaestle & Allen, 2011; Laumann et al., 1994). People want to know if they are normal for wanting to touch themselves in a sexual way (Cornog, 2004). Masturbation is not only a safer sex alternative, but a means to sexual pleasure (Coleman, 2003; Kaestle & Allen, 2011; Kinsey et al., 1953; Leiblum & Backmann, 1988). The only purpose of the clitoris is pleasure. How can it be wrong? Counselors are perfect to assist those who wish to explore shame and anxiety associated with masturbation, just like any other concern.

The understanding and education of masturbation are often linked to one's cultural background and childhood upbringing (Kaestle & Allen, 2011). This history is more influential to a person than the overarching stigma of masturbation itself. The mere discussion of masturbation, along with societal perceptions of its taboo, naturally reinforces the stigma that there is something wrong with it (Shelton, 2010). Although masturbation is commonly linked to adolescence, a study conducted by Lindau et al. (2007) found that among participants ages 57 to 64, 63% of men and 32% of women reported masturbating within a year prior to the study. Nevertheless, Shelton (2010) postulated that masturbation continues to be viewed as an unfulfilling means of sexual expression, despite the distinct advantages of being pleasurable, accessible, inexpensive, and safe. Because masturbation has no link to reproduction, in some cultures it may be deemed unnatural. Talking about masturbation publicly not only allows for safer sex practices, but it also allows practitioners to demystify the myths, fallacies, and shame often associated with masturbation (Kaestle & Allen, 2011). After all, sexual pleasure in the absence of shame leads to . . . more pleasure!

Debunking Myths Around Masturbation

Myths about masturbation are pervasive, and just about every culture has some belief about it. *Masturbation* is defined as "erotic stimulation especially of one's own genital . . . organs commonly resulting in orgasm and achieved by manual . . . or other bodily contact exclusive of sexual intercourse, by instrumental manipulation . . . , occasionally by sexual fantasies, or by various combinations of these agencies" (Merriam-Webster, n.d.). As with most sexuality topics, masturbation carries a stigma of shame, which results in the creation of myths. Following are some of the most common myths and how we would debunk them:

Myth 1: Manually stretching the penis by hand or with a penis pump can help the penis lengthen in size permanently.

Fact: A penis, which is primarily made of sponge-like erectile tissue, changes in size because of blood flow, not muscle bulk. In fact, there are no muscles in the penis. There is no known way to increase penis size through manual stimulation. The firmness of an erection can change as a result of blood flow, the health of associated veins, illness, and quality of brain signal response (Gerbild et al., 2018). Penis pumps may help with erection, but there is no evidence to suggest they help to lengthen the penis.

Myth 2: If a person masturbates, they will get hairy palms, and everyone will know.
Fact: Hair typically does not grow on palms unless there is a genetic disorder called *circumscribed hairy dysembryoplasia*, which is a rare genetic disorder (Martel et al., 2020). Simply stated, masturbation does not cause a person to grow hair on their palms, despite what their grandma may have told them.

Myth 3: Masturbation can ruin sexual experiences with another person and masturbation can cause infertility!
Fact: A person who masturbates typically understands how to pleasure themself. As such, folks who masturbate are better able to communicate personal needs and teach their partners how to stimulate them in a pleasurable way. For those who produce semen, masturbation can decrease sperm count; however, it also increases sperm quality by decreasing the amount of dead sperm present in an ejaculation (Kendall@Planned Parenthood, 2011). For those who ovulate, masturbation has no effect on ovulation (Bokaie et al., 2016).

Myth 4: People can become addicted to masturbation and addicted to a vibrator because of overstimulation or may experience nerve damage.
Fact: Although sexual acts such as masturbation can be used as coping mechanisms, they are categorized as maladaptive behaviors (vs. addictions) when they negatively impact a person's life. Nerve endings continually grow and replenish unless severely damaged. Nerves can be overstimulated, but this is temporary. Despite the myth, research supports the medical benefits of vibratory stimulation to treat erectile dysfunction, ejaculatory dysfunction, anorgasmia, and pelvic floor dysfunction (Rullo et al., 2018). People who use vibrators and sexual devices may become accustomed to experiencing pleasure in one way, which can inhibit orgasm from other forms of pleasure. Although the clitoris can become conditioned to respond only to intense stimulation, if one takes a break from such activity, the need for intensity may decrease. In this chapter, the term *sexual devices* is used in place of sex toys to be inclusive of those who need supportive tools to facilitate pleasure and to convey the importance of access to such devices to support pleasure experiences for all people regardless of ability.

Outside of behavioral and bodily myths, there are also sociocultural beliefs regarding relationships and masturbation. For some people in relationships, masturbation can be a difficult topic. In a society where discussions about sexuality are often taboo and occur only in hushed tones, discussing masturbatory practices can be difficult and is often easily avoided. For couples, there can even be a feeling of betrayal akin to cheating.

Myth 5: Masturbation is no longer necessary once a partner is involved in the relationship because a partner is supposed to fulfill all the needs for a person, especially sexually.
Fact: Masturbation is about self-pleasure and agency and is not always about partnered connection. Masturbatory practices vary from person to person and relationship to relationship. It is important for couples to have a conversation about masturbatory needs and desires in order to explore any potential beliefs that may negatively impact the relationship. Mutual masturbation can be so enjoyable and intimate as it requires a higher level of communication about personal needs, physical closeness, and intimacy.

Myth 6: Losing semen causes men to lose energy and fluid.

Fact: Masturbation supports sound sleep, decreases the stress hormone cortisol, and increases the feel-good hormones dopamine and oxytocin. About 3 milliliters of fluid are expelled during an ejaculation, which is primarily composed of sperm, fatty acids, fructose, and proteins (Gerbild et al., 2018). The amount may be less if the body is dehydrated. Simply stated, semen loss does not equate to a loss in energy or fluid.

Approaches to Masturbation

Use of hands and/or sexual devices can alert a person to the more sensitive pleasure areas of their genitals, which could help with expressing desire and achieving pleasure in partnered interactions in the future. It is also important that during this sexual exploration, lubricants are used no matter which body part is being stimulated. During the arousal phase of sexual desire, most vaginal canals start to relax and lubricate. Vaginal lubrication amounts vary depending on the person and their arousal level, age, body health, and even level of hydration. Despite the vagina's ability to lubricate during arousal, this lubrication can wane over time and decrease as a result of friction. With dissipating lubricant of the area, the vaginal and vulvar tissue are at risk for microscopic tears, which can be painful and open sites for bacteria to enter the body. Lubricant helps to decrease the risk of a microtear and helps to enhance manual stimulation. Lubricant is also important as the vagina is the only genital that self-lubricates. The nipple, penis, and anus are not self-lubricating and are also at risk for microtears and chaffing. Therefore, when engaging in sexual stimulation, use a body-safe, water-based lubricant to enhance pleasure, reduce the risk of harm, and prolong gratification. An additional myth is that masturbation must occur one way, when in fact there are various ways to masturbate.

There are many different approaches to masturbation. For this discussion, we will focus on two: solo and mutual. *Solo masturbation*, also known as solo sex, is conducted individually by one person. This can be done manually or with devices and even with another person present. *Mutual masturbation* is conducted with another partner or partners. Each person is stimulating another person or themselves simultaneously. Like solo sex, mutual masturbation can be completed manually or with sexual devices, as well as with or without lubricants. With all these facts about masturbation, the most important fact to remember is that it can be done in many ways that are up to the individual.

Sex Positive Approach to Masturbation

Sex positive can be defined as an attitude toward human sexuality that regards all consensual sexual activities as fundamentally healthy and pleasurable, encouraging sexual pleasure and experimentation (Gabosch, 2014). Thus, a sex positive approach is one which the counselor advocates and accepts their client's individual sexual experience (Kimmes et al., 2015). Before engaging in conversations about masturbation with clients, a sex positive counselor first needs to examine their own beliefs, biases, and assumptions. As a result of this reflective exploration, a sex positive counselor is better able to approach the topic with an openness to meeting the client where they are with the presenting issue. Regardless of where the client is, a sex positive counselor encourages exploration for the sake of pleasure. Every one of us has opinions, thoughts, and feelings and has been socialized around sexuality-based ideas. As helping professionals, dissecting our own notions around self-pleasure is integral for supporting others through their journey. Some people have been and are shamed for masturbatory practices and interests. This often results in a person feeling bad and wrong for natural urges and pleasure. Being sex positive as a counselor does not mean that the counselor is advocating for sexual play, such as masturbation (although we can and will when therapeutically appropriate); instead, a counselor who supports sex positivity follows the lead of the client as they explore personal beliefs and feelings surrounding masturbation and sexual play and is advocating for the client's empowered sexual agency.

A golden rule when it comes to sex positivity is "don't yuck my yum." This rule reminds us as professional counselors that people masturbate in all sorts of ways and that it is not up to us to judge how they enact this behavior. This includes not judging the use of sexually explicit material, sexual devices, positionality, frequency, or length of time—if the client does not find it problematic. To be sex positive means that counselors may have to confront their own sexual attitudes to support clients on their own journey. With all the myths and potentially conflicting feelings surrounding masturbation, a sex positive counselor may approach masturbation with permission (or consent), limited information, and specific suggestions, as we will describe.

Annon's (1976) PLISSIT model offers a sex positive approach to counseling on all topics regarding sexuality, including masturbation. In this chapter, we will apply the stepwise progression of the model, focusing on the first five letters. As a reminder, P stands for permission, whereby permission means to give clients permission to bring up sexual topics. However, we point out that the permission step of the model can also be used to gain consent. Making permission-giving reciprocal supports client autonomy and provides explicit consent for the counselor to ask about and discuss sexuality. Therapeutically modeling a consensual relationship supports how the client can build connections in the future and how they might want others to obtain consent when building relationships. Once permission is given or gained, the counselor can move to the next step, LI, by helping the client access limited information.

Limited information offers the client the opportunity to ask questions and gain specific information regarding masturbation. At an assessment stage, counselors are able to ask questions regarding the specific needs and desires of the client. During this stage, counselors invite clients to ask questions about masturbation and receive information pertinent to masturbation. This way a client is not inundated with unnecessary information and is able to satiate curiosity. At this stage, counselors can dispel commonly held myths, reduce stigma, and help reduce harm from exploratory behaviors. For example, a teenager may not know to use lubricant during masturbation and suffer microtears and abrasions as a result. During the limited information stage, a counselor may inform the client of the benefits of lubrication during masturbation as a means to prevent microtears, prevent abrasions and potential infection, and help to increase pleasure.

The next step in Annon's model is specific suggestions, or SS, whereby more detailed information and follow-up questions are explored. In this step, a counselor can offer a client specific interventions to help with masturbation challenges. These suggestions, which can range anywhere from a discussion of methods to negotiating how to obtain privacy in the home, are intended to support the experience of sexual pleasure for the client who is facing challenges. The suggestion can be as simple as using a lubricant, investing in a device, or giving oneself permission to explore the genitals sexually. When issues regarding masturbation and sexuality overall are not resolved through these steps, the counselor may have to implement the last step, intensive therapy or IT.

Treatment Approach and Practice Issues

With masturbation, there can be quite a few challenges that specific suggestions can help resolve, thus ensuring that a counselor is able to support a client before having to refer out. Following are some examples of issues that may be addressable with some specific suggestions:

1. **A client is masturbating in public spaces or around others, for example, by touching their genitals at the dinner table, during bath time, in class, or at the grocery store.**
   The specific suggestion may be "private things in private spaces." When people are engaging in self-pleasure, they may not notice that this is taking place in the presence of others. This may occur especially with children, people with loss of cognitive function, and some neurodiverse individuals. Taking a sex positive approach means not shaming a person for their behavior, even though it can make others very uncomfortable, and instead educating (and reminding) a client that this behavior is for a private space. This also means that a counselor is going to need to explain, and test that the client understands, what a private space is and what it is not. Do this by explaining that privacy means a space and time when a person is alone. A counselor might also have to talk to parents and caregivers to ensure that there is a time and space where privacy can take place for someone to take time to masturbate. For adults and even couples who masturbate, establishing how to ask for privacy and give privacy might be some of the work counselors must do.
2. **A client is having genital discomfort from masturbation.**
   Genital discomfort is always concerning, and more information is needed to understand the extent. When the issue is chafing or microtears—often indicated by a burning sensation during urination—it is quite possibly a result of too little lubricant used. Although counselors should recommend clients speak to a medical provider to discuss genital comfort, counselors are able to discuss lubricant as a means to prevent chafing or microtears. A water-based, nonflavored lubricant is the preferred suggestion when this issue is present. Additionally, if there is genital discomfort that develops in the form of a fish-smelling discharge, it may be an indication there is a bacterial infection for which a doctor should be consulted. If the anus is being used in masturbatory exploration, it is imperative that any object being used has a flared base to prevent being sucked into the anal cavity and that a lube is being used because the anus is not self-lubricating. Furthermore, patch-testing lubricant on a small patch of skin prior to placing it on genitals can help to ensure the lubricant is safe to use on other parts of the body that tend to be more sensitive.
3. **Client is concerned about cleanliness around masturbation.**
   Masturbation can be messy. There are often fluid excretions from genitals when there is arousal, and when a lubricant is added, it is easy to understand why there can be stains on sheets, socks, laundry. When this is happening, it is important to take a sex positive approach that is shame free. Hygiene regulation is a part of

creating and maintaining body health; this also means cleaning your space and not sharing body fluids in places where others have not consented to be exposed to those fluids. A counselor might suggest to a client to have something ready to clean up after a masturbation experience, which would also include washing hands before and after genital stimulus and washing clothing and sheets regularly.

4. **Sexual desire in the presence of body dysmorphia or a body shift.**
   Body dysmorphia is a disorder where a person obsesses over a perceived body part defect that others may not see or may be minor. This angst can be so strong that it causes social anxiety and avoidance. Those with body dysmorphia tend to avoid looking at their body or touching their body. When this body part is a genital, there can be an aversion to sexual pleasure regarding that organ. Specific suggestions for those who struggle with body dysmorphia include permission giving, whereby a counselor would give permission to explore a variety of masturbatory practices. There are plenty of ways to masturbate, and no one way is correct. By normalizing the varied ways to masturbate, the counselor is helping to encourage the client to find what works best for them so that they can integrate their perceived flaw into their pleasure narrative. This suggestion also holds true for those who have body shifts.

   Clients with *body shifts* such as weight fluctuation, body autonomy changes, permanent changes (e.g., loss of testicle, loss of breast), and temporary changes (e.g., needing a brace or cast, healing from surgery) may benefit from specific suggestions similar to those for body dysmorphia. One non-shame-based specific suggestion is for exploration without expectation. Client exploration would include shifting positions, possibly using helpful tools (i.e., pillows, lubricants, sexual devices, use of voice, and sexual stimulus that can be visual, auditory, or sensory), and taking the time to explore the new body. A sensory exploration without performance expectations may help the client reconnect with their body and rewrite their sexual script or erotic template. Masturbation is not just about genitals. It is a sensory experience that can be done using the mind and all five senses. It is important when helping a client navigate their body to expand the potential of masturbation to include sight, touch, smell, sound, and even taste.

5. **Out-of-the-box situations.**
   There are plenty of situations regarding masturbation that will be out of the box. People who masturbate can be "caught" in the act so to speak, sexual devices exist and can be pleasurable when used appropriately, and there is always the question of when to have a conversation with children regarding masturbation. Having a conversation about sexuality does not encourage the behavior. Instead, it helps to equip a person with knowledge, validate the experience and desire as normal, and teach them how to navigate an experience safely. The values of the individual and family a counselor is working with are important to consider when it comes to specific suggestions.

   For example, consider the case of a mother who rewards her 14-year-old son by putting money on his very own controlled debit card. When a package arrives for him at home, his mother opens it to find that he has ordered a masturbation sleeve, a sexual pleasure device. The mother is unsure if this is age-appropriate behavior. She has a lot of questions, one of which is whether she should take it or let him keep it. In these types of out-of-the-box situations, it is not the counselor's position to determine what is or is not appropriate for this family. By offering specific suggestions, rather than being the decision maker, the counselor can give the family access to various methods to solve a challenging masturbation problem for themselves.

6. **A parent notices their child is masturbating and wonders if something is wrong with the child.**
   Children discover that masturbation and self-play feels good to them as early as 2 to 3 years of age. It is important to understand that at this phase, the genital stimulation is not specifically for orgasm, it is more of a pleasurable exploration—like how children dig in their noses. Although it may be surprising, arousal responses such as erections or vaginal lubrication occur as early as in utero and are completely normal. This may concern parents and caregivers or trigger survivors of sexual assault if they are not familiar with healthy childhood sexual development. Conversing with parents to normalize these reactions and masturbation behavior is key to destigmatizing masturbation and promoting positive sexual experiences.
   No parent wants their child to have horrible sexual experiences. Parents may want to delay or remain unaware of their child's sexual proclivities, but we have not seen any documented evidence to suggest they purposely want their children to have negative and harmful sexual experiences. Educating the parents on what to say and how to teach children about healthy sexual boundaries, such as private places in private spaces, will help in destigmatizing masturbation and promoting positive sexual development.

Masturbation as an Intervention for Sexual Barriers

To help clients overcome a sexual barrier, as counselors we need to be able to normalize masturbation and promote positive benefits of its use. We also need to be able to teach proper technique, along with variations and tools through appropriate sexual education. Last, addressing the pleasure of masturbation along with the safer-sex benefits is equally important. When we take a sex positive approach to these discussions, we are better equipped to serve our clients.

The ethics chapter in this book (see Chapter 3) offers an adapted PLISSIT ethical decision-making matrix to identify whether a counselor is within scope of practice to make specific suggestions. Please consider reviewing this prior to engaging in PLISSIT with clients. If the counselor is within scope, they may suggest the client explore masturbation as a possible treatment for various sexual problems. For example, to treat issues with orgasm, counselors may invite women to explore their bodies and masturbate. The use of this method allows women to become comfortable with touching their own body (Buehler, 2017; McCabe, 2009). You may give more detailed instructions, such as creating a relaxed scene, beginning with a bath while touching herself, and fantasizing about sex. This experience may happen over time, rather than all at once. A client may also be informed of the positive benefits of including lubricants when masturbating to increase comfort and relaxation. The hope is that over time, she will gradually find her orgasm, but it is the permission of touching herself that is critical. Of course, this exploration can be single or partnered.

Additionally, counselors may instruct clients to introduce vibrators as a means of masturbation. Vibrators are often used when manual stimulation is not enough to obtain an orgasm (Buehler, 2017; Ramage, 2007). When introducing sexual devices to couples and individuals, it is important to also explore values around sexual devices and educate them on the ways to use sexual devices. Be mindful that partners may feel threatened by the client's use of a sexual device. It is important to discuss the importance of masturbation as a means to individual fulfillment in addition to the fulfillment received in the relationship. Buehler (2017) recommends that counselors explain the differences in the sexual anatomy structures of a vulva, vagina, and clitoris, for example, and that vibrators be used to enhance the sexual experience, not to replace it.

Counselors may also direct men and folks with penises to masturbate as a means of ejaculatory control. Techniques such as stop/start, the squeeze technique, and mindful masturbation have been beneficial in helping folks with penises address various orgasmic disorders (Buehler, 2017). Using tools such as the vaginal sleeve helps to simulate intercourse where the client can use their imagination to achieve orgasm (Metz & McCarthy, 2004).

Masturbation and Out-of-Control Sexual Behaviors

Although masturbation has been shown to be beneficial in the treatment of sexual dysfunctions, its purpose and function may be misinterpreted, resulting in problems within relationships (Coleman, 2003; Michael et al., 1994). This may include being inaccurately linked to out-of-control sexual behaviors (OCSB), such as excessive masturbation (Braun-Harvey & Vigorito, 2016; Coleman, 2003). With so many conflicting views and the negative stigma surrounding hypersexuality and addiction, there is no consensus on whether sex addiction actually exists (Buehler, 2017; Giordiano & Cashwell, 2018). OCSB was defined by Braun-Harvey and Vigorito (2016) as a sexual health problem where an individual's thoughts and behaviors feel out of control. This definition allows counselors to view the problem through a social and constructivist lens while also maintaining a sex positive approach.

In practice, this may look like a counselor receiving a call from a potential client or their partner stating that they may be addicted to masturbation. Given what we now know about OCSB, it is important for the counselor to respond not from a place of shame or disgust, but rather from a place of warmth, empathy, and understanding (Buehler, 2017). By first exploring the sexual script and the thoughts and practices surrounding masturbation of all parties, the counselor will have a more comprehensive picture of how masturbation is practiced and the thoughts and feelings surrounding masturbation. Second, before making a decision to refer the client out, the counselor must assess the client to rule out any substance problems, relationship problems, level of risk or harm, and the person's ability to function. If there is inherent risk of harm and other confounding factors that prove to be outside of the counselor's scope, the counselor should refer the client to a sex therapist for further assessment or treatment.

Red Flags in Counseling Regarding Children and Masturbation

Earlier in this chapter, we addressed the fact that masturbation begins at birth and continues through life. However, children are not exempt from the stigma surrounding masturbatory practices. When parents find younger children masturbating, they may fear the worst. Although it is not uncommon for children ages 2 to 6 years to masturbate, it may be scary for a parent to find their child masturbating in public. Consider the family of a 4-year-old child who was found masturbating in the local supermarket. When approached by the parent, the child stated that it made them feel good. Because the parent was not versed in normal childhood sexual behavior, given the stigma of masturbation, the parent feared that the child may have been a victim of sexual abuse. In a case like this, it is important for the counselor to teach the parent about healthy childhood sexual behaviors, normalizing masturbation at this age. As well, the counselor will need to rule out abuse, and can do so while maintaining sex positivity using the PLISSIT approach described above. The counselor can teach the parent how to explain private places in private spaces while teaching body safety (Healthychildren.org, 2016). Given the delicate nature of masturbation, it is necessary that we also address other points that may come up in the counselor-client relationship.

Conclusion

Masturbation leads to a higher potentiality of sexual pleasure and overall health. Masturbation is known to improve sexual health, strengthen pelvic floor and anal muscles, decrease pain from menstrual cramping, enhance relaxed mood, reduce stress, treat sexual issues, promote intimacy among couples, and boost the immune system. Masturbation can also be used as an exploratory tool for people to safely find out what and how they enjoy pleasure with their bodies. This is especially important for women, since it is far less likely that women as children were encouraged to explore their bodies or their pleasure. Moreover, agency is also cultivated and strengthened as a result of engaging in masturbation. For example, women are far more likely to communicate how they like to be touched if they have taken the time to identify their erogenous zones before engaging with others. Masturbation can be a healing and pleasurable experience for all, and like with most things, moderation and mindfulness are imperative to the level of pleasure experienced.

Case Example

When clinical cases involve masturbation, it can be hard to decipher how to approach the topic using a sex positive approach and clinical lens. For example, consider doing family therapy with a family where there is a 13-year-old male client who identified as sexually fluid. His parent found out that he was using the handle end of a plunger to stimulate and penetrate his anus during masturbation. The parent was able to discern something was happening with the plunger due to an odor emanating from the plunger handle. Outraged, confused, disgusted, and shocked, the parent confronted the youth with disgust and accused him of debauchery during your family session.

A sex positive clinician would take the necessary steps to develop therapeutic rapport and provide developmentally appropriate psychoeducation on safe masturbatory practices. Engaging in the PLISSIT model, the counselor would first address permission by talking with the family about consent to discuss masturbation. As a counselor, clients might look to you for all the answers, and parents may not want you to provide all those answers. Therefore, to take a sex positive approach, gaining consent and information from the caregivers is pertinent. Once consent is agreed upon, the counselor may ask for permission to discuss medically accurate facts about masturbation.

With limited information, it is important to normalize and describe sexual exploration inclusive of anal play in masturbation practices. It is also important to note that a family household tool is not a private sex device for personal use. While offering limited information, facts are important to deliver. Facts are without bias and are ideal to help discourage sexual shame and increase validation. Sharing facts about the anus and the potential for anal pleasure may further calm the parent's fear about the son's desire to explore his anus. For example, it would be important to inform the family of the pleasurable nerve endings located in the anus, or how masturbation and exploration are normal parts of puberty, or even how during puberty, an influx of hormones and spontaneous arousal are normal. Additionally, safety education would be important in this case scenario. For example, the son would benefit from knowing that using an unlubricated wooden handle for anal stimulation may increase the risk of anal tearing, splinters, and serious injury or infection. Once this limited information is delivered, the next step is specific suggestions.

For this case, discussing specific suggestions can help ease the angst of multiple people in this situation. First and foremost, to reduce harm, techniques regarding sexual exploration of the anus with objects are pertinent. The client would benefit from knowing the importance of lubricant when engaging in anal play, because the anus is not self-lubricating. Moreover, the client would benefit from learning about safe sexual devices, such as a flared base anal plug, to ensure anything inserted into the anus is body safe and not going to cause harm. Furthermore, specific suggestions might also include discussions around privacy and strategies for having effective sexual discussions and communicating needs around sexuality-based topics. Ideally, this will help reduce the number of sexual topic confrontations, promote a healthy place where the family can ask questions, and bring information and explore how to have everyone's needs met within their own family value system. If you must progress to individual therapy, it may be beneficial to refer to a sex therapist or seek out sex therapy supervision.

Reflective questions to consider include:

1. What are your initial reactions to the case scenario?
2. What is the true client presenting issue and how might you best treat it from a sex positive framework?
3. Do you feel consultation is necessary and why? If so, who might you consult with?

Questions You Always Wanted to Ask

Every counselor has had burning questions for which they or their clients have always wanted answers. Following are some of the most common questions we hear, and our answers to those questions. It is our hope that this will help guide the work you do with your clients when addressing their questions and concerns.

1. **What is the difference between water-based and silicone-based lubricants?** Lubricant is amazing! Although people may worry or experience shame for needing lubricant, there is nothing wrong with lubricant. Lubricant adds to pleasure, decreases friction and microtears, and allows for the sexual act to go on as long as the person desires. Water-based lubricants are made with water, and many people find that it is easier to clean up after sexual activity. Water-based lubricants tend to evaporate quicker than silicone-based lubricants. Silicone-based lubricants are made with silicone (silicone varies in quality so be sure to review possible products before suggesting to a client) and have more of an oil-based feel to them. People find that silicone-based lubricants feel silky and last longer but can be harder to clean up. Silicone-based lubricants are often prescribed by the physician to people with vaginas who may be experiencing menopause and may be unable to naturally lubricate (or experience a reduction

in ability to lubricate) on their own during sexual activity. With silicone-based lubricants, it is important to ensure that they are not used on silicone-based devices or near fire and flame.

2. **What do I need to know about safety and care of lubricants?**
The directions on the container should be followed. You want to make sure that lubricants designed for vaginal use and anal use are stored properly and used properly on the body. This is important for external and internal body safety. Unless the lubricant is designed for internal use, it should not be placed inside the vagina or anus. As mentioned in the facts section above, use of body-safe lubricants is imperative to healthy sexual experiences.
3. **What type of sexual devices exist?**
There are a variety of masturbatory devices, including lubricant, vibrators, masturbation sleeves, masturbation gloves, and insertion style devices for vaginas and the anus. These devices also can serve and be specific to genitalia that might not fit the mainstream phenotype depictions or for those who are transgender or intersex. Anything that aids in sexual pleasure is a sexual device. For people who are differently abled, a sexual device can also have added handles, remote controls, or larger buttons for ease of use and accessibility. Sexual devices also range in cost, size, and material, which can make the experience of seeking out a device seem daunting. Rather than recommending a sexual device, a counselor may choose to involve a sex educator as part of treatment to help guide the client to find the best device for their specific needs.
4. **What type of batteries are best to use? What about rechargeable devices?**
It is best to use batteries that stop when the power is turned off. Certain battery brands and rechargeable batteries are not ideal in any battery-operated device as they continue working when the power is removed. It is best to check with the manufacturer of the product or the distributor for specific information for your device. Many devices are rechargeable and are ideal because most charge in the same way as a cell phone.
5. **Where should I go to buy my devices and lubricants? Is it safe to purchase online?**
To ensure the safety of you and/or your partner, it is best to purchase your device from a reputable company with a distributor. If your device is battery operated, we advise that you turn on the device before walking away to ensure that it works, as sexual devices are nonreturnable. You can review various sources online for reputable companies. People who purchase sexual devices online are likely to leave feedback about the product. It may be advantageous to review the feedback about specific sexual devices prior to purchasing them.
6. **What do I need to know about care and safety of sexual devices?**
Any toys or objects used for pleasure should be used according to the instructions on the label. Prior to use and between uses, sexual devices should be cleaned properly. Cleaning recommendations vary by type of material, such as porous or nonporous. Porous materials include latex; rubber; wood; and Ultra-Realistic 3.0, also known as UR3, a thermal plastic material made up of polyvinyl chloride and silicone that is meant to feel like human skin. Nonporous materials include glass, silicone, metal, medical grade stainless steel, and hard plastic. Cleaning sexual devices helps to prevent infection. Bacteria may also break down the material of the sexual device. Motorized devices made

of silicone, steel, or wood may be cleaned with mild antibacterial soap and a toy cleaner. Nonmotorized devices made of silicone or steel may be placed in the dishwasher without using a dish detergent. If you are penetrating an orifice with the toy, you want to be sure to clean it off before inserting the same device into another orifice. This ensures that bacteria are not transferred from one orifice to another. For more information on how to clean a sexual device, Brown University has a comprehensive list of items and cleaning procedures at https://www.brown.edu/campus-life/health/services/promotion/content/whats-best-way-clean-sex-toys.

Resources

For clients or counselors looking to gain more information on masturbation, toys, and devices, we suggest the following resources:

Bockting, W. O., & Coleman, E. (Eds.). (2002). *Masturbation as means of achieving sexual health.* Haworth.

The Center for Sexual Pleasure and Health at https://www.thecsph.org.

Dodson, B. (1996). *Sex for one: The joy of self-loving.* Harmony.

Nagoski, E. (2015). *Come as you are: The surprising new science that will transform your sex life.* Simon & Schuster.

Rowan, E. L. (2000). *The joy of self-pleasuring: Why feel guilty about feeling good?* Prometheus.

Stengers, J., & Van Neck, A. (2001). *Masturbation: The history of a great terror* (K. Hoffmann, Trans.). St. Martin's Press.

We also suggest the following online resources:

Advocates for Youth
Guidelines for educators and best practices regarding teaching sex education to youth at
https://www.advocatesforyouth.org/

Afrosexology
Black sexuality educators catering to 18+ Black people at
https://afrosexology.com/

Ask Goody
A sex educator for the 18+ crowd who teaches how to achieve maximum pleasure at
https://askgoody.com/

Cripping Up Sex With Eva
A sex educator teaching about sexuality and disability for all at
https://crippingupsexwitheva.com/ **Sex Positive Families**
A family-friendly website of resources and webinars at
https://sexpositivefamilies.com/

Dirty Lola
A sexuality educator for ages 18+ that discusses range of safer sex practices at
https://dirtylola.com/

Jane Fleishman
Discusses aging, queerness, and sexual pleasure. Best for professionals, at
https://janefleishman.com/

Joan Price
Discusses navigating sexuality and aging. Best for professionals, at https://joanprice.com/

Marla Renee Stewart of Velvet Lips
A professional sex educator, author, and intimacy coach for adults at https://velvetlipssexed.com/

Nadine Thornhill
A certified sex educator and speaker helping adults teach kids about consent, bodies, and relationships at https://nadinethornhill.com/

The Pleasure Mechanics
A website dedicated to creation and sharing of erotic touch, pleasure, and compassionate relationships for people 18+ at https://thepleasuremechanics.com/

Scarleteen
Inclusive, comprehensive, supportive sexuality and relationships information for teens and emerging adults at https://scarleteen.com/

References

Annon, J. S. (1976). The PLISSIT model: A proposed conceptual scheme for the behavioral treatment of sexual problems. *Journal of Sex Education and Therapy, 2*(1), 1–15.

Bancroft, J., Herbenick, D., & Reynolds, M. (2002). Masturbation as a marker of sexual development: Two studies 50 years apart. In J. Bancroft (Ed.), *Sexual development in childhood* (pp. 134–155). Indiana University Press.

Bokaie, M., Simbar, M., Ardekani, S. M. Y., & Majd, H. A. (2016). Women's beliefs about infertility and sexual behaviors: A qualitative study. *Iranian Journal of Nursing and Midwifery Research, 21*(4), 379–384. https://doi.org/10.4103/1735-9066.185579

Braun-Harvey, D., & Vigorito, M. A. (2016). *Treating out of control sexual behavior: Rethinking sex addiction.* Springer Publishing

Buehler, S. (2017). *What every mental health professional needs to know about sex* (2nd ed.). Springer Publishing.

Carnes, P. (2001). *Out of the shadows: Understanding sexual addiction.* Hazelden.

Coleman, E. (2003). Masturbation as a means of achieving sexual health. *Journal of Psychology & Human Sexuality, 14*(2–3), 5–16. https://doi.org/10.1300/J056v14n02_02

Cornog, M. (2004). The decloseting of masturbation? *The Journal of Sex Research, 14*(3), 310–312. https://www.jstor.org/stable/4423788

Gabosch, A. (2014, December 8). *A sex positive renaissance.* https://allenagabosch.wordpress.com/2014/12/08/a-sex-positive-renaissance/

Gerbild, H., Larsen, C. M., Graugaard, C., & Areskoug Josefsson, K. (2018). Physical activity to improve erectile function: A systematic review of intervention studies. *Sexual Medicine, 6*(2), 75–89. https://doi.org/10.1016/j.esxm.2018.02.001

Giordano, A. L., & Cashwell, C. S. (2018, August). Addicted to sex? *Counseling Today,* pp. 40–45.

Healthychildren.org. (2016). *Sexual behaviors in young children: What's normal, what's not?* American Academy of Pediatrics. https://www.healthychildren.org/English/ages-stages/preschool/Pages/Sexual-Behaviors-Young-Children.aspx

Kaestle, C. E., & Allen, K. R. (2011). The role of masturbation in healthy sexual development: Perceptions of young adults. *Archives of Sex Behavior, 40*, 983–994. https://doi.org/10.1007/s10508-010-9722-0

Kendall@Planned Parenthood. (2011, September 14). *Will masturbation affect sperm count and fertility?* Planned Parenthood. https://www.plannedparenthood.org/learn/teens/ask-experts/will-masturbating-affect-sperm-count-or-fertility

Kimmes, J. G., Mallory, A. B., Cameron, C., & Köse, Ö. (2015). A treatment model for anxiety-related sexual dysfunctions using mindfulness meditation within a sex-positive framework. *Sexual and Relationship Therapy, 30*(2), 286–296. https://doi.org/10.1080/14681994.2015.1013023

Kinsey, A. (1953). *Sexual health in the human female.* Indiana University Press.

Kinsey, A., Pomeroy, W., Martin, C., & Gephard, P. (1953). *Sexual behavior in the human female.* W.B. Saunders.

Lacquer, T. W. (2003). *Solitary sex: A cultural history of masturbation.* Zone Books.

Laumann, E. O., Gagnon, J. H., Michael, R. T., & Michaels, S. (1994). *The social organization of sexuality: Sexual practices in the United States.* University of Chicago Press.

Leiblum, S., & Backmann, G. (1988). *Principles and practice of sex therapy* (2nd ed.). Guilford.

Lindau, S. T., Schumm, L. P., Laumann, E. O, Levinson, W., O'Muircheartaigh, C. A., & Waite, L. J. (2007). A study of sexuality and health among older adults in the United States. *New England Journal of Medicine, 357*(8), 762–774. https://doi.org/10.1056/NEJMoa067423

Martel, J. L., Miao, J. H., & Badri, T. (2020). *Anatomy, hair follicle.* StatPearls [Internet]. Retrieved August 15, 2020, from https://www.ncbi.nlm.nih.gov/books/NBK470321/

Masters, W. H., & Johnson, V. E. (1966). *Human sexual response.* Bantam Books

McCabe, M. P. (2009). Anorgasmia in women. *Journal of Family Psychotherapy, 20*(2–3), 177–197. https://doi.org/10.1080/08975350902970055

McCarthy, B., & McCarthy, E. (2012). *Sexual awareness* (5th ed.). Routledge.

Merriam-Webster. (n.d.). Masturbation. In *Merriam-Webster.com dictionary.* Retrieved May 23, 2022, from https://www.merriam-webster.com/dictionary/masturbation

Metz, M. E., & McCarthy, B. W. (2004). *Coping with erectile dysfunction: How to regain confidence and enjoy great sex.* New Harbinger.

Michael, R., Gagnon, J., Laumann, E., & Kolaa, G. (1994). *Sex in America.* Little Brown & Company.

Penner, J. J., & Penner, C. L. (2005). *Counseling for sexual disorders* (G. R. Collins, Ed.).

Ramage, M. (2007). Female sexual dysfunction. *Psychiatry, 6*(3), 105–110. https://doi.org/10.1016/j.mppsy.2006.12.003

Rullo, J. E., Lorenz, T., Ziegelmann, M. J., Meihofer, L., Herbenick, D., & Faubion, S. S. (2018). Genital vibration for sexual function and enhancement: A review of evidence. *Sexual and Relationship Therapy, 33*(3), 263–274. https://doi.org/10.1080/14681994.2017.1419557

Shelton, J. D. (2010). Masturbation: Breaking the silence. *International Perspectives on Sexual and Reproductive Health, 36*(3), 157–158. https://www.jstor.org/stable/20775353

Soble, A. (2003). Kant and sexual perversion. *The Monist, 86*(1), 55–89. https://ssrn.com/abstract=2324025

They Hurt Me and I Didn't Ask Them To: Healing After Sexual Violence

Jared S. Rose

The sheer litany of unwanted nonconsensual verbal and physical acts that operate against an individual's sexuality is vast and must be organized and understood first as forms of sexual violence. The World Health Organization (WHO) defines *sexual violence* as "any sexual act, attempt to obtain a sexual act, unwanted sexual comments or advances, or acts to traffic, or otherwise directed against a person's sexuality . . . by any person regardless of their relationship to the victim, in any setting" (WHO, 2014, p. 76). Terms such as "sexual assault" and "rape" have legal connotations for both perpetrator and survivor, which in the United States vary from state to state (Rape, Abuse & Incest National Network [RAINN], n.d.), and do not include verbal or otherwise nonphysical acts that can also be harmful. Conceptualizing all such acts as sexual violence brings to focus that anything nonconsensual against one's sexuality is a violent act. Such acts range from noncontact (e.g., harassment, threats, quid pro quo offers) to contact (e.g., touching, groping) to intercourse (i.e., penetration of an orifice by a body part or object). Sexual violence can happen to anyone, regardless of age, sex, gender, sexuality, affectionality, or any other characteristics. It is, however, overwhelmingly committed by cisgender (identity and gender align with biological birth sex), heterosexual (or *cishet*, meaning cisgender and heterosexual) men against women more so than any other demographic dyad (RAINN, 2020a).

Specific, accurate epidemiological rates of sexual violence are difficult to know because reporting it is fraught with challenges. Individuals who have been victimized are often embarrassed, ashamed, scared, under someone else's control, want to avoid dealing with legal matters, or otherwise unempowered to step forward. Sometimes an individual may not know or consider their experience to be that of sexual violence (e.g., flashed by an exhibitionist, marital rape, having been frottaged) or perhaps it has happened to them so often that they do not consider it worthy of reporting. In the United States, we live in a *rape culture* (Harding, 2015), meaning that sexual violence, including rape, is so prevalent it is normalized, which contributes to being overlooked and underreported. Rape culture minimizes perpetrator responsibility by imposing little-to-no criminal punishment, while simultaneously increasing victim blaming (e.g., citing clothing or alcohol intake as reasoning for the sexual violence). Rape culture focuses on telling people what not to do to be harmed and blames them if they are, instead of focusing on telling people not perpetrate it. These issues further contribute to underreporting. Based on information collected from four federal government studies, RAINN (2020b) identified that two thirds of sexual violence acts go unreported. We are therefore left with what statistics are available and acknowledging that sexual violence is even more prevalent that what is known.

In the United States, someone is sexually assaulted (a type of contact sexual violence) every 73 seconds (RAINN, 2020a). One study found that over 80% of women and girls report being subjected to noncontact sexual violence at least once in their lifetime (Stop Street Harassment, 2018). A culmination of studies suggests that the lifetime prevalence rates for contact sexual violence to be around 44% for women and 23% for men (Office for Victims of Crime, 2018). Estimates further indicate that 1 in 3 women and 1 in 4 men will have been victimized by contact and/or intercourse sexual violence at some point in their life (Centers for Disease Control and Prevention [CDC], n.d.-c). These counts do not include trans and gender-expansive individuals, who experience sexual violence at higher rates; 1 in 2 will experience contact and/or intercourse sexual violence in their lifetime (Human Rights Campaign [HRC], 2016; National Sexual Violence Resource Center [NSVRC], 2012). Oftentimes, contact and intercourse sexual violence are viewed and reported differently than specific types of ongoing abuse; thus, such statistics often do not account for additional considerations, such as marital rape or child sexual abuse. According to the CDC (n.d.-a.), child sexual abuse occurs before adulthood for 1 in 4 girls and 1 in 13 boys. Prevalence rates for lesbian, gay, bisexual, trans/gender-expansive, queer/questioning, and other non-cishet identities (LGBTQ+) are difficult to properly estimate because child sexual abuse is consistently reported in context of the victim's biological sex.

Culminating data from a variety of research, the CDC (n.d.-b) estimates nearly 20 people a minute (over 10 million per year) experience intimate partner violence. Intimate partner violence can entail a variety of emotional, physical, and mental abuse, including sexual violence. About 1 in 4 women and 1 in 10 men in cishet couples experiencing intimate partner violence has been subjected to contact and intercourse forms of sexual violence (CDC, n.d.-b). The prevalence of intimate partner violence involving trans and gender-expansive individuals is largely unknown. Because they experience higher levels of threats and coercion to remain silent about abuse (National Coalition Against Domestic Violence [NCADV], 2018), they often feel unempowered to reach out for help and report their abuse. Couples involving lesbian, gay, and bisexual individuals are estimated to experience intimate partner sexual violence at rates ranging from 43% to 61% for women and 25% to 37% for men (NCADV, 2018).

There is also a staggering incidence of sexual violence in the U.S. military. The U.S. Department of Defense (DOD, 2021) estimated over 20,500 service members a year experiencing sexual violence of contact or intercourse, at a rate of 56 per day. Over 30% have been victimized by noncontact sexual violence, and escalation from noncontact to contact and eventual intercourse is a known, likely progression in the military (DOD, 2021; Morral et al., 2015). The prominent sexual violence environment is known by those who serve in the military, yet over 75% do not report because of feeling like either nothing will be done or they will be discharged, as 1 in 3 are discharged within 7 months of reporting (DOD, 2021; Morral et al., 2015).

Of all the discussed forms of sexual violence, human sex trafficking remains one of the most prominent yet is far too often overlooked. The Victims of Trafficking and Violence Protection Act of 2000 and subsequent reauthorizations defined *human trafficking* as labor, services, or commercial sex through the use of force, fraud, or coercion. Human trafficking involves specific actions, means, and purposes relating to the buying and selling of people (National Human Trafficking Resource Center, 2012). After drug trafficking, human trafficking is the second- to third-largest criminal industry in the world, and the fastest growing (Global Financial Integrity, 2017; Office on Drugs and Crime, 2009; UNICEF USA, 2017).

Human sex trafficking, more specifically, involves commercial reproductive and sexual exploitation for things such as forced prostitution, pornography, and entertainment (e.g., live webcam, exotic dancing, massage parlor). Sex trafficking involves the selling and purchasing of children, women, men, and trans and gender-expansive individuals, with children being the number one commodity (Thorn, 2018; UNICEF USA, 2017; WHO, 2012). The average age of minors who are sex trafficked domestically has been estimated between 12 and 14 years old, yet this varies by state and an accurate average age remains unclear (Polaris, 2016). What is known is that young children are sold for sex—highlighting the deplorable nature of selling children into repeated sexually violent situations. Those being victimized can be of any age, race, socioeconomic status, gender, sexuality, or other characteristic. The common variable that puts someone at risk of being trafficked is vulnerability. Intersectional and minority-status identities, such as female, Black, Latinx, LGBTQ+, varied ability level, being in foster care, and having run away or been "thrown away," put some at higher risk (Hannan et al., 2017; Lillie, 2013; Office to Monitor and Combat Trafficking in Persons, 2019; Polaris, n.d., 2018; Thorn, 2018; Xian et al., 2017).

The continuum of sexual violence types and ways it can happen is immeasurable. A sex positive approach recognizes that sex, sexuality, and gender are inherent to all humans and are present regardless of other multicultural- or identity-related dynamics. Everyone, including those who identify as asexual, has a sex, a sexuality, an affectionality, a gender identity, and ways of expressing gender. Maslow (1942, 1962) recognized this with his hierarchy of needs so much so that he included both the act of sex (i.e., physiological base) and sexual intimacy (i.e., love/belonging mid-tier). When critics challenged this view, Maslow (1964) insisted that an individual's progression for well-being and self-actualization has to include sexual considerations because these are universal and essential to the human condition. The very nature of sexual violence violates these personal and intimate areas of one's self identity. As the prevalence rates discussed demonstrate, sexual violence is very common and an issue to the health of not only individuals but also the public. Sexual violence is so prominent that the question is not *if* a counseling professional will work with a survivor, but *when*.

Therapeutic Techniques

Counselors and other mental health professionals use a variety of therapeutic techniques in clinical treatment. As counselors, we gravitate toward the theory and techniques we expect to be best for those we help; however, any number of them can be beneficial in helping those who have experienced sexual violence. An intentional, person-centered approach should be one of the pillars for clinical treatment. An individual with a sexual violence past needs to experience high levels of empathy, positive regard, and empowerment from their therapist. The following sections describe five core elements that can be incorporated into therapy to maximize healing from sexual violence: Assessment, Language, Engagement, Roles, and Trauma Treatment. These form what will be referred to in this chapter as the ***sexual violence ALERT points***. (A quick reference guide to the ALERT is available online https://www.moosecounseling.com/Desk-Reference_SV-ALERT-Points.pdf.)

Assessment

Although initial and periodic assessments are routine in counseling practice, it is important for counselors to also evaluate the frequency and type(s) of sexual violence, and the impact such violence has had on a client. Understanding the full history and sexually violent events a person has lived through is crucial; however, clients may not disclose all information until strong rapport and trust have been established.

In addition to understanding their client's history, counselors need to consider diagnostic impressions from considerations of the sexually violent experience(s). For example, sustained, chronic, or complex trauma during childhood may contribute to the development of extreme personalities (e.g., personality disorders). Sexual violence survivors, like people with different experiences or conditions, may turn to using substances as a coping mechanism (e.g., substance use disorders). Mood disorders, such as depression and anxiety, or even the need to control one's environment (e.g., obsessive-compulsive disorder) are also possible consequences of sexual violence. Mental health professionals need to understand the environmental and developmental nature of clients' pathology. A person-centered approach will conceptualize diagnoses from the perspective that the presenting issue may be the symptom, but the sexual violence is the cause. Time and care should be taken during the assessment phase to tease out what is really going on and causing a client's issues. If sexual violence is the cause, focusing treatment on that rather than on the symptoms may lead to more positive outcomes for the client's well-being.

Language

The language surrounding sexual violence, and the lived experiences of clients, must be understood by the counseling professional and client alike. From a constructivism standpoint, how sexual violence is understood, described, and discussed can have positive impact on treatment. Language used by a client informs their counselor how the client thinks, feels, and behaves as a result of their circumstances. Conversely, a counselor can assist a client not only in recognizing these interactions, but also in gaining empowerment through understanding core language associated with sexually violent acts and events.

Power and Control

Counselors should first consider, and later help their clients understand, how sexual violence at its core is about wielding power and control over another person (WHO, 2014). Those who commit sexual violence use it to threaten, elicit, or force domination, regardless of the sexual or affectional orientations, age, race, or other characteristic of themselves or their victims. Like the bully on the playground who is acting out because of their own issues, sexual offenders are often acting out of their own psychological pain, past trauma, or perceived social expectations and the normalization of sexual violence in the culture. Understanding this does not mean that behavior that violates the rights of others is excused, but it should be considered when providing treatment to those who have committed sexual offenses.

Counselors and other mental health providers should be ever mindful that the individual who was harmed was invalidated in very intimate ways. Everyone wants to be validated for who they are. Having their own sexual power and control ripped away can leave individuals feeling deeply invalidated and with embedded psychological scars; their sexual and gender identity was used by someone else without consent. Mental health providers can work with clients to establish their own sense of power and control over their own varied sex, sexuality, affectionality, and gender identities by affirming, validating, and strengthening the client's sense of self.

Sexual Scripts

As suggested earlier, to provide effective treatment and supportive services for sexual healing—in fact, to be sex positive at all—counseling professionals must first and foremost be person centered. The client and their experiences must be viewed, considered, and understood from their perspective. Clients do not, however, develop their considerations about sex and sexuality in a vacuum; rather, they are taught and operate from sexual scripts. Gagnon and Simon (1973) were the first to propose *sexual script theory*, stating that sexual behaviors are socialized and learned interactions and, in a later work (Simon & Gagnon, 1986), that sexual behaviors are not mere expressions of biology, but rather have social, cultural, and historical connotations.

Rutagumirwa and Bailey (2018) wrote that "fundamental to sexual script theory is the notion that sexual scripts are inherently embedded in a cultural context in which cultural norms provide guidelines for appropriate behaviours, emotions, and cognitions . . . in sexual experiences" (p. 654). Sexual script theory helps to further conceptualize and understand rape culture. When a culture perpetuates contact and intercourse sexual violence, it becomes part of the social consciousness and constructivism, which suggests it is part of the norm (Harding, 2015; Ryan, 2011). Assumption that sexual violence is part of a culture contributes to offenders acting in ways they see as normal and acceptable, regardless of the violation of rights it poses to others.

Those commonly victimized (e.g., females), conversely, become indoctrinated into assuming it will happen, and in fact it often already has, which reinforces this knowledge and belief. The standard script of sexual violence is most assumed from a cishet perspective. Additionally, in some cishet male circumstances, performing a violent sexual act is seen as a rite of passage or as a way to prove one's manhood (Griffin, 2015). Moreover, such cishet views can lead to noncishet victims being unheard or not believed when reporting sexual violence (Javaid, 2017; Levin 2017). The cishet sexual violence script is so prominent that some studies have suggested many females struggle with believing they can say no to unwanted sexual activity or become so inundated by sexually violent experiences that they just stop responding altogether (Frith, 2013; Frith & Kitzinger, 2001; Lonsway & Archambault, 2020).

Following from sexual script theory comes structured, operationalized sexual scripts. Although many have been proposed and used as guides, Schneider and Gould's (1987) structure is clear and appropriate across all sex, sexuality, and gender identities. They proposed a four-part sexual script: (a) Who has sex with whom? (b)

What is the range of sexual acts? (c) When is sex? and (d) Why have sex? Those subjected to sexual violence have had their internalized sexual script destroyed in one to all of these areas at the time of the violent event. Working with survivors, counselors need to be mindful of how the client's personal script is constructed (e.g., past and current environments, upbringing, religious beliefs), maintained, and impacted by the sexual violence. They can work with such clients to help them reconstruct their personal sexual script from a place of not only healing but also empowerment, in how they have survived and how they can reclaim control of their own sexuality.

Many individuals have not reflected on how their views of sex and sexual behavior have developed. Most just accept what they have been taught over time. Counseling professionals can provide clients with a safe space to consider this development, challenge it where harmful, and learn how it is largely socially constructed—a construction that the individual need not just blindly accept as their own truth. Rather, individuals can reconceptualize and, when needed, rebuild their own personal sexual script. For counselors, this may mean helping individuals learn or relearn that they have a fundamental right to their own self and to who, how, when, and in what way(s) they will engage in sexual behaviors. This will inevitably mean a vast continuum of individualized needs and possible sexual acts to be considered.

A common concern often arises around the idea of virginity. A *virgin* is defined by Merriam Webster's (n.d.) dictionary as "a person who has not had sexual intercourse." The definition does not make clear what is meant by "sexual intercourse." Does intercourse mean only vaginal or does it consider oral or anal intercourse? As any clinician who has worked with youth is aware, it is common for adolescents to consider it to be vaginal and will engage in oral and anal intercourses to have sex yet still be "a virgin." If only vaginal, then would not some individuals go through their life with healthy, positive sex lives yet still be virgins (e.g., gay males)? Virginity is also largely concerned with females. The sexual script for this is common, to the point where the dictionary has four delineations for virgin, three of which specifically reference only females (Merriam Webster, n.d.). Virginity is further (a) highly misogynistic as a means to exert power and control over females and (b) embedded as a sexual script through many religions. These issues surrounding virginity lead many to wonder if they are still virgins after intercourse sexual violence.

In cases of vaginal intercourse sexual violence, where the hymen has been stretched, perhaps to the point of tearing, females may feel this is the end of their virginity. Here again counselors have the ability to help clients address their views of virginity and what it means for them in their personalized sexual script. The client's views and emotions surrounding the topic are paramount. They would benefit from learning, through psychoeducation and processing their thoughts and emotions, that their virginity can still be retained if they so choose. For one, intercourse sexual violence is based on lack of consent. This includes the legal considerations whereby most state laws regarding rape include language related to lack of, or inability to provide, consent. Sexual *consent* is defined as freely given, reversible, informed, enthusiastic, and specific (Planned Parenthood, n.d.). Not consenting to activity means one did not agree to give their virginity. This may be a thin technicality to some people. It is nonetheless true.

The sexual script around virginity not only includes consent, but also the thoughts and emotions that go along with giving of one's virginity. A first sexual partner being special, unique, and pivotal is a strongly held element of sexual scripts. This includes trust, conscious decision-making, and emotional investment. Those elements are not present in cases of sexual violence. A client can relearn how those elements associated with giving of their sexual self to another person remain until such time as they do so by choice and with full consent. Helping clients through this rewriting of virginity (or any) sexual script is accomplished as it would be with other faulty or harmful thinking by a client, such as from a person-centered approach with psychoeducation, and cognitive restructuring.

Trauma

The next piece of appropriate language and understanding that should be considered is that of *trauma* versus *Trauma*. Trauma with a big "T" may be used to refer to single events that cause the symptoms of posttraumatic stress disorder (PTSD), whereas trauma with a small "t" may refer to events that are disturbing and had an impact, but are not at a level that results in PTSD or long-lasting symptomatology. For example, compare a Trauma from violent intercourse sexual violence versus the trauma of being fondled. Working with survivors of sexual violence, mental health professionals must recognize that, although these conceptualizations of trauma may be accurate for some, they are not the only possibilities for differences in level of trauma. The impact of events on individuals varies greatly based on their personal history, resiliency, environment, and more. What is traumatic for one person may not be for another. It may also be the case that what is Trauma for one person may be only trauma for another. For example, a single instance of catcalling while walking down the street may cause no trauma response to one person, but it could be extremely Traumatic to another.

Number of events should also be taken into consideration. An individual, for example, who has a life history of child sexual abuse may experience chronic or complex Trauma, whereas certain single episodes within that history may have elicited only an acute trauma for the person. What matters is the full history of the individual and how they conceptualize and have felt about their circumstances. What a counselor may view as Traumatic, a client may see as traumatic or not traumatic at all. Moreover, some clients may be so numb to their experiences, they do not view their circumstances through a trauma lens; rather, they see such events as just part of life. The level of an initial trauma may be high enough to numb the individual to other events like it. To aid in healing from sexual violence, the client's thoughts and feelings regarding their experiences must be considered and addressed in treatment.

Trauma is stored in the brain, mind, and body. The amygdala, two small almond-shaped nuclei clusters, holds emotions associated with visual memory. It is also what activates the fight-flight-or-freeze response. The amygdala, however, does not understand time (Hull, 2002). Therefore, when a traumatic memory, conscious or unconscious, is activated, the amygdala does not know how to differentiate between the threat in the past and what is happening in the present. This contributes to triggers such as flashbacks, intrusive thoughts, and hyper- or hypo-arousal. When presented with new stimuli that remind the brain, mind, and/or body of the past traumatic event, either consciously or unconsciously, the individual's system reacts accordingly. Such a response may result from interpreting the information as the original event happening again or as a new incident, but with a similar expected outcome. In short, the past is the present; our brains, minds, and bodies hold past events, and if these are not processed and integrated in healthy ways, we may react strongly to situations that remind us of what has happened previously. Although the amygdala reacts with emotion, the brain's frontal lobe is responsible for rational decision-making. In normal circumstances, the frontal lobe processes data in a way that allows us to act in cognitive, rational ways. However, in cases of trauma, *amygdala hijacking* (Moyer, 2019) may occur with an intense emotional reaction, such as fear, anxiety, or dread.

Trauma responses are not limited to the brain or mind; the body is also likely to respond. The body responds physically to the fight-flight-or-freeze response. The body also retains the physical pains endured during sexual violence (van der Kolk, 2015). Trauma becomes imbedded in bodily tissue such as muscle (Cutler, n.d.; Substance Abuse and Mental Health Services Administration [SAMHSA], 2014b). Physical bodies react when someone is triggered and, if left untreated and unreleased, the physical self can worsen over time as well. Another effect of sexual violence trauma stored in the body can come in the form of body parts not functioning in expected ways, such as erectile dysfunction, genito-pelvic pain/penetration disorder, or disruptions to orgasm cycle. Counselors may need to assess physical sensations and complaints when working to help heal sexual violence. It may be necessary to differentiate sexual violence trauma impacting sexual health from medical causes of sexual dysfunctions. For example, a female intercourse sexual violence survivor experiences pelvic pain during otherwise healthy and consensual vaginal intercourse. Is the pain associated with physical health or psychological causes from sexually related trauma? Counseling professionals recognize the mind-body connection and must remember when treating clients who have experienced sexual violence trauma or Trauma that healing the psychological can also heal the physical, but they must attend to both.

Victim, Survivor, Thriver

The other core language elements that must be understood and respected by mental health professionals are those of the self-thoughts, conceptualization, and terms used by those who have experienced sexual violence. These most often fall within three areas: victim, survivor, and thriver. "Victim," for example, is what professionals have been taught to say and consider for someone who has been victimized by other people, be it through sexual violence or other types of abuse. It is a term often used while abuse is being sustained, after abuse has stopped, or both. Such a term, however, can be invalidating and degrading if used improperly or callously. Many clients are uncomfortable with or otherwise reject this term, expressing "I don't think of myself as a victim," "I am no one's victim," or "I'm not a victim, he doesn't mean to do it. He loves me." These or similar phrases indicate a client's rejection of the term. Counseling professionals need to meet clients where they are and affirm their views and thoughts about themselves in relation to sexual violence. This does not entail discarding that victimization has occurred (or still is occurring); rather, it means validating the client in how they view themselves and their circumstances.

They may prefer the term "survivor." Survivor is a common term to reflect that while victimization has happened in the past, an individual has survived it and is able to move forward. It is intended to validate and honor an individual while acknowledging the past and addressing the symptoms and circumstances the past has caused. Here too, however, clients may be uncomfortable with such a term being used. "Survivor?! I haven't survived anything! I live with this pain every day" is an example of such a client's expression.

Finally, "thriver" is a term used to reflect the progress an individual has made from surviving past victimization to thriving in life (e.g., significant symptom management, reduction, or elimination; prospering in school or work). Although it is often used for those who have gotten "out of the life" of human sex trafficking, it has merit and benefits for any type of healing from sexual violence. Although many may feel empowered by such terminology, others may find it is uncomfortable or a misfit for them. Exploration of terms and concepts the individual is comfortable using is vitally important not only for their improvement, but for the therapeutic relationship itself. With helpful and supportive treatment, an individual should see changes in their circumstances and thoughts about their past, making language changes over time likely. Clinicians should take note of these changes, validate the client's perceptions when positive, and take note of what it means for the treatment progression.

Engagement

A strong, helpful therapeutic relationship is necessary, but not sufficient, to positive client healing and outcomes. In sexual violence work, a strong engagement in the therapeutic relationship is crucial for both professional and client. Remembering the impact sexual violence has had on an individual's feeling of validation, trust, and needing safety to address their intimate details, mental health professionals must be intentional in developing and maintaining the therapeutic relationship. This may take time and patience to build than it does with other clients. This may mean recognizing that even with the best intentions and perfect treatment toolbox, a counselor may not be the best fit for some clients. A male counselor, for example, may not be the best fit for a female client who has experienced sex trafficking by a male trafficker. A female counselor who reminds the client of their mother that committed child sexual abuse against them while growing up is another example of how the relationship can be hindered. These are but a few examples of transference that may be experienced by a client who has experienced sexual violence. While professional training often indicates that transference must be addressed and handled within the counseling office, for those who have experienced sexual violence, it is appropriate to avoid such opportunities for transference when possible. Transparent dialogue with a client about transference may be appropriate. Referral to another clinician who is less likely to cause transference is also an appropriate option when in the best interest of the client.

Countertransference and other thoughts about a client that impede an appropriate therapeutic relationship must also be monitored. Although countertransference can happen with any client, in situations of sexual violence, it can occur when the counseling professional has experienced such violence themselves. It is not the case that such countertransference will always happen. In fact, thrivers may be particularly equipped to help others with similar experiences. One must be mindful, however, that hearing situations of sexual violence can initiate countertransference, or even a trauma response, in a provider. Negative or ill-informed thoughts can also pose potential for harm. It is harmful to believe the myth that past child sexual assault results in a client's sexual or affectional orientation (James, 2006; Parents, Families, and Friends of Lesbians and Gays, 2022). Assuming a male cannot be raped by a female is also harmful. Thinking a young female's manner of clothing or alcohol consumption is what caused her to be assaulted is another example of harm. Bracketing one's own attitudes, values, and beliefs is vitally important if a professional is going to be of assistance working with those who have a sexual violence history.

Roles

There is strong therapeutic benefit for individuals who have experienced sexual violence in recognizing how certain broadly considered concepts impact their daily thoughts, feelings, and behaviors. Negative messages they receive from society and their support systems are easily internalized in unhelpful, harmful, or even dysfunctional ways. Working with them to better understand and reframe metacognitive concepts and their impact can better serve the individual's overall well-being. This is particularly true for meaning making and therapeutic forgiveness.

Meaning Making

Highly constructivist in approach, meaning making for clients who have experienced sexual violence is important. In 1946, Austrian neurologist Viktor Frankl first introduced the idea of psychotherapeutic meaning making from experiencing traumatic events (Frankl, 1946/2006). Having survived multiple Nazi concentration labor camps where the rest of his family perished, Frankl identified how important it is to find meaning in one's life events. He founded logotherapy (*logos* is the Greek word for meaning and reason) because he recognized that humans cannot avoid pain and suffering but can decide how to make sense of it, incorporate it, and move forward positively from it. Although Frankl did not specifically use the term meaning making, his views on incorporating meaning into psychotherapy grew in psychology to the meaning-making models we now know.

Meaning, in the therapeutic sense, is how "people attribute significance to life events in relation to their broader understanding of their lives . . . the interaction of the meanings people give to traumatic events and the meanings they have accrued or built in their lives" (Steger & Park, 2012, p. 172). Various meaning-making models have been proposed for issues such as grief, educational experiences, spirituality, child sexual abuse, and trauma (Ignelzi, 2002; Marotta-Walters, 2015; Neimeyer & Thompson, 2014; Park, 2013; Park & Al, 2006; Wright et al., 2007). Meaning-making models include both (a) the situational, or the event(s) that happened; and (b) the global, which is the individual's orientation to the world, place within it, attitudes, values, and beliefs. Steger and Park (2012) noted that humans naturally seek meaning coherence, and when events are incongruent with this need, it causes distress. The process is an adaptive one, whereby individuals typically adapt in one way or another to their experiences and find meaning in those experiences and their place within the global perspective. Counseling professionals can assist victims of sexual violence in finding and reconciling the meaning they associate with their lived experiences. Individuals can reestablish well-being by finding meaning in what happened and incorporating it into their sense of the world. Meaning-making models are widely available and help facilitate this from a technique standpoint. When working with sexually violated clients, counselors should use a model that has been designed for that specific type of sexual violence (e.g., child sexual abuse); however, it may also be appropriate to adapt a general sexual violence or trauma meaning-making model.

Forgiveness

Pioneers of forgiveness therapy, Enright and Fitzgibbons (2000), define therapeutic *forgiveness* as a person's willingness to

> abandon resentment and related responses (to which they have a right), and endeavor to respond to the wrongdoer based on the moral principle of beneficence, which may include compassion, unconditional worth, generosity, and moral love (to which the wrongdoer, by nature of the hurtful act or acts, has no right). (p. 29)

Forgiveness does not mean justifying, rationalizing, or excusing sexual violence. Rather, it accepts that the event(s) happened and that holding on to negative thoughts and emotions about the perpetrator can impede the survivor's healing.

Social constructs, such as "forgive and forget," and religious views, such as "turn the other cheek" or "God forgave you, so you should forgive them," can make forgiveness in therapy a challenging topic to bring up and address. Clients may feel they are required by either social pressure or religious tenets to forgive their abuser (Geiger, 2019; Tener & Eisikovits, 2015). Such perceived or actual demands on a client can increase negative, harmful mood and symptomatology.

Yet, there is a long history of forgiveness as part of impactful and successful work in cases of sexual violence (Freedman & Enright, 2017; Morton et al., 2018). As mental health professionals already know, continuing to hold on to anger or resentment toward someone who has inflicted pain causes and maintains problems such as anxiety, depression, and interpersonal relationship struggles that can block client progress. Addressing the role of forgiveness relating to sexually violent perpetrators should be, at a minimum, brought up and discussed with clients. A simple search for psychotherapy resources will deliver dozens of books, workbooks, and handouts for how to facilitate forgiveness in therapy.

Forgiving the offender should not, however, be demanded or required of a client as part of treatment. Researchers, providers, and survivors alike have indicated that successful treatment is possible without forgiving the perpetrator, and insisting on forgiveness can break the therapeutic relationship and even cause harm to the client (Altmaier, 2019; Maraschak, 2013; Rapske et al., 2010; Walton, 2005). Intrapersonal forgiveness, however, whereby clients learn how to forgive themselves for what happened to them, is paramount (Enright & Fitzgibbons, 2000; Phillips, 2017). Clients cannot move forward in healing from sexual violence without addressing the negative cognitions and emotions of blaming themselves. Despite any victim blaming by those around them or by the culture as a whole, they are not at fault for what happened to them. Counseling professionals should help them recognize and believe this for themselves.

Trauma Treatment

As discussed previously, trauma or Trauma is a likely effect of sexual violence. The treatment foundations discussed in the last section are appropriate regardless of whether trauma is present with a client. Given the prevalence of trauma generally in today's world, counselors should investigate and gain further continuing education on providing services through a trauma-informed care lens. Helping professionals need to be ever mindful of the experiences clients have had that contribute to their thoughts, feelings, and behaviors. Trauma can have a pervasive, significant impact across the life span and directly influence a client's functioning. SAMHSA (2014a) defines *trauma-informed care* as follows:

> A program, organization, or system that is trauma-informed realizes the widespread impact of trauma and understands potential paths for recovery; recognizes the signs and symptoms of trauma in clients, families, staff, and others involved with the system; and responds by fully integrating knowledge about trauma into policies, procedures, and practices, and seeks to actively resist re-traumatization. (p. 9)

SAMHSA (2014a) goes on to elaborate on six guiding principles for trauma-informed care: safety; trustworthiness and transparency; peer support; collaboration and mutuality; empowerment, voice, and choice; and cultural, historical, and gender issues. Even if sexual violence has not risen to the level of trauma for a client, these principles are still beneficial in following when providing care to any survivor. When the sexual violence has had traumatic impact, trauma-specific treatment is essential. Supportive therapies such as art therapy, animal-assisted therapy, and group work are all beneficial and helpful in sexual violence work, but they do not facilitate true trauma recovery. Such treatment will address the symptoms of sexual violence and may even be necessary to help stabilize a client. But they do not treat the cause—the trauma itself.

Triphasic Model

Since created by Herman (1992), the triphasic model of trauma recovery has been adapted and enhanced; yet, it continues to consist of three basic phases. The first phase involves stabilization of the client by helping them reestablish a sense of safety and trust. In this phase, a counselor helps to ensure the client feels safe in the therapeutic relationship, has skills to use when work becomes painful, and is secure enough for difficult treatment work. The actual trauma work, using a trauma-specific treatment, begins in the second phase with a process of desensitizing, reprocessing, and resolving the trauma. In the third phase, the client works on their ability to refocus and reconnect with themselves and their future.

Regardless of the selected approach to treat trauma resulting from sexual violence, this three-phase process is strongly recommended. Far too often mental health professionals want to immediately address the trauma itself, when survivors really need to establish safety, security, and the resources to use (phase one) before addressing the trauma directly (phase two). Neglecting to ensure stability for clients first can lead not only to poor outcomes but to harm (e.g., retraumatizing). Sometimes, a future focus (phase three) is overlooked, which can impede clients' ability to move forward positively, possibly with meaning making and forgiveness. Although there are numerous trauma-specific treatments available for use in counseling, some are intentionally triphasic in their approach, evidence-based, and frequently used in relation to sexual violence.

Trauma-Focused Cognitive Behavioral Therapy

Trauma-focused cognitive behavioral therapy (TF-CBT) is a trauma-focused treatment that counselors commonly turn to when working with trauma recovery. This is likely because, as the name suggests, it is based on CBT, with which most mental health professionals are already familiar. TF-CBT overlays CBT with specific trauma-sensitive elements. It is evidenced-based for children and adolescents (ages 3–21 years) and includes parents/caregivers in treatment. It is grounded not only in CBT, but also in family systems theory (The National Child Traumatic Stress Network [NCTSN], 2012b). It is component-based and ensures readiness by clients prior to addressing the traumatic experience(s) directly. This is important not only for any trauma treatment but for TF-CBT specifically, because TF-CBT introduces elements of exposure therapy by gradually exposing clients, when ready, to triggering reminders (Cohen & Mannarino, 2008).

TF-CBT is facilitated through 10 progressive stages, each with techniques, activities, and assignments. The components of treatment are referred to by the acronym PRACTICE, in which letters represent the following:

- Psychoeducation about child trauma and trauma reminders
- Parenting component including parenting skills
- Relaxation skills individualized to youth and parent

- Affective modulation skills tailored to youth, family, and culture
- Cognitive coping: connecting thoughts, feelings, and behaviors
- Trauma narrative and processing
- In vivo mastery of trauma reminders
- Conjoint youth-parent sessions
- Enhancing safety and future developmental trajectory
- Traumatic grief components (NCTSN, 2012a, p. 2)

TF-CBT research has reported symptom improvement for depression, anxiety, externalizing behavior issues, shame, interpersonal relationships, and social functioning (Cohen & Mannarino, 2008). Because it is effective with children as young as 3 years of age and is widely used for children of all ages, TF-CBT is viewed as the gold standard for treating children with PTSD (Cisler et al., 2016). Yet reviews of the literature have suggested effect sizes for treatment outcomes vary greatly, depending on the type of trauma, clinician, conditions of administration, and type of symptom reduction (Ascienzo et al., 2020; Cary & McMillen, 2012). Training in TF-CBT is required to facilitate it properly and to maximize positive outcomes for clients. Information on certification is available from the TF-CBT National Therapist Certification Program (see https://www.tfcbt.org).

Eye Movement Desensitization and Reprocessing

Eye movement desensitization and reprocessing (EMDR) is a memory-based therapy that is evidence-based not only for trauma, but also for a wide range of mental and emotional disorders (EMDR International Association [EMDRIA], n.d.). Incorporating novel techniques and protocols, it is an integrative psychotherapeutic approach that focuses on level of disturbances about events and the negative cognitions associated with those events. For trauma treatment, it is less concerned with what type or level of trauma has occurred and more with the "long-lasting negative effect upon self and psyche" (Shapiro, 2001, p. 4). The theoretical basis for EMDR is adaptive information processing (AIP; Shapiro, 2001, 2017). Freud (1955) and Pavlov (1927) both contended that information is processed by individuals in ways that find balance within self and the world. The AIP model accepts this and further posits that when the brain cannot make sense of events and experiences (such as in traumatic situations), it places disturbing sensory input about that event, or multiple events of similar impact to the psyche, aside in a stored neural network, which can then become disengaged from more productive adaptive processing. EMDR's focus is to bring the maladaptive neural network into alignment with the rational brain.

EMDR can be used in a variety of ways depending on the problem or traumatic event(s). The standard protocol follows a triphasic model by building in specific phases within each step. The eight phases of the standard protocol are history, preparation, assessment, desensitization, installation, body scan, closure, and reevaluation (Shapiro, 2001, 2017). These protocols may vary depending on the issue being treated, number of events experienced, and time elapsed since the event(s) happened, but the triphasic model is always used. One of the core elements that makes EMDR different from other treatments is the use of bilateral stimulation (BLS). BLS consists of rhythmic stimulation on alternating sides of the body, causing the brain to give focus to both sides of the body. This can be facilitated through auditory (e.g., alternating sounds in headphones), tactile (e.g., tapping on knees, gentle buzzing through hand-held paddles), or visual (e.g., eye movement) methods. When EMDR was first developed, only eye movements were used, hence the therapy's name. Since that time, however, EMDR has been evidence-based with a variety of other BLS techniques (Shapiro, 2017). The developer, psychologist Francine Shapiro, has demonstrated how BLS activates the information processing system to allow reprocessing and eventual resolution to take place (Shapiro, 2001, 2017). More than that, BLS strengthens positive cognitions, grounding effects, and calming effects when implemented in slower, shorter intervals.

EMDR is endorsed as a treatment of choice for trauma by many national and international organizations, including the National Institute for Health and Care Excellence (2018), the U.S. Department of Veterans Affairs (2017), SAMHSA (2014b), and the WHO (2013). EMDRIA recognizes two levels of training: EMDR trained and EMDR certified therapist. Basic training consists of core foundations of EMDR with practice during training. For certification, advanced training, in-field practice, and supervision are required. Ongoing continuing EMDR-specific education is required to maintain certification. Information on EMDR training and certification is available from EMDRIA (see https://www.emdria.org).

Case Example Using the Sexual Violence ALERT Points

To illustrate the finer features of incorporating sexual violence ALERT points into psychotherapy, consider the case of Brianna (Bri). Bri is a 19-year-old Black female who has been referred to Alyssa (Aly), a 26-year-old licensed clinical mental health counselor. Bri was brought into treatment by her foster mother, Chris, who is the third foster mother Bri has had since entering into the foster system at the age of 12. Chris says she does not know much about Bri's family of origin, only that she was placed in foster care because of her biological parents abusing her, because Bri has always refused to discuss the details. Chris reports Bri is highly emotional and temperamental, one minute getting along well with Chris, her husband, and the other children in the home and the next minute being distant, cold, and sometimes violent toward them. Chris also reports Bri has been acting out at school. She notes that Bri's teachers say Bri is hostile and angry at other students, breaks rules regularly, is attention seeking in class, and is generally disruptive to the learning environment. Chris indicates that Bri tends to have close friends and then suddenly wants nothing to do with those friends, claiming that they have wronged her in some fashion. Bri has had, Chris goes on to indicate, three past psychotherapists, but as soon as they do anything Bri doesn't like, Bri refuses to work with them further and demands a new counselor. Chris indicates these interpersonal relationship patterns are consistent with Bri and, in fact, is why she was removed from the other two foster homes. Chris notes that Bri's first foster mother, Diane, once told Chris that Bri is "an angry, manipulative girl who tried to seduce my husband, and she lies about everything." Bri was only in that home for 1 year between the ages of 12 and 13 before being moved to her next foster family.

Aly, having experience working with adolescents, recognizes that Bri is at particularly high risk of past sexual violence because she is female, adolescent, and in the foster care system. Aly begins clinical treatment of Bri with this in mind. Using the sexual violence ALERT points, Aly proceeds as follows:

Assessment: Aly takes additional time for the assessment, beyond what is standard for intake procedures. Aly focuses on Bri's sense of safety and comfort. She inquires about interpersonal relationships and recognizes patterns of behavior as indications of possible borderline personality disorder. She recognizes that extreme personalities are developmental in nature, and likely coming from self-protection and defense mechanisms. Aly assesses for self-harm and suicidality, both of which Bri endorses as having struggled with previously. Although the assessment takes more sessions than usual, taking this time allows Bri to feel more comfortable opening up about her past. She reports to Aly that her biological parents lost custody of her because they had both sexually abused her for as long as she can remember, and she is pretty sure it was happening before she was able to retain memory. Bri later goes on to report that her first foster father was drunk with his friend one night, and they both violently raped her. She reported the incident to Diane, but instead of helping her, Diane kicked her out of the house, saying that she made the whole thing up.

Language: Aly takes time with Bri to provide psychoeducation about power and control, explores how Bri describes her personal sexual scripts, and does some general exploration of how Bri views her level of trauma. Aly also takes note of Bri's use of the word "victim" when describing herself. Aly incorporates all of this into her usual method of treatment. She first plants the seeds of these issues and then discusses them fully when Bri is able, but she also notes for herself to spend more time on them later in Bri's treatment when dealing with the trauma more specifically.

Engagement: Aly focuses more than usual on building a strong therapeutic relationship with Bri. For example, she lets Bri exert more control of the session than she might otherwise allow a client, while maintaining and modeling healthy boundaries for Bri and keeping the treatment focus intentional. Aly also opens the conversation regarding the cultural differences between them, allowing Bri the space to consider and discuss her thoughts and any concerns she may have. Aly reflects regularly on the engagement between them and adapts where she feels it is clinically appropriate. She helps Bri understand, given her past exposure to such sexual violence, that trauma treatment is appropriate, but she wants to make sure Bri is clinically ready for that when the time comes. Bri, who was previously quite specific in noting she didn't want to talk about the past abuse, softens her stance when she realizes she will not be forced and has power to be part of the decision-making. Being told she had to talk about it when she wasn't ready to do so, Bri reports, is part of why she left each of her past counselors.

Roles: In addition to her established tools for helping clients learn, practice, and implement new coping strategies, Aly introduces the notions of meaning and forgiveness to Bri. She provides psychoeducation on these concepts but does not push them, instead allowing Bri to conceptualize and consider for herself. Aly, having worked with emotional and physically abused youth previously, already has worksheets for both meaning making and forgiveness and is able to use them with Bri. Here again, Aly spends time on these issues but knows she will need to address them again and more specifically with Bri during trauma treatment, and she makes sure Bri knows this as well.

Trauma treatment: Aly has past training on working with abuse survivors but has not previously worked with someone with Bri's level of past sexual violence. Recognizing she needs to increase her competency in this area, she obtains training in TF-CBT. She does so while still laying groundwork with Bri so that she can keep Bri's treatment moving forward. Aly also identifies a specialist in sexual violence trauma in her area and makes contact for potential consultation. After preparing for the structured intervention and ensuring that Bri reports feeling safe and with resources to fall back on when dealing with the past becomes painful, Aly implements TF-CBT with Bri. Because of their foundational work addressing the sexual violence ALERT points, Aly views Bri's prognosis as good. Aly is confident that Bri will be able to move forward in healthier, more positive ways after treatment.

Conclusion

A sex positive approach recognizes that all sexual activity must include full and proper consent by all those involved in the sexual activities. In sexually violent events, individuals have had their consent ripped from them and are deeply, intimately violated. Sexual violence is so prominent in today's culture, it is assumed and expected. Sex positive professional counselors take on the responsibility not only of advocacy and social justice against this rape culture, but also of supporting and providing treatment to those who have survived such violent acts. Such counselors can assistant these individuals by integrating key evidence-based methods into their existing treatment modalities. The sexual violence ALERT points encapsulate such foundations in a sex positive context for psychotherapists as they work aiding sexual violence survivor healing.

References

Altmaier, E. M. (2019). *Promoting positive processes after trauma*. Elsevier. https://doi.org/10.1016/C2016-0-02551-2

Ascienzo, S., Sprang, G., & Eslinger, J. (2020). Disseminating TF-CBT: A mixed methods investigation of clinician perspectives and the impact of training format and formalized problem-solving approaches on implementation outcomes. *Journal of Evaluation in Clinical Practice, 26*(1), 1–12. https://doi.org/10.1111/jep.13351

Cary, C. E., & McMillen, J. C. (2012). The data behind the dissemination: A systematic review of trauma-focused cognitive behavioral therapy for use with children and youth. *Children and Youth Services Review, 34*(4), 748–757. https://doi.org/10.1016/j.childyouth. 2012.01.003

Centers for Disease Control and Prevention. (n.d.-a). *Child abuse and neglect prevention*. https://www.cdc.gov/violenceprevention/childabuseandneglect/index.html

Centers for Disease Control and Prevention. (n.d.-b). *Intimate partner violence*. https://www.cdc.gov/ViolencePrevention/intimatepartnerviolence/index.html

Centers for Disease Control and Prevention. (n.d.-c). *Preventing sexual violence*. https://www.cdc.gov/violenceprevention/sexualviolence/fastfact.html

Cisler, J. M., Sigel, B. A., Kramer, T. L., Smitherman, S., Vanderzee, K., Pemberton, J., & Kilts, C. D. (2016). Modes of large-scale brain network organization during threat processing and posttraumatic stress disorder symptom reduction during TF-CBT among adolescent girls. *PLOS ONE, 11*(8), Article e0159620. https://doi.org/10.1371/journal.pone.0159620

Cohen, J. A., & Mannarino, A. P. (2008). Trauma-focused cognitive behavioural therapy for children and parents. *Child and Adolescent Mental Health, 13*(4), 158–162. https://doi.org/10.1111/j.1475-3588.2008.00502.x

Cutler, N. (n.d.). *Learning how to unlock tissue memory.* Integrated Physical Therapy & Wellness. https://www.iptmiami.com/news/Learning_How_to_Unlock_Tissue_Memory

EMDR International Association. (n.d.). *About EMDR therapy.* https://www.emdria.org/about-emdr-therapy

Enright, R. D., & Fitzgibbons, R. P. (2000). *Helping clients forgive: An empirical guide for resolving anger and restoring hope.* American Psychological Association. https://doi.org/10.1037/10381-000

Frankl, V. E. (2006). *Man's search for meaning.* Beacon Press. (Original work published 1946).

Freedman, S., & Enright, R. D. (2017). The use of forgiveness therapy with female survivors of abuse. *Journal of Women's Health Care, 6*(3), 1–6. https://doi.org/10.4172/2167-0420.1000369

Freud, S. (1955). An infantile neurosis and other works. In J. Strachey (Ed. & Trans.), *The standard edition of the complete psychological works of Sigmund Freud (Vol. 17, 191–1919).* The Hogarth Press.

Frith, H. (2013). Sexual scripts, sexual refusals and rape. In M. Horvath & J. Brown (Eds.), *Rape: Challenging contemporary thinking* (pp. 99–124). Routledge.

Frith, H., & Kitzinger, C. (2001). Reformulating sexual script theory: Developing a discursive psychology of sexual negotiation. *Theory & Psychology, 11*(2), 209–232. https://doi.org/10.1177/0959354301112004

Gagnon, J. H., & Simon, W. (1973). *Sexual conduct: The social sources of human sexuality* (2nd ed.). Aldine. https://doi.org/10.4324/9781315129242

Geiger, T. J., II. (2019). Forgiveness is more than platitudes: Evangelical women, sexual violence, and casuistic tightening. *Rhetoric Society Quarterly, 49*(2), 163–184. https://doi.org/ 10.1111/j.1475-3588.2008.00502.x

Global Financial Integrity. (2017). *Transnational crime and the developing world.* https://www.gfintegrity.org/wp-content/uploads/2017/03/Transnational_Crime-final.pdf

Griffin, S. (2015). *Rape: The politics of consciousness.* Open Road Media.

Hannan, M., Martin, K., Caceres, K., & Aledort, N. (2017). Children at risk: Foster care and human trafficking. In M. Chisolm-Straker & H. Stoklosa (Eds.), *Human trafficking is a public health issue* (pp. 105–121). Springer. https://doi.org/10.1007/978-3-319-47824-1_7

Harding, K. (2015). *Asking for it: The alarming rise of rape culture and what we can do about it.* Da Capo Press.

Herman, J. L. (1992). *Trauma and recovery.* Basic Books.

Hull, A. M. (2002). Neuroimaging findings in post-traumatic stress disorder: Systematic review. *British Journal of Psychiatry, 181*(2), 102–110. https://doi.org/10.1192/bjp.181.2.102

Human Rights Campaign. (2016). *Sexual assault and the LGBTQ community.* https://www.hrc.org/resources/sexual-assault-and-the-lgbt-community

Ignelzi, M. (2002). Meaning-making in the learning and teaching process. *New Directions for Teaching and Learning, 2000*(82), 5–14. https://doi.org/10.1002/tl.8201

James, W. H. (2006). Two hypotheses on the causes of male homosexuality and pedophilia. *Journal of Biosocial Science, 38*(6), 745–761. https://doi.org/10.1017/S0021932005027173

Javaid, A. (2017). Giving a voice to the voiceless: Police responses to male rape. *Policing: A Journal of Policy and Practice, 11*(2), 146–156. https://doi.org/10.1093/police/paw035

Levin, E. C. (2017). Sexual scripts and criminal statutes: Gender restrictions, spousal allowances, and victim accountability after rape law reform. *Violence Against Women, 24*(3), 322–349. https://doi.org/10.1177/1077801216687876

Lillie, M. R. (2013, October 10). *An unholy alliance: The connection between foster care and human trafficking* [Paper presentation]. Fifth Annual Interdisciplinary Conference on Human Trafficking 2013, Lincoln, NE, United States. https://digitalcommons.unl.edu/humtrafcon5/4/

Lonsway, K. A., & Archambault, J. (2020). *Victim impact: How victims are affected by sexual assault and how law enforcement can respond.* End Violence Against Women International. https://evawintl.org/wp-content/uploads/Module-2_Victim-Impact.pdf

Marotta-Walters, S. A. (2015). Spiritual meaning making following clergy-perpetrated sexual abuse. *Traumatology, 21*(2), 64–70. https://doi.org/10.1037/trm0000022

Marschak, M. (2013, January 11). *Do I need to forgive to heal from sexual abuse?* Colorado Coalition Against Sexual Assault. https://www.ccasa.org/do-i-need-to-forgive-to-heal-from-sexual-abuse/

Maslow, A. H. (1942). A theory of human motivation. *Psychological Review, 50*(4), 370–396. https://doi.org/10.1037/h0054346

Maslow, A. H. (1962). *Toward a psychology of being.* John Wiley & Sons.

Maslow, A. H. (1964). A theory of human motivation. In H. J. Leavitt & L. R. Pondy (Eds.), *Readings in managerial psychology* (pp. 6–24). University of Chicago Press.

Merriam-Webster. (n.d.). Virgin. In *Merriam-Webster.com dictionary.* Retrieved June 18, 2020, from https://www.merriam-webster.com/dictionary/virgin

Morral, A. R., Gore, K. L., & Schell, T. L. (Eds.). (2015). *Sexual assault and sexual harassment in the U.S. military: Volume 2. Estimates for Department of Defense service members from the 2014 RAND Military Workplace Study.* RAND Corporation National Defense Research Institute. https://apps.dtic.mil/sti/pdfs/ADA616051.pdf

Morton, K. R., Tanzini, L., & Lee, J. W. (2018). Adult life satisfaction and the role of forgiveness after childhood sexual abuse: Evidence from a Seventh-Day Adventist cohort. *Journal for the Scientific Study of Religion, 58*(1), 138–152. https://doi.org/10.1111/jssr.12575

Moyer, N. (2019, April 22). *Amygdala hijack: When emotion takes over.* https://www.healthline.com/health/stress/amygdala-hijack

National Child Traumatic Stress Network. (2012a). *TF-CBT: Trauma-focused cognitive behavioral therapy.* https://www.nctsn.org/sites/default/files/interventions/tfcbt_fact_sheet.pdf

National Child Traumatic Stress Network. (2012b). *Trauma-focused cognitive behavioral therapy.* https://www.nctsn.org/interventions/trauma-focused-cognitive-behavioral-therapy

National Coalition Against Domestic Violence. (2018, June 6). *Domestic violence and the LGBTQ community*. https://ncadv.org/blog/posts/domestic-violence-and-the-lgbtq-community

National Human Trafficking Resource Center. (2012). *The action means purpose model*. Human Trafficking Hotline. https://humantraffickinghotline.org/sites/default/files/AMP%20Model.pdf

National Institute for Health and Care Excellence. (2018). *Post-traumatic stress disorder: NICE guideline* (NG116). https://www.nice.org.uk/guidance/ng116

National Sexual Violence Resource Center. (2012). *Sexual violence & individuals who identify as LGBTQ*. https://www.nsvrc.org/sites/default/files/Publications_NSVRC_Research-Brief_Sexual-Violence-LGBTQ.pdf

Neimeyer, R. A., & Thompson, B. E. (2014). Meaning making and the art of grief therapy. In B. E. Thompson & R. A. Neimeyer (Eds.), *Grief and the expressive arts: Practices for creating meaning* (pp. 3–13). Routledge/Taylor & Francis.

Office for Victims of Crime. (2018). *Sexual violence* [Fact sheet]. U.S. Department of Justice. https://ovc.ojp.gov/sites/g/files/xyckuh226/files/ncvrw2018/info_flyers/fact_sheets/2018NCVRW_SexualViolence_508_QC.pdf

Office on Drugs and Crime. (2009). *Global report on trafficking in persons*. United Nations. https://www.unodc.org/unodc/en/human-trafficking/global-report-on-trafficking-in-persons.html

Office to Monitor and Combat Trafficking in Persons. (2019). *2019 trafficking in persons report*. U.S. Department of State. https://www.state.gov/reports/2019-trafficking-in-persons-report/

Parents, Families, and Friends of Lesbians and Gays. (2022, April 19). *The problem with the belief that child sexual abuse causes homosexuality/bisexuality*. https://www.pflagatl.org/the-problem-with-the-belief-that-child-sexual-abuse-causes-homosexuality-bisexuality/

Park, C. L. (2013). The meaning making model: A framework for understanding meaning, spirituality, and stress-related growth in health psychology. *The European Health Psychologist, 15*(2), 40–47. https://ehps.net/ehp/index.php/contents/article/view/ehp.v15.i2.p40

Park, C. L., & Al, A. L. (2006). Meaning making and growth: New directions for research on survivors of trauma. *Journal of Loss and Trauma, 11*(5), 389–407. https://doi.org/10.1080/15325020600685295

Pavlov, I. P. (1927). *Conditioned reflexes: An investigation of the physiological activity of the cerebral cortex*. Oxford University Press.

Phillips, L. (2017, April). The selfish act of forgiving. *Counseling Today*. https://ct.counseling.org/2017/04/self%E2%80%8Aish-act-forgiving/

Planned Parenthood. (n.d.). *Sexual consent*. https://www.plannedparenthood.org/learn/relationships/sexual-consent

Polaris. (n.d.). *Recognizing human trafficking*. https://polarisproject.org/recognizing-human-trafficking/

Polaris. (2016, January 5). *The average age of entry myth*. https://polarisproject.org/blog/2016/01/the-average-age-of-entry-myth/

Polaris. (2018, August 15). *Individuals with disabilities may face increased risk of human trafficking*. https://polarisproject.org/blog/2018/08/individuals-with-disabilities-may-face-increased-risk-of-human-trafficking/

Rape, Abuse & Incest National Network. (n.d.). *Public policy & action.* https://www.rainn.org/ public-policy-action

Rape, Abuse & Incest National Network. (2020a). *About sexual assault.* https://www.rainn.org/about-sexual-assault

Rape, Abuse & Incest National Network. (2020b). *The criminal justice system: Statistics.* https://www.rainn.org/statistics/criminal-justice-system

Rapske, D. L., Boon, S. D., Alibhai, A. M., & Kheong, M. (2010). Not forgiven, not forgotten: An investigation of unforgiven interpersonal offenses. *Journal of Social and Clinical Psychology, 29*(10), 1100–1130. https://doi.org/10.1521/jscp.2010.29.10.1100

Rutagmumirwa, S. K., & Bailey, A. (2018). "The heart desires but the body refuses": Sexual scripts, older men's perceptions of sexuality, and implications for their mental and sexual health. *Sex Roles, 78*(9), 653–668. https://doi.org/10.1007/s11199-017-0822-3

Ryan, K. M. (2011). The relationship between rape myths and sexual scripts: The social construction of rape. *Sex Roles, 65*, 774–782. https://doi.org/10.1007/s11199-011-0033-2

Schneider, B. E., & Gould, M. (1987). Female sexuality: Looking back into the future. In B. B. Hess & M. M. Ferre (Eds.), *Analyzing gender: A handbook of social science research* (pp. 120–153). SAGE Publications.

Shapiro, F. (2001). *Eye movement desensitization and reprocessing (EMDR): Basic principles, protocols, and procedures* (2nd ed.). Guilford Press.

Shapiro, F. (2017). *Eye movement desensitization and reprocessing (EMDR): Basic principles, protocols, and procedures* (3rd ed.). Guilford Press.

Simon, W., & Gagnon, J. H. (1986). Sexual scripts: Permanence and change. *Archives of Sexual Behaviour, 15*, 97–120. https://doi.org/10.1007/BF01542219

Steger, M. F., & Park, C. L. (2012). *The creation of meaning following trauma: Meaning making and trajectories of distress and recovery.* In R. A. McMackin, E. Newman, J. M. Fogler, & T. M. Keane (Eds.), *Trauma therapy in context: The science and craft of evidence-based practice* (pp. 171–191). American Psychological Association. https://doi.org/10.1037/13746-008

Stop Street Harassment. (2018). *2018 study on sexual harassment and assault.* http://www.stopstreetharassment.org/our-work/nationalstudy/2018-national-sexual-abuse-report/

Substance Abuse and Mental Health Services Administration. (2014a). *SAMHSA's concept of trauma and guidance for a trauma-informed approach.* https://ncsacw.samhsa.gov/userfiles/files/SAMHSA_Trauma.pdf

Substance Abuse and Mental Health Services Administration. (2014b). *A treatment improvement protocol: Trauma-informed care in behavioral health services* (TIP 57). https://www.ncbi.nlm.nih.gov/books/NBK207201/

Tener, D., & Eisikovits, Z. (2015). Torn: Social expectations concerning forgiveness among women who have experienced intrafamilial child sexual abuse. *Journal of Interpersonal Violence, 32*(16), 2496–2514. https://doi.org/10.1177/0886260515593296

Thorn. (2018). *Child sex trafficking is a cycle of abuse.* https://www.thorn.org/child-trafficking-statistics/

UNICEF USA. (2017). *End trafficking.* https://www.unicefusa.org/sites/default/files/assets/pdf/End-Child-Trafficking-One-Pager.pdf

U.S. Department of Defense. (2021). *Department of Defense annual report on sexual assault in the military. Fiscal year 2020.* https://www.sapr.mil/sites/default/files/DOD_Annual_Report_on_Sexual_Assault_in_the_Military_FY2020.pdf

U.S. Department of Veterans Affairs. (2017). *VA/DOD clinical practice guideline for the management of posttraumatic stress disorder and acute stress disorder* (Version 3.0). https://www.healthquality.va.gov/guidelines/MH/ptsd/VADoDPTSDCPGFinal012418.pdf

van der Kolk, B. (2015). *The body keeps the score: Brain, mind, and body in the healing of trauma.* Penguin Books.

Victims of Trafficking and Violence Protection Act of 2000, Pub. L. No. 106–386, 114 Stat. 1464 (2000). https://www.govinfo.gov/content/pkg/PLAW-106publ386/pdf/PLAW-106publ386.pdf

Walton, E. (2005). Therapeutic forgiveness: Developing a model for empowering victims of sexual abuse. *Clinical Social Work Journal, 33*, 193–207. https://doi.org/10.1007/s10615-005-3532-1

World Health Organization. (2012). *Understanding and addressing violence against women.* http://apps.who.int/iris/bitstream/handle/10665/77394/WHO_RHR_12.42_eng.pdf

World Health Organization. (2013, August 6). *WHO releases guidance on mental health care after trauma* [Press release]. https://www.who.int/news/item/06-08-2013-who-releases-guidance-on-mental-health-care-after-trauma

World Health Organization. (2014). *Global status report on violence prevention 2014.* https://www.who.int/publications/i/item/9789241564793

Wright, M. O., Crawford, E., & Sebastian, K. (2007). Positive resolution of childhood sexual abuse experiences: The role of coping, benefit-finding and meaning-making. *Journal of Family Violence, 22*(7), 597–608. https://doi.org/10.1007/s10896-007-9111-1

Xian K., Chock S., & Dwiggins, D. (2017). LGBTQ youth and vulnerability to sex trafficking. In M. Chisolm-Straker & H. Stoklosa (Eds.), *Human trafficking is a public health issue* (pp. 141–152). Springer. https://doi.org/10.1007/978-3-319-47824-1_9

I Still Yearn for Connection: Illness and Chronic Pain

Jessica Z. Taylor and Leslie E. Davis

Six in 10 U.S. adults live with a chronic disease, and four in 10 have two or more chronic diseases, according to the National Center for Chronic Disease Prevention and Health Promotion (NCCDPHP, 2019). The primary chronic diseases causing death and disability in the United States include heart disease, cancer, chronic lung disease, stroke, Alzheimer's disease, diabetes, and chronic kidney disease (NCCD-PHP, 2019). Chronic disease and illness can affect individuals in a variety of ways across the life span. This chapter will focus on the potential influences of chronic illness on individuals' sexual wellness, describe a sex positive approach for counseling individuals whose sexual wellness is affected by chronic illness, provide a case scenario applying such a sex positive approach, guide sex positive counseling treatment for clients living with chronic illness, and provide a summary of practice points for counselors working with this population. First, an overview of chronic illness and its possible impact on sexual wellness will be discussed.

Chronic Disease and Illness

Living with a chronic illness can be challenging to manage because it changes so many different aspects of one's life, both intrapersonally and interpersonally (Webster, 1997). These changes may occur gradually over time, and so a person may have little awareness of changes in their sexual wellness until a significant problem is presented (Katzin, 1990). When one's physical ability to engage in sexual behaviors has been affected by a medical illness, it may be difficult to separate psychosocial influences and consequences from the physical impact of the illness on sexual functioning (Steinke, 2013).

According to Searight (2019), psychosocial influences on psychosexual difficulties and disorders may have a more significant impact than biological influences on one's perceived sexual abilities. For example, men experiencing erectile dysfunction due in part to the influence of a medical illness may experience feelings of anxiety, anticipatory thoughts of sexual failure, and feelings of sadness when thinking about engaging in sexual behaviors. When a counselor is working with a client who reports erectile dysfunction and discussing its effect on sexual wellness and satisfaction, it is crucial to obtain a physical assessment by a medical professional to ascertain whether a chronic illness, such as type 2 diabetes or cardiovascular disease, is present and affecting the client's physical sexual capabilities (Searight, 2019).

In addition to affecting one's physical capability to engage in certain sexual behaviors, chronic illness may also lead to pain with certain sexual behaviors (Searight, 2019) and a reduction in desire for sexual activity—such as with ulcerative colitis or inflammatory bowel disease—or lead to psychosocial difficulties associated with sexual activity. In a qualitative study of 81 women living with a chronic illness, Kralik et al. (2001) found that living with the chronic illness had changed the way the participants understood their sexuality—namely, regarding changes in their bodies, changes in being able to meet others' sexual needs, and changes in their approaches to expressing sexuality.

Effects of chronic illness may also affect an individual's relationships and quality of life. In a study of 138 women living with interstitial cystitis, Webster (1997) found that participants expressed changes in their sexual relationships in terms of how their experiences living with chronic illness had affected their maintained relationships. Furthermore, in a study of approximately 1,000 individuals living with a chronic disease (e.g., chronic obstructive pulmonary disease or diabetes), approximately one third of respondents reported diminished quality of life as a result of sexual challenges, with over 70% of participants desiring "some help for the problem" (Lemaire et al., 2010, p. 310). Clearly, one's perception of sexuality and sexual wellness can be affected by a variety of chronic illnesses in various ways.

Pain

One way chronic illness may affect one's sexuality and sexual wellness is through pain. Because chronic illnesses vary in how they physically impact individuals, counselors should learn how a client perceives their illness as impacting their sexual capacity. For example, an individual living with arthritis may experience challenges with their ability to masturbate due to arthritis in their hands (Katzin, 1990). An individual living with chronic low back pain may experience challenges engaging in sexual activity as a result of their back pain. In a study of 100 individuals with chronic low back pain, 81% reported sexual difficulties related to chronic low back pain (Bahouq et al., 2013). Of those, 14.8% reported a decrease in libido and 97.5% reported pain with intercourse positioning, with the supine position being ranked as the most painful intercourse position due to back pain (Bahouq et al., 2013).

Chronic illness may result in pain in the genital or pelvic area. Much of the literature on genital pain in individuals living with chronic illness is focused on women, but it is important to remember that men also may experience genital pain from chronic illness (Searight, 2019). Women experiencing vulvovaginal or pelvic floor pain may encounter difficulties with penetrative intercourse because of involuntarily tightening of their pelvic muscle. Searight (2019) discussed how this physical impact of chronic illness may affect one's relationship with a partner and lead to conflicts. In men living with the effects of testis cancer and its treatment, chronic pain in the genital region could impact sexual functioning and perceptions of their sexuality (Pühse et al., 2012).

Cancer

Cancer and its treatment often involve changes in sexuality (Steinke, 2013). Women being treated for gynecological cancer may struggle with their perception of themselves as sexual beings and their desire for sex (Steinke, 2013). Even if the type of cancer is not associated with the genital region, the effects of cancer treatment can be detrimental to any client's physical ability and confidence to engage in sexual activity or behavior. Young adults with cancer, in particular, may experience difficulties with sexual functioning as a result of medical treatment. Katz (2015) described young adulthood as a time of sexual exploration and experimentation and when romantic relationships are formed and cemented. Changes in sexuality and sexual functioning may have a significant impact on young adult relationships. Studying the counseling preferences of young adults with cancer, Taylor and Kashubeck-West (2017) found that they are significantly more likely to want to discuss these concerns in individual counseling versus group counseling with other young adults with cancer or in couples/family counseling.

Mental Illness

Mental illness is a different type of chronic illness, with an organic basis, that may affect individuals' sexuality and sexual well-being. This may be especially detrimental to individuals living with mental illness because many consider sexually intimate relationships to be an important part of their path to recovery (Boucher et al., 2016). In addition to desiring a sexually romantic relationship, individuals with mental illness may encounter challenges expressing their sexuality in socially prescribed ways, or they may struggle with weight and body image as a result of the side effects of psychotropic medications (Davison & Huntington, 2010). Individuals living with mental illness may also experience stigmatic responses to their experiences and work hard to find potential partners who also live with mental illness or are able to accept their mental illness experience without judgment (Davis & Huntington, 2010).

Individuals may use psychotropic medications to cope with mental illness and take additional medications for other chronic illnesses. Psychotropic medications, alone or interacting with other medications, may contribute to physical sexual challenges (Searight, 2019). The use of SSRI medications by individuals with major depressive disorder is widely known to affect sexual well-being. Specifically, SSRIs may lead to anorgasmia, lowered sexual desire, or diminished sexual responsiveness to intimate behavior (Searight, 2019).

Schizophrenia, another mental illness conceptualized as chronic, may have significant effects on one's sexual relationship. Östman and Björkman (2013) qualitatively studied individuals with schizophrenia and their partners to explore the influence of schizophrenia on sexuality. The study identified themes of concern related to the relationship taking on a different feel than a sexual relationship, unknowns about one's sexual ability, lowered sexual desire, and reduced communication about sexual issues. Additionally, participants in the study described experiences with psychiatric services as erasing their sense of themselves as sexual individuals with sexual needs (Östman & Björkman, 2013).

Caregiving

Caregiving for an individual living with chronic illness can also be a relevant area of concern, especially when the caregiver is also in the role of intimate partner. An individual who is in a relationship with someone who is living with, and whose sexuality has been affected by, a chronic illness may naturally contribute to a cyclical situation in which the sexuality of both partners is affected (Searight, 2019). Importantly, Searight (2019) emphasized the need to approach sexuality as more than just biological functioning and to consider the intimate and communicative aspects of a relationship and how they affect one's sexuality.

Obviously, a caregiving partner's sexual needs and concerns are important to consider. Steinke (2013) discussed how partners of individuals living with chronic illness often experience challenges in balancing their roles as a caregiver versus a sexual partner. A caregiving partner may need time to grieve the loss of how the sexual relationship used to be and may also need time to make modifications to sexual activities to support the partner with illness. Working with partners to help them process concerns related to "anxiety, fear, changes in body image, and depression" (Steinke, 2013, p. 25) for both them and their partner is important.

Perhaps one of the best ways to support caregivers and their partners with chronic illness is to enhance their communication. Steinke (2013) discussed how transparent communication about sexual needs and related concerns normalizes those needs and concerns and is crucial to a healthy sexual relationship. Without open communication, hostility and uncertainty about remaining in the relationship may lead to sexual issues such as delayed ejaculation (Searight, 2019).

Unfortunately, caregivers may sometimes elect to leave relationships with individuals living with chronic illness due in part to developed negative feelings about the relationship. Frequently, mental health providers do not ask caregivers about their sexuality or intimacy concerns, and so caregivers do not disclose them (Brotman et al., 2016). Brotman et al. (2016) discussed that counseling for caregivers of individuals living with chronic illness "should involve addressing issues such as internalized stigma, self-esteem, and identity-role changes as well as sex education" (p. 268). Counselors may also recommend couples counseling so caregivers and their partners living with chronic illness may learn effective communication skills for expressing their needs and concerns (Taylor et al., 2019).

Theoretical Framework(s)

Sperry (2006) proposed a biopsychosocial therapeutic approach for treating chronic illness. This approach conceptualizes chronic illness as being managed through a combination of treating biological, psychological, and social concerns. Biologically, individuals living with chronic illness experiencing concerns with their sexuality may benefit from medication or medical treatments. However, this approach can benefit from the addition of a psychosocial assessment to better understand how they perceive their own sexual concerns and what level of knowledge they have about sexual functioning and the modifications that are possible (Searight, 2019).

Psychologically, Searight (2019) recommended the use of cognitive behavior therapy (CBT) "for distorted beliefs about sexuality and to manage pain" (p. 289) as well as the use of "mindfulness-based treatment" (p. 289) to manage emotional feelings and responses to sexual concerns. Drawing from Steinke's (2013) discussion about challenging cognitive beliefs with individuals diagnosed with cancer and how their sexuality has been impacted, *coping flexibility* is a useful construct applicable to the idea that individuals living with chronic illness may find other ways to derive sexual satisfaction than just solely sexual intercourse.

Interventions

Various modifications to enhance sexual satisfaction may be possible, depending upon the effect chronic illness has on a client's sexual capabilities. Medications may be available, but they should always be discussed in collaboration with a client's health care provider(s) to avoid overstepping one's bounds of competence as a counselor (Taylor et al., 2019). Additional physical approaches, which should also always be discussed in collaboration with a client's health care provider(s), may involve use of vaginal dilation (Searight, 2019; Steinke, 2013), vaginal lubricants (Steinke, 2013), directed masturbation (Searight, 2019), squeeze technique (Searight, 2019), or vacuum devices and other sexual aids (Steinke, 2013).

Approaches to modifying planning and positioning may also be discussed with clients living with chronic illness. As Katzin (1990) stated, "Planning ahead for sexual activity is essential" (p. 56) when living with chronic illness. Katzin recommended exploring different times of day for sexual activity when clients feel at their physical best, modifying room temperature to be most comfortable, physically stretching ahead of time to assist with range of motion, and taking a warm shower beforehand to promote relaxation. Modifying positioning for sexual activity can also improve sexual satisfaction between individuals living with chronic illness and their partners (Steinke, 2013). Katzin recommended exploring positions that may allow for easier breathing, as well as having pillows available to reduce bodily discomfort and provide additional support. Specific to chronic low back pain, avoiding the supine position has been recommended (Bahouq et al., 2013).

Individuals with chronic illness may choose to position themselves on a partner's lap, depending upon height differences and comfortability, with or without penetration (Kaufman et al., 2007). Using not only a bed but also different styles of furniture can also be beneficial when searching for pleasurable positioning. As an example, partners may take turns leaning over couches, sitting in chairs, or laying on the side of an ottoman. Individuals can try different heights and angles, in addition to adding different pillow or wedge placements, in order to alleviate back pain or lift pelvises for increased support and pleasure (Kaufman et al., 2007). The use of an array of toys can be positioned on different parts of the body, depending on what feels the most comfortable at the time of sexual activity.

Individuals living with chronic illness may find the use of mobility aids, such as wheelchairs or walkers, helpful or even necessary. For individuals using mobility aids, it is important to be mindful of positions that allow for kissing and other forms of intimate touching that do not impede breathing or blocking of the nose. Taking turns in supportively leaning over chairs when kissing or touching reachable parts of the body for a short period of time can allow for enjoyable and arousing foreplay (Kaufman et al., 2007). If an intimate partner has any bodily areas with minimal or absent sensation, and that individual is positioned beneath another intimate partner, it is important to be careful that their legs or other body parts are not being crushed (Kaufman et al., 2007).

Intimacy, separate from focused sexuality, may also help improve sexual satisfaction. Physical contact need not always result in sexual intercourse. Holding hands while on a walk may improve intimacy and increase a sense of relational satisfaction among intimate partners (Steinke, 2013). As an individual's body changes due to a chronic illness, a focus on pleasure instead of sex can encourage physical exploration at a safe pace so each partner feels comfortable and understands how one's needs may be met in other ways (Steinke, 2013). *Sensate focus*, an intentional approach to slowing down physical exploration, may benefit individuals living with chronic illness and their partners (Searight, 2019; Taylor et al., 2019). Furthermore, purposefully slowing down physical exploration to focus on pleasure may also reduce emotional fears and anxiety related to physical touch and the worry of inadvertently harming one's partner (Katzin, 1990).

Success Outcomes

Success outcomes for addressing sexual well-being for clients living with chronic illness will likely depend upon their specific concerns. If their concerns relate more to physical outcomes of duration (e.g., time maintaining an erection or time toward orgasm), then these outcomes may be quantified and tracked over time. Levels of pain may be quantified on a 1-to-10 scale and tracked over time. Success outcomes focused more on psychosocial improvement may include intentionally selected measures of quality of life, health-related quality of life specific to the type of chronic illness, body image satisfaction, or relationship satisfaction.

The Functional Assessment of Chronic Illness Therapy Measurement System (Cella & Nowinski, 2002) contains a variety of brief measures and items that can be used to assess the particular health-related quality of life needs of clients. Categories of brief measures include general measures, cancer-specific measures, cancer-specific symptom indexes, treatment-specific measures, symptom-specific measures, financial toxicity measures, disease-specific measures, palliative care and spiritual well-being measures, treatment satisfaction measures, utility indexes, and pediatric measures (see https://www.facit.org/facit-measures-searchable-library). The general measure's Social/Family Well-Being subscale includes an item asking about level of satisfaction with sex life, which provides counselors with a direct way to broach conversation about this topic with clients. Overall, listening to what the client wants from treatment is imperative in selecting the most appropriate outcome measures for success.

Transference and Countertransference Issues

As discussed previously about the importance of taking the initiative to ask caregivers about their sexual or intimacy concerns, so must we take the initiative to ask about sexual or intimacy concerns of clients living with chronic illness (Lemaire et al., 2010). Unfortunately, if counselors lack comfort in discussing sexual or intimacy concerns with clients, they may completely ignore these needs and not ask about them (Taylor et al., 2019). Additional factors that may lead to counselors having discomfort in discussing sexuality or intimacy needs with clients are being of a younger age, being relatively newer to the counseling field, or being uncomfortable with their own sexuality (Brotman et al., 2016).

In addition to a general level of comfort in discussing sexuality and intimacy, counselors also need competency in addressing these concerns in appropriate ways. If counselors have not achieved a level of competency in this area, they may suggest treatments that align with their own personal value system rather than that of the client. Comfort and competency are necessary to appropriately address sexual and intimacy concerns with clients who are living with chronic illness as well as their partners (Taylor et al., 2019).

Multicultural Issues

Just as it is important for counselors to have competency and comfort in discussing clients' sexual or intimacy concerns, so is it important to have multicultural competency and comfort in discussing how sexuality is perceived from the client's worldview. This requires discussion with clients about their cultural expectations regarding sexuality; their own personal perceptions, beliefs, and value systems about sexuality; and how their thoughts on sexuality may lead to challenges with their partners' thoughts on sexuality. Searight (2019) discussed how different cultures may have different expectations for sexual performance or duration, emphasizing that little is known about sexual dysfunction in non-Western cultures. As with other culture-related issues in counseling, the influence of culture on a client's beliefs about sexuality should be approached calmly, openly, and with acceptance.

Crisis Issues

Crisis issues may be relevant for a client, depending upon the recency of the diagnosis of chronic illness, experience of any additional complications, or escalating relationship challenges. Sperry (2006) discussed four phases of chronic illness, with the first phase being conceptualized as more of a crisis stage upon initial diagnosis. An initial diagnosis of chronic illness may affect individuals differently, with some perceiving the diagnosis as a threat to their wellness and others perceiving the diagnosis with relief at finally understanding what has been wrong with their health. For counselors who are not familiar with de-escalating clients in crisis, Roberts and Ottens's (2005) seven-stage crisis intervention model and Granello's (2010) article with practical ideas at each of the seven stages are helpful places to start obtaining familiarity with a crisis intervention approach.

A Sex Positive Approach

Sex positive approaches aim to facilitate counseling that moves away from behaviors and attitudes of sex shaming and pathologizing in sessions (Burnes et al., 2017). One of the ways to implement a sex positive approach is to identify negative influences on the client's sexuality and understanding of sex. When a counselor practices a sex positive approach, they do not overlook, dismiss, or minimize the client's understanding of their sexual experiences (Burnes et al., 2017). Sex is another part of the client's lived experience, similar to how they understand and form meanings around constructs such as familial relationships, food, and spirituality. The client's understanding of sex is met with an affirming and accepting counselor. At times, the counselor may need to provide sexual education or reframes if negative or false information has shaped the client's conceptualization of sex. Sex can often be seen as a taboo, but in sex positive counseling, it is a counselor's job to provide a safe place to process all client topics. Shame is never to be a part of the counseling experience, particularly in regard to sex, when counseling from a sex positive framework.

It is not uncommon for those living with chronic illness to feel invalidated, even in a counseling setting. If a client's chronic illness is not visible, counselors might assume they are not significantly impacted by their health condition, including their sense of sexuality and intimate behaviors. Even if a counselor does validate a client's chronic illness, the counselor still may be uncomfortable bringing up the topic of sex or believe it to be irrelevant. A sex positive counselor understands that for all clients, sexuality is just as important a lived dimension as is someone's family, relationships, and cultural influences.

Relevant Inclusive and Affirming Language

In approaching clients living with chronic illness in a sex positive way, a few terms to promote inclusivity and affirm their lived experiences as valid are relevant. First, the term *spoonie* must be understood as a way some individuals with chronic illness refer to themselves. This term comes from writer and activist Christine Miserandino's *spoon theory*, which describes the limited energy level experienced by many individuals living with chronic illness and how different activities, including sexual activities, require varying amounts of energy (Fisher, 2019; Miserando, n.d.). If any client refers to themself as a spoonie or describes their energy level by how many spoons they have remaining, they are referring to spoon theory.

Similarly, someone who is *unchargeable* is someone who is not finding success in refueling their energy level, no matter what self-care activities they engage in. The perceived difference between a spoonie and a *chargie* (i.e., an unchargeable person) may be in whether individuals with chronic illness perceive waking up with all their energy (i.e., spoons) or still drained with an empty battery. Not only is it important for a counselor to be aware of these terms, they can also be useful in assisting with communication between clients and their partners about sexual concerns.

An additional relevant term is flare. Chronic illness *flares* are "peaks of symptoms, followed by remission periods, while others might live with constant symptoms" (Beatty & Joffe, 2006, p. 182). Specific symptoms of flares may look different depending upon the chronic illness and within groups of individuals with any given chronic illness. It is important for counselors to listen to clients and understand how they experience and manage their flares before offering suggestions for mitigating challenges to their sexual wellness.

Counselor Attitudes and Behaviors to Exhibit

One of the first, and most important, attitudes and behaviors for counselors to exhibit is a willingness to create space and initiate discussion about relevant sexual wellness concerns for clients with chronic illness (Brotman et al., 2016). Clients often can discern when a counselor is uncomfortable speaking about a topic, so counselors should strive to open discussion calmly, nonjudgmentally, and with a sense of hope and confidence that things have potential to improve. Additionally, specific to individuals living with chronic illness, counselors must approach conversation with an attitude of understanding that a client's health situation may always be changing, with concerns arising intermittently depending on other life factors and health management.

Counselors should exhibit an attitude of welcoming interdisciplinary collaboration with the client's team of health care providers (Taylor et al., 2019). Although counselors are not medical experts and should not step outside of their scope of competency by attempting to speak as medical experts, they can empower clients to advocate for their needs with health care providers by modeling that sort of conversation through interdisciplinary collaboration on the client's behalf (Taylor et al., 2019). Counselors serve on clients' interdisciplinary teams as the team member who assists the client in processing psychosocial concerns and experiences related to living with their chronic illness and its effects on well-being. Specific to sexual wellness, counselors can assist clients with redefining their sexual script to gain a new understanding and awareness of themselves as sexual beings. In doing so, counselors are mindful of staying within the health care team's medical guidelines for what behaviors clients may safely engage in, given the impact of the chronic illness. In addition to being comfortable discussing sexual wellness issues with clients, counselors must also be comfortable discussing sexual wellness issues with clients' health care teams, which normalizes the presence of sexual concerns and the potential for solutions through reasonable modifications (Taylor et al., 2019). Following is a case scenario in which the counselor, applying a sex positive approach, demonstrates these attitudes and behaviors in working toward sexual satisfaction with a client living with chronic illness.

Case Example

A 35-year-old lesbian female client, Janet, has sought out counseling because of concerns with her sex life being negatively impacted by her fibromyalgia pain. Janet is in a monogamous relationship with her girlfriend Chelsea. Janet expresses that she is beginning to fear for her relationship because she has been consistently avoiding sex over the past month. It is discovered that Janet is avoiding sex with her partner because of spikes in pain from her fibromyalgia. Janet explains how her fibromyalgia manifests in severe inflammation causing full-body pain and chronic fatigue. Sometimes, she is able to locate her pain to one spot, but at other times, the flare-ups are in multiple parts of her body.

After connecting Janet's sporadic and painful flare-ups with her avoidance of sex, the counselor openly inquires about what sex has been like with her partner leading up to the session. Janet discloses that she is unsure where she will have pain and how intense it will be each day. For example, sometimes she has intense pain on her inner thighs, whereas other days her mouth can feel extremely sensitive and sore. Janet used to decline sex with her partner only if the pain was too intense near her genital areas, but now she is avoiding all sex and feeling guilty for rejecting Chelsea. Janet is also aware that if she does choose to engage in sex she will more than likely be in residual pain for days after.

Janet also expresses a decline in self-care, such as showering, when she feels exhausted from pain. This has had a ripple effect of her not feeling sexy or desirable.

One of the major feelings Janet verbalizes is fear. Janet feels fear of many things, including her body choosing to not "function properly," her partner leaving her, not fulfilling her sexual obligations in the relationship, never wanting to have sex again, and the pain that may be intensified through intimate and sexual behaviors. Janet has been feeling isolated from others who do not struggle with these chronic pains and do not seem to understand her fluctuating pain and motivation levels. Her pain is not visible, so others often assume she is exaggerating her symptoms. As such, she perceives having a limited support system.

As the counselor calmly continues to explore these fears, it is discovered that Janet was raised in a Christian home that was highly involved in their religious community—and still is to this day. Janet expressed that she was only given "the talk" about sex at age 9, and the message was that her body belonged to God. There were many implicit rules regarding sex, and it was considered highly offensive and taboo to have conversations about sex. Self-pleasure was considered a sin and sex was only for the purposes of procreation or to pleasure your opposite-sex spouse. Janet felt a great deal of pressure not only to remain "pure" for the view of herself, but also for her family and their image in the church. Janet disclosed that her family does not know about the intimate nature of her relationship with Chelsea, describing it more as a roommate situation with a friend than a romantic relationship. Although Chelsea states that she understands Janet's reasoning for concealing these details from her family, Janet feels ashamed about her self-described cowardice in openly disclosing her relationship to her family. This is an additional reason Janet is afraid Chelsea will end the relationship. Janet admits it is hard to talk about her sexual concerns with the counselor because of the guilt and shame she feels about the topic, as well as the invalidation she typically experiences when discussing her health situation with others.

Treatment: A Specific Approach

When working with Janet, the first, and arguably the most important, goal is to build therapeutic alliance in addition to vocalizing the counselor's sex positive approach. This will inform Janet that the counselor is comfortable discussing sexual topics, in addition to a willingness to aid her in processing sex-related stressors.

Once there is an alliance formed, and Janet trusts that the counselor has no intention of minimizing or shaming her about sex, it is important to conduct a sexual assessment. Some things that will be assessed are Janet and Chelsea's relationship dynamics, Janet's relationship with her own sexuality and body, Janet's relationship with self-pleasure, what the pain is like the day following a sexual encounter, and possible shame surrounding sex and her body. At this stage, it may also be important to provide psychoeducation around different types of sexual and intimate activities, ways to communicate her needs to reduce pain related to her fibromyalgia, and the importance of ongoing and dynamic consent within her relationships.

When collecting this type of assessment information, it is important to pay attention to multicultural factors that could also be impacting Janet's perception of sex, in addition to the barriers created by her chronic illness. The counselor will want to identify if there are any internalized heteronormative sexual biases, negative core beliefs, developmental or current experiences causing guilt or shame, cooccurring mental health symptoms, catastrophic thinking, or other cognitive distortions. Some examples of possible negative core beliefs might be "I am a burden," "I am broken/my body is against me," "I am helpless/hopeless," "I am not good enough," "I don't deserve pleasure," "I am out of control (of my body)," or "I am unlovable/undesirable." These are just a few possible examples—the sex positive counselor should remain open to collaboratively exploring Janet's negative core beliefs related to sex or intimacy.

After the counselor has taken time to collect as much assessment information as possible, in addition to aiding Janet in increasing introspective work, the goals will then be to increase desire while extinguishing shame. For example, Janet is not feeling desirable due to poor hygiene practices because of the pain and increased depressive symptoms. Treatment goals will be to increase normalization of sex-based conversations, empathy and compassion for both partners, body positivity and acceptance, somatic awareness around pain and pleasure, and flexibility with how and when sex can take place.

By normalizing desire and lack of desire, Janet will be able to feel reduced levels of guilt and shame surrounding her chronic illness and its influence on her sexuality and relationship with Chelsea. This new ability to practice self-compassion can increase her awareness of her negative core beliefs and their possible origins across her life span (e.g., the influence of societal gendered messages, her religious community, and systemic heteronormative shame). Janet will be able to reframe what intimacy and sex life can look like for her and Chelsea while shedding conventional, heteronormative, and societal expectations.

The counselor can use interventions to aid Janet in tracking her pain and feeling empowered to decide if she wishes to have sex on a given day. It will be important to support Janet's exploration in considering sexual positions that may feel comfortable depending on where her pain is that day, increase the focus of fun intimacy and pleasure instead of just the outcome of achieving orgasm, eliminate pressures of obligatory sexual participation, consider sexual enhancement products that are safe for her body while avoiding triggering ingredients, and increase somatic awareness to more clearly identify what bodily areas are in pain. Increased somatic awareness would enhance Janet's ability to engage in sex, while avoiding kissing or rubbing certain areas of her body that may be more likely to experience discomfort. Other therapy types that may be helpful could be somatic experiencing to process trauma her body may be holding, eye movement desensitization and reprocessing to reprocess negative core beliefs, acceptance and commitment therapy, or CBT.

Practice Issues for Approaching the Topic With Clients

When first initiating counseling with clients living with chronic illness, counselors should include sexual satisfaction and wellness needs in the opening intake discussion. Additionally, when talking about relationship satisfaction concerns and needs, counselors should include sexual wellness concerns in the discussion, as the two often go hand in hand. Many clients will not voluntarily bring up sexual wellness concerns with their health care providers (Krebs, 2007), and so it may be expected that clients will be unlikely to voluntarily bring up sexual wellness concerns with counselors either unless invited. When counselors do choose to broach sexual wellness concerns, they should ask questions directly rather than try to use euphemisms or talk about sexual wellness concerns in an abstract, roundabout way (Katzin, 1990).

For counselors working with clients living with chronic illness, it is important for counselors to try to understand the client's unique experience of living with the illness. Chronic illnesses, especially rare diseases, can present with a wide variety of symptoms. As such, counselors should try to learn enough about the illness to be familiar with it, while also being open to listening to clients share their individual experiences, so counselors can help the client learn to modify their own way of living life with the illness, rather than provide generic suggestions (Taylor et al., 2019).

Logistics of setting up an office should be approached intentionally when working with clients who are living with chronic illness. Some effects of chronic illness are not visible, so counselors should proactively arrange their office to be a safe and comforting setting, even without knowing specifics of the client's situation. For example, any available food should be free from common food allergens and sensitivities. Furniture and pillows should be selected carefully so as to not aggravate clients with textile sensitivities. Candles and incense should be avoided because of chemical sensitivities.

Hand soap, sanitizer, and lotions should be hypoallergenic, made for sensitive skin, and free from fragrance. Clients may not always know all of their flare triggers, so counselors should strive to make their office as free from common flare triggers as possible.

When discussing physical sensations of living with chronic illness, clients may have previously developed ways of disconnecting from bodily sensations to lower their perception of pain and discomfort. Counselors can use mindfulness meditation and somatic experiencing to assist clients in learning how to reconnect with their bodies in safe and comfortable ways. As counselors explore sensations related to intimate body areas, conversation should start broad and then gradually narrow in on more sexual areas of the body as the client's comfort level allows. Genital puppets can also be a helpful way for clients to visually connect feelings of genital pain to physical parts of their body and explore possible physical modifications for reducing associated pain.

Practice Issues for Advocating for a Sex Positive Environment

When advocating for a sex positive environment for clients living with chronic illness, it is important that counselors keep in the forefront of their minds that someone's sex life is not over because they have a chronic illness. Through open discussion and client exploration, many clients with chronic illness can regain sexual satisfaction through lifestyle, positional, and relational modifications (Steinke, 2013). This may involve engaging in physician-approved physical activity to improve stamina or lung capacity, adding support props or changing positions with intimate activities, or learning to communicate more effectively with intimate partners. Always keep in mind that chronic illnesses may present differently in different clients, so avoid general suggestions and understand the client's unique sexual concerns before considering potential solutions (Steinke, 2013). Although framed as a practice issue for counselors, interdisciplinary collaboration with the client's health care team is of the utmost importance to stay within one's professional scope of competence, as well as to avoid suggesting anything harmful or inadvisable to clients (Taylor et al., 2019).

One important aspect of advocating for a sex positive environment may also involve attending to clients' partners. Counselors can provide their clients with resources for their partners about support programs for partners of individuals with chronic illness so their concerns can be heard and supported (Brotman et al., 2016). For some chronic situations, such as for a client with schizophrenia, the client and partner may desire for the partner to be a part of treatment in addressing sexual wellness concerns, since they are both affected and already closely involved with managing life around schizophrenia symptoms (Östman & Björkman, 2013). Counselors should ask their clients with chronic illness if they would like their intimate partners, or intimate partner caregivers, to be a part of conversations discussing sexual wellness concerns. Doing so advocates for a sex positive approach to normalizing the need for sexual intimacy, even when managing a chronic illness.

Questions You Always Wanted to Ask

1. **I want to incorporate a sex positive approach into my sessions, but it seems pretty overwhelming to have so much to learn. Where do I start?**
   One way to help incorporate a sex positive approach in sessions is to first check your own biases, in addition to examining countertransference. This will be similar to going through ethics trainings but focused on attitudes toward sex and illness.

2. **So, check my biases. Got it. That doesn't seem like enough. What else should I be thinking about?**
   You have probably taken a multicultural class. It is important to consider intersectionality or maybe even reference the ADDRESSING model (Hays, 2016) to better understand your influences and the influences the client may have experienced when it comes to their perception of sex, sex education, and sex positivity.
   A helpful question to ask yourself if you feel conflicted in bringing a sex positive attitude into counseling is, "Is it my moral dilemma or is it theirs?" If you are a straight counselor working with the LGBTQ+ population, it is also important to avoid heteronormative assumptions, in addition to understanding that there are many forms of sex, pleasure, and paraphilias.
3. **How should I respond when clients reveal their many forms of sex, pleasure, and paraphilias to me?**
   When a client discloses specific acts, desires, or kinks, it is important not to react in a shocked or judgmental manner. Two acronyms used in kink play are SSC for safe, sane, and consensual and RACK for risk-aware consensual kink. Working with kink clients is another application of sex positivity in counseling. The important takeaway is that in a sex positive framework, the counselor meets the client with openness and willingness to aid in processing sex-related stressors without the intention to pathologize or further stigmatize. It is important to be aware of your nonverbal expressions and personal biases while addressing intimate topics with clients pertaining to the influence of their chronic illness on their intimate behavior preferences. See Chapter 19 for more on the topic of kink.
4. **I think I understand the type of attitude I need to bring to sex positive counseling work. How do I initiate bringing conversations of sex into my clinical practice?**
   When first working with clients, it is common practice to ask about activities of daily living. When asking about sleep, appetite, and other self-care topics, sexual health can also be a topic of that conversion. A person's sex life can be a large indicator of what is happening for them emotionally, physically, and interpersonally. It is a piece of someone's overall wellness, so approach it through the lens of it being a normal aspect of their lived experience.
5. **Wow, that sounds like it gets pretty personal pretty quickly. Won't that scare away my client?**
   Although sexual health is a natural part of someone's overall wellness, it is still important to assess comfortability with the topic of sex, self-pleasure, and pleasure with partners. Clients can usually tell if you're uncomfortable with this conversation and they may respond with the appeasing response to help you in your discomfort. When clients shy away from the topic, it is often due to a perception of the counselor's discomfort, rather than client discomfort.
6. **How is sex positivity relevant to my counseling work with clients living with chronic illness?**
   When working with chronic illness, it is important not to assume the client is asexual because they experience pain or are avoiding sex. If a client tells you they are not interested in sex, it is vital to further explore their experience to assess whether it is due to a lack of interest or due to an influencing symptom

of their chronic illness. Some counselors may avoid this conversation in order to relieve their own discomfort with processing sex with clients. In addition, the counselor should have some understanding of the asexuality spectrum to avoid mislabeling or invalidating their client.

7. **I'm not a medical health professional. Isn't any focus on chronic illness symptoms within sessions outside of my scope of competence?**
   Once a client has disclosed their diagnosis, it is important to do research on the client's specific illness to better understand their experience and how it could be impacting sex. However, remember the individual's experience matters most. Also, try to get a signed release of information from the client to collaborate with their health care team. This way, you can better understand what is medically ill-advised for your client depending on their unique medical situation.
8. **Anything else I should be thinking about in approaching sex positive counseling with clients living with chronic illness?**
   Finally, make sure to assess possible attributions that the client may make about themselves because they have chronic illness and how it may be impacting how they have sex. There may be underlying negative cognitive schemas influencing their felt bodily sensations.

References

Bahouq, H., Fadoua, A., Hanan, R., Ihsane, H., & Najia, H.-H. (2013). Profile of sexuality in Moroccan chronic low back pain patients. *BMC Musculoskeletal Disorders, 14*, 63–69. https://doi.org/10.1186/1471-2474-14-63

Beatty, J. E., & Joffe, R. (2006). An overlooked dimension of diversity: The career effects of chronic illness. *Organizational Dynamics, 35*, 182–195. https://doi.org/10.1016/j.orgdyn.2006.03.006

Boucher, M., Groleau, D., & Whitley, R. (2016). Recovery and severe mental illness: The role of romantic relationships, intimacy, and sexuality. *Psychiatric Rehabilitation Journal, 39*, 180–182. https://doi.org/10.1037/prj0000193

Brotman, S., Drummond, J., Silverman, M., Sussman, T., Orzeck, P., Barylak, L., & Billette, V. (2016). Talking about sexuality and intimacy with women spousal caregivers: Perspectives of service providers. *Health & Social Work, 41*, 263–270. https://doi.org/10.1093/hsw/hlw040

Burnes, T. R., Singh, A. A., & Witherspoon, R. G. (2017). Sex positivity and counseling psychology: An introduction to the major contribution. *The Counseling Psychologist, 45*, 470–486. https://doi.org/10.1177/0011000017710216

Cella, D., & Nowinski, C. J. (2002). Measuring quality of life in chronic illness: The Functional Assessment of Chronic Illness Therapy Measurement System. *Archives of Physical Medicine and Rehabilitation, 83*, S10–S17. https://doi.org/10.1053/apmr.2002.36959

Davison, J., & Huntington, A. (2010). "Out of sight": Sexuality and women with enduring mental illness. *International Journal of Mental Health Nursing, 19*, 240–249. https://doi.org/10.1111/j.1447-0349.2010.00676.x

Fisher, C. (2019). Counseling connoisseur: Revisiting the spoon theory. *Counseling Today.* https://ct.counseling.org/2019/07/counseling-connoisseur-revisiting-the-spoon-theory/

Granello, D. H. (2010). A suicide crisis intervention model with 25 practical strategies for implementation. *Journal of Mental Health Counseling, 32*, 218–235. https://doi.org/10.17744/mehc.32.3.n6371355496t4704

Hays, P. A. (2016). *Addressing cultural complexities in practice: Assessment, diagnosis, and therapy* (3rd ed.). American Psychological Association.

Katz, A. (2015). *Meeting the need for psychosocial care in young adults with cancer.* Oncology Nursing Society.

Katzin, L. (1990). Chronic illness and sexuality. *American Journal of Nursing, 90*, 54–59. https://doi.org/10.2307/3426228

Kaufman, M., Silverberg, C., & Odette, F. (2007). *The ultimate guide to sex and disability: For all of us who live with disabilities, chronic pain, and illness* (2nd ed). Cleis Press.

Kralik, D., Koch, T., & Telford, K. (2001). Constructions of sexuality for midlife women living with chronic illness. *Journal of Advanced Nursing, 35*, 180–187. https://doi.org/10.1046/j.1365-2648.2001.01835.x

Krebs, L. U. (2007). Sexual assessment: Research and clinical. *Nursing Clinics of North America, 42*, 515–529. https://doi.org/10.1016/j.cnur.2007.07.004

Lemaire, A., Alexandre, B., & Blond, D. (2010). Chronic illness and sexuality: Patients' perception. *Journal of Men's Health, 7*(3), 310. https://doi.org/10.1016/j.jomh.2010.09.092

Miserando, C. (n.d.). *The spoon theory.* https://butyoudontlooksick.com/articles/written-by-christine/the-spoon-theory/

National Center for Chronic Disease Prevention and Health Promotion. (2019). *Chronic diseases in America.* Centers for Disease Control and Prevention. https://www.cdc.gov/chronicdisease/pdf/infographics/chronic-disease-H.pdf

Östman, M., & Björkman, A. (2013). Schizophrenia and relationships: The effect of mental illness on sexuality. *Clinical Schizophrenia & Related Psychoses, 7*, 20–24. https://doi.org/10.3371/CSRP.OSBJ.012513

Pühse, G., Wachsmuth, J. U., Kemper, S., Husstedt, I. W., Evers, S., & Kliesch, S. (2012). Chronic pain has a negative impact on sexuality in testis cancer survivors. *Journal of Andrology, 33*, 886–893. https://doi.org/10.2164/jandrol.110.012500

Roberts, A. R., & Ottens, A. J. (2005). The seven-stage crisis intervention model: A road map to goal attainment, problem solving, and crisis resolution. *Brief Treatment and Crisis Intervention, 5*, 329–339. https://doi.org/10.1093/brief-treatment/mhi030

Searight, H. R. (2019). *Health and behavior: A multidisciplinary perspective.* Rowman & Littlefield.

Sperry, L. (2006). *Psychological treatment of chronic illness: The biopsychosocial therapy approach.* American Psychological Association.

Steinke, E. E. (2013). Sexuality and chronic illness. *Journal of Gerontological Nursing, 39*, 18–27. https://doi.org/10.3928/00989134-20130916-01

Taylor, J. Z., & Kashubeck-West, S. (2017). Counseling preferences of young adults with cancer. *The Professional Counselor, 7*, 259–271. https://doi.org/10.15241/jzt.7.3.259

Taylor, J. Z., Lewis, C. L., & Davis, L. E. (2019). Sexual wellness and rare disease considerations: A behavioral case conceptualization and approach to counseling treatment. *Journal of Counseling Sexology & Sexual Wellness, 1*, 96–104. https://doi.org/10.34296/01021018

Webster, D. C. (1997). Recontextualizing sexuality in chronic illness: Women and interstitial cystitis. *Health Care for Women International, 18*, 575–589. https://doi.org/10.1080/07399339709516313

Healthy While Sexual: Preventing and Living With Sexually Transmitted Infections

J. Richelle Joe and John T. Super

Many of us can probably recall a discussion about sex and sexually transmitted infections (STIs) that was vague, awkward, or utterly terrifying. Our aim is for the discussion in this chapter to be none of those things. Here, we will explore sexual health topics in detail to provide clear and accurate information. Although some aspects of what we discuss will be unpleasant, the aim is not to scare you, but rather to inform you, so you are well equipped to support your clients in being healthy while sexual. We will provide an overview of multiple STIs with a specific focus on HIV and the misconceptions that persist around that condition. We will also share practical information about how to support clients through testing, diagnosis, treatment, and the experience of living well after contracting an STI.

In this chapter, we are mindful of the language we use and the way we talk about STIs because we recognize that STIs and HIV are weighty topics that can expose moral biases and stigma. For example, we discuss prevention without using terms like "safe sex" or "protection," both of which connote danger or something to fear. Although most believe a common goal is to avoid contracting an STI, we do not have to stigmatize illnesses or people living with those illnesses in the process. By taking this approach, we hope that this chapter will be informative while also providing the language to use with clients to decrease stigma and engage in sex positive conversations about sex and prevention.

STIs: Nomenclature and Trends

STIs were once commonly referred to as *sexually transmitted diseases* (STDs); however, the terminology used by experts in medicine and public health has evolved to reflect that (a) infections occur prior to any symptoms of a disease appearing and (b) most infections have no symptoms and do not reach disease state (Anderson, 2019; Lederer & Laing, 2017).

Knowledge of STIs, including transmission, prevention, and treatment, is critical to maintaining sexual health. Of course, abstinence from sexual activity is the only way to absolutely prevent an STI; however, abstinence may not be desirable or possible for some people. Thus, for individuals who want to be sexual, being equipped with accurate knowledge and tools will help them to also remain healthy.

Although anyone engaging in sexual activity has the potential to contract an STI, knowledge and prevention tools are especially important for groups that are most affected by STIs, such as youth and young adults, gay and bisexual men, and pregnant women (Centers for Disease Control and Prevention [CDC], n.d.-k). If undetected and untreated, STIs can have long-term medical effects including other pelvic and abdominal conditions, cancer, and fertility issues. In the following discussion, we provide overviews of the STIs that are common in the United States: chlamydia, genital herpes, gonorrhea, human papillomavirus (HPV), syphilis, trichomoniasis, and HIV/AIDS (see Table 14.1).

Chlamydia

Exposure to the bacteria *chlamydia trachomatis* leads to chlamydia, which affects an estimated 2.68 million people in the United States every year (CDC, n.d.-c).

Table 14.1

Sexually Transmitted Infections (STIs) at a Glance

STI	*Transmission*	*Prevention Methods*	*Treatment and Prognosis*
Chlamydia	Contact with penis, vagina, mouth, or anus	Abstinence, proper condom use, proper dental dam use	Can be cured with antibiotics
Genital herpes	Contact with herpes lesions or from genital and oral secretions containing the virus	Abstinence, proper condom use, proper dental dam use	No cure; however, antiviral medication can prevent or shorten outbreaks and reduce likelihood of transmission
Gonorrhea	Sexual contact with penis, vagina, mouth, or anus	Abstinence, proper condom use, proper dental dam use	Can be cured with proper medication
Human immunodeficiency virus (HIV)	Transmitted via blood, semen, preseminal fluids, vaginal fluids, rectal fluids, and breast milk	Abstinence, proper condom use, proper dental dam use, PrEP, PEP	No cure; however, ART can reduce viral load and likelihood of transmission
Human papillomavirus (HPV)	Vaginal, anal, or oral sex	Abstinence, HPV vaccine, proper condom use, proper dental dam use	No cure or treatment for the virus
Syphilis	Contact with a syphilitic sore in or around the penis, vagina, anus, rectum, or mouth	Abstinence, proper condom use, proper dental dam use	Can be treated and cured with appropriate administration of penicillin
Trichomoniasis	Sexual contact with the penis or vagina	Abstinence, proper condom use, proper dental dam use	Can be cured with antibiotics

Note. ART = antiretroviral therapy; PrEP = preexposure prophylaxis; PEP = postexposure prophylaxis.

Two thirds of new chlamydia cases occur among youth and young adults ages 15 to 24 years. Transmission of chlamydia occurs through sexual contact with the penis, vagina, mouth, or anus. Proper use of latex condoms and dental dams (CDC, n.d.-d) can reduce the likelihood of transmission. Often the infection is symptom free, so chlamydia can go untreated for years. Left untreated, chlamydia can cause significant damage to the cervix, uterus, and fallopian tubes, causing pelvic inflammatory disease and infertility. Additionally, chlamydia can also cause urethral discharge, testicular pain, and rectal discharge and/or bleeding. Fortunately, chlamydia can easily be cured with antibiotics. Thus, it is important that individuals engage in regular screenings for chlamydia and receive treatment before the bacteria spreads and causes permanent damage.

Genital Herpes

Annually, about 776,000 people in the United States contract genital herpes through contact with herpes lesions, genital secretions, or oral secretions that contain the herpes simplex virus (HSV; CDC, n.d.-e). HSV causes herpes lesions or small blisters around the genitals, rectum, or mouth that can last 2 to 12 days after exposure. Additionally, an initial outbreak may be accompanied by fever, body aches, and swollen lymph nodes. Outbreaks of genital herpes can occur multiple times, but over time, they typically occur for shorter and less intense periods. There is no cure for genital herpes; however, antiviral treatments can shorten or prevent future outbreaks and reduce the likelihood of transmission to others.

Gonorrhea

The bacterium *Neisseria gonorrhoeae* causes gonorrhea in 1.14 million people in the United States each year (CDC, n.d.-g). Transmitted via sexual contact with the penis, vagina, mouth, or anus, gonorrhea can affect the cervix, uterus, fallopian tubes, and urethra. Symptoms of gonorrhea include unusual discharge from the penis, vagina or anus; testicular pain; anal itching, soreness, or bleeding; and vaginal bleeding not associated with menstruation. Gonorrhea can be cured with the appropriate medical treatment; however, if left untreated, it can lead to pelvic inflammatory disease and infertility.

HPV

HPV, the most common STI, is a virus typically spread through vaginal and anal sex, although it can be transmitted via oral sex (CDC, n.d.-f). Most people who contract HPV show no symptoms or develop symptoms only years after contracting the virus. Thus, the source of transmission is more difficult to identify. For most people, HPV goes away without causing any other health problems. However, over time, it can cause genital warts and cancer of the cervix, vulva, vagina, penis, or anus. Early detection and monitoring of HPV via cervical examinations is critical to the prevention of cervical cancer. For individuals under the age of 26, CDC recommends HPV vaccination at age 11 or 12, regardless of gender identity. HPV is currently the only STI for which there is an approved vaccine.

Syphilis

Treponema pallidum, the bacterium causing syphilis, is transmitted by direct contact with a sore or chancre found on or around the genitals or anus, in the vagina or rectum, or in or around the mouth (CDC, n.d.-l). Treatment for syphilis includes a regimen of penicillin; however, if untreated, syphilis can progress through multiple stages. Initial symptoms of syphilis include the appearance of one or more chancres that may go unnoticed and can heal without treatment. As syphilis progresses, however, other symptoms may include skin rashes in multiple areas such as the palms of the hands or the soles of the feet; lesions in the mouth, vagina, or anus; or other symptoms such as fever, swollen lymph glands, hair loss, weight loss, muscle aches, and fatigue. There is a latent stage of syphilis where there are no visible signs or symptoms; however, again, if left untreated, syphilis can damage multiple organ systems (e.g., nervous system, cardiovascular system, bones and joints) and ultimately be fatal.

Trichomoniasis

Trichomoniasis is caused by the parasite *Trichomonas vaginalis* and is a common, curable STI (CDC, n.d.-m). The parasite rarely infects the hands, mouth, or anus; therefore, trichomoniasis is most commonly spread from penis to vagina, from vagina to penis, or from vagina to vagina. Symptoms of trichomoniasis include itching or irritation of the genitals (both penis and vagina), unusual discharge from the penis or vagina, discomfort during urination, and discomfort during ejaculation. Effective medication for trichomoniasis exists, and treatment of this STI is critical because it can increase the risk of contracting or transmitting another STI, including HIV.

HIV/AIDS

HIV (human immunodeficiency virus) and AIDS (acquired immunodeficiency syndrome) were first identified in the 1980s, and over the last 5 decades, scientific knowledge about them has increased dramatically. In 2020, there were approximately 37.7 million people living with HIV worldwide (World Health Organization, n.d.), including nearly 1.2 million people in the United States (HIV.gov, 2021). Although there is currently no cure for HIV/AIDS, effective testing, prevention, and treatment efforts have slowed the spread and made the possibility of living with HIV realistic. Still, in the United States, HIV/AIDS continues to disproportionately affect vulnerable and marginalized populations, including gay and bisexual men, Black/African American and Hispanic/Latina women, transgender women, and individuals living in high-poverty and rural communities (HIV.gov, 2021). Multiple social determinants of health account for HIV/AIDS health disparities, including varied access to health care, including prevention and treatment; geographic location and physical barriers to care; social and cultural beliefs about sexuality; racism, sexism, homophobia, and transphobia; and stigma.

Early references to HIV as "gay cancer" or "gay-related immune deficiency" shaped the initial perception of HIV/AIDS as an illness affecting only gay men (HIV.gov, n.d.). The resulting stigmatizing beliefs about HIV/AIDS reflected social and cultural biases about sex and sexuality that associated same-sex relationships with immorality. Stigma persisted with the discovery that HIV could be transmitted via shared injection-drug paraphernalia. Despite increasing scientific understanding of HIV transmission and acceptance of individuals in the LGBTQ+ community, HIV remains among the most stigmatized medical conditions.

HIV Basics

HIV is a virus that can be transmitted from person to person by certain bodily fluids; knowing which bodily fluids can transmit the virus is critical to understanding HIV. Blood, semen, preseminal fluids, vaginal fluids, rectal fluids, and breast milk can all carry the virus, and direct contact with these fluids can result in transmission of HIV (HIV.gov, 2019). It is important to note that transmission of HIV occurs when any of the fluids mentioned enter into another person's bloodstream through a mucous membrane, open cut or sore, or direct injection. Mucous membranes can be found in the vagina, tip of the penis, rectum, and mouth, which is why HIV is most commonly transmitted via sexual contact (HIV.gov, 2019). Additionally, anal sex has the highest risk of HIV transmission because of the consistency of the mucous membrane in the rectum.

Although fragile outside of the human body, HIV is a virus that can take a significant toll on the body once it has entered the bloodstream. It attacks the immune system by taking over the body's healthy CD4 cells, which are the white blood cells that help the body fight off disease and infection (CDC, n.d.-a). After taking over a CD4 cell, the virus duplicates itself, and each duplicated cell seeks out other CD4 cells to take over, thus spreading the virus throughout the body. If untreated, the virus continues to multiply until a person's immune system is of little to no use in protecting the body from illness. However, with treatment, a person's viral load (i.e., the amount of the virus in the body) can decrease and their CD4 count can increase. This is an ideal scenario, with the goal being an undetectable viral load and a healthy immune system. With an undetectable viral load, an individual would be considered virally suppressed, would experience the benefits of overall better health, and would be extremely unlikely to transmit HIV to another person via sexual contact (National Institute of Allergy and Infectious Disease, n.d.).

Conversely, without treatment, a person's viral load would increase and their CD4 cell count would decrease, making them susceptible to opportunistic infections (i.e., other conditions that their immune system is unable to adequately address). In such a case, a person's medical condition would worsen and could ultimately progress to the point that medical professionals would diagnose them with AIDS (CDC, n.d.-a). An AIDS diagnosis is given if a person's CD4 cell count drops below 200 (normal cell count ranges from 500 to 1500) or that person develops certain opportunistic infections. Once an AIDS diagnosis is given, an individual's immune system has been badly compromised, making them vulnerable to almost any illness, including the common cold or flu. With treatment, an individual *can* experience a boost in CD4 cells and decline in viral load to ultimately return to a healthier state. However, if adequate treatment is not provided in time, an individual might die from one of those opportunistic infections. Fortunately, medical advancements in HIV treatment have reduced the fatality rate from AIDS-related illnesses since the 1980s.

HIV Prevention and Treatment

As for other STIs discussed in this chapter, the most effective prevention for HIV is abstinence. However, for people who enjoy sex and want to engage in it, proper use of either internal or external latex condoms or dental dams during all sexual encounters reduces the risk of transmitting or contracting HIV. In addition to proper condom use, there are medicinal methods of preventing HIV that are novel and exciting, and for people living with HIV, adherence to effective treatment of HIV is another method of reducing the likelihood of HIV transmission.

Pre- and Postexposure Prophylaxis

For individuals who have not tested positive for HIV, preexposure prophylaxis (PrEP) involves taking one pill a day to prevent contraction of the virus. With proper adherence,

PrEP has demonstrated 99% effectiveness in preventing HIV transmission via sexual contact even when other preventive methods (e.g., condoms) are not used (CDC, n.d.-h, n.d.-j). Hence, in addition to using condoms, individuals concerned about contracting HIV have this method of prevention at their disposal. This is particularly important for someone whose partner is living with HIV or for individuals who engage in sex work where condom negotiation might be difficult.

In addition to PrEP, postexposure prophylaxis (PEP) is available to individuals who were exposed or think they were exposed to HIV. Like the morning-after contraceptive pill, PEP is an emergency prevention method that must be started within 72 hours of possible exposure to HIV (CDC, n.d.-h). The PEP regimen consists of 28 days of medication taken either once or twice daily. It is effective in preventing HIV, but it is not 100% effective. PEP is particularly important in instances of sexual assault or condom failure.

It is important to note that HIV is the only STI for which there is an approved medication that can prevent transmission. Additionally, although a vaccine is not presently available, research efforts are underway to develop one in the coming years.

Antiretroviral therapy

Treatment for HIV has improved in effectiveness since the 1980s. The standard of care for HIV is antiretroviral therapy (ART), which, when adhered to as prescribed, slows the spread of the virus within the body (CDC, n.d.-i). ART reduces the presence of HIV, allowing for CD4 cells to recover and protect the body from other illnesses. For some people living with HIV, ART involves a combination of medications; however, advancements in HIV treatment have resulted in the possibility of individuals taking only one pill a day—making adherence much more manageable. Adherence is key to living a healthy life with HIV. By adhering to treatment, people living with HIV may experience the benefits of an undetectable viral load, a stronger immune system and healthier body, and reduced concern about transmitting HIV to their sexual partners.

Multiple studies have confirmed that when an individual achieves and maintains an undetectable viral load, they cannot sexually transmit HIV to their partners. Undetectable = untransmittable is a critical element of HIV prevention. People living with HIV should be supported in their efforts to adhere to ART to maintain their own health and to prevent the spread of HIV. This is also known as treatment as prevention (National Institute of Allergy and Infectious Disease, n.d.).

HIV and the other STIs discussed in this chapter are illnesses that can affect an individual's physical and mental health. In some cases, they can have long-lasting effects; however, all are conditions with which one can live and live well. Access to accurate information about these STIs, methods of prevention, and treatment can help individuals make wise decisions about their sexual health. Additionally, open, honest dialogue about sex, sexuality, and STIs is critical to decreasing stigma and normalizing these topics within families and relationships.

Communicating About Sex, Sexuality, and STIs

When teaching sexuality classes for counselors, we hear students commonly share their belief that communicating about sex is important for all people. As humans, students believe parents should be talking to children about sex, children should be talking to parents about sex, partners should be talking to each other about sex, and society should be talking about sex as a topic. Yet, as students often realize, sex is talked about far less than it should be, which raises the question, "Why are people not talking about sex as much as they need to?" That question is a bigger topic than we can fully address in this chapter, but often the subject is avoided for many reasons which we will discuss (Murray et al., 2017). Those reasons can be cultural, social, contextual, interpersonal, intrapersonal, or the result of previous experiences.

Why Are Sexuality and STIs Difficult to Talk About?

Most agree that sex should be discussed in relationships. Ironically, however, in long-term relationships sex is often treated as something to be done rather than talked about (Buehler, 2017). If sexuality and STIs are difficult to discuss for a couple with a lengthy shared history, imagine how difficult it can be for those partners with shorter histories. Additionally, parents who struggle to talk to each other about sex may also struggle to talk to children about sex or STIs.

Avoidance Begins Early

Ideally, discussing sexuality should begin with young children and continue as they grow. However, the frequency of this happening is surprisingly low (Fisher et al., 2020), and for adolescents, learning how to talk about STIs with a partner rarely occurs in their schools or homes. Those between the ages of 15 and 24 are at the highest risk of contracting an STI; yet, they are often uninformed about STI communication (Brannon & Rauscher, 2019) and unengaged in learning how to talk with a partner (Fisher et al., 2020). Adolescents are less likely to be proactive in STI prevention but often become more educated and proactive after an STI diagnosis (Fisher et al., 2020). There may be many reasons for this, but one of the most prevalent is that sex is thought to be a private matter and discussing STIs with a partner can appear as being overly sexual or unfaithful. Either perception can be difficult during a stage of life that places a high value on external perceptions (Brannon & Rauscher, 2019) and both perceptions promote silence.

Society Influences Silence

Society is the collection of people living together giving some sort of structure or order to their lives. Societal beliefs reflect many cultures and often amplify the messages of individual cultures throughout the greater population. The overall message many receive from society is to avoid discussing STI diagnoses or testing. The evidence of the message was seen in a study of over 4,000 participants between the ages of 15 and 24 who lived in the United States (McFarlane et al., 2015). Of the study participants, over 60% tested positive for HIV or an STI; yet, only 23% discussed it with a health care worker, and only 18% with a sexual partner. The result for such a large sample indicates the prevalence of society's message of avoiding discussing personal sexual topics such as STI testing and diagnosis.

The individualist or collectivist beliefs held within a particular society may also affect silence on the subjects of sexuality and STIs. In an individualistic society, greater emphasis is placed on individual freedoms and protection of self, whereas collectivistic cultures value protecting fellow citizens and maintaining social respect. People with an individualistic worldview may prioritize privacy and thus avoid discussions related to STI testing, prevention, and diagnosis. Conversely, due to social influences, those with a collectivist cultural view are less likely to discuss testing or a diagnosis (McFarlane et al., 2015). In a collectivistic worldview, a core belief is that the actions of one will reflect on that person's family, friends, and ancestors and may bring shame to their collective group. Hence, feeling shame and desiring to retain social respect inhibit discussing STIs when testing positive. Understanding the worldview of the client, particularly in terms of individualism and collectivism, is critical to exploring their readiness to discuss sex and STIs.

Religion

Historically, organized religions have strongly influenced the values and beliefs that humans hold about sex, often supporting silence around sexuality. As a result, a deep-rooted belief exists that sex should be more covert, deeply personal, and a topic to be avoided. Additionally, some religious beliefs are heteronormative and emphasize sex only within the context of heterosexual marriage. Such beliefs can communicate stigmatizing and shame-based messages about sexuality and STIs. Even those not considering themselves religious share some of these values, which have been learned through social messages. Thus, if an assimilated societal message is to avoid talking about sex, it becomes easier to understand how those living in the society are reluctant to talk about STIs.

How to Talk About STI Prevention and Diagnoses

Discussing an STI diagnosis can be difficult, especially for those with a recent positive diagnosis, because there can be many thoughts and feelings occurring at the same time. Some common emotions after a positive diagnosis can be shock, shame, sadness, anger, confusion, or loneliness. For some, the diagnosis is overwhelming, and finding a starting point from which to move forward is difficult. Often the starting point is finding hope for the future. Someone newly diagnosed may need greater education on their condition, how it will physically affect them, and how it can be transmitted to a partner. Ideally, the medically focused conversations should happen with a trained health care professional, but the mental health care professional may also be a part of an integrated care team that supports the client. Thus, when clients present in the therapeutic space with multiple and complex thoughts and feelings, the clinician's primary aim is to validate and explore these feelings. As time passes and the client experiences empathy within the therapeutic space, the common thoughts and emotions regarding a new diagnosis generally reduce and the person adjusts emotionally.

Whether a client is newly diagnosed or has lived with a diagnosis for some time, there are questions worth considering when thinking of discussing the diagnosis with a potential partner. First, how ready is the person to share their diagnosis? Do they need more information to know how to answer their partner's questions? Are they emotionally ready to have that conversation? If they decide to disclose their status, there are ways to make the process easier. Clinicians can offer the following tips to support their clients who are considering how to discuss their diagnosis with a partner:

- Be direct with information.
- Be honest.
- Approach the discussion as calmly as possible. A partner hearing the news for the first time might be struggling with their own emotions, and the calm is helpful.
- Be clear about the facts. Have resources available for your partner to learn more.
- Tune in to how your partner is reacting.
- Express your concerns for your partner's health. Concern will help reduce defensiveness and encourage conversation.
- When ready, plan to discuss how this diagnosis will affect future sexual activity.
- Obtain consent before any and all sexual activity.

For some, discussing an STI diagnosis is daunting. By using these simple tips, the process can be clearer and less stressful. When considering how to tell a partner about a diagnosis, it is important for the client to accept that a perfect way to share the news is improbable, but the value in having the conversation is immense.

When to Have the Conversation

When a client is living with an STI diagnosis, discussing the diagnosis with a partner before being sexually active is recommended to reduce the likelihood of transmission. Additionally, there may be legal ramifications for individuals living in states that have laws related to HIV or STI disclosure (see https://www.hivlawandpolicy.org). Although it seems common sense to discuss STIs and prevention methods prior to sexual contact, oftentimes individuals find this conversation difficult to have with their partners. In some cases, individuals may assume things about their own STI status, as well as that of their partner, and may not be concerned about transmitting or contracting an STI. In other cases, discussing STIs and prevention may seem awkward or accusatory, and individuals may fear offending their partners. It is common to hear of perceived or actual shame experienced when having a conversation on STIs. Such fears may be stronger for individuals who feel less empowered in their relationships than their partners—for instance, if intimate partner violence or some other unequal power dynamic exists within the relationship (Joe et al., 2020). Individuals living with HIV or another STI may experience internalized stigma as a barrier to disclosure and discussion of prevention and sexual wellness. In all of these cases, clinicians can empower clients to self-advocate and initiate conversations and sexual activity on their own terms, within a timeline that maximizes efforts to prevent both transmission and contraction.

It is important to note that communication about sexuality and STIs occurs both verbally and nonverbally. Ideally, verbal communication about the STIs or a diagnosis is direct, using clear language that avoids jargon or euphemisms. For instance, a partner may state their interest in both partners getting tested for specific STIs prior to sexual contact. They might even declare testing a requirement. This discussion of testing can open up the conversation to allow either or both partners to disclose an STI diagnosis clearly and directly. To avoid sending conflicting messages, the verbal communication should also include congruent nonverbal communication, such as facial expressions, tone of voice, and observable behaviors (Levand, 2019). For example, a client who discusses an STI diagnosis in a nonchalant manner or while already engaged in sex may send conflicting messages to their partner about the seriousness of the discussion and the importance they place on their diagnosis. Clinicians can help clients understand the value of clear, congruent communication about STIs, and they can support clients' efforts to initiate and engage in such conversations as part of the consent process.

How Can Counseling Support Communication?

Counselors should be active in engaging clients in the topic of sexuality. Opening the door to issues in an affirming, open, and direct way promotes the discussion of STI prevention or diagnosis. Many clients hesitate or avoid discussing sex or STIs with their counselor because they are unsure of the counselor's attitudes or judgments (Cruz et al., 2017). Sex and sexuality are among the topics that counselors-in-training identify as challenging topics that might affect a counselor's comfort in discussing an

STI, specifically HIV (Joe et al., 2019). Hence, as clinicians, we must evaluate our own thoughts, feelings, and biases before approaching the topic. We also should be aware of our own heteronormative assumptions and language that may be off-putting to clients. Individuals who do not identify as part of a heteronormative majority are more reluctant to discuss an STI diagnosis and prevention with health care workers (Jahn et al., 2019). Therefore, we must be inquisitive about affectional orientation and gender identity when discussing STIs, rather than operating on our own assumptions. For example, emphasizing that a client should be using condoms during sex if one member of the couple is not a cisgender male could rupture the therapeutic rapport.

A counselor's support for a client who desires to discuss STIs can take many forms. As mentioned, a counselor may explore a client's thoughts and feelings about STI testing and prevention, diagnosis disclosure, or a recent STI diagnosis. A counselor may also engage a client in role-playing activities to provide the space to practice the discussions they want to have and to receive feedback from the counselor. The counselor and the client may discuss the client's knowledge around the STI and help expand what is known about the diagnosis. The counselor may also help the client assess their readiness to share the diagnosis with others and explore the benefits and drawbacks of both sharing and not sharing a diagnosis. Finally, a counselor can connect their client with human resources, such as local clinics and organizations that focus on STIs, and informational resources such as accurate up-to-date information verified by the CDC or the U.S. Department of Health and Human Services.

Currently, STIs are among the most common infectious diseases in the United States (Brannon & Rauscher, 2019). Yet, learning to talk about STIs is rare or missing in many homes and schools. Research supports the importance of more discussions on prevention and diagnosis of STIs in encouraging risk-reducing activities (Sales et al., 2008). Specifically, communicating about an STI diagnosis with a partner is associated with use of prevention methods such as condoms (Ha et al., 2019; Noar et al., 2006).

Discussing sexuality should begin early and be expanded through adolescence given that nearly half of newly diagnosed STIs occur in the 15- to 24-year-old age group (CDC, n.d.-b). Within this age group, individuals believe that learning about sexuality in easily understood and relatable language should occur in schools, homes, the media, and among their friends (Fisher et al., 2020). Ideally, discussions about sexuality and STIs should continue through high school into college and encourage open communication about STI testing and diagnosis. Although more young people (ages 15–24) have an STI than talk about it to their partners, studies show media encouraging testing and discussions about STIs increase the number of conversations had with partners (McFarlane et al., 2015). Social cognitive theory suggests a behavior is repeated if it is supported socially (Wilkerson et al., 2014). Hence, more frequent positive social messages about sexuality and STIs can increase communication.

Case Example: Christian and Felicia

Christian and Felicia are in their 20s and at an early stage of their relationship. To their surprise, their friendship grew quickly as they found common ground in their personal interests, life goals, and general perspectives on life. Although Christian was more established in his career than Felicia was in hers, they both shared a common vision for the future, including romance. Within the first month, they began discussing a long-term commitment. Although they were open with each other about many aspects of their lives, within that month, they had never seriously discussed sex. Their physical interactions had been close but not sexual, despite the obvious attraction between them. Felicia worried that sharing with Christian her positive HIV status would end their developing relationship but knew she had to share this before their relationship became sexual. A counselor helped her understand that she needed to be direct with Christian; be clear, honest, calm, understanding, and sensitive to Christian's thoughts and feelings; and discuss how this would affect their sexual activity. Felicia learned that having the conversation in person with Christian was preferred and to find a space that would offer them both some confidentiality and privacy. She met with Christian the next day, and although Christian was understanding, he said he felt afraid to continue their relationship and was concerned about trust between the two of them. The conversation ended with them agreeing to meet with a counselor.

In their meeting with the counselor, they explored their individual thoughts and feelings and what Christian learning of the HIV diagnosis meant to the future of their relationship. Christian shared he was afraid of contracting HIV and wondered if he could trust Felicia to be honest with him in other areas of their relationship. The counselor facilitated a discussion between Felicia and Christian about medication adherence, viral load, PrEP, and the chance of transmission should they engage in sexual activity. She then asked the couple to role-play reversing roles and discuss their thoughts and feelings as the other person. The couple reported they felt more connected and secure about the future of their relationship. They also agreed to continue learning about ways to reduce the risk of transmission to Christian through professional medical advice.

In this case example, a mental health professional was able to support Felicia in her decision to disclose her HIV status to Christian and to facilitate dialogue between the two to help them address emotions, concerns, and thoughts for the future. As this couple moves forward, the counselor will want to consider power dynamics within the couple, the individual psychological wellness of each partner, and the challenges that the couple may face as a unit. Specifically, the counselor will want to explore how the couple will handle potential stigma among their family members and friends and what the couple will do if they desire to expand their family beyond the two of them. Additionally, the counselor will want to explore holistic wellness for both Christian and Felicia, as they will be living with an illness that has both physical and psychosocial effects.

Reflections About the Case Example

After reading this case example, consider the following questions:

1. How would you approach the case and treatment?
2. What resources might you need to pull for yourself to be properly prepared to treat the couple?

Conclusion

Counselors may encounter clients who are living with an STI or who are interested in available methods to prevent contracting HIV or any number of STIs. To provide effective services to these clients, counselors need to know current and accurate information about prevention, transmission, prognosis, and treatment, and they need to know how to engage clients in meaningful conversations about this information. Counselors also should use language that communicates a sex positive approach to discussing STIs that avoids stigma related to sex, sexuality, STIs generally, and HIV specifically. It is also important for counselors to have current, accurate information about the prevalence of STIs in United States, address misconceptions about HIV/AIDS, and have knowledge about methods of preventing HIV and other STIs, such as PrEP. The case example at the end of the chapter and the suggestions for facilitating discussions about STIs provide guidance regarding ways to normalize these difficult conversations with clients and their sexual partners.

Questions You Always Wanted to Ask

1. **Can a woman living with HIV give birth to a healthy baby?**
   Yes! Fortunately, routine HIV testing of pregnant women has allowed medical professionals to treat HIV during pregnancy so that mothers themselves can be healthy and so that their children can be born without HIV. Early detection of HIV and adherence to treatment are critical to prevent transmission of HIV in utero or in childbirth.
2. **How long can someone live with HIV?**
   People can live a long, healthy life after an HIV diagnosis, provided they have access to care and adhere to treatment. Unfortunately, individuals who face multiple challenges in daily living, such as poverty, unemployment, homelessness, and food insecurity, may experience a decline in their health that may result in an AIDS diagnosis and eventually death. Additionally, prevalence statistics indicate that people living with HIV in the South have higher rates of AIDS diagnoses and mortality from AIDS-related illnesses. These are examples of social determinants of health that can affect the health outcomes for people living with HIV.
3. **How can you tell if someone has HIV?**
   There are no external markers that an individual has contracted HIV. In fact, some people do not have any symptoms of the virus for years. This is why regular HIV testing is important to detect and treat the virus early.
4. **Is there a cure for HIV?**
   Although there are effective treatments to suppress HIV within the body, there currently is not a cure. Additionally, there is not currently a vaccine for HIV, although there are global research efforts to develop one.

References

Anderson, J. B. (2019). *STD (sexually transmitted disease) or STI (sexually transmitted infection): Should we choose?* American Sexual Health Association. http://www.ashasexualhealth.org/pdfs/STDI.pdf

Brannon, G. E., & Rauscher, E. A. (2019). Managing face while managing privacy: Factors that predict young adults' communication about sexually transmitted infections with romantic partners. *Health Communication*, *34*(14), 1833–1844. https://doi.org/10.1080/10410236.2018.1536951

Buehler, S. (2017). *What every mental health professional needs to know about sex* (2nd ed.). Springer Publishing Company.

Centers for Disease Control and Prevention. (n.d.-a). *About HIV*. https://www.cdc.gov/hiv/basics/whatishiv.html
Centers for Disease Control and Prevention. (n.d.-b). *Adolescents and young adults*. https://www.cdc.gov/std/life-stages-populations/adolescents-youngadults.htm
Centers for Disease Control and Prevention. (n.d.-c). *Chlamydia—CDC fact sheet (detailed)*. https://www.cdc.gov/std/chlamydia/stdfact-chlamydia-detailed.htm
Centers for Disease Control and Prevention. (n.d.-d). *Dental dam use*. https://www.cdc.gov/condomeffectiveness/Dental-dam-use.html
Centers for Disease Control and Prevention. (n.d.-e). *Genital herpes—CDC fact sheet (detailed)*. https://www.cdc.gov/std/herpes/stdfact-herpes-detailed.htm
Centers for Disease Control and Prevention. (n.d.-f). *Genital HPV infection—Fact sheet*. https://www.cdc.gov/std/hpv/stdfact-hpv.htm
Centers for Disease Control and Prevention. (n.d.-g). *Gonorrhea—CDC fact sheet (Detailed version)*. https://www.cdc.gov/std/gonorrhea/stdfact-gonorrhea-detailed.htm
Centers for Disease Control and Prevention. (n.d.-h). *HIV prevention*. https://www.cdc.gov/hiv/basics/prevention.html
Centers for Disease Control and Prevention. (n.d.-i). *HIV treatment*. https://www.cdc.gov/hiv/basics/livingwithhiv/treatment.html
Centers for Disease Control and Prevention. (n.d.-j). *Safer sexual behaviors*. https://www.cdc.gov/actagainstaids/campaigns/pic/talks/safer-sex.html
Centers for Disease Control and Prevention. (n.d.-k). *The state of STDs in the United States*. https://www.cdc.gov/std/statistics/2020/infographic-html.htm
Centers for Disease Control and Prevention. (n.d.-l). *Syphilis—CDC fact sheet (detailed)*. https://www.cdc.gov/std/syphilis/stdfact-syphilis-detailed.htm
Centers for Disease Control and Prevention. (n.d.-m). *Trichomoniasis—CDC fact sheet*. https://www.cdc.gov/std/trichomonas/stdfact-trichomoniasis.htm
Cruz, C., Greenwald, E., & Sandil, R. (2017). Let's talk about sex: Integrating sex positivity in counseling psychology practice. *Counseling Psychologist*, *45*(4), 547–569. https://doi.org/10.1177/0011000017714763
Fisher, C. M., Kerr, L., Ezer, P., Kneip Pelster, A. D., Coleman, J. D., & Tibbits, M. (2020). Adolescent perspectives on addressing teenage pregnancy and sexually transmitted infections in the classroom and beyond. *Sex Education*, *20*(1), 90–100. https://doi.org/10.1080/14681811.2019.1618257
Ha, M. M., Belcher, H. M. E., Butz, A. M., Perin, J., Matson, P. A., & Trent, M. (2019). Partner notification, treatment, and subsequent condom use after pelvic inflammatory disease: Implications for dyadic intervention with urban youth. *Clinical Pediatrics*, *58*(11–12), 1271–1276. https://doi.org/10.1177/0009922819852979
HIV.gov. (n.d.). *A timeline of HIV and AIDS*. https://www.hiv.gov/hiv-basics/overview/history/hiv-and-aids-timeline
HIV.gov. (2019, June 24). *How is HIV transmitted?* https://www.hiv.gov/hiv-basics/overview/about-hiv-and-aids/how-is-hiv-transmitted
HIV.gov. (2021, June 2). *U.S. statistics*. https://www.hiv.gov/hiv-basics/overview/data-and-trends/statistics
Jahn, J. L., Bishop, R. A., Tan, A. S. L., & Agénor, M. (2019). Patient–provider sexually transmitted infection prevention communication among young adult sexual minority cisgender women and nonbinary assigned female at birth individuals. *Women's Health Issues*, *29*(4), 308–314. https://doi.org/10.1016/j.whi.2019.01.002

Joe, J. R., Heard, N. J., & Yurcisin, K. (2019). Entering the discomfort zone: Counseling trainees' perspectives on counseling clients with HIV/AIDS. *International Journal for the Advancement of Counselling, 41*(4), 1–14. https://doi.org/10.1007/s10447-018-9340-4

Joe, J. R., Norman, A. R., Brown, S., & Diaz, J. (2020). The intersection of HIV and intimate partner violence: An application of relational-cultural theory with Black and Latina women. *Journal of Mental Health Counseling, 42*(1), 32–46. https://doi.org/10.17744/mehc.42.1.03

Lederer, A. M., & Laing, E. E. (2017). What's in a name? Perceptions of the terms sexually transmitted disease and sexually transmitted infection among late adolescents. *Sexually Transmitted Diseases, 44*(11), 707–711. https://doi.org/10.1097/OLQ.0000000000000682

Levand, M. A. (2019). Consent as cross-cultural communication: Navigating consent in a multicultural world. *Sexuality and Culture, 24*, 835–847. https://doi.org/10.1007/s12119-019-09667-7

McFarlane, M., Brookmeyer, K., Friedman, A., Habel, M., Kachur, R., & Hogben, M. (2015). GYT: Get yourself tested campaign awareness: Associations with sexually transmitted disease/HIV testing and communication behaviors among youth. *Sexually Transmitted Diseases, 42*(11), 619–624. https://doi.org/10.1097/OLQ.0000000000000361

Murray, C., Pope, A. L., & Willis, B. (2017). *Sexuality counseling: Theory, research and practice*. Sage Publications.

National Institute of Allergy and Infectious Disease. (n.d.). *HIV undetectable = untransmittable (U=U), or treatment as prevention*. https://www.niaid.nih.gov/diseases-conditions/treatment-prevention

Noar, S. M., Carlyle, K., & Cole, C. (2006). Why communication is crucial: Meta-analysis of the relationship between safer sexual communication and condom use. *Journal of Health Communication, 11*(4), 365–390.

Sales, J. M. D., Salazar, L. F., Wingood, G. M., DiClemente, R. J., Rose, E., & Crosby, R. A. (2008). The mediating role of partner communication skills on HIV/STD-associated risk behaviors in young African American females with a history of sexual violence. *Archives of Pediatrics and Adolescent Medicine, 162*(5), 432–438. https://doi.org/10.1001/archpedi.162.5.432

Wilkerson, J. M., Fuchs, E. L., Brady, S. S., Jones-Webb, R., & Rosser, B. R. S. (2014). Correlates of human immunodeficiency virus/sexually transmitted infection (HIV/STI) testing and disclosure among HIV-negative collegiate men who have sex with men. *Journal of American College Health, 62*(7), 450–460. https://doi.org/10.1080/07448481.2014.917654

World Health Organization. (n.d.). *HIV/AIDS*. https://www.who.int/health-topics/hiv-aids/#tab=tab_1.

PART 5

Sexual Agency

"Yes, We Can and We Will!" Sexuality in Later Life

Angela M. Schubert, Theresa L. Keown, Anastasia Canfield, Sarah Richards, Melissa Franzen, and Sharon Gerstein

Aging is a reality—dare we say, an opportunity. Because life is perceptually and sequentially experienced, one can surmise that only during the older stages of life is it possible to truly appreciate our body's story, our innermost desires, and our sexual capabilities. True to all reality across the life span, we can choose to be aware of our bodies' needs or not. Sensual sexual experiencing requires intention and attention. Age offers the opportunity to embrace the changes and seasoned awareness of sensual experiences beyond that of traditional sexual activity. As a result, we are able to manifest a sexual script that is authentically us. If we mindfully seek to explore and expand our sexual script, we will create one that is intentionally unique and free from any misconceptions or biases we may have absorbed growing up. A *sexual script* is informed by our own biology, our experiences, our culture, and all the messages we have ever received about sex and sexuality. And like our own life, our sexual script is not static; therefore, we are all capable of changing the way we view our sexual selves, our bodies, and our perspective on the human sexual experience. Again, it requires intention and attention.

From the time we are born to the day we pass, sexuality is in a constant state of change. Older sexuality is no different. In fact, sexual desire fluctuates across the life span for a myriad of reasons and yet remains an important aspect of life to the last breath. There are many contributing factors that reinforce and challenge human sexual behavior, including how we respond to our aging body and our own sexual script. However, it is when we expand our horizon of sexual experiences beyond penetrative sexual activities that we start to understand the true potential for human connection and intimacy. Unfortunately, there remain barriers that prevent older adults and society from respecting and honoring older adult sexual expression. In *Older, Wiser, Sexually*

Smarter: 30 Lessons for Adults Only, Brick et al. (2009) explained that "the expectation that older men and women will not be sexual is probably responsible for more sexual problems than physical changes" (p. iii). Although sexual problems increase in frequency as a result of physiological aging, the presence of sexual behaviors, as well as interest in sex and sexual expression and desire, remains active among older adults (Lindau et al., 2007; Pope & Schulz, 1990; Schubert & Pope, 2020). This chapter will address the barriers and myths surrounding older adult sexuality and explore a sex positive approach to counter each barrier. This chapter will further expand on how adults change and adapt to their bodies and sexual functioning, and how vitality and resiliency support sexual needs and expression.

Barriers and Solutions

Barrier: "I Can't Get It Up"

The nature of sexual functioning is predicated on the biological reality of the person and may be influenced by "intrapersonal, interpersonal, cultural, and psychological factors" (King, 2014, p. 12). As the body ages, the physiological response to sexual engagement changes. Rather than chronological age, the general health of the human body plays a significant role in quality of sexual health. For example, the primary contributing factor of erectile difficulties (inability to achieve or maintain a penile erection of varying severity) is related not so much to age but to a problem in the vascular system (Ferrini et al., 2017). Such erectile difficulties can be experienced by people across their life span. In a large study ($N = 3,005$) by Lindau et al. (2007), erectile and ejaculatory difficulties were the most common physiological problems reported by older adult male participants.

Solution: Rule Out and Redefine

In the words of counselor educator and sex researcher Robert Zeglin (2019), "Sometimes penises are finicky." Unfortunately, this continued decrease in rigidity stands as a major challenge to sexual functioning for some. And yet, there are solutions. Sex positive counselors can support the needs of their clients by first asking them whether they have had a medical evaluation. As earlier mentioned, there are a number of medical reasons why erectile difficulties occur. Advocating for the client to seek out medical advice might help the client rule out physiological issues such as neurological causes, medication side effects, and issues with blood flow.

As medical issues are ruled out and/or treated, the sex positive counselor might explore possible psychological causes. Performance anxiety, depression, and stress are common causes for psychogenic erectile difficulties. A sex positive counselor would best serve the client by exploring how sexual acts are experienced by the person and to what degree anxiety is present leading up to and during the sexual act. An ideal goal would be to help the client focus on the somatic, sensual experience of the sexual act, rather than on performance. Sex is meant to be fun and does not require an erect penis, or a penis at all. Counselors can help to expand the sexual script to include playfulness, mindfulness, and presence versus an overfocus on performance, rigidity, and penetration.

Barrier: "I'm Too Dry. It's Not Fun Anymore"

The biological makeup of the human being undergoes complex changes throughout the life span. Older women most commonly report a noticeable decrease in vaginal lubrication (Lindau et al., 2007). Vaginal dryness is the result of decreased estrogen production. Such a decrease can be caused by certain medications, breastfeeding, chemotherapy, menopause, and ovary removal (Bachmann & Santen, 2020). Other physiological changes in older women include decreased amounts of estrogen and progesterone, shrinking of the external genitalia, loss of pubic hair, decrease in duration of orgasm, inability to achieve orgasm, loss of elasticity, and thinness of vaginal wall (Croft, 1982; Hayes & Dennerstein, 2005; Lindau et al., 2007; Willert & Semans, 2000).

Solution: It's Not Over Until You Say It's Over

Let's go back to the sexual script. If sex is believed to be only a penetrative activity, vaginal dryness might make having sex impossible for some. Vaginal dryness, issues with elasticity, and health of the vaginal lining can cause great discomfort and pain if left untreated. Estrogen is a key hormone ally of the vagina. Estrogen lubricates the vagina, maintains the thickness of the vaginal lining, and helps to maintain the health and elasticity of the vaginal tissue (Bachmann & Santen, 2020). Counselors can approach the issue by advocating for the client to first seek out medical assistance. Treatment for vaginal dryness may include vaginal moisturizers and vaginal estrogen such as estrogen creams, tablets, and the vaginal estrogen ring (Bachman & Santen, 2020). Counselors might also explore clients' sexual beliefs surrounding lubricants and penetrative sex. Education about sexual lubricants might alleviate concerns the client has regarding sex and may create immediate relief for the person. Encouraging clients to give themselves permission to explore sexual acts outside of penetration can help cultivate a new interpretation of sexual expression and their own sexual script as a result.

Barrier: "I'm Too Old"

Although biological and hormonal changes contribute to desire, psychosocial dynamics appear to be the primary reason for loss in desire among older adults (Maciel & Laganà, 2014). Cultural factors such as conservative attitudes, gender roles, outlook on life, and perception of self as a sexual being influence individual desire and can be further complicated by social messaging around sexuality (Nappi et al., 2007; Schubert & Pope, 2020). Like younger adults, older adults are concerned about the way they look, as well as perform, and are just as likely to believe their body must *pass* societal standards of beauty, in order to be sexual or desirable. To add to this concern, there exists a social belief that older adults are nonsexual beings. As such, older adults may not be able to guard themselves from internalizing such messages. As Schubert and Pope (2020) wrote, "In societies where messages of beauty, health, and sex are ascribed to young people, older adults are challenged with their own sense of beauty and sexuality" (p. 37).

Older adults might find themselves conflicted as their own sexual desires are challenged by social mores. Some may resign their desires and refrain from seeking out physical intimacy in order to maintain moral and social connections with family (Muzacz & Akinsulure-Smith, 2013; Schubert & Pope, 2020).

Solution: Too Old for What Though?

There are countless ways to engage in intimacy and physical acts with self and with another person(s). The only limitations are those presented by the body and the mind. By virtue of exploring the beliefs, assumptions, and personal experiences surrounding sexuality, counselors are better able to foster authentic sexual exploration with the client. In many cases, psychoeducation is a critical element in understanding the sexual script of the client and how they might best support their own sexual desires and needs. Engaging in a respectful and curious conversation about masturbation might help the person better understand their own sexual agency and sexual potential. For example, if a client believes they must have penetrative sex with a penis, we help them process what that means to no longer have penetrative sex. Limited beliefs about penetrative sex are correlated with low or inhibited desire (Schubert & Pope, 2020). The quality of mental health, including presence of stress, anxiety, depression, negative body image, and low self-esteem, also negatively influences desire, especially since sexuality is perceived as primarily a physical experience (Maciel & Laganà, 2014).

Counselors are in an optimal position to explore the client's sexual script and educate clients on the different types of intimacy and sexual expression that stretch far beyond what is typically understood. As we continue to grow and evolve, so must our ability to see ourselves as sexual beings. Simply because others might view older sexual expression in a negative light does not mean that we need to subscribe to that belief. Desire continues across the life span. It makes no sense to act as if we no longer desire just because we turn a certain age. Similar to a child who desires to explore their genitals to the young adult who enjoys multiple partners to the older adult who desires to *dry hump* (or to rub genitals against another person's body), it is all relative—there is no yum to yuck. That is to say, sexuality in all of its expressions are valid.

Barrier: "I'm Not as Healthy as I Used to Be"

Health is considered a main predictor of sexual engagement and interest, regardless of age. People of any age who experience sexual difficulties due to illness may experience negative psychological side effects, including anxiety, depression, and lowered self-esteem (Schubert & Pope, 2020; Twitchell et al., 2019). For those in later stages of life, experiences of illness or pain may push sexual needs, desires, and expression to the background (Gentili & Mulligan, 1998; Lindau et al., 2007; Willert & Semans, 2000). Common health issues related to the digestive system, the urinary system, and the bowel system heavily influence sexual interest and enjoyment. For example, lower urinary tract symptoms (e.g., incontinence), bowel symptoms (e.g., constipation), and pelvic organ prolapse are common barriers to sexual satisfaction among women (Cameron et al., 2018). Findings of the Lindau et al. (2007) study suggested a strong relationship between continued interest or disinterest in sexual activity and self-reported physical health. Those who rated their health as being "fair" or "poor" had a higher prevalence of sexual issues, including disinterest in sex, decreased experience of pleasure, decreased interest in masturbation, erectile difficulties, delayed onset and/or continued presence of self-created lubrication, and pain. Specific health issues, such as diabetes and arthritis, were more positively associated with sexual disinterest among women who reported those issues compared with women who did not.

Health of a partner is also considered a barrier to continued interest or engagement in sexual expression (Lindau et al., 2007). Female-identified participants ranging from 65 to 85 years of age who were involved in relationships identified the male partner's physical health as the main reason for sexual inactivity (Lindau et al., 2007). As a result of a partner's health issues, a shift in identity may result—from intimate partner to caregiver—consequently forcing an "outsider" perception of self and partner. As a means of coping, the healthy partner might write off sexual expression as irrelevant, pushing all sexual interest aside (Drummond et al., 2013). In some cases, partners who desire to be sexually intimate are met with rejection, either as a result of the new role of caregiver or because the partner with health issues refuses or denies the sexual invitation (Drummond et al., 2013).

Solution: Grieve, Embrace, and Celebrate

As a person ages, it is reasonable to expect age-related changes in health. Those not already impacted by health might find themselves in an emotional flux as they come to understand their new health status and any subsequent changes to desire or sexual interest. As these changes increase, the individual and couple alike are inevitably affected. Counselors can help clients explore both the barriers and the opportunities during this time of transition and beyond, beginning with an open, compassionate conversation. Cognitive, sexual, and physical illness can be seen as a major barrier to those who desire physical intimacy with self or with another person (Gott & Hinchliff, 2003; Schubert & Pope, 2020). Illness and the perception of self as a result of illness can itself become an obstacle to overall sexual satisfaction (Maciel & Laganà, 2014).

In cases of changes in health (physical/sexual/cognitive) or relational dynamic, counselors can facilitate conversations with the client and their loved ones surrounding any potential grief or loss of previous sexual health, intimacy, or quality of relationship in relation to the changes. For example, a couple presents with issues surrounding communication after one is diagnosed with Parkinson's disease. After a thorough first interview of exploring each person's conceptualization of the problem, the counselor works toward identifying ways for each party to explore their grief. By honoring the clients where they are, counselors are better able to help them explore ways to embrace their new health statuses and identify new, and possibly improved, ways to celebrate their sexuality.

Barrier: "I No Longer Have Rights Over Myself. My Children Are My Power of Attorney, and I Live in a Nursing Home"

As a person gets older and mental or physical health issues arise, it can become a challenge for older adults to balance autonomy and independence with the negative consequences of these problems. As a result, sometimes a person (e.g., family member, friend, ally) might be legally designated as guardian or holder of power of attorney for the older adult. This can be extremely helpful for the older adult as this power of attorney allows the holder to act on their behalf in legal and financial matters. Unfortunately, this places the holder of the power of attorney in a position of new power over the older adult, which is sometimes to the detriment of the older adult. In cases where an older adult is transitioned into a nursing home or retirement community, the older adult loses even more autonomy and independence. As a result, the older adult may feel less inclined to engage in independent sexual activity out of fear of being rejected, disciplined, or losing status in the family.

Depending on the attitudes of caregivers, residents may be restricted from having partners, restricted from engaging in sexual activities, and denied privacy (Bentrott & Margrett, 2011; Hajjar & Kamel, 2004; Lindau et al., 2007; Pope & Schulz, 1990). Residents may feel torn as a result because of their social need to stay connected to their family and primary caregivers; therefore, these individuals may refrain from freely expressing themselves. For example, adult children, who have power of attorney over their mother who resides in a nursing home, may request privacy to be denied to their mother for sexual engagements with another resident. Laflin (1996) stated that "grown children of divorced and widowed older Americans often discourage their parents from behaving as sexual beings" (p. 46).

Familial and caregiving support can be more complex for residents who identify as nonheterosexual. Although each person may struggle throughout their life with community and connection, there is a greater chance that lesbian, gay, bisexual, transgender, queer plus other identities (LGBTQ+) individuals have gone through multiple challenges finding support and establishing a community. As a result, such residents may be less inclined to take any unnecessary risks when it directly involves potentially losing a caregiver or other forms of help (Laflin, 1996).

Solution: Let Us Help You Help Them

In cases where family is involved in the care of the older adult client, counselors are in a great position to advocate on behalf of the client's needs. Counselors can offer psychoeducation to caregivers, clients, and staff on the topic of healthy sexuality, autonomy, and safe sex practices. Individual counseling could focus on grief surrounding loss of autonomy and identifying concerns related to sexual needs, as well as exploring ways to effectively communicate needs and desires with the person holding the power of attorney. Family therapy may also be an effective intervention to support the needs of the client and to help family members and/or the person holding the power of attorney understand the client better. Developing educational opportunities can empower older adults, staff, and family to embrace optimal sexuality in older adults (Kleinplatz et al., 2013).

Barrier: "My Partner Died"

Although the experience of aging and sexuality can feel complicated, questions that can come up for many individuals include "How will my sexuality change after my partner's death?" and "What does sex and sexuality even look like after my partner dies?" This can feel overwhelming and quite complex for people, as the answers can be quite layered with desire, loss, grief, and so much more. Adapting to the loss and thriving sexually after a partner dies requires patience, understanding, and awareness of the potential complexity. It is important to identify the grief aspect first before diving into the sexual component. Broken down, grief is essentially all of the thoughts, feelings, and body reactions a person has after someone has died, and it is necessary to acknowledge that everyone grieves differently.

It is important to acknowledge where a person is on their grief journey because this will impact where they are on their sexual journey. A person's desire to have sex may fluctuate because it relates to what emotions they are experiencing with grief. Whereas one day they may feel sadness that brings a decreased sense desire for sex, the next day they may feel happiness that allows them to feel more sexually exploratory. Some people may have an increase in sexual desire during sadness as a way to cope. Both sadness and relief are categories of grief that may impact one's sexual functioning.

Sadness

Sexual bereavement, or the mourning of the loss of one's sexual intimacy with the deceased, is a phenomenon that is often overlooked by loved ones and society

(Radosh & Simkin, 2016). Unfortunately, some are too embarrassed or afraid to burden others with any discussion about sadness and mourning regarding sex with lost lovers (Radosh & Simkin, 2016). For the same reason, individuals are also less inclined to openly discuss the sex lives of widowed friends and family members. Consequently, the surviving partner may be left processing their grief alone—a silent and isolated endeavor. The sexual response of a surviving partner varies, ranging from a fervent desire to engage in sexual acts immediately to denying sex as a possibility (Price, 2019). Some report feeling guilt for sexual longing (Schubert & Pope, 2020). Like any other ending to a chapter in one's life, a person can experience grief, or sexual bereavement, when a partner dies. In this state of sexual bereavement—grief tied to the loss of sexual intimacy with a long-term partner (Radosh & Simkin, 2016)—some refrain from engaging in sexual activity entirely.

Sadness can greatly ebb and flow during the grieving process, and some people may experience this throughout their life. When a person is experiencing this, it can greatly affect their desire to have sex and their ability to be physically ready for sex. Sex could also become a trigger for sadness, and they may need to take a break from the relationship or talk with their new partner about what they are experiencing. When a person is grieving, they may be unsure as to how to facilitate a discussion surrounding sex with a potential new partner or how to explain mixed feelings of desire and sadness. Moreover, sex could be used as a coping mechanism to alleviate the feelings of sadness for a period of time. This could help to mitigate some of the increased cortisol hormones that a person may have due to their grieving process. Additionally, a person may try to hide some of their sadness and grief behind a sexual experience and to try to pretend that things are not as bad as they may be.

Relief

Relief is generally less discussed by bereaved people because they fear others will not understand it or because they feel guilt and shame to be experiencing relief in their grieving process. However, there actually can be many experiences when relief is felt. Relief may come as a result of processing the positive aspects of the former relationship. From day-to-day love rituals to who bought the groceries, even the tiniest of gestures can be celebrated. Counselors may provide opportunities for the client to explore the beauty and wonder of their deceased lover and the former relationship. Relief may also come as a result of a new instilled sense of freedom.

Maybe a partner no longer has to worry about physical concerns the deceased had, and they now can feel free to explore sexually. For some, perhaps the deceased partner hindered aspects of the surviving lover's sexual identity, and they had to conform to their partner's needs versus supporting their own needs and desires. Relief might come as a result of formerly feeling "unsafe" to be true to their own sexual desires and wants. Some people report relief if they have been in an abusive relationship they believed they could not leave, and now that the person is deceased, they may feel free to not only explore emotional and physical safety but sexual safety as well.

Relief may very well change the way in which a person views relationships and/or their sexual identity or orientation. A person may be free to explore the potential of an ethically nonmonogamous relationship, whereas previously they may have been bound to monogamy. Relief surrounding gender identity and sexual orientation may come into play as a result of changes in societal attitudes toward the LGBTQ+ community. A person may also experience increased safety as a result of overall acceptance toward self, their sexuality, and/or their orientation. Whereas once they may have felt hindered by the confines of societal stigma, relief may exist as a result of this newfound freedom to explore their sexual story in a deeper, human-centered way.

Solution: Cultivating a New Sexual Identity

While reflecting on these concepts, it may be important for the widow/widower to explore their sexual story and reevaluate which aspects of their sexual identity and sexual script they wish to let go of and which aspects to reclaim. Some people may focus on the desire for companionship, whereas others are focused on sex without feelings or connection. There could also be a desire to find a new partner completely different from the deceased in order to either eliminate potential emotional triggers or foster a new aspect of the person's identity that wasn't explored previously. Others may enjoy the idea of romance, but when it comes to a deep connection or sexual intimacy, it may be too much for them after the death loss and the challenges of having to recreate their identity.

Inviting clients to explore and process triggers allows for clients to understand emotions and thoughts that surface when engaging in sexual exploration. Being cognizant of triggers is crucial to take into account when creating a new sexual identity. Triggers may include the death, past sexual trauma, sexual acts they experienced while with the deceased, and their sexual story when their partner was alive. Other people may prefer a partner who is able to explore similar sexual experiences they once had with their past partner. No matter what, it is important to approach this new identity with grace, exploration, caution, and patience as they slowly rebuild a new identity—a revised sexual story that embodies both dignity and pleasure.

In light of the aforementioned stressors and barriers, it is imperative for counselors to navigate conversations that are inclusive of sex positive psychoeducation that involves an assessment and reevaluation of the individual's sexual story. What once worked may not anymore, but that does not mean the older adult is doomed to live out the rest of their days devoid of love, intimacy, compassion, touch, and pleasure.

Dignity and Pleasure

Fostering a meaningful dialog about autonomy and agency with all clients is imperative to the work we do. When it comes to sexuality, one of the goals may be to help older adults see themselves, their sexuality, and their body as viable and worthy of pleasure. This part of the reflective journey is part of adaptation and requires radical acceptance of self. In reality, many of us do not feel older, and there are times we may even deny that we are aging. It is typical to disengage from the chronological age until we are met with health issues, loss of a loved one, or quite possibly, not recognizing the person in the mirror.

How do we learn to accept that our body is not behaving the way we expect it to, in or out of the bedroom? Age is cognitively perceived as constant and yet, when the self is observed in a mirror or in action, there is a possibility that loss, pain, or exhaustion is experienced. Facilitating conversations with clients about their individual desires and how they wish to best fulfill themselves sexually is one of the ways we can increase individual dignity and self-esteem. What are the possible outcomes for sexual experiences and growth? The work of helping individuals mourn functioning, accept the self, and adapt to a new and changing sexual experience and expression is where this journey begins.

Dignity, which can be encompassed in subjective well-being, "refers to the intrinsic value of each human life and has been described as nothing less than a central feature of our humanity" (Harper & Fernee, 2022, p. 1). *Hopefulness* can be integral to having dignity and seeing oneself as a sexual being. As Cotten (2005) described in a review of the film *Still Doing It*, it is vital that people move beyond viewing sexuality as a youth-oriented culture and explore with openness the possibilities for their sexual selves and the intimacy opportunities available to them as a population. Equally as important is confronting stereotypes about virility, vitality, and sin, thus allowing sexual beings to explore positive effects of aspects of humor, being older, and being more comfortable (Cotten, 2005).

Creating a satisfying sexual life is a vital component in the life quality of older individuals and cannot be discounted as only necessary for young people. The more positively connected we are in our relationships, our own sexuality, and our willingness to explore mental and physical realms of touch and intimacy, the more positive outcomes can occur and the more likely the possibility of sexual satisfaction (Byers & Rehman, 2014; Chao et al., 2011; Griebling, 2006; Sánchez-Fuentes et al., 2014; Stephenson & Meston, 2011; Tsang et al., 2012). As helping professionals and guests in the lives of these individuals, we can help them explore how to think about sex and to prime their minds by exploring thoughts and fantasies along with their bodies, understanding their limitations, and then moving out of the box to explore ways of touching, kissing, snuggling, and even involving themselves in love-note writing and other fun fantasy moments.

Reframing the Script

Some people believe that you need to have a partner in order to be sexual. Consequently, when a partner dies, sex is considered unattainable. However, expressing the sexual self is quite possible if intention and attention are given. Masturbation is quite often overlooked; yet, it is one of the most intimate ways to connect with our body and our sexual self. Exploring beliefs and thoughts surrounding sex is important to identify those aspects of our desire that we wish to keep and those that we wish to surrender. The sexual script can also include things that are beyond the physical expression of sexual acts. Our five senses may be included and highlighted to explore our sexual desires—a sexy smell, a lingering musical note, a perfect breeze, a rich flavor, all of which can be revered in a way that honors our sexual script.

Case Example

Dorothy is a 60-year-old multiracial, cisgender female of African American, European, and Mexican decent. Dorothy works as a teacher at an elementary school. After 2 years of abstinence upon the death of her husband of 35 years, Dorothy has for 3 years been involved with Alfredo. She sought counseling initially for grief work to help cope with the loss of her husband. Recently, she has been experiencing issues with menopause, loss of sexual interest, anxiety, some minor pain upon penetration, as well as concerns about incontinence. She is a mother of four and has been suffering some level of incontinence for several years, but it has recently worsened. Dorothy has become very depressed about aging and doesn't feel like she can get help because previously her doctor had been dismissive of her health concerns. As a result, she doesn't want to share her recent sexual concerns and incontinence issues, even though they are taking a toll on her relationship with Alfredo, as well as her own self-esteem.

Dorothy discusses with her counselor her current concerns and seems to feel more at ease as the counselor acknowledges and validates her symptoms and fears. Given that Dorothy struggles with incontinence and vaginal pain during sex, the counselor believes an integrated team approach to her care would be most helpful. The counselor encourages Dorothy to seek out a pelvic floor specialist. While Dorothy receives medical attention for the pain and incontinence, she and the counselor will explore issues surrounding sexual disinterest and decreased self-esteem.

Reflections About the Case Example

After reading this case example, consider the following questions:

1. How would a sex positive counselor approach health, safety, and boundaries with this client?
2. How might a counselor best support Dorothy in evaluating and exploring her sexual script?
3. How might a counselor help Dorothy explore her sexual needs and desires, and later, communicate her struggle with desire with her partner?

Conclusion

Sexuality is part of our lives. It just doesn't come at you when there is someone else in your life. Safe abandon, or the ability to communicate sexual needs with trust and an instilled sense of safety, is paramount to reframing the sexual script, regardless of age. In the counseling space, counselors can model safe places for sexual conversations to occur. In this space, clients can explore and redefine their sexual script to meet them where they are physically, emotionally, and possibly spiritually. Counselors can assist the client in identifying a list of things that embrace desire, celebrate personal sensuality, and honor those things that internally delight the individual. Counselors can help clients become more keenly aware of the little joys in their lives and then connect with those memories of things that bring joy. Once counselors begin to connect clients to this bigger idea of who they are, counselors are better able to help them become more aware of this delicious abandonment. We can take it a step further by asking them what sexuality means to them, when they last felt sexual (if at all), how did that feel when there wasn't anyone to make them feel bad about it (if that ever was a reality), and how do they imagine this could be brought back into their life right now.

Let us reflect on you, the reader, and your personal experience. Where does sexuality, desire, connection, and intimacy fall in the list of priorities of your everyday life? Perhaps you are actively engaging in all aspects, to the best of your ability and to the best of your interest, or perhaps not. What do you need to experience "delicious abandonment" in your life? How might you best support your clients in helping them experience the same?

Questions You Always Wanted to Ask

1. **How can I best support the needs of my older adult clients who reside in the nursing home?**
   Ideally, it would be great to involve the caregivers/powers of attorney, the nursing home, and the local ombudsman. Each may need to receive psychoeducation regarding the importance of honoring said concerns, but it is important regard-

less. Local ombudsmen are specifically trained to advocate for the needs of residents of long-term care facilities.

2. **How can I find out if the long-term care facility is sex positive?**
   Nursing homes have policies that are made available to potential residents and involved parties. It would be helpful to request access to their policies and procedures manual in order to find out what the rules are regarding sexual activity, privacy for intimacy, and consent. Moreover, it would behoove you to look into resident rights, LGBTQ+ rights, and expectations of residents. If there are no rules or policies in place to support the private, intimate needs of residents, be sure to ask to have something written in the contract IF the client feels it is necessary.

References

Bachmann, G., & Santen, R. J. (2020, June 7.). *Patient education: Vaginal dryness (beyond the basics)*. UpToDate. https://www.uptodate.com/contents/vaginal-dryness-beyond-the-basics

Bentrott, M. D., & Margrett, J. A. (2011). Taking a person-centered approach to understanding sexual expression among long-term care residents: Theoretical perspectives and research challenges. *Ageing International, 36*, Article 401. https://doi.org/10.1007/s12126-011-9110-7

Brick, P., Lunquist, J., Sandak, A., & Taverner, B. (2009). *Older, wiser, sexually smarter: 30 lessons for adults only*. Planned Parenthood of Greater Northern New Jersey.

Byers, E. S., & Rehman, U. S. (2014). Sexual well-being. In D. L. Tolman & L. M. Hamilton (Eds.), *APA handbook of sexuality and psychology* (Vol. 1, pp. 317–337). American Psychological Association.

Cameron, A. P., Smith, A. R., Lai, H. H., Bradley, C. S., Liu, A. B., Merion, R. M., Gillespie, B. W., Amundsen, C. L., Cella, D., Griffith, J. W., Wiseman, J. B., Kreder, K. J., Kenton, K. S., Helmuth, M. E., Fraser, M. O., Clemens, J. Q., Kirkali, Z., Kusek, J. W., Siddiqui, N. Y., & LURN Study Group. (2018). Bowel function, sexual function, and symptoms of pelvic organ prolapse in women with and without urinary incontinence. *Neurourology and Urodynamics, 37*(8), 2586–2596. https://doi.org/10.1002/nau.23587

Chao, J.-K., Lin, Y.-C., Ma, M.-C., Lai, C.-J., Ku, Y.-C., Kuo, W.-H., & Chao, I.-C. (2011). Relationship among sexual desire, sexual satisfaction, and quality of life in middle-aged and older adults. *Journal of Sex & Marital Therapy, 37*(5), 386–403. http://doi.org/10.1080/0092623X.2011.607051

Cotten, A. L. (2005). Still doing it: The intimate lives of women over 65 [Review]. *Sexual and Relationship Therapy, 20*(4), 483–484. https://doi.org/10.1080/14681990500296081

Croft, L. H. (1982). *Sexuality in later life: A counseling guide for physicians*. Bristol-Wright.

Drummond, J. D., Brotman, S., Silverman, M., Sussman, T., Orzeck, P., Barylak, L., & Wallach, I. (2013). The impact of caregiving: Older women's experiences of sexuality and intimacy. *Affilia, 28*(4), 415–428. https://doi.org/10.1177/0886109913504154

Ferrini, M. G., Gonzalez-Cadavid, N. F., & Rajfer, J. (2017). Aging related erectile dysfunction-potential mechanism to halt or delay its onset. *Translational Andrology and Urology, 6*(1), 20–27. https://doi.org/10.21037/tau.2016.11.18

Gentili, A., & Mulligan, T. (1998). Sexual dysfunction in older adults. *Clinics in Geriatric Medicine, 14*(2), 383–394. https://doi.org/10.1016/S0749-0690(18)30123-X

Gott, M., & Hinchliff, S. (2003). How important is sex in later life? The views of older people. *Social Science & Medicine, 56*(8), 1617–1628. https://doi.org/10.1016/s0277-9536(02)00180-6

Griebling, T. L. (2006). The impact of urinary incontinence on sexual health in older adults. *Journal of the American Geriatrics Society, 54*(8), 1290–1292. http://doi.org/10.1111/j.1532-5415.2006.00864.x

Hajjar, R. R., & Kamel, H. K. (2004). Sexuality in the nursing home, Part 1: Attitudes and barriers to sexual expression. *Journal of the American Medical Directors Association, 5*(2), S43–S47. https://doi.org/10.1016/S1525-8610(04)70092-4

Harper, N. J., & Fernee, C. R. (2022). Unpacking relational dignity: In pursuit of an ethic of care for outdoor therapies. *Frontiers in Psychology,* Article 766283. https://doi.org/10.3389/fpsyg.2022.766283

Hayes, R., & Dennerstein, L. (2005). The impact of aging on sexual function and sexual dysfunction in women: A review of population-based studies. *The Journal of Sexual Medicine, 2*(3), 317–330. https://doi.org/10.1111/j.1743-6109.2005.20356.x

King, J. H. (2014, February). Deconstructing the *DSM-5*: Assessment and diagnosis of sexual and gender related disorders. *Counseling Today*, 12–15.

Kleinplatz, P. J., Ménard, A. D., Paradis, N., Campbell, M., & Dalgleish, T. L. (2013). Beyond sexual stereotypes: Revealing group similarities and differences in optimal sexuality. *Canadian Journal of Behavioural Science, 45*(3), 250–258.

Laflin, M. T. (1996). Promoting the sexual health of geriatric patients. *Topics in Geriatric Rehabilitation, 11*(4), 43–54. https://doi.org/10.1097/00013614-199606000-00008

Lindau, S. T., Schumm, L. P., Laumann, E. O., Levinson, W., O'Muircheartaigh, C. A., & Waite, L. J. (2007). A study of sexuality and health among older adults in the United States. *New England Journal of Medicine, 357,* 762–774. https://doi.org/10.1056/NEJMoa067423

Maciel, M., & Laganà, L. (2014). Older women's sexual desire problems: Biopsychosocial factors impacting them and barriers to their clinical assessment. *BioMed Research International, 2014*, Article 107217. https://doi.org/10.1155/2014/107217

Muzacz, A., & Akinsulure-Smith, A. (2013). Older adults and sexuality: Implications for counseling ethnic and sexual minority clients. *Journal of Mental Health Counseling, 35*(1), 1–14. https://doi.org/10.17744/mehc.35.1.534385v3r0876235

Nappi, R. E., Albani, F., Valentino, V., Polatti, F., Chiovato, L., & Genazzani, A. R. (2007). Invecchiamento e sessualità nelle donne [Aging and sexuality in women]. *Minervaginecologica, 59*(3), 287–298.

Pope, M., & Schulz, R. (1990). Sexual attitudes and behavior in midlife and aging homosexual males. *Journal of Homosexuality, 20*(3–4), 169–177. https://doi.org/10.1300/J082v20n03_11

Price, J. (2019). *Sex after grief: Navigating your sexuality after losing your beloved.* Mango Publishing Group.

Radosh, A., & Simkin, L. (2016). Acknowledging sexual bereavement: A path out of disenfranchised grief. *Reproductive Health Matters, 24*(48), 25–33. https://doi.org/10.1016/j.rhm.2016.11.005

Sánchez-Fuentes, M. M., Santos-Iglesias, P., & Sierra, J. C. (2014). A systematic review of sexual satisfaction. *International Journal of Clinical and Health Psychology, 14*(1), 67–75. https://doi.org/10.1016/S1697-2600(14)70038-9

Schubert, A., & Pope, M. (2020). Sexuality beyond young adulthood: Affordances and barriers to sexual expression in the nursing home. *Journal of Counseling Sexology & Sexual Wellness, 2*(1), Article 5. https://doi.org/doi:10.34296/02011022

Stephenson, K. R., & Meston, C. (2011). The association between sexual costs and sexual satisfaction in women: An exploration of the interpersonal exchange model of sexual satisfaction. *Canadian Journal of Human Sexuality, 20*, 31–40.

Tsang, A. K. T., Fuller-Thompson, E., & Lai, D. W. L. (2012). Sexuality and health among Chinese seniors in Canada. *Journal of International Migration and Integration, 13*, 525–540. https://doi.org/10.1007/s12134-011-0221-5

Twitchell, D. K., Wittmann, D. A., Hotaling, J. M., & Pastuszak, A. W. (2019). Psychological impacts of male sexual dysfunction in pelvic cancer survivorship. *Sexual Medicine Reviews, 7*(4), 614–626. https://doi.org/10.1016/j.sxmr.2019.02.003

Willert, A., & Semans, M. P. (2000). Knowledge and attitudes about later life sexuality: What clinicians need to know about helping the elderly. *Contemporary Family Therapy, 22*, 415–435.

Zeglin, R. J. (2019, February 7–10). *Human sexuality counseling competency for college populations: Applying the life course health development model* [Conference session]. 2019 American College Counseling Association Conference, San Diego, California, United States.

The Queer Crip

Julie Lynn Williams and Virginia Ogletree

In this chapter, we will review current research on sexuality and disability at the intersection of the queer and crip. Counselors will learn how to support clients to embrace both their disability and their lesbian, gay, bisexual, transgender, and queer plus other (LGBTQ+) identities. We also introduce sex surrogacy as a healing and valid intervention for queer-crip communities.

The queer crip is the intersectional human experience that produces pervasive silence among the heteronormative and temporarily able-bodied community, resulting in painful invisibility for those who hold disabled bodies and queerness. *Queer crip* refers to the community of people who challenge cis-heteronormativity and disrupt systems that able-ize sexuality. Use of the terms "queer" and "crip" reclaims labels that were once hurtful, recentering them with pride and political agency.

It is no wonder the queer-crip community is largely invisible, given that cisgenderism and ableism are framed predominantly by heteronormative binaries and able-bodied images. Ableist images portray beauty and attractiveness in bodies that are symmetrical and move with volitional control and fluidity. Ableist and cis-heteronormative narratives suggest that to be sexual, one must perform within a narrow set of physiological functions. Furthermore, the absence of disabled bodies in LGBTQ+ literature amplifies the silence and invisibility of sexual expression for the disabled. Likewise, the rejection of LGBTQ+ individuals within the disability community renders their experiences and perspectives invisible. Where does that leave the queer crip? Erased and absent from professional literature. Therefore, this chapter will center queerness and cripness.

The framing of this chapter is both professional and personal. I, coauthor Julie Lynn Williams, am writing this chapter at the age of 55 and from the voice of a dwarf, queer, hard-of-hearing, White and cisgender professor of psychology and clinical psychologist who practices liberatory and affirming therapies. It is here I wish to pay homage to my chosen family from queer-crip communities. To all the crips and queers who have come before me and are with me now, I love you all, and I strive to bring authenticity and healing to our narratives. Call me out if I fall short and then call me back in as I continue to challenge myself and the world of professional counselors to get it right as they work to see us, hear us, and join us on our journeys toward our sexual freedom. Peace and solidarity.

I, coauthor Virginia Ogletree, am writing this at the age of 48 and from the voice of a currently nondisabled, lesbian, White and cisgender woman from a low socioeconomic status background. I appreciate and am grateful for the opportunity to participate in the authorship of this chapter and this endeavor to help counselors and other mental health providers be more culturally humble, competent, and inclusive in their work with queer-crip clients. This work can be challenging, but I promise you will likely find it rewarding, as I have, if you are open and receptive to these experiences.

The Literature

Normative sexual and ability paradigms result in the marginalization and the suffering of the disabled. Normative paradigms leave us with a narrow conceptualization of all that brings pleasure and connectedness with our bodies and each other. In this chapter, we will introduce and expand the dialogue, offer liberatory and healing interventions, and suggest systemic changes. These are lofty goals for a chapter. To this end, we will deconstruct the oppressive narratives of normalcy that shroud ability and sexuality and offer an expanded truth and pathway for mental health providers who have the honor and privilege to provide mental health care at the intersections of queerness and cripness. Furthermore, we will strive to bring evidence to and extend the works of those who have bravely shared their cripness and queerness, expertise, and lived experience at the 2015 and 2017 Breaking Silences, Demanding Crip Justice: Sex, Sexuality, and Disability conferences hosted by Wright State University School of Professional Psychology in Dayton, Ohio (see https://corescholar.libraries.wright.edu/breaking_silences).

The Breaking Silences conference presenters' work represents a proud claiming of disability identity as a natural and normal human experience that enhances, rather than diminishes, one's sexuality. Many of the ideas shared within Breaking Silences have been considered radical, because when asked anonymously about their "real" thoughts on disability, people generally describe disability as something that is abnormal, tragic, and to be pitied. Classified in this way, disability becomes something to treat, cure, or correct. Furthermore, when curative measures are not possible, disability becomes something to tolerate, prevent, or eliminate—the ultimate erasure of us. But it does not have to be this way. Mental health providers with disabilities or temporarily without disabilities have a pivotal role to play to eradicate this pain and break silences.

A chapter that brings together sexuality and disability in and of itself is critical to the counseling world, which is charged with addressing and alleviating human suffering and doing so in a culturally humble and competent manner. Addressing the needs of the queer crip in an academic manuscript is nothing short of revolutionary as evidenced by its absence in professional mental health literature. The absence is problematic as the intersectional appreciation of diversity as a professional competency is now a mandate within our human services professions. For example, the American Psychological Association (APA, 2017) has released *Multicultural Guidelines: An Ecological Approach to Context, Identity, and Intersectionality*, which emphasize multicultural inclusivity in services (Guideline 6) and call for social activism when social and political forces are creating and maintaining human suffering (Guideline 9). APA's (2022) *Guidelines for Assessment and Intervention with Persons with Disabilities* provided information on how psychologists could improve their competency in disability-related matters, make their practices more accessible and disability-sensitive, and implement more effective assessments for persons with disabilities—all of which are relevant to people at the intersection of queer and crip.

Within the 2022 APA disability guidelines, research is provided that illuminates disparities and struggles within the disability community. Specific to sexuality and intersectionality, research on women with disabilities found that women with disabilities experience depression and low self-esteem (Hughes et al., 2015; Niemeier, 2008; Nosek et al., 2001). This was further linked to social isolation, quality of intimate relationships, pain, and higher risk of abuse (Nosek et al., 2001). The gendering of disabilities and unique differences has been highlighted in Marini's (2001) research, which found that men with disabilities may experience psychological distress ranging from threats to sexual identity and masculinity to concerns about self-reliance, independence, and employment.

Yet, the coverage of the intersection of lesbian, gay, bisexual, transgender with disability in mental health literature is scarce. Olkin (2009) indicated that these communities are more likely to be ostracized by their own families as well as from queer communities that do not embrace disabilities. The culmination of these intersections is invisibility, silence, and barriers to finding sexual expressions, body positivity, and even partner(s). *Intersectionality theory*, as defined by Kimberlé Crenshaw (1989), refers to the interconnection of multiple identities in which the identities overlap and are linked in a prejudicial, discriminatory, and oppressive system. All identities (e.g., gender, race, class, sexual orientation, ability status) are affected. For example, a Black woman will face racism and misogyny, but the racism she faces will differ from the racism a Black man faces, and the misogyny she faces will differ from the misogyny a White woman faces. If she is also disabled, the ableism she faces will be influenced by racism and misogyny and so will differ from the ableism faced by a White man, for example. Likewise, the ableism faced by a poor, gay, White man will differ from the ableism faced by an affluent, straight, Black woman.

In providing affirming and liberatory services to members of the queer-crip community, it is worthwhile to adopt an intersectional mindset so as to best understand the interdependent, overlapping oppressive systems that contribute to their lived experiences. When considering intersectionality theory and systemic contributions, mental health professionals can better understand sexual freedoms as a human rights issue for both the queer and disabled communities, rather than as a medical or psychological problem (McRuer, 2018). Conceptualizing sexuality as a human right further creates a sense of urgency to not only become competent mental health professionals to those with disabilities on an individual level but also to offer healing systemic changes as we become aware of and challenge our own biases and ultimately disrupt the systems that create the suffering. As you are reading this, you may be asking yourself "What does this look like?"

We will begin the unpacking of the queer-crip experience by reviewing the current status of sexual disparities universally experienced by the disability community as connected to disability civil rights. Research shows that individuals with disabilities often are left with little to no information about their sexual health, and the information they do obtain is often irrelevant or unhelpful (Kaufman et al., 2007). On an individual level, counselors and other mental health professionals can offer access to information and resources and connect the client to affirming communities. On a systemic level, they can advocate for institutional policies favorable to the development of sex-inclusive education, intersectional understandings of LGBTQ+ crip communities, and improved training of sexual health providers to work with a diversity of bodies. In addition, understanding sexuality as a disability civil rights issue is critical; sexual freedoms are rarely considered within the Americans With Disabilities Act (ADA) of 1990 or the ADA Amendments Act of 2008. The ADA addresses fundamental rights across important life domains, but it does not address sexual health rights specifically or societal attitudinal beliefs that cultivate the grounds for sexual oppression. For example, in cases of sexual abuse, if one is not seen as sexual, then one is not seen as a target for sexual abuse. This creates an absence of prevention/detection efforts and responses to sexual abuse when it involves persons with disabilities and particularly when the abuse involves disability service providers such as personal care attendants (PCAs).

As a society, we have language and laws that address interpersonal violence, and we have advocacy systems (albeit, still fighting for their place in criminal justice systems) that offer services to victims of interpersonal violence. However, we have no language or system to address situations in which interpersonal violence and sexual assault are perpetrated by PCAs. This leaves the disabled victim without much-needed advocacy and emotional support. The cumulative impact increases the vulnerability to abuse, extends the length of abuse, creates a rationale for the denial of reproductive rights, lowers sexual esteem, and reduces sexual satisfaction. This is another systemic space where mental health professionals can advocate for language and legal systemic responses that consider the interpersonal relationship and power dynamics that can play out between the disabled and their PCAs as perpetrators of sexual violence. On an individual level, narrative exposure therapy for trauma (Schauer et al., 2011) is the preferred intervention for the authors of this chapter as it allows for a processing and holding of an abuse story that may involve chronic, repetitive abuse and possibly from a multitude of abusers.

Another important experience related to trauma as many have written about (Williams & Colvin, 2016) is that having a disability exposes the disabled body to potential wanted and unwanted medical touch that can be appropriate and inappropriate. Regardless of whether it is wanted and appropriate or not, medical touch and interventions are inherently intrusive to the body. Therefore, the trauma narrative may involve reliving and processing somatic memories the disabled body holds. The work of Levine (1997) offers reparative talk and body work to address the able-ized trauma the body holds. Mental health professionals may refer to Levine's (1997) pivotal book, *Waking the Tiger*, as a resource. Trauma impacts how one connects safely and finds pleasure within the body; therefore, given the prevalence of trauma within the disability community from both perpetrators and as a consequence of medical interventions, assessing for and providing room for trauma work can be an important first step in undertaking affirming and liberatory therapies.

Conceptually, restorative justice and reparative justice may further deepen the work mental health professionals do with queer-crip communities. These models consider the invisibility of intersectional communities and oppressive impacts as social constructs that require an understanding of "How did we get here?" and the identification of who has been harmed and how such harm might be repaired individually and collectively. I, author Williams, in 2013 was approached by disability providers presenting a concern for sex awareness for college students with disabilities. The suggestion was to bring in a speaker to talk to disabled college students about "sex appropriate behaviors." At that time, I was admittedly annoyed. "Who and what are we fixing?" I asked. "And who is being given the power to be the fixer?" This is when the concept of having a sex and disability conference began to take shape in my head. Although I continue to provide individual and group interventions to clients from an affirming and liberatory framework, no work I have ever done has had the same healing and liberatory effect as bringing together the community of crips and queers that I love, care for, and live within.

The review that follows will unpack how queerphobic, ableist narratives have formed, have done harm, and thus can be healed in direct-care modalities. The review will start with identification and descriptions of disability-related sexual myths, historical disability models, and prevailing attitudes toward queer-crip communities. And finally, we will describe what liberators are doing to correct and heal.

A comprehensive list of sexual myths for the disabled is found in the book *The Ultimate Guide to Sex and Disability* by Kaufman et al. (2007). We recommend that every counselor obtain this resource, which describes some common myths about persons with disabilities (PWD) and sex as follows:

- PWD cannot have sex
- PWD are asexual and asexuality is not a form of sexuality
- PWD have more important things to worry about
- PWD are not desirable
- Sex must be spontaneous
- PWD can't have real sex
- PWD are pathetic partner choices
- PWD who have sex are perverted
- People living in institutions should not have sex
- Sex is private
- PWD will hurt themselves
- PWD don't need sex education
- PWD are not sexually assaulted

On review of these myths, it is not hard to consider how these beliefs lead to systemic sexual health disparities in the form of poor and/or limited sexual health information, violation of reproductive rights, and even inaccessible medical offices (Silvers et al., 2016). Again, if the disabled body is not seen as a sexual body, then it is not seen as needing sexual health services, reproductive rights, and sexual pleasure or as a potential location of sexual assault. According to Human Rights Watch (2011), forced sterilization of girls and women with disabilities continues to occur and to be "justified by governments, legal, medical and other professionals, and family members and carers as being in the 'best interests' of women and girls with disabilities" (para. 4). Questioning parenting abilities of disabled parents is real. And while annual Pap smear examinations are suggested for the temporarily able-bodied world, accessibility has been used to deny and or discourage annual pelvic examinations for disabled people, further disempowering them and depriving them of needed information and preventive care in matters of cancer detection and more. The perception that sexual pleasure in the LGBTQ+ community can only be obtained through perversion, or the perception that all queer sexual activity is perverted, further pathologizes the community and creates fertile ground for the internalization of self-loathing.

Unpacking sexual myths further requires a quick journey into disability history for a moment as it relates to common disability attitudinal themes and prevalent models of disabilities that have framed the lived experience of disability across time and currently. Again, we are asking ourselves to understand the queer-crip experience by asking ourselves, "How did we get here?" An important pathway to getting us here has been linked to embracing Puritan (or generally Christian or religious) attitudes toward human sexuality, specifically that sexual pleasure is inherently sinful/dirty/shameful and that the only acceptable type of, and reason for, sexual activity is reproduction (Friedman, 2018; Livneh, 1982). This then easily translates to the idea that sex between men and sex between women is perverse/disgusting/evil and that sex with or between disabled people is also perverse/disgusting/evil, because we certainly do not want them making more disabled bodies.

Research has offered that attitudes toward disability in general are negative (Livneh, 1982). Disability attitudes often reflect a theme of inferiority in mind, body, and spirit. In this way, PWD are seen as burdens, second-class citizens, and unattractive. Feelings of pity expressed by nondisabled people, although not viewed as macroaggressive, nonetheless are perceived by PWD as patronizing microaggressions. People who are not yet disabled often assume that disabled people exist in a state of perpetual suffering. Another common belief is the *spread effect*, which suggests that if one is disabled in one dimension, one must be disabled in other or all dimensions. The spread effect is often seen when the assumption of one's competency is questioned as a rule until proven otherwise. The impact of *assumed incompetency* is confirmed in literature that shows that parenting rights and reproductive rights are questioned more often and without cause in disabled parents. Disabled people who report a sexual assault are often not believed and do not receive appropriate access to help, particularly if they are Deaf, cognitively different, or have a psychiatric disability (Browne et al., 2016; Harrell, 2014; Lund, 2011). *Hero worship* occurs when a disabled person is viewed as particularly super-human simply for surviving. What is known in the disabled community as *inspiration porn* is media that portrays a disabled person demonstrating a valued ability, such as a blind skier or a one-armed swimmer. Inspiration porn objectifies the accomplished disabled person and holds them up to nondisabled people as if to say, "See how lucky you are?" or "If this person can run a marathon on prosthetic legs, what's your excuse?" The person who is supposedly in a state of perpetual suffering has somehow found a noble way to cope with their suffering.

Offering a useful perspective on how attitudes form, disability models have been offered as ways to understand how attitudes form, function, and posture the disabled community within society and as sexual beings. Olkin (2002) outlines the disability models and discusses how they impact the disabled experience. First, the *moral model of disability* holds that disability is divine retribution for sin and/or a test of faith and that the cure for it lies in faith. In this model, the disabled person and/or their family is responsible for them being disabled. Society responds with charity, prayer, blame, and/or forgiveness. Second, the *medical or normalcy model*, which is the prevailing model in use today, holds that disability is a bodily defect or abnormality that needs to be cured so the disabled person can function in society. Society responds with efforts to correct, eliminate, and/or prevent disability. This manifests as medical interventions to create or restore functionality for disabled people, abort fetuses that show signs of disability, and forcibly sterilize disabled people. Disabled people are expected to try to be as "normal" as possible. Finally, the *minority, minority group, or social model* holds that disability is a social construct and is defined and maintained by sociopolitical factors. Society responds by embracing disability as natural, promoting disabled perspectives and empowerment, assuming competence in disabled people, and working to achieve inclusivity.

Disabled sexuality under the moral model is considered perversion. Disabled sexuality under the medical model is largely ignored, as disabled people are perceived as neither wanting nor being able to have sexual experiences. The social model embraces and seeks to facilitate disabled sexuality, while also acknowledging and honoring that asexuality is a legitimate sexual orientation.

As you go forward in your career as a mental health professional, it will be important to bear in mind the prevalence of the medical model and the ways in which it has impacted the lived experience of your clients with disabilities. Sexually oppressive beliefs about disabled people are widely held by people who provide services to the disabled community, whether they are parents, children, siblings, or spouses functioning as caregivers or whether they are medical or mental health professionals. A 2018 study by Chou et al. found that university students showed more positive attitudes toward their peers with disabilities than did parents and disability professionals. The researchers concluded that parents and professionals needed education and awareness of sexual health needs of children with intellectual disability, especially girls (Chou et al., 2018). The irony of this study's findings is that attitudinal acceptance of sexuality within disability communities was lower in those who had central roles in the lives of disability community members.

What Can Be Done: Disability Justice/Crip Culture Speaks

"Do You First"; Yep, I Said It

Typically, a discussion of population-specific needs involves describing the interventions. Although this of course is critical, author Williams, who writes as a self-identified crip, queer, hard-of-hearing, cisgender, dwarf, activist ally offers a first step that involves engaging in hard and honest self-reflection around personally held beliefs about disability and sexuality. Consistent with APA (2022) Guideline 2, psychologists strive to examine their beliefs and emotional reactions toward various disabilities and determine how these may influence their work. Within this guideline, mental health professionals of all ability statuses should

a. examine preconceptions, beliefs, and emotional reactions toward persons with disabilities;
b. consider how disability-related and other life experiences, separately or together, might be related to the client's current problems;
c. assess the client's strengths and weaknesses and incorporate them into interventions;
d. emphasize the client's realistic possibilities rather than limitations in social, vocational, and educational endeavors;
e. integrate disability-related case material and topics into professional discussions, study groups, courses, and seminars;
f. contact professionals in the community who can provide consultation and/or supervision; and
g. become familiar with disability resources in the community and explore opportunities to strengthen engagement. (APA, 2022, Guideline 2, pp. 8–9)

Immersion in Queer-Crip Communities

In addition to following the APA (2022) guidelines, a mental health professional is encouraged to find experts in the field and engage in immersive experiences with these communities. As this chapter is being written, we are restricting our movements due to the COVID-19 pandemic. Therefore, immersion experiences can be restricted to virtual engagements. Queer-crip communities have long used virtual forums for engagement, education, and affinity. Virtual platforms offer expanded access and connections to communities that are often fragmented from one another. Virtual platforms to consider include such platforms as Sins Invalid (https://sinsinvalid.org), Krip Hop Nation (kriphopnation.com), and Andrew Gurza's *DisabilityAfterDark* podcast (see http://www.andrewgurza.com/home) and other works that have brought queer-crip experiences to the mainstream.

Additionally, consider engaging with disability rights organizations such as ADAPT (adapt.org) that are on the front line challenging and offering liberating narratives and trainings from the community of disabilities, celebrating persons of color, queer, nonbinary, and more. Many of these organizations and the individuals involved with them can be found on social media.

Acquire Knowledge

Just as it is important to examine your beliefs and attitudes toward sexuality and disability, the acquisition of knowledge is important. Professional journals and organizations for a variety of disciplines exist that focus on disability-related issues, including sexuality. Organizations available for psychologists include divisions in the APA, such as Division 22 (Rehabilitation Psychology), Division 27 (Society for Community Research and Action), and Division 33 (Intellectual and Developmental Disabilities). Furthermore, the APA Committee on Disability Issues in Psychology is available to offer consultation and mentorship to professionals with disability and those striving to develop competency in disability work (APA, n.d.). Organizations specifically for counselors include the American Counseling Association and its many divisions, such as the American Rehabilitation Counseling Association; Counselors for Social Justice; and the Society for Sexual, Affectional, Intersex, and Gender Expansive Identities. Organizations for social workers include the National Association of Social Workers and the Clinical Social Work Association. Many of these organizations also publish scholarly journals.

We include a caveat here for mental health professionals: When seeking sources of guidance to inform your practice, defer to those sources that are written and researched by those who live the life of disability or have identified evidence of their allyship if they are not yet disabled. There is a saying in the disability community that there should be "nothing about us without us."

Disability Justice and Crip Theory

Conceptually, it is also important to understand disability justice paradigms as movements that emphasize healing that can be manifested in mental health treatment work. In this way, mental health professionals can learn from disability justice workers about the healing to queer communities as a function of building communities; celebrating and promoting wholeness; working within crip and queer movements; providing sexual education, dialogues, and information relevant to the queer-crip narrative; and ultimately breaking the silence and bringing visibility to the intersections. *Disability justice* refers to a need for solidarity across disability groups and within disability groups, the promotion of wholeness, and inclusion and solidarity with other marginalized groups. In the words of Mia Mingus, a member of the queer-crip community, activist, and liberator,

> Disability justice deals with the oppression of disability, but at the same time deals with other systems of oppression and injustice—it is a "multi-issue politic." It moves beyond rights- and equality-based approaches, beyond access and inclusion in unjust systems, instead working towards collective justice and liberation, towards transforming society as a whole. (MacDougall, 2013, 13:39)

Finally, crip theory offers another way to conceptualize mental health approaches to queer-crip communities. As stated by Bennett (2007) reviewing the work of McRuer (2018), "Crip theory is concerned with the ways in which neoliberal capitalism (the dominant economic and cultural system as driven by market priorities) has imagined and composed sexual and embodied identities" (Bennett, 2007, para. 1). Much of McRuer's work parallels the work of queer theory.

The Language We Use

Language is another powerful intervention that can promote or injure. Wright (1983, 1987) proposed in her scholarship that an important pathway to affirmative healing is by bringing awareness to the objectifying disability language used historically and the move toward liberatory language relevant today to queer-crip communities. Wright described the inhumane treatment of the disabled when identified solely as their impairment resulting in the erasure of them as a whole person (Dunn & Elliott, 2005). Research supports the reality that when disability is visible and present, onlookers erase all other aspects of the person's identity (Rohmer & Louvet, 2009).

In the 1990s, the movement toward "people first" language emerged. With this approach to language, an individual was not "spinal cord injured" but rather "a person with a spinal cord injury." More recently, an argument has been made for "Say the Word" (Andrews et al., 2019). Similar to other movements within marginalized communities, there has been a reclaiming of those terms, including disability names, that have been used in a damaging manner. As mental health professionals, the forms we develop and the intake and assessments we use and administer need to be consistent with progressive crip and queer communities. Pronouns need to be inclusive of nonbinary identities and included on intake forms, with space for disability labels as defined by our clients and sexual inclusive terms reflecting all bodies and human experiences represented by LGBTQ+. Perhaps there might even be open spaces for the client to simply explain and name self.

The use of the terms crip and queer goes beyond saying the word. It is important to distinguish between the political intentions behind the linguistics of Say the Word and liberatory language. Say the Word refers to an attempt to erase the shame associated with descriptive disability terms. The use of the words "crip" and "queer," previously derogatory terms used against LGBTQ+ and disability communities, represents a political taking back and centering of the pride and power of the disability and queer communities. Put this way it is not a mere naming but a celebration of and act of resistance. In a sense, it is a pushing back against the verbal weapons of ableist, cisgender heteronormativists. In therapeutic settings, clients struggling with the impacts of oppressed genders, sexualities, and disabilities may not own these identities or words as valid and something that gives them strength. Eli Clare (1999) offers the following statement that captures the complexity of the intersection: "Gender reaches into disability; disability wraps around class; class strains against abuse; abuse snarls into sexuality; sexuality folds on top of race . . . everything finally piling onto a single human body" (p. 123). Put this way, the client may have internalized all that is negative and injurious, and therefore, therapy offers a space potentially to unpack and bring awareness and strategies to address internalized negative self-beliefs. Therapy therefore can be a process of discovery and birth to new and unrealized identities. Sins Invalid refers to this in the ending of their performance as "we are coming home" (Milbern, 2011).

Affirming Therapies

Affirming therapies were initially introduced to mental health professionals as a corrective therapy for the gay community, known as gay-affirming treatment (Kort, 2008). Olkin (2009) later, using gay-affirming therapy tenets, applied affirmative therapy conceptually to the disability community. Olkin (2009) defined disability-affirmative therapy (D-AT) as therapy that "considers the political, legal, economic, financial, social, educational, familial, as well as the personal impact of disability in a cultural and historical context" (p. 367) and introduced strategies to offer affirming therapy within the context of direct services. Such strategies include understanding the client's developmental history and the relevant disability model that best informs their experience. Olkin (2009) also offered special attention to accessibility of clinical services, including such considerations as access to office, mobility barriers, paperwork, and inclusivity of questions asked. She also shared disability-specific issues related to the experience of trauma beyond typical understandings, such as assaults, and included trauma that may have occurred in the course of intrusive medical and/or personal care. Her work was the first to take into consideration the sociopolitical context of disability to inform assessment, interventions, and the clinical environment.

D-AT is considered pantheoretical and it conceptualizes sexuality as an important domain to explore with all clients. Olkin (2009) offered the following questions to consider when exploring sexuality and intimacy with the disabled client:

- Does the client feel they choose partners as much as the partners choose them?
- Is acceptance of the client as a person with a disability a salient feature of the client's partners?
- Does the client have adequate sexual knowledge relevant to disability and/or otherwise?
- How does disability play a role in relationships?

Case Example

We will use a case example to discuss affirming and liberatory approaches to intersectional process issues. The case example offered is that of an individual with spastic cerebral palsy, impacting speech and volitional control of arms and legs. The client, Jasper, identifies as a gay Black man. He has never dated or experienced a sexual encounter.

The presenting problem is a young adult who is struggling with virginity and wishing to be engaged in a sexual relationship with another individual. The client experiences body shame and self-loathing. Jasper has a long-term goal of finding a committed relationship. He identifies a troubling memory that appears to be a significant trauma secondary to medical treatment and interventions that were not painful or life threatening but were not needed and placed Jasper in spaces of humiliation. A common memory for adults with disabilities who were treated as children in academic medical institutions is that of being stripped naked for doctors in training and examined by a team of doctors looking on, touching, and discussing their body. This has been a repetitive experience for many young children, leaving them with feelings of aversion to touch, shame, and loss of control over one's body. The message conveyed can be a profound belief that "my body is not my own."

Jasper, the client in this case example, has had these experiences in the context of being gay, Black, and a boy/man. The impacts of Jasper's sexual orientation, race, and gender on his life experiences generally, and on his experiences as a disabled person specifically, intersect in ways that may compound the harm done by being subjected to the ideals, norms, and expectations of society. Being gay alone may have "othered" him in his family, at school, in his community, at work, and in society at large, and/or been a source of shame or fear. Being Black alone may have led to him having been mistreated by teachers, employers, law enforcement officers, medical professionals, and the general public. Being a man alone may mean he was socialized to always be tough, constrict his experience and expression of emotion, and avoid intimacy and vulnerability.

Inclusive Spaces

D-AT and sex positivity begin the moment the client arrives at the counseling clinic, before the actual interventions commence. Before treating clients, we suggest that mental health professionals take a long look at their office space and clinical process. Is it inclusive? Are the forms accessible? Are the questions asked on intake inclusive to queer and crip communities? Will clients receive welcoming messages when they enter the clinical space? Will they see images that represent them? Will it be comfortable? Will it be safe? And how will you know? Prior to working with queer-crip communities, consider inviting experts to audit your office and clinic. Go beyond the requirements of the ADA accessibility checklist. Remember, this work is about honoring wholeness and inclusivity, not merely compliance. Ask for honest and direct feedback on problems with access and inclusivity, and then fix them! Leah Lakshmi Piepzna-Samarasinha (2018) described the profound meaning of transformative inclusivity:

> I mean that when we reach for each other and make the most access possible, it is a radical act of love. When access is centralized at the beginning dream of every action or event, that is radical love. I mean that access is far more to me than a checklist of accessibility needs—though checklists are needed and necessary. I mean that without deep love and care for each other, for our crip body minds, an event can have all the fragrance-free soap and interpreters and thirty-six-inch-wide doorways in the world. And it can still be empty. I've been asked to do disability and access trainings by well-meaning organizations that want the checklists, the ten things they can do to make things accessible. I know that if they do those things, without changing their internal worlds that see disabled people as sad and stupid, or refuse to see those of us already in their lives, they can have all the ASL [American Sign Language] and ramps in the world, and we won't come where we're not loved, needed, and understood as leaders, not just people they must begrudgingly provide services for. (p. 76) . . . When disabled people get free, everyone gets free. More access makes everything more accessible for everybody. (p. 78)

D-AT works toward eradication of internalized shame around disability and gay identification. Creating a space of nonjudging and collaborative exploration of sexuality and body awareness can set the stage for successive approximations to the goal of sexual intimacy in the form of behavioral experiments with self, sensate focus work, and even perhaps joining a social group meetup virtually or in person with queer-crip communities. Other behavioral experiments can involve low intensity, such as inviting a coworker to a movie, or high intensity, such as the adjunctive use of relational surrogacy.

Partner Surrogacy: What Is It? How Does It Work? When Should You Refer? Is It Legal?

Love Poem to No-One in Particular

Let me touch you with my words
for my hands lie limp as empty gloves
let my words stroke your hair
slide down your back
and tickle your belly
for my hands, light and free flying as bricks
ignore my wishes and stubbornly refuse to carry out my quietest desires
let my words enter your mind
bearing torches
admit them willingly into your being
so they may caress you gently
within.

— Mark O'Brien
(poet, activist, disabled, deceased)

Mark O'Brien, poet, activist, lover, and sexual being with a disability wrote these words. His story was the subject of the 2012 movie *The Sessions* (Lewin, 2012), which depicted his quest for love, intimacy, his first sexual experience, and ultimately, a life partner. His journey involved the support of what was then called a "sex surrogate." Although *The Sessions* was popular and certainly groundbreaking for many, it is important to know that the specific steps and understandings of partnership surrogacy were not well defined in that movie.

Sex surrogacy refers to the use of another to explore one's body and relational possibilities. The current terminology is *partner surrogacy*, whereby the emphasis is not restricted to "sex" but rather is relational (see, for example, https://www.healthline.com/health/healthy-sex/sex-surrogate). The International Professional Surrogates Association (IPSA, n.d.) describes surrogate partner therapy as a therapeutic team comprising a client, a licensed therapist, and a surrogate partner who work together to "build client self-awareness and skills in the areas of physical and emotional intimacy" (para. 1).

A brief overview will be provided below about surrogate partnership parameters, referral processes, certifications, ethics, and how to become a surrogate partner. First, the distinction between sex therapy and surrogacy is important. In short, sex therapy involves the talk, and surrogacy involves the talk, experiential activities, and touch. Again, surrogacy does not just mean sexual contact but can involve sexual intercourse. Surrogacy may involve relaxation, mindfulness, communication, and sensual and sexual touch exercises. Exactly which services are provided is determined by the treatment goals. As such, the goals of partner surrogacy will vary from client to client and will be determined by a collaboration between client, licensed professional, and surrogate. Typically, the licensed clinical professional is in regular communication with the partner surrogate and while the client is engaging in individual talk therapies and separate partner surrogate meetings. Treatment goals can involve addressing virginity, developing a greater understanding and awareness of one's body, struggles with body shame, and /or recovery from abuse.

The potential benefit of partner surrogate is vast. As someone comes to know their body, there can be a greater sense of personal agency and power, reducing anxiety and possibly reducing the client's vulnerability to abuse or at least increasing their empowerment to report abuse. As someone confronts a history of abuse and learns to know the difference between safe touch and hurtful touch as well as pain versus pleasure, one can again begin to process the somatic and emotional "holding" of abuse one may have experienced. In the case of virginity, for someone who has had limited access to dating and has come to believe they are not "datable," or who has internalized feelings of body loathing, partner surrogacy can challenge those beliefs with experiential activities such as "mirroring," in which the client and surrogate look at their naked bodies in front of a mirror and take turns identifying what they like and what they do not like and where they struggle. The partner surrogate models a nonjudging approach to body acceptance and body neutrality.

Another resource to consider is viewing the 2017 episode "Sexual Healing" of *This Is Life with Lisa Ling* (Dennett, 2017). This is a 25-minute video in which two individuals work with a surrogate to address two very different sets of clinical issues. Ling interviews the clients and the surrogate and then observes a partner surrogacy session. Although brief in duration, the segment serves to demystify and correct stigmas and invisibility of the disabled.

A common question about partner surrogacy is whether it is legal. It is legal; yet, there is evidence of misrepresentation and exploitation. It is costly and limited in availability. It is important for mental health professionals to confirm certification, supervision, and background of partner surrogates before referring. Organizations such as IPSA and the American Association of Sexuality Educators, Counselors, and Therapists may be able to provide helpful resources on partner surrogacy.

After reading this chapter, we hope you (a) are better positioned to identify the sources of and impact of ableism at the intersection of sexuality and disability identity; (b) have learned how disability models have historically oppressed sexual freedoms and expression for queer crips; (c) have a deeper understanding of the denial of sexual freedom as a human rights violation within queer-crip communities; and (d) can now identify disability-affirming and liberatory strategies, including partner surrogacy, to promote wholeness. It has been an honor to write this chapter. We appreciate the opportunity to help inform future mental health professionals about the "dos and don'ts" of providing services to a population that is quite large but has long been invisible and underserved by our fields.

Conclusion

The prioritization of treatment issues, of course, is driven by the client and collaborative exchange between mental health professional and client. When trauma memories are present and appear to be blocking movement, addressing trauma may be an important issue to process early in the therapeutic process. Authentic efforts to establish trust, nonjudging, and a sense of self-efficacy can open the door to psychoeducation that brings awareness to the impact of medical interventions as trauma experiences. The body that has experienced multiple medical interventions remembers and needs release (Levine, 1997). This awareness and release can be a catalyst for the healing process and offer opportunities to normalize and empower the client to understand they have rights to control who touches their body, how, and when. It can also begin the journey of understanding medical touch as different from soft, sensual, and pleasurable touch.

D-AT, as described in this chapter, is pantheoretical. Other theoretical interventions can be integrated to challenge internalized shame and oppression. Using cognitive behavioral strategies to explore core beliefs, feelings, and behaviors can offer points of interventions. Jasper, in our case example, could have expressed feelings of shame, humiliation, and anxiety as, "I am ugly, broken, and unlovable; I am not a real man." These feelings drive a protective response to withdraw and avoid all opportunities to engage even in an intimate exploration of one's own body, much less an intimate relationship with another. Interventions to combat and weaken internalized self-deprecating beliefs can involve cognitive reframing, behavioral experiments, and introductions to images of competing messages of disability pride and body celebration from disabled queer bodies. Introducing the client to disability members in the form of video and prose can provide the client an opportunity to find community and competing narratives, particularly those from the voices of queer-crip communities.

It is also suggested to assess your client's beliefs about these identities before proceeding with sharing liberating images and narratives. As Olkin (2009) recommended, assessing for the disability model the client subscribes to and meeting them there is an important step of conveying understanding. Likewise, assessing where the client is and what attitudes they hold toward their sexual identities can promote trust and safety. Introducing a client to "messages of disability pride" prematurely could lead to rupture. It can be difficult for a clinician who has worked hard to be culturally competent and been steeped in social justice work in their education and training have a client who says they hate being gay or disabled or Black and that their fondest wish is to be straight or cured or White. Meeting clients here is not agreeing or colluding with self-hatred; rather, it is opening the door for understanding and reparative work. The final take as always is to never assume readiness to embrace a reparative journey but to meet self-hatred in the same way we meet readiness to make change models of care.

Questions You Always Wanted to Ask

1. **How can I immerse myself in queer-crip communities virtually if not directly due to COVID-19 restrictions?**
   We suggest the following:
   - Robin M. Eames is a queer-crip writer, artist and historian who is genderqueer and uses they/them pronouns. See https://robinmeames.org/about
   - Sky Cubacub (they/them) at https://www.rebirthgarments.com
   - Tovah on Autostraddle at https://www.autostraddle.com/author/tovah/
   - Ashley Volion, "The Adventures of a Mis/identified Queer Crip" on POC Zine Project at https://issuu.com/poczineproject/docs/taoamiqc_ashleyvolion_zine_readonly
   - Edward Ndopu, "Musings From a Queercrip Femme Man of Color," on BGD at https://www.bgdblog.org/2013/01/201312musings-from-a-queercrip-femme-man-of-color/

2. **What should I read?**
Read everything mentioned in the chapter text and in the references below. In particular, we recommend *Care Work: Dreaming Disability Justice* by Lambda Literary Award-winning writer and disability justice activist Leah Lakshmi Piepzna-Samarasinha. This work explores the politics and realities of disability justice, a movement that centers the lives and leadership of sick and disabled queer, trans, Black, and Brown people, with knowledge and gifts for all. As described by the publisher, Arsenal Pulp Press (n.d.), *Care Work* is "a mapping of access as radical love, a celebration of the work that sick and disabled queer/people of color are doing to find each other and to build power and community, and a toolkit for everyone who wants to build radically resilient communities of liberation where no one is left behind. Powerful and passionate, *Care Work* is a crucial and necessary call to arms" (para. 2).
We also recommend *The Body Is Not an Apology* by Sonya Renee Taylor. The book and associated resources are online at https://thebodyisnotanapology.com.
3. **Are there critics of crip theory?**
Yes. Kirstin Marie Bone wrote an article, "Trapped Behind the Glass: Crip Theory and Disability Identity," published in *Disability & Society* in 2017. The article is online at https://doi.org/10.1080/09687599.2017.1313722.
4. **Where can one go for sex toys inclusive for disability and queer communities?**
The Come as You Are cooperative (www.comeasyouare.com) is an option. Check it out.
5. **How can I learn more about disability history?**
We suggest the documentary film *Lives Worth Living* (see https://www.pbs.org/independentlens/documentaries/lives-worth-living) and ADAPT's account of the disability rights movement, "We Will Ride! The Gang of 19," at https://adapt.org/we-will-ride-the-gang-of-19.

References

ADA Amendments Act of 2008, 42 U.S.C. § 12101 et seq. (2008).

American Psychological Association. (n.d.). *Committee on disability issues in psychology*. https://www.apa.org/pi/disability/committee

American Psychological Association. (2017). *Multicultural guidelines: An ecological approach to context, identity, and intersectionality*. http://www.apa.org/about/policy/multicultural-guidelines.pdf

American Psychological Association. (2022). *APA guidelines for assessment and intervention with persons with disabilities*. https://www.apa.org/pi/disability/resources/assessment-disabilities

Americans With Disabilities Act of 1990, 42 U.S.C. § 12101 et seq. (1990). https://www.ada.gov/pubs/adastatute08.htm

Andrews, E. E., Forber-Pratt, A. J., Mona, L. R., Lund, E. M., Pilarski, C. R., & Balter, R. (2019). #SaytheWord: A disability culture commentary on the erasure of "disability." *Rehabilitation Psychology, 64*(2), 111–118. https://doi.org/10.1037/rep0000258

Arsenal Pulp Press. (n.d.). *Care work: Dreaming disability justice*. https://arsenalpulp.com/Books/C/Care-Work

Bennett, A. (2007). Robert McRuer. Crip theory: Cultural signs of queerness and disability [Book review]. *Disability Studies Quarterly, 27*(4). https://dsq-sds.org/article/view/60/60

Browne, A., Agha, A., Demyan, A., & Beatriz, E. (2016). *Examining criminal justice responses to and help-seeking patterns of sexual violence survivors with disabilities* [Report submitted to the U.S. Department of Justice]. Vera Institute of Justice. https://www.ojp.gov/pdffiles1/nij/grants/250196.pdf

Chou, Y.-C., Lu, Z. J., & Lin, C.-J. (2018). Comparison of attitudes to the sexual health of men and women with intellectual disability among parents, professionals, and university students. *Journal of Intellectual and Developmental Disability, 43*(2), 164–173. https://doi.org/10.3109/13668250.2016.1259465

Clare, E. (1999). *Exile and pride: Disability, queerness and liberation.* South End Press.

Crenshaw, K. (1989). Demarginalizing the intersection of race and sex: A Black feminist critique of antidiscrimination doctrine, feminist theory and antiracist politics. *University of Chicago Legal Forum, 1989*, Article 8. http://chicagounbound.uchicago.edu/uclf/vol1989/iss1/8

Dennett, D. (Director). (2017, October 1). Sexual healing (Season 4, Episode 1) [TV series episode]. In L. Ling, A. Bucher, & D. S. Smith (Executive Producers), *This is life with Lisa Ling.* Part2 Pictures.

Dunn, D. S., & Elliott, T. R. (2005). Revisiting a constructive classic: Wright's physical disability: A psychosocial approach. *Rehabilitation Psychology, 50*(2), 183–189. https://doi.org/10.1037/0090-5550.50.2.183

Friedman, C. (2018). Aversive ableism: Modern prejudice towards disabled people. *Review of Disability Studies, 14*(4). https://rdsjournal.org/index.php/journal/article/view/811

Harrell, E. (2014). *Crime against persons with disabilities, 2009–2012—Statistical tables.* Bureau of Justice Statistics. http://www.bjs.gov/index.cfm?ty=pbdetail&iid=4884

Hughes, R. B., Nosek, M. A., & Robinson-Whelan, S. (2015). Correlates of depression in rural women with physical disabilities. *Journal of Obstetric, Gynecologic, & Neonatal Nursing, 36*(1), 105–114. https://doi.org/10.1111/j.1552-6909.2006.00122.x

Human Rights Watch. (2011, November 10). *Sterilization of women and girls with disabilities: A briefing paper.* https://www.hrw.org/news/2011/11/10/sterilization-women-and-girls-disabilities#

International Professional Surrogates Association. (n.d.). *What is surrogate partner therapy.* https://www.surrogatetherapy.org/what-is-surrogate-partner-therapy

Kaufman, M., Silverberg, C., & Odette, F. (2007). *The ultimate guide to sex and disability: For all of us who live with disabilities, chronic pain, and illness.* Cleis Press.

Kort, J. (2008). *Gay affirmative therapy for the straight clinician: The essential guide.* W. W. Norton & Co.

Levine, P. A. (with Frederick, A.). (1997). *Waking the tiger: Healing trauma.* North Atlantic Books.

Lewin, B. (Director). (2012). *The sessions* [Film]. Such Much Films.

Livneh, H. (1982). On the origins of negative attitudes toward people with disabilities. *Rehabilitation Literature, 43*, 338–347.

Lund, E. M. (2011). Community-based services and interventions for adults with disabilities who have experienced interpersonal violence: A review of the literature. *Trauma, Violence, & Abuse, 12*(4), 171–182. https://doi.org/10.1177/1524838011416377

Marini, I. (2001). Cross cultural counseling issues of males who sustain a disability. *Journal of Applied Rehabilitation Counseling, 32*(1), 36–44. https://doi.org/10.1891/0047-2220.32.1.36
MacDougall, G. (2013, November 30). *Beyond access: Mia Mingus on disability justice (video interview)*. EquitableEducation.ca. https://equitableeducation.ca/2013/mia-mingus-disability-justice
McRuer, R. (2018). *Crip times: Disability, globalization, and resistance*. NYU Press. https://doi.org/10.2307/j.ctt1pwt9nj
Milbern, S. (2011, April 6). *"My body is not a liability"—Interview with Leah Lakshmi Piepzna-Samarasinha*. Sins Invalid. https://www.sinsinvalid.org/blog/%E2%80%9Cmy-body-is-not-a-liability%E2%80%9D-%E2%80%93-interview-with-leah-lakshmi-piepzna-samarasinha
Niemeier, J. P. (2008). Unique aspects of women's emotional responses to disability. *Disability and Rehabilitation, 30*(3), 166–173. https://doi.org/10.1080/09638280701532169
Nosek, M. A., Foley, C. C., Hughes, R. B., & Howland, C. A. (2001). Vulnerabilities for abuse among women with disabilities. *Sexuality and Disability, 19*, 177–189. https://doi.org/10.1023/A:1013152530758
Olkin, R. (2002). Could you hold the door for me? Including disability in diversity. *Cultural Diversity and Ethnic Minority Psychology, 8*(2), 130–137. https://doi.org/10.1037/1099-9809.8.2.130
Olkin, R. (2009). Disability-affirmative therapy. In I. Marini & M. A. Stebnicki (Eds.), *The professional counselor's desk reference* (pp. 355–369). Springer.
Piepzna-Samarasinha, L. L. (2018). *Care work: Dreaming disability justice*. Arsenal Pulp Press.
Rohmer, O., & Louvet, E. (2009). Describing persons with disability: Salience of disability, gender and ethnicity. *Rehabilitation Psychology, 54*(1), 76–82. https://doi.org/10.1037/a0014445
Schauer, M., Neuner, F., & Elbert, T. (2011). *Narrative exposure therapy: A short-term treatment for traumatic stress disorders* (2nd ed.). Hogrefe and Huber Publishing.
Silvers, A., Francis, L., & Badesch, B. (2016). Reproductive rights and access to reproductive services for women with disabilities. *AMA Journal of Ethics, 18*(4), 430–437. https://doi.org/10.1001/journalofethics.2016.18.4.msoc1-1604
Williams, J., & Colvin, L. (2016). Coming together to end violence against women and girls with disabilities. In S. E. Miles-Cohen & C. Signore (Eds.). *Eliminating inequities for women with disabilities: An agenda for health and wellness* (pp. 243–262). American Psychological Association.
Wright, B. (1983). *Physical disability: A psychosocial approach* (2nd ed.). Harper & Row.
Wright, B. (1987). Human dignity and professional self-monitoring. *Journal of Applied Rehabilitation Counseling, 18*, 12–14.

Embracing Our Sex, Race, and Ethnicity

Kim Lee Hughes, Roseina Britton, Cheryl D. Walker, L. Allen Crosby, and Nicole Woodcox Bolden

This chapter is written from each of our perspectives as an individual author. We chose to write this way because as individuals we cannot and will not speak on behalf of all races and all ethnicities. We will not portend to speak for all Black women.

We do recognize there are similarities in the way people of color have been marginalized, objectified, vilified, and sexualized but our experiences are each those of our own. Some of us chose to write of our personal experiences and some chose to write on behalf of what our community has experienced. We are Black women scholars, Black researchers, Black mothers, Black lovers, Black therapists. We represent Black womanhood.

Voices of Black Girl Magicians

Everything Comes to the Light: The Voice of Kim Lee Hughes

As I began to write this essay and think about the ways in which we as Black women have had our sexuality denied or distorted, I became angry. Toni Morrison (1987) stated through the character Sethe in her novel *Beloved*, "Love is or it ain't. Thin love ain't love at all" (p. 194). We can no longer tread on thin ice. We want to love and be loved in return. As such, we are speaking our truths individually because we are not a monolith. We are sisters, though, and our love represents our actualization. We are bursting forth in full bloom.

We believe in our right to experience sexual pleasure. We profess that the power within will unfurl because everything comes to the light . . . eventually. I am your tour guide on this excursion through the love and sex positive rituals of Black Girl Magicians (see Bond, 2018). Why me? Well, I am not only a member, but I am also The Black Girl Magic Representative (spoken with a Biggie Smalls flow). I am bodacious because there is no room here for shame or apology. Our love is often fraught in pain and trauma. Truth is, you can take shit and use it to fertilize your own garden, and that is what we do.

I have been distraught lately, yet productive, determined, available to others, and emotionally bereft. It has been a struggle to stay focused and harness the beauty that is Black love in my own life. I am inundated with it. I live in a multigenerational home with my husband, stepdaughter and her significant other, and our grandson. Stepparenting was a challenge, and those patterns ooze into the next generation. I remain optimistic that the role of Nana will open doors that remain closed.

Simultaneously, I teach at a historically Black college or university (HBCU). My students intentionally chose to attend an HBCU for "the love." Intuitively they sense that we, Black professors, love them, and we do. We love them helicopter-parent style. Black love, all of it, near and dear to my purpose. I am managing it all undaunted, and that gives me a hard-on. My yin to lead has transformed my sexual pleasure-seeking style. I am not afraid to take the lead, which is not very ladylike of me.

At age 53, I have the audacity to speak my mind, and the intelligence to separate my opinions from facts. Seems simple, right? Honestly, it is a silent scream to be mansplained at most professional intersections even when men are not present. The pandemic has meant that my social interactions are limited. If I can have it delivered, I do. My extrovert has inverted. I no longer connect to mainstream interpretations of what is "real." I refine reality for me, sifting through to retain that which sustains. I am flowing in my own current these days, poetic about my peace and unfurling my kundalini with my life partner. I am building a paradise for queer Black girls because we need to dig our toes in the sand.

A Queer Black Girl's Adventures in Paradise

I am on fire.
It's a smolder not a burn.

I am yearning.
It's a calling not an urge.

I am curious.
It's instinctive not distracted.

I am bold.
It's authentic no need for show.

I am fearless.
Random hugs no sticks or stones.

I am a voice.
Resounding in an echoing whisper.

I am transformed.

In my perspective, it's all rainbows, hummingbirds, and moonbeams.
I've got dust on my shoes from mountain tops and hard labor creeks.
I've quenched my thirst on Niagara waterfalls and local brews.
Gazing upon sunsets on Waikiki Beach

I am liberated from an opposite attract kind of quest.
Invested in synchronicity over success.
Aligning the positive with the positive
Creating affinity to generate flow.

In the smallness of this moment, I feel expansion in my soul.

"Don't crush the flower." A mantra, a prayer, and a caution
Not to lose my balance with assumption and conjecture
I can do good work with an open heart as I keep stretching.
Hell, it's my story I can tell it like I please. I'm going to let it breath.
It's a queer Black girl's adventure in paradise—who's a better narrator than me?

(Hughes, 2015, pp. 142–143)

I am the narrator on this excursion through the intimacy patterns of Black Girl Magicians. Read it like an incantation, one story blurring into the next. Shake it like a kaleidoscope between each entry, then taste it like a red-velvet cupcake, rich, deep, chocolate, and lip-smacking sweet. Please know that our alliance is forged in the blood of our ancestors. Listen. We are speaking.

The Impact of Stereotypes: The Voice of Cheryl D. Walker

What you think about us matters. No, you do not define us, and your margins confine our possibility because we are Black and female. The most feared mother on the planet still breastfeeding, even without giving birth.

I grew up hating my body. My metabolism was extremely high, and my tall physique made me an ideal candidate for basketball and volleyball. I was the total opposite of the ideal body type, despite the unwanted attention for my potential. When I was an '80s child living in the South, female fashions were bold, colorful, and flattering if you possessed the right body. The images in society entailed curvaceous Black bodies that could bring any person to their knees. Enter self-loathing. Fortunately for me, religion spared me the embarrassment of exposing the lackluster curves of my body.

Media in the 1980s offered a variety of the Black experience that stretched across several mediums. Popular television series depicted Black families in a range of socioeconomic statuses with several family dynamics. Black publications reported on issues that resonated with me while showcasing skin that mirrored my own. Music channels blasted videos of Black artists, displaying a portion of our rhythmic and composition flair. As a young child raised in a predominantly Black community, I did not find the stories and images foreign. The dissonance for me was in how my body compared with other Black bodies, and consequently, how I internalized this into an unhealthy relationship with my body. I despised my long legs, lanky arms, big feet, lengthy neck, and "pecans" for a chest. My closest friends possessed the hips, butt, thighs, and chests that were highly favored by our male counterparts. Ironically, my school required us to wear uniforms, so I strategically wore items that deflected attention from those areas of my body. I continuously found myself limiting my dating pool based on height, but more deleterious, I did not appreciate or value my body.

The perfect storm for disaster includes raging adolescent hormones, someone struggling with self-esteem issues, and a longing to be desired. My sexual history dances between violations of consent, an absence of empowerment, and a disgust of my natural God-given form. The number of partners were pale in comparison to their possibilities, considering the depths of disdain and disconnect that plagued my interpretation of how I occupied space. There were a select few in my past who offered a glimpse of what I failed to see, but it was not enough to convince me of my worth. My transition to college presented new surroundings, a new narrative, and new opportunities to wield agency. These attempts were met with accolades from girlfriends who admonished my self-loathing and challenged me to embrace every nook and cranny of my body. The metamorphosis to self-compassion and self-acceptance occurred on a microlevel, beginning with a realization that I could ultimately define beauty, and guided by supportive friends and partners who, similarly to me, liked to challenge the maladaptive standards of society.

The marvels of motherhood championed another set of stereotypes aimed at Black bodies. The joys of pregnancy negated most, if not all, of the assumptions. I was not concerned with the look or shape of my belly, the thickness of my ankles, or the swell of my breasts. My only concern was the health of the life inside me and how my habits contributed to its development. To be honest, I was more concerned about the gender. I was not far removed from the sexist malarkey of society and questioned whether I could protect and empower little Black girls. Fast forward those concerns to four daughters later. One of the most humbling experiences lies in admitting your vulnerabilities to someone who looks to you for all the answers. I shared accounts detailing the "isms" that burdened me and the impact of stereotypes on my wellness. No topic was too mature or inappropriate, and no inquiry was too childish or too basic. From an early age, I celebrated everything about their little Black bodies, from the curl of their hair to the stubbiness of their toes. My husband and I constantly emphasize consent and how expectations of others have no validity in personal self-expression. The decision for ear piercing serves as a prime example. Contrary to popular beliefs in my culture, I chose to refrain from ear piercing until the age of 10. I speak so heavily about consent that it seems hypocritical of me to impose my decision onto their bodies. When my daughters were able to coherently identify a want for ear piercing, I honored their request. Parenting ushers in the best and worst of an individual, but if I can offer reprieve from worldly expectations, cultural stereotypes, and toxic relationships, my parenting efforts look promising.

The onslaught of stereotypes did not cease because I chose to ignore and challenge them. Some things were so internalized that I would make simple decisions without rhyme or reason based on my conditioning. Motherhood provided countless benefits, including the curves that I longed for throughout my adolescent and young adult life. My body now illustrated the stereotypes of Black bodies that I admired; however, I wanted to keep my curvaceous secrets to myself. As I saw it, society did not deserve to see the fullness of my breasts or the plumpness of my butt. More than half of my life was spent with self-deprecating thoughts about my body. I ruminated over images that were "doctored" and produced to feed into a heteronormative system of self-interested narratives. Why on earth would I share my beautiful body with a non-deserving public? But then the answer came to me—because I can.

Stereotypes exist in the absence of awareness and are often perpetuated by people who fear something different from themselves. Stereotypes also restrict the richness of the human experience and create narratives to satisfy the egos and intentions of others. The flawed effects reverberate across generations and require a myriad of approaches to refute them. At the most basic level, parents can uplift and empower their children to accept their bodies, and not just with words. Allowing children to be creative and expressive through movement and dress gives them permission to define their own standards of beauty. Toy and book selections also influence self-perceptions during a child's formative years. Representation matters across our identified culture and with exposure to other cultures through books, toys, playdates, and television shows.

As sure as there are people who dispute science, truth, and humanity, so will stereotypes persist. My decision to mask my curves entailed a long, sorted history with stereotypes, wearing a muumuu was not going to change that. Change occurs internally through self-acceptance and the realization that in a paradoxical way, I perpetuated the stereotypes. Many beautiful variations of Black bodies exist, but if society fails to see the full spectrum of body types, the stereotypes gain legitimacy. I am proud of my body and even more proud of the fact that my body is capable of great things. I refuse to allow convoluted beliefs to dictate my story and prevent an expression of Black beauty. Human sexuality is everywhere, yet we still whisper about it in the dark corners of society. Sadly, the harshness of negativity outweighed the echoes of affirming messages. But there is one poem that resonates as I continue to embrace my definition of beauty. The words of Maya Angelou (1978) succinctly described the beauty of my contours and perfect imperfections. Her poem "Phenomenal Woman" eloquently challenges what is "pretty" and reminds me of the special bond I have with my own body. My body does not fit the societal mold of an ideal form, and yet there is a spiritual and quiet pride that elucidates from my body.

The Cost of Phenomenology: The Voice of Roseina Britton

Yes, all this "phenomenal-ness" is true; yet, for centuries, we have been depicted as loud, ugly, sapphire or matriarch, materialistic, the strong Black woman, the mammy, variations of the term bitch, and hypersexualized. The sexual health of Black American women has been compromised, primarily by racism and discriminatory health care practices, from slavery to the present day (Prather et al., 2018). Although many Black women have fought against these stereotypes or distortions of Black womanhood through literature, art, and music, the negative representation still exists. This phenomenon, also known as gendered racism, is rooted in stereotypes of Black women (Watson et al., 2019). Gendered racism against Black women and girls in the United States has resulted in racial trauma for many Black women and girls. Racial trauma stems from a person experiencing or witnessing actual or perceived racial discrimination. This can take many forms, including physical abuse, threats of harm, humiliation, or shaming (Comas-Díaz, 2016; Gómez & Gobin, 2019). The racial trauma and gendered racism experienced by Black women and girls from the slave era to the present time are a direct determinant of sexual health disparities (Prather et al., 2018).

Gendered racism has depicted Black women in films as an obedient mammy, as seen in the Academy Award–winning film, *Gone With the Wind* (Fleming, 1939). Within the film, the character "Mammy" is a large, dark-skinned, unattractive, asexual woman who is an obedient caretaker and servant (Watson et al., 2019). The mammy has been a racial caricature of an African American woman, often depicted on souvenirs (e.g., postcards) as a cheerful servant willing to protect her slave owner. On the opposite end of the spectrum, Black women have also been characterized as the "Jezebel," which is a sexually promiscuous and manipulative woman (Collins, 2000; Watson et al., 2019). The negative Black woman stereotypes were made in contrast to the stereotypes of White women, which include prim, ladylike, and proper (Collins, 2000; Watson et al., 2019). The stereotype Jezebel deemed Black women as hypersexual and treated as commodities by White slave owners. For example, an enslaved South African woman Saartje "Sarah" Bartmann, also known as Hottentot Venus, was used in this manner (Ashley, 2021). Portrayed as the Jezebel of her time, Bartmann was exploited and toured around European countries in the early 1800s to display her voluptuous body. As a result of the negative images of Black women over the years, those who display their sexual freedom are considered the modern-day Jezebel (Collins, 2004).

Overview of Sexual Health of Black Women

Historically, sexual violence such as forced breeding, rape, and sexual assault by slave owners were some of the struggles experienced by Black enslaved women (Moultrie, 2018). Black enslaved women were sold and bought as commodities because of their reproductive and sexual features (Holmes, 2016). The objectification of the Black woman's body dates back to slavery when Black women were on auction blocks.

During the slave era (1619–1865), Black people were perceived as hypersexual and uncivilized and were dehumanized and sexually exploited (Holmes, 2016). Apprehensive colonizers deemed African culture primitive and uncivilized; however, it was mesmerized by the culture and turned into a spectacle enterprise (Collins, 2004). Many Europeans believed Black people were subhuman and conducted scientific studies to support the inhumane treatment of Black women (Holmes, 2016). For example, narratives from Thomas Jefferson in *Notes on the State of Virginia* suggest Black men are "more ardent after their female: but love seems with them to be more eager desire, than a tender delicate mixture of sentiment and sensation" (Jefferson, 1788, p. 137). Jefferson's writing suggested that Black women had unquenchable sexual appetites and considered them "unrapable" because of their lack of standards when choosing sexual partners (Holmes, 2016). Jefferson's assertions laid a fundamental foundation for hegemonic masculinity and White supremacist authority in our nation's origins. Racism is bedrock in the foundation of the United States.

Race-based trauma spans across eras and has a current impact on Black women's sexual health (Prather et al., 2018). Black women have experienced health care disparities from the slave era to the post–civil rights era (Prather et al., 2018). During the Jim Crow era (1865–1965), Black women experienced rape, genital mutilation, and sterilization. During this time, Black women did not have access to adequate health care—if they received any "care" at all. Black women rarely received adequate health care and were often subjected to nonconsensual medical experimentation (Prather et al., 2018). Institutional racism and racial discrimination manifested race-based mistreatment and racial health disparities that marginalized Black women in the United States. Black women continue to experience disproportionate rates of sexual exploitation and abuse rooted in reproductive control and hypersexualization (Holmes, 2016).

The Black woman's sexuality has been objectified and contributes to the gendered racism faced today. This lived reality is compounded with institutional racism when considering racial health disparities. Among the many health disparities experienced in the United States, Black women have been disproportionately affected by sexually transmitted infections (STIs) and HIV/AIDS (Crooks et al., 2020). In 2018, Black adolescents and adults made up about 92% of new HIV diagnoses (Centers for Disease Control and Prevention, n.d.). Additionally, as of 2018, Black women were 5 times more likely than White women to have chlamydia, 7.7 times more likely to have gonorrhea, and 4.7 times more likely to have syphilis. The sexual health disparities for Black women are not mere coincidence. Racism is the fundamental determinant of these health inequities (Prather et al., 2018).

Relationships and Sexual Health Disparities

Black American culture is inherently collectivistic. Therefore, as Black people we have a strong sense of kinship, communalism, and unity (Gómez & Gobin, 2020). Marriage, for a Black enslaved woman, was for the purpose of procreating and producing more property (Watson et al., 2019). During slavery, Black women were not free to choose whom they had sexual relations with because it was determined by the potential for profit (Prather et al., 2018). To date, Black sexual networks have an imbalanced ratio of males to females that limits the pool of potential sexual partners for many women (Crooks et al., 2020). As a result, multiple co-occurring sexual partnerships develop, resulting in the rapid spread of STIs and HIV. According to Cipres et al. (2017), Black women are more likely to encounter a partner who has an STI or has had multiple sex partners in the past year.

In addition to having a limited pool of sexual partners, Black women also have a limited pool of marriage-oriented male partners (Moultrie, 2018). Moultrie (2018) defined marriage-oriented among young, urban, Black males as the choice to commit to monogamy. However, Black men are more likely to be serial monogamous, have back-to-back monogamous exclusive partners, or have concurrent partnerships (Towner et al., 2015). A double standard within this phenomenon encourages the acceptance of Black men having concurrent partnerships, whereas Black women are expected to remain monogamous in relationships (Towner et al., 2015).

The Voice of Nicole Woodcox Bolden

Sex and sexuality are concepts that American culture has weaponized and perverted, especially for those who have not historically had control over the dominant narrative. Sexuality has a few elements, but to me, understanding sexuality in America for people who are members of the *global majority* (i.e., people who have historically been considered minorities in America) should start with a conversation of identity and how that is connected to behavior. There are numerous theories on identity development and on identity development specifically for each race/culture. To only begin the conversation, we will be using the concepts of structural symbolic interaction and identity salience.

Sheldon Stryker utilized George Herbert Mead's "I" and "Me" to create the structural symbolic interaction framework that says that "society shapes self shapes social interaction" (Stets & Burke, 2014, p. 58). Identity salience discusses how we organize the various identities we have in society, and which ones we have committed to the most. This concept also helps us recognize that each identity has its own societal expectations. Therefore, the identities we have committed to the most will determine our behaviors in relationship with others and self (Brenner et al., 2014). I acknowledge that there are numerous studies and debates around the dominant culture in America. For the purposes of this conversation, dominant American culture will be understood as White Anglo-Saxon Protestant. So, taking this basic understanding of identity and understanding that American societal expectations are typically based on that dominant culture, one can already start to see how the journey to understand self and sexuality can be complicated for non-White-identifying Americans.

How can a beautiful exploration of self and sexuality occur with ease and peace when the society you live in has been determined, for many generations, to dictate who you are and even who your family will be?

Everyone's Story Begins With a Birth Story

As therapists, many of us tend to focus on the story of a specific hurt, but might we consider the most important story of all—a person's birth story? Such is the story of what was passed down, what was buried, what went unspoken in the family when that person was born. A person's birth story provides a window to some of the intergenerational trauma that may be present in their life. This will guide us in knowing when cognitive behavior therapy is not going to be the most useful tool to start with, but maybe internal family systems would be the most powerful start.

An estimated 9% of women (1 out of every 11) experience postpartum posttraumatic stress disorder (Postpartum Support International, n.d.). Up to 20% of Black women (1 in 5) experience a postpartum mood disorder. Unfortunately, there are not yet many statistics on nonbinary birthing people. Birth is an event that truly impacts the well-being of the entire family. Because of the vulnerability involved, birth stirs up fears, hurts, and aspirations. Birth causes a major shakeup of the identity saliency in a person. When we, as mental health practitioners, can assist our client in getting back to the root of their self, we can remind them that there are no bad parts, only patterns that were created for survival. When there are no bad parts, we can invite the freedom to be. This freedom to be is necessary to owning one's sexuality.

The Voice of L. Allen Crosby

As a Black woman, I can painfully recall when I first learned about the value of my body. I was 10 years old. It first started with colorism when I was called "red" because my skin tone was lighter than many members of my family. Not understanding a thing about colorism, I knew I was experiencing something different than what I observed for others. This felt isolating.

As children, we quickly learn the importance of inclusivity and the human longing to fit in with others, particularly when we are on the outside of this experience. The next lesson I learned about my body was that I was too thin. This was affirmed when the neighborhood boys refused to play our sexually charged rite-of-passage touching games like "Freaky Friday" or "Hot Bread and Butter" with me because I was too skinny. Around this same time, I started my period—the perfect opportunity for a young woman to learn about her body, right? Nope. Even then, I did not receive "the talk."

Growing up on the inner-city streets of Washington, DC, I was raised primarily by women. However, I do not recall receiving lessons from them regarding my development from girl to young woman and young woman to adult. Often, I heard comments such as, "You're starting to smell yourself" or "Don't get too big for your britches." In hindsight, these comments were more of an observation of my attitude, and not commentary about the development of my body. The next lesson I received about my body was a hard one. I became pregnant at age 15, bearing the responsibility for another without first even understanding myself. Without the benefit of context, I had to quickly learn. The lessons I connected to my body were rooted in shame.

Crenshaw's (1991) intersectionality theory posits that Black women are encumbered with at least two undervalued identities in the United States. As such, we are unable to freely exist in our bodies without fear of judgment. Shame is negative judgment of the self. As a Black woman, I have felt pain from fractured connections between women in my family leading to disbelief in myself. Even in silence, the women in my family are resilient. Through their self-protective behaviors, they often manifest strength, toughness, and excellence. It was in this space that I started reclaiming my body, who I allowed access to it, and how I expressed my sexuality.

Final Thoughts of Stereotyping and the Black Female Experience

As the primary narrator of these stories of Black Girl Magicians, I (Kim Lee Hughes) want to speak to another stereotype that is intimate, personal, and political. Do Black woman like oral sex? As a queer Black woman, yes, we are thumbs up with the idea of giving and receiving oral sex. The extent to which we are comfortable discussing our experiences and preferences is also generational. Black women in my generation were shamed for admitting that they gave and or received sexual pleasure orally. In fact, a young woman accused of "sucking dick" was not marriage material.

I attended a women's college, which was across the street from a men's college. Tradition urged the students to seek a suitable mate from within the college community.

We were partnered with a brother during our orientation week. It was ceremonial, and you and your brother were introduced and presented to the community. I was 18 years old when I met my brother, and eventually that connection did lead to a sexual encounter. We had oral sex. I will add that he is not my husband. We did not date for a long period of time in college either.

I was raised by single Black women who celebrated their sexuality. My mother's mother had a subscription to *Playboy* magazine on our hallway credenza. Sex positive was called "free love" when I was a young woman, and it was attached to counterculture movements. Attending an HBCU meant a relentless effort to represent the race with honor and decorum. I will share that giving and receiving head was not discussed openly in polite circles.

I have always been comfortable exploring issues left in the dark. I am called to upend taboos. Sex in Black communities in the 1970s and early 1980s was hyperbolic, thanks to "Blaxploitation" films that again attached our sexuality to stereotypes. As the civil rights and women's movements gave way to the capitalist 1980s, Black women were advancing in educational and career pursuits. Controlling our financial well-being increased our ability to explore our sexual pleasure-seeking styles. Simultaneously, the rate of female-led households continued to rise, and new narratives of the emasculating Black woman gained momentum.

The new stereotype gave Black women the opportunity to take charge in heterosexual relationships in ways that middle-class White women desired. Thus, the "strong Black woman" prototype became the new stereotype of a Black woman from the United States. Like all stereotypes, the strong Black woman stereotype has parameters, and Black women have blurred these lines to take an active and overt role in our sexual pleasure seeking that led us to the unapologetic pursuit of valuing our orgasm. In this context, we can include behaviors that were once forbidden and frequently hidden.

Black women across the sexual spectrum are engaging in our countrywide sexual evolution. From high school to senior residential facilities, oral sex is on the menu being served and received. Our sexual orientation is not the discussion. Our sexual pleasure is at the center, and we are willing to seek counseling interventions to discuss ways to address negative patterns of belief that inhibit our zeal. Counselors who are sexually affirmed can guide and support Black women to finding relief from societal stress by reclaiming and seeking their orgasms using oral sex as a main menu item.

Case Example

Brittani is a 34-year-old upwardly mobile employee at a Fortune 500 company in a major metropolitan city, which is also her hometown. Brittani reported that she was at a crossroad in her professional life that may have major ramifications for her personal relationships. Brittani decided to find a counselor to discuss how the decision to earn her Master of Business Administration (MBA) would affect her grandmother, her significant other Rick, and her job satisfaction.

Brittani has a job opportunity in another state, and she is seeking counseling to determine her next steps. Brittani lives with Rick, and they have been dating for 2 years. Brittani believes that Rick has become complacent in the relationship, and he does not want to attend couples counseling because, as he said, "You are the one getting 'new' in the relationship." Brittani and her two brothers assist with care for their aging grandmother Pearl. Pearl raised Brittani and her brothers in a middle-class neighborhood after gaining custody when Brittani was in elementary school. Brittani's older brothers left for college when Brittani was in middle school, and Brittani decided to stay close to home to attend college because she wanted to stay close to Pearl.

As Brittani was completing her coursework toward her MBA, Pearl was diagnosed with dementia. Pearl's insurance covers the cost of long-term care in a residential facility and Brittani visits her every Sunday. Rick uses these Sunday visits as time to hang out with the guys. On a weekly basis, Pearl asks if Brittani is engaged yet, because she wants some great-grandchildren. Pearl closes every visit with "I hope this is the year that I get to walk you down the aisle."

Brittani has shared this comment with Rick and expressed to him that she always dreamed of her grandmother giving her away. He laughed, saying that she is willing to do anything to say "Yes to the dress." Brittani is starting to doubt if Rick wants to marry her. Although he says that he is committed to the relationship, he does not believe that marriage makes a bond stronger. Brittani does not want a child without the commitment of marriage. Lately, she and Rick have been avoiding each other in their apartment and their conversations have become either short and shallow or long and argumentative.

As Brittani approaches her MBA graduation, she wants to prioritize her vision, and she is seriously considering leaving her hometown for a director of marketing career opportunity in Chicago. She is hesitant to lose Rick because he is the best lover she has ever experienced. He is a generous lover who is committed to Brittani experiencing orgasm during sex. Her girlfriends tease that she is "dicknotized."

Questions About the Case Example

After reading this case example, consider the following questions:

1. What theoretical approach would allow Brittani to move forward without unearthing painful patterns from her childhood loss?
2. How could the counselor support Brittani with a focus on her own empowerment, while balancing the concerns she has for her grandmother's well-being?
3. What narratives or recollections does Brittani have around sexual exploration and fulfillment?
4. How does Brittani's career efficacy fuel and connect with her drive for a relationship partnership?
5. If Brittani takes the job in Chicago, what are the potential benefits of having some distance from her grandmother? Aside from distance, what other losses might she experience in moving away from her grandmother?

Conclusion: Blooming Into the Light

We are rising because we were buried to bloom. The gardener does not determine the fate of the seedling. The seedling has its divine nature to reach. We are rising because we are innately attuned. We are "cumming" too because the motherland is in our hips. This is the shimmy that rocks the boat and turns the tide.

Coming into this sex positive era in our society has marked dividends for Black women and girls across the life span. Black women are intersectional, and our beliefs about sharing our sexual experiences, desires, fantasies, and fears vary widely, too. Establishing therapeutic rapport with a Black woman will require looking beyond the "presenting problem" and quickly identifying signs of resilience. In essence, you must find the magic for the genie to leave the bottle. It will not be enough to articulate your sentiments in words. Black women will want to see evidence of the connection between words and results before they commit to the goal of the therapy.

Postmodern theories may be better short-term therapeutic approaches than solution-focused theory. As a counselor educator teaching counseling skills and group counseling courses, I (Kim Lee Hughes) lead robust discussions about the cost of counseling and the need to be cognizant that Black women need viable options and choices for appropriate interventions. As mental health providers, we are ethically responsible for designing treatment plans that are malleable and client directed. Black women are ensnarled in a macroaggressive system that is racist and sexist. The therapeutic relationship is a safe harbor in the turbulent, yet ever fluid, lives of your Black female clients.

Questions You Always Wanted to Ask

1. **What might I need to do to best do the work?**
   To become a counselor who is able to provide holistic support that addresses diverse needs and identities, it is necessary to understand the various aspects of trauma and embodied awareness. When we study trauma and embodied awareness with openness, rather than simply checking off a requirement box, it helps us build a deeper relationship with ourselves. It is not essential that counselors strive for perfection, but we must strive to be more connected with ourselves. This inner connection supports our being able to hear and see our clients and colleagues as whole people walking a journey with us, rather than as a broken minority needing a savior. People of the global majority (see https://regenerative.medium.com/im-embracing-the-term-people-of-the-global-majority-abd1c1251241) need support that encourages them to truly trust themselves and feel safe in being their true self, rather than being the representative that White society wants. Intergenerational trauma has instilled in many people, especially Black and Latinx people, that it is not safe to be seen, to feel, or to take up too much space in their own minds. For resources and training, see the Inclusive Therapists website (https://www.inclusivetherapists.com/resources). We also recommend a PBS video on decolonizing mental illness (see https://www.pbs.org/video/dr-vivian-jackson-decolonizing-mental-health-1o3e4k).
2. **How can White counselors best support the needs of their clients and colleagues of color?**
   White counselors can best support the needs of their Black women clients through continuous education about diversity in their own community. It is important to know who grew up in the areas where you practice as well as the populations that transferred or immigrated and their reasons for doing so. Antiracism is about spending time and staying engaged with your neighbors who have varying intersectionality markers while exercising your clinical acumen in healing and advocacy. Advocacy is the hand inside of the glove of mental health practitioners. Your practice should include active engagement, starting with visiting various communities and participating in commerce in those areas. A strong therapeutic alliance is essential, and often authenticity is reflected through the company you keep voluntarily. Do you live in a diverse community? Do you have diverse friends and colleagues? Do you and members of your family actively engage with the client populations that you serve? Answering these questions earnestly is a great starting point, while planning a way to engage more actively if needed.

3. **What are some resources to become more knowledgeable about the sexual concerns of Black women clients?**
   Sexual health and well-being for Black women have many crossovers with the majority population. Organizations like Planned Parenthood and the National Partnership for Women & Families are good, generalized resources when referring women to pursue a broad range of sexual concerns from birth control to mammography and pregnancy. Even so, Black women experience disparities in health and health care, such as increased risk of uterine fibroids (see Stephanie Tubbs Jones Uterine Fibroid Research and Education Act of 2021). Likewise, in 2018 Black women suffered infant mortality at twice the rate of White women (Office of Minority Health, n.d.), As such, organizations such as the Resilient Sisterhood Project (https://rsphealth.org/) and Black Women's Health Imperative (https://bwhi.org/) exist to help close these gaps.
4. **What can I do to advocate for my university/institution/employer/agency to do better at advocating for and supporting folx of color?**
   At your universities, institutions, jobs, or agencies, you can join and lead groups that advocate for important intersections for Black women, such as a Black faculty and staff group. You can offer to coteach a course in the African American or Women's Studies departments. A more direct way is to treat your Black students, faculty members, coworkers, and colleagues with the same level of deference and respect you expect for yourself. Simply stated, treat Black women like you want to be treated, with an awareness that you make a tremendous impact simply doing what mental health professionals do—we show empathy. If you want to go beyond advocacy to inclusion, show compassion by acting beyond your paid commitment and volunteer to be an agent of change.

References

Angelou, M. (1978). *And I still rise: A book of poems by Maya Angelou*. Random House.

Ashley, R. R. (2021, July 15). How Sarah Baartman's hips went from a symbol of exploitation to a source of empowerment for Black women. *The Conversation*. https://theconversation.com/how-sarah-baartmans-hips-went-from-a-symbol-of-exploitation-to-a-source-of-empowerment-for-black-women-160063

Bond, B. (Ed.). (2018). *Black girls rock! Owning our magic. Rocking our truth.* 37INK Atria.

Brenner, P. S., Serpe, R. T., & Stryker, S. (2014). The causal ordering of prominence and salience in identity theory. *Social Psychology Quarterly*, *77*(3), 231–252. https://doi.org/10.1177/0190272513518337

Centers for Disease Control and Prevention. (n.d.). *Health disparities in HIV, viral hepatitis, STDs, and TB: African Americans/Blacks.* https://www.cdc.gov/nchhstp/healthdisparities/africanamericans.html

Cipres, D., Rodriguez, A., Alvarez, J., Stern, L., Steinauer, J., & Seidman, D. (2017). Racial/ethnic differences in young women's health-promoting strategies to reduce vulnerability to sexually transmitted infections. *Journal of Adolescent Health*, *60*(5), 556–562. https://doi.org/10.1016/j.jadohealth.2016.11.024

Collins, P. H., (2000). *Black feminist thought: Knowledge, power, and the politics of empowerment.* Routledge.

Collins, P. H. (2004). *Black sexual politics: African Americans, gender, and the new racism.* Routledge.

Comas-Díaz, L. (2016). Racial trauma recovery: A race-informed therapeutic approach to racial wounds. In A. N. Alvarez, C. T. H. Liang, & H. A. Neville (Eds.), *The cost of racism for people of color: Contextualizing experiences of discrimination* (pp. 249–272). American Psychological Association. https://content.apa.org/doi/10.1037/14852-012

Crenshaw, K. (1991). Mapping the margins: Identity politics, intersectionality, and violence against women. *Stanford Law Review, 43*(6), 1241–1299. https://www.jstor.org/stable/1229039

Crooks, N., Wise, A., & Frazier, T. (2020). Addressing sexually transmitted infections in the sociocultural context of Black heterosexual relationships in the United States. *Social Science & Medicine*, *263*, Article 113303. https://doi.org/10.1016/j.socscimed.2020.113303

Fleming, V. (Director). (1939). *Gone with the wind* [Film]. Selznick International Pictures.

Gómez, J. M., & Gobin, R. L. (2020). Black Women and bgirls & #MeToo: Rape, cultural betrayal, & healing. *Sex Roles, 82*, 1–12. https://doi.org/10.1007/s11199-019-01040-0

Holmes, C. M. (2016). The colonial roots of the racial fetishization of Black women. *Black & Gold*, *2*(1), Article 2.

Hughes, K. L. (2015). *The experiences queer college women of color have of friendship* [Doctoral dissertation, University of Georgia].

Jefferson, T., (1788). *Notes on the state of Virginia.* Lilly and Wait.

Morrison, T. (1987). *Beloved.* Vintage Books.

Moultrie, M. (2018). Putting a ring on it: Black women, Black churches, and coerced monogamy. *Black Theology*, *16*(3), 231–247.

Office of Minority Health. (n.d.). *Infant mortality and African Americans.* U.S. Department of Health and Human Services. https://www.minorityhealth.hhs.gov/omh/browse.aspx?lvl=4&lvlid=23

Postpartum Support International. (n.d.). *Postpartum post-traumatic stress disorder.* https://www.postpartum.net/learn-more/postpartum-post-traumatic-stress-disorder/

Prather, C., Fuller, T. R., Jefferies W. L., IV, Marshall, K. J., Howell, A. V., Belyue-Umole, A., & King, W. (2018). Racism, African American women, and their sexual and reproductive health: A review of historical and contemporary evidence and implications for health equity. *Health Equity, 2*(1), 249–259. https://doi.org/10.1089/heq.2017.0045

Stephanie Tubbs Jones Uterine Fibroid Research and Education Act of 2021, H.R. 2007, 117th Cong. (2021). https://www.congress.gov/bill/117th-congress/house-bill/2007

Stets, J. E., & Burke, P. J. (2014). The development of identity theory. *Advances in Group Processes, 31*, 57–97. https://doi.org/10.1108/s0882-614520140000031002

Towner, S. L., Dolcini, M. M., & Harper, G. W. (2015). Romantic relationship dynamics of urban African American adolescents: Patterns of monogamy, commitment, and trust. *Youth & Society*, *47*(3), 343–373. https://doi.org/10.1177/0044118X12462591

Watson, L. B., Lewis, J. A., & Moody, A. T. (2019). A sociocultural examination of body image among Black women. *Body Image*, *31*, 280–287. https://doi.org/10.1016/j.bodyim.2019.03.008

CHAPTER 18

You Want Me to Feel Ashamed? The Influence of Religion on Sexuality

M. N. Barringer and Ethan L. Bratt

Mainstream religious traditions, sometimes referred to as "mainline" in academic papers, are defined as the dominant, culturally established faiths held by most people (Roof & McKinney, 1987). Given the cultural, social, and political power of American religious traditions, it is no surprise that these traditions shape individuals' beliefs and understandings of sexuality. Counselors and other mental health clinicians who already appreciate the role of religion in identity formation will find their practice further strengthened by learning to navigate the nuanced differences that exist between the various mainstream religious traditions and how clients are likely to form a personal identity that is consistent with their religious tradition's normative attitudes and behaviors (Gay et al., 1996). Therefore, the purpose of this chapter is to provide a brief overview of the dominant religious traditions (evangelical Protestantism, mainline Protestantism, historically Black Protestant traditions, Roman Catholicism, Judaism, and Mormonism) and how affiliation with a particular religious tradition, or a non-religious affiliation, may impact clients' attitudes and views on sexuality. This chapter also discusses religious sexual shame and provides counselors with a case example to highlight the impact of spirituality on sex therapy and support sexual health discussions.

Defining Religion

Before discussing the impact that religion can have on any area, including sexuality, the term must be clearly defined. In research, religion has often been understood from two perspectives: substantive (e.g., creeds, beliefs, rites) versus functional (e.g., what the religious belief does, such as providing context for death). Although a substantive definition of religion has been critiqued for missing the nuance required for cross-cultural application, we believe a substantive definition of religion is more helpful in addressing our topic—namely, what are the beliefs and practices of the primary, mainstream, U.S. religious traditions that may impact an adherent's sexual beliefs, attitudes, and behaviors?

From a substantive view, religions function as an organized system of beliefs, ceremonies, and rules used to worship a god or gods. Within that definition are two distinct facets on which religions can be explored: orthodoxy and orthopraxy.

Orthodoxy is a uniformity (*ortho-*) of established beliefs or doctrine (*-doxy*). The doctrine of a religious tradition often expounds upon, for example, what deity exists, the nature of that deity, the role of that deity in life, the purpose of life, and what happens after death. Religions vary in the degree to which followers must hold consistent and uniform doctrinal beliefs.

Orthopraxy, the uniformity of practice (*-praxy*), is generally derived from the orthodoxy (e.g., deriving Sabbath-day observance practices from beliefs about a Sabbath day). A religion's orthopraxy dictates the behavior of its followers. It appears as both prescriptive and restrictive rules that adherents are expected to follow. Violations of orthopraxy may be addressed with varying levels of intensity that range from self-monitoring and self-correction to authority-based interventions, such as leaders publicly disclosing a follower's unacceptable behavior to the congregation and expelling them from the congregation or religion.

It is important for counselors to be aware of the distinction between orthodoxy and orthopraxy in the clinical setting. Clients may have distinct and important struggles taking place in either or both areas. Clients may struggle with reconciling personal beliefs with the orthodoxy of their religion (e.g., gender orientation) or personal behavior with orthopraxy (e.g., birth control and abortions). If a counselor assumes that a client's beliefs or practices are perfectly in line with their religion's orthodoxy or orthopraxy, the counselor will likely miss substantial and even defining issues that the client may be facing.

Lastly, counselors should be cautious about a client too easily dismissing how religion affects them regarding their sexuality. Clients who identify with a religious tradition, especially those who were raised in that religion, are likely so acculturated to that religion that they may not be immediately aware of the influence it has on their beliefs and understandings of sexuality. Clients who are not religious in adulthood nor raised in nonreligious households as children may still have received religious messages about sexuality (e.g., purity culture, abstinence before marriage, prejudice toward gender and sexual minorities) from mainstream American culture. Messages regarding sexuality norms may also be learned from peers, media, romantic or sexual partners, medical professionals, and educational institutions.

Shame, Sexual Shame, and Religious Sexual Shame

While many religious adherents may follow their religion's orthopraxy out of belief or devotion, there are some negative reinforcement mechanisms that are used by many religions to enforce orthopraxy and/or orthodoxy among adherents. Such approaches include restricting access to rites or sacraments; isolation, alienation, and exclusion (e.g., the practices of disfellowship or excommunication); and the use of fear of eternal consequences following death. Another mechanism of religious control is religious sexual shaming.

Brené Brown (2007), perhaps one of the most well-known researchers and educators on shame, defines shame as "the intensely painful feeling or experience of believing we are flawed and therefore unworthy of acceptance and belonging" (p. 5). She distinguishes this from guilt in noting that guilt is focused on whether one's actions (or inactions) are in line with one's internal moral beliefs and values. Shame is an assessment of one's self, rather than one's behavior, as lacking. The experience of shame has been shown to correlate with significant negative impacts on mental and emotional well-being, including, but not limited to, feelings of inferiority, hopelessness, depression, reduced self-esteem, and aggression.

Sexual shame overlaps with but has distinct features from general shame. Noel Clark (2017) proposed the following definition of sexual shame:

> Sexual shame is a visceral feeling of humiliation and disgust toward one's own body and identity as a sexual being, and a belief of being abnormal, inferior and unworthy. This feeling can be internalized but also manifests in interpersonal relationships having a negative impact on trust, communication, and physical and emotional intimacy. Sexual shame develops across the lifespan in interactions with interpersonal relationships, one's culture and society, and subsequent critical self-appraisal (a continuous feedback loop). There is also a fear and uncertainty related to one's power or right to make decisions, including safety decisions, related to sexual encounters, along with an internalized judgment toward one's own sexual desire. (p. 87)

Sexual shame is frequently encountered by sex therapists in the therapy room. Clients may feel sexual shame due to familial, regional, or ethnic culture. Religion is a common contributing factor to sexual shame among clients as religious teachings are used to regulate sexuality. Given the number of clients who experience sexual shame due to religious teachings, Tina Schermer Sellers (2017) coined the term "religious sexual shame" to identify shame that "is prompted by particular religious messages about the sexual self, innate sexual desire, natural sexual curiosity, natural sexual thoughts, and sexual actions" (p. xxiv). Religious sexual shame can be particularly toxic because the underlying standard against which one's sexuality is being measured has implications for rejection or acceptance by their deity and eternal consequences, compared with purely social or cultural consequences. It is often experienced by clients as a literal pitting of their sexuality against their redemption, salvation, exaltation, or liberation.

Sellers (2019) notes that "this combination of fear, shame, and silence wrapped in a religious context of 'This is of God' is what produces religious sexual shame that can manifest as symptoms of childhood sexual abuse in adults" (p. xxiv). Sellers notes that religious sexual shame also presents as sexual dysfunction as well as depression and anxiety. The silence Sellers references often means that access to sexual health information is restricted and curiosity about the body or sexuality is condemned.

Sellers outlines a protocol for the treatment of religious sexual shame. Although Sellers presents this protocol within the context of a general Christian perspective, this protocol can be appropriately adapted to other religious frameworks. Sellers's treatment for religious sexual shame calls for medically accurate, sexual health knowledge referencing the use of the PLISSIT (Permission, Limited Information, Specific Suggestions, and Intensive Therapy; Annon, 1976) model; claiming and celebrating your body; naming your story and sharing it with someone, which addresses the past up to that point of treatment; and constructing and living your new sexual legacy, which is both present- and future-oriented.

Counselors should also pay close attention to issues with cisgender and transgender women and religious traditions' views toward gender issues. Historically, religious traditions discuss gender and sexuality within a patriarchal framework. Although some religious traditions have worked to dismantle the patriarchal structures, other religious traditions have yet to address patriarchy and continue to discuss sexuality within the hierarchical relationship of cisgender and heterosexual men over women. Religious patriarchy tends to minimize, dismiss, or actively undermine the sexual autonomy and pleasure of women. Religious women may carry significant religious sexual shame around issues of self-pleasure, limiting the number of children they have (if any), using birth control, and/or turning down their husband's sexual advances.

Religious Traditions and How They Shape Beliefs and Understandings of Sexuality

Research (e.g., Barringer et al., 2013) shows that individuals' attitudes toward sexuality vary by religious traditions in the United States. Beyond identifying with a religious tradition, the extent to which individuals engage in religious communities and hold group membership will also affect their beliefs and attitudes on sexuality (Sherkat, 2014). Messages of rejection and sexual shame within religious contexts are associated with individuals struggling to accept one's sexual identity, internalized homonegativity, depression, psychological distress, and lower self-esteem. Therefore, it is important for counselors to be familiar with the different mainline religious traditions and how religious socialization may influence clients' attitudes and internalized beliefs.

Protestantism: Three Traditions

Protestantism in the United States is best understood as three distinct traditions—evangelical Protestantism, mainline Protestantism, and historically Black Protestantism—given that each tradition is composed of numerous denominations and congregations which share similar histories, beliefs, and practices (Pew Research Center, 2015). Protestantism differs from other religious traditions, such as Catholicism or Mormonism, in that practitioners appeal to the Bible as the ultimate source of authority on understanding God's will and doctrine, rather than to a central authority figure such as a pope/prophet (Melton, 2005).

Although the religious landscape in the United States continues to change, the majority of Americans identify with Protestantism (46.6%), with 25.4% identifying as evangelical Protestant, 14.7% identifying as mainline Protestant, and 6.5% identifying with the historically Black church (Pew Research Center, 2015). Given that these Protestant traditions demonstrate different subcultural characteristics, it is important to discuss these three Protestant traditions separately as clients are likely to form a personal identity consistent with the religious tradition's normative attitudes (Gay et al., 1996).

Evangelical Protestantism

Evangelical Protestantism is one of the most influential religious groups in the United States (Wellman, 2008). Evangelical Protestants (e.g., Southern Baptists) in the United States tend to interpret the Bible as the literal word of God (i.e., biblical literalism), have higher religious involvement (e.g., attend church more frequently, pray often), and describe themselves as "born-again" and/or "evangelical" (e.g., Perry & Whitehead, 2016; Sherkat, 2014). As the term born again lost popularity among some conservative Christians, the term evangelical took its place to denote a religious group with an orientation toward *proselytizing*, which in this context is defined as the act of attempting to convince someone to adopt a particular religious belief (Sherkat, 2014).

However, it should be noted that the term evangelical is included in the names of denominations that do not proselytize and would be considered mainline Protestant in the sense that they are more theologically liberal (e.g., the Evangelical Lutheran Church of America). Additionally, evangelical Protestant denominations distinguish themselves from other religious traditions by invoking the power of scripture when discussing sexuality in contrast to mainline Protestant denominations, which tend to frame issues of sexuality using less religiously distinctive arguments (Kapinus & Kraus, 2010).

Masturbation and Sexually Explicit Material

Evangelical Protestants tend to view and discuss sexually explicit material and self-pleasure (i.e., masturbation) as morally problematic given that they violate direct commands against nonmarital sex (Grubbs & Perry, 2019). Evangelical pastors largely conclude that masturbation should be avoided (Regnerus, 2007). Research shows individuals often feel a sense of shame, guilt, and moral incongruence (e.g., the experience of violating one's scared or deeply held values) surrounding the usage of sexually explicit material, particularly among evangelicals as they are collectively opposed to it (Grubbs & Perry, 2019; Perry, 2018). However, individuals may seek out covert outlets for sexual expression within disapproving religious communities (Whitehead & Perry, 2018). For instance, research has shown that states with higher percentages of evangelical Protestants have a higher proportion of searches for online sexually explicit material (Whitehead & Perry, 2018). Because of the shame and guilt surrounding sexually explicit material, religious people are more likely to believe they are addicted to it as well (Grubbs et al., 2015).

Gender Identity and Sexual Orientation

Evangelical religious leaders remain the primary opponents of gender and sexual minorities rights in the United States (Olson et al., 2006). Religious leaders typically discuss gay men and lesbian women's sexual orientation as an individual choice that is not innate, but rather is controllable (Stokes & Schewe, 2016). In turn, evangelical Protestants tend to view sexual minorities less favorably because they believe their sexual behavior/attraction is in direct, willful violation of religious doctrine and can be altered through religious discipline (Whitehead, 2010). Research examining evangelical pastors' sermon transcripts has found that pastors frame their discussion of gender and sexual minorities negatively and justify their stance against couples who are lesbian, gay, bisexual, transgender, queer, plus other identities (LGBTQ+) by using biblical passages, potential health hazards, and individual choice narratives (Stokes & Schewe, 2016). Thus, creating a clear in-group (cisgender, heterosexual evangelicals) versus out-group (gender and sexual minorities) identity along moral boundaries is prevalent among evangelical Protestant denominations (Roger, 2019; Stokes & Schewe, 2016).

Extramarital Sexual Activity

There is a substantial amount of evangelical literature (e.g., self-help literature, sex manuals) that describe sexual expression from a conservative, prescriptive narrative in which heterosexual marriage is the essential and necessary element (e.g., Gresh, 2012). More recently, these narratives coupled with the evangelical purity movement have gained popularity among mainstream social media sites (e.g., blogs, YouTube, Instagram) as young adult cisgender, heterosexual women have been creating blogs and vlogs detailing their heterosexual marriages and purity promises to remain virgins until marriage. These storylines center around the idea that women will suffer if they have premarital heterosexual sex and provide misinformation as to why women should live chastely, suggesting for example that women become "chemically bonded" to their first sexual partner and that "having sex will cause heartbreak" (Oldfield, 2018, para. 3).

Birth Control

Evangelical Protestant denominations tend to be less supportive of family planning and agree that the widespread access and availability of contraceptives will lead to increased nonmarital sexual activity (Barrett et al., 2014; Ellison & Goodson, 1997). Many evangelical Protestants are concerned about the moral ramifications of fostering nonmarital sexual activity through contraceptive access and usage (Barrett et al., 2014). This is not surprising given that clergy members' understanding of human sexuality is rooted in the belief that the Bible is the Word of God (Ellison & Goodson, 1997).

Mainline Protestantism

Mainline Protestants (e.g., United Methodist Church, Lutheran Church, U.S. Presbyterian Church) typically do not describe themselves as born again and are not as theologically conservative as evangelical Protestant denominations. Mainline Protestants tend to hold more progressive and accepting attitudes regarding sexuality (Sherkat, 2014). Many mainline Protestant denominations tend to advocate on their churches' websites, and within their religious communities, for open dialogues about sexuality and assert that sexual morality is based on consensual and caring sexual relationships (Kapinus & Kraus, 2010).

Masturbation and Sexually Explicit Material

Mainline Protestant denominations may not openly advocate for their members to engage in masturbation practices, but they typically do not discuss masturbation within a negative context compared with evangelical Protestants (Regnerus, 2007). Mainline Protestants tend to be less morally concerned about sexually explicit materials and less likely to exhibit sexual shame because it may not conflict with their religious beliefs compared with conservative Christian traditions (Perry, 2018).

Gender Identity and Sexual Orientation

Research shows mainline Protestants have called for inclusivity when discussing sexuality, including same-sex relationships (Olson & Cadge, 2002). Mainline Protestants hold more favorable attitudes toward gender and sexual minorities compared with other Protestants (Perry & Whitehead, 2016; Sherkat, 2014).

However, counselors should be aware that conflicts over same-sex marriage and ordaining openly gay clergy members have resulted in divisions among mainline Protestant denominations (see Haxby, 2008). Although some mainline Protestant denominations have stated that gay and lesbian sexual orientations are morally incompatible with Christian doctrine, these denominations have simultaneously supported the civil rights of sexual and gender minorities (Cadge et al., 2008). This stands in contrast to evangelical and Black Protestants, who are less supportive of both same-sex marriage and same-sex relations (Barringer et al., 2013; Harris, 2010).

Extramarital Sexual Activity

Research shows that mainline Protestants denominations are comfortable with discussing responsible premarital sex, both among heterosexuals and sexual minorities (Sherkat, 2014). Mainline Protestants tend to hold more accepting and progressive attitudes toward extramarital sexual activity compared with other Protestant traditions (Gay et al., 1996).

Birth Control

In contrast with evangelical Protestant denominations, which believe widespread access to contraceptives will lead to increased nonmarital sex, official mainline Protestants' statements have supported contraception (see The United Methodist Church, 2022). Although some attitudes may vary among mainline Protestant denominations regarding birth control and family planning, mainline Protestants are not as theologically conservative as other Protestant traditions.

Historically Black Protestant Tradition

The Black church, or historically Black Protestant tradition, tends to take a theologically conservative stance toward sexuality. Research (e.g., Harris, 2010) has shown that the Black church has traditionally had difficulty reconciling sex and sexuality with religious beliefs. Historically Black Protestant denominations take conservative stances toward gender and sexual minorities, same-sex marriage, and premarital sex (Harris, 2010). Although it is outside the scope of this chapter to delve into the history of the Black church, it is important for counselors to know that the Black church plays a pivotal role in the Black community, where it remains the most influential institution in shaping attitudes and beliefs among members (e.g., Harris, 2010). Pastors in predominantly Black churches provide members with spiritual guidance as well as information regarding social, political, and health issues (Campbell et al., 2007).

Masturbation and Sexually Explicit Material

Research shows religious leaders in Black churches do not typically discuss sex and sexual health in their congregations (Williams et al., 2014). When topics such as masturbation are discussed, the messages are typically framed as immoral acts (Williams et al., 2014). Research shows that Black Protestants have not taken a particularly strong moral stance against sexually explicit material (Perry & Schleifer, 2019).

Gender Identity and Sexual Orientation

Given the influence religion has in many Black Americans' lives, counselors should be aware that the negative effects of sexual shaming and stigmatization may be amplified for gender and sexual minorities (Quinn et al., 2016). Black churches tend to view gay men and lesbian women's sexual orientation as acquired through socialization (Roberts & Yamane, 2016). The messages preached by religious leaders in Black churches tend to condemn and stigmatize (Pitt, 2010). Religious leaders may use pejorative or code words (e.g., punk, sissy) when referring to Black gay men (Pitt, 2010). Although the term "homosexual" is typically used throughout religious theology and religious nomenclature, the term itself is loaded as it has been used to denigrate and ostracize the gay community over the years (see Peters, 2014). Additionally, GLAAD (2022), a dynamic media force for LGBTQ+ acceptance and equality, has listed the term "homosexual" as offensive. Therefore, we recommend that counselors refrain from using the term in their practice as well. Counselors also may want to be aware of the language used in the pulpit to describe sexual minorities, as clients may repeat those terms. Recent research shows that Black Protestants' attitudes regarding sexual minorities' civil liberties have become increasingly tolerant, which may indicate members distinguish between issues of personal morality and civil liberties regarding sexual minorities (Ledet, 2017).

Extramarital Sexual Activity

Discussions regarding heterosexual sexuality are limited in Black churches. Typically, when pastors discuss extramarital sexual activity, it is in the context of heterosexual married couples (Williams et al., 2014).

Birth Control

Research shows that pastors of Black church denominations typically believe it is appropriate to teach abstinence-only to their congregations and do not discuss contraceptive usage and other sexual practices (Williams et al., 2014).

Roman Catholic Church

The Roman Catholic Church is a highly structured, centralized organization with its doctrines explained and defined by the pope. Currently, 20% of the U.S. population identifies as Roman Catholic (Pew Research Center, 2019). The Roman Catholic Church teaches that sexuality is the expression of a person's belonging to the "bodily and biological world" and that sexuality only becomes "personal and truly human" when expressed in heterosexual marriage.

Masturbation and Sexually Explicit Material

Lust is viewed as a "disordered desire" and the seeking of sexual pleasure, even within marriage, in a way that does not have the potential for reproduction to happen is "morally disordered" (Catholic Church, 2019, para. 2351–2352). Consequently, masturbation is seen as sinful. The Roman Catholic Church teaches that sexually explicit material "offends against chastity because it perverts the conjugal act, the intimate giving of spouses to each other." They also teach that "civil authorities should prevent the production and distribution of pornographic materials."

Gender Identity and Sexual Orientation

The Roman Catholic Church denounces the idea of gender identity as being the product of an ideology that "denies the difference and reciprocity in nature of a man and woman" (Synod of Bishops, 2015, Chapter 1, Cultural Contradictions section, para. 2 [Section 8 in original]) and affirms that a person's sex is a structural determinant of male or female identity. The Roman Catholic Church has remained consistent in its stance against affirming same-sex relations (Fassin, 2010). The official stance on same-sex relations is mixed, as the Catholic Church makes a clear distinction between same-sex behavior (i.e., morally wrong) and same-sex orientation (i.e., not morally wrong so long as individuals do not engage in same-sex intimate relations; Maher et al., 2008). This distinction between behavior and orientation could be one of the reasons why recent research indicates that Catholics' attitudes are aligning more with those of mainline Protestants rather than conservative evangelical Protestants (Sherkat et al., 2010).

Extramarital Sexual Activity

The Roman Catholic Church continues to teach to their members that sexual intercourse, sometimes referred to by Catholics as the conjugal embrace, is reserved for men and women within the confines of heterosexual marriage (Catholic Church, 2019).

Birth Control

As any form of contraception separates the reproductive possibility from the seeking of sexual pleasure, all birth control is considered sinful. Additionally, sexual intercourse among those who are infertile or for women who are postmenopausal is not seen as sinful because it is believed that God can still cause conception to happen if it is his will. The Roman Catholic Church condemns any form of reproductive assistance that involves another person outside of a heterosexual marriage (e.g., donating sperm or eggs, surrogacy) and holds that artificial insemination involving only the married couple is morally unacceptable because it separates the act of sex from reproduction (Catholic Church, 2019).

Judaism

Over the last 10 years, the number of U.S. adults who identify with the Jewish tradition has remained steady, with about 2% of the population identifying as Jewish (Pew Research Center, 2019). Modern Judaism in the United States is typically divided into the three major movements, also referred to as branches, streams, or denominations—Orthodox, Conservative, and Reform (My Jewish Learning, n.d.). Orthodox Judaism generally tends toward a strict interpretation of *halakha* (Jewish law), whereas Conservative Judaism is viewed as a balance of traditional Jewish law and progressive understanding, along with its egalitarianism, which sets it apart from Orthodox Judaism (Holzer, 2020). Reform Judaism tends to be the more progressive movement because it also acknowledges the diversity of Reform Jewish beliefs and practices. Counselors should be aware that much of the existing religious and social science literature does not parse out the three movements in examinations of attitudes toward sexuality. Some scholars also have noted differences in all the movements between what is practiced versus what is preached. For example, Jewish individuals may hold more liberal and progressive beliefs than those expressed in the direct interpretations of their rabbis (Holzer, 2020). Overall, Jewish people tend to hold progressive outlooks regarding issues of sexuality, such as same-sex marriage, compared with other religious traditions (Pew Research Center, 2013).

Masturbation and Sexually Explicit Material

There are many opinions on male masturbation across the three movements of Judaism. Orthodox Judaism considers male masturbation a sin, whereas the Reform and Conservative movements have been more accepting (My Jewish Learning, n.d.). Reform Judaism teaches that male masturbation is not sinful or harmful, and some Conservative rabbis have recently suggested that male masturbation is morally preferable compared to premarital sex (My Jewish Learning, n.d.). Female masturbation is less problematic in Jewish traditions because there are no concerns regarding the spilling, or wasting, of seed (male sperm), and some rabbis do not object to female masturbation (My Jewish Learning, n.d.).

Traditional Jewish law is firmly opposed to sexually explicit material (My Jewish Learning, n.d.). Orthodox Judaism forbids consuming sexually explicit materials. Conservative rabbis have raised concerns about issues of exploitation with the production of sexually explicit material, whereas Rabbi Jonathan Crane for the Reform movement recently suggested that textual tradition would support Jewish people to produce and consume forms of sexually explicit material (My Jewish Learning, n.d.).

Gender Identity and Sexual Orientation

Among the Jewish movements, there are varying attitudes toward same-sex relations. Orthodox Judaism is characterized by a traditional interpretation of Jewish law, which views same-sex relations and marriage in direct violation of God's laws. However, more recently, there have been a growing number of Modern Orthodox rabbis performing same-sex weddings, and there's an increased acceptance of gender and sexual minorities within Modern Orthodox communities (Dolsten, 2020). Conservative and Reform Jewish people have been welcoming to sexual minorities in their communities and both sanction same-sex marriage (Ariel, 2007; Moon, 2014; Roberts & Yamane, 2016). Overall, those who identify as Jewish in the United States have been more accepting of LGBTQ+ people compared to other religious traditions (Olson et al., 2006).

Extramarital Sexual Activity

Research has found that Jewish people tend to hold more favorable and accepting attitudes toward extramarital sex and do not view it as wrong compared to other religious traditions (Gay et al., 1996; Sherkat, 2014). However, Conservative and Reform rabbis continue to uphold Judaism's traditional preference that sex is reserved for marriage, whereas the Orthodox movement strictly forbids sex outside of marriage (My Jewish Learning, n.d.).

Birth Control

The practice of birth control usage among Jewish people has been prevalent. Jewish law permits methods of contraception that do not damage the sperm or prevent it from getting to its intended destination (i.e., oral contraceptive pills; Rosner, 2001). The Conservative movement generally permits the use of contraceptives within marriage (Berkowitz & Popovsky, 2010). The Reform movement generally supports Jewish women's decision to use contraceptives for a wide range of reasons. Although the Orthodox movement is more restrictive than the other movements, Orthodox Jewish women are permitted in some circumstances to use some forms of contraceptives, whereas contraceptive usage for men is not allowed (Feldman, 1992). Modern Orthodox Judaism permits the use of birth control under some circumstances, such as when pregnancy/childbirth could harm the woman or to space out having children, but not to avoid having any children (Rosner, 2001).

Mormonism

Mormonism, formally known as the Church of Jesus Christ of Latter-day Saints, is a highly centralized religion similar in this way to Roman Catholicism. The percentage of Mormons in the United States has remained steady at 2% over the past decade (Pew Research Center, 2019). Mormonism teaches that heterosexuality is of divine origins and that "physical intimacy between husband and wife is intended to be beautiful and sacred. It is ordained of God for the creation of children and for the expression of love between husband and wife" (Church of Jesus Christ of Latter-day Saints [LDS], 2011, p. 35)

Masturbation and Sexually Explicit Material

Mormonism has taught that "prophets have condemned [masturbation] as a sin throughout the ages" (LDS, 1985, p. 36). However, there is no record of any church leader commenting about masturbation prior to the 1900s, and masturbation is not addressed in any official canon of scripture. It was taught that masturbation caused nonheterosexual orientations and that with enough conviction and prayer that one can rid themselves of masturbation. Mormonism has consistently condemned all forms of sexually explicit material as sinful and has also taught that sexually explicit material is "one of the approaches" to nonheterosexual orientations (Kimball, 1974,

p. 8). It teaches that sexually explicit material is "a plague like we have never seen," is addictive, and cautions that it will lead to "evil actions" (LDS, 2014, 0:04). Mormons have shown support for making sexually explicit material illegal (Sherkat, 2014).

Gender Identity and Sexual Orientation

Mormonism teaches that gender is "an essential characteristic of [an] individual" (LDS, 1995, para. 2) not just during this life but also before we were born and will be such after death. Mormonism has taught that this eternal gender is the person's "biological sex at birth" (LDS, 2019, President Dallin H. Oaks section, para. 5). Regarding transgender issues, the Mormon church has eschewed the term transgender in favor of "gender incongruence" but does not take a position on the cause of someone being transgender. Transgender individuals who have transitioned, even just socially, experience restrictions on their participation in the Mormon church. They do not address the issue of intersex individuals who may disagree with their assigned gender except to direct questions to central church leadership

Mormonism has at times taught that nonheterosexual orientations are a learned behavior caused by poor family background, poor peer relationships, or early homosexual behaviors and that behaviors, thoughts, and desires "can be overcome" (LDS, 1981, p. 2) and that no one is "born that way" (p. 5). Many Mormons still carry these beliefs despite the church's current handbook now stating that they do not have a position on the cause of "same-sex attraction" (LDS, 2021, Section 38.6.15). The Mormon church's handbook (LDS, 2021) also notes that all homosexual behavior is sinful and that only those who abstain from any physical expression of their homosexual orientation can fully participate in the church. The Mormon church condemns same-sex marriage as "sinful and [undermining of] the divinely created institution of the family" (LDS, 2021, Section 38.6.16).

Extramarital Sexual Activity

The Mormon church condemns all "sexual relations" (LDS, 2021, Section 38.6.16) outside of heterosexual marriage. The church outlines clearly the expectations around chastity in a pamphlet distributed to all Mormon children ages 12 to 18 years old. "Before marriage, do not participate in passionate kissing, lie on top of another person, or touch the private, sacred parts of another person's body, with or without clothing. Do not do anything else that arouses sexual feelings. Do not arouse those emotions in your own body" (LDS, 2011, p. 36). Research shows that individuals raised as Mormon and those who currently identify as Mormon have the lowest rates of premarital sex compared to other religious traditions (Sherkat, 2014).

Birth Control

Although the Mormon church has at times condemned all birth control for preventing offspring as a "heinous crime," "a grievous sin," or a violation of the "covenant of marriage," the Mormon church's official handbook states that "the decision of how many children to have and when to have them . . . should be left between the couple and the Lord" (LDS, 2021, Section 38.6.4) and that the church "strongly discourages" (Section 38.6.4) surgical sterilization.

Nonreligious/Religious Nones

The Pew Research Center in 2019 reported that the nonreligious or religiously unaffiliated population, also referred to as "religious nones," rose from 17% in 2009 to

26% over the previous decade and was continuing to grow in size. The religiously unaffiliated can include those who identify as atheist, agnostic, spiritual but non-religious (SBNR), or describe their religion as "nothing in particular" (Pew Research Center, 2019, para. 1). The majority of religious nones were raised in a religious tradition but dropped their religious identity in adulthood (Lipka, 2015). The religious nones are not uniformly nonreligious, as most religious nones report they believe in God and that religion plays a somewhat important role in their lives (Lipka, 2015). However, the religious nones are becoming increasingly secular in their attitudes and beliefs (Lipka, 2015). Although outside the scope of this chapter, counselors should note that there are nuanced differences in social and political attitudes within the broad category of religious nones when controlling for those who are privately religious and spiritual (Baker & Smith, 2009).

Masturbation and Sexually Explicit Material

Overall, nonreligious individuals tend to hold more favorable attitudes toward sexually explicit material and masturbation compared to religious individuals (Ahrold et al., 2011). Recent research finds that states with larger proportions of religious nones show that searches for online sexually explicit material are less popular (Whitehead & Perry, 2018). Given that nonreligious individuals are typically not immersed within a religious community, seeking out sexually explicit material may not be necessary as they have other opportunities for sexual exploration without sexual shame and religious monitoring (Whitehead & Perry, 2018).

Gender Identity and Sexual Orientation

Religious nones as a group have held supportive attitudes toward same-sex marriage and gender and sexual minorities for some time in the United States (Fingerhut, 2016). Religious nones tend to hold more favorable attitudes toward gender and sexual minorities compared with other religious traditions (Frame, 2020).

Extramarital Sexual Activity

Nonreligious individuals are less inclined to view extramarital sexual activity as wrong compared to individuals who identify with a religious tradition (Sherkat, 2014). Again, religious nones are less likely to be immersed within a religious community that sexually shames and problematizes extramarital sexual activity.

Birth Control

Nonreligious individuals are likely to view birth control as acceptable and that contraceptives should be accessible and affordable. Research has shown that nonreligious parents are more likely to believe birth control to be safe and effective and, consequently, more likely to discuss with teenagers where to obtain birth control. This contrasts with their religious counterparts, who are more likely to view birth control as less effective or safe and to instead discuss with teenagers the negative consequences of nonmarital sex (Swain et al., 2006).

Case Example: Erin and Don

Erin and Don were selected as our case example because religion played a dual role for them as a significant source of distress and shame as well as a valuable strength that was utilized in their therapeutic work.

Case History

Background

Don is a 23-year-old Caucasian, cisgender, heterosexual male presenting in good physical health and denying any substance use. He obtained a bachelor's degree and is employed full-time. He is the oldest of two children born into an intact, cisgender, heterosexual marriage that continues to date. He reports feeling close to his family members, who are highly religious nondenominational Christians, which is how he currently identifies.

Don first learned of sex at around the age of 8 after asking his father about masturbation. He was discouraged from learning about sexuality and was told "just don't." His first exposure to sexually explicit material was via the internet at the age of 11. Curiosity drove further exploration of sexually explicit material despite intense feelings of shame after each episode. His parents discovered his activities and confronted him at which time he simply shut down and didn't engage. He did have one non-intercourse sexual experience in high school and experienced the same intense shame response. In college, sexually explicit material use increased. He became involved in Christian "porn recovery programs" where he learned that his sexuality was something to be feared, that he had to protect his girlfriend from himself, and that if he wanted sex then he wouldn't be able to stop himself. He was taught that sexually explicit material was addicting, was evil, and would corrupt his sexuality.

Erin is a 24-year-old Caucasian, cisgender, heterosexual female presenting with several health issues including irritable bowel syndrome and vocal cord dysfunction, two conditions that can be caused by trauma. She has one to two alcoholic drinks a few times a month and denies recreational drug use. She is currently enrolled in a master's degree program.

She is the younger of two children born into an intact, cisgender, heterosexual marriage that has since ended. Notable family history includes multigenerational alcoholism, her father growing up in an abusive household, his mother being diagnosed with bipolar disorder and schizotypal personality disorder, his own diagnosis of bipolar disorder, and his refusal of treatment for his disorder. Her family was not religious.

She reports that she is a survivor of childhood sexual, physical, and emotional abuse by her father. Sexual abuse began before she can remember and included penetrative rape. She was subjected to brutal, life-threatening violence in response to any resistance during the abuse. Sexual abuse continued until about the start of middle school. She reports that she also endured neglect through the denial and withholding of food and appropriate clothing during her early teenage years. In her mid-teens, her mother finally left her father, taking Erin with her.

Erin received mental health counseling during her later high school years and into college, including eye movement desensitization and reprocessing for her trauma. She reports decreased intrusive thoughts, nightmares, and dissociation. She reports that dance has been an incredibly important part of her healing as it helps her to reconnect with her body.

Erin reports that she learned about sex from her sister at a very young age. She was told that sex is shameful, bad, and to be kept secret, all messages that were reinforced by the family's reaction to her sister's sexual activities in high school. By middle school, Erin reports that sexuality was "a box that was shut off and put aside" and that she did her best to shut off and "disown" her sexuality. She notes that touching and kissing have always been uncomfortable and that she had never kissed anyone prior to Don.

Erin and Don met while both were undergraduate students. During this time, Erin "found Jesus," converted to nondenominational Christianity, and began attending Don's church. They dated for the next 3 years and had no sexual contact prior to marriage for religious reasons. Premarital counseling did not address sexuality. Erin anticipated difficulty with sex after an unsuccessful pap smear due to vaginismus.

At the time of intake, they have been married for less than 2 years. During their honeymoon, Don nearly drowned while swimming in the ocean and was rescued by Erin. Don was resuscitated and hospitalized. Don did five sessions of mental health counseling ending just a few months prior for his acute trauma but still deals with posttraumatic stress disorder.

Presenting Problems

Erin and Don report being unable to have penetrative intercourse due to intense tightness at the vaginal opening. Attempts at penetration cause Erin significant pain. She also experiences deep shame following any sexual engagement, regardless of whether they attempt penetration. "I feel disconnected from my body [but I try to] push through." She has begun avoiding sex. Don reports that his distress over the sexual issues and relationship generally is resulting in sleep disturbances, hopelessness about their situation, and anger. Erin's distress and frequent rejections have left him disinterested in initiating sex. Their experiences and lack of intercourse have left them both feeling lonely and frustrated.

Also, Don reports being "addicted to pornography" and has attended several Christian "pornography recovery" programs/retreats aimed at curing his "addiction." He notes that he has been able to reduce his usage but not eliminate it over the last 5 years. The culmination of the above issues and his trauma have resulted in a recent increase in usage to about once every 2 weeks. His usage contributes to a lack of trust and vulnerability in the relationship around matters of attraction, desire, and intimacy. He and Erin have tried limiting his opportunities to view sexually explicit material with little success.

Diagnoses

Erin was given a primary diagnosis of posttraumatic stress disorder, 309.81 (F43.10). Secondary diagnoses and descriptive codes included genito-pelvic pain or penetration disorder, 302.76 (F52.6); relationship distress with spouse or intimate partner, V61.10 (Z63.0); encounter for mental health services for victim of child sexual abuse by parent, V61.21 (Z69.010); and personal history (past history) of sexual abuse in childhood, V15.41 (Z62.810).

Don's primary diagnosis was also posttraumatic stress disorder, 309.81 (F43.10), with a secondary diagnosis of relationship distress with spouse or intimate partner, V61.10 (Z63.0).

Treatment Summary

Therapeutic Goals

The clients' goals were identified as eliminating Don's viewing of sexually explicit material; healing the distress, distrust, and disconnection they are experiencing in response to Don's sexually explicit material usage; treatment of Erin's penetration disorder so that they can engage in penetrative intercourse; and building a healthier sexual relationship focused on mutual pleasure and authenticity. The clients agreed that the first two goals were the most immediately pressing for them.

Therapeutic Treatment

We began addressing Don's use of sexually explicit material by dispelling myths about it being addictive or corruptive of sexuality. Interest in sexual stimulation, desire for pleasure, and his use of sexually explicit material for that purpose were depathologized. Unwanted use of sexually explicit material was identified as a maladaptive coping skill used in times of emotional distress (e.g., when feeling rejection, loneliness, overwhelm, sadness, or disconnection). We explored alternative coping and emotion regulation skills that better aligned with his morals and values.

Religious sexual shame as cultivated in his church and recovery group experiences was identified and explored. Don's religious ideas of growth (using the religious metaphor of "milk before meat"; 1 Corinthians 3:2 The New King James) and imperfection as essential to a relationship with God (Paul's "thorn in the flesh"; 2 Corinthians 12:6–7) were used to reframe his efforts as a process of improvement rather than a shame-based dichotomy of recovery or relapse. Rather than perceiving cutoff from God and loss of worth, Don could maintain connection with God and see himself as an imperfect but good Christian.

Erin's experiences were also heavily impacted by religious sexual shame. Having been taught that Don looked at sexually explicit material because he was choosing other women over her, Erin saw his behaviors as evidence that she was insufficient as a woman and that she would never "measure up." Consequently, his usage left her feeling inadequate and betrayed.

Sexually explicit material was reframed as depictions of fantasy that were not intended to be realistic, similar to how action or science-fiction movies may be exciting but don't represent reality. Erin began to let go of sexually explicit material as a standard she was failing to meet. Don began to reaffirm Erin's attractiveness and his desire for her, which reduced her feelings of inadequacy and betrayal.

Focus of treatment shifted to their interpersonal sexuality. Erin's sense of shame and failure regarding penetration issues was again explored, normalized, and subsequently challenged. Sexual performance was deemphasized in her self-assessment framework, and other areas that she was proud of and confident in were emphasized. The growth mindset was again applied, which allowed for greater acceptance of self-compassion and compassion from Don.

We explored the "good enough sex" model (Metz & McCarthy, 2007), which emphasizes a pleasure-oriented instead of performance-oriented paradigm. This model allowed them to focus on what they liked about their sex life, rather than what wasn't working. They identified sexual activities Erin was capable of and open to engaging in and that they both would enjoy. We identified three areas in which Erin specifically struggles: desire to engage, fear of having trauma reactions, and experiencing pleasure.

Erin experienced conflict about engaging sexually. She believed sex with her husband was a good and desirable thing and yet she would experience anxiety, fear, and other trauma reactions when attempting to engage. She prioritized her belief and attempted to ignore her body's reactions by forcing sexual activity anyway, which resulted in more negative experiences.

We discussed the principles of consent and honesty from the six principles of sexual health (Braun-Harvey & Vigorito, 2016) in the context of how she engages with herself. Her abuse history had taught her that her desire to engage in sex or not didn't matter. She concluded that honesty would require her being transparent about her desire for sex or not and that she had the right to give or withhold consent. She and Don agreed to take attempts at penetration off the table temporarily to reduce Erin's anxiety about Don's expectations.

As Erin began paying attention to her body and sexuality, she noticed significant resistance. Her body's resistance to sexuality and her trauma reactions left her feeling betrayed by her body. She also realized that "my body doesn't trust me to keep it safe," in reference to how she had been hurt during abuse and when she had ignored her body's messages and forced sexual experiences with Don.

Her body's reactions were reframed as it attempting to protect her from what it understood sex to be: abuse and harm. This new paradigm created space for compassion and appreciation for her body and a willingness to work with her body rather than fight against it. Dissociation was addressed through grounding exercises. Narrative and self-talk exercises were used to reinforce to herself and her body the differences between the unwanted sexual abuse and the consensual experiences that she did want.

Consent was revisited. Erin's generalization that "nonconsent is what sex is all about" was reframed to "nonconsent is what abuse is all about." We identified that her abuse and rape met none of the six principles (Braun-Harvey & Vigorito, 2016), including consent, while Don's actions in their experiences met all of them. Don affirmed that consent meant she could say stop at any time. They were assigned a green light/red light exercise where Erin could practice giving and withdrawing consent for the type of touch she did or didn't want. During this, Don was able to fill a practical, supportive role in Emily listening to her body. They reported back that the experience was very connecting and pleasurable, and that Erin having the power to say no or to stop an experience at any time freed her to be able to say yes more easily. Green (go) and red (pause) were expanded to include yellow (slow down) and "engines off" (stop everything) to allow Erin to keep communication simple but expand her options. This exercise created the base framework that they would use for sexual activity throughout treatment.

As Erin continued to stay in tune with her body, attend to its reactions, discern between traumatic abuse and consensual sexual engagement, and exercise control through consent, she felt progressively less anxious about her body's reactions, which were becoming more infrequent and manageable.

During her childhood, Erin had endured the withholding of food, being forced to wear clothes that were much too small, physical abuse, and shaming of any pleasures or comforts she did have. This had resulted in her now experiencing guilt and shame with all forms of pleasure including food, comfortable clothing, and enjoyable activities including leisure, recreation, and sexuality.

We examined the discrepancy between her reactions of pleasure being bad and her current beliefs about pleasure. She identified examples in her belief system of Jesus Christ meeting people's needs for pleasure and comfort in the Bible, including feeding those who were hungry and comforting or healing those in pain. We discussed her belief in the divine design of the human body and the significance of the clitoris, a structure whose sole purpose is sexual pleasure. These ideas served as the basis from which she began to challenge her persistent thoughts about pleasure being something that is bad or that makes her bad.

Two other issues were identified as obstructing her progress. First, Erin disclosed a fear that Don would become so sexually excited that he would lose self-control and not stop even if she said stop, a belief born from the messages that Don had received from religious leaders that his sexuality was uncontrollable and to be feared. We identified this as a myth and deconstructed the flawed reasoning in what Don was taught (Ley, 2014).

Second, they both felt broken and shameful for having conflicting desires for sex: Erin for wanting to stop sex at different times and Don for wanting sex at all. They saw this as violating 1 Corinthians 7:4, which says that one's body belongs to the spouse. We explored discrepancies in how they saw this verse with sexuality versus anything else with the body such as eating, elimination, exercise, and sleeping. They reframed this verse as being about sexual fidelity and commitment rather than about not being allowed to have differing desires at times.

With religious sexual shame confronted and managed, a sexual health framework in place, a stronger sense of connection built, and Erin having a greater sense of trust and cooperation with her body, we returned to the specific goal of penetrative sex.

Treatment focused on education about vulvar anatomy, pelvic floor physiology, and the role that trauma can play in vaginismus. Erin was referred to a pelvic floor physical therapist for evaluation and dilator therapy. This was also framed as an opportunity to practice consent, as the therapist consistently asked permission before engaging in any physical work or touch. After four sessions, Erin began dilator work at home with Don handling the dilators at her request. They used the same red light/green light framework as before. Shortly after, they also began attempting digital penetration.

Erin experienced shame reactions both if she did allow digital penetration (due to lingering trauma reactions) and if she didn't (due to religious messages about "good wives" submitting to their husbands). Shame was challenged based on her new values that pleasure and touch are positive things and her new belief that being a "good wife" isn't defined by patriarchal ideas of female sexual submission but is about working together to meet needs.

Over the coming months, Erin began using the dilators herself, working her way up in sizes. When she reached the dilator that was comparable in size to Don's penis, they attempted penetrative intercourse. Despite quickly discontinuing penile penetration attempts due to her anxiety, they celebrated this step. Don reported feeling dramatically more hopeful about their relationship. Erin reported that much of what had felt stuck internally had "loosened up" and also that her irritable bowel syndrome had dramatically improved.

Religious sexual shame notably persisted around their experience of sexual fantasies and interests. These were not in alignment with their church's teachings about what sex is "supposed" to be. Diversity of sexual fantasy and interests was normalized, and they were referred to literature that talks about the commonality of many sexual interests and fantasies. Based on his understanding of Matthew 5:27–28 condemning lust as infidelity, Don believed that even having a sexual fantasy or desire that wasn't about his wife made him a bad Christian. We explored religious interpretations (Staples, 2009) of that verse that create room for passing thoughts and fantasies but still condemn actions. This view allowed him to begin working on claiming his individual sexuality while still being faithful to his wife and his Christian beliefs.

Don also had to work through his fear of uncontrollable sexual behavior. Don had been taught that if you want something, then the action is inevitable. We explored the differences between desire, intention, and action and reinforced this new understanding by referencing times where he may have wanted to continue a sexual engagement with Erin but chose not to because she said stop.

They began to explore with one another the fantasies and desires they each had. Anxiety and fears of rejection or judgment were tempered by the new sexual values they had claimed, including honesty, authenticity, pleasure, and acceptance. Fears about being pressured or coerced to participate in the other's fantasies quelled with reaffirmations of values around consent, safety, mutual pleasure, and respect.

As a result of all of her work, Erin was more confident that she could manage anxiety about penetration and have greater control over her pelvic floor muscles and felt ready to attempt penetrative intercourse again. We explored the setting and context for their next attempt, including finding time with no outside pressure or obligation, lighting in the room, sexual positions to afford her the greatest sense of safety and control, a review of the red/yellow/green lights and what they meant within this specific context, and how they wanted to proceed if penetration was or wasn't successful.

In their next session, they reported that the experience was challenging due to Erin having waves of anxiety at times. Despite this, they had been successful at her being able to be penetrated 3 inches by his penis and him being able to thrust several times before she decided to stop.

After several more months of work, they were able to experience full penetration, then full penetration with thrusting, and then full penetration with him achieving orgasm. Concurrently, they also incorporated clitoral stimulation into penetrative activities and Erin was able to experience orgasm while penetrated.

Questions You Always Wanted to Ask

1. **Can someone be a member of a particular religion and be a sexual minority?**
   Many people live as closeted sexual minorities in various religions. Being open about a sexual minority status can result in restrictions in participation, social ostracism, or excommunication depending on the religion. Openly engaging in behaviors consistent with the status (e.g., same-sex romantic relationships, gender-affirming transitions) broadens the number of religions in which such levels of exclusion would be experienced.
2. **Can I counsel someone from a different religion than I have?**
   Yes. There is nothing inherently unethical in treating someone from another religion. However, there are a few points to keep in mind. First, meet the client where they are with their beliefs. Religious people may be concerned that you will judge, condemn, or attempt to tear down their beliefs. Counselors should be very sensitive to this and reassuring that religious beliefs will be treated with respect. Any attempts at reframing or appropriate challenging should be reserved until after a solid relationship of trust has been established. Second, being culturally competent requires that you seek out information and consultation around the religion at the general level. The client's responsibility of educating you should be limited as much as possible to their interpretation and understanding of their religion, not the religion itself. Lastly, be aware of your personal reactions to their beliefs. If you find your reactions to be getting in the way, seek consultation and refer out as necessary and appropriate.
3. **Masturbation is not an uncommon intervention for some sexual issues, but many religious people object to this even if it is the best approach. How do I help them?**
   If you clarify their values about masturbation, you may find a way to work with them in their values. What is it about masturbation that is problematic for them?

For example, their objection could be fantasizing about other people (fantasize about their spouse instead), experiencing sexual pleasure without their spouse (masturbation with a spouse present may be an option instead), or the lack of procreation potential (perhaps use masturbation as part of sexual play with them finishing with vaginal intercourse to meet the need for the potential of conceiving).

4. **How can I help my very conservative clients feel more comfortable asking one another for sexual activities beyond missionary position vaginal intercourse?**
Start by exploring with them whether they have ever talked about sexual fantasies with one another and how they think their relationship might be different if they did. Then help them identify what gets in the way of them talking about those things. Take time to address the concerns that come up (often they will center around fear of judgment and rejection by their partner) and invite them to create values for how they want their fantasies to be received by each other including nonjudgment (not "yucking someone's yum" or "yumming someone's yuck"). Then move into negotiating consent for particular acts.
5. **How can I be more inclusive and supportive of LGBTQ+ individuals who may be struggling to define their religious and sexual selves?**
Start with solid basic practices, such as including questions about gender identity, pronouns, sexual orientation, and religious affiliation/beliefs, as well as noting on your practice materials and website that you are LGBTQ+ affirming or that your practice is an LGBTQ+ safe space. Avoid assuming how clients feel about their sexuality and religiosity. Normalize their struggle to reconcile these components of themselves: their sexuality and their beliefs. Give them space to not have answers and affirm their right to not make choices until they are ready to make those choices. Lastly, ask them how they best want to be supported. Even if they don't know, you are showing them that their needs are the most important thing to you and you have the opportunity to reassure them that you will discover that together in the therapy process.

References

Ahrold, T. K., Farmer, M., Trapnell, P. D., & Meston, C. M. (2011). The relationship among sexual attitudes, sexual fantasy, and religiosity. *Archives of Sexual Behavior*, *40*(3), 619–630. https://doi.org/10.1007/s10508-010-9621-4

Annon, J. S. (1976). The PLISSIT model: A proposed conceptual scheme for the behavioral treatment of sexual problems. *Journal of Sex Education and Therapy*, *2*(1), 1–15.

Ariel, Y. (2007). Gay, Orthodox, and trembling: The rise of Jewish Orthodox gay consciousness, 1970s–2000s. *Journal of Homosexuality*, *52*(3/4), 91–109. https://doi.org/10.1300/J082v52n03_05

Baker, J. O., & Smith, B. (2009). None too simple: Examining issues of religious nonbelief and nonbelonging in the United States. *Journal for the Scientific Study of Religion*, *48*(4), 719–733. https://doi.org/10.1111/j.1468-5906.2009.01475.x

Barrett, J. B., DaVanzo, J., Ellison, C. G., & Grammich, C. (2014). Religion and attitudes toward family planning issues among US adults. *Review of Religious Research*, *56*(2), 161–188. https://doi.org/10.1007/s13644-013-0136-z

Barringer, M. N., Gay, D. A., & Lynxwiler, J. P. (2013). Gender, religiosity, spirituality, and attitudes toward homosexuality. *Sociological Spectrum*, *33*(3), 240–257. https://doi.org/10.1080/02732173.2013.732903

Berkowitz, M., & Popovsky, M. (2010). *Contraception*. The Rabbinical Assembly. https://www.rabbinicalassembly.org/sites/default/files/public/halakhah/teshuvot/20052010/Contraception%20Berkowitz%20and%20Popovsky.pdf
Braun-Harvey, D., & Vigorito, M. A. (2016). *Treating out of control sexual behavior: Rethinking sex addiction*. Springer Publishing Company.
Brown, B. (2007). *I thought it was just me: Women reclaiming power and courage in a culture of shame*. Gotham.
Cadge, W., Olson, L. R., & Wildeman, C. (2008). How denominational resources influence debate about homosexuality in mainline Protestant congregations. *Sociology of Religion*, *69*(2), 187–207. https://doi.org/10.1093/socrel/69.2.187
Campbell, M. K., Hudson, M. A., Resnicow, K., Blakeney, N., Paxton, A., & Baskin, M. (2007). Church-based health promotion interventions: Evidence and lessons learned. *Annual Review of Public Health, 28*(1), 213–234. https://doi.org/10.1146/annurev.publhealth.28.021406.144016
Catholic Church. (2019). The vocation to chastity. In *Catechism of the Catholic Church* (2nd ed., 2351–2352). Libreria Editrice Vaticana.
Church of Jesus Christ of Latter-day Saints. (1981). *Homosexuality* (2nd ed.). https://mormonleaks.io/wiki/documents/4/4c/Homosexuality-1981.pdf
Church of Jesus Christ of Latter-day Saints. (1985). *A parent's guide*. https://www.churchofjesuschrist.org/study/manual/a-parents-guide
Church of Jesus Christ of Latter-day Saints. (1995). *The family: A proclamation to the world*. https://www.churchofjesuschrist.org/study/scriptures/the-family-a-proclamation-to-the-world/the-family-a-proclamation-to-the-world
Church of Jesus Christ of Latter-day Saints. (2011). *For the strength of youth*. https://www.churchofjesuschrist.org/study/manual/for-the-strength-of-youth
Church of Jesus Christ of Latter-day Saints. (2014, August 20). *Overcoming pornography addiction: The healing power of Jesus Christ* [Video]. YouTube. https://www.youtube.com/watch?v=iXXQpTgSSD8
Church of Jesus Christ of Latter-day Saints. (2019, October 2). *General conference leadership meetings begin* [Press release]. https://newsroom.churchofjesuschrist.org/article/october-2019-general-conference-first-presidency-leadership-session
Church of Jesus Christ of Latter-day Saints. (2021). *General handbook: Serving in the Church of Jesus Christ of Latter-day Saints*. https://www.churchofjesuschrist.org/study/manual/general-handbook/title-page
Clark, N. (2017). *The etiology and phenomenology of sexual shame: A grounded theory study* [Doctoral dissertation, Seattle Pacific University]. Digital Commons @ SPU. https://digitalcommons.spu.edu/cpy_etd/25
Dolsten, J. (2020, October 29). Small but growing number of Orthodox rabbis are officiating gay weddings. *The Jerusalem Post*. https://www.jpost.com/judaism/small-but-growing-number-of-orthodox-rabbis-are-officiating-gay-weddings-647279
Ellison, C. G., & Goodson, P. (1997). Conservative Protestantism and attitudes toward family planning in a sample of seminarians. *Journal for the Scientific Study of Religion*, *36*(4), 512–529. https://doi.org/10.2307/1387687
Fassin, E. (2010). National identities and transnational intimacies: Sexual democracy and the politics of immigration in Europe. *Public Culture*. *22*(3), 507–529. https://doi.org/10.1215/08992363-2010-007.
Feldman, P. (1992). Sexuality, birth control and childbirth in orthodox Jewish tradition. *Canadian Medical Association Journal*, *146*(1), 29–33.

Fingerhut, H. (2016, May 12). *Support steady for same-sex marriage and acceptance of homosexuality.* Pew Research Center. https://www.pewresearch.org/fact-tank/2016/05/12/support-steady-for-same-sex-marriage-and-acceptance-of-homosexuality/

Frame, N. (2020). Intragroup differences of the non-religious: Attitudes towards same-sex marriage and same-sex adoption in the United States. *Journal of Homosexuality, 68*(13), 2285–2300. https://doi.org/10.1080/00918369.2020.1736430

Gay, D. A., Ellison, C. G., & Powers, D. A. (1996). In search of denominational subcultures: Religious affiliation and "pro-family" issues revisited. *Review of Religious Research, 38*(1), 3–17. https://doi.org/10.2307/3512537

GLAAD. (2022). *GLAAD media reference guide* (11th ed.). https://www.glaad.org/reference

Gresh, D. (2012). *And the bride wore white: Seven secrets to sexual purity.* Moody Press.

Grubbs, J. B., Exline, J. J., Pargament, K. I., Hook, J. N., & Carlisle, R. D. (2015). Transgression as addiction: Religiosity and moral disapproval as predictors of perceived addiction to pornography. *Archives of Sexual Behavior, 44*(1), 125–136. https://doi.org/10.1007/s10508-013-0257-z

Grubbs, J. B., & Perry, S. L. (2019). Moral incongruence and pornography use: A critical review and integration. *Journal of Sex Research, 56*(1), 29–37. https://doi.org/10.1080/00224499.2018.1427204

Harris, A. C. (2010). Sex, stigma, and the Holy Ghost: The Black church and the construction of AIDS in New York City. *Journal of African American Studies, 14*(1), 21–43. https://www.jstor.org/stable/41819234

Haxby, D. (2008, December 29). Episcopal Church splits over gay equality. *The Nation.* https://www.thenation.com/article/archive/episcopal-church-splits-over-gay-equality/

Holzer, J. (2020, November). Notes from foundations of Judaism. *Your Neighborhood Cantor's Corner.* https://hazzanholzer.com/upcoming-events/notes-from-foundations-of-judaism/

Kapinus, C. A., & Kraus, R. (2010). Excluding inclusivity: Protestant framing of homosexuality. *Interdisciplinary Journal of Research on Religion, 4*(6), 1–22.

Kimball, S. W. (1974, November). God will not be mocked. *Ensign, 4*(11). https://www.churchofjesuschrist.org/study/ensign/1974/11/god-will-not-be-mocked

Ledet, R. (2017). Competing claims: Religious affiliation and African Americans' intolerance of homosexuals. *Journal of Homosexuality, 64*(6), 786–803. https://doi.org/10.1080/00918369.2016.1236580

Ley, D. J. (2014). *The myth of sex addiction.* Rowman & Littlefield.

Lipka, M. (2015, November 11). *Religious "nones" are not only growing, they're becoming more secular.* Pew Research Center. https://www.pewresearch.org/fact-tank/2015/11/11/religious-nones-are-not-only-growing-theyre-becoming-more-secular/

Maher, M. J., Sever, L. M., & Pichler, S. (2008). How Catholic college students think about homosexuality: The connection between authority and sexuality. *Journal of Homosexuality, 55*(3), 325–349. https://doi.org/10.1080/00918360802345065

Melton, J. G. (2005). *Encyclopedia of Protestantism.* Facts on File.

Metz, M. E., & McCarthy, B. W. (2007). The "good-enough sex" model for couple sexual satisfaction. *Sexual and Relationship Therapy, 22*(3), 351–362. https://doi.org/10.1080/14681990601013492

My Jewish Learning. (n.d.). *Judaism and sex: Questions and answers.* https://www.myjewishlearning.com/article/judaism-and-sex-questions-and-answers/

Moon, D. (2014). Beyond the dichotomy: Six religious views of homosexuality. *Journal of Homosexuality, 61*(9), 1215–1241. https://doi.org/10.1080/00918369.2014.926762
Oldfield, A. (2018, October 15). The real truth about YouTube's obsessive purity subculture. *Bitch Media.* https://www.bitchmedia.org/article/youtube-purity-vloggers
Olson, L. R., & Cadge, W. (2002). Talking about homosexuality: The views of mainline Protestant clergy. *Journal for the Scientific Study of Religion, 41*(1), 153–167.
Olson, L. R., Cadge, W., & Harrison, J. T. (2006). Religion and public opinion about same-sex marriage. *Social Science Quarterly, 87*(2), 340–360. https://doi.org/10.1111/j.1540-6237.2006.00384.x
Perry, S. L. (2018). How pornography use reduces participation in congregational leadership: A research note. *Review of Religious Research, 61*(1), 57–74. https://doi.org/10.1007/s13644-018-0355-4
Perry, S. L., & Schleifer, C. (2019). Race and trends in pornography viewership, 1973–2016: Examining the moderating roles of gender and religion. *Journal of Sex Research, 56*(1), 62–73. https://doi.org/10.1080/00224499.2017.1404959
Perry, S. L., & Whitehead, A. L. (2016). Religion and public opinion toward same-sex relations, marriage, and adoption: Does the type of practice matter? *Journal for the Scientific Study of Religion, 55*(3), 637–651. https://doi.org/10.1111/jssr.12215
Peters, J. W. (2014, March 21). The decline and fall of the 'H' word. *The New York Times.* https://www.nytimes.com/2014/03/23/fashion/gays-lesbians-the-term-homosexual.html
Pew Research Center. (2013). *A portrait of Jewish Americans: Findings from a Pew Research Center survey of U.S. Jews.* https://www.pewresearch.org/wp-content/uploads/sites/7/2013/10/jewish-american-beliefs-attitudes-culture-survey-overview.pdf
Pew Research Center. (2015, May 12). *America's changing religious landscape.* https://www.pewforum.org/2015/05/12/americas-changing-religious-landscape/
Pew Research Center. (2019, October 17). *In U.S., decline of Christianity continues at rapid pace.* https://www.pewforum.org/2019/10/17/in-u-s-decline-of-christianity-continues-at-rapid-pace/
Pitt, R. N. (2010). "Still looking for my Jonathan": Gay Black men's management of religious and sexual identity conflicts. *Journal of Homosexuality, 57*(1), 39–53. https://doi.org/10.1080/00918360903285566
Regnerus, M. D. (2007). *Forbidden fruit: Sex & religion in the lives of American teenagers.* Oxford University Press.
Roberts, K. A., & Yamane, D. A. (2016). *Religion in sociological perspective.* SAGE Publications.
Roger, B. A. (2019). *Conditionally accepted: Christians' perspectives on sexuality and gay and lesbian civil rights.* Rutgers University Press.
Roof, W. C., & McKinney, W. (1987). *American mainline religion: Its changing shape and future.* Rutgers University Press.
Rosner, F. (2001). *Biomedical ethics and Jewish law.* Ktav Publishing House.
Sellers, T. S. (2017). *Sex, God, and the conservative church: Erasing shame from sexual intimacy.* Routledge/Taylor & Francis Group.

Sellers, T. S. (2019, September 12). *How the purity movement causes symptoms of sexual abuse.* https://www.tinaschermersellers.com/post/how-the-purity-movement-causes-symptoms-of-sexual-abuse
Sherkat, D. E. (2014). *Changing faith: The dynamics and consequences of Americans' shifting religious identities.* New York University Press.
Sherkat, D. E., de Vries, K. M., & Creek, S. (2010). Race, religion, and opposition to same-sex marriage. *Social Science Quarterly*, *91*(1), 80–98. https://doi.org/10.1111/j.1540-6237.2010.00682.x
Staples, J. (2009, August 20). "*Whoever looks at a woman with lust*": *Misinterpreted Bible passages #1.* https://www.jasonstaples.com/bible/most-misinterpreted-bible-passages-1-matthew-527-28/
Stokes, E., & Schewe, R. (2016). Framing from the pulpit: A content analysis of American conservative evangelical Protestant sermon rhetoric discussing LGBT couples and marriage. *Journal of Communication & Religion*, *39*(3), 59–75.
Swain, C. R., Ackerman, L. K., & Ackerman, M. A. (2006). The influence of individual characteristics and contraceptive beliefs on parent-teen sexual communications: A structural model. *Journal of Adolescent Health*, *38*(6), 753.e9–753.e18. https://doi.org/10.1016/j.jadohealth.2005.08.015
Synod of Bishops. (2015, October 24). *The vocation and mission of the family in the church and in the contemporary world: The final report of the synod of bishops to the Holy Father, Pope Francis.* https://www.vatican.va/roman_curia/synod/documents/rc_synod_doc_20151026_relazione-finale-xiv-assemblea_en.html
The United Methodist Church. (2022). *Faith & facts: Maternal health and family planning.* https://www.umcjustice.org/documents/25
Wellman, J. K., Jr. (2008). *Evangelical vs. liberal* (1st ed.). Oxford University Press.
Whitehead, A. L. (2010). Sacred rites and civil rights: Religion's effect on attitudes toward same-sex unions and the perceived cause of homosexuality. *Social Science Quarterly*, *91*(1), 63–79.
Whitehead, A. L., & Perry, S. L. (2018). Unbuckling the Bible Belt: A state-level analysis of religious factors and Google searches for porn. *Journal of Sex Research*, *55*(3), 273–283. https://doi.org/10.1080/00224499.2017.1278736
Williams, T. T., Dodd, D., Campbell, B., Pichon, L. C., & Griffith, D. M. (2014). Discussing adolescent sexual health in African American churches. *Journal of Religion and Health*, *53*(2), 339–351. https://doi.org/10.1007/s10943-012-9632-7

PART 6

Approaches to Sexual Divergence

CHAPTER 19

Beyond Awareness: Becoming a Kink-Affirming Counselor

Megan Speciale and Stacey Diane Arañez Litam

If you have ever wondered what a kinkster might look like, perhaps you can take a peek in the mirror! Many of us engage in kink without even knowing it. Gentle (or not so gentle) spanking, hair pulling, and role play are all considered kinky forms of erotic expression. The spectrum of healthy sexual desire is broad and includes behaviors, identities, and communities viewed within and outside of the narrow slice of what is considered "normal" or appropriate in society. Societal views about sex are constantly changing, and so too are the bounds of what is considered normal. People across all cultural and demographic groups can practice kink, so with no way to immediately determine who is and who is not kinky, professional counselors working in all settings should be prepared to meet the therapeutic needs of clients with diverse forms of erotic expression.

We use *kink* in this chapter as an umbrella term to describe behaviors, identities, and communities that stand in contrast to, or outside of, socially and culturally normative sexualities, including BDSM, paraphilias, and fetishes (Popp & Kaldera, 2014; Taormino, 2012). BDSM is an overlapping abbreviation, representing bondage and discipline (BD), dominance and submission (DS), and sadism and masochism (SM). BDSM typically involves sexual and nonsexual behaviors that feature restraint, pressure, intense sensation, and components of power exchange between consenting persons. Although kink and BDSM can represent distinct identities and communities, they are often used interchangeably. We also use the term *kinkster* to refer to clients who practice kink and/or belong to the kink community and *vanilla* to refer to nonkinky sex and relationships. Although we use these terms to delineate cultural norms, research findings, and counseling implications, it is important to note that sexual desire comprises a vast and nuanced spectrum, and the majority of people fall somewhere between these two poles.

A Cultural View of Kink

Similar to other cultural groups, the kink community has established its own set of rituals and hierarchies, belief systems, values, social norms, practices, customs, ceremonies, and ways of understanding themselves, others, and the world (Moore et al., 2018). Becoming kink competent requires professional counselors to expand their awareness of the terms, practices, and values endorsed by kinksters. Becoming familiar with basic kink terminology is a great place to start!

Individuals who practice kink or BDSM often begin their kink play by carefully planning out scenes (Moore et al., 2018). *Play* refers to the actual practice and use of skills, and *scenes* are formal sessions in which play partners plan the anticipated physical, emotional, psychological, and spiritual interactions that will occur in a specified time. Within a scene, individuals may embody specific roles associated with power exchange, such as a *top*, *Dom/me* (dominant), *bottom*, or *sub* (submissive). Tops and dom/mes are typically those who give direction and/or sensation in a scene, while bottoms and subs typically receive direction and/or sensation in a scene. Although the direction of the scene tends to be led by the dom/me, the details of the power exchange are prenegotiated, consented upon, and subject to amendment or revocation at any time. Although the dom/me may perform acts of direction, subjugation, and/or punishment within a scene, the scene is ultimately controlled by the submissive partner, who precedes the scene with active and ongoing consent. Once a scene comes to a close, the process of *aftercare* begins. During aftercare, play partners engage in gentle and honest communication about the scene, the emotions that arose during play, and the elements they would like to change in the future. The importance of aftercare amplifies as the physical and emotional intensity of the scene increase. More pain, more aftercare. More manipulation, more aftercare. Aftercare is not seen as optional within the BDSM community, and play partners are expected to care for one another following each and every scene.

Ethics of Kink and BDSM

Although the best-selling book *Fifty Shades of Grey* (James, 2012) offered many people around the world an intriguing and surprisingly titillating peek into the world of kink, kinksters everywhere breathed a collective sigh of disappointment that the kink community was not consulted before the writing and directing of the subsequent trilogy and film (Freeburg & McNaughton, 2017). The books and film displayed behaviors and communication that are in stark contrast to the core values of the kink community. Kink culture upholds important shared values including radical honesty, open communication, expressed and enthusiastic consent, safety, trust, and full knowledge and disclosure of physical and psychological risks (Moore et al., 2018; Pitagora, 2013; Taormino, 2012; Tripodi, 2017). Before participating in a scene, all parties involved must voluntarily provide affirmative, enthusiastic consent. If a person uses dishonesty or manipulation to obtain consent (i.e., "I will never have feelings for you unless you let me do what I want to your body"), that is not consent. Enthusiastic consent is offered freely, actively, and voluntarily, without the presence of coercion or duress. Consent is obtained before and throughout each scene and may be revoked or amended at any time (Fanghanel, 2019). Did you hear that, Christian Grey?

The kink community has developed several frameworks to describe the multiple factors of consent. Safe, sane, and consensual (SSC) and risk aware consensual kink

(RACK) are frameworks that emphasize the importance of safety and consent; however, individuals who engage in kink and BDSM practices are beginning to phase out SSC terminology in favor of RACK because the term "sane" pathologizes BDSM practitioners who currently face or have a history of mental illness (Williams et al., 2014). The RACK framework emphasizes the kink community's core values of radical honesty, communication, and safety for all parties involved. At the core of RACK, individuals cannot consent to kinky practices without fully understanding the possible physical, emotional, and psychological risks that may arise during a scene, through the exchange of power dynamics, or from other forms of erotic expression. As the BDSM community has evolved, so has its frameworks for conceptualizing consent. A third framework, caring, communication, consent, and caution (the 4 Cs), expands upon the RACK framework by emphasizing the quintessential components of open communication and emotional well-being.

Professional counselors who understand the consent process are in a better position to assist all clients (not just kinksters!) in navigating sexual relationships. In what may be regarded as one of the core strengths of this community, kinksters prioritize direct, honest, and detailed consent communication. Before the specific details of a scene are negotiated, *surface consent* is obtained through the initial "Yes, I am interested" or "No, I am not" following a play proposition. Once surface consent has been granted, scene consent may begin. *Scene consent* involves the active planning, negotiating, and preparation of the play that will occur before, during, and after the scene, and includes a plan of action for withdrawing or amending consent throughout the encounter. Scene consent also outlines details for the aftercare process and the establishment of a safe word. In the event that scenes are loud or safe words may not be clearly audible, other nonverbal indicators (snapping fingers or winking) may be established. Once the scene has been planned, all parties involved must remain mindful of *deep consent*. Deep consent is a more ambiguous process and relates to each person's capacity to communicate distress and withdraw consent during the entirety of a scene. The ability to provide deep consent is influenced by a myriad of factors, including the person's level of BDSM experience, the level of trust and safety established between partners, and the level of specificity achieved during the scene consent process. Professional counselors are in a prime position to help clients explore their individual desires and abilities to provide each level of consent. Counselors may also empower clients to explore the motivations, boundaries, and emotional responses that lead to more informed consent decisions and greater sexual fulfillment.

Kink and Mental Health

Kinky practices have historically been viewed by the mental health profession as symptoms of mental pathology, sexual trauma, and insecure relational attachments (Yates & Neuer-Colburn, 2019). Thus, it is unsurprising that many counselors and laypeople alike view kink and BDSM with squeamishness and skepticism (Waldura et al., 2016; Yates & Neuer-Colburn, 2019), despite ongoing research that suggests kink is a common variance of normal sexual desire. In a move toward depathologization, the fifth edition of the *Diagnostic and Statistical Manual of Mental Disorders* (*DSM-5*; American Psychiatric Association, 2013) updated the diagnostic criteria for a paraphilic disorder, requiring the presence of nonconsent and/or significant client distress, anxiety, guilt, shame, and/or obsessions surrounding the symptoms. Paraphilic desires may also qualify as a disorder if they interfere with important areas of functioning. Despite these updates, many professional counselors are still unaware that nondistressing and consensual paraphilias are no longer classified as mental disorders (Williams et al., 2014). As such, stigma and bias related to BDSM, kink, and individuals within the community are still quite common among professional counselors and other helping professionals, which may lead to unethical and/or harmful practice (Bezreh et al., 2012; Connolly, 2006; Gemberling et al., 2015; Waldura et al, 2016; Wismeijer & van Assen, 2013).

Despite this history of pathologization, research has demonstrated that kinky individuals do not display higher levels of mental illness, previous abuse/trauma, or clinical distress related to their sexual practices (Connolly, 2006; Richters et al., 2008). In fact, there is evidence to suggest that individuals may access mental and emotional benefits through the practice of kink (Speciale & Khambatta, 2020; Wismeijer & van Assen, 2013). Wismeijer and van Assen (2013) found that kinksters, when compared with a group of nonkinky adults, displayed less neuroticism, more extraversion, more openness to new experiences, more conscientiousness, less rejection sensitivity, and had higher scores of subjective well-being. Although the researchers were unsure of how these favorable characteristics developed, many kinksters reported experiencing a broad array of mental health benefits associated with their kink practice, such as personal healing of previous traumas, increasing communication skills, decreasing body shame, increasing feelings of sex positivity, and pleasure fulfillment (Lindemann, 2011; Pitagora, 2017; Speciale & Khambatta, 2020).

Distinguishing BDSM From Abuse

The enduring belief that BDSM is a form of abuse is among the most common stigmas and misconceptions about kink. Professional counselors who are unable to distinguish the differences between healthy BDSM and abuse are at risk of aliening otherwise healthy clients and potentially failing to support clients who are in fact in abusive environments (Waldura et al., 2016). Healthy, consensual BDSM can be distinguished from abuse by observing the following criteria:

- Does the client display fear or anxiety related to BDSM involvement, boundary setting, and/or consent negotiation?
- Has the client established safety guidelines with play partners, such as safe words and aftercare?
- Does the client differentiate between kink scenes and everyday life? In other words, are there temporal and/or spatial boundaries to the BDSM play?
- Does the client feel isolated socially?
- Does the client experience emotional volatility that typically accompanies relationship violence?
- Do power imbalances exist between the client and their partner(s) that persist in everyday life?
- Does the client engage in clear negotiation before scenes with partners?

Problems with one or more of the above factors do not conclusively determine presence of abuse. It is possible that people engaged in consensual BDSM—especially those new to kink/BDSM—may be struggling with protective practices, such as negotiation and safety communication, simply because they are uninformed or unskilled at enacting those behaviors with partners. The counseling practice may thus be the perfect space for the client and counselor to work together to build skills and confidence with asserting one's desires, boundaries, and limits. It is also possible that a person can unwittingly remain in an abusive BDSM relationship simply because they do not know the warning signs of abuse. Again, therapy can be an opportune place to explore the boundaries of healthy relationships and empower the client to distinguish for themself whether their relationships are healthy or abusive. Professional counselors may also guide clients to explore what changes they would like to see in their current and future relationship configurations.

Becoming a Kink-Affirming Counselor

How would you respond if a client disclosed heightened sexual responses when popping balloons? Or if your client had bruising on their thighs from being flogged in a recent scene? Are you prepared to support clients who experience feelings of shame and disconnect following the postscene aftercare process? Becoming a kink-affirming counselor extends beyond increasing one's awareness of kink culture and encompasses one's willingness to recognize and celebrate alternate forms of erotic and sexual expression. Cultivating an identity as a kink-affirming counselor begins with recognition of the historical stigma and pathologizing of individuals who practice BDSM from mental and medical health institutions. Kink-affirming counselors acknowledge the deleterious effects of stigmatizing labels and actively work to nurture therapeutic counseling spaces characterized by openness, warmth, compassion, and nonjudgmental attitudes. Stigmatizing beliefs toward individuals who engage in BDSM and kink include myths that BDSM- and kink-oriented individuals are deviant or mentally ill, tend to be violent or emotionally unstable, perpetuate the subjugation of women, lack stable and healthy relationships, or are uneducated (Bezreh et al., 2012; Gemberling et al., 2015; Lin, 2016). Professional counselors must examine whether they hold preexisting bias or prejudice within themselves or others to promote ethical practice (American Counseling Association, 2014).

An important first step to becoming a kink-affirming counselor is engaging a process of deep self-reflection through which one identifies and challenges any underlying biases, notions, or unhelpful beliefs about the kink community, BDSM practitioners, or individuals with paraphilias. Kink-affirming counselors understand that BDSM practices may have deep and meaningful purposes in the lives of participants and seek to illuminate the unique ways through which each client individually experiences and benefits from engaging in play. It is especially important for kink-affirming counselors to recognize that their client's presenting concerns may or may not be related to their alternate sexual practices and avoid stigmatizing, shaming, or making assumptions about clients who practice BDSM or kink. Taking the initiative to learn more about kink culture, BDSM practices, paraphilias, and aspects of consent is of paramount importance for professional counselors who strive to become kink-affirming practitioners. Ultimately, BDSM practices, kinky behaviors, and the use of paraphilias exist on the normal spectrum of healthy sexual expression.

The Case of Mariana and Shelby: "But We're Feminists!"

Mariana and Shelby are coming to counseling to work on their relationship. Mariana is a 25-year-old Latina, cisgender, bisexual woman, and Shelby is a 30-year-old

Black, cisgender, lesbian woman. They have been together for 3 years, and overall, the couple agree that they have a generally heathy and happy relationship, although they have felt a steady decline in their sexual intimacy over the past 2 years. This is their first time in counseling together; however, Mariana and Shelby have tried several things to jump-start their sex life, including going to intimacy workshops at their local sexuality resource center, reading self-help books, and watching erotic films together. These strategies seemed to be helpful for a week or so, but then the couple fell back into a pattern of lower sexual intimacy. Both partners struggle to initiate sex, a problem that Shelby attributes to internalized religious shame in both of their upbringings. Mariana describes that as a bisexual woman who has dated mostly men, she never really had to bother with initiating sex and now feels sheepish and unskilled in doing so.

After a couple of sessions, Mariana tells Shelby that she has been having recurrent fantasies about being tied up, spanked, and penetrated against her will. Her fantasy involves Shelby forcefully waking her up from a nap and binding her to the bed frame with leather straps. In the fantasy, Mariana wants Shelby to continue spanking and having sex with her despite Mariana's cries for her to stop. Shelby is shocked and immediately expresses discomfort with the idea of role-playing a "rape-like" scenario and tries to convince Mariana that her fantasy is related to internalized misogyny learned in her upbringing. "But we're feminists!" she exclaims to Mariana, who, expressing deep shame, struggles to reconcile her values of being a strong Latina woman with her desire to be physically and sexually dominated by Shelby. At Mariana's urging, Shelby attempts to reconsider her initial reaction and be open to exploring these new desires. After some thought, Shelby agrees that the role-play idea is "kinda hot, actually," but she feels unprepared emotionally and physically to step into a role of dominance.

Kink-Affirming Treatment Strategies

Foremost, the counselor listening to the couple navigate the conversation should be mindful of the internal responses arising as Mariana describes her fantasy of being dominated, as well as Shelby's initial reaction of disgust. What feelings arise in you as you hear Mariana's fantasy? How are these feelings manifesting in your physical body? Which client do you feel more empathy for or agreement with? From this initial internal scan, the counselor can observe their triggers and respond with established bracketing and grounding techniques to deal with the countertransference. Slow, deep breathing, open palms resting on the tops of the thighs, and acknowledging and setting aside personal values can all be helpful ways of recentering back to the client. Ultimately, the counselor's comfort and openness talking about sex is instrumental to clients' feelings of safety and confidence in the counseling process.

As a kink-affirming counselor, it is important to also normalize the existence of new, surprising, and complex desires. Simply sharing with the couple that it is quite normal for people (even feminists!) to have desires of being ravished, as well as to have conflicting feelings about unequal power dynamics in sexual relationships, can set a tone of nonjudgment and assuage the couple's fears about being odd or perverse. The counselor should affirm the relevance of the conversation, acknowledge the vulnerability and courage required to speak openly about forbidden desires, and invite continued dialogue about the couple's thoughts and feelings about the conversation. It may also be helpful to share with clients that asymmetrical sexual desires are extremely common and do not necessarily signify an unsolvable problem in the relationship.

Using a multicultural approach, the counselor will then encourage each partner to reflect on how their cultural identities play a role in the new fantasy. What messages did the clients learn about sex growing up? How does this fantasy conflict with or confirm those messages? How might members of their cultures view this sexual experience? What values are at the core of those cultural beliefs? Are these shared values? If not, how are the clients' values different? From this conversation, each partner will have increased insight into the shared and differing issues that arise with relation to their unique cultural backgrounds, facilitating increased empathy and awareness for one another. Intentional and appropriate self-disclosure may be helpful in this conversation, as the counselor may be able to normalize the challenge of growing up in a sex negative household and society, as well as confirm to the clients that countering and unlearning sex negativity is difficult, ongoing work.

Kink-affirming counseling also hinges upon dispelling myths and providing accurate kink information, so the counselor may use psychoeducation to describe the existence of kink culture (if the clients are unaware that one exists), explore the ethics of kink (including consent, negotiation, safe words, and aftercare), and deconstruct common myths about kink using relevant research with the clients. Psychoeducation should be dynamic and invitational rather than didactic to encourage clients to also share whatever knowledge they have learned related to sex and kink. The counselor may also ask the clients if they are interested in receiving resources that may help them navigate this new experience. During or after the session, the counselor can share websites, blogs, books, films, and/or social media accounts that offer a sex positive, kink-affirming perspective and can help the clients learn more about the wide world of kink. The counselor may also invite the clients to create a homework assignment for themselves related to better understanding one another, exploring kink resources, or practicing safe intimacy. The hope is that as the clients return in future sessions, they may look to the counseling room as a space to explore their evolving sexual desires, gain new information, and experience an integrated and affirming approach to their sexual desires, relational satisfaction, and mental health.

Conclusion

Despite the common occurrence and increasing mainstream acceptance of alternative sexual desires, mental health professionals seldom receive formal training on kink and BDSM. Accordingly, many counselors feel unprepared to treat the unique issues faced by this population. Kelsey et al. (2013) discovered that although 76% of mental health professionals reported treating at least one client within the kink community, only 48% felt they were competent in this area. Lack of training also contributes to professional counselors' discomfort working with kink and BDSM clients, as well as counselors' use of harmful practices that pathologize kink and BDSM practice (Ford & Hendrick, 2003; Lawrence & Love-Crowell, 2007). This is corroborated by a study conducted by the National Coalition of Sexual Freedom (2008), which found that 49% of participants (N = 3,058) reported discrimination from a medical professional and 39% reported discrimination from a mental health professional. This evidence suggests that kinky clients may face additional barriers to mental health related to the iatrogenic effects of therapy—that is, a well-intentioned yet unprepared and pathologizing counselor may run the risk of further harming the client.

Questions You Always Wanted to Ask

1. **How do I invite the conversation of alternative sexual desires with a client without coming across as inappropriate—or worse, creepy?**
   We get that it can feel a little awkward to ask a client about their specific sexual desires, so you might be pleased to know that, in most cases, it is probably not necessary to ask. The key is to set a tone of kink affirmation right at the start, so your clients have no question about your ability to accept their diverse sexual identities, desires, and relationships. Include language on your website or counseling profile that you are kink-affirming, and list any related trainings you have received in this area. Include books on the topics of sex, kink, and BDSM on the shelves of your office. In your informed-consent procedures, explicitly state that the counseling office is a safe place to discuss sex and desire in all their diverse forms. Educate clients about the connection between sexual health and mental health. Include questions on your intake forms that assess the client's sexual satisfaction and access to safe and meaningful intimacy, pleasure, and desire. If a client mentions sex, hold space and stay present. Encourage the client to explore their personal meanings related to sex and how it relates to their presenting issues. If it is clinically relevant to ask about specific sexual desires, be sure to explain to the client (a) why you are asking the question (i.e., why is it clinically relevant?) and (b) that they are free to not answer, should they feel uncomfortable.
2. **What if my client shares a sexual desire that makes me uncomfortable?**
   Imagine a client shares with his counselor that he and his wife role play a father and daughter relationship during sex. In this role play, he describes playing "daddy" while his wife pretends to be a 5-year-old girl. Despite being kink-affirming, the counselor immediately feels disgust, skepticism, and fear while listening to the client's disclosure. Her first instinct is to launch into questioning to determine the presence of abuse or a paraphilic disorder. Before she speaks, she takes a deep breath, grounds herself, and realizes she is feeling triggered. She remembers her kink training and chooses a different route. Instead of assuming pathology or criminality, she commends the client for sharing a taboo and invites the client to say more about how this scene impacts his relationship with his wife. Through her invitational and affirming questioning, she learns that the role play was an idea brought forth by his wife to help her process early childhood neglect. He shares that the role play has done wonders for their intimacy, trust, and individual healing. He also shares that he feels quite a bit of shame about role-playing an incest situation, which the counselor is able to respond to with validation and normalization.

   Remember that the broad spectrum of acceptable sexual behaviors includes all behaviors that are enacted consensually and without coercion between individuals capable of giving consent. The possibilities are limitless. It's time we unlearn our judgments about sexualities that look different from ours, or what we believe is normal or "right."
3. **How can I learn more about kink culture and BDSM?**
   Professional counselors who want to learn more about BDSM and kink can do so in a variety of ways. We believe that one of the best ways to learn about a community is to build relationships with its members, so we suggest exploring in your own hometown! Try searching for public kink/BDSM events, take an

in-person or virtual tour of a dungeon, and attend a munch, which is a social gathering usually in a coffee shop or other public space meant to help those who are new to or curious about kink learn more about the community. Following are a few websites we recommend:

- KinkyKarrot (a YouTube education series) at www.youtube.com/c/KinkyKarrot and Pan Eros at www.pan-eros.org both offer resources regarding consent policies, power exchange statements, consent statements, strategies to navigate consent violations, and ways to distinguish BDSM from abuse.
- REKINK at https://rekink.com is a website that offers comprehensive how-to guides on the practice of kink and BDSM, as well as a full online store for kink and BDSM accoutrements.
- *Scarleteen* at https://www.scarleteen is a website that provides comprehensive, inclusive, and supportive information about sex and relationships to teenagers, emerging adults, and adults looking for ways to address these topics with youth.

Following are some books we recommend:

Exhibitionism for the Shy: Show Off, Dress Up, and Talk Hot by Carol Queen (2009)
The New Bottoming Book by Janet Hardy and Dossie Easton (2001)
The New Topping Book by Dossie Easton and Janet Hardy (2003)
Safe, Sane, and Consensual: Contemporary Perspectives on Sadomasochism by Darren Langdridge and Meg Barker (2007)
When Someone You Love Is Kinky by Dossie Easton and Catherine A. Liszt (2000)
Wild Side Sex: The Book of Kink: Educational, Sensual, and Entertaining Essays by Midori (2005)

References

American Counseling Association. (2014). *ACA code of ethics.* https://www.counseling.org/resources/aca-code-of-ethics.pdf

American Psychiatric Association. (2013). *Diagnostic and statistical manual of mental disorders* (5th ed.). https://doi.org/10.1176/appi.books.9780890425596

Bezreh, T., Weinberg, T. S., & Edgar, T. (2012). BDSM disclosure and stigma management: Identifying opportunities for sex education. *American Journal of Sexuality Education, 7*(1), 37–61. https://doi.org/10.1080/15546128.2012.650984

Connolly, P. H. (2006). Psychological functioning of bondage/domination/sadomasochism (BDSM) practitioners. *Journal of Psychology & Human Sexuality, 18*(1), 79–120. https://doi.org/10.1300/J056v18n01_05

Fanghanel, A. (2019). Asking for it: BDSM sexual practice and the trouble of consent. *Sexualities, 23*(3) 269–286. https://doi.org/10.1177/1363460719828933

Ford, M. P., & Hendrick, S. S. (2003). Therapists' sexual values for self and clients: Implications for practice and training. *Professional Psychology: Research and Practice, 34*(1), 80–87. https://doi.org/10.1037/0735-7028.34.1.80

Freeburg, M. N., & McNaughton, M. J. (2017). Fifty shades of grey: Implications for counseling BDSM clients. *VISTAS Online,* Article 13. https://www.counseling.org/knowledge-center/vistas/by-year2/vistas-2017/docs/default-source/vistas/counseling-bdsm-clients

Gemberling, T. M., Cramer, R. J., & Miller, R. S. (2015). BDSM as sexual orientation: A comparison to lesbian, gay, and bisexual sexuality. *Journal of Positive Sexuality, 1*, 37–43.

James, E. L. (2012). *Fifty shades of grey*. Bloom Books.

Kelsey, K., Stiles, B. L., Spiller, L., & Diekhoff, G. M. (2013). Assessment of therapists' attitudes towards BDSM. *Psychology & Sexuality, 4*(3), 255–267. https://doi.org/10.1080/19419899.2012.655255

Lawrence, A. A., & Love-Crowell, J. (2007). Psychotherapists' experience with clients who engage in consensual sadomasochism: A qualitative study. *Journal of Sex & Marital Therapy, 34*(1), 67–85. https://doi.org/10.1080/00926230701620936

Lin, K. (2016). The medicalization and demedicalization of kink: Shifting contexts of sexual politics. *Sexualities, 20*(3), 302–323. https://doi.org/10.1177/1363460716651420

Lindemann, D. (2011). BDSM as therapy? *Sexualities, 14*(2), 151–172. https://doi.org/10.1177/1363460711399038

Moore, L., Pincus, T., & Rodemaker, D. (2018). *What professionals need to know about BDSM*. https://www.ncsfreedom.org/images/stories/pdfs/Activist/What_Professionals_Need_to_Know_About_BDSM_1.pdf

National Coalition for Sexual Freedom. (2008). *Second national survey of violence & discrimination against sexual minorities*. https://ncsfreedom.org/wp-content/uploads/2019/12/Violence-Discrimination-Against-Sexual-Minorities-Survey.pdf

Pitagora, D. (2013). Consent vs. coercion: BDSM interactions highlight a fine but immutable line. *The New School Psychology Bulletin, 10*(1), 27–36.

Pitagora, D. (2017). No pain, no gain? Therapeutic and relational benefits of subspace in BDSM contexts. *Journal of Positive Sexuality, 3*(3), 44–54. https://journalofpositivesexuality.org/wp-content/uploads/2017/10/No-Pain-No-Gain-Therapeutic-and-Relational-Benefits-of-Subspace-in-BDSM-Pitagora.pdf

Popp, S., & Kaldera, R. (2014). *Unequal by design: Counseling power dynamic relationships*. Asphodel Press.

Richters, J., De Visser, R. O., Rissel, C. E., Grulich, A. E., & Smith, A. M. A. (2008). Demographic and psychosocial features of participants in bondage and discipline, "sadomasochism" or dominance and submission (BDSM): Data from a national survey. *Journal of Sexual Medicine, 5*, 1660–1668. https://doi.org/10.1111/j.1743-6109.2008.00795.x

Speciale, M., & Khambatta, D. (2020). Kinky & queer: Exploring the experiences of LGBTQ+ individuals who practice BDSM. *Journal for LGBT Issues in Counseling, 4*(4), 341–361. https://doi.org/10.1080/15538605.2020.1827476

Taormino, T. (2012). *The ultimate guide to kink: BDSM, role play and the erotic edge*. Cleis Press.

Tripodi, F. (2017). Fifty shades of consent? *Feminist Media Studies, 17*(1), 93–107. https://doi.org/10.1080/14680777.2017.1261846

Waldura, J. F., Arora, I., Randall, A. M., Farala, J. P., & Sprott, R. A. (2016). Fifty shades of stigma: Exploring the health care experiences of kink-oriented patients. *The Journal of Sexual Medicine, 13*(12), 1918–1929. https://doi.org/10.1016/j.jsxm.2016.09.019

Williams, D. J., Thomas, J., & Prior, E. (2014). From 'SSC' and 'RACK' to the '4Cs': Introducing a new framework for negotiating BDSM practice. *Electronic Journal of Human Sexuality, 17*, 1–13.

Wismeijer, A. A. J., & van Assen, M. A. L. M. (2013). Psychological characteristics of BDSM practitioners. *The Journal of Sexual Medicine, 10*(8), 1943–1952. https://doi.org/10.1111/jsm.12192

Yates, S. M., & Neuer-Colburn, A. A. (2019). Counseling the kink community: What clinicians need to know. *Journal of Counseling Sexology & Sexual Wellness, 1*(1), Article 4. https://doi.org/10.34296/01011007

You Want to Do What? Treating Paraphilic Disorders Through a Sex Positive Framework

Robert J. Zeglin and Angela M. Schubert

This I can say for certain: If you go to war with your sexuality, you will lose and end up in more trouble than before you started.

—Jack Morin,
The Erotic Mind: Unlocking the Inner Sources of Passion and Fulfillment

DSM-5 Approach to Paraphilias

The most recent iteration of the *Diagnostic and Statistical Manual of Mental Disorders, Fifth Edition* (5th ed.; *DSM-5*; American Psychiatric Association [APA], 2013) separated what were previously and collectively called sexual and gender identity disorders (APA, 2000) into three distinct chapters: gender dysphoria, sexual dysfunctions, and paraphilic disorders. The last of these, paraphilic disorders, though undergoing relatively few structural changes to the diagnoses themselves, did receive notable philosophical attention and refinement. Most notably, the *DSM-5* spends considerable effort in distinguishing between *paraphilias* and *paraphilic disorders.* Paraphilias are, according to the *DSM-5*, "any intense and persistent sexual interest other than sexual interest in genital stimulation or preparatory fondling with phenotypically normal, physiologically mature, consenting human partners" (APA, 2013, p. 685). This definition makes especially clear that having a nontypical *sexual interest* is what epitomizes a paraphilia. However, a nontypical sexual interest is not ipso facto diagnosable as a mental illness. The *DSM-5* specifically notes that paraphilias do not "necessarily justify or require clinical intervention" (APA, 2013, p. 686). However, one must have a paraphilia to be diagnosed with a paraphilic disorder, as a paraphilia is "a necessary but not a sufficient condition for having a paraphilic disorder" (APA, 2013, p. 687). The sine qua non for applying a paraphilic disorder diagnosis is the presence of distress, dysfunction, or danger as a result of the paraphilia and/or when "harm, or risk of harm, to others" (APA, 2013, p. 685) results from the satisfaction of the paraphilia. In the absence of these factors, the paraphilia is not disordered and therefore requires neither diagnosis nor treatment.

There have been significant critiques of the *DSM-5*'s (APA, 2013) paraphilic disorder chapter, both with respect to specific criteria (Balon, 2016; Fedoroff et al., 2013) and to the general philosophy of including paraphilias in the *DSM-5* (Downing, 2015; Giami, 2015; Moser, 2019). The former set of critiques focuses primarily on perceived inconsistencies, contradictions, and gaps in the specific diagnostic criteria for the disorders. To be frank, similar criticisms exist for nearly every diagnosis in the *DSM-5*, from major depressive disorder to schizophrenia. The latter set of critiques, however, and more to the point of the current chapter, questions the validity of discussing so-called non-normophilic sexual interests within the context of mental illness at all. There are, in general, three major points raised by these critiques that warrant repeating through a sex positive perspective.

First, the hetero- and repro-normativity (i.e., the normativity of sexual practices that are both heterosexual and lead to reproduction) perpetuated by even considering non-genital-related sexual interests and activities non-normophilic is problematic. This approach shines a spotlight on the values of the *DSM-5* authors being heavily weighted toward vanilla sex (i.e., typically conventional positions during penetrative sex that conform to cultural expectations). As Fedoroff et al. (2013) pointed out, the *DSM-5* only defines paraphilia by describing its inverse (i.e., it is non-normophilic) without detailing what precisely *is* paraphilic. This is especially salient considering that research has found that the prevalence of paraphilic interests is higher than would be considered truly unusual (Joyal, 2015; Joyal & Carpentier, 2017). Such an approach to conceptualizing paraphilias produces a moving target, whereby the same behavior or interest could become normophilic simply through more people identifying with the behavior or interest. It cannot be emphasized enough how important it is to consider cross-cultural variations when pathology is questioned; however, it seems a futile endeavor considering there is no universal consensus on what constitutes normative sexual behavior and interest (Moser, 2019). For example, "female nipples" (Tiktok, 2022, Adult Nudity and Sexual Activities section) or "female-presenting nipples" (Tumblr, 2020, Adult Content section) are considered sexual content, and therefore censored, because of a generally accepted social sexualization of this part of the anatomy (Bock et al., 2019; Ruberg et al., 2019). Sexual play and fantasy involving the breasts and nipples would therefore be considered normophilic. Contrastingly, feet are not a generally socially accepted target of sexualization, despite being the most frequently endorsed fetish (Scorolli et al., 2007), and are thus not censored. By extension, the censorship of sexual play and fantasy involving feet is, rather than being applied to the part of the body in question (as with nipples), instead applied to the owner of the sexual desire, pathologizing their behavior and interest as paraphilic. Alternatively, from a sex positive framework, any sexual play and fantasy is valid and worthwhile, providing that all participants consented. As such, arbitrarily designating certain behaviors and interests as paraphilic is antithetical to a sex positive approach and potentially harmful to clients.

The second general point raised by criticisms of the paraphilic disorders chapter of the *DSM-5* (APA, 2013) lies with the lack of utility in diagnosing paraphilias as disordered. This is the only chapter in the *DSM-5* where the target of distress is ultimately labeled as the problem rather than the distress itself. For example, if a devout Catholic client falls unexpectedly in love with a Jewish classmate at university, and subsequently experiences marked anxious distress over what they experience as a deeply intrapersonal values conflict (i.e., religious tenets vs. true love), nary a clinician would consider diagnosing the client with a religious disorder. Instead, the clinician would probably diagnose an anxiety disorder and assist the client in processing that internal struggle. However, in a congruent situation involving paraphilias, and as predicted by Foucault (1985), the client's sexuality is problemized. For example, if a client experiences marked distress over having sexual fantasies involving minors, the client's sexual desire is the focus rather than the client's distress, rendering a stigmatized pedophilic disorder diagnosis (Fedoroff et al., 2013; Jahnke, 2018). Even in the rare circumstances where a client with a paraphilia seeks to satisfy their desire with a nonconsenting person, thus causing harm and meeting criteria for a paraphilic disorder, there is an argument that the *DSM-5* already provides diagnostic language to account for this presentation (e.g., antisocial personality disorder, disruptive and impulse-control disorders) without needing to pathologize the client's sexuality (Balon, 2016; Moser, 2019). This is congruent with the justification offered in the *DSM-5* for changing the name of gender identity disorder to gender dysphoria: "The current term is more descriptive than the previous DSM-IV term *gender identity disorder* and focuses on dysphoria as the clinical problem, not identity per se" (APA, 2013, p. 451).

Third and finally, the conceptualization of paraphilias in the *DSM-5* (APA, 2013) perpetuates a false dichotomy that a person either has or does not have a paraphilia. Sex positive practice, on the other hand, views all sexual behavior and interest along a continuum of intensity rather than as falling into discrete categories of normophilic or paraphilic. For example, lightly and consensually tugging on one's partner's hair during sexual activity, whether to take momentary control or to elicit transient discomfort, is a form of sexual sadism, albeit at the more vanilla end of any spectrum thereof. As one moves along that spectrum through handcuffing one's partner's hands to the bed, through light spanking on the buttock, to flogging one's partner with a cat-o'-nine-tails while they are gagged, it is impossible, from a sex positive perspective, to discern exactly where the activity magically transforms from normophilic to paraphilic. For sex positive clinicians and educators, there is but one relevant question: Is it consensual? (Coppens et al., 2020; Russell & Zeglin, 2020; Wright, 2010).

In summary, a sex positive approach to treating paraphilias is, at its core, one that does not aim to eradicate the underlying paraphilia, as there is limited evidence that such an aim is fruitful. Sex positive treatment of paraphilias seeks first to educate clients on the complexity of sexuality and the variety of sexual interests, behaviors, fantasies, and identities that comprise one's sexuality (World Health Organization, 2006), validating the client's sexuality whenever possible (Annon, 1976; Evans, 2013; Kleinplatz, 2012). Instead, sex positive clinicians seek to reduce the distress, dysfunction, and/or danger resulting from the behavior or interest. For example, distress may be the consequence of internal values conflicts related to the sexual behavior or interest; dysfunction may be evidenced by relational angst as a result of the sexual interest or behavior; and danger may be posed to others because the client has heretofore only been able to identify means of satiating their sexual behavior or interest involving nonconsenting persons. It will likely and largely be a fool's errand to clinically attack the underlying paraphilia, frustrating both client and clinician. Yes, even the most controversial paraphilias would not be the direct treatment target; sex positive clinicians would instead investigate the client's relationship with the paraphilia. The remainder of this chapter will provide concrete examples of how clinicians can conceptualize and treat the eight paraphilic disorders listed in the *DSM-5* (APA, 2013) through such a sex positive framework. This is not an exhaustive or comprehensive treatment planner, but rather a guide to help clinicians refocus their work with clients presenting with possible paraphilic disorders.

Voyeuristic Disorder

Conceptualization

Voyeurism is a paraphilia involving the desire to watch and observe others (APA, 2013; Långström, 2010). Freud (1905/2017) hypothesized that voyeurism, or what he called *scopophilia*, was an innate experience of the libido within personality, shared more or less commonly among all people. There is a pleasure in watching and seeing that which one finds sexually appealing or interesting. Vision, as with all the senses, is a critical part of the sexual experience (Schwarz, 2010; Wehrum et al., 2013). For example, consenting partners may exchange sexual photos, watch while the other undresses, observe the other masturbating, or watch as the other engages in sexual activity with another person altogether, all as a means by which to satiate their scopophilic drive. This libidinal drive to observe that which is sexual is therefore rather normophilic (Stoléru, 2014). However, some clients may find it particularly interesting or arousing to observe nonconsenting persons. The desire to do so, the paraphilia, is simply and only that—a fantasy. The paraphilia does not, unto itself, require diagnosis or treatment, and it should be conceptualized as purely a part of the client's own unique sexuality. If, on the other hand, the voyeuristic desire produces distress, dysfunction, and/or danger, a diagnosis of voyeuristic disorder may be warranted, and treatment should be administered to alleviate the distress, dysfunction, and/or danger.

Treatment

Distress as a result of a voyeuristic desire may be the consequence of guilt and shame stemming from a values set that admonishes such fantasies. Values conflicts are not unusual in the clinical space and can often be alleviated with standard therapeutic practices used to explore any other values conflicts. Distress can also be the result of emotional unrest over the perceived impropriety of the desire and/or its consequences to one's life (e.g., relationships). Simple psychosexual education, congruent with Annon's (1976) PLISSIT model (see Chapter 3), can help ease these worries.

Dysfunction as a result of a voyeuristic desire can manifest as relationship discord with sexual partners who may not wish to be observed even consensually (e.g., the partner denies the client's requests for a striptease). Conflict resolution training and relationship negotiation skills building, common interventions for relationship therapists, can aid in ameliorating relational conflicts. In extreme cases, dysfunction can also be the result of extraordinary time being spent attempting to satiate the desire to the detriment of the client's other life roles (e.g., work). Treatment of such a presentation can largely follow traditional treatments of impulsivity or compulsivity.

Finally, danger may be present if the client succeeds in observing a nonconsenting person in a sexual capacity. Consent is of paramount importance in sex positive practice and, as such, treatment aiming to eliminate the danger in voyeuristic disorder means increasing consent of the observed. That is to say that sex positive clinicians should work with these clients to identify means by which to safely satiate the voyeuristic desire wherein the person being observed has consented to being seen or watched. Such solutions will likely be less than perfect for the client, as the lack of consent was part of the appeal, but sex positive clinicians do not advocate for nonconsensual behavior, even for clients. Examples of such less-than-perfect but clinically appropriate outlets may be websites where users have consented to being watched, adult clubs with nude or seminude performers (as local laws allow), legal nude beaches, or consensual role play with a partner. Part of this treatment will include working with the client to process any dissatisfaction or disappointment with these less-than-perfect solutions. Having a sexual desire 75% safely satiated is a better clinical goal than a desire being either 0% satiated or repressed, and therefore causing even more distress, or being 100% satiated via unsafe means and potentially causing nearly intractable dysfunction within the client's life.

Exhibitionistic Disorder

Conceptualization

Exhibitionism is a paraphilia wherein an individual desires to be observed by others during sexual activity or becomes sexually aroused as a result of exposing their genitals to another person. The desire to be observed during sexual or erotic activity is not, by itself, pathological. In fact, Hopkins et al. (2016) explained that "viewing others and exposing oneself is an integral part of the normative sexual experience" (p. 6). This may be because of a powerful sensuality experienced by the exhibitionist via acute awareness of one's body by both self and others in the moment of its observation, as a central feature of sensual experiences is body awareness (Dailey, 1981). Rarely, if ever, during the normal course of life is one's body simply observed for pleasure's sake (Ellis, 2004). Having a consenting person willingly drink from the scopophilic well-being presented before them is erotic to the exhibitionist (Freud, 1905/2007). Furthermore, engaging in exhibitionism can result in positive mental health. Hugh-Jones et al. (2005) conducted a qualitative study exploring self-perceptions of six women who identified as exhibitionists and identified three phenomena: (a) positive effects of exhibitionism on self-esteem and an increased sense of self-fulfillment, (b) a moral responsibility to know their "audience" and to entertain rather than shock, and (c) experienced social support of and consent to exhibitionism by loved ones and observers.

However, some individuals who engage in exhibitionism may desire to be observed by a nonconsenting person or people. Oswald et al. (2020) noted that almost half of the male participants in the sample sent unsolicited "dick pics" as a means to "sexually excite" the recipient and in hopes that the recipient may "feel attractive" as a result. This is consistent with Ellis's (2004) supposition that individuals who engage in nonconsenting exhibitionism often do so with the anticipation that it will be a pleasurable experience for the nonconsenting recipient. Motivations aside, however, and as previously mentioned, a sex positive approach prioritizes consent. Therefore, exhibitionistic behavior toward a nonconsenting person is contrary to sex positivity and a sex positive approach. If the desire for exhibitionism and/or if fulfilled exhibitionism causes distress, dysfunction, or danger to self or others, a diagnosis of exhibitionistic disorder may be necessary and treatment warranted. The aim of such treatment would be, congruent with sex-positive practice, to alleviate the distress or dysfunction and to promote safety and consent.

Treatment

Distress related to exhibitionism may result from intrapersonal conflict rooted in values associated with nudity, particularly if the client's values stipulate that nudity is reserved only for intimate partners. There may be some cultural values that, even when with intimate partners, suggest modesty and temperance when nude. This obviously is in conflict with the client's exhibitionistic desire. Similar to any value conflict presented by a client, clinicians are in an optimal position to help the client explore and process the competing values, seeking resolution and harmony (Vyskocilova et al., 2015). For example, a female exhibitionist may report feeling guilty after engaging in the exhibitionistic behavior because of a values conflict regarding wanting to be seen while, at the same time, morally questioning whether it perpetuates the objectification of women. Such a presentation lies squarely in the wheelhouse of a sex positive clinician. Narrative therapy and acceptance commitment therapy may also be used to help the client explore their story for potential conflict between value and desire. Distress may also occur as a result of the possible secrecy surrounding the desire to engage in exhibitionism. The embarrassment or, worse, shame in such secrecy can exacerbate distress symptomatology and should be a focus of clinical work for clinicians working with exhibitionists experiencing distress as a result of their desires. Mindfulness-based cognitive therapy may be used to reduce rumination and shame and to increase self-compassion (Proeve et al., 2018). Finally, distress can result from clients' suppressing their desires and thus showing up unauthentically in their relationships, always feelings slightly disconnected from their partner. Many clients who struggle with exhibitionism desire to be seen and often report feeling invisible to the world (Cannon, 2021).

Dysfunction as a result of exhibitionism can manifest as sexual avoidance. Individuals avoiding or repressing sexual desires may avoid or struggle engaging in other sexual activities. This, of course, can also cause or co-occur with relationship discord. In rare cases, one might go to great lengths to fulfill exhibitionistic desires, thus interfering with daily life activities. In any case, sex positive clinicians should be mindful to target their interventions toward the dysfunctional and disruptive consequences of satiating the paraphilic desires and not on the paraphilic desires themselves.

There is potential risk of danger associated with exhibitionism if, as mentioned before, the act is performed on a nonconsenting person, including in a public space or public online forum. If there is an intrigue to expose oneself in either a public space or online forum, basic education on how to do this safely could alleviate both danger and distress. For example, clients may benefit from attending private nudist venues, sex clubs, erotic dungeons, the Folsom Street Fair in San Francisco, and/or nudist events such as World Naked Bike Ride Day (in states where such activities are legal). Participating in online forums, such as Omegle and Chatroulette, facilitates a consensual space wherein the exhibitionist may engage in exhibitionistic behavior, largely without limit. Additionally, exhibitionistic clients may find it arousing to discretely use sexual devices in public spaces (e.g., a small remote-controlled vibrator hidden in one's underwear while at dinner). However, in these circumstances, the potential for nearby persons to unknowingly become passive participants in the sex play raises difficult questions related to consent; thus, any such public play should be well considered with respect to the exhibitionist's ability to keep the play completely discrete. In essence, so long as no laws are broken and each participant in the exhibitionistic play has consented to observing the exhibitionist's body or pleasure, there is no reason for a sex positive clinician to assume the presence of danger.

Frotteuristic Disorder

Conceptualization

Frottage derives from the French verb *frotter*, meaning "to rub." At a very early age, people begin to explore their bodies by touching, rubbing, and pulling on their body parts, including their genitalia. Natural, healthy exploration is typically inclusive of both touching one's own body and touching and rubbing others (Healthchildren.org, n.d.). It is also considered developmentally appropriate, albeit less common, for children to hump or grind inanimate objects such as pillows, a favorite stuffed octopus, or a bed post (Wurtele & Kenny, 2011). As children grow up, they are socialized on how to navigate touch with self and with others within the confines of established social mores. According to McCarthy and McCarthy (2009), engaging in rubbing and grinding is a satisfying form of erotic nonintercourse touch and can be considered a precursor to intercourse or the main sexual event itself. In either case, rubbing and grinding can be considered a pleasurable aspect of outercourse. Those who enjoy grinding or rubbing up against another may engage in "dry humping" in the bedroom, grinding on the dance floor, giving/receiving a lap dance, or even a subtle rubbing up against the buttock of a lover in a crowded elevator—to name a few. In each of these examples, all involved persons are consenting to the contact. Freund (1990) described frotteurism, along with exhibitionism, voyeurism, and preferential rape, to be an anomaly of the natural pattern of human courtship. Freund (1990) argued that frotteurism was an expression of courtship disorder during the tactile stage of human sexual interaction between people. By itself, there is nothing pathological about these desires. Moreover, if sexual arousal is not present at the time of the frottage (whether consent is present or not), technically the individual does not have a paraphilic disorder (Moser, 2016). For some with frotteuristic urges, the desires and behaviors can cause significant distress, dysfunction, or danger. In these cases, and congruent with the *DSM-5* (APA, 2013), a diagnosis of frotteuristic disorder may be warranted.

Treatment

Distress for the client may exist as a result of the social stigma and discrimination of nonnormophilic desires and behaviors, including frotteurism. Annon's (1976) PLISSIT model would communicate to the client that the counseling session is a safe place to express their sexual desires. Distress may surface as a result of unresolved conflict with the individual's erotic template (Cannon, 2021). Exploring the messaging, values, and beliefs associated with the template would be beneficial to create a script that better aligns with the person's values and beliefs. Moreover, a client may benefit from engaging in internal family systems (Schwartz & Southern, 2017) to explore and communicate with the protective part (potentially the fetish), the wounded part (potentially the exile that needs the frottage), and the manager part (potentially the part that wants to eradicate the fetish) linked to the unresolved conflict associated with the erotic template.

Dysfunction may exist as a result of severe anxiety tied to and impairing social interactions with attracted parties. Treatment may include social skills building and traditional approaches to anxiety reduction. Dysfunction may also exist as a result of out-of-control sexual behavior (OCSB). Braun-Harvey and Vigorito (2016) developed an innovative sex positive sexual health model for assessing and treating OCSB. Instead of focusing on behavior or mental illness, Braun-Harvey and Vigorito defined OCSB as a sexual health disorder "in which an individual's consensual sexual urges, thoughts, and behaviors *feel* out of control" (Braun-Harvey & Vigorito, 2016, p. 11). Rather than using the sex addiction model in which the focus is on disorder or disease, Braun-Harvey and Vigorito (2016) focused on the presence of "internal conflicts and self-discrepancies when deciding to provide OCSB assessment and treatment" (p. 11). The OCSB model is based on six sexual health principles: (a) consent; (b) nonexploitation; (c) protection against HIV, sexually transmitted infections, and unwanted or unplanned pregnancy; (d) honesty; (e) shared values; and (f) mutual pleasure (Braun-Harvey & Vigorito, 2016).

Danger exists if a nonconsenting person is involved. Moser (2016) suggests that this is the only circumstance under which a frotteuristic disorder diagnosis should be considered. Although the exact prevalence of nonconsensual frotteurism is unknown, the most commonly reported locations have occurred on public transportation vehicles (e.g., buses, trains, trams) and in crowded places such as malls, elevators, bars, and concert venues. Rubbing or touching a person without their consent may result in legal consequences and may not only harm the victim who is being touched but also those who witness the act. Traditional behavioral and cognitive behavioral therapy can be effective treatments to help the client learn how to control the impulse to touch or rub nonconsenting persons. It may also be possible to employ the 75% satiation approach discussed above, whereby the client identifies opportunities to satiate their frottage desires 75% completely but 100% consensually. Examples include dancing closely with a partner, purchasing legal performances at adult clubs, and obtaining consent and identifying boundaries and opportunities for frottage behavior with a partner.

Sexual Masochism Disorder

Conceptualization

Sexual masochism, or deriving sexual pleasure from experiencing pain, is one possible iteration of so-called "kink" sex (Pillai-Friedman et al., 2015; Yates & Neuer-Colburn, 2019; Zeglin et al., 2018). Kink sex tends to encompass all possible manifestations of BDSM, including bondage, discipline, dominance, submission, sadism, and masochism (see Chapter 19). For the purposes of this discussion, masochism will be used to represent some overlapping features of several of these manifestations, taken to mean sexual enjoyment of one's own pain, subjugation, humiliation, and other positions of powerlessness in relation to and at the hand of a sexual partner(s). Approximately two thirds of women and half of men report masochistic fantasies (Brown et al., 2020). The relationship between power/pain and sexual enjoyment has been long contemplated, with Richard von Krafft-Ebing coining the terms "sadism" and "masochism" in the late 1800s (Ortmann & Sprott, 2013). Havelock Ellis (as cited in Robinson, 1973) conceptualized masochism as sadism's dance partner as the two seek to navigate power dynamics during sexual encounters. Ellis (as cited in Robinson,

1973) also suggested that masochism is simply a linear extension of the natural *energy of fear* present when animals mate. Ellis seems to have done the work, then, for us, offering a clear sex positive conceptualization of masochism: It is an intense expression of the energy of fear present during sex, perhaps one intentionally manifested as to gain control over it (Labrecque et al., 2021).

A sex positive approach to sexual masochism is one where the enjoyment of the practice is respected. Especially as science has yet to clarify the etiology of that enjoyment, no presumptions of underlying pathology, trauma, or deficit should be made (Labrecque et al., 2021; Moser, 2011, 2019). Fundamentally, by disclosing a masochistic interest, a client has disclosed enjoying the exploration and manipulation of power and fear in their sexual encounters. Consent to do so, freely given by all parties, is the central concern of a sex positive clinician (Moser, 2011, 2019). Only if the client is experiencing distress, dysfunction, or danger as a result of their masochistic desire and/or their attempts to satiate their desire, a diagnosis of sexual masochistic disorder may be applied and treatment strategies explored.

Treatment

Distress as a result of sexual masochism can, as with other paraphilias, result from a client's perceived incongruence between these masochistic desires and their personal values and identities. This can be especially true when themes of masculinity, femininity, and gender roles are salient (Bartky, 2015; Yates & Neuer-Colburn, 2019). Congruent with the PLISSIT model (Annon, 1976), simply providing the space for the client to explore and process this conflict can ameliorate a sizable portion of their distress. Because of sexual masochism's position at the intersection of power and gender (Bartky, 2015; Robinson, 1973), two additional contextual features should be considered when treating client distress: (a) lesbian, gay, bisexual, transgender, queer and other identities (LGBTQ+) positionality and (b) societal norms, pressures, messages, and realities. A sex positive clinician is aware of the lived experiences of their clients as sexual persons in a largely heteronormative and hegemonic society, thus forcing clients to navigate their power, their gender, and the interaction of the two on a daily basis. Processing dynamic, intertwining, and conflicting identities and values is not an uncommon task for counselors and should be approached no differently when treating sexual masochistic disorder than when treating other identity and values conflicts.

Dysfunction as a result of sexual masochism can frequently manifest as relationship discord and/or dissatisfaction. Often, one partner may identify with a masochistic sexuality while their partner does not. Or, in other instances, the negotiated limits of the power play between them are notably disparate (e.g., client requests to be consensually choked during sex, but their partner is uncomfortable with this and prefers nothing more than light bondage). In nearly all of these cases, the limits of the client's (and their partner's) imagination are the culprit and should be explored, perhaps via the use of a "yes-no-maybe" list to spur creativity and ingenuity. By doing so, more overlap between partners' comfort zones can be identified and explored. This includes the possibility of consensual nonconsent (Morse, 2019), whereby the client role plays not having consent at all (although always retaining the ultimate power). Also, sensate focus (Weiner & Avery-Clark, 2014, 2017) can be employed to help the partners (re)gain awareness of and appreciation for bodily sensations, thus increasing access to these (new) sensations as targets of consensual power play (e.g., ice on breasts) and breaking through stalemates between partners. Throughout these interventions, exploration and building of trust and vulnerability between partners should be prioritized, especially when that trust might have been damaged, eroded, or dubious, as trust is a central component of sexual encounters involving masochism (Labrecque et al., 2021; Turley, 2011; Zeglin et al., 2018).

Danger as a result of masochism is quite clearly when a client's attempts to satiate their masochistic sexual desires puts them directly at risk for death or debilitating injury. The *DSM-5* (APA, 2013) includes a specifier for whether the diagnosis includes erotic asphyxiation, an ostensibly more dangerous facet of kink sex. There is always a delicate balance in assessing risk in any voluntary and consensual activity in which clients may choose to engage (e.g., cliff jumping, sky diving, playing contact sports, swimming with sharks, sword swallowing, fire dancing, driving). Each of the examples provided require training and orientation to the activity. The best guidance we can offer to clinicians is to ask themselves three derivative questions: (a) Is the client aware of the danger involved with the activity? (b) Does the client have the requisite training, skills, knowledge, or orientation to safely engage in the activity? and (c) Is it unlikely that the client would be permanently injured or die from engaging in this behavior? A sex positive counselor, if the answer to any of the questions is "no," aims to increase safety rather than reduce the activity (see Bloom et al., 2019). This can be accomplished by providing education if the counselor is qualified to do so and/or by providing a referral to or seeking consultation with a qualified professional (e.g., sex educator, sex therapist).

Sexual Sadism Disorder

Conceptualization

The conceptualization of sexual sadism is nearly identical to the conceptualization of sexual masochism, expect in the inverse. *Sadism*, or the sexual enjoyment of inflicting pain, is one possible manifestation of kink sex and is the counterpart to masochism, its metaphorical dance partner (Pillai-Friedman et al., 2015; Yates & Neuer-Colburn, 2019; Zeglin et al., 2018). For the purposes of this discussion, sadism will stand to mean sexual enjoyment of causing pain, subjugation, humiliation, and other positions of powerlessness to one's sexual partner(s). Approximately 60% of men and 47% of women report fantasizing about dominating sexual partners (Brown et al., 2020). After Richard von Krafft-Ebing coined the terms "sadism" and "masochism" in the late 1800s (Ortmann & Sprott, 2013), Havelock Ellis (as cited in Robinson, 1973) suggested that sadism is an extension of the natural *energy of anger/aggression* present during animal mating. Moser (1999) cited Alfred Kinsey as identifying two dozen species of mammal that intentionally inflict pain during coitus. Unlike in the wild animal world, however, among humans, consent is paramount in conceptualizing sexual encounters. Sexual sadists experience as erotic the consensual offering of complete trust by their partner (Turley, 2011; Zeglin et al., 2018). Ellis, again, seems to have done the heavy lifting for us, offering a sex positive conceptualization of sadism as an intense expression of the energy of aggression naturally present during sex, perhaps one intentionally manifested in a context where the "aggressor" can experience receiving intense trust from their partner (Turley, 2011). If sadistic fantasies and behaviors exist devoid of distress, dysfunction, or danger, a diagnosis of sexual sadistic disorder would be inappropriate. However, if distress, dysfunction, or danger is, in fact, reported, sexual sadistic disorder may be an appropriate diagnosis to consider and treatment strategies should be explored.

Treatment

Distress as a result of sexual sadism, much like with sexual masochistic disorder, is frequently a by-product of a values conflict whereby the sexual desire to make a partner powerless is in conflict with an identity or value that admonishes such dynamics. The PLISSIT model (Annon, 1976) suggests to first provide an open space for clients to nonjudgmentally explore and process these intrapersonal conflicts. Social gender roles and norms, again, influence clients' values and schemas related to power and should be intentionally broached as part of this treatment, including LGBTQ+ identity (Bartky, 2015; Bauer, 2014; Chaline, 2010; Yates & Neuer-Colburn, 2019). Counselors are experienced at inviting clients to explore and process intrapersonal conflicts, there need not be an exception made when that conflict involves sexual sadism. Counselors need only be careful not to, through bias, indict the sexual sadism-related desire as the root cause of the conflict (and thus be the one targeted for exorcism). A sex positive counselor's job is simply to aid in processing the conflict.

Dysfunction as a result of sexual sadism is, as with sexual masochism, often the result of relationship dissatisfaction that has spurred from (ostensibly) mismatched comfort zones between partners. When negotiated limits between partners appear irrevocably disparate (e.g., client wishes to blindfold their partner, but their partner is not comfortable with having their vision obstructed), resentment and distrust may brew. Trust, as previously discussed, is a necessary component of sexual encounters involving sexual sadism. As such, traditional therapeutic practices aimed at increasing and maintaining trust between partners may prove beneficial. Open communication skills, perhaps elicited through "yes-no-maybe" lists and sensate focus exercises (Weiner & Avery-Clark, 2014, 2017), can help establish or reestablish the secure trust necessary for sexual sadism play during sexual encounters. Moreover, "yes-no-maybe" lists and sensate focus have the added advantage of helping to spur creativity between partners, possibly inviting new avenues for power play that land squarely within the partners' overlapping comfort zones.

Danger as a result of sexual sadism most directly involves the infliction of pain on a nonconsenting partner. Let us be perfectly clear: Sadism without consent is sexual assault. Period. Sex positive clinicians recognize that it is the lack of consent, rather than the presence of the sadistic behavior, that makes it sexual assault. Also, sex positive counselors recognize that the desire to inflict pain on a nonconsenting partner is strictly fantasy and not therefore pathological. If a client is imminently at risk of acting on that desire, and since no clinician should advocate for nonconsensual sexual activity, the clinician is left to offer only less-than-perfect solutions. As discussed with other paraphilias, a 75% perfect solution is preferred over a 100% solution that is illegal and leads to harm for both client and others or a 0% solution that can lead to repression and unanticipated consequences. Consensual nonconsent, a type of role play, is a viable solution in these circumstances (Morse, 2019). The ultimate power of the "nonconsenting" partner should be established and prioritized. In the absence of a partner who is comfortable playing the nonconsenting role, ethically produced pornography with sadism themes (wherein the consent of the actors/actresses is obtained and communicated) can be an exciting sexual stimulus. Finally, as with sexual masochism, sometimes clients will unwittingly put themselves and their consenting partners in danger as they seek to satiate their sexual desires. Again, we encourage sex positive clinicians to ask themselves three derivative questions: (a) Is the client aware of the danger involved with the activity? (b) Does the client have the requisite training, skills, knowledge, or orientation to safely engage in the activity? and (c) Is it unlikely that the client would cause permanent injury or death if engaging in this behavior? If the answer to any of these questions is "no," clinicians should aim to increase safety rather than reduce the activity (Bloom et al., 2019). As with sexual masochism, education (if the counselor is qualified) and/or a referral to or consultation with a qualified professional (e.g., sex educator, sex therapist) can be helpful here.

Pedophilic Disorder

Conceptualization

Perhaps the most controversial of the paraphilias, the mental health field's clinical understanding of pedophilia is hampered by a poor understanding of language and by unchecked bias. First, *pedophilia* technically refers to sexual attraction to prepubescent children specifically, whereas *hebephilia* and *ephebophilia* refer to sexual attraction to peripubescent and postpubescent children, respectively (Rind, 2017; Seto, 2017). Nonetheless, the *DSM-5* (APA, 2013) consolidates these into one paraphilia: pedophilia. Moreover, it is important to note that these terms only connote the attraction, not resulting behavior. The great majority of people with attraction to minors do not act on that attraction and are rather secretive about their attraction (Cantor & McPhail, 2016). To further cloud the relationship between attraction and behavior, many child sexual abusers commit the abuse for reasons other than sexual attraction, meaning they are not, in fact, pedophiles at all (i.e., they have no sexual attraction to children; Hall & Hall, 2007; Schiffer & Vonlaufen, 2011; Strassberg et al., 2012).

There continues to exist a conflation of "pedophile" with "abuser." These two groups are distinct (although there is considerable overlap) and should be conceptualized as such. This is an important point, as even counselors may fall victim to assuming that a self-disclosed pedophile must have, must want to, and/or certainly will sexually abuse a child (Jahnke, 2018; Levenson et al., 2019; Walker et al., 2021). As we move forward in our discussion, we will approach this paraphilia as we have all others, through a sex positive lens that affirms all sexualities by default. That is to say that we will discuss people with pedophilia, or who we shall call minor-attracted people (MAP; Freimond, 2013; Levenson et al., 2019), by placing their attraction at the center of our discussion.

To appropriately conceptualize MAPs, counselors must first acknowledge and process their own biases against this population. Approximately 54% of helping professionals would report a self-disclosed MAP to police, even if the client had not committed a crime (Walker et al., 2021). This unwarranted breach of client confidentiality is often driven by fear on the part of the counselor of civil litigation, with society and the legal system offering little resistance to violating these clients' right to privileged communication (Cantor, 2014; Jahnke, 2018). There may actually be malicious intent in some of these breaches of confidentiality, as 40% of mental health professionals report feeling angry when thinking of MAPs (Jahnke et al., 2015). In fact, Koops et al. (2016) found that almost a third of therapists agree that MAPs should be preemptively incarcerated. This is untenable and contrary to the *ACA Code of Ethics* (American Counseling Association [ACA], 2014). Furthermore, there is no evidence that this strategy achieves the goal of protecting children. As Jahnke (2018) stated, "Even though it is common and tempting to believe otherwise, ostracizing [MAPs] is unlikely to help keep children safe" (p. 150).

There is still a great deal that is unknown about MAPs, particularly because nearly all research on MAPs is conducted with samples of participants who have been convicted of child abuse (and sometimes incorrectly labeled as pedophiles, as discussed above). However, emerging research indicates that minor attraction is (a) developed early in life (Grundmann et al., 2016; Houtepen et al., 2016), (b) stable across the life span (Cantor, 2012; Grundmann et al., 2016), (c) biologically based (Shim et al., 2014; Tenbergen et al., 2015), and (d) dimensional versus taxonomic (i.e., exists on a continuum for all people rather than as a discrete category of people; Sea & Beauregard, 2018; Stephens et al., 2017). For these reasons, there is a growing support for conceptualizing minor attraction, in clinical and scientific discourse exclusively, as a sexual orientation (Berlin, 2014; Grundmann et al., 2016; Jahnke, 2018; Seto, 2012).

In summary, sex positive counselors should view client disclosures of minor attraction as a unique component of a client's sexuality, one that requires neither celebration nor reproval. There may be some clinical virtue in commending the disclosure of minor attraction, as therapeutic responses to such disclosure may facilitate better treatment outcomes (Grady et al., 2019; Jahnke, 2018; Jain et al., 2022; Levenson & Grady, 2019; Levenson et al., 2019). Furthermore, and perhaps most controversially, sex positive counselors should avoid attempting to decrease or weaken the attraction, as there is limited evidence that such is even possible and it may frustrate the therapeutic process in irrevocable ways (Cantor, 2018; Cantor & McPhail, 2016; Levenson & Grady, 2019). If, through processing the client's sexuality and the role/history that minor attraction plays within it, the client does not express distress, dysfunction, or danger as a consequence of their minor attraction, then no diagnosis of pedophilic disorder should be applied (Berlin, 2014; Jahnke, 2018; Levenson & Grady, 2019).

Treatment

Distress as a result of minor attraction frequently results from shame compounded by the inability to find mental health professionals who are willing to work with MAPs nonjudgmentally (Grady et al., 2019; Jahnke, 2018; Levenson & Grady, 2019; Levenson et al., 2019; Lievesley et al., 2020). This stigma has been associated with increased suicidal ideation among MAPs (Cohen et al., 2020). Consequently, much of the research on (sex positive) treatment of minor attraction focuses on reducing the internalized stigma that MAPs experience (Berlin, 2014; Jahnke, 2018; Walker, 2017). By doing so, MAPs are better able to access and leverage coping mechanisms, social supports, and resilience strategies, all of which can help prevent illegal behavior (Berlin, 2014; Jahnke, 2018; Jain et al., 2022; Walker, 2017). Levenson et al. (2019) details 10 helpful considerations when treating distress in MAP client.

Dysfunction, most notably "interpersonal difficulties" (APA, 2013, p. 697), as a result of minor attraction can be expected to manifest as discord within major interpersonal relationships in the client's life. This includes losing jobs and friends if their attraction were discovered (Freimond, 2013). Severe relationship ruptures are not unfamiliar presenting problems for counselors and can be approached with similar skills and interventions already used in such situations. However, counselors should be mindful of the very real likelihood that these relationships will be irrevocable because of the profound stigmatization that the client now faces; attempts to repair and renew these relationships may prove fruitless and frustrating and thus should be done only after the client has been given the time and space to process this possibility.

Finally, and perhaps most importantly, danger as a result of minor attraction manifests clearly as endangering the well-being and safety of children. Let us be clear in stating that child-adult sexual activity is illegal, consistently evidenced to be harmful, should not be endorsed by counselors, and must be reported by the counselor to authorities as guided by the *ACA Code of Ethics* (ACA, 2014) and the applicable state law. However, treating pedophilic disorder from a sex positive framework does mean acknowledging that the attraction alone poses no danger to children (Berlin, 2014; Cantor, 2014; Cantor & McPhail, 2016; Jahnke, 2018; Levenson et al., 2019). As such, counselors should first be sure to properly assess potential danger, rather than relying on bias, self-preservation, or alarmism (Berlin, 2014; Koops et al., 2016; Walker et al., 2021). If, in the honest assessment of the counselor, the client is an imminent threat to harm a child, the counselor should implement strategies up to and including reporting the client to the authorities. This may include client disclosures of viewing child pornography, as viewing child pornography facilitates the abuse of the child depicted in the pornography (Berlin, 2014; Heasman & Foreman, 2019). Importantly, the reporting of these latter clients to authorities remains a point of debate in some states (e.g., Wallin & Klarich, 2020), and counselors should therefore review their state's requirements carefully.

If, however, the client is not posing an imminent threat to harm a child, the counselor must seek other treatment methods to mitigate any potential risk from emerging. This, as has been discussed with other paraphilias, may require the exploration of 75% solutions. These solutions aim to help the client satiate their fantasies in such a way as to mitigate the risk to those around them, most especially children, and are congruent with harm-reduction strategies. "By taking a harm reduction approach, clinicians are promoting client autonomy and seeking to do good by preventing nonoffenders from becoming offenders" (Heasman & Foreman, 2019, p. 271). As such, the aim of these harm-reduction strategies is always to prevent the client from (although still recognizing that not all MAPs even desire) sexually abusing a child. These can include solo activity like fantasy play (e.g., the internal visual recreation during masturbation of appealing stimuli), partnered activity like age play (e.g., a consenting adult partner role plays as a younger age during sexual activity; see Tiidenberg & Paasonen, 2019), and viewing legally and ethically produced nonpornographic visual stimuli (e.g., clothing advertisements). The use of computer-generated virtual pornographic visual stimuli depicting children (i.e., similar to that of video game characters) remains contentious, despite a 2002 U.S. Supreme Court ruling (*Ashcroft v. Free Speech Coalition*) that virtual child pornography, in contrast to actual child pornography, "records no crime and creates no victims by its production" (p. 236) and is "an alternative and permissible" (p. 251) medium. Nonetheless, because of the inconsistencies in interpreting this ruling (see Kravets, 2009), counselors should proceed with great caution on this front.

Fetishistic Disorder

Conceptualization

In his essay, "Le fétichisme dans l'amour," Alfred Binet (1887) described fetishism as the act of becoming sexually aroused as a result of engaging sexually with inanimate objects. Von Krafft-Ebing (1886/1998) and Havelock Ellis (1927/2004) theorized the origin of fetishism to be a result of developmental associative experiences tied to emotions, physical sensations, and arousal. That is to say that fetishes develop as a result of repeated and/or intense actual or symbolic co-occurrences of arousal, satisfaction or other positive emotions, and the object. In the *DSM-5* (APA, 2013), the modestly revised version of fetishistic disorder included clinical distress or impairment as a result of recurrent sexual arousal from the use of inanimate objects (e.g., leather-bound books) or a hyperfocus on a body part considered non-erogenous (e.g., elbows). The fetishized object becomes an extension of the person or their partner, becoming sensual and therefore erotic. This extension of the sensual is to conceptualize the client's pleasure derived from, say, stroking the underside of a stiletto as taxonomically indistinguishable from the pleasure derived from stroking their partner's inner thigh. The act itself is one of sensual contact, pleasure, and arousal—only, in the case of fetishes, by extension. Congruent with sex positive clinicians' avoidance of judging the sensual experiences of clients, the eroticism that fetishistic clients experience with inanimate or nonerogenous extensions to their sensuality should be equally free from judgment.

Fetishistic desires and behaviors are best conceptualized along a continuum (Dant, 1996; Rees & Garcia, 2017; Wiederman, 2003). In the first type, *Type 1–Inclusive*, the presence of the fetishized object/part is not necessary for a sexually satisfying encounter and may not even be thought of during the entirety of the sexual encounter. That is to say that a person with a Type 1 leather fetish can have completely satisfying sexual encounters without ever thinking about or wishing leather to be included in the encounter. However, a Type 1 fetishized object/part will consistently and predictably heighten the person's sexual enjoyment and satisfaction if presented into the sexual encounter. This latter point is actually what separates a paraphilic fetish from a normophilic preference, as including a preferred but not fetishized object into a sexual encounter would occasionally and inconsistently heighten sexual satisfaction and pleasure. This is all to say that the defining feature of a fetishized object is that it always (or very nearly always) elicits heightened pleasure and satisfaction. For somebody with a fetish of the second type, *Type 2–Necessity*, the fetishized object/part must be present and included in the sexual encounter for the person to experience sexual satisfaction and pleasure. For example, a person with a lingerie fetish would need to have lingerie involved in the encounter, perhaps worn by either partner during sex or perhaps focusing on the experience of removing the lingerie during foreplay. As with any type of fetish, the exact manifestation is unique and idiosyncratic to the person with the fetish. In the final type of fetish, *Type 3–Substitution*, the fetishized object/part is directly substituted into the role of sexual partner. For example, a person with a shoe fetish may begin masturbating with shoes (e.g., thrusting their penis into the soles, inserting the heel of a shoe into their vagina). This does not always but often can mean that there is a preference for sexual activity with the fetishized object/part over sexual activity with human partners.

According to Bad Girls Bible (Adriana, n.d.), there are 239 sexual fetishes and kinks, yet even that list was met with numerous responses suggesting necessary additions. Nearly anything can be fetishized, for it is not about the object itself as much as the sensual association connected to the object for the person. Enjoying sexual experiences involving the body and/or fetishized objects (sensual extensions of the body) is the sexual equivalent of enjoying both the music of one's favorite band and their album covers, the latter as a sensual (visual) extension of their aural body.

Occasionally, the fetishistic client may report distress, dysfunction, or danger as a result of their fetishizing desires or behaviors. It is important to note, and possibly even to explain to the client (Annon, 1976), that the clinical issue lies not with the fetish itself (as one's sensuality—even an extended sensuality—is inherently nonproblematic) but with the undesirable consequences derived therefrom. In such cases, a diagnosis of fetishistic disorder may be appropriate, and treatment may be justified. When studying fetishes, one might be met with language of "levels of fetish." We opt instead for "types of fetish," as the use of the word "level" can connote severity. The three types discussed above do not represent varying severity of fetish, but rather simply varying manifestations of fetishism. This means that somebody with a Type 3 fetish would warrant neither a diagnosis nor treatment if there is no resulting distress, dysfunction, or danger, whereas a person with a Type 1 fetish may warrant diagnosis and treatment if experiencing distress, dysfunction, or danger as a result thereof.

Treatment

Distress from fetishism may occur as the result of shame, embarrassment, anxiety, and isolation experienced by an individual for wanting to engage in the fetishistic behavior. It is not within the sex positive clinician's role to tell someone what is and what is not socially acceptable or sexually appropriate. For example, individuals whose erotic script includes adult baby and diaper lover (AB/DL) identities are noted to experience higher rates of shame, embarrassment, anxiety, and guilt than the general population because of society's admonition, fear of rejection by partner, judgment of the fetish by loved ones (Lipscomb, 2014; Zamboni, 2018), or historical parental rejection (Lasala et al., 2020). Clinicians may help the client explore unmet core emotional needs (e.g., safety, compassion, nurturance, acceptance) associated with the shame and rejection by focusing on self-acceptance, compassion, and attachment. Such interventions may provide corrective emotional experiences that facilitate emotional growth, change, and contentedness, all without ever reducing the fetishistic desires or behaviors. Furthermore, a sex positive approach may also support the client's desire to connect and be accepted by identifying safe spaces to explore their fetishistic desires, identity, and behavior, including in groups on FetLife, local sex/kink clubs, or conferences/meetups (e.g., TeddyCon, Tomkat, CAPCon).

Dysfunction may manifest as relationship discontent wherein the client's partner does not agree with or wish to entertain the client's fetish and/or admonishes or mocks it. For example, a husband may desire to lick his spouse's feet as part of foreplay; however, the spouse finds this idea repulsive. In this case, the couple can experience emotional and sexual gridlock (Cannon & Holmberg-Sasek, 2020). Similarly, if one partner with a Type 3 fetish is frequently opting to engage in sex play with the fetishized object without including their partner, this can lead to significant relationship discord. Neil Cannon's heartfelt-hearing approach may be useful in helping the couple listen to each other's needs and cultivate compassion as a result (Cannon & Holmberg-Sasek, 2020). The approach is a highly structured process where each person takes turns speaking, listening, and being heard. For couples it may also be beneficial to have them read *Decoding Your Kink* by Galen Fous (2015) or *When Someone You Love Is Kinky* by Dossie Easton and Catherine A. Liszt (2000). Although kinks and fetishes are not the same thing, the conversations and negotiations between partners that they often require are quite similar.

Danger can, in some cases, be present as a natural by-product of the fetish, if, for example, the client's fetish is one that requires the presence or use of a dangerous object (e.g., knife). Engaging in such fetishes can be extremely satisfying for the individual, as there can be a thrill rooted in the primal pleasures associated with being vulnerable with a partner in such an intimate way (Ellis, as cited in Robinson, 1973; Fous, 2015).

As with sexual sadism and masochism, the sex positive clinician seeks only to increase the client's risk awareness. This can include assessing the client's familiarity with the danger of the fetish in question. Discussing boundaries and hard limits, identifying safe words and/or gestures to signal when to stop, and ensuring that all involved understand the risks may be helpful to these clients. What is important here is for the clinician to avoid relying on their own neophyte understanding of the dangers, often informed by bias and prejudice. The knowledge-based decision-making matrix (see Chapter 3) may be helpful in guiding the clinician in these situations. A sex positive clinician may also use a "yes-no-maybe" list with the couple to identify those fetishistic acts they approve and those they do not approve.

Transvestic Disorder

Conceptualization

Transvestitism is, in general terms, the sexual gratification as a result of cross-dressing (i.e., wearing the clothes traditionally worn by another gender; Allen, 2014; APA, 2013; Blanchard, 2010). There is an important note to be made here: Transvestitism is not drag and is not gender identity/gender expression. For cross-dressing behavior to qualify as paraphilic transvestitism, the person must experience sexual gratification from it (APA, 2013; Blanchard, 2010). Cross-dressing for entertainment, performance, or drag would not qualify (Allen, 2014; Blanchard, 2010). Similarly, clients who wear clothing traditionally worn by other genders either because they desire to present as more masculine, feminine, or androgynous than they are (i.e., gender expression) or because they inwardly and personally identify as that gender (i.e., gender identity) would not qualify (Allen, 2014; APA, 2013; Blanchard, 2010). One must always keep in mind the overarching definition of paraphilia, which prioritizes the sexual satisfaction of the desires and behaviors. Because transvestic desires can be easily satiated, even without a partner and even in public (e.g., wearing the underwear traditionally worn by another gender), it is remarkably unclear how prevalent transvestitism truly is, as there is no clear data among the population (Moser, 2016). By extension, there is limited available evidence to help narrow the possible means by which to conceptualize a client with transvestic desires. Nonetheless, because sex positivity considers all sexual desires healthy and acceptable by default, the burden experienced by the mental health field to clinically conceptualize a perfectly benign behavior is purely fictional at best.

Not wanting to leave this section devoid of helpful guidance, we can provide a framework through which a sex positive counselor can explore a client's transvestic desires. The circles of sexuality model (Dailey, 1981; Gochros, 1972, 1974) outlines five components of sexuality: (a) intimacy, (b) sensuality, (c) sexual identity, (d) sexual health and behavior, and (e) sexualization. A client's transvestic desires may be a manifestation of one or more of these circles and are always personal and unique (Hauk & Holliday, 2019). Table 20.1 provides examples of each. In any case, only if the client reports distress, dysfunction, or danger as a result of their transvestic desires should a diagnosis of transvestic disorder be explored and treatment considered.

Treatment

Distress from transvestic desires may be the result of an intense and persistent fear of being discovered to be wearing clothing nontraditional for the client's gender. Of

Table 20.1

Examples of Transvestic Motivations Across the Circles of Sexuality

Circle of Sexuality	*Example Transvestic Motivation*
Intimacy	The vulnerability and risk of wearing another gender's clothing, particularly in public, can be risqué and erotic.
Sensuality	The physical feel of the clothing material may be gratifying and erotic.
Sexual identity	The navigation of one's femininity and masculinity, and the social lines drawn around them, can be taboo and erotic.
Sexual health and behavior	The physiological interaction with the clothing in one's erogenous zones can be stimulating and erotic.
Sexualization	The ability to "pass" as another gender in public, drawing the gaze of a different population, may be exhilarating and erotic.

course, this may speak more to society's own discomfort with fluid gender norms; however, the acuity is experienced by the client and can be distressing. Counselors regularly work with clients who present with some social anxiety about potentially embarrassing traits, behaviors, or facts being noticed or discovered; the interventions and approaches used to reduce anxiety in those cases can be confidently applied here as well. Notably, counselors must avoid working to relegate the transvestic behavior to the client's home if that is not the client's goal. Strengthening coping rather than weakening desire should be a sex positive counselor's aim. Relatedly, as with other paraphilias, distress can be the consequence of a conflict in values or identities. Sex positive counselors work with clients to explore and process the conflict, without laying their thumb upon the scales in either direction.

Dysfunction as a consequence of transvestic behaviors has not been documented in the research (Blanchard, 2010; Moser, 2016). It is challenging to foresee how transvestitism could cause "impairment in social, occupational, or other important areas of functioning" (APA, 2013, p. 702). However, as with several other paraphilias, dysfunction can manifest as relationship discord, particularly if a client's partner is less than understanding toward the transvestic desires and behaviors. Sex positive counselors should be mindful not to overeagerly suggest reducing the transvestic behavior as a means of (re)harmonizing the relationship. This cautionary statement is true, however, for any relationship discord and is not altogether foreign to counselors working with couples (Christensen et al., 2015; Nelson, 2020). As such, traditional interventions aimed at improving communication, mutual respect, and emotional vocabulary in couples can be applied here with confidence. An additional component of psychosexual education may also be a justifiable supplemental intervention, exploring with all parties the language of transvestitism. If this is outside the bailiwick of the counselor, a sex educator or sex therapist can be consulted.

Finally, danger as a result of transvestic desires and behaviors also has not been documented in the research (Blanchard, 2010; Moser, 2016). Moser (2016) noted that nonconsent is a nonissue with transvestitism because, as mentioned earlier, this paraphilic desire can be fully satiated even without a partner. In light of this, there is no salient concern toward which we feel the need to call clinicians' attention with respect to transvestitism. However, each client is unique and may articulate a heretofore unanticipated component of risk in their transvestic behaviors. Sex positive clinicians are not naïve to this possibility, but are mindful to properly place the ethos of any risk. For example, it is not transvestitism-derived risk if a client is selling drugs to supplement their income enough to support their clothing purchases. Nor is it a transvestitism-derived risk for children to see a person wearing the clothing traditionally worn by another gender, despite the societal pearl-clutching that may catalyze this worry (Andrade, 2020; Dickson, 2020). Only in the former example is there some level of risk, and, with respect to transvestitism, the risk lies elsewhere (i.e., in the illicit drug market). Although a counselor may choose to work with such a client to reduce any risk in this case, they would do so without a transvestic disorder diagnosis being applied.

Conclusion

The paraphilic disorders, perhaps more than nearly any other class of diagnoses in the *DSM-5*, conjure for counselors both a clinical confusion and a moral misgiving. This intersection often either compels them to or provides refuge when they attempt to treat these disorders from their own (often limited) personal understanding of sexuality and sexual appropriateness. This is an inadequate, unhelpful, unethical, and sex negative approach to treating paraphilic disorders. Alternatively, paraphilic disorders should be fundamentally viewed as a client's subjective experience of distress about a paraphilia, with paraphilias being unto themselves neither diagnosable nor in need of treatment. Sex positive counselors should prioritize the treatment of the client's distress, as is the ethical standard in the field across diagnoses, cultural identities, clinical presentations, or interpersonal disruptions. Even the most controversial paraphilic disorders offer at their core an opportunity to live up to Rogers's (1995) call for empathy, genuineness, and unconditional positive regard.

Case Example

Gregory is a 31-year-old White cisgender male who came to counseling with the encouragement of his wife Sasha. Gregory initially explained he did not need counseling and that his wife Sasha was "overreacting." During the initial interview, Gregory explained that he and Sasha had been together for 10 years and married for 5 years. When asked why Sasha might want him to pursue counseling, Gregory explained that he felt "down" and "depressed" for the past several months and reported difficulty sleeping. He clarified that he had often struggled to fall asleep and stay asleep, leaving him with only a few hours of restless sleep a night for the past few weeks. He stated that he spent the time awake "thinking" and "worrying." He acknowledged that some of his worries included stress about work and thoughts that he reported were "too much." Although he did not share what those thoughts were, he explained that they caused him a great deal of distress.

During the initial intake, Gregory explained that he is an only child who grew up in a home with both parents who are still presently married. Gregory has lived with Sasha for the past 8 years. Gregory explained that he has an "awesome job" as a business administrator at a local nonprofit. He shared that he likes to play Frisbee golf with Sasha, participates in the local whiskey-tasting club with another friend, and attends a spiritual center. Gregory indicated there was no history of counseling. He noted that he has always wanted to go to counseling but was concerned about not finding "the right counselor." Gregory explained that he casually drinks with his wife and one friend and stated no history or current use of drugs. He reported no history of mental illness, sexual abuse, or physical abuse. Over the course of the session, Gregory shared that he sometimes felt like he was "better off dead." A suicide assessment revealed that Gregory's passive suicidal thoughts began around the age of 12, with no history of active suicide attempts.

Gregory acknowledged that feeling down has affected his life intermittently since he was younger. He explained that it is currently affecting his relationship with Sasha. Gregory noted that he has not been interested in physical intimacy with Sasha, stating, "We are in a rut, or maybe it is me. She wants to, but I am just not 'into it.' I just haven't been in the mood." He stated that his sleepless nights are affecting his ability to focus at work. Gregory shared that he has difficulty talking about feelings but reported feeling "lonely." When prompted, Gregory explained, "I love kids, but I am not sure if I should have them."

This initial session marked the beginning of Gregory's journey in counseling. The counselor focused on therapeutic rapport, trust building, and remained client-centered in focus. Gregory was encouraged to lead the counseling sessions and as such, he wished to explore his loneliness, depression, and his concerns about having children. Over the course of several sessions, Gregory was able to increase sleep by engaging in meditation and journaling before and after he went to bed. He was also able to explore values associated with his identity as a spouse, a worker, and a spiritual being. Gregory was asked to write about what it meant to be a father. At the next session, Gregory arrived clearly anxious, covering his face and bent over with his elbows resting on his knees. He reported not sleeping at all the night before. At this time, Gregory shared that he was afraid of himself because he was attracted to children.

Gregory explained how he first noticed he liked girls who were younger than him when he was around 11 years old. At first, he thought it was not a big deal because they were close in age but as he grew older, his attraction for younger girls remained. He explained that he was also attracted to girls his age and continued to date casually within his peer group throughout high school and college, but the attraction for younger girls seemed differently more appealing. Gregory began to weep as he shared that he had never interacted with a child in a sexual way and explained, "I would never hurt a child. I just wish I were not attracted to little girls. I want to be normal." Gregory went into further detail about how he had tried to tell his mother when he professed his love for his neighbor's younger daughter, who was 7 when he was 11. He explained that his mother brushed off his feelings but did warn him to always stay in a public space with the girl. He reported battling his feelings for the neighbor and the feelings only worsened when she moved. He noted that he was sure they moved because "I think they thought it was weird for me to hang out with their daughter." From this point, he explained that he tried to "shut off" any feelings and thoughts when it came to younger girls. Instead, he focused on his schoolwork and school clubs. He dated, but his attraction for younger girls never went away.

Gregory reported that he surprised himself when he fell in love with Sasha. He explained, "She is wild and free and is always open to new adventures. She usually is the one who takes the lead when it comes to our sex life. I want to share everything with her, but I am pushing her away. I do not know how she will handle this. I don't know where to go, but it's eating me up inside."

Reflections About the Case Example

After reading this case example, consider the following questions:

1. Regarding minor attraction, the primary error made by counselors is the belief that clients seeking treatment has or will molest a child. What are your current beliefs regarding the client's minor attractions?

2. As you read the case example, what thoughts and feelings came up for you?
3. What might you need to do to best prepare to work with individuals who struggle with minor attraction?
4. What are the clinical concerns in the case example: distress, danger, and/or dysfunction?
5. How might you best approach treatment with Gregory?

Questions You Always Wanted to Ask

1. **What resources are available for therapists preparing to work with clients with minor attraction?**
   Following are some resources that may benefit mental health professionals working with clients with minor-attraction concerns.
   - B4U-ACT at https://www.b4uact.org advocates for compassionate mental health services, promotes competent and effective professional services and resources for individuals, and offers guidelines and resources to mental health professionals.
   - Global Prevention Project at http://theglobalpreventionproject.org/maps offers scholarly resources and support to therapists interested in supporting the needs of minor-attracted persons and support to those attracted to minors.
   - Virtuous Pedophiles at https://www.virped.org/ is a website for non-offending, anticontact pedophiles.
2. **What fetish services are available for clients interested in joining a particular community?**
   There are many safe places for clients to find community, support, and connection. Fetishdirectory.com offers a variety of venues to interested parties, including Fetish Easter Weekend, Florida Fetish Weekend, Fetish Con, and Shibari Conference—to name a few.
3. **How do I best prepare to treat individuals experiencing distress related to a paraphilia?**
   Simply stated, educate yourself about yourself. One of the most informative ways to learn how to be a sex positive counselor is to go through a sexual attitude reassessment (SAR) intensive group training. The goal of the SAR is to help attendees examine personal attitudes, values, biases, and assumptions associated with sex, sexuality, and their erotic template. The American Association of Sexuality Educators, Counselors, and Therapists (AASECT.org) offers an updated list of upcoming SAR events along with other training opportunities. The Association of Counseling Sexology & Sexual Wellness also offers training events on their website: www.counselingsexology.com.

References

Adriana. (n.d.). The complete list of 239 sexual fetishes and kinks. *Bad Girls Bible*. https://badgirlsbible.com/list-of-kinks-and-fetishes

Allen, S. (2014). Whither the transvestite? Theorising male-to-female transvestism in feminist and queer theory. *Feminist Theory, 15*(1), 51–72.

American Counseling Association. (2014). *ACA code of ethics*. https://www.counseling.org/resources/aca-code-of-ethics.pdf

American Psychiatric Association. (2000). *Diagnostic and statistical manual of mental disorders* (4th ed., text rev.).

American Psychiatric Association. (2013). *Diagnostic and statistical manual of mental disorders* (5th ed.). https://doi.org/10.1176/appi.books.9780890425596

Andrade, S. (2020, December). What the hell happened: Candace Owens upset by Harry Styles' dress. *The Harvard Crimson*. https://www.thecrimson.com/article/2020/12/8/wthh-candance-owens-harry-styles/

Annon, J. S. (1976). The PLISSIT model: A proposed conceptual scheme for the behavioral treatment of sexual problems. *Journal of Sex Education and Therapy, 2*(1), 1–15.

Ashcroft v. Free Speech Coalition, 535 U.S. 234 (2002). https://supreme.justia.com/cases/federal/us/535/234/case.pdf

Balon, R. (Ed.). (2016). *Practical guide to paraphilia and paraphilic disorders*. Springer International Publishing.

Bartky, S. L. (2015). *Femininity and domination: Studies in the phenomenology of oppression*. Routledge.

Bauer, R. (2014). *Queer BDSM intimacies: Critical consent and pushing boundaries*. Springer.

Berlin, F. S. (2014). Pedophilia and *DSM-5*: The importance of clearly defining the nature of a pedophilic disorder. *Journal of the American Academy of Psychiatry Law, 42*, 404–407.

Binet, A. (1887). Le fétichisme dans l'amour [Fetishism in love]. *Revue Philosophique. 24*, 143–167, 252–274.

Blanchard, R. (2010). The *DSM* diagnostic criteria for transvestic fetishism. *Archives of Sexual Behavior, 39*(2), 363–372.

Bloom, Z. D., Blount, A. J., Dillman Taylor, D. L., & Lipkin, G. (2019). The sexual values and behaviors discrepancy model. *Journal of Counseling Sexology & Sexual Wellness, 1*(2), 69–79. https://doi.org/10.34296/01021025

Bock, M. A., Pain, P., & Jhang, J. (2019). Covering nipples: News discourse and the framing of breastfeeding. *Feminist Media Studies, 19*(1), 53–69.

Braun-Harvey, D., & Vigorito, M. A. (2016). *Treating out of control sexual behavior: Rethinking sex addiction*. Springer Publishing Company.

Brown, A., Barker, E. D., & Rahman, Q. (2020). A systematic scoping review of the prevalence, etiological, psychological, and interpersonal factors associated with BDSM. *The Journal of Sex Research, 57*(6), 781–811.

Cannon, N. (2021, January 9). *Treating kinky couples with competence & compassion with Dr. Neil Cannon* [Webinar]. Denver Family Institute. https://denverfamilyinstitute.org/product/treating-kinky-couples-with-competence-compassion-with-dr-neil-cannon/

Cannon, N. P., & Holmberg-Sasek, A. (2020). Relationship counseling and sex therapy with kinky clients. In T. Nelson (Ed.), *Integrative sex & couples therapy: A therapist's guide to new and innovative approaches*, (pp. 99–122). PESI Publishing & Media.

Cantor, J. M. (2012). Is homosexuality a paraphilia? The evidence for and against. *Archives of Sexual Behavior, 41*(1), 237–247.

Cantor, J. M. (2014). "Gold-star" pedophiles in general sex therapy practice. *Principles and Practice of Sex Therapy, 19*, 219–234.

Cantor, J. M. (2018). Can pedophiles change? *Current Sexual Health Reports, 10*(4), 203–206.

Cantor, J. M., & McPhail, I. V. (2016). Non-offending pedophiles. *Current Sexual Health Reports, 8*(3), 121–128.

Chaline, E. R. (2010). The construction, maintenance, and evolution of gay SM sexualities and sexual identities: A preliminary description of gay SM sexual identity practices. *Sexualities, 13*(3), 338–356.

Christensen, A., Dimidjian, S., & Martell, C. R. (2015). Integrative behavioral couple therapy. In A. S. Gurman, J. L. Lebow, & D. K. Snyder (Eds.), *Clinical handbook of couple therapy* (pp. 61–94). The Guilford Press.

Cohen, L. J., Wilman-Depena, S., Barzilay, S., Hawes, M., Yaseen, Z., & Galynker, I. (2020). Correlates of chronic suicidal ideation among community-based minor-attracted persons. *Sexual Abuse, 32*(3), 273–300.

Coppens, V., Ten Brink, S., Huys, W., Fransen, E., & Morrens, M. (2020). A survey on BDSM-related activities: BDSM experience correlates with age of first exposure, interest profile, and role identity. *The Journal of Sex Research, 57*(1), 129–136.

Dailey, D. M. (1981). Sexual expression and aging. In F. J. Berghorn, D. E. Schafer, & Associates (Eds.), *The dynamics of aging: Original essays on the processes and experiences of growing old* (pp. 311–330). Westview Press.

Dant, T. (1996). Fetishism and the social value of objects 1. *The Sociological Review, 44*(3), 495–516.

Dickson, E. J. (2020, December). Why conservatives are so threatened by Harry Styles in a dress. *Rolling Stone*. https://www.rollingstone.com/culture/culture-news/harry-styles-dress-conservatives-threatened-1097874/

Downing, L. (2015). Heteronormativity and repronormativity in sexological "perversion theory" and the *DSM-5*'s "paraphilic disorder" diagnoses. *Archives of Sexual Behavior, 44*(5), 1139–1145.

Easton, D., & Liszt, C. A. (2000). *When someone you know is kinky*. Greenery Press.

Ellis, H. (2004). *Studies in the psychology of sex* (Vol. 5). The Project Gutenberg eBook, Studies in the Psychology of Sex. (Original work published 1927) https://www.gutenberg.org/files/13614/13614-h/13614-h.htm

Evans, D. T. (2013). Promoting sexual health and wellbeing: The role of the nurse. *Nursing Standard, 28*(10), 53–57. https://doi.org/10.7748/ns2013.11.28.10.53.e7654

Fedoroff, J. P., Di Gioacchino, L., & Murphy, L. (2013). Problems with paraphilias in the *DSM-5*. *Current Psychiatry Reports, 15*(8), 363.

Foucault, M. (1985). *Use of pleasure* (Vol. 2). Random House.

Fous, G. (2015). *Decoding your kink: Guide to explore share and enjoy your wildest sexual desires*. Create Space Publishing.

Freimond, C. M. (2013). *Navigating the stigma of pedophilia: The experiences of nine minor-attracted men in Canada* [Doctoral dissertation, Simon Frasier University].

Freud, S. (2017). *Three essays on the theory of sexuality: The 1905 edition*. Verso Books. (Original work published 1905)

Freund, K. (1990). Courtship disorders: Toward a biosocial understanding of voyeurism, exhibitionism, toucherism, and the preferential rape pattern. In L. Ellis & H. Hoffman (Eds.), *Crime in biological, social, and moral contexts* (pp. 100–114). Praeger.

Giami, A. (2015). Between *DSM* and *ICD*: Paraphilias and the transformation of sexual norms. *Archives of Sexual Behavior, 44*(5), 1127–1138.
Gochros, H. L. (1972). Sexual problems in social work practice. In H. L. Gocros & L. G. Schultz (Eds.), *Human sexuality and social work* (pp. 82–84). Association Press.
Gochros, H. L. (1974). A concentration in social work practice with sex-related problems. *Journal of Education for Social Work, 10*(2), 40–46. https://doi.org/10.1080/00220612.1974.10672308
Grady, M. D., Levenson, J. S., Mesias, G., Kavanagh, S., & Charles, J. (2019). "I can't talk about that": Stigma and fear as barriers to preventive services for minor-attracted persons. *Stigma and Health, 4*(4), 400–410.
Grundmann, D., Krupp, J., Scherner, G., Amelung, T., & Beier, K. M. (2016). Stability of self-reported arousal to sexual fantasies involving children in a clinical sample of pedophiles and hebephiles. *Archives of Sexual Behavior, 45*(5), 1153–1162.
Hall, R. C., & Hall, R. C. (2007). A profile of pedophilia: Definition, characteristics of offenders, recidivism, treatment outcomes, and forensic issues. *Mayo Clinic Proceedings, 82*(4), 457–471.
Hauk, S., & Holliday, B. (2019). *Living with crossdressing: Discovering your true identity* (J. Swain, Ed.). Charles Ingersoll.
Healthychildren.org. (n.d.) *Sexual behaviors in young children: What's normal, what's not?* American Academy of Pediatrics. https://www.healthychildren.org/English/ages-stages/preschool/Pages/Sexual-Behaviors-Young-Children.aspx
Heasman, A., & Foreman, T. (2019). Bioethical issues and secondary prevention for nonoffending individuals with pedophilia. *Cambridge Quarterly of Healthcare Ethics, 28*(2), 264–275.
Hopkins, T. A., Green, B. A., Carnes, P. J., & Campling, S. (2016). Varieties of intrusion: Exhibitionism and voyeurism. *Sexual Addiction & Compulsivity, 23*(1), 4–33.
Houtepen, J. A., Sijtsema, J. J., & Bogaerts, S. (2016). Being sexually attracted to minors: Sexual development, coping with forbidden feelings, and relieving sexual arousal in self-identified pedophiles. *Journal of Sex & Marital Therapy, 42*(1), 48–69.
Hugh-Jones, S., Gough, B., & Littlewood, A. (2005). Sexual exhibitionism as 'sexuality and individuality': A critique of psycho-medical discourse from the perspectives of women who exhibit. *Sexualities, 8*(3), 259–281. https://doi.org/10.1177/1363460705049576
Jahnke, S. (2018). The stigma of pedophilia: Clinical and forensic implications. *European Psychologist, 23*(2), 144–153.
Jahnke, S., Philipp, K., & Hoyer, J. (2015). Stigmatizing attitudes towards people with pedophilia and their malleability among psychotherapists in training. *Child Abuse & Neglect, 40*, 93–102.
Jain, S., Forrest, T. B., Baum, C., Curry, C., Bogomaz, M., Schubert, A. M., & Zeglin, R. J. (2022, February 17–20). *Group therapy for minor attracted persons* [Conference session]. Association of Specialists in Group Work, Atlantic Beach, FL, United States.
Joyal, C. C. (2015). Defining "normophilic" and "paraphilic" sexual fantasies in a population-based sample: On the importance of considering subgroups. *Sexual Medicine, 3*(4), 321–330.

Joyal, C. C., & Carpentier, J. (2017). The prevalence of paraphilic interests and behaviors in the general population: A provincial survey. *The Journal of Sex Research, 54*(2), 161–171.

Kleinplatz, P. J. (Ed.). (2012). *New directions in sex therapy: Innovations and alternatives.* Taylor & Francis.

Koops, T., Turner, D., Jahnke, S., Märker, V., & Briken, P. (2016). Stigmatisierung von Menschen mit sexuellem Interesse anKindern unter Sexualtherapeuten in Russland [Stigmatization of people with a sexual interest in children among sex therapists in Russia]. *Zeitschrift für Sexualforschung, 29,*131–146. https://doi.org/10.1055/s-0042-107735

Krafft-Ebing, R. (1998). *Psychopathia sexualis: With especial reference to the antipathic sexual instinct: A medico-forensic study.* Arcade Publishing. (Original work published 1886)

Kravets, D. (2009, May 28). U.S. manga obscenity conviction roils comics world. *Wired.* https://www.wired.com/2009/05/manga-porn/

Labrecque, F., Potz, A., Larouche, É., & Joyal, C. C. (2021). What is so appealing about being spanked, flogged, dominated, or restrained? Answers from practitioners of sexual masochism/submission. *The Journal of Sex Research, 58*(4), 409–423.

Långström, N. (2010). The *DSM* diagnostic criteria for exhibitionism, voyeurism, and frotteurism. *Archives of Sexual Behavior, 39*(2), 317–324.

Lasala, A., Paparo, F., Senese, V. P., & Perrella, R. (2020). An exploratory study of adult baby-diaper lovers' characteristics in an Italian online sample. *International Journal of Environmental Research and Public Health, 17*(4), Article 1371.

Levenson, J. S., & Grady, M. D. (2019). Preventing sexual abuse: Perspectives of minor-attracted persons about seeking help. *Sexual Abuse, 31*(8), 991–1013.

Levenson, J. S., Grady, M. D., & Morin, J. W. (2019). Beyond the "ick factor": Counseling non-offending persons with pedophilia. *Clinical Social Work Journal, 48*(4), 380–388.

Lievesley, R., Harper, C. A., & Elliott, H. (2020). The internalization of social stigma among minor-attracted persons: Implications for treatment. *Archives of Sexual Behavior, 49*(4), 1291–1304.

Lipscomb, R. (2014). *The clinical mental health experience of persons with paraphilic infantilism and autonepiophilia* [Doctoral dissertation, The American Academy of Clinical Sexologists]. https://understanding.infantilism.org/surveys/rjl_doctoral_dissertation.php

McCarthy, B. W., & McCarthy, E. (2009). *Discovering your couple sexual style.* Routledge.

Morse, E. (2019). Your guide to consensual non-consent. *Sex w/ Emily.* https://sexwithemily.com/consensual-non-consent/

Moser, C. (1999). The psychology of sadomasochism (S/M). In S. Wright (Ed.), *SM classics* (pp. 47–61). Harrington Park Press.

Moser, C. (2011). Yet another paraphilia definition fails. *Archives of Sexual Behavior, 40*(3), 483–485.

Moser, C. (2016). *DSM-5* and the paraphilic disorders: Conceptual issues. *Archives of Sexual Behavior, 45*(8), 2181–2186.

Moser, C. (2019). *DSM-5*, paraphilias, and the paraphilic disorders: Confusion reigns. *Archives of Sexual Behavior, 48*(3), 681–689.

Nelson, T. (Ed.). (2020). *Integrative sex & couples therapy: A therapist's guide to new and innovative approaches.* PESI Publishing & Media.

Ortmann, D., & Sprott, R. (2013). *Sexual outsiders: Understanding BDSM sexualities and communities.* Rowman & Littlefield Publishers.

Oswald, F., Lopes, A., Skoda, K., Hesse, C. L., & Pedersen, C. L. (2020). I'll show you mine so you'll show me yours: Motivations and personality variables in photographic exhibitionism. *The Journal of Sex Research, 57*(5), 597–609.

Pillai-Friedman, S., Pollitt, J. L., & Castaldo, A. (2015). Becoming kink-aware—A necessity for sexuality professionals. *Sexual and Relationship Therapy, 30*(2), 196–210.

Proeve, M., Anton, R., & Kenny, M. (2018). Effects of mindfulness-based cognitive therapy on shame, self-compassion and psychological distress in anxious and depressed patients: A pilot study. *Psychology and Psychotherapy, 91*(4), 434–449. https://doi.org/10.1111/papt.12170

Rees, G., & Garcia, J. R. (2017). All I need is shoe: An investigation into the obligatory aspect of sexual object fetishism. *International Journal of Sexual Health, 29*(4), 303–312.

Rind, B. (2017). Hebephilia and other chronophilic puzzles. *Archives of Sexual Behavior, 46*(1), 47–51.

Robinson, P. (1973). Havelock Ellis and modern sexual theory. *Salmagundi, 21*(Winter), 27–62.

Rogers, C. R. (1995). *On becoming a person: A therapist's view of psychotherapy.* Houghton Mifflin Harcourt.

Ruberg, B., Cullen, A. L., & Brewster, K. (2019). Nothing but a "titty streamer": Legitimacy, labor, and the debate over women's breasts in video game live streaming. *Critical Studies in Media Communication, 36*(5), 466–481.

Russell, A., & Zeglin, R. J. (2020, March 2). *Sex from A to Z LIVE—K is for kinky hormones* [Video podcast]. https://www.youtube.com/watch?v=WHTwcGoUZZo

Schiffer, B., & Vonlaufen, C. (2011). Executive dysfunctions in pedophilic and nonpedophilic child molesters. *The Journal of Sexual Medicine, 8*(7), 1975–1984.

Schwartz, M. F., & Southern, S. (2017). Recovery from sexual compulsivity. *Sexual Addiction & Compulsivity, 24*(3), 224–240. https://doi.org/10.1080/10720162.2017.1350229

Schwarz, O. (2010). Going to bed with a camera: On the visualization of sexuality and the production of knowledge. *International Journal of Cultural Studies, 13*(6), 637–656.

Scorolli, C., Ghirlanda, S., Enquist, M., Zattoni, S., & Jannini, E. A. (2007). Relative prevalence of different fetishes. *International Journal of Impotence Research, 19*(4), 432–437.

Sea, J., & Beauregard, E. (2018). The hebephiliac: Pedophile or teleiophiliac? *International Journal of Offender Therapy and Comparative Criminology, 62*(9), 2507–2526.

Seto, M. C. (2012). Is pedophilia a sexual orientation? *Archives of Sexual Behavior, 41*(1), 231–236.

Seto, M. C. (2017). The puzzle of male chronophilias. *Archives of Sexual Behavior, 46*(1), 3–22.

Shim, G., Lee, J. W., Lee, T., Lee, Y., & Lee, J. (2014). Research on the etiology of pedophilia through monozygotic twins with pedophilia: A case report. *Journal of Korean Neuropsychiatric Association, 53*(3), 186–190.

Stephens, S., Leroux, E., Skilling, T., Cantor, J. M., & Seto, M. C. (2017). Taxometric analyses of pedophilia utilizing self-report, behavioral, and sexual arousal indicators. *Journal of Abnormal Psychology, 126*(8), 1114–1119.

Stoléru, S. (2014). Reading the Freudian theory of sexual drives from a functional neuroimaging perspective. *Frontiers in Human Neuroscience, 8*, Article 157.

Strassberg, D. S., Eastvold, A., Kenney, J. W., & Suchy, Y. (2012). Psychopathy among pedophilic and nonpedophilic child molesters. *Child Abuse & Neglect, 36*(4), 379–382.

Tenbergen, G., Wittfoth, M., Frieling, H., Ponseti, J., Walter, M., Walter, H., Beier, K. M., Schiffer, B., & Kruger, T. H. C. (2015). The neurobiology and psychology of pedophilia: Recent advances and challenges. *Frontiers in Human Neuroscience, 9*, Article 344.

Tiidenberg, K., & Paasonen, S. (2019). Littles: Affects and aesthetics in sexual ageplay. *Sexuality & Culture, 23*(2), 375–393.

Tiktok. (2022, February). *Community guidelines.* https://www.tiktok.com/community-guidelines

Tumblr. (2020, July 16). *Community guidelines.* https://www.tumblr.com/policy/en/community

Turley, E. (2011). *"It started when I barked once when I was licking his boots!": A phenomenological study of the experience of bondage, discipline, dominance & submission, and sadism & masochism (BDSM)* [Doctoral dissertation, University of Huddersfield].

Vyskocilova, J., Prasko, J., Ociskova, M., Sedlackova, Z., & Mozny, P. (2015). Values and values work in cognitive behavioral therapy. *Activitas Nervosa Superior Rediviva, 57*(1-2), 40–48.

Walker, A. (2017). *Understanding resilience strategies among minor-attracted individuals* [Doctoral dissertation, City University of New York]. https://academicworks.cuny.edu/cgi/viewcontent.cgi?article=3317&context=gc_etds

Walker, A., Butters, R. P., & Nichols, E. (2021). "I would report it even if they have not committed anything": Social service students' attitudes toward minor-attracted people. *Sexual Abuse, 34*(1), 52–77. https://doi.org/10.1177/1079063221993480

Wallin & Klarich. (2020, February 6). Supreme Court sides with therapists on child pornography reporting law. *Southern California Defense Blog.* https://www.southerncaliforniadefenseblog.com/2020/02/supreme-court-sides-with-therapists-on-child-pornography-reporting-law.html

Wehrum, S., Klucken, T., Kagerer, S., Walter, B., Hermann, A., Vaitl, D., & Stark, R. (2013). Gender commonalities and differences in the neural processing of visual sexual stimuli. *The Journal of Sexual Medicine, 10*(5), 1328–1342.

Weiner, L., & Avery-Clark, C. (2014). Sensate focus: Clarifying the Masters and Johnson's model. *Sexual and Relationship Therapy, 29*(3), 307–319.

Weiner, L., & Avery-Clark, C. (2017). *Sensate focus in sex therapy: The illustrated manual.* Taylor & Francis.

Wiederman, M. W. (2003). Paraphilia and fetishism. *The Family Journal, 11*(3), 315–321.

World Health Organization. (2006). *Defining sexual health.*

Wright, S. (2010). Depathologizing consensual sexual sadism, sexual masochism, transvestic fetishism, and fetishism. *Archives of Sexual Behavior, 39*(6), 1229–1230.

Wurtele, S. K., & Kenny, M. C. (2011). Normative sexuality development in childhood: Implications for developmental guidance and prevention of childhood sexual abuse. *Counseling and Human Development, 43*(9), 1–24.
Yates, S. M., & Neuer-Colburn, A. A. (2019). Counseling the kink community: What clinicians need to know. *Journal of Counseling Sexology & Sexual Wellness, 1*(1), 14–22. https://doi.org/10.34296/01011007
Zamboni, B. D. (2018). Experiences of distress by participants in the adult baby/diaper lover community. *Sexual Relationships Therapy, 33,* 470–486. https://doi.org/10.1080/14681994.2018.1434312
Zeglin, R. J., Van Dam, D., & Hergenrather, K. C. (2018). An introduction to proposed human sexuality counseling competencies. *International Journal for the Advancement of Counselling, 40*(2), 105–121.

You Can Have Too Much Sex? The Line Between Sexual Expression and Addiction

Reginald W. Holt

Sex is a natural, healthy, and enjoyable part of life. Having sexual desires, thoughts, and fantasies and engaging in sexual behaviors are biologically occurring components of the human experience. And, as sexual health, sexual expression, and sexual freedom carve a pathway toward a more progressive and open society whose viewpoints are not as closely aligned with puritanical attitudes, people are now more than ever able to acknowledge their sexual practices and preferences. This pathway is not wide, however, nor is it traveled by all.

Sexuality is a complicated subject that is not easily embraced by everyone. Societal traditions, religious dogmas, cultural beliefs, individual prejudices, and clinical discrepancies have conditioned many people to consider sex as something that is taboo, distasteful, forbidden, or pathological. Deconstructing sexuality and grouping its practices into nice, tidy categories of "healthy and normal" versus "unhealthy and abnormal" is a problematic and risky task because there is no definitive standardized diagnostic agreement on recognizing when the line is crossed.

Not everyone participates in the same sexual practices, and those individuals whose safe and legal erotic predilections fall outside "customary" behaviors may be maligned by others or labeled as a clinical problem when evaluated against a traditional substance addiction model. Should the counselor (who is considered to be the expert in the art and science of counseling) or the client (who is considered to be the expert in their own life) differentiate nonconforming sexual activities from sex-related problems, or is it the aggregate of the two? How do counselors effectively navigate between a sex positive approach and a pathology-based model? What are the decisions counselors should make upon deliberating how to effectively work with clients who approach them with concerns related to their sexual interests and activities? It is anticipated that by the end of this chapter, the reader will have a newfound perspective that helps inform the answers to these questions.

The Neuroscience of Pleasure

With the possible exception of adults who engage in consensual sexual behaviors such as bondage, discipline, dominance, submission, sadism, and masochism (BDSM), an existential dilemma of humans is that we want to experience pleasure and avoid pain. Although the desire of obtaining pleasure and shunning pain can lead to suffering (Low, 2000), humans nonetheless want to feel good, and sex undeniably fits the bill! The reinforcement properties of pleasure are rooted in the brain's reward pathway, whereby an increase in dopamine, a neurotransmitter that makes a person feel good, occurs when natural rewards such as food and sex are presented (Veach & Moro, 2018), thus helping the brain to remember and encouraging repetition of the pleasurable activity (National Institute on Drug Abuse, 2020). Sex also feels good for another primary reason—the excitement that is experienced in anticipation of sex, the arousal that arises during sex, and the euphoria that occurs at the peak of sex are all powerful motivators designed to ensure survival of the species (Georgiadis & Kringelbach, 2012). In fact, neuroscience offers evidence that engaging in sexual behaviors provides sensory pleasure by hitting hedonic hot spots in the brain, and the greater the "hedonic impact" (Peciña et al., 2006, p. 500) that a behavior has, the more likely we are to repeatedly pursue and excessively participate in that behavior. The same psychological components of *liking* (hedonic impact of the reward), *wanting* (motivation for the reward), and *learning* (conditioning for future rewards) involve the same brain circuits regardless of whether the route to pleasure is food, drugs, or sex (Berridge & Kringelbach, 2011).

Nosological Classification Constraints

The neuroscience of pleasure forms the foundation of one paradigm that postulates addiction is a brain-based disease (Volkow et al., 2016). Although natural rewards such as having sex or eating food are less addictive than drugs (National Institute on Drug Abuse, 2020), research involving neuroimaging indicates that various activities that result in feeling pleasure all impact the brain's reward network in overlapping and similar patterns (Berridge & Kringelbach, 2015). Regardless of this assertion, the only formal diagnostic language in the *Diagnostic and Statistical Manual of Mental Disorders* (5th ed.; *DSM-5*; American Psychiatric Association [APA], 2013) that has been conceptualized to identify addiction pertains to substance-related addictive disorders and gambling disorder. These circumscribed inclusions appear to be, in part, because "there is insufficient peer-reviewed evidence to establish the diagnostic criteria and course descriptions needed" (APA, 2013, p. 481) to identify sex addiction as a mental disorder. And, despite gambling disorder being the only non-substance-related addictive disorder in the *DSM-5*, sexual addiction is a term that is commonly applied when discussing the condition of people who feel their sex-related urges, thoughts, and behaviors are out of control (Braun-Harvey & Vigorito, 2016).

Assorted nomenclatures are interchangeably used when referring to sex addiction. These include hypersexuality, sexual compulsivity, sexual impulsivity, and out-of-control sexual behavior. Although hypersexual disorder, a nonparaphilic mental disorder promoted by Kafka (2010), was excluded from the *DSM-5* because an operational definition and associated diagnostic criteria could not be uniformly agreed upon (Halpern, 2011), "sex addiction" is a frequently used descriptor in clinical settings. The proposed diagnostic criteria for hypersexual disorder was as follows:

A. Over a period of at least 6 months, recurrent and intense sexual fantasies, sexual urges, or sexual behaviors in association with 3 or more of the following 5 criteria:
  A1. Time consumed by sexual fantasies, urges or behaviors repetitively interferes with other important (non-sexual) goals, activities and obligations.
  A2. Repetitively engaging in sexual fantasies, urges or behaviors in response to dysphoric mood states (e.g., anxiety, depression, boredom, irritability).
  A3. Repetitively engaging in sexual fantasies, urges or behaviors in response to stressful life events.
  A4. Repetitive but unsuccessful efforts to control or significantly reduce these sexual fantasies, urges or behaviors.
  A5. Repetitively engaging in sexual behaviors while disregarding the risk for physical or emotional harm to self or others.
B. There is clinically significant personal distress or impairment in social, occupational or other important areas of functioning associated with the frequency and intensity of these sexual fantasies, urges or behaviors.
C. These sexual fantasies, urges or behaviors are not due to the direct physiological effect of an exogenous substance (e.g., a drug of abuse or a medication)
  Specify if:
    Masturbation
    Sexually explicit material
    Sexual Behavior with Consenting Adults
    Cybersex
    Telephone Sex
    Strip Clubs
    Other: _______

(Kafka, 2010, p. 379)

Although the *DSM-5* does not formally acknowledge addiction to sex-related behaviors, it devotes an entire category to paraphilic disorders. *Paraphilia*, which is defined as "any intense and persistent sexual interest other than sexual interest in genital stimulation or preparatory fondling with phenotypically normal, physically mature, consenting human partners" (APA, 2013, p. 685), is distinguished from a *paraphilic disorder*, which is described as "a paraphilia that is currently causing distress or impairment to the individual or a paraphilia whose satisfaction has entailed personal harm, or risk of harm, to others" (APA, 2013, pp. 685–686). It is interesting that the *DSM-5* denotes that the existence of a paraphilia is not fully sufficient to warrant a diagnosis of paraphilic disorder, nor does simply having a paraphilia necessitate the need for clinical services. As critiqued by Moser (2016), a brief 6-month timeframe of experiencing distress related to a paraphilia could potentially transition it into a paraphilic disorder, but the APA offers no rationale to explain this distinction. Adding to this inconsistency, considering that people without paraphilic interests commonly experience distress yet are not candidates for a psychiatric diagnosis, what makes the impairment associated with a paraphilia different from the impairment that is not so associated (Moser, 2016)? If the *DSM*-5 specifies that having a paraphilia is not enough to justify the existence of a mental disorder, counselors should be informed so they will not unknowingly harm their clients by basing their diagnosis and intervention on the duration and impact of the client's sexual interests and behaviors.

Another attempt by the APA (2013) to offer a clarifying definition is that "there are also specific paraphilias that are generally better described as *preferential* sexual interests than as intense sexual interests" (p. 685). The *DSM*-5 does not provide a rationale and there is a lack of research to offer supporting evidence that clearly distinguishes why sexual interest in genital stimulation or preparatory fondling with a mature and consenting partner is not a paraphilia but having sexual interest in a nongenital body part (e.g., the feet) with a mature and consenting partner automatically meets the definition of a paraphilia, and because of this, it can be easily implied that any sexual interest outside what is considered "normal" is therefore anomalous (Moser, 2016). The *DSM-5*'s conceptualization may inadvertently lead some counselors to pathologize clients if they strictly base their clinical decisions on the APA's interpretation of "unusual" sexual practices.

Despite its exclusion as a non-substance-related addictive disorder in the *DSM-5*, various theories exist regarding so-called "excessive" nonparaphilic sexual behaviors, including paradigms based on (a) obsessive-compulsive disorder, (b) impulse-control disorder, (c) out-of-control excessive sexual behavior, and (d) sexual addiction (Garcia & Thibaut, 2010). Braun-Harvey and Vigorito (2020) described four pathology-based models to categorize sexual behaviors that deviate from healthy sexual expression: (a) sexual addiction, (b) sexual impulsivity, (c) sexual compulsivity, and (d) hypersexual disorder. Non-pathology-based models of sexual dysregulation include it being a symptom of (a) a pre-existing medical or psychiatric condition, (b) moral incongruence, or (c) a psychosexual problem (Braun-Harvey & Vigorito, 2020).

The World Health Organization (WHO) defined *compulsive sexual behavior disorder* in the 11th revision of the *International Classification of Diseases* (*ICD-11*) as

> a persistent pattern of failure to control intense, repetitive sexual impulses or urges resulting in repetitive sexual behaviour. Symptoms may include repetitive sexual activities becoming a central focus of the person's life to the point of neglecting health and personal care or other interests, activities and responsibilities; numerous unsuccessful efforts to significantly reduce repetitive sexual behaviour; and continued repetitive sexual behaviour despite adverse consequences or deriving little or no satisfaction from it. The pattern of failure to control intense, sexual impulses or urges and resulting repetitive sexual behaviour is manifested over an extended period of time (e.g., 6 months or more), and causes marked distress or significant impairment in personal, family, social, educational, occupational, or other important areas of functioning. Distress that is entirely related to moral judgments and disapproval about sexual impulses, urges, or behaviours is not sufficient to meet this requirement. (WHO, 2022, Description section)

Although the *ICD-11* offers a diagnostic classification system for compulsive sexual behavior disorder, it falls under the parent category of impulse control disorders because, again, there is a lack of strong evidence to support that its characteristics are comparable to the processes observed in the formation of substance use and addictive disorders (Kraus et al., 2018).

Clinical Considerations

The first description of hypersexuality made comparisons to excessive sexual behavior with excessive drinking and gambling (Orford, 1978). Carnes (1983, 2001) took this further by describing sex addiction as a pathological-based condition that can be viewed in parallel with substance addiction: "The addict substitutes a sick relationship to an event or a process for a healthy relationship with others. The addict's relationship with a mood-altering experience becomes central to his life" (Carnes, 2001, p. 14). Carne's sexual addiction model is exemplified by a four-phase sequence that becomes amplified after each pass through the cycle: (a) preoccupation, (b) ritualization, (c) compulsive sexual behavior, and (d) despair. According to Carnes (2001), sexual addiction originates from the person's faulty belief system that causes impaired thinking and paves the way for entering the four-step addiction cycle that ultimately results in the unmanageability of the person's life.

The initial Sexual Addiction Screening Test (SAST) was developed by Carnes (1989), who later offered a revised version (SAST-R; Carnes et al., 2010) that was more relevant to gender and sexual orientation. The SAST-R, a 45-item nondiagnostic screening tool that assesses the addictive dimensions of preoccupation, loss of control, and relationship and affect disturbances, is designed for individuals to subjectively identify potential sexually compulsive or addictive behavior. Readers are encouraged to review all 45 items in the SAST-R and the full description of the scoring system (Carnes et al., 2010); however, the following are some sample items:

28. I have subscribed to or regularly purchased or rented sexually explicit materials (magazines, videos, books or online sexually explicit material).
37. I have maintained multiple romantic or sexual relationships at the same time.
39. I have regularly engaged in sadomasochistic behavior.

Critics of the SAST-R ask clinicians to consider if they want to use such criteria "to determine whether or not [clients] are 'sex addicts'" (Klein, 2003, p. 9), especially considering some items may imply that using sexually explicit material, having sex with strangers or multiple partners, and/or searching the internet to romantically or sexually connect with others are warning indicators of having a sexual addiction. It is therefore important for counselors to be mindful of who and what guides their clinical judgments when assessing and defining the sexual health of their clients; otherwise, they risk causing iatrogenic injury when basing decisions on models that claim pathology for forms of sexual expression that differ from traditional and established sociocultural and political doctrine. In the case of assessing for sexual addiction, *iatrogenesis* specifically refers to the possibility of inadvertently manufacturing a condition that is founded on narrow diagnostic procedures or limited case conceptualization skills. To mitigate this threat, Braun-Harvey and Vigorito (2020) recommend completing a comprehensive biopsychosocial assessment, conducting a qualitative client interview that includes an examination of values conflict, and using non-pathology-based scales to explore what "out-of-control" sexual behaviors signify for the client. Such scales may include the Sexual Symptom Assessment Scale (Raymond et al., 2007), the Hypersexual Behavior Consequences Scale (Reid et al., 2012), or the Sexual Inhibition/ Sexual Excitation Scales (Janssen et al., 2002). Additional reviews and recommendations are offered by Womack et al. (2013), who identified an extensive list of 32 measures comprising clinical interviews as well as self-report questionnaires of general symptoms and consequences associated with hypersexual behavior.

Carnes (2001) promoted sexual addiction recovery on work modeled after the 12 Steps of Alcoholics Anonymous, whereby treatment includes participating in a support group and being mentored by a sponsor. One such group is Sexaholics Anonymous (SA), whose "only requirement for membership is a desire to stop lusting and become sexually sober" (SA, n.d.-b, para. 1). SA (n.d.-b) defines sexual *sobriety* for the married sexaholic as

> having no form of sex with self or with persons other than the spouse. In SA's sobriety definition, the term "spouse" refers to one's partner in a marriage between a man and a woman. For the unmarried sexaholic, sexual sobriety means freedom from sex of any kind. And for all of us, single and married alike, sexual sobriety also includes progressive victory over lust. (para. 4)

Upon reviewing the tenets of SA, it appears that anyone outside a monogamous heteronormative legal union is excluded from its fellowship. This condition inherently pathologizes and shames people who have open relationships, and perhaps more grievously, any individual who is part of the lesbian, gay, bisexual, transgender, queer plus other identities (LGBTQ+) community. Gay and lesbian people already experience sexual stigma (Salvati et al., 2018), which negatively affects their mental health by causing depressive symptoms (Lewis et al., 2003), social anxiety (Pachankis et al., 2018), and psychological distress (Hatzenbuechler et al., 2009). Additionally, various research has been cited (Cook & Cottrell, 2021) indicating gay men are often stigmatized because of being labeled as sexually promiscuous; however, the attitudes of men regarding sex are generally more open than those of women, including being more accepting of and having fewer conditions for participating in casual sex.

SA (n.d.-a) advocates that "any form of sex with one's self or with partners other than the spouse is progressively addictive and destructive . . . and true sobriety includes progressive victory over lust" (para. 2). And although SA offers a caveat that they can only speak for themselves, this viewpoint continues to perpetuate the belief that any form of sexuality or sexual expression that falls outside the arena built by conventional values and societal/cultural mores is improper and potentially injurious. It is important to understand that sexual health is "not merely the absence of disease, dysfunction or infirmity" (WHO, n.d., para. 1). Expecting people to refrain from sexual behaviors is not equivalent to promoting abstinence from substances any more than it would be to advise persons with eating disorders to give up food: Humans do not have to drink alcohol or use drugs to survive, but being sexual is a fundamental part of human growth and development.

Other Perspectives

Marty Klein, considered a leader in the field of sex therapy as well as an advocate of sex positive sexual health, is a critic of the sex addiction movement who believes their objective is to "put everyone in the missionary position" (Klein, 1998, Summary section, para. 3). In a 2003 article, Klein outlined suppositions of the sex addiction model that contrast with the views of many sexologists:

> sex and sexual desire are dangerous
> there is only one "best" way to express sexuality
> sex that enhances "intimacy" is the best sex
> imagination has no healthy role in sexuality
> people need to be told what kinds of sex are wrong/bad
> if you feel out of control, you are out of control
> laws and social norms define sexual health. (p. 8)

Klein (2003) also indicated that because of these assumptions, the sex addiction model is pathology-oriented (which also pertains to nonproblematic behavior), clinically incomplete, culturally bound, without individual and situational context, and politically exploited.

As a replacement for the sex addiction model, Klein (2003) encouraged a sex positive clinical model that does not stigmatize diverse sexual practices. Characteristics of this sexual health model require counseling professionals to consider the subjective context (including the client's perspective), have clinical sophistication (including differential diagnostic conceptualizations), place an emphasis on personal agency (including how people can be empowered to make individual changes), and have cross-cultural insight (including recognizing how culture influences sexual expression). To illustrate this concept, Table 21.1 displays the specific way Klein (2003, p. 10) compared assessments of client behaviors by two types of clinicians: those who follow a sex addiction model, and those who take a more sex positive approach.

Adding to the argument that caution should be exercised when considering sex addiction as an actual diagnosable disorder is the view that sex-related problems may be a manifestation of a primary mental disorder or attributed to attempts to manage negative affect states (Kraus et al., 2016). A central theme exists within the various criteria for the *ICD-11* compulsive sexual behavior disorder (WHO, 2022) and the *DSM-5* paraphilic disorders (APA, 2013) that do not include criminal sexual acts involving nonconsenting persons or children (i.e., sexual masochism disorder, fetishistic disorder, transvestic disorder). This diagnostic motif specifies that sexual impulses, fantasies, urges, or behaviors must result in negative consequences, distress, or impairment in functioning in order to meet criteria for the disorder (APA, 2013).

It has been suggested that some of the distress experienced by individuals may be related to the shame and guilt brought on by violating societal, cultural, or religious mores (Grubbs et al., 2015) or internalized judgments related to conflicts with personal values (Braun-Harvey & Vigorito, 2020). It is plausible that core issues such as depression, anxiety, unprocessed trauma, relationship dissatisfaction, and social discomfort may better explain why a person presents with sex-related problems. This view is best supported by Moser (2013), who challenged the hypersexual disorder proposal:

Table 21.1

The Sexual Addiction Model (SAM) Compared Against the Clinical Sexology (CS) Perspective

Behavior	*SAM Diagnosis*	*CS Possible Diagnosis*
Masturbates twice daily	Sex addict	Not necessarily a problem
Extramarital affairs	Sex addict	Existential dilemma
Wants partner sex daily	Sex addict	Not necessarily a problem; personality disorder
Enjoys sadomasochism	Sex addict	Not necessarily a problem
Uses inappropriate come-ons	Sex addict	Socially inept; narcissism
Exhibitionism	Sex addict	Obsessive compulsive disorder
Wants non-monogamy	Sex addict	Borderline; adventurous
Married but cruises bathrooms	Sex addict	Tormented about sexual orientation
Fetish behavior	Sex addict	Self-aware
Commercial sex	Sex addict	Committed to marriage; social anxiety
Uses internet porn	Sex addict	Depression; dissatisfied with sexual partner

> There are individuals who perceive their sexual behavior "as out of control" and there is no dispute that some of these individuals could benefit from psychiatric intervention. Nonetheless, the individual's perception of the problem may not be an accurate assessment or the "problem" may not be an actual problem. Appropriate clinical evaluation may demonstrate that their sexual behavior is a symptom or a result of another disorder (which should become the focus of treatment rather than their sexual behavior) or that the individual's behavior is within normal limits. (p. 49)

If clients obtain pleasure and reward through sex as a coping strategy to ease biopsychosocial difficulties related to larger, unaddressed problems, it is crucial that their counselors assess all potential underlying issues and address them accordingly, rather than using standard addiction recovery-based models (i.e., being abstinent while working a 12-step program).

This is not to suggest that recovery communities and 12-step programs are not beneficial or valuable. Countless people have found their way to a healthier lifestyle through the fellowship and support offered by these groups. When counselors consider these as a viable resource, it is essential to keep in mind each client's individual experiences, characteristics, and needs. Compared with SA, Sexual Compulsives Anonymous (n.d.) is a more affirmative 12-step group that allows individuals to define their own sexual sobriety as well as design their own recovery plan without attempting to inhibit sexuality. Sexual Compulsives Anonymous is open to all sexual orientations and there are no predefined admission requirements.

Not only does the absence of a distinct and universally accepted term with an accompanying definition for "sex addiction" represent a clinical conundrum when attempting to discern the client's issues and conditions, another significant shortcoming exists when counselors casually base their assessment and diagnosis of problematic sexual behaviors on traditional models of substance addiction criteria. The *DSM-5* outlines the features and criteria needed to diagnose substance-related and addictive disorders, which can include lack of control, experience of cravings, development of tolerance, and occurrence of withdrawal (APA, 2013), but that does not mean counselors should overlay these onto a possible behavioral addiction that is not yet clearly identified and understood.

Although not considered a formal framework to diagnose addiction, Volkow et al.'s (2016) neuroscientific model includes three stages where each correlates with a neural and behavioral feature. The first stage, *binge and intoxication*, is when an addictive substance is ingested, and the person subsequently experiences its pleasurable, rewarding, and euphoric effect. The next stage, *withdrawal and negative affect*, is when the pleasurable effect has dissipated, and the person subsequently experiences a negative emotional and/or physical state in the absence of the addictive substance. The third stage, *preoccupation and anticipation*, is when the person craves the effect of the addictive substance after a period of abstinence and begins planning or obsessing to obtain it.

Bearing in mind the characteristics of addiction as described in the *DSM-5* and in Volkow et al.'s model, the basic application of clinical features, diagnostic criteria, and conventional treatments for substance use disorders with clients who are in conflict with their sexual behaviors is perplexing. A discrepancy that adds to this confusion is the presence of tolerance and withdrawal that are included in many of the *DSM-5* addictive disorders, such as alcohol, cannabis, and opioid use disorders (APA, 2013), are said to not conclusively exist for sex (Kraus et al., 2016; Prause et al., 2017).

Although research has shown a positive correlation between sexually explicit material cravings and sexual compulsivity (Rosenberg & Kraus, 2014), more work is needed to examine whether cravings (another criterion listed in the *DSM-5* for substance use disorders) have a role in problematic sex-related behaviors (Kraus et al., 2016).

The Intersection of Sexuality and Substance Addiction

Up to this point in the chapter, attention has been placed on comparing unconventional forms of sexual expression against unestablished models of sexual addiction. It would be remiss, however, to not briefly mention the influence of substance-related addiction on sexuality. The damaging effects of acute and chronic abuse of alcohol and drugs on sexual health and wellness are numerous and well known. The harmful outcomes, which are partly related to impaired judgment, lowered inhibitions, and dysregulated emotions, include engaging in risky sexual behaviors (e.g., unprotected sex), committing acts of sexual assault and violence (e.g., nonconsensual sex), contracting sexually transmitted infections (e.g., viral hepatitis via needle sharing), experiencing sexual dysfunction (e.g., reduced libido/sexual desire, impotence), and having relationship difficulties (e.g., infidelity, lack of intimacy).

Binge and long-term abuse can lead to pernicious behavioral, emotional, physical, and relational outcomes, all which need to be a focus of treatment when a correlation exists between unhealthy sexual expression and substance-related addiction. Braun-Harvey (2011) coined the term "sex/drug-linked behavior" (p. 4) because a client's sexual life may be intertwined with their individual pattern of alcohol and drug use. For example, a person may engage in the practice of *chemsex* to lower inhibitions and increase arousal and pleasure while participating in lengthy sexual sessions with multiple partners. Taking part in this sexual activity while intentionally being under the influence of drugs may create an indistinguishable relationship between sexual expression and substance use (Braun-Harvey & Vigorito, 2016).

The pattern of sexual activities and substance-related addictive behaviors should be assessed by the counselor in order to identify the impact they have on a client's overall level of functioning as well as understand the relationship between the two. Equally important is the need to discuss how to achieve sexual health while concurrently engaging in the addiction recovery process. A common addiction treatment intervention is to advise clients to be celibate outside a committed relationship throughout the initial year of sobriety. Although the *Big Book* (Alcoholics Anonymous World Services, 2001) does not directly instruct newcomers to avoid dating and sexual intimacy, such is the standard recommendation colloquially known in recovery circles as the "one-year rule."

This guidance is offered due to various beliefs that romantic or sexual relations may trigger a relapse for the vulnerable newcomer, including the fear they may interfere with the person maintaining a primary focus on their recovery or the belief they may possibly lead to a cross addiction. Granted, these may be valid concerns for certain individuals who will need to address these factors within their relapse prevention plan, but room must be left to consider if recovery can be achieved while concurrently engaging in sex. It is important for addiction counselors to allow space for this alternate view, considering that sexuality is part of being human and that avoiding sex does not disrupt sex/drug-linked behaviors (Braun-Harvey & Vigorito, 2016).

The need to help clients with acute degrees of sex/drug-link behaviors develop individualized relapse prevention strategies that enable them to achieve a healthy sexual life without using substances has been emphasized (Braun-Harvey, 2011; Braun-Harvey & Vigorito, 2016). It goes without saying that addiction counselors should be well versed in traditional substance-related recovery models and interventions. But what needs to be noted is that they should also be comfortable discussing the client's sexuality, assessing for sex/drug-linked behavior, addressing sexual issues that may interfere with addiction recovery, and helping the client establish healthy sexual expectations and relationships (both in treatment and while in recovery).

Case Example

Derrick is a 24-year-old single, gay cisgender man who presented for individual counseling. Other than stating he was previously involved in therapy with another clinician, he did not readily talk about his past during the initial phase of counseling, preferring instead to generally vent about his day-to-day experiences. He was highly guarded and easily irritated anytime the counselor attempted to deepen the conversation and more fully understand his experiences. Once the therapeutic alliance became stronger and Derrick believed he could possibly trust the counselor, he gradually opened up and began sharing his history. Over time, especially in the past year, he reported becoming increasingly angry and resentful because he "expects rejection" from others. As a result, he isolates at home when not at work. He stated that anger "rages" inside of him because he feels hurt, misunderstood, and betrayed by his former therapist. He admitted he was initially reluctant to reveal to the present counselor that he was gay because he feared condemnation—a worry he regularly experiences in both his personal and professional life. The present counselor gave Derrick space to tell his story, which progressively unfolded over several sessions.

Derrick was raised in a small, Midwest town by his biological parents. His mother was deeply religious and maintained strict beliefs about what behaviors she considered to be morally "right and wrong." His father, whom Derrick called a "working class man's man," maintained conservative political views. Instead of providing various details regarding his early life, Derrick said he needed to talk about a certain subject that he has been struggling with for several years: his sexuality. He began by informing his counselor that his first sexual experience occurred at the age of 15 when he had intercourse with a 16-year-old female classmate. Before and after the encounter, he was uncomfortable when he thought about having sex with girls. He felt attraction only to other boys but did not admit this to others. He occasionally overheard comments made by family members, especially his father, that gay people are "sick and destined for hell." To alleviate his fear about possibly being gay, he adopted a counterphobic attitude and had consensual sex with as many girls as possible throughout high school (he estimated at least nine different girls, if not more, during his junior and senior years). His father, who regularly called Derrick a "sissy" during late childhood and early adolescence, began bragging to his friends about his son's sexual bravado with the "ladies." Derrick's interpretation of his father's proud accolades was that heteronormative sex resulted in acceptance and recognition because he was now "a real man."

Once he left home at the age of 18 to attend college in another state, Derrick continued to suppress his feelings of attraction to men; however, this was becoming more difficult with the passing of time. While living in the dorm at the university, he would become sexually aroused when other men would go in and out of the community shower stalls. He relieved these feelings by regularly masturbating while watching straight sex videos on free internet porn websites. After recognizing he focused more on the male actors than the female ones, he soon transitioned to the gay sexually explicit material channels. This was when he realized he needed to experience live man-to-man sexual contact.

Now that Derrick was far away from his childhood environment, including the repressive attitude of his hypermasculine father, he mustered the courage to enter a local park that was rumored to be an after-dark cruising spot for men who want to have sex with other men. It was not long before he was noticed by another man who approached and propositioned him for oral sex. Although Derrick felt anxiety about this exchange, the sexual excitement he experienced overruled his fear. With this one encounter, he felt more pleasure than any of the times he had sex with girls in high school. After years of struggling with his sexual identity, he allowed himself to internally acknowledge that he was "probably" gay, but instead of feeling relief, he experienced guilt when he considered his recent behaviors. He refused to tell anyone, because he believed he would be kicked out of the all-male dorm, expelled from the university, or worse, rejected by his family and friends.

Over the next few years, Derrick began secretly going to gay nightclubs in a nearby city. He initially drank alcohol to lower his anxiety about doing this but soon learned that he was also less sexually restrained when under the influence. There were times when Derrick became so intoxicated and uninhibited that he could not remember if he or his partners wore condoms. He would have sex with a different man (and sometimes a group of men) each time he went to the bar, either having sex in a bathroom stall, the parking lot, or a stranger's apartment. On a few occasions, Derrick "hooked up" with men that he met through online gay social networking apps. He realized he particularly felt empowered during moments of pursuing other men, especially when he assumed the role as "the dominant."

Although he recognized that having sex with men was more fulfilling and sexually rewarding for him than with women, he felt tremendous shame about his sexual orientation. He sporadically tried to conquer his sexual feelings by avoiding gay bars or deleting his hookup apps, but he eventually returned to having anonymous gay sex, which, he assumed, was his only available option apart from trying to deny his true sexual feelings. He dreamed of having a "real" relationship with another man but believed he would be shunned by his family (and possibly his extended community) if he truly tried to live an authentic life. In addition, he was tormented with existential anxiety of permanently being alone, because he predicted no one would be in a long-term, romantic partnership with him once they heard of his past sordid sexual escapades. Although he previously turned away from the teachings and beliefs of his church, he prayed to be "normal" and wished he was sexually attracted to women instead of men. He felt worthless as a man and started hating himself for being gay. His lack of focus, motivation, and energy began impacting the quality of his work. It was at this point that Derrick became very depressed and scheduled an appointment to see a therapist.

Derrick provided an account of his sex-related experiences and problems during the first session with this therapist. After administering the SAST-R, the therapist informed Derrick that he seemed to have an addiction to sex and needed to attend therapy sessions on a regular basis while concurrently participating in SA. Derrick was caught off guard by this diagnosis, but he was becoming convinced that he must be a sex addict after answering "yes" to many items on the SAST-R and hearing the professional recommendations of the therapist. Based on the same interventions used for other types of addiction, the therapist prescribed a treatment plan of abstaining from sexual behaviors of any kind while Derrick learned to manage his sexual urges. Although he had a lot of work to do, he felt relief because now there was language to identify his problem as well as a corresponding plan to address it.

Derrick visited the website of SA to locate a nearby meeting. While there, he noticed the description of their fellowship, whereby men and women help each other achieve and maintain sexual sobriety through a collective sharing of experiences; their definition of sexual sobriety and recommendations for recovery; and their explanation of the term spouse to mean a married man and woman. Derrick immediately had trepidations but thought that if he wanted to get better, he needed to follow the recommendations of his therapist. Derrick attended his first SA group within the week. He was apprehensive about disclosing intimate details of his personal life to a room full of people he had never met (especially since he still needed clarity about this recovery group's intention and expectations); however, he felt more at ease once he walked in and was immediately greeted by two men who welcomed him to the meeting. He was offered a seat and informed that he could listen to the group discussion or talk about whatever he wanted to share; there was no pressure to do anything he did not want to do. As he settled in, he noticed a poster on the wall that listed the 12 Steps of SA. He noticed statements such as being "powerless over lust" and turning your life "over to the care of God." He became more confused as well as uneasy as these words triggered memories of being raised by a religious mother and how immoral he felt because of his sexuality. He wondered whether he had made a mistake in coming to the group, whether it was for straight people only, if he would have to suppress his sexuality in order to feel better, and whether there was any hope for his recovery or if he was a "lost cause." As he listened, he could not help but wonder if he would be judged by the group if he told his story of having clandestine sex with men and being promiscuous with random strangers. He heard his father's voice whisper in his ear, "Of course they will. You're nothing but a perverted homo!" Derrick stayed for the duration of the meeting but quickly exited after it ended.

The following week he saw his therapist for a follow-up appointment. Derrick informed that he did not intend to return to SA meetings, stating, "They seem like very nice people who want to help and I don't begrudge anyone, but it's just not for me." The therapist suggested that Derrick may be misinterpreting the group's purpose as well as allowing his discomfort regarding his diagnosis to interfere with complying with his prescribed treatment protocol. The therapist advised Derrick to focus on managing his sex addiction by working on a recovery plan or his life would inevitably remain "unmanageable." Derrick was uncertain and remained hesitant. After a lengthy back-and-forth debate occurred between the two, the therapist finally indicated that he does not typically work harder than his clients, so Derrick should come back when he was ready. Even though Derrick felt like he was being reprimanded for not agreeing, he indicated he would consider these recommendations. Derrick left the session feeling worse than he did before entering therapy. He felt rejected by the therapist when he did not readily cooperate with the treatment plan, which only added to the guilt Derrick already experienced. He remained confused, misunderstood, and, for the first time, angry and resentful. Derrick canceled his next appointment, believing therapy could not help.

Over the next several months, Derrick continued to be depressed and his resentment escalated. Other than going to work, he withdrew from others believing this was the only way he could avoid sex with men as well as be protected from rejection. When he started thinking about how he would be better off dead, he decided he should try therapy one more time but with a different provider. This is where a return to the beginning of this case scenario occurs. Derrick's new counselor listened with patience and compassion until he finished telling his story and then asked Derrick's permission before offering a different interpretation of his experiences.

Derrick actively listened as the counselor proposed that the familial, religious, and societal influences in Derrick's background more than likely contributed to his conflict about being gay. And because he feared being disowned by his family, punished by God, and disregarded by society, he developed internalized homophobia as a defensive reaction. Derrick had sex with many girls during high school hoping that he could change. Although this plan ultimately did not work, he inadvertently received praise and positive attention from his father for the first time in his life (which unfortunately only reinforced Derrick's desire to be straight). Derrick attempted to subdue his feelings toward men but because being a human involves sexual feelings and experiences, he initially found an outlet through gay sexually explicit material. When his sexual desire intensified to needing actual intimate human contact, it was understandable that he chose covert ways to find pleasure while protecting his privacy. Once he discovered various ways to secretly meet men, he experienced a period of hypersexuality, which the counselor normalized by explaining this is a common outcome for some people who did not have a supportive coming out process.

Derrick's sex/drug-linked patterns were also assessed by the counselor. Derrick's abuse of alcohol was possibly a coping strategy that offered him the courage to have sex with men while providing temporary relief from negative feeling states. And despite the sex being stimulating and rewarding, Derrick felt guilty afterward, because needing to get drunk before having promiscuous sex with strangers was in conflict with his core values. When the counselor indicated it is feasible to integrate sexual health into life without abusing substances, Derrick requested to incorporate this as a goal within his overall treatment plan.

When Derrick initially went to therapy to sort through his concerns, he was pathologized and labeled as a sex addict by a therapist who did not explore alternate perspectives or underlying reasons for his behaviors and moods. And because this diagnosis was based upon a limited review and narrow standpoint, he was prescribed a treatment plan that did not fully correspond with his primary needs. Derrick's fear of rejection became something of a self-fulfilling prophecy when he did not meet the criteria outlined by SA and when his former therapist gave him only one option to consider. These occurrences only exacerbated his feelings of depression, anxiety, and anger.

His present counselor acknowledged that although Derrick regularly and frequently engaged in risky and potentially harmful sexual practices, this does not conclusively confirm that he has a sexual addiction. It is conceivable that Derrick enjoyed taking a dominant role during sex with other men because it made him feel powerful (something he did not experience around his father or in other parts of his life). Because Derrick's new counselor affirmed his experiences in an empathic and nonjudgmental manner while looking at his problems through another lens, he felt a burden had been lifted from his shoulders.

The new counselor offered another meeting should Derrick want to continue the assessment process and mutually identify the core issues that require their focus, including factors that may place Derrick at ongoing risk for sex-related difficulties and substance abuse problems. Derrick expressed a desire to reconcile with his sexual orientation so he can be emotionally, physically, socially, and sexually healthy without suppressing his true sexuality or abusing substances. Ideally, Derrick hoped to develop a positive attitude toward same-sex behavior and find ways to be empowered even when facing possible rejection from his family because he is gay. And should he choose to have random sex with other men or enjoy erotic practices involving dominance, it will be because it is an authentic source of consensual sexual pleasure—not a symptom of addiction to sex, an unhealthy coping mechanism to manage negative emotions, or an ineffective way to compensate for a perceived lack of power.

Final Remarks

It is beyond the scope of this chapter to provide an exhaustive comparison of the various forms of healthy sexual expression with terms such as hypersexuality, sexual compulsivity, sexual addiction, and out-of-control sexual behaviors, including the assessment and counseling approaches relevant to each. Interested readers are encouraged to explore strength-based and sex positive resources offered by the American Association of Sexuality Educators, Counselors and Therapists (see https://www.aasect.org), a professional training and certification organization supporting sexual health and sexual freedom without pathologizing consensual sexual behaviors. Readers also may find it illuminating to review Braun-Harvey and Vigorito's (2016) book *Treating Out of Control Sexual Behavior: Rethinking Sex Addiction*, which offers a reconceptualization of sexual behavior problems and a comprehensive overview of clinical strategies for working with men in individual and group settings. Last, it may be helpful to explore the work of Marty Klein (see martyklein.com), who advocates sex positive models of sexual health.

Sexuality is an intrinsic yet diverse part of the human experience. Judgment should be suspended irrespective of how many people value the traditional expression of sex compared to those who enjoy BDSM, fetish, or kink-related activities with varied and numerous partners. When approached by clients who express concern over their sexual experiences, counselors should carefully examine all angles and perspectives (including their own beliefs, attitudes, and biases) before assigning pathology. As stated by Ortmann (2020), "Sex therapists can help individuals and relationships deepen their sexual connection and pleasure by accepting, sharing, and embracing their sexuality rather than hiding, shaming, or eliminating it" (p. 299).

Problems and harm resulting from sexual thoughts, urges, and practices occur, but should a client immediately be branded as a sex addict if the criteria used to make this determination of addiction are based on paradigms developed for substance use disorders? The debate over the existence of sexual addiction is not over; there are too many inconsistent conceptualizations and treatment approaches. Counselors take a risk if they simply rely on the diagnostic criterion that the individual must be experiencing significant distress or impairment in functioning as a result of sexual behaviors. They may inadvertently overlook the possibility that a client's felt distress may be related to several factors such as being stigmatized when judged against societal and cultural values (e.g., with fetishistic arousal; see Chapter 20), disgraced when labeled as being sexually deviant or perverse (e.g., men who have sex with men), or conflicted when experiencing cognitive dissonance because their sexual fantasies and consensual erotic practices contrast with the moral model's conceptualization of "normal" sexual expression and sexual health (e.g., dominance and submission; see Chapter 19).

Finding meaning, experiencing happiness, achieving well-being, and establishing relationships are all existential goals, and there is a positive correlation between sex and life satisfaction (Prause et al., 2017). It is incompatible for the term *hedonia* to refer to a state of psychological pleasure that contributes to our well-being (Berridge & Kringelbach, 2011) if the word *hedonism* becomes a pejorative connotation when used to describe pleasure attained through sexual behaviors beyond what is considered socially acceptable or achieved outside romantic love or a committed relationship (Fulle et al., 2016). Within this contradiction lies another example of how experiencing sensory pleasure can be distorted into a stigmatized connotation when applied to sexuality. As long as erotic practices and sexual behaviors do not violate mutually agreed upon rules of consent established between mature human partners, can we be brave enough to widen our conceptualization of what is means to be sexually healthy, thereby creating a more inclusive and welcoming world? If you need the permission to accept, the courage to change, or the wisdom to understand, consider the words of perhaps the greatest feminist advocate of sexual expression and sexual freedom, "Express yourself, don't repress yourself. . . . I'm not your bitch don't hang your shit on me" (Madonna, 1994).

Questions You Always Wanted to Ask

1. **What are the diagnostic criteria for sexual addiction?**
   Sexual addiction is not recognized as a formal diagnosis in the *DSM-5* (APA, 2013) because there is not enough evidence to develop the diagnostic criteria and affiliated features to classify sex addiction as a mental disorder. The WHO (2022) included compulsive sexual behavior disorder in the *ICD-11*; however, this disorder is categorized as an impulsive control disorder rather than as a disorder due to substance use or addictive behaviors.
2. **Am I limited in what I can do as a counselor if sexual addiction is not a diagnosable disorder per the *DSM-5*?**
   Even though there is a debate regarding the existence of sex addiction, problems related to sexual behaviors exist. Counselors should, however, be careful to not base their assessment and interpretation of sexual problems on pathology-based models of sexuality that are influenced by societal, cultural, political, or religious conventions. Counselors, in collaboration with their clients, are encouraged to conduct a comprehensive biopsychosocial assessment to explore the scope of the problem as well as consider underlying influences for the various ways that sexuality is expressed. Example influences for sexual behavior may include but are not limited to personal desire, sexual preference, compulsive behavior, or a secondary symptom of a primary problem (e.g., depression, social stigma, relationship difficulties). The subjective voice of the client is just as important, if not sometimes more, than solely relying on psychological measures and inconsistent clinical paradigms. Once the counselor and client coconstruct the narrative, any concern that requires an actual intervention can be addressed accordingly. Any jointly identified goals should be identified through motivational interviewing methods (Miller & Rollnick, 2012) and developed in line with the transtheoretical model of behavior change (Prochaska et al., 2006).

3. **Is there a reason I should not treat my client's hypersexual behaviors using the same approach that I take with a client who has a substance addiction?**
   As previously indicated, there is no universal consensus on the actual existence of sexual addiction. Out-of-control sexual behaviors can manifest, but the diagnostic features of tolerance, withdrawal, and cravings that are seen in substance use disorders are not fully established for problems ostensibly related to sex addiction. Furthermore, traditional recovery methods involve maintaining complete abstinence from alcohol and drugs. Although being sexually healthy does not equate to being sexually abstinent, it is probably unrealistic to expect abstinence from sexual thoughts and behaviors considering sexuality is a central part of what is means to be a human.
4. **What should I be mindful of as I work with clients who share their sexual practices during counseling sessions?**
   Be courageous enough to recognize and address your own internal biases, judgments, and opinions regarding sexuality. Regardless of the client's presenting issues or problems, counselors are ethically bound to avoid imposing their personal values, attitudes, and beliefs onto their clients (American Counseling Association, 2014). It is paramount that counselors not allow their clinical assessment and counseling approach to be prejudiced just because erotic desires and practices of the client fall outside conventional customs or because they conflict with the counselor's personal beliefs or opinions.
5. **Should I advise newly sober clients who are not in a committed relationship to avoid becoming sexually and/or romantically involved during the first year of their recovery?**
   Although this recommendation is commonly known as the one-year rule in the addiction recovery community and field, counselors should base their treatment plan interventions on each client's unique history, pattern, and sex- or drug-linked behavior. There are many variables to consider, including those related to clients who habitually and consistently link sex with substance use, whose sobriety is directly threatened by sex-related triggers, and/or whose sex- or drug-linked relapse risk is high. It may be clinically appropriate for some clients to primarily focus on their initial recovery from substance-related addiction rather than being preoccupied with new relationships or having sex to fill a void left by alcohol or drugs. Conversely, it is equally appropriate to help clients develop a healthy sex life while concurrently achieving sobriety and sustaining recovery. For more information regarding how to address sexuality with clients in addiction treatment, counselors are encouraged to consider Braun-Harvey's (2011) book, *Sexual Health in Recovery: A Professional Counselor's Manual.*
6. **What does it mean to be sexually healthy?**
   According to the WHO (n.d.), sexual health is defined as

   > a state of physical, emotional, mental and social well-being in relation to sexuality; it is not merely the absence of disease, dysfunction or infirmity. Sexual health requires a positive and respectful approach to sexuality and sexual relationships, as well as the possibility of having pleasurable and safe sexual experiences, free of coercion, discrimination and violence. For sexual health to be attained and maintained, the sexual rights of all persons must be respected, protected and fulfilled. (para. 1)

7. **What resources are recommended if I want to learn more about sex positivity and sex positive counseling approaches?**
Recommended resources include the following:

American Association of Sexuality Educators, Counselors and Therapists (AASECT) at https://www.aasect.org
Braun-Harvey, D., & Vigorito, M. A. (2016). *Treating out of control sexual behavior: Rethinking sex addiction.* Springer Publishing.
Burnes, T.R., Singh, A. A., & Witherspoon, R. G. (2017). Sex positivity and counseling psychology: An introduction to the major contribution. *The Counseling Psychologist*, *45*(4), 470–486. https://doi.org/10.1177/0011000017710216
Hall, K., & Binik, Y. M. (Eds.). (2020). *Principles and practices of sex therapy* (6th ed). The Guilford Press.
International Society for Sexual Medicine at https://www.issm.info
Dr. Marty Klein's website at https://www.martyklein.com/
Ley, D. J. (2012). *The myth of sex addiction.* Rowman & Littlefield Publishers.
Ortmann, D. M., & Sprott, R. A. (2013). *Sexual outsiders: Understanding BDSM sexualities and communities.* Rowman & Littlefield Publishers.

References

Alcoholics Anonymous World Services. (2001). *Alcoholics Anonymous: The story of how many thousands of men and women have recovered from alcoholism* (4th ed.).
American Counseling Association. (2014). *ACA code of ethics.* https://www.counseling.org/resources/aca-code-of-ethics.pdf
American Psychiatric Association. (2013). *Diagnostic and statistical manual of mental disorders* (5th ed.). https://doi.org/10.1176/appi.books.9780890425596
Berridge, K. C., & Kringelbach, M. L. (2011). Building a neuroscience of pleasure and well-being. *Psychology of Well-Being*, *1*(1), 1–3. https://doi.org/10.1186/2211-1522-1-3
Berridge, K. C., & Kringelbach, M. L. (2015). Pleasure systems in the brain. *Neuron, 86*(3), 646–664. https://doi.org/10.1016/j.neuron.2015.02.018
Braun-Harvey, D. (2011). *Sexual health in recovery: A professional counselor's manual.* Springer Publishing.
Braun-Harvey, D., & Vigorito, M. A. (2016). *Treating out of control sexual behavior: Rethinking sex addiction.* Springer Publishing.
Braun-Harvey, D., & Vigorito, M. A. (2020). Out-of-control sexual behavior. In K. S. K. Hall & Y. M. Binik (Eds.), *Principles and practices of sex therapy* (6th ed., pp. 269–293). The Guilford Press.
Carnes, P. (1983). *Out of the shadows: Understanding sexual addiction.* CompCare Publishers.
Carnes, P. (1989). *Contrary to love: Helping the sexual addict.* CompCare Publishers.
Carnes, P. (2001). *Out of the shadows: Understanding sexual addiction* (3rd ed.). Hazelden.
Carnes, P., Green, B., & Carnes, S. (2010). The same yet different: Refocusing the Sexual Addiction Screening Test (SAST) to reflect orientation and gender. *Sexual Addiction & Compulsivity*, *17*, 7–30. https://doi.org/10.1080/10720161003604087

Cook, C. L., & Cottrell, C. A. (2021). You don't know where he's been: Sexual promiscuity negatively affects responses to both gay and straight men. *Psychology of Men & Masculinities, 21*(1), 63–76. https://doi.org/10.1037/men0000270

Fulle, A., Chang, I. J., & Knox, D. (2016). Female sexual hedonism: Navigating stigma. *College Student Journal, 50*(1), 29–34.

Garcia, F. D., & Thibaut, F. (2010). Sexual addictions. *The American Journal of Drug and Alcohol Abuse, 36*, 254–260. https://doi.org/10.3109/00952990.2010.503823

Georgiadis, J. R., & Kringelbach, M. L. (2012). The human sexual response cycle: Brain imaging evidence linking sex to other pleasures. *Progress in Neurobiology, 98*(1), 49–81. https://doi.org/10.1016/j.pneurobio.2012.05.004

Grubbs, J. B., Exline, J. J., Pargament, P. I., Hook, J. N., & Carlisle, R. D. (2015). Transgression as addiction: Religiosity and moral disapproval as predictors of perceived addiction to pornography. *Archives of Sexual Behavior, 44*, 125–126. https://doi.org/10.1007/s10508-013-0257-z

Halpern, A. L. (2011). The proposed diagnosis of hypersexual disorder for inclusion in the *DSM-5*: Unnecessary and harmful. *Archives of Sexual Behavior, 40*, 487–488. https://doi.org/10.1007/s10508-011-9727-3

Hatzenbuehler, M. L., Nolen-Hoeksema, S., & Dovidio, J. (2009). How does stigma "get under the skin"? The mediating role of emotion regulation. *Psychological Science, 20*(10), 1282–1289.

Janssen, E., Vorst, H., Finn, P., & Bancroft, J. (2002). The Sexual Inhibition (SIS) and Sexual Excitation (SES) Scales: I. Measuring sexual inhibition and excitation proneness in men. *Journal of Sex Research, 39*(2), 114–126.

Kafka, M. P. (2010). Hypersexual disorder: A proposed diagnosis for *DSM-V*. *Archives of Sexual Behavior, 39*, 377–400. https://doi.org/10.1007/s10508-009-9574-7

Klein, M. (1998, March 5). Sexual addiction is NOT a useful diagnosis—and why it matters. *Sex Therapist's Couch, Sexual Intelligence Blog*. https://www.martyklein.com/why-sexual-addiction-is-not-a-useful-diagnosis-and-why-it-matters/

Klein, M. (2003). Sex addiction: A dangerous clinical concept. *SIECUS Report, 31*(5), 8–11. https://siecus.org/wp-content/uploads/2015/07/31-5.pdf

Kraus, S. W., Krueger, R. B., Briken, P., First, M. B., Stein, D. J., Kaplan, M. S., Voon, V., Abdo, C. H. N., Grant, J. E., Atalla, E., & Reed, G. M. (2018). Compulsive sexual behaviour disorder in the ICD-11. *World Psychiatry, 17*(1), 109–110. https://doi.org/10.1002/wps.20499

Kraus, S. W., Voon, V., & Potenza, M. N. (2016). Should compulsive sexual behavior be considered an addiction? *Addiction, 111*(2), 2097–2016. https://doi.org/10.1111/add.13297

Lewis, R. J., Derlega, V. J., Griffin, J. L., & Krowinski, A. C. (2003). Stressors for gay men and lesbians: Life stress, gay-related stress, stigma consciousness, and depressive symptoms. *Journal of Social and Clinical Psychology, 22*(6), 716–729. https://doi.org/10.1521/jscp.22.6.716.22932

Low, J. (2000). The structures of suffering: Tibetan Buddhist and cognitive-analytic approaches. In G. Watson, S. Batchelor, & G. Claxton (Eds.), *The psychology of awakening: Buddhism, science, and our day-to-day lives* (pp. 250–270). Samuel Weiser.

Madonna. (1994). Human nature [Song]. On *Bedtime stories*. Maverick; Sire; Warner.

Miller, W. R., & Rollnick, S. (2012). *Motivational interviewing: Helping people change*. Guilford Press.

Moser, C. (2013). Hypersexual disorder: Searching for clarity. *Sexual Addiction & Compulsivity*, *20*, 48–58. https://doi.org/10.1080/10720162.2013.775631

Moser, C. (2016). *DSM-5* and the paraphilic disorders: Conceptual issues. *Archives of Sexual Behavior*, *45*, 2181–2186. https://doi.org/10.1007/s10508-016-0861-9

National Institute on Drug Abuse. (2020, July). *Drugs, brains, and behavior: The science of addiction*. https://www.drugabuse.gov/publications/drugs-brains-behavior-science-addiction/drugs-brain

Orford, J. (1978). Hypersexuality: Implications for a theory of dependence. *British Journal of Addiction*, *73*, 299–310.

Ortmann, D. (2020). The pleasure of power: Sex therapy in the BDSM community. In K. S. K. Hall & Y. M. Binik (Eds.), *Principles and practices of sex therapy* (6th ed., pp. 294–316). The Guilford Press.

Pachankis, J. E., Sullivan, T. J., Feinstein, B. A., & Newcomb, M. E. (2018). Young adult gay and bisexual men's stigma experiences and mental health: An 8-year longitudinal study. *Developmental Psychology*, *54*(7), 1381–1393.

Peciña, S., Smith, K. S., & Berridge, K. C. (2006). Hedonic hots spots in the brain. *The Neuroscientist*, *12*(6), 500–511.

Prause, N., Janssen, E., Georgiadis, J., Finn, P., & Pfaus, J. (2017). Data do not support sex as addictive. *Lancet*, *4*(12), 30441–30448. https://doi.org/10.1016/S2215-0366(17)30441-8

Prochaska, J. O., Norcross, J. C., & DiClemente, C. C. (2006). *Changing for good: A revolutionary six-stage program for overcoming bad habits*. Collins.

Raymond, N. C., Lloyd, M. D., Miner, M. H., & Kim, S. W. (2007). Preliminary report on the development and validation of the Sexual Symptom Assessment Scale. *Sexual Addiction & Compulsivity*, *14*(2), 119–129. https://doi.org/10.1080/10720160701310856

Reid, R. C., Garos, S., & Fong, T. (2012). Psychometric development of the Hypersexual Behavior Consequences Scale. *Journal of Behavioral Addictions*, *1*(3), 115–122. https://doi.org/10.1556/jba.1.2012.001

Rosenberg, H., & Kraus, S. (2014). The relationship of "passionate attachment" for pornography with sexual compulsivity, frequency of use, and craving for pornography. *Addictive Behaviors*, *39*(5), 1012–1017. https://doi.org/10.1016/j.addbeh.2014.02.010

Salvati, M., Pistella, J., & Baiocco, R. (2018). Gender roles and internalized sexual stigma in gay and lesbian persons: A quadratic relationship. *International Journal of Sexual Health*, *30*(1), 42–48. https://doi.org/10.1080/19317611.2017.1404542

Sexaholics Anonymous (n.d.-a). *What is a sexaholic and what is sexual sobriety?* https://www.sa.org/sexaholic/

Sexaholics Anonymous. (n.d.-b). *What is Sexaholics Anonymous?* https://www.sa.org/sa/

Sexual Compulsives Anonymous. (n.d.). *Our purpose*. https://sca-recovery.org/WP/

Veach, L. J., & Moro, R. R. (2018). *The spectrum of addiction: Evidenced-based assessment, prevention, and treatment across the lifespan*. SAGE.

Volkow, N. D., Koob, G. F., & McLellan, A. T., (2016). Neurobiological advances from the brain disease model of addiction. *The New England Journal of Medicine*, *374*, 363–371. https://doi.org/10.1056/NEJMra1511480

Womack, S. D., Hook, J. N., Ramos, M., Davis, D. E., & Penberthy, J. K. (2013). Measuring hypersexual disorder. *Sexual Addiction & Compulsivity*, 20, 65–78. https://doi.org/10.1080/10720162.2013.768126

World Health Organization. (n.d.). *Sexual health and well-being*. https://www.who.int/teams/sexual-and-reproductive-health-and-research-(srh)/areas-of-work/sexual-health

World Health Organization. (2022). 6C72. Compulsive sexual behaviour disorder. *ICD-11 for mortality and morbidity statistics* (Version: 02/2022). https://icd.who.int/browse11/l-m/en#/http://id.who.int/icd/entity/1630268048

PART 7

Relationships

Sex and Love: What's Love Got to Do With It?

H. L. Brostrand, V. A. Dansereau, and James P. Ahearn

Since the beginning of time, humans have sought intimacy with one another. Today, there are many options from brief, sexual encounters to intimate long-term relationships, from expensive matchmakers to free smartphone applications, for increasing the chances of meeting that special person. Poetry and ballads, letters carried by the Pony Express, personal ads in the newspaper, telephone calls, and now the internet—our ways of meeting have evolved over time. The form of meeting an intimate partner may have changed, but the function remains the same. The desire for connection and to be successful in relationships, as well as the pros and cons of dating, still exist. As the nuances of courtship have entered the digital age, counselors and other mental health therapists face new opportunities to assist clients with navigating these online relationship challenges.

Evolution of Connecting

During the 18th century in America, suitors and courtship were generally arranged for and supervised by relatives (Baldwin & Baldwin, 2018). Marriage fulfilled a polite society's requirement for sanctioned sexual relationships; and without a spouse, sexual relationships could lead to a loss in social status or harsher consequences. The focus was on heterosexual unions beneficial to the family or community. The individual preferences of the potential spouse(s) played little part in these unions. Not until the 1800s did romance and love become a consideration in budding relationships. Couples were more likely to interact outside of the formal parlor of the woman's home. Social outings, as a pair, were more acceptable, allowing for more in-depth conversation and expressions of affection.

With the Roaring Twenties came the concept of dating. No longer were matches made and supervised by family members. Men and women could initiate conversation and activities with members of the opposite sex. Couples could go to jazz clubs, the theater, the park, and other places without being under the watchful eye of a chaperone. The young adults could get to know each other personally and could date many people before tying the knot (Baldwin & Baldwin, 2018).

In the 1950s, the most common ways for heterosexual couples to meet was through family, in church, or in the community (Rosenfeld et al., 2019). Due to potential criminal consequences and the lack of legal protection and socially sanctioned avenues for developing intimate relationships, same-sex couples were less likely to engage in formalized or public courtship, although such relationships did exist away from the public's gaze (Baldwin & Baldwin, 2018).

The sexual revolution of the 1970s brought a dramatic change to the activities of dating (Baldwin & Baldwin, 2018). Partners could now engage in sexual intercourse before marriage without devastating social stigma and risk of unwanted pregnancy. Physical intimacy with or without emotional intimacy and/or commitment became acceptable. As men and women engaged in more sex without marriage, "hookups" became more common. A *hookup* suggests sexual intimacy without emotional attachment or commitment. Relaxation of social regulations also allowed men and women to interact one-on-one in most settings. They now worked, studied, and played together, thus offering more dating and sexual opportunities.

Over the last 2 decades, we have seen dating services evolve from the use of videocassettes to a rise in popularity for personal interest chat rooms, to phone apps where people can connect with anyone, anywhere, anytime. In 2017, more heterosexual couples met online than through friends (Rosenfeld et al., 2019). With the advent of the website browser Internet Explorer in 1995, smartphones in 2007, and literally hundreds of online dating platforms by 2020, cyber daters began to experience greater accessibility, affordability, and anonymity (Barrada et al., 2019; Choudhary, 2019; Orchard, 2019; Potts, 2018). As the types of opportunities for human connection expanded, so did the terminology used to describe them.

New Vocabulary

Words describing activities relating to this new technological platform for dating may be unfamiliar. We recommend counselors learn to "speak the client's language" by becoming familiar with terms they commonly use, and which we define using sources such as the Urban Dictionary (www.urbandictionary.com) as follows:

casual sex: having sexual contact with another person with no plans for a long-term or committed relationship.
catfishing: hiding who you really are to lure someone into an online relationship using social media, dating platform, or by cell phone.
cyberporn: pornography found online.
cybersex: a virtual sex encounter in which two or more persons connect remotely.
dating app: an online platform where people meet virtually, usually with the intention of ultimately meeting in person.
doxing: publicly exposing on the internet someone else's real name or address.
friends with benefits: friends who are engaged in sexual activity with each other.
fuck buddies: people who have sexual contact without friendship or other relationship.
ghosting: when a person cuts off all communication, with no warning or notice.

hookup: any form of intimacy with a member of the preferred sex who is not a significant other.
revenge porn: nude pictures or videos which are publicly shared, usually for the purpose of spiteful humiliation.
troll: someone who posts a deliberately provocative message with the intention of causing maximum disruption and argument.
video cam: camera, often on the computer or internet device, which streams directly online.

Let's Talk About Sex, Baby

From our therapeutic perspective, online sexual activity (OSA) generally falls into two types of interactions: those that are focused on intimacy by getting to know each other and forming a relationship online before sexual activity, and those internet-facilitated connections that are focused on uncommitted or "no strings attached" sexually based encounters. Regardless of the category, the internet provides a common way to create these connections. According to the Pew Research Foundation (Anderson et al., 2020), almost a third of Americans have used an app or dating site to meet someone new. Forty percent of those meetings developed into a committed relationship. Almost half of adults in their 20s have used a dating site. Two thirds of these found matches who shared their interests, were attractive, and/or were someone they would like to meet face-to-face (Anderson et al., 2020).

Cyber dating, OSA, and online relationships can be beneficial or productive in many ways. Counselors, rather than avoiding or marginalizing this mode of relationship building, can help clients use these means of connecting to support their personal goals. Overall, it is easier and more efficient for many people to meet someone with common interests online. Written communication allows a client an opportunity to get to know someone better before meeting in person. It may also be easier for clients to screen out and screen in those with dissimilar and similar values and goals. Clients can feel physically safe while vetting perspective suitors and/or sexual partners (Rosenfeld et al., 2019). Clients can access more people and people who are not likely to be in their everyday environment and can search for potential partners whether they are 5 miles or 500 miles away, thus widening the dating pool (Barrada et al., 2019; Liu & Zheng, 2020). Nevertheless, in heterosexual cyber dating, geographic proximity seems to be the leading factor in first dates (Bruch & Newman, 2019).

Online connections remove physical barriers for people who have mobility issues, geographic limitations, or other complications around being physically present. Long-distance relationships can be enhanced and strengthened with instantaneous communication and live exchange using not only video but applications designed for real-time sexual interaction, such as an application that sends signals to a vibrator worn by someone miles away (Nixon & Dusterhoft, 2018). Flirting, entertainment, pleasure, exploring different ways of being, anonymity, learning about different perspectives, learning about the same perspectives, connecting with a thriving subculture such as 12-step addiction recovery communities, the kink community, the evangelical Christian community, and others can occur with the click of a mouse. Researchers are also seeing less racial segregation in online platforms. Jackson (2018) pointed out that 79% of people on Tinder went out with someone from a different ethnicity. The possibilities for social engagement are endless.

The internet is the ultimate level playing field in that people with disabilities may use online communication as an accommodation. Individuals living in rural areas can increase their pool of potential intimate partners. An individual with body or self-image issues can remove their appearance from the initial impression to be disclosed at a time of their choosing. Tiidenberg (2018) suggested that women can even be empowered by sharing sexy selfies on their own terms and at their own discretion. Shy or introverted people can set their own pace for getting to know someone (Bray, 2018). Barrada et al. (2019) found that healthy use of OSA was associated with more satisfaction and self-esteem as a sexual partner. Someone from a particular religion, a specific sexual orientation, a certain age, or a particular culture can use the internet to overcome barriers and limitations when building relationships (see, for example, Chapter 16). The client's involvement in cyber dating allows for unique opportunities for therapeutic intervention, providing the therapist is competent to meet the client where they are at. As individual counselors, our attitudes about sex without commitment, infidelity, intimacy, trust, honesty, or disclosure may differ from the attitudes of our clients. Before we explore these relationship issues with clients, it behooves us to determine our own values and attitudes. When we do so, we are better prepared to advocate for the client's personal exploration surrounding relationships.

Counselor Values Around OSA

Without introducing a discourse on how counselor values should not interfere with therapy, the more common "issues" with cyber dating will be reviewed. The function of relationship counseling remains the same; however, counselors need to be familiar with the multitude of technological platforms on which dating occurs. Some misunderstandings between clients and counselors regarding online dating and cybersex can be attributed to clinicians' unfamiliarity with OSA. The sex positive counselor, as a professional and as a person, must recognize the client's values to avoid pushing their own agenda on clients' dating activities. We have included a chart of cybersex and cyber dating websites (see Table 22.1) in the hope that you will personally review sites where your clients may be surfing.

Guidelines developed by the Multicultural Counseling Competencies Revisions Committee (2015) of the Association for Multicultural Counseling and Development offer some assistance in navigating the cyberworld. These guidelines inform us as to how counselors should engage with clients from an informed position related to the intersecting client identities that remain ever present in the client-counselor relationship. These guidelines require us, as counselors, to be aware of our own beliefs and biases while simultaneously holding space for our clients' own worldviews. Myths and stereotypes about online dating and OSA can serve as a barrier to an otherwise beneficial therapeutic alliance and may leave the counselor ill-equipped to be of benefit to clients traversing the world of online romance and sexual activity. Above all other ethical principles, client autonomy should be of paramount concern to the therapist. Beauchamp and Childress (2019) recommended embracing people's "right to hold views, to make choices, and to take actions based on their values and beliefs" (p. 104). Attitudes and actions that "ignore, insult, demean or are inattentive" (Beauchamp & Childress, 2019, p. 104) to our clients' choices do not support client autonomy and may damage the therapeutic relationship. Although we each may have our own "knee-jerk" reaction to the expanding world of OSA, we should strive to withhold judgment and see these experiences through our clients' eyes.

Table 22.1

Summary of Online Mingling Applications and Cyber Dating Sites

Application Name	*Targeted Demographic*	*Dating*	*Hookup*
Adam4adam	Gay/bi men	X	X
AsianDating	Asian, hetero, match-making	X	
AtheistPersonals	All orientations; all genders; atheists	X	
Bumble	All orientations; all genders	X	X
Coffee Meets Bagel	All orientations; all genders	X	X
Culture Crush	African American/Black	X	
EHarmony	All orientations; all genders	X	
EliteSingles	All orientations; all genders; affluent	X	
FaceBook Cyberdating	All orientations	X	X
FaithLife	Christian	X	
FarmersOnly	All orientations; agricultural	X	
Fetlife	Kink and poly identifying	X	X
FreeThinkerMatch	Agnostic	X	
GreenSingles	Vegans, vegetarians, and environmentalists	X	
Grindr	Gay/bisexual men	X	X
Happn	African American/Black	X	
Her	Lesbian/bisexual women	X	X
Hinge	All orientations; all genders	X	
Jacked	Gay/bisexual men	X	X
Jerkmate	All orientations; all genders		X
JSwipe	Jewish religion and ethnicity	X	
KIK	All orientations; all genders		
Match	All orientations; all genders	X	
Onlyfans	All orientations; all genders; amateur porn		
OurTime	Older adults	X	
Positive Singles	HSV, HIV, etc.	X	
ProgressiveSingles	Progressives	X	
RepublicanPeopleMeet	All orientations; politically conservative	X	
Scruff	Gay; male identifying only, some nonbinary	X	X
Second Life	All orientations; all genders; virtual reality	X	X
SilverSingles	All orientations; older adults	X	X
Tinder	All orientations; all genders		X
Zoosk	All orientations; all genders	X	

A sex positive therapist works "toward helping their clients attain greater pleasure and less pain and suffering in living" (Cohen & Cohen, 1999, p. 90). Therapeutic competence—the skills, abilities, and qualifications to address the problem effectively—underlies the moral principle of beneficence. This includes having a basic understanding of OSA and being aware of available resources for our clients (Cohen & Cohen, 1999), so we can support them in moving forward with their relationship goals. Without professional knowledge of or personal experience in cyber dating, a counselor is at a disadvantage when working with internet daters. Our clients' desires may range from abstinence until marriage to anonymous one-night stands. As the helper, we can facilitate our clients' healthy behaviors, in whatever form that may take.

Therapeutic Use of Cyber Activities

In addition to dating and OSA, our clients can gain therapeutic benefits from online communication. Many clients need to develop and improve their interpersonal skills, learn to set appropriate boundaries, practice assertive communication, confront appropriately, increase self-efficacy, overcome shyness or social anxiety, and sometimes even learn to flirt. As knowledgeable and informed counselors, we can use the internet as a tool in our therapeutic toolbox. If clients want to become comfortable using the web for connecting with people they might never meet in person, we can help them learn. If we want to use the internet to help them navigate dating and intimate, assertive interpersonal communication, we can teach them using the internet.

Murray et al. (2017) pointed out that 70% of therapeutic change is accounted for by extratherapeutic factors that exist in addition to the therapeutic counseling relationship. For example, exploring the client's perceptions of what they see online is facilitated by a knowledgeable, experienced therapist who is open to intimate discussion. We can expect the client's perception of therapeutic rapport and the circumstances beyond our theory of choice will have the greatest impact on client progress. By understanding and fully utilizing the internet and cyber communications, we can tailor interventions and techniques to stretch outside of our session and into the clients' real-life experiences. Interventions such as client education, cognitive restructuring, skills training, homework assignments, and mindfulness training can be accomplished in the therapeutic setting using online platforms already familiar to our clients (Murray et al., 2017).

Sex positive counselors can help clients with appropriate self-disclosures, boundary setting, intimate communication, and improving the quality of a budding relationship. A skilled counselor can also help clients recognize potential blind spots as well as practice assertive and respectful communication (Green & Flemons, 2018). Some counselors may choose to use the internet to expose a client to certain stimuli during a session, while providing therapeutic support and reframing. For example, the counselor can ask the client to pull up a comment or reply online that they found hurtful or anxiety producing. Together, the two can work through the client's perceptions, feelings, and reactions. Cognitive restructuring and healthy coping skills can be taught and practiced. Creative use of clients' online personas can invigorate the goals and objectives in counseling. For example, with the counselor's guidance, perhaps in session or as homework, clients can learn and practice their social and interpersonal communication skills.

Some people have difficulty initiating conversation and making that first contact, and the internet can overcome isolation, be it geographical, physical, or attitudinal. There are thousands of online special-interest, sex-related communities that can serve to normalize those feelings, particularly for those individuals who identify as part of a nonmainstream culture. In his review of *Sex in the Digital Age*, Kerpen (2019) accentuated how cybersex can "facilitate community and belonging for those engaging in marginalized practices, but also provide important opportunities for accessing information and engaging in discussions around sexual ethics to empower practitioners to negotiate personal boundaries and develop safe and healthy consensual practice" (p. 2028).

Safety Measures and OSA

Although the counselor cannot protect the client from all possible complications, some basic safety tips should be reviewed with the client. Numerous websites offer advice for safe and fulfilling online dating. The following are a few suggestions a counselor might offer to the client to cyber date safely:

- Before meeting someone in person for the first time, chat by phone or, better yet, chat by video. This way, you know that the person you are talking to is the same person who shows up for coffee.
- It is not necessary to give out your personal phone number. Google Voice, for example, provides free phone numbers.
- Get your date's first and last name, so that you can look them up online beforehand. For your first meeting, go to a public place and drive yourself, use rideshare, or take public transportation rather than getting into your date's car.
- Keep your personal information to yourself until you get to know each other better.
- Have a friend who has all the details and is scheduled to follow up with you during or after your meet and greet.
- Plan to go home alone after your first meeting. This is not only a safety precaution, but it will allow you to "sleep on it" and process your thoughts and feelings.

These recommendations are important for self-care and personal safety. The counselor can support the client in developing healthy and positive techniques for dating online.

Finding love and sexual relationships online can be advantageous and fulfilling for so many people. Although the internet can provide bountiful opportunities to find that special someone, be it Mr. Right or Mr. Right Now, there can be a darker and uglier side to finding romance through the internet. It is imperative for clinicians to be aware of what dangers can lurk behind the screen. In the following section, we will discuss concerns affiliated with online dating and OSA, such as physical, sexual, financial, and emotional exploitation, and dating addiction.

Like most tools, the internet can be used for nefarious purposes, and with the ease of access to many people with little effort, we as clinicians need to be aware of the potential dangers facing our clients. Along with the rise of internet use, experiences of internet-facilitated sexual assault have been a growing social concern. Rowse et al. (2020) completed an audit of sexual assault forensic examinations with consideration given to the "relationship to offender" and the demographic information (i.e., age, sex, race) about both the perpetrator and the victim. The researchers additionally audited which online platform was used to facilitate the meeting, whether the assault occurred during the first meeting, and the location of the assault. Of the 76 identified sexual assault cases, 14.5% of cases involved meeting the perpetrator through a dating application. Of these cases, 100% of the victims were women, and 100% of perpetrators were men, with 72% of the women being under the age of 30. Rowse et al. (2020) further reported that the sexual assaults were more likely to occur in the evening or late night (81%), more likely to occur in the perpetrator's private residence (54%), and more likely to occur during the first face-to-face meeting (82%). Such data highlight the importance for clinicians to be aware of the very real risk factors evident in online dating. Scannell (2019) further emphasized that perpetrators have an effective way of finding victims with an online platform, particularly if an individual is lonely and more vulnerable. This poses a unique risk to college-age students, people moving to a new area, or people who struggle with interpersonal skills.

Data from the Pew Research Center (Anderson et al., 2020) showed that on an online dating app or website, 60% of cisgender women ages 18 to 34 reported that someone they had connected with continued to contact them, despite making their disinterest known. In this same demographic, 57% received an unsolicited sexually explicit image or message, 44% were called an offensive name, and 19% received threats of physical harm. When compared with cisgender men in the same age bracket, 27% had a "match" continue to contact them after expressing they were not interested, 28% received an unsolicited sexually explicit image or message, 23% were called an offensive name, and 9% received threats of physical harm. Although the prevalence of these interactions decreased among those over the age of 35, there continued to be a notable disparity between the incidences for women compared to men. The Pew data also showed that lesbian, gay, and bisexual users of online dating were more likely (56%) than heterosexual users (32%) to receive unsolicited sexually explicit messages. Additionally, 17% of the lesbian, gay, and bisexual users reported being threatened with physical harm, compared with 7% of heterosexual users. Counselors need to understand the potential dangers of online dating and be able to educate their clients about making informed decisions before diving into the world of cyber dating.

Doxing is another concern for online daters. Identifying and disseminating private information about a person with the intent to threaten, intimidate, or harass is not uncommon (Jones, 2016). Anyone active online is at risk as anyone can use resources such as Google reverse image search, White Pages, and Facebook to reveal another person's identity and address through screenshots, emails, or phone numbers. With modern technology, pictures taken with smartphones can be geotagged and the location where the picture was taken easily identified. This poses an immediate safety concern for anyone who uses an online platform for dating, hooking up, and sending pictures. The motivation for doxing varies, ranging from attitudes of power assurance (e.g., "Look at how smart I am") to threat of physical and sexual harm.

Risks

From photo-shopped images to manipulated videos, not everything on the internet is as it seems. With almost unlimited access to photos, profiles, and personal information, some online users have taken on a life different from their own: Enter the catfish. Catfishing occurs when an individual creates a fake persona online with intent to facilitate a relationship with another person under false pretenses. The risk of emotional and financial exploitation through catfishing sheds light on the ugly side of online dating. Catfish establish an online romantic relationship with their victim and offer promises of love or marriage, with a picturesque life together, and sweep their victim off their feet. However, the catfish then begins to take advantage of their victim by gaining financial support using faked emergencies or promises to visit the victim (FBI, n.d.; Federal Trade Commission, 2020). As of 2019, $201 million had been stolen in these romance scams. The average victim lost approximately $2,600—seven times the average amount lost in other fraud schemes.

Thanks to the ease of maintaining anonymity online, romance scams can easily occur on social media and dating websites, especially if the victim feels isolated and lonely. According to the Federal Trade Commission (2020), the catfish may profess their love very early on, may claim to be a member of the military, and would often provide numerous explanations for the lack of real-time interaction such as video chatting. The catfish usually has one goal in mind—money. An investigative article identified that romance scammers generally prey on vulnerable women who are older, single, or widowed (Dellinger, 2019). The catfish can build an intense connection and make promises of love seem like a dream come true. Unfortunately for the victim, catfish are rarely monogamous in their schemes and likely to be speaking to multiple victims at one time to up the odds of a successful scam. The catfish often use stolen pictures of people considered to be attractive, may create an entire social media profile to appear convincing, and may even have others participating in the scheme.

Counselors must be wary as clinicians when clients discuss their online romances. Hearing a client discuss some of these red flags should alert us that things may not always be as they seem. Using this as a resource, it will be beneficial for the emotional and financial safety of the client to be on alert for these warning signs and to help the client see these warning signs for themselves. Clients whose potential love interest provides only photos that appear outdated, is never available for a live video chat, or has a suspect social media profile (e.g., with few friends, few posts, and minimal activity) may benefit from questioning how well they truly know this person.

In a 2016 survey of 5,500 singles in America, the dating website Match.com (n.d.) found that millennials were 125% more likely to admit an addiction to finding a love connection when compared with other generations. With the availability and accessibility of online dating apps, it can feel easy to get "pulled in." The ability to swipe right and match with another person provides an immediate validation of one's appearance and existence. Yet when does the use of dating apps cross the line and become problematic? Coduto et al. (2020) examined the compulsive use of online dating in the context of social anxiety, loneliness, and preference for online social interaction. Compulsive online dating is strongly connected to feelings of loneliness. Preference for online social interaction can occur in the context of problematic internet usage that can interfere with daily functioning, as "online life" takes precedence over "offline life." Coduto et al.'s study indicated that those with higher social anxiety are more likely to have a preference for online social interaction. In addition to this, compulsive users of online dating apps tend to experience more negative than positive outcomes. These negative outcomes include elements such as missing work, classes, or other offline obligations to engage with apps. Counselors can help clients recognize the underlying motivations and needs behind their use and explore ways to enforce boundaries around limiting how often and to what extent users engage with online dating apps. As with many things in life, anything done to excess tends to become problematic.

Is Your 3 O'Clock "The One"?

With over 100 million downloads on dating apps such as Tinder, there is no guarantee that we as counselors can avoid an online interaction with our clients (LeFebvre, 2018) if we are dating online. The *ACA Code of Ethics* (American Counseling Association [ACA], 2014) mandates that counselors "respect the privacy of their clients' presence on social media unless given consent to view such information" (ACA, 2014, Section H.6.c.). In the age of technology, keeping an inquisitive mind from exploring a client's online presence poses new challenges as the boundary between the professional and private spheres blurs. Kolmes and Taube (2014) found that of the psychotherapists surveyed, 49% reported intentionally seeking out client information online, which raises a question about the extent to which counselors choose to abide by their ethical obligation of respecting the privacy of clients' online presence. Although the ethical expectation is that counselors should avoid delving into a client's profile and to maintain that privacy, clients by contrast may choose to explore counselors' personal lives in the digital world.

Kolmes and Taube (2016) found that although 69.9% of clients surveyed reported finding personal information about their counselor, only about a quarter of clients who sought personal information about their counselor online disclosed that fact in therapy. Counselors should take the same precautions we urge our clients to take—that is, limit personal disclosure until you can confirm the identity of the other individual, withhold private images until real-time communication has verified the identity of the intended recipient, and control who may access your personal pages and how that access will occur. If possible, take advantage of online anonymity by not using your real name in this venue. Cybersafety applies to everyone.

When working within any client's multicultural issue or working with a client who lives in a culture different from that of one's own, there exists an obligation for the counselor to do some work to become culturally competent. Counselors would be well served by completing a little research into how various apps function, the intention behind each app, and who is likely to be using a certain app or site. Counselors can miss the mark by basing their clinical practice on anecdotes from friends, other clients, or their own experiences. In summary, the benefits of cyber dating and OSA to our clients, and to our therapeutic relationship, can be realized. Counselors should be culturally competent by understanding the nuances and risks of online dating. We as individuals may not be avid users of a particular platform, but we can help our clients navigate the challenges of online relationships.

Case Example

Margo is a 29-year-old woman whom you as a counselor have been treating for approximately 5 months. She has been working on assertiveness, setting boundaries, and overcoming her fear of commitment. She has a good job and owns her small condo in the city.

Margo has been chatting on KIK with Elliot, whom she met on Fetlife.com. Elliot is into BDSM, and Margo is excited about it but hasn't tried BDSM before. She wants to talk about setting and holding her boundaries and about becoming physically and emotionally intimate with Elliot. She plans to meet him in person for coffee next week.

As her counselor, some topics for you to address with Margo might include the following:

- What is the setting for the coffee meeting going to be?
- Does anyone know you are meeting with Elliot?
- Have you had a video chat or other interaction to verify that Elliot is who he says he is?
- Is Elliot comfortable with you requesting verification of his identity?
- How long has Elliot been a member of FetLife?
- What are his friends' profiles like?
- What groups from FetLife is Elliot a part of?
- What has Elliot posted on FetLife (e.g., pictures, writings, statuses)?
- Are there any potential red flags that arise in conversations with Elliot or from viewing his profile?
- Is Elliot comfortable with you "vetting" him—that is, asking his online friends about his demeanor and behavior?

- Is Elliot a paid member of the site? (Having provided financial information to a dating site affords an extra level of identification verification.)
- Have you read the FetLife community guidelines?

Reflections About the Case Example

After reading this case example, consider the following questions:

1. What is your initial reaction after reading this vignette?
2. What are your opinions and beliefs about kink and BDSM?
3. What do you need to learn before you initiate a dialogue with Margo? (This can include cultural competency, knowledge of tools to navigate the conversation, or research as to the experiences of others in a similar circumstance.)
4. How would you define and establish boundaries prioritizing health and safety?
5. How would you facilitate a discussion with Margo about setting and communicating her boundaries and limits?
6. Examine Margo's values. How does she envision this relationship with Elliot developing?
7. For Margo, what would a physically intimate connection look like with Elliot?
8. How does Margo communicate her wants, needs, and desires?

If you do not feel competent to counsel Margo in this area, it may be helpful to explore our recommended resources and also to be open with your clients about your lack of direct experience with this community and activity. You may decide you need to refer, but you may decide, through conversation with your client, consultation, and other resources, to proceed.

Conclusion

It is just as important to maintain the delicate balance of encouraging and supporting healthy online dating and/or hooking up while providing education as to the risk factors present in online dating and OSA and promoting safety and consent. We have provided basic safety tips for the novice online dater. Considering the risk factors we have discussed, there is a benefit in asking yourself about your own attitude toward online dating and how that potential bias may influence the clients you serve.

As clients embark on their first foray into the realm of online relationships—be it romantic, sexual, or otherwise—the innumerable online apps and sites provide a myriad of hazards and dangers of which novice users may not be aware. For counselors, the challenge remains: How do we navigate these issues while maintaining professional ethics in an arena where new questions and dilemmas can be ample? In addition to the ethical issues evident in the new world of online dating and OSA, we also must meet the universal expectation of counselors to be culturally competent within the interweaving identities of our clients. With the ever-growing list of sites and applications marketed to certain targeted populations, counselors need to be educated and informed as to the cultural complexity existing in online dating/sexual activity.

Adolescents, just like adults, seek the opportunity to have and engage in sexual relationships; however, unlike adult clients, legal issues come front and center when considering how adolescents participate in OSA. As the internet achieves a near omnipresence in the lives of teenagers, counselors need to navigate the balance of client confidentiality and client welfare especially with regard to privacy and confidentiality. Most young adults are using electronic communication, which can include sexting and cybersex (Van Ouytsel et al., 2020). Those working with clients under 18 (minors) would benefit from establishing clear parameters as to how issues such as sex and sexuality will be approached, as well as gaining the unique cultural competencies needed to navigate adolescent love and sexual activity (see Chapter 24).

References

American Counseling Association. (2014). *ACA code of ethics.* http://www.counseling.org/docs/ethics/2014-aca-code-of-ethics.pdf

Anderson, M., Vogels, E. A., & Turner, E. (2020). *The virtues and downsides of online dating: 2. Users of online dating platforms experience both positive—and negative—aspects of courtship on the web.* Pew Research Center. https://www.pewresearch.org/internet/2020/02/06/users-of-online-dating-platforms-experience-both-positive-and-negative-aspects-of-courtship-on-the-web/

Baldwin, J., & Baldwin, J. (2018, March). *The history of dating in America.* SexInfo Online. https://sexinfoonline.com/the-history-of-dating-in-america

Barrada, J. R., Ruiz-Gomez, P., Correa, A. B., & Castro, A. (2019, February 26). Not all online sexual activities are the same. *Frontiers in Psychology.* https://doi.org/10.3389/fpsyg.2019.00339

Beauchamp, T. L., & Childress, J. F. (2019). *Principles of biomedical ethics* (8th ed.). Oxford.

Bray, B. (2018, December). Finding love in a "swipe left" universe. *Counseling Today,* 22–27.

Bruch, E. E., & Newman, M. E. J. (2019). Structure of online dating markets and US cities. *Sociological Science 6,* 219–234. https://doi.org/10.15195/v6.a9

Choudhary, A. (2019). Cybersex. In R. T. Gopalan (Ed.), *Intimacy and developing personal relationships in the virtual world* (pp. 201–212). IGI Global. https://doi.org/10.4018/978-1-5225-4047-2.ch011

Coduto, K. D., Lee-Won, R. J., & Baek, Y. M. (2020). Swiping for trouble: Problematic dating application use among psychosocially distraught individuals and the paths to negative outcomes. *Journal of Social and Personal Relationships, 37*(1), 212–232. https://doi.org/10.1177%2F0265407519861153

Cohen, E. D., & Cohen, G. S. (1999). *The virtuous therapist.* Brooks/Cole Wadworth.

Dellinger, A. J. (2019). Anatomy of a scam: Nigerian romance scammer shares secrets. *Forbes.* https://www.forbes.com/sites/ajdellinger/2019/11/25/anatomy-of-a-scam-nigerian-romance-scammer-shares-secrets/#7a4eb1a07638

FBI. (n.d.). *Scams and safety: Romance scams.* Federal Bureau of Investigation. https://www.fbi.gov/scams-and-safety/common-scams-and-crimes/romance-scams

Federal Trade Commission. (2020, February 12). *New FTC data show consumers reported losing more than $200 million to romance scams in 2019* [Press release]. https://www.ftc.gov/news-events/press-releases/2020/02/new-ftc-data-show-consumers-reported-losing-more-200-million

Green, S., & Flemons, D. (2018). *Quickies: The handbook of brief sex therapy* (3rd ed.). W. W. Norton & Company.

Jackson, C. K. (2018). The data on dating. *Essence, 48*(11), 96–96. https://www.essence.com/love/online-millenial-dating-stats-you-need-know/

Jones, A. (2016). "I get paid to have orgasms": Adult webcam models' negotiation of pleasure and danger. *Journal of Women in Culture and Society, 42*(1), 227–256. http://doi:0097-9740/2016/4201-0011

Kerpen, S. (2019). Digital empowerment: Who's empowerment? On the limits of gender and sexuality in the digital age [Review of the book *Sex in the digital age* by P. G. Nixon & I. K. Dusterhoft]. *Information, Communication & Society, 22*(13), 2024–2029. https://doi.org/10.1080/1369118X.2019.1604786

Kolmes, K., & Taube, D. O. (2014). Seeking and finding our clients on the internet: Boundary considerations in cyberspace. *Professional Psychology: Research and Practice, 45*(1), 3–10. https://doi.org/10.1037/a0029958

Kolmes, K., & Taube, D. O. (2016). Client discovery of psychotherapist personal information online. *Professional Psychology: Research and Practice, 47*(2), 147–154. https://doi.apa.org/doi/10.1037/pro0000065

LeFebvre, L. E. (2018). Swiping me off my feet: Explicating relationship initiation on Tinder. *Journal of Social and Personal Relationships, 35*(9), 1205–1229. https://doi.org/10.1177%2F0265407517706419

Liu, Y., & Zheng, L. (2020). Relationships between the Big Five, narcissistic personality traits, and online sexual activities. *Personality and Individual Differences, 152,* Article 109593. https://doi.org/10.1016/j.paid.2019.109593

Match.com. (n.d.). *Singles in America: Over-connection = no connection.* [Infographic]. https://www.match.com/dnws/cpx/en-us/singlesinamerica/2017/#millennial

Multicultural Counseling Competencies Revisions Committee. (2015). *Multicultural and social justice counseling competencies.* Association for Multicultural Counseling and Development. https://www.counseling.org/docs/default-source/competencies/multicultural-and-social-justice-counseling-competencies.pdf

Murray, C., Pope, A., & Willis, B. (2017). *Sexuality counseling: Theory, research, and practice.* Sage.

Nixon, P. G., & Dusterhoft, I. K. (Eds.). (2018). *Sex in the digital age.* Routledge.

Orchard, T. (2019). *Encyclopedia of sexuality and gender* (A. D. Lynkins, Ed.). Springer.

Potts, H. (2018, February). "You can always press delete": Should we keep playing the game of love? Hannah Potts wonders. *Psychologist,* 46–49.

Rosenfeld, M. J., Thomas, R. J., & Hausen, S. (2019). Disintermediating your friends: How online dating in the United States displaces other ways of meeting. *PNAS, 116*(36), 17753–17758. https://doi.org/10.1073/pnas.1908630116

Rowse, J., Bolt, C., & Gaya, S. (2020). Swipe right: The emergence of dating-app facilitated sexual assault. A descriptive retrospective audit of forensic examination caseload in an Australian metropolitan service. *Forensic Science, Medicine and Pathology, 16,* 71–77. https://doi.org/10.1007/s12024-019-00201-7

Scannell, M. J. (2019). Online dating and the risk of sexual assault to college students. *Building Healthy Academic Communities, 3*(1), 34–43. http://doi.org/10.18061/bhac.v3i1.6688

Tiidenberg, K. (2018). Visibly ageing femininities: Women's visual discourses of being over-40 and over-50 on Instagram. *Feminist Media Studies, 18*(1), 61–76, https://doi.org/10.1080/14680777.2018.1409988

Van Ouytsel, J., Punyanunt-Carter, N. M., Walrave, M., & Ponnet, K. (2020). Sexting within young adults' dating and romantic relationships. *Current Opinion in Psychology, 36,* 55–59. https://doi.org/10.1016/j.copsyc.2020.04.007

Flipping the Scarlet Letter: A New Approach to Infidelity

Molly Eames and Shannon Shoemaker

Many people, including counselors, struggle with the concept of infidelity in relationships, especially values around right and wrong. Unresolved countertransference issues may interfere with the therapeutic process that could negatively affect clients. As you read through this chapter, we encourage you to have an open thought process around your values and biases toward infidelity, how it's defined, and what it means to you.

Counseling Theories and Research

Counseling theories for years have discussed the value of intimacy and its importance in human relationships and sexual functioning (Bowlby, 1983). Developmentally, Erikson (1950) included intimacy as a central task to be completed for young adults for healthy functioning. Specifically, Erikson's stage of intimacy versus isolation focuses on developing a long-term commitment with other humans outside of the family of origin. Sexual intimacy within a relationship carries with it many expectations around the dynamics of intimacy and the roles that partners may take. Dandurand and Lafontaine (2013) discussed the importance of intimacy within sexual relationships as a predictor of physical and mental health in an individual. Although intimacy has been shown to be important, monogamy and intimacy are not synonymous. Intimacy can be had in both sexual and nonsexual relationships. Most of the counseling research, however, focuses on romantic or sexual intimacy as being between only two individuals in a committed (monogamous) relationship, suggesting that sexual intimacy cannot happen outside of these restraints (Murray et al., 2017).

Although research has focused primarily on monogamous heterosexual relationships, cohabitation, same-sex relationships, and consensual nonmonogamy (CNM) are other types of sexual, romantic, and/or emotional relationship choices. A *monogamous* relationship is defined as two individuals engaged in an exclusive relationship both sexually and emotionally (Conley et al., 2012). This is the most common type of relationship in the United States. CNM can encompass a broad range of relationships in which partners agree to have extra-dyadic sexual or romantic partners and is roughly estimated to comprise about 4%–5% of research-identified samples (Conley et al., 2012; Matsick et al., 2014). CNM relationship structures include polyamorous or open relationships, swinging, polygamy, bigamy, and others (Conley et al., 2012; Matsick et al., 2014; Murray et al., 2017).

In *polyamory* structures, multiple partners are engaged in a sexual relationship that typically has a romantic or emotional component (Matsick et al., 2014). People engaging in this relationship style may have several simultaneous relationships that could be intimate in multiple ways for longer term commitments. These agreements could be made up of primary partners with secondary partners who are invited into forming triads or quads (Matsick et al., 2014).

Swinging relationships are similar to polyamorous in that there are multiple partners; however, swinging typically involves couples with a strictly sexual component, even if the sexual relationship is maintained for a longer period of time (Matsick et al., 2014). Behaviors characteristic of this relationship could include couples exchanging partners or a third partner being invited into a couple (Matsick et al., 2014). Sklar reported in 2010 that there were more than 7 million profiles on the website Swingers Date Club (https://sdc.com), which provides resources to people who engage in this particular arrangement.

The broader category of *open* relationships includes partners who engage in sexual relationships separate from the primary partnership that do not include an emotional or relational component (Matsick et al., 2014).

Bigamy and/or *polygamy* are defined as being legally married to one person while also marrying another. When women have multiple husbands, this is known as polyandry, and when husbands have multiple wives, this is known as polygyny.

The configuration of individual relationships will differ in terms of how these defined characteristics and involvements are enacted at the level of sexual or emotional commitment (Matsick et al., 2014). Both monogamous and CNM relationships can exist in cohabitating, heterosexual, and same-sex partnerings; however, within a CNM relationship, both the individuals and the relationship itself are seen as deeply stigmatizing and of less value than a monogamous relationship (Conley et al., 2012). In a study by Conley et al. (2012), participants assumed that monogamous individuals were better citizens than those in CNM relationships.

It is important to note that CNM is distinct from infidelity, otherwise known as *nonconsensual nonmonogamy*. In infidelity, a partner has broken the understood agreed-upon rules and roles of the relationship configuration to which they have previously committed. Infidelity can include not only nonmonogamy when monogamy has been agreed to but also emotional attachments to others in an open relationship in which only sexual attachments are acceptable. Although infidelity is often seen as a pivotal event, it is actually the symptom of a much larger relational concern. Just as there are many types of relationships, there are many variations of infidelity, including type of affair (e.g., cyber, sexual, or emotional), number of affairs (one single affair versus multiple affairs), and the time or length of an affair. The gender identification of each partner in the group, as well as type of relationship, also factors into how infidelity is defined and how it is addressed with the clients.

The most current research on infidelity is out of the evolutionary behavioral sciences field, which focuses on sex and gender differences in responses to both sexual and emotional infidelity (Walsh et al., 2019), mate abandonment versus mate retention when there has been an affair (Millar & Baker, 2017), disclosure of the primary relationship status when seeking an extra partner (Hughes & Harrison, 2018), and men's tolerance of women's same-sex infidelity (Apostolou, 2019). For example, men tend to be more distressed than women by sexual infidelity because of the possibility of spending costly resources on a child that is genetically unrelated, whereas women are more distressed by relational infidelity because they depend on their partners for resources and do not want to risk losing that relationship (Walsh et al., 2019). The common theme is the effect of infidelity on parenting and resources and the practical costs for both sexes to the evolutionary goal of procreation of the species (Apostolou, 2019; Hughes & Harrison, 2018; Ijzerman et al., 2014; Millar & Baker, 2017; Walsh et al., 2019). Although evolutionarily this may be important, it is known that humans engage in sexual behavior for a wide variety of reasons and in many different relationship patterns. Procreation is no longer the sole purpose of sexual relations.

There is little recent counseling research specifically concerning the concept of infidelity (LaBrecque & Whisman, 2017). The research that does exist posits infidelity as being the most damaging transgression in a relationship "second only to physical abuse" (Fife et al., 2013, p. 344). Fife et al. (2013) lists the potential consequences, such as disease transmission and harming the primary partner in some way. This exemplifies that infidelity is typically conceptualized as a sexual-only issue in the literature rather than acknowledging the range of problems surrounding infidelity or the multiple types of infidelity that exist and how they alter depending on the relationship configuration. Esther Perel, a noted couples therapist, has said, "If we just pretend that this betrayal tops all others . . . I think we do a disservice to honesty and to marriage" (Rock, 2017, para. 20). Research acknowledges that infidelity is a common issue in committed relationships and the most common reason for divorce, while reporting negative consequences of infidelity both personally and for the marriage (Cornish et al., 2020). Outcomes of an affair as well as treatment for an affair are also foci in the counseling research. Typically, these outcomes are either about remaining together in the primary relationship or about separation, but rarely do they discuss other alternatives, such as open relationships, swinging, or polyamory. Other outcome research looks at the negative consequences of the affair, such as shame, jealousy, reduction in trust, increased conflicts, depression, anxiety, and symptoms of posttraumatic stress disorder (Balderrama-Durbin et al., 2012; Bendixen et al., 2018; Cornish et al., 2020; DeWall et al., 2011; Heintzelman et al., 2014; Marin et al., 2014; McNulty et al., 2018; Negash et al., 2018). Despite these negative outcomes, posttraumatic growth is a possible positive outcome of an affair (Heintzelman et al., 2014). Interestingly, disclosure of the affair is not necessarily an assurance of a positive outcome (Marin et al., 2014).

Infidelity Defined

A narrow definition of infidelity is no longer culturally appropriate and exemplifies the White, westernized ideals of romantic love that focus on monogamy and continue to guide the research (Conley et al., 2012). Similarly, theories and research of infidelity within the professions of counseling and psychology focus on how infidelity affects monogamous relationships and epitomizes ideas of typical human development and attachment as only monogamous dyadic pairings (Conley et al., 2012). Perel has pointed out that not only do many people who deal with infidelity in their relationship stay but that, in fact, staying is the "new shame":

> When you are shamed for staying, you are in a double bind—I have been betrayed by my partner and I have to lie about it to protect him so that other people won't judge him to such an extent that I will lose them. So now I can't talk to anybody. That's the new shame. (Rock, 2017, para. 4)

This also leaves individuals feeling isolated, subsequently increasing negative emotions and mental health concerns. Marin et al.'s (2014) research on married couples and infidelity actually found that marital stability for couples that remained together did not differ from couples that had not experienced an affair, which suggests that affairs do not need to be the death knell that society believes them to be.

Treatment for infidelity focuses on the effectiveness of couples therapy for this specific relationship issue, measuring effectiveness as to whether or not the couple stay together. The most frequently cited option for treatment is the trauma-based model of forgiveness (Gordon & Baucom, 1998), which presents a three-stage model. Negash et al. (2018) suggested that emotionally focused therapy and eye movement desensitizing and reprocessing could be helpful from a trauma perspective. Other approaches include the intersystems approach (Fife et al., 2013) and relationship enhancement couples therapy (Scuka, 2012).

Avoiding Victimizing or Blaming Language

As a counselor, it is imperative for you to know how your client couple views and defines infidelity, as it will have a different meaning to each couple, regardless of what kind of relationship they are operating within (Skurtu, 2018). Although the agreements in every relationship are different, each partner suffers when it comes to infidelity—there are no winners. To help remove victimizing language and feelings of blame or unworthiness, it is best to identify and conceptualize the couple as the "hurt partner," or the individual who has been affected by their partner's infidelity, and the "unfaithful partner," the individual who has actively stepped outside of their agreements (Spring, 2012).

Preparing for Infidelity Work

There is something engaging about the word infidelity and how it lands in human beings. Americans, in particular, have been conditioned by cultural and religious values to respond negatively toward the idea of an "affair" or "infidelity"; however, this response is not universal. Relationships do not always end as a result of an affair, which is considered normal in some cultures (Perel, 2017). As counselors, it is important for us to assess our personal biases surrounding infidelity. Do you have firsthand experience of being the unfaithful or the hurt partner? Has a family member or dear friend gone through a long, drawn-out divorce that was miserable to watch? Does your religion or culture of origin have specific values surrounding infidelity?

Take notice of what is happening in your body when considering these experiences. Is there a tightening of the chest or a turn in the stomach? With a curious and open mind, explore that feeling, because it is potentially triggering to work with infidelity.

Self-care needs to be a priority in such situations. Make sure there are rituals and methods in place to help you distinguish between your work life and your home life.

Allow yourself 30 minutes to transition from work to home each day. Listen to a song or musical genre that helps release whatever emotions are coming up for you or take time to journal and "brain dump" (an exercise of writing down whatever comes to your mind and not attaching judgment or meaning to it) after a day of sessions. It can be easy to slip into having negative thoughts about our current partnership or begin to question motives within our own relationships. To counter this, it can be helpful to end your workday by offering gratitude to your personal relationships. Remember that personal relationships are sacred, and continue to touch base with your partner surrounding your own needs within the relationship.

In this modern day, marriage is not what it used to be, and a better understanding of the history of marriage and how technology plays a role in relationships and in affairs is essential. Perel speaks of these changes in her book *The State of Affairs* (2017), proposing that the greatest difference in modern marriage practices is that individuals tend to marry for "love," rather than for financial security or social stability. Getting divorced in the 1950s was very different compared with divorcing in the modern era. This cultural shift has given women more voice and agency when it comes to advocating for their livelihood. However, technological advancements have created a multitude of virtual social networks for individuals to explore, which provides the presentation for a sense of connection for individuals and an opportunity to stray. This coupled with a second cultural shift toward individualism and entitlement creates a potential narrative for the unfaithful partner to justify why they sought intimacy outside of the relationship.

Affairs occur in every type of relationship. Although it would be easier to blame technology and the current culture, individuals have choice and free agency; therefore, infidelity is a choice. Although drunken, intoxicated, and "it didn't mean anything" affairs do happen, more often the unfaithful partner usually has some need that is not being met in their current relationship. However, it is the meaning behind the affair and attached to the affair that is important to flush out in therapy; this is where the stories of self-discovery, growth, expansion and journey to claim a new or lost identity are found (Perel, 2017). The goal as a therapist is to be a neutral third party who can advocate for the best outcome for the couple—that is, stay committed to the partnership or part ways.

The crisis of the affair is truly an existential crisis for both the unfaithful and hurt partner. Once a couple is successfully out of the crisis phase, the next question (Perel, 2017) could be, "Are you prepared to create a new relationship?" This could be a powerful and empowering question for a couple who is navigating questions of values, needs, and desires. Once the affair occurs, trust is broken. The agreements that bound the relationship are null and void. Whatever was will never be again, and that can be a difficult concept for both partners. In particular, when individuals get married young, they are often unsure of how to negotiate or ask for certain things within the relationship and rarely possess the vocabulary to do so. The foundation of a relationship consists of communication, compromise, and commitment. This is an opportunity for forgiveness, compassion, reflection, and creation. Not only for each partner, but for the foundation of a new relationship; a new relationship with agreements that honor each partner and hold space for growth and expansion.

Therapeutic rapport and having a plan to guide a clinician's actions is essential to successful healing. Counselors often "ride the emotional wave" with their clients and that makes having a guide to the process crucial. To help facilitate rapport building with both partners (hurt and unfaithful), taking a 2-1-1-2 approach is best, with additional one-on-one (1:1) sessions with each partner if needed (Skurtu, 2018). The 2-1-1-2 approach supports seeing the couple together (2) in the first session, followed by individual sessions with each partner (1:1), and uniting the couple (2) in the fourth session. The 1:1 sessions provide an opportunity to understand established relationship patterns and to connect with the vulnerability of each partner (Skurtu, 2018).

Secrets may reveal themselves in these sessions, and clinicians should know how to address these ethical concerns ahead of time. If the unfaithful partner reveals that they are actively engaged in the affair, it makes it difficult for them to fully commit to therapy—which is necessary for successful couples therapy (Skurtu, 2018). However, this is an opportunity to explore with the unfaithful partner why they are choosing to stay in the affair and perhaps help create a plan for disentanglement, to officially let their partner know that the relationship is over, or perhaps address the possibility of opening up the relationship (Perel, 2017). Secrets are not always best shared, and sometimes the clinician will hold information that is only known by one partner. When contemplating whether to reveal secrets, counselors should consider three questions (Perel, 2017): Is it honest, is it helpful, and is it kind? What will it be like for a partner to receive this piece of information? Each counselor will have to find what feels most authentic and ethical to them when it comes to sharing partner secrets, but keep in mind the context as cultural norms vary and some secrets may have far greater consequences, if revealed, than others.

Three Phases of Healing

The timeline for healing from infidelity varies greatly, but there are three phases and various milestones and accomplishments that can be referenced to help conceptualize the path (Perel, 2017). Throughout these phases, clinicians can teach the unfaithful and hurt partners to lean toward each other and recognize that the best way to heal is to heal together, regardless of the outcome. Each partner will also benefit from having an identified individual outside of their relationship who can be the safe space to turn when they need to vent or talk about their feelings. The three phases are crisis management, meaning making, and visioning or relationship by design (Perel, 2017; Skurtu, 2018).

Phase One: Crisis Management

The first phase of healing is crisis management (Perel, 2017). The first milestone usually occurs 3 months after the unfaithful partner has disclosed the last piece of "new" information from their affair (Skurtu, 2018). Clinicians should expect to deescalate, normalize the emotional rollercoaster of feelings for the hurt partner (which tend to vacillate between love, hate, and self-loathing), and learn about the grief cycle; teach communication skills for the couples to use outside of session; and encourage both partners to not make any major decisions. It is essential that the unfaithful partner can acknowledge the basic "who, what, when, and where" details of their affair and the pain that the affair caused the hurt partner. Perel (2017) suggests helping the hurt partner explore the reason behind their curiosity if they desire more information; the details of the affair do not often help the situation, but understanding the larger emotional needs, feelings, and thoughts is paramount to the hurt partner's healing.

Using the dialectical behavior therapy (DBT) technique of both/and is a strong way of offering validation (for each partner's feelings) while also suggesting change (the most positive choices) when discussing topics throughout the phases (Skurtu, 2018). Actively defining what an affair is and helping each partner create the meaning of what the affair is to them is another milestone. This signifies the transition from the crisis phase to the meaning-making phase.

Phase Two: Meaning Making

Whereas the first phase of healing deals with the crisis (e.g., the fallout, the lies, the hurt feelings), the second phase explores the why—that is, the meaning of the affair, the motives, and the experience of the infidelity as a whole (Perel, 2017). By exploring these various questions, each partner will begin to accept that their partner, like all of humanity, has flaws and can begin to identify the various vulnerabilities that existed within their relationship that created space for the affair. Each partner has a responsibility to the relationship, and taking ownership of their actions and thoughts is necessary for recovery. As Perel (2017) stated, "Infidelity is not just about broken contracts, it is about broken hearts" (p. 98).

Jealousy is a strange emotion, but it can be considered the "shadow of love," which allows us as counselors to provide a powerful reframe when jealousy issues arise (Perel, 2017). The word "jealousy" can be traced back to the Greek word for zeal, which honors both the suffering and vulnerability that exist within jealousy (Perel, 2017). This acknowledgment frees the hurt partner from victimhood and the sense of being part of a failed system, placing them instead as the "protagonist in their own forlorn love story" (Perel, 2017, p. 99).

Throughout this phase, it can be highly effective to use techniques such as the Love Map by John and Julie Gottman (see Lisitsa, n.d.); DBT's both/and approach; and systems theory, which explains why healing must be done as a team, rather than as individuals alone (Skurtu, 2018). Major milestones to address during the meaning-making phase are choosing whether to stay in the relationship or separate, repairing unresolved issues in the relationship, and rebuilding trust in the relationship (Skurtu, 2018). This first round of "should I stay or should I go" can be difficult to navigate. For some hurt partners, the decision will be an easy one: The offense is so shocking and painful that there is no option for repair. Others, however, fall into the "previously happy" (no prior relationship or sexual issues) or "chronic issues"' (the relationship has ongoing issues that have not been addressed) categories with their relationship. Looking for contextual factors within the relationship that led to the affair is helpful for those individuals who existed in a previously happy relationship. Otherwise, exploring 1:1 sessions with each partner to assess for any mental health issues, chronic pain, and understanding the relationship dynamic pre-affair is useful (Skurtu, 2018). If both partners decide to remain committed to the relationship, the counselor can focus on rebuilding trust and helping the unfaithful and hurt partner develop perspective.

Trust covers many realms: financial duties, coparenting responsibilities, career, household chores, emotional needs, and sexual needs—to name only a few. To rebuild trust, the unfaithful partner needs to understand that earned trust takes time; there will be a period of time where the hurt partner will need to witness the unfaithful partner saying and doing exactly what they said they would. This is the only way to gain trust and rebuild the connection, and it can be done in many different ways. Effective interventions include creating clear boundaries (request for action and how the partner will respond), helping the unfaithful partner identify relationship vulnerabilities and make a plan for avoiding them, redefining privacy and setting up new types of accountabilities, and helping the couple with language for boundary-setting conversations (Skurtu, 2018). This marks the transition to the third phase of healing, which is visioning and creating for the future (Perel, 2017).

Phase Three: Visioning

The final stage of healing from infidelity is an exciting space for visioning and creation. This is the space for delving into all things related to sexuality, intimacy, and relationships (Perel, 2017). Visioning and creation is imagining the kind of relationship, partnership, and experiences that the couple wants to have in the future—the possibilities are endless! It is about couples designing their ideal relationship and figuring out how to obtain it. Many people in the United States have not received adequate guidance on how, why, when, and where to talk about sex. It is therefore a counselor's job to teach and coach them through this crucial development (Perel, 2017). The milestones in this phase are redefining the relationship, reclaiming healthy sex, and forgiveness (Skurtu, 2018).

Infidelity does not have to be a forever scarlet letter. The question to ask the couple at this venture is "Would you like to create a new relationship?" (Perel, 2017, p. 17). Part of redefining the relationship is to redefine how the couple celebrates special moments and holidays that are different from their last relationship, but also to help each partner explore and identify what kind of relationship they want to be engaged in. What shared values, experiences, and expectations do they desire to call into their new relationship? How can each partner use other sources to strengthen this new connection (e.g., five love languages, erotic blueprint [see www.missjaiya.com])? What kind of rituals or routines could be put into place to help ease the fears of the hurt partner, while respecting the unfaithful partner (or vice versa)? There will be good days and bad days as each partner reflects on their individual needs, wants, and desires, but this is also an opportunity for unity. Although the unfaithful and hurt partners are learning how to communicate about their needs, they are also negotiating and working together to create the relationship that best fits them.

Additionally, the couple is learning how to discuss sex and their desires throughout this final healing phase. The milestone of reclaiming a healthy sex life is about assessing for any trauma triggers and learning about what feels good in their body. Criticism cannot be part of these conversations. Sex should to be discussed in a nonjudgmental, playful, curious, open-minded way. Teach grounding techniques if they are needed. Mindfulness is a great tool to teach throughout all three phases, but it can be particularly helpful with sexual connection. The good enough sex model can help in assessing areas that need continued sexuality education, as well as provide an outline for a healthy sexual relationship (Metz & McCarthy, 2012). This model supports a focus on intimacy rather than performance and/or penetration, and suggests healthy sexual connection stems from honest dialogue, reflection, realistic expectations, and an understanding that sexuality is always evolving. Eroticism often comes up in these discussions, and couples who are able to share these thoughts without shame experience a "growing acceptance that they both feel is one of the strongest protectors against future betrayal" (Perel, 2017, p. 211).

The final milestone of healing is forgiveness (Skurtu, 2018). Forgiveness takes time. Forgiveness and compassion are perhaps the most difficult to facilitate for ourselves, and forgiveness is not always achieved. Skurtu (2018) created five steps to help clients understand and conceptualize forgiveness: (a) make an intentional choice to work on forgiveness, (b) empathize with your partner and develop a sense of understanding as to how an individual could have made such a mistake, (c) acknowledge the moments when you are hurting and feeling triggered by your partner (and remember to be kind to yourself!), (d) intentionally shift your thoughts to more positive aspects of your relationship, and (e) remember that forgiveness takes time.

The answer to the question "How do you affair-proof a marriage?" is simple: Create a relationship by your design that is so incredible and amazing that you are willing to fight for it every day (Skurtu, 2018). This is not done by having extensive rules and regulations for your partner (or lack of rules). Perel (2017) states that helping couples create a "tolerance for ambiguity and uncertainty [creates an] open space for exploration, in which they could more deeply connect" (p. 295). Every relationship will look different, because each partner has their own unique needs and desires. Perel (2017) suggests that allowing each partner to experience a sense of freedom within the relationship actually helps the couple to feel more connected and less likely to seek excitement outside of their designated relationship. The erotic exists within that sense of freedom, and that contributes to keeping the sexual spark alive (Perel, 2017).

The foundation of a healthy relationship is communication, compromise, and commitment. Infidelity can be a moment of empowerment and exploration for the unfaithful and hurt partner—an opportunity to create the life and relationship that allows each partner to feel fully seen, recognized, and appreciated. Gone are the days of saying infidelity destroys your life; rather, infidelity closes chapters, although sometimes very painfully. But through that pain is growth, a true moment of rising from the ashes and reclaiming a life and relationship that is so worthwhile, it is intentionally nurtured. Love is an intentional choice. Successful relationships require communication about needs even when the conversation is difficult, compromise because somebody always has to lead the dance, and commitment to always show up and fight for each other.

Case Example

Cecil, a 46-year-old cisgender male, and Adria, a 44-year-old cisgender queer female, have been cohabitating for over 20 years, have no children, and are upper middle class. They met in their middle 20s, sharing a deep passion for the arts, and later they became business owners together. The couple continues to run a small art gallery, stating that they are truly "compatible at business." Cecil handles the finances and back end of business, while Adria builds relationships with local artists and travels occasionally looking for unique pieces and artists who have a story. Adria does not believe in the "institution of marriage"; therefore, she and Cecil call each other "life partners." In lieu of rings or jewelry as a symbol of their chosen union, they each have a tattoo on their left wrist that is symbolic to them. Both partners had heteronormative sexual experiences prior to meeting and state that for most of their relationship, sex has been "fantastic."

Three years prior to counseling, Adria had an emotional affair with Elaine, a local artist whom Cecil and Adria had grown close to as a couple. Adria first met Elaine 7 years earlier at her graduate school's end-of-year art show, where Elaine was showcasing her photography. By the end of the summer, Cecil, Adria, and Elaine had become fast friends. Over the course of the next few years, Elaine becomes a regularly shown artist in the couple's art gallery.

As Adria neared age 38, she and Cecil decided to try "more aggressively" to procreate, which meant tracking Adria's period, taking ovulation tabs, changing diets in hopes of creating a better sperm count, and having sex at specific times. Adria and Cecil struggled for 2 more years until she became pregnant, just before her 41st birthday. The couple was elated and immediately named it the "miracle nut." Due to unforeseen circumstances, Adria miscarried the child in the middle of her second trimester.

Adria remembers "hating" sex after the miscarriage. Although she was eager for the physical connection with Cecil, the thought of losing another child far outweighed the pleasureful side of sex. Adria and Cecil struggled with intimacy issues for several years.

Adria felt alone and abandoned after her miscarriage. She hoped therapy would help assuage her intense feelings of guilt about the loss, but believes Cecil benefited more from it. She felt "unseen" in session and "unseen" at home. Adria turned to Elaine for support.

Cecil soon began noticing how much time Elaine and Adria were spending together and stated his unhappiness about how he was feeling "left out." Adria reassured him that Elaine was just needing some "good girl time" and called Cecil "paranoid."

Adria states in counseling that she was aware of how close she was becoming to Elaine and calls it an "emotional affair." After 2 years of this "emotional affair," Elaine had kissed Adria. Adria remembers the evening with wistfulness and deep regret. She states that in that moment she felt "alive" and like she had been transported back to her "younger days." Although always identifying as queer, Adria had never been with a woman before and enjoyed the "connection" of another woman's body. She states that the sex was "primal yet nurturing" but felt "deep shame" when it was over. She knew she had crossed a boundary and decided to never tell Cecil, ending the relationship with Elaine a week later. By the end of the following year, Elaine was no longer an artist being shown at the couple's art gallery.

Cecil expresses in counseling that he is angry that he has been "duped." It does not matter that Adria ended the affair over a year ago; he had been lied to and honesty was their number one rule of the relationship. He had suspicions and when Adria told him that she no longer wanted to show Elaine's photography, he figured the two women had an argument and would eventually work it out. Cecil was cleaning the office at the art gallery when he stumbled upon a photograph of Adria, taken by Elaine, with a note attached. Cecil states he felt "gut punched" and "saw red." He immediately confronted Adria, who acknowledged the affair and shared the timeline of her indiscretion.

The first step in treatment planning is crisis management. Neither partner should rush into any major decisions while emotions are flying high. Educating Cecil and Adria on what to expect in terms of a timeline of recovery is helpful to normalize the emotional rollercoaster of feelings that Cecil is experiencing and to alert the couple that healing takes time. After the initial intake session, the counselor should schedule 1:1 sessions with each partner to help develop rapport, check for emotional regulation, and gain the trust of the unfaithful partner. Throughout the beginning stages of seeing the couple, educating Cecil and Adria on healthy communication techniques, such as the gentle start-up and "I" statements, helps give the couple a roadmap of how to start communicating about the infidelity and how to appropriately ask for their needs. Cecil and Adria took to these techniques quickly and set aside 30 minutes each day to discuss their needs post affair. During our 1:1 sessions, Adria is able to acknowledge the hurt that she has caused Cecil and the reasons she turned toward

Elaine in the first place. By addressing these issues, Adria was able to connect with Cecil in session and take responsibility for her actions. Likewise, Cecil identified the pain that their miscarriage had caused for Adria and acknowledged that he turned toward their art gallery for solace instead of turning toward his partner for support. Cecil expressed his hurt feelings in a letter and acknowledged how his actions contributed to Adria not feeling "seen" anymore in their relationship. The letter was read aloud during session and the couple cried as they revisited the details of how the affair started. Affairs are common after a loss, and this knowledge was comforting to the couple. By defining the affair and assigning meaning to it, Cecil and Adria are able to identify the factors in their relationship that led to Adria finding comfort in Elaine. Cecil and Adria also took the time to properly acknowledge and grieve the loss of their child, an event that was identified as the starting point of the infidelity.

The couple was asked if they are interested in saying goodbye to their old relationship and yes to creating a new relationship that honors who they are now. They accepted the offer. The couple begins to create a plan for rebuilding trust that includes redefining boundaries, accountability systems, the "benefit of the doubt," and privacy. They also spend time individually reflecting on their values and exploring what kind of relationship would ultimately make them happiest. Each partner explored their physical, mental, spiritual, and sexual well-being, and together in session Adria and Cecil created a new set of shared values and a plan for the future. This plan includes knowing how to talk if one of them feels like they may be interested in cheating and an honest discussion about opening up their relationship, with an agreed-upon set of parameters for how that will happen.

Questions You Always Wanted to Ask

1. **There are so many relationship options right now—how do I keep up with them all?**
   It's best to let your clients define their relationship status for you. Providing a blank space on your intake form for a short, written response allows your clients the fluidity to describe their relationship in their own words, which helps you build rapport.
2. **What if I use the wrong language in a session?**
   As you let clients define their relationship status, also follow their lead when defining other aspects of their identity such as gender identification and/or sexual/affectional identity. Occasionally, you may use language that could offend a client, but paying attention to their nonverbal cues and interpreting them correctly could allow you to bring this up in session and build a stronger therapeutic rapport by allowing for open dialogue and a sharing of power in the counseling room.
3. **How do I handle asexual or celibate clients discussing affairs?**
   Often, we think that affairs can only be sexual in nature. Instead, broadening our definition of what an affair is can be helpful in working with clients from all backgrounds and cultural contexts that we may not be familiar with. Committing to doing internal work around your own values and beliefs of what an affair is and its meaning to you personally will help you to separate your own biases from those of your clients.

4. **What if I have personally experienced infidelity as a clinician and am biased?** As most people have been in committed, monogamous relationships at least at one time in their lives, it is almost certain that they have experienced affairs, which means that you have also most likely experienced infidelity at some point in either role. We all have biases around these types of value-laden experiences, and we need to be aware of them so that we can ensure we are not imposing our values onto our clients as that is an ethical concern. Being open with yourself and engaging in individual therapy is a great starting point for this process.
5. **Why do people cheat?** People have affairs for a number of reasons, many of which have nothing to do with their partner and instead reflect an unmet need in themselves. It is better to make sure you work with each client individually to understand their particular circumstance without making assumptions or judgments about why the infidelity occurred.
6. **How do you affair-proof a marriage?** The answer is simple: Create a relationship by your design that leaves you feeling so fulfilled and seen that you are willing to fight for that relationship every day (Skurtu, 2018).
7. **What if my definition of an affair is different from my clients'?** Often your definition of an affair will be different from that of your clients because the definition of an affair is very individualized. Seeing your client as the expert on their own life and allowing them to define what an affair is for themselves and/or their relationship—and respecting that definition rather than allowing your own values to impede the process—is the ethical stance.
8. **What is the best treatment for an affair?** There are various techniques that have been found effective, from DBT to emotion-focused therapy, cognitive behavior therapy, and mindfulness. Treatment planning is best conceptualized in stages: crisis management, meaning making, and visioning/relationship by design.
9. **How do I handle secrets in session?** Secrets happen, and it is best practice to include your policy on your informed consent form. Some counselors have a hard "no secrets" policy, believing it is best to be transparent because keeping secrets may result in one partner feeling like the clinician is taking sides (Skurtu, 2018). Others prefer to allow secrets but only for a limited amount of time so they can explore the "why" with the partner who holds the secret, perhaps offering assistance in ending the affair and/or clarifying that the unfaithful partner is not interested in remaining committed to the original relationship (Perel, 2017).

References

Apostolou, M. (2019). The evolution of same-sex attraction in women. *Journal of Individual Differences 40*(2), 104–110. https://doi.org/10.1027/1614-0001/a000281

Balderrama-Durbin, C. M., Rhoades, G. K., & Allen, E. S. (2012). Demand and withdraw behaviors in couples with a history of infidelity. *Journal of Family Psychology, 26*(1), 11–17. https://doi.org/10.1037/a0026756

Bendixen, M., Kennair, L. E. O., & Grontvedt, T. V. (2018). Forgiving the unforgivable: Couples' forgiveness and expected forgiveness of emotional and sexual infidelity from an error management theory perspective. *Evolutionary Behavioral Sciences, 12*(4), 322–335. https://doi.org/10.1037/ebs0000110

Bowlby, J. (1983). *Attachment* (2nd ed.). Basic Books.
Conley, T. D., Moors, A. C., Matsick, J. L., & Ziegler, A. (2012). The fewer the merrier? Assessing stigma surrounding consensually non-monogamous romantic relationships. *Analyses of Social Issues and Public Policy, 13*(1), 1–30. https://doi.org/10.1111/j.1530-2415.2012.01286.x
Cornish, M. A., Hanks, M. A., & Gubash Black, S. M. (2020). Self-forgiving process in therapy for romantic relationship infidelity: An evidence-based case study. *Psychotherapy, 57*(3), 352–365. https://doi.org/10.1037/pst0000292
Dandurand, C., & Lafontaine, M. F. (2013). Intimacy and couple satisfaction: The moderating role of romantic attachment. *International Journal of Psychological Studies, 1*(5), 74–90. https://doi.org/10.5539/ijps.v5n1p74
DeWall, N. C., Lambert, N. M., Slotter, E. B., Pond, R. S., Jr., Deckman, T., Finkel, E. J., Luchies, L. B., & Fincham, F. D. (2011). So far away from one's partner, yet so close to romantic alternatives: Avoidant attachment, interest in alternatives, and infidelity. *Journal of Personality and Social Psychology, 101*(6), 1302–1316. https://doi.org/10.1037/a0025497
Erikson, E. (1950). *Childhood and society.* Norton.
Fife, S. T., Weeks, G. R., & Stellberg-Filbert, J. (2013). Facilitating forgiveness in the treatment of infidelity: An interpersonal model. *Journal of Family Therapy, 35*, 343–367. https://doi.org/10.1111/j.1467-6427.2011.00561.x
Gordon, K. C., & Baucom, D. H. (1998). Understanding betrayals in marriage: A synthesized model of forgiveness. *Family Process, 37*(4), 425–449. https://doi.org/10.1111/j.1545-5300.1998.00425.x
Heintzelman, A., Murdock, N. L., Krycak, R. C., & Seay, L. (2014). Recovery from infidelity: Differentiation of self, trauma, forgiveness, and posttraumatic growth among couples in continuing relationships. *Couple and Family Psychology: Research and Practice, 3*(1), 13–29. https://doi.org/10.1037/cfp0000016
Hughes, S. M., & Harrison, M. A. (2018). Women reveal, men conceal: Current relationship disclosure when seeking an extrapair partner. *Evolutionary Behavioral Sciences, 13*(3), 272–277. https://doi.org/10.1037/ebs0000133
Ijzerman, H., Blanken, I., Brandt, M. J., Oerlemans, J. M., Van den Hoogenhof, M. M. W., Franken, S. J. M., & Oerlemans, M. W. G. (2014). Sex differences in distress from infidelity and early adulthood and later life: A replication and meta-analysis of Shackelford et al. (2004). *Social Psychology, 45*(3), 202–208.
Labrecque, L. T., & Whisman, M. A. (2017). Attitudes toward and prevalence of extramarital sex and descriptions of extramarital partners in the 21st century. *Journal of Family Psychology, 31*(7), 952–957. https://doi.org/10.1037/fam0000280
Lisitsa, E. (n.d.). The sound relationship house: Build love maps. *The Gottman Relationship Blog.* https://www.gottman.com/blog/the-sound-relationship-house-build-love-maps/
Marin, R. A., Christensen, A., & Atkins, D. C. (2014). Infidelity and behavioral couple therapy: Relationship outcomes over 5 years following therapy. *Couple and Family Psychology: Research and Practice, 3*(1), 1–12. https://doi.org/10.1037/cfp0000012
Matsick, J. L., Conley, T. D., Ziegler, A., Moors, A. C., & Rubin, J. D. (2014). Love and sex: Polyamorous relationships are perceived more favourably than swinging and open relationships. *Psychology & Sexuality, 5*, 339–348. https://doi.org/10.1080/19419899.2013.832934

McNulty, J. K., Meltzer, A. L., Makhanova, A., & Maner, J. K. (2018). Attentional and evaluative biases help people maintain relationships by avoiding infidelity. *Journal of Personality and Social Psychology, 115*(1), 76–95. https://doi.org/10.1037/pspi0000127

Metz, M. E., & McCarthy, B. W. (2012). The good enough sex model. In P. J. Kleinplatz (Ed.), *New directions in sex therapy: Innovations and alternatives* (2nd ed., pp. 213–229). Routledge.

Millar, M. G., & Baker, A. (2017). Behavioral reactions to emotional and sexual infidelity: Mate abandonment versus mate retention. *Evolutionary Behavioral Sciences, 11*(4), 336–340. https://doi.org/10.1037/ebs0000091

Murray, C., Pope, A., & Willis, B. (2017). *Sexuality counseling: Theory, research and practice*. SAGE.

Negash, S., Carlson, S. H., & Linder, J. N. (2018). Emotionally focused therapy and eye movement desensitization and reprocessing: An integrated treatment to heal the trauma of infidelity. *Couple and Family Psychology: Research and Practice, 7*(3 & 4), 143–157. https://doi.org/10.1037/cfp0000107

Perel, E. (2017). *The state of affairs: Rethinking infidelity*. Harper Collins.

Rock, L. (2017, October 28). Esther Perel on affairs: Do you break up or can you make up? *The Guardian*. https://www.theguardian.com/lifeandstyle/2017/oct/28/esther-perel-the-relationship-guru-who-thinks-infidelity-isnt-all-bad

Scuka, R. F. (2012). Repairing a relationship imperiled by infidelity: Combining individual work, relationship enhancement couple therapy, and guided visualization to break through and emotional impasse. *Sexual and Relationship Therapy, 27*(4), 335–343. https://doi.org/10.1080/14681994.2012.735768

Sklar, H. L. (2010, March 17). Meet the swingers. *Self Magazine*. https://www.self.com/story/meet-the-swingers

Skurtu, A. (2018). *Helping couples overcome infidelity: A therapist's manual*. Routledge.

Spring, J. A. (2012). *After the affair: Healing the pain and rebuilding trust when a partner has been unfaithful* (2nd ed.). William Morrow.

Walsh, M., Millar, M., & Westfall, R. S. (2019). Sex differences in response to emotional and sexual infidelity in dating relationships. *Journal of Individual Differences, 40*(2), 63–70. https://doi.org/10/1027/1614-0001/a000277

PART 8

Education

Adolescents Do It Too! Sex Education in America

Karen O'Hearn

"Where do babies come from?" This is a question that many children ask—and most adults dread answering. It may be preceded by other sex-related inquiries, such as "Mommy, why do you have those bumps?" "Why is daddy's so much bigger than mine?" and "Why do boys have one of those?" It is logical to assume that these obvious physical differences have generated the same questions throughout history, but today's answers to these childhood curiosities are usually much different from those provided just a generation ago. Because of the scientific research into sexual development by physicians, sex educators, sexologists, and child-development experts, adults are now able to provide children and adolescents with fact-based answers that promote healthy sexual development.

The acceptance, development, and implementation of sex education have continually evolved over the last century and are still changing to meet the challenges of inclusion, new technologies, diseases, and the persistent obstacles presented by sexual moralists. By improving communication between primary caretakers and educators, adults and students will be better able to understand the validity, developmental appropriateness, purpose, and usefulness of sex education during family discussions on sex-related topics. A dialogue based on facts will result in healthier psychological, physical, and relationship outcomes for everyone.

Opposing Viewpoints: Morality Versus Science

Just as Darwin's theory of evolution has continually been disputed by believers in creationism, theories regarding sexual development and behavior are constantly being challenged around the world by centuries-old religious beliefs and social mores regarding human sexuality. Science may not care what people believe, but that does not mean everyone will be easily convinced to replace their traditional religious and cultural norms with science-based research findings. Sex educators have a duty to respectfully, but persuasively, present science-based information even when it contradicts students' existing belief systems.

According to Breuner et al. (2016):

> Sexuality education is defined as teaching about human sexuality, including intimate relationships, human sexual anatomy, sexual reproduction, sexually transmitted infections, sexual activity, sexual orientation, gender identity, abstinence, contraception, and reproductive rights and responsibilities. Developmentally appropriate and evidence-based education about human sexuality and sexual reproduction over time provided by pediatricians, schools, other professionals, and parents is important to help children and adolescents make informed, positive, and safe choices about healthy relationships, responsible sexual activity, and their reproductive health. (para. 1)

There are currently two predominant viewpoints on sex education available to educators when developing curricula: *abstinence only sex education* (AOSE), which is sometimes referred to in the literature as *abstinence only until marriage* (AOUM); and *comprehensive sexuality education* (CSE). A less common approach is termed *abstinence plus education* (APE). These approaches have been thoroughly evaluated through fact-based research to determine how effectively each provides children and adolescents with the information necessary for a lifetime of healthy sexual development. Through an understanding of the theoretical basis for each viewpoint, a review of the related research, and an understanding of the impact of the cultural and political environments, sexuality educators can develop and defend their curriculum content.

Abstinence Only Approach

To understand AOSE, there must be a clear understanding of what is meant by abstinence as it applies to this theory. *Abstinence* is simply the act or practice of restraining oneself from indulging in sexual activity, including sexual intercourse. The primary objective of federally funded AOSE programs, as defined in the Social Security Act, is for students to remain celibate until marriage to ensure sexual health and positive relationships (U.S. Department of Health and Human Services, 2007). This objective is based on the AOSE proponents' premise that married couples are safe from the physical and psychological concerns of nonmarried sexually active persons. Therefore, in practice, AOSE does not assist sexually active adolescents and adults in regulating, exploring, or enjoying sex before or during marriage. Such programs in the schools instruct adolescents and unmarried adults to suppress all sexual desire and activity until marriage. This approach fosters fear of the possible negative consequences of engaging in nonmarital sex and guilt for not meeting the AOSE program expectation of complete chastity.

AOSE is based on long-term cultural and religious beliefs that nonmarital sex is immoral and that marital sex is the only proper type of sex. In spite of a traditional basis for this position, it has been difficult to defend philosophically, legally, or scientifically. People who are married have no guarantees that their sexual activities will always be consensual, nonviolent, or legal. Conversely, nonmarital sex often results in no damage to its voluntary participants who are of full capacity and not coerced by undue influence.

Marriage offers little protection from rape and other forms of sexual abuse within or outside of the marriage. It is also no guarantee of protection from sexually transmitted infections (STIs), which would require both marital partners to successfully achieve lifelong sexual fidelity. Abstinence until marriage is a religious tenet for most evangelicals (religious fundamentalists), who assume it will result in stronger marital relationships. In a study conducted for the Council on Contemporary Families (Baylor University, 2014), it was reported that, in fact, evangelical Christians have a higher-than-average divorce rate, marry at a younger-than-average age, and require their potential partners to profess faith in Jesus and a willingness to abstain from sex until marriage. Dainton (2011) conducted a study that identified conversation, intimacy, relaxation, ambition, philosophy, interests, respect, and passion, among others, as compatibility factors important for relationship maintenance. Abstinence until marriage was not specifically identified as an important relationship maintenance factor.

For several decades, AOSE educators and conservative legislators referred to their sex-education viewpoint as "abstinence only sex education," but then later as "abstinence centered education." Now, it is sometimes referred to as "sexual risk avoidance" (SRA) education. Grossu and Sprigg (2014) described SRA as

> an approach to sex education that focuses on risk-avoidance instead of sexual risk-reduction (SRR) or "comprehensive sex education" when it comes to sexual activity. The term . . . communicates how this approach mirrors other public health models designed to encourage avoidance instead of reduction of risky behavior, such as underage drinking or the use of illegal drugs. SRA education teaches that avoiding sexual activity before marriage is the surest way to avoid its risks. It also encourages youth to pursue good decision-making skills. (p. 1)

Although the primary emphasis of AOSE (or SRA) is on eliminating nonmarital sexual activity, SRA education is the descriptor used by many AOSE practitioners (Grossu & Sprigg, 2014). Previous constitutional challenges to the government funding of the morality-based AOSE program are lessened by reframing its primary objective of abstinence until marriage to emphasizing the negative risks associated with sexual behavior outside of marriage. AOSE theory places the personal responsibility of abstinence until marriage on the individual. It instructs students on how to make decisions that avoid, resist, and discourage situations that might cause them to become sexually active, while rejecting the appropriateness of many forms of legal sexual expression as harmful.

Grossu and Sprigg (2014) supported AOSE's mission to condemn all adolescent nonmarital sexual activity while disregarding and devaluing safer-sex practices. They justify this "just say no" strategy by citing its alignment with established drug and alcohol use prevention programs that condemn all illegal drug and underage alcohol use. Unlike sex, recreational drug use and underage drinking are not normal or necessary bodily functions, and sexual activity is not exclusively a health risk. Sex is natural for all living organisms and a necessary element of the human reproductive system. McCammon (2017) quoted Laura Lindberg, a researcher at the Guttmacher Institute, who argued that Grossu and Sprigg's comparison is nonsensical: "We tell people not to drink and drive. . . . We don't teach them not to drive. . . . We would never withhold information about seat belts because they wouldn't know how to protect themselves" (para. 16).

In a 6-year follow-up study of participants who took chastity pledges and participated in a 4-year AOSE program during high school, Ott and Santelli (2007) determined that 88% of these students had participated in vaginal intercourse before marriage, and their instances of STIs were no less than those of students who had not participated in an AOSE program. This study disregarded the data provided by the

AOSE program regarding participants' sexual activity, because these data were found to be lacking in completeness and scientific integrity.

In a comprehensive review of abstinence only policies and programs and their impact in the United States, Santelli et al. (2017) found that

> programs that promote abstinence-only-until-marriage (AOUM) or sexual risk avoidance are scientifically and ethically problematic and—as such—have been widely rejected by medical and public health professionals. Although abstinence is theoretically effective, in actual practice, intentions to abstain from sexual activity often fail. . . . Promotion of AOUM policies by the U.S. government has undermined sexuality education in the United States and in U.S. foreign aid programs. . . . AOUM programs, as defined by U.S. federal funding requirements, inherently withhold information about human sexuality and may provide medically inaccurate and stigmatizing information. Thus, AOUM programs threaten fundamental human rights to health, information, and life. Young people need access to accurate and comprehensive sexual health information to protect their health and lives. (p. 273)

Fox et al. (2019) found that conservative states, which are more likely to utilize government funds provided for AOSE, have higher teen birth rates than states that do not take full advantage of this funding. Regarding teen pregnancy rates among AOSE students, their research concluded that

> the millions of dollars spent on abstinence-only education has had no effect on adolescent birthrates, although conservative states, which experience the greatest burden of adolescent births, are the most responsive to changes in sexuality education–funding streams. (Fox et al., 2019, p. 497)

Sex positivity, positive body-image development, and the normalizing of sexual desire are unaddressed or discouraged in AOSE. It does not recognize the rights of children and adolescents, at every developmental stage, to have access to age-appropriate information regarding sexual activity, sexual health, pregnancy prevention, sexual orientation, and gender diversity to inform their sexual decision-making.

Comprehensive Approach

The impact of the worldwide HIV/AIDS pandemic in the 1980s required the focus of sexuality education to be shifted away from the traditional morality-based methods to CSE, which democratically offers universal sexuality education based on scientific data (People for the American Way Foundation, 1996). The Guttmacher Institute (n.d.) stated that an objective of CSE is to educate men and women on the proper and consistent use of condoms for sexual health. A study by the U.S. Agency for International Development (2015) found that condom use had led to a significant reduction in the HIV/AIDS virus's morbidity and death rates.

The United Nations Educational, Scientific, and Cultural Organization (UNESCO, 2018) has defined CSE as a

> curriculum-based process of teaching and learning about the cognitive, emotional, physical and social aspects of sexuality . . . [that] aims to equip children and young people with knowledge, skills, attitudes and values that will empower them to: realize their health, well-being and dignity; develop respectful social and sexual relationships; consider how their choices affect their own well-being and that of others; and understand and ensure the protection of their rights throughout their lives. (p. 16)

By this definition, CSE includes all or nearly all aspects of sexuality education, thus answering sexual questions and concerns of all students. By contrast, AOSE does not address sexual activity when discussing abstinence or sexuality.

The Guttmacher Institute (Panchaud & Anderson, 2016) supports the work of the African Population and Health Research Center, World Health Organization, Johns Hopkins University Bloomberg School of Public Health, and many other research-based professionals in the field of human sexuality and is committed to promoting sexual health and reproductive rights through the implementation of CSE. The Guttmacher Institute also endorses and distributes the International Planned Parenthood Federation's (IPPF) Seven Essential Components of Comprehensive Sex Education in its essential handouts, which are used by many sex educators when developing their CSE curricula and practices (Guttmacher Institute, n.d.). It also emphasizes the importance of age appropriateness for CSE topics, with an emphasis on providing services that are "youth-friendly" (Guttmacher Institute, 2022, para. 1). CSE allows students to generate curriculum topics that are based on their own environment, experiences, and identified needs.

The IPPF Seven Components (Guttmacher Institute, n.d.) specify the types of information that must be included in a curriculum for it to be called a CSE program, as follows:

1. *Gender*: Difference between gender and sex; exploring gender roles and attributes; understanding perceptions of masculinity and femininity within the family and across the life cycle; society's changing norms and values; manifestations and consequences of gender bias, stereotypes, and inequality (including self-stigmatization).
2. *Sexual and reproductive health and HIV*: Sexuality and the life cycle (e.g., puberty, menopause, stigma, sexual problems); anatomy; reproductive process; how to use condoms and other forms of contraception (including emergency contraception); pregnancy options and information; legal and safe abortion; unsafe abortion; understanding HIV and other [STIs], including transmission and symptoms; HIV and STI prevention, treatment, care, and support; voluntary counseling and testing for HIV; antiretroviral therapy and living with HIV; prevention of mother-to-child transmission; injection drug use and HIV; virginity; abstinence and faithfulness; sexual response; social expectations; self-esteem and empowerment; respect for the body; myths and stereotypes.
3. *Sexual rights and sexual citizenship*: Knowledge of international human rights and national policies, laws, and structures that relate to people's sexuality; rights-based approach to sexual and reproductive health; social, cultural, and ethical barriers to exercising rights related to sexual and reproductive health; understanding that sexuality and culture are diverse and dynamic; available services and resources and how to access them; participation; practices and norms; diversity of sexual identities; advocacy; choice; protection; negotiation skills; consent and the right to have sex only when you are ready; the right to freely express and explore one's sexuality in a safe, healthy, and pleasurable way.
4. *Pleasure*: Having a positive approach to young people's sexuality; understanding that sex should be enjoyable and consensual; understanding that sex is much more than just sexual intercourse; sexuality as a healthy and normal part of

everybody's life; the biology and emotions behind the human sexual response; gender and pleasure; sexual well-being; safer sex practices and pleasure; masturbation; love, lust, and relationships; interpersonal communication; the diversity of sexuality; the first sexual experience; consent; alcohol, drugs, and the implications of their use; addressing stigma associated with pleasure.

5. *Violence*: Exploring the various types of violence toward men and women and how they manifest, particularly gender-based violence; nonconsensual sex and understanding what is unacceptable; rights and laws; support options available and seeking help; community norms and myths regarding power and gender; prevention, including personal safety plans; self-defense techniques; understanding the dynamics of victims and abusers; appropriate referral mechanisms for survivors; preventing the victim from becoming a perpetrator; men and boys as both perpetrators and allies in violence prevention.
6. *Diversity*: Recognizing and understanding the range of diversity in our lives (e.g., faith, culture, ethnicity, socioeconomic status, ability/disability, HIV status, sexual orientation); a positive view of diversity; recognizing discrimination and its damaging effects and being able to manage it; developing a belief in equality; supporting young people to move beyond just tolerance.
7. *Relationships*: Different types of relationships (e.g., family, friends, sexual, romantic); that relationships are constantly changing; emotions; intimacy (emotional and physical); rights and responsibilities; power dynamics; recognizing healthy and unhealthy or coercive relationships; communication, trust, and honesty in relationships; peer pressure and social norms; that love and sex are not the same. (pp. 2–3)

The United Nations Population Fund (UNFPA, 2022) has endorsed the implementation of CSE and provided the following explanation in its overview publication on sex education:

> Comprehensive sexuality education enables young people to protect their health, well-being and dignity. . . . And because these programmes are based on human rights principles, they advance gender equality and the rights and empowerment of young people. UNFPA works with governments to implement comprehensive sexuality education, both in schools and outside of schools through community-based training and outreach. UNFPA also promotes policies for, and investment in, sexuality education programmes that meet internationally agreed standards. (para. 2)

CSE is a rights-based, gender-focused, age-appropriate approach to sex education that evolves with the students' comprehension levels and needs. It provides fact-based contraception, STI (including HIV) prevention strategies, and pregnancy and birth information. It requires students to examine personal and societal values, gender roles, gender equality, sexual violence, human rights, and relationships (UNFPA, 2022). Properly trained CSE educators and counselors have knowledge of the overall sexual environment in which children and adolescents live and accept input from students in determining group and individual needs.

UNESCO (2018) issued technical guidance on sexuality education, stating that

> a significant body of evidence shows that CSE enables children and young people to develop: accurate and age-appropriate knowledge, attitudes and skills; positive values, including respect for human rights, gender equality; and diversity, and, attitudes

> and skills that contribute to safe, healthy, positive relationships. . . . CSE is also important as it can help young people reflect on social norms, cultural values and traditional beliefs, in order to better understand and manage their relationships with peers, parents, teachers, other adults and their communities. (p. 12)

CSE theory focuses on teaching children and adolescents their rights related to sexuality and provides them with the tools necessary to exercise those rights while maintaining lifelong sexual health, sex positivity, and enjoyment that is appropriate for their intellectual, emotional, and physical capacities. It is inclusive and encourages an understanding of the many choices related to sexuality and how to best prevent physical, emotional, social, or legal damage to themselves or others, based on current scientific research, while exercising their sexual rights. CSE presents abstinence as a viable choice throughout life, without imposing guilt, shame, or fear for persons who do not choose to be celibate. CSE's ultimate outcomes for its participants are sexual awareness and healthy lifelong sexual fulfillment.

Abstinence Plus Approach

A third viewpoint on sex education mentioned in the literature, APE, requires sex educators to strongly encourage abstinence before marriage but allows for some instruction regarding birth-control methods and disease prevention tools. CSE proponents reject it as thinly veiled AOSE because of verbiage that presents abstinence as the preferred choice for unmarried individuals (Advocates for Youth, 2009). Although APE offers some practical information to students who are sexually active, it still includes the primary components of AOSE, which are a judgmental preference for premarital abstinence over other options for maintaining sexual health and wellness, a devaluation of nonmarital sexual activity, and a disregard of the issues of gender identity and diversity.

Comparison of AOSE and CSE

A major critic of CSE is the Center for Family & Human Rights (C-Fam), previously known as the Catholic Family and Human Rights Institute. A briefing paper published on the C-Fam website by Gennarini et al. (2018) presents many of AOSE's reasons for rejecting CSE. In summary, their primary claims are that CSE (a) does not provide guidance to children, only information that often conflicts with the beliefs of many parents regarding sexuality education; (b) will not reduce teen pregnancy, sexual violence, or STIs; and (c) does not provide age-appropriate guidelines for curriculum development. However, there is ample research to counter these C-Fam claims against CSE.

CSE Encourages Awareness of Beliefs and Influences

CSE directs sexuality educators to consider students' beliefs and cultural influences over their own, whereas AOSE imposes adherence to abstinence over the personal freedom of students and possibly their family's belief systems. UNESCO (2018) conducted a scientific study that found curriculums developed using CSE guidelines recognized students' traditional cultural and religious beliefs in regard to understanding and regulating relationships. This study also determined that CSE allows each child to personalize and utilize this information in their decision-making process.

Kantor and Levitz (2017) found that most parents support the learning objectives of CSE despite their political identity. In their survey of parents from both political parties, 93% of respondents supported CSE in public schools. The American College of Obstetricians and Gynecologists (2020) has encouraged families to support CSE in order to reduce adolescent sexual activity, STIs, and teen pregnancies. CSE provides children and adolescents with the knowledge necessary to cross-generationally communicate their sexuality-related questions and concerns with parents, counselors, and medical professionals.

Children, adolescents, and their parents (guardians) may not have the same moral requirements for total abstinence before marriage that AOSE requires. CSE provides adolescents who exercise their freedom to be sexually active (with or without their parents' knowledge) with information that promotes sexual wellness. CSE supports both students who choose to remain abstinent and students who make the choice to be sexually active now or in the future.

CSE Provides Adolescents With Knowledge and Tools

It is a fact that complete sexual abstinence until marriage, as encouraged by AOSE, is 100% effective in preventing pregnancy and STIs, if achieved. The problem remains that safe sexual practices are not discussed for those who cannot, or do not want to, maintain sexual abstinence. CSE prepares children and adolescents for current or eventual sexual activity, even as married adults, which aids in the prevention of unplanned pregnancies and the achievement of lifelong sexual health.

For adults who participated in AOSE, it might prove difficult to remain celibate for 10 or more years before marriage and even more difficult for those who never marry. Even abstinent adolescents need CSE instruction on STI prevention and treatments to prepare for healthy adult sexual activity. Ott and Santelli (2007) found that 88% of AOSE participants had vaginal sex before marriage. This study confirms that promoting abstinence is not sufficient to prevent sexual activity, unintended pregnancies, or STIs.

Using an extensive ethnographic study of college students, Santelli et al. (2018) examined the postsecondary risk factors for penetrative sexual assault (PSA). The researchers found that teaching consent-and-refusal strategies during postsecondary sex education programs decreased the participants' likelihood of PSA, and teaching CSE (which addresses consent and refusal) before college further protects students against PSA. In addition, the study found that AOSE, which does not teach consent-and-refusal communication strategies, was found not to reduce college PSAs. Except in the case of social isolation, AOSE students cannot design or control their environment to the extent that they will never need the ability to communicate refusal to unwanted sexual activity.

The U.S. House of Representatives Committee on Government Reform (2004) found that AOSE verbiage reinforces gender stereotypes by undermining girls' achievement, presenting girls as weak and in need of protection, and reinforcing boys' sexual aggressiveness. Santelli et al. (2018) recognized that stereotypes are often related to an increased risk of violence against women and girls, stating that "risk factors for perpetrating PSA include attitudes associated with hostility towards women, rape myth acceptance, hypermasculinity, traditional gender roles, and acceptance of violence" (p. 2). CSE curricula encourage the fundamental principles of respect for diversity, recognition of gender roles, and violence prevention as strategies for reducing the incidence of PSAs.

Sexual violence risks vary by age, gender, environment, and other variables that CSE curricula address, whereas AOSE usually avoids these contributing risk factors and implies that students are personally responsible (or partially responsible) for their own sexual victimization. Schneider and Hirsch (2018) examined CSE using the National Sexuality Education Standards and determined that CSE's discussion of age-appropriate sexual violence risks, and its consideration of multiple contributing factors, decreased the incidences of sexual violence. AOSE places too much responsibility on girls and women for the sexual violence perpetrated against them by boys and men. It expects females to repress sexual interests and to construct social environments in which males will not be tempted or allowed to act on their sexual urges. This perpetuates the *rape myth*, that women who experience sexual violence are somehow responsible, and it excuses male sexual aggression as a natural consequence of being a man (Kay & Jackson, 2008).

Grant et al. (2011) reported that 78% of transgender students in Grades K–12 said they had been exposed to harassment, 35% to physical assault, and 12% to sexual assault. The comprehensive premise is that CSE not only assists in preventing sexual violence against women, it also addresses this disproportionate occurrence of harassment and sexual violence against lesbian, gay, bisexual, transgender, and queer (LGBTQ+) youth (Peterson, 2013). AOSE is not suggested as a strategy for reducing the risks of sexual violence and gender-related discrimination (Naide, 2020). CSE teaches that it is the responsibility of all sexual participants to gain mutual, legal, clear, and ongoing consent before proceeding with any sex-related activity.

AOSE programs do not specifically discuss oral or anal sex and inaccurately claim that the use of condoms is ineffective as a disease protection tool. They mistakenly profess that CSE encourages adolescent sexual activity, and it increases STIs by providing information on disease protection and treatments. Again, these claims are based on the unproven assumption that AOSE students will faithfully follow the abstinence directive. Santelli et al. (2017) adds that when abstinence fails, the adolescent may experience a level of guilt that causes them to postpone seeking assistance with STI symptoms—especially if they have violated a chastity pledge. Lack of reporting because of guilt complicates effective disease contact tracing. CSE's lessons on the prevention, symptoms, and medical treatments for STIs contribute to its participants being better protected from the risks of STIs.

CSE Provides the Framework for Curriculum Development

To establish lesson readiness, CSE expects educators to familiarize themselves with their students' culture and environment as it relates to sexual activities and to communicate with students to determine their individual sex-related educational needs. CSE provides the flexibility necessary to meet the needs of individual students of different cultures at every age. The National Sex Education Standards (Future of Sex Education, 2020) have been endorsed by many organizations and individuals with expertise in CSE. These standards provide a basic framework for CSE practitioners to refer to during curriculum development.

What Is the Status of Sex Education in Schools Today?

Sexuality educators need to familiarize themselves with the legal environment in their state and realize that sexuality education is an ever-evolving area of law subject to each state's current political influences. Many U.S. legislators do not rely on scientific research findings when addressing sexuality education policies. The World Population

Review (n.d.) reported in 2022 that 19 states were AOSE states. Five of those states had the highest rates of teen pregnancy and also did not mandate any information on contraception or disease prevention instruction.

Educators, including counselors, are often restricted by state statutes or district policies from presenting CSE concepts to students including information about contraception, STI prevention, inclusive gender support, and abortion. These policies are continually in flux, as they are dependent on the political viewpoints of the legislatures at any given time. A National Conference of State Legislatures (NCSL, 2020) report on state policies on sex education in schools found the following:

- Thirty states and the District of Columbia require public schools teach sex education; 28 of these mandate both sex education and HIV education.
- Thirty-nine states and the District of Columbia require students receive instruction about HIV.
- Twenty-two states require that if provided, sex and/or HIV education must be medically, factually, or technically accurate. State definitions of "medically accurate" vary, from curriculum be based on information from "published authorities" upon which medical professionals rely.

The NCSL (2020) report also provided data on how states define parents' rights concerning sexual education as follows:

- Twenty-five states and the District of Columbia require school districts to notify parents that sexual or HIV education will be provided.
- Five states require parental consent before a child can receive instruction.
- Thirty-six states and the District of Columbia allow parents to opt out on behalf of their children.

Parents, adolescents, teachers, and counselors have begun to question why anti-choice Christian groups are presenting sex education lessons in public schools (Munz, 2017). After numerous objections by CSE proponents across the country concerning these presentations, abstinence-educator groups are repackaging their morality-and-religion-based approach by simply removing the more objectionable ideas, ignoring gender identity issues, and avoiding their more judgmental claims. They are unable, however, to remove the moralizing and shame that undergird the entire AOSE program.

Sexuality education is sometimes incorporated into other subjects, such as human body systems and biology (Marshall, 2018). This may result in only a few hours of dedicated teaching time from teachers who might not be comfortable with the subject of sex. Fortunately, most schools are designed to meet the needs of students by offering a community of professionals that include teachers, counselors, administrators, school psychologists, social workers, resource officers, and nurses. Communication within this network, and an awareness of each agent's responsibilities and strengths, will enable sexuality educators to better utilize this expertise.

U.S. teacher and school counselor education programs sometimes lack enough emphasis on human sexuality to enable educators to effectively and confidently address the subject matter with students and parents (Eisenberg et al., 2013). In order to effectively implement CSE curricula and strategies, teachers and counselors must recognize their own sex-related biases and become comfortable with discussing sexuality topics. They need to be confident enough in their knowledge base to communicate the curriculum and advocate for CSE implementation.

Because of the personal nature of sexuality education, its practitioners might gain knowledge of abusive (or potentially abusive) situations (Goldfarb & Lieberman, 2021). Knowledge of organizational procedures and laws defining the reporting responsibilities of medical and educational professionals is legally and professionally required to protect children and persons who serve children and adolescents. The federal Child Abuse Prevention and Treatment Act (Children's Bureau, n.d.), Title II, 42 U.S.C. §5106a(b)(2)(B)(i), establishes each state's legal responsibility to enact state statutes and enforcement procedures for reporting child endangerment/abuse and identifies mandatory reporters as being all counselors, teachers, administrators, doctors, nurses, and any others (including volunteers) who are assigned to protect the well-being of children and adolescents. It requires the reporter to be protected from workplace (organizational) retaliation. Confidentiality concerns in these cases will not excuse educators from the duty to follow laws requiring them to report abuse that might harm any person(s) even when discovered during counseling sessions (Cornell Law School Legal Information Institute, 2022).

States and districts may also have legislation or guidelines regarding adherence to sexuality education content, approved supplemental materials, and referral processes (Washburn, 2019). As an educator, it is always wise to seek approval from an administrator before inviting guest speakers, making referrals to outside professionals, or introducing materials that have not been district approved for use in a particular curriculum. Also, parent requests regarding curriculum changes usually require administration approval before implementation.

Because the United States does not have a national policy regulating sex education, state guidelines are often nondirective, inconsistent, inadequate, and vague. States that have adopted CSE policies have found that its effective implementation is dependent on teachers, administrators, counselors, individual school districts, and patrons to provide the support necessary to fully adhere to the curricula over the long term (Lindberg et al., 2016). The over-politicization of sexuality education has led to inconsistencies and confusion regarding its content. Politicians and educators who are not knowledgeable and comfortable with sex-education subject matter may not be able to provide students and families with the tools necessary to effectively respond to sex-related concerns.

While an examination of scientifically collected data as to the efficacy of sex education methodologies provides the most accurate program assessments, the moral codes, beliefs, and opinions of a few vocal community members, administrators, and legislators are still impacting the political environment that funds and controls sex education curriculums. AOSE's influence is directly tied to its political and religious alliances, financial strength, and the vocal activism of its proponents and financial beneficiaries.

Sexuality educators are never bored. They are constantly challenged to stay relevant, effectively communicate, and democratically advocate for the sexuality education rights of students. By staying aware of current sexuality research, educators can be proactive regarding the future sexuality education topics of concern for children and adolescents. Sexting, virtual sex, human papillomavirus vaccinations, giving and obtaining consent, sexual and gender minority issues, and addressing the sexuality educational needs of students with disabilities are a few of the more recent issues being addressed by educators.

The evidence is starkly clear. Comprehensive sexuality education works. Goldfarb and Lieberman (2021) reviewed 3 decades of research on the outcome of CSE and found evidence for the following:

- *Enhanced appreciation of sexual diversity*, such as lower homophobia; reduced homophobia bullying; expanded understanding of gender/gender norms; and recognition of gender equity, rights, and social justice;
- *Dating and intimate partner violence prevention*, including improved knowledge and attitudes toward and reporting of dating violence (DV) and intimate partner violence (IPV); decreased DV and IPV penetration and victimization; and increased bystander intentions and behaviors;
- *Healthy relationships*, such as increased knowledge, attitudes, and skills related to healthy relationships; and improved communication skills and intentions;
- *Child sex abuse prevention*, including improved knowledge, attitudes, skills, and social-emotional outcomes related to personal safety and touch; and improved disclosure skills and behaviors; and
- *Enhancements in social-emotional learning and media literacy*, although these were not included directly in the CSE curriculum.

As Goldfarb and Lieberman (2021) concluded, we know that academic achievement is related to the physical and emotional health of young people, as healthier students are more likely to stay in school and achieve their educational potential. If students are able to avoid early pregnancy, STIs, sexual abuse, and interpersonal violence and harassment, while feeling safe and supported within their school environment, they are more likely to experience academic success.

Sexuality education curriculum committees need to meet frequently in order to assess the effectiveness of the curriculum and to support any necessary revisions with fact-based data. By inviting the input of all parents and students and involving them in the curriculum development process, educators are more likely to avoid the one-sided impact of an oppositional vocal minority on the implementation of research-based CSE curricula. It is important to communicate research findings and related data that build public confidence in the effectiveness of CSE subject matter. Sexuality educators who strive to form professional alliances with parents (guardians), scientists, teacher educators, school counselors, school psychologists, school nurses, medical professionals, and school district patrons will be able to provide children and adolescents with the sexuality education necessary for them to achieve a lifetime of healthy sexual relationships and experiences. It is a fight worth fighting.

References

Advocates for Youth. (2009, January 28). *Sex education programs: Definitions & point-by-point comparison.* https://advocatesforyouth.org/resources/fact-sheets/sex-education-programs-definitions-and-point-by-point-comparison

American College of Obstetricians and Gynecologists. (2020, November). *Comprehensive sexuality education* (Committee Opinion No. 678). https://www.acog.org/clinical/clinical-guidance/committee-opinion/articles/2016/11/comprehensive-sexuality-education

Baylor University. (2014, February 5). *Evangelicals have higher-than-average divorce rates, according to a report compiled for Baylor for the Council on Contemporary Families* [Press release]. https://www.baylor.edu/mediacommunications/news.php?action=story&story=137892

Breuner, C. C., Mattson, G., Committee on Adolescents, & Committee on Psychological Aspects of Child and Family Health. (2016, August). Sexuality education for children and adolescents. *Pediatrics, 138*(2). https://pediatrics.aappublications.org/content/138/2/e20161348

Children's Bureau. (n.d.). *The Child Abuse Prevention and Treatment Act as amended by P.L. 115-271.* U.S. Department of Health and Human Services. https://www.acf.hhs.gov/sites/default/files/documents/cb/capta.pdf

Cornell Law School Legal Information Institute. (2022). *42 U.S. Code § 5106a—Grants to states for child abuse or neglect prevention and treatment programs.* https://www.law.cornell.edu/uscode/text/42/5106a

Dainton, M. (2011). Linking theoretical explanations for the use of marital maintenance: Equity, uncertainty, attachment, and reciprocity. *Acta de Investigación Psicológica, 1*, 352–374.

Eisenberg, M. E., Madsen, N., Oliphant, J. A., & Sieving, R. E. (2013). Barriers to providing the sexuality education that teachers believe students need. *Journal of School Health, 83*(5), 335–342. https://doi.org/10.1111/josh.12036

Fox, A. M., Himmelstein, G., Khalid, H., & Howell, E. A. (2019, March). Funding for abstinence-only education and adolescent pregnancy prevention: Does state ideology affect outcomes? *American Journal of Public Health, 109*(3), 497–504. https://ajph.aphapublications.org/doi/abs/10.2105/AJPH.2018.304896

Future of Sex Education Initiative. (2020). *National sex education standards: Core content and skills, K-12* (2nd ed.). https://siecus.org/wp-content/uploads/2020/03/NSES-2020-2.pdf

Gennarini, S., Orlandi, M., & Oas, R. (2018, August). *Seven reasons to reject "comprehensive" sexuality education* (Briefing Paper No. 16, 2-18). International Organizations Research Group. https://c-fam.org/wp-content/uploads/CSE-Briefing-Paper-8.26.18.pdf

Goldfarb, E. S., & Lieberman, L. D. (2021). Three decades of research: The case for comprehensive sex education. *Journal of Adolescent Health, 68*(1), 13–27. https://doi.org/10.1016/j.jadohealth.2020.07.036

Grant, J. M., Mottet, L. A., & Tanis, J. (with Harrison, J., Herman, J. L., & Keisling, M.). (2011). *Injustice at every turn: A report of the National Transgender Discrimination Survey.* National Center for Transgender Equality. https://www.transequality.org/sites/default/files/docs/resources/NTDS_Report.pdf

Grossu, A., & Sprigg, P. (2014, April). *Sexual risk-avoidance education* [Issue brief]. Family Research Council. https://downloads.frc.org/EF/EF14D14.pdf

Guttmacher Institute. (n.d.). *A definition of comprehensive sexuality education* [Informational handout]. https://www.guttmacher.org/sites/default/files/report_downloads/demystifying-data-handouts_0.pdf

Guttmacher Institute. (2022, May). *United States teens.* https://www.guttmacher.org/united-states/teens

Kantor, L., & Levitz, N. (2017, July 3). Parents' views on sex education in schools: How much do Democrats and Republicans agree? *PLOS ONE, 12*(7) Article e0180250. https://doi.org/10.1371/journal.pone.0180250

Kay, J. F., & Jackson, A. (2008). Sex, lies, and stereotypes: How abstinence-only programs hurt women and girls. *Legal Momentum.* https://hrp.law.harvard.edu/wp-content/uploads/2013/03/sexlies_stereotypes2008.pdf

Lindberg, L., Santelli, J., & Desai, S. (2016). Understanding the decline in adolescent fertility in the United States, 2007–2012. *Journal of Adolescent Health, 59*, 577–583. https://www.jahonline.org/article/S1054-139X(16)30172-0/pdf

Marshall, K. (2018, September 24). Teaching sex education: 7 key questions. *Phi Delta Kappan.* https://kappanonline.org/marshall-sex-education/

McCammon, S. (2017, August 23). Abstinence-only education is ineffective and unethical, report argues. *NPR.* https://www.npr.org/sections/health-shots/2017/08/23/545289168/abstinence-education-is-ineffective-and-unethical-report-argues

Munz, M. (2017, March 6). Christian anti-abortion group is providing sex ed at area public schools: Parents and students wonder if that's a good idea. *St. Louis Post-Dispatch.* https://www.stltoday.com/lifestyles/health-med-fit/health/christian-anti-abortion-group-is-providing-sex-ed-at-area/article_65cb9e4e-6671-53c2-b4a2-5d1c87912a4a.html

Naide, S. (2020, January 15). *State lawmakers say yes to consent education.* Guttmacher Institute. https://www.guttmacher.org/article/2020/01/state-lawmakers-say-yes-consent- education

National Conference of State Legislatures. (2020, October 1). *State policies on sex education in schools: Why is sexual education taught in schools?* https://www.ncsl.org/research/health/state-policies-on-sex-education-in-schools.aspx

Ott, M. A., & Santelli, J. S. (2007). Abstinence and abstinence-only education. *Current Opinion in Obstetrics & Gynecology, 19*(5), 446–452. https://doi.org/101097/GCO.0b013e3282efdc0b

Panchaud, C., & Anderson, R. (2016, July). *Demystifying data: Using evidence to improve young people's sexual health and rights.* Guttmacher Institute. https://www.guttmacher.org/report/demystifying-data-workshop-toolkit

People for the American Way Foundation. (1996, September). *Teaching fear: The religious right's campaign against sexuality education.* https://www.pfaw.org/report/teaching-fear-the-religious-rights-campaign-against-sexuality-education/

Peterson, N. (2013, November). *The health and rights of transgender youth: Understanding and support are critical for this highly marginalized group.* Advocates for Youth. https://www.advocatesforyouth.org/wp-content/uploads/storage//advfy/documents/the%20health%20and%20rights%20of%20transgender%20youth.pdf

Santelli, J. S., Grilo, S. A., Choo, T., Diaz, G., Walsh, K., Wall, M., Hirsch, J. S., Wilson, P., Gilbert, L., Khan S., & Mellins, C. A. (2018). Does sex education before college protect students from sexual assault in college? *PLOS ONE, 13*(11), Article e0205951. https://journals.plos.org/plosone/article?id=10.1371/journal.pone.0205951

Santelli, J. S., Kantor, L. M., Grilo, S. A., Speizer, I. S., Lindberg, L. D., Heitel, J., Schalet, A. T., Lyon, M. E., Mason-Jones, A. J., McGovern, T., Heck, C. J., Rogers, J., & Ott, M. A. (2017). Abstinence-only-until-marriage: An updated review of U.S. policies and programs and their impact. *Journal of Adolescent Health, 61*, 273–280. https://doi.org/10.1016/j.jadohealth.2017.05.031

Schneider, M., & Hirsch, J. S. (2018, May 2). Comprehensive sexuality education as a primary prevention strategy for sexual violence perpetration. *Trauma, Violence, & Abuse*, *21*(3), 439–455. https://doi.org/10.1177/1524838018772855

United Nations Educational, Scientific, and Cultural Organization. (2018). *International technical guidance on sexuality education: An evidence informed approach.* https://unesdoc.unesco.org/ark:/48223/pf0000260770

United Nations Population Fund. (2022). *Comprehensive sexuality education.* https://www.unfpa.org/comprehensive-sexuality-education#readmore-expand

U.S. Agency for International Development. (2015, April). *Condom fact sheet.* https://www.usaid.gov/sites/default/files/documents/1864/condomfactsheet.pdf

U.S. Department of Health and Human Services. (2007, April 12). *Impacts of four Title V, Section 510 abstinence education programs.* https://aspe.hhs.gov/reports/impacts-four-title-v-section-510-abstinence-education-programs-1

U.S. House of Representatives Committee on Government Reform. (2004). *The content of federally funded abstinence-only education programs.* https://spot.colorado.edu/~tooley/HenryWaxman.pdf

Washburn, D. (2019, May 9). California approves new guidance for teaching sex education. *EdSource.* https://edsource.org/2019/california-approves-new-guidance-for-teaching-sex-education/612169

World Population Review. (n.d.). *Abstinence only education states 2022.* https://worldpopulationreview.com/state-rankings/abstinence-only-education-states

Human Sexuality Is Not an Elective: Why Sexuality Education in Counseling Is an Ethical Imperative

Frances L. McClain and Lisa Salvadore

Sexuality is an essential aspect of the human experience. It is socially constructed and is impacted across the life span, touching all cultures, races, ethnicities, religions, genders and gender expressions, socioeconomic statuses, and physical abilities. An individual's sexual well-being is a critical factor in their overall health and quality of life (Giami 2002; Higgins et al., 2006; McCabe et al., 2010; Southern & Cade, 2011). Despite the significance of sexuality in people's lives, the directives for training counselors around issues related to sexuality are vague (Zeglin et al., 2018). Historically ignored in counselor education, human sexuality has received more consideration in the recent past (Dermer & Bachenberg, 2015; Fyfe, 1980; Sanabria & Murray, 2018; Southern & Cade, 2011). There is no shortage of research indicating that sexuality education and training of clinicians yields increased comfort in addressing sexuality-related issues with clients as well as greater levels of confidence in working with sexuality-related presenting concerns (e.g., Haboubi & Lincoln, 2003; Hanzlik & Gaubatz, 2012; Harris & Hays, 2008; Juergens et al., 2009; Russell, 2012). However, graduates entering the counseling profession are ill prepared to provide adequate care to people around issues of sexuality. The failure of counselor education to comprehensively address sexuality education and training has left graduates with significant knowledge and skill deficits.

Research has indicated anywhere from 30% to 50% of couples in the United States may experience some sexually related problems at some point in their relationship (Flynn et al., 2015), and up to half of men and women experience sexual dysfunction at some point in their lives (Heiman, 2002; Simons & Carey, 2001). Given those statistics, it is ethically imperative that counselor education programs adopt comprehensive sexuality education and training into the curriculum. Additionally, sexuality-related issues are interwoven with other mental and physical health concerns, such as depression, anxiety, substance use, and chronic pain conditions. It is also important to address sexuality with people who have physical limitations, are neurodivergent, or have other developmental disabilities. People who have disabilities of any kind are generally viewed as asexual or unable to engage in sexual relationships (see Chapter 16), so are even less likely to be educated or given opportunities to talk about their sexuality-related issues. The counseling profession can no longer ignore this vital aspect of life, which impacts clients' overall health and well-being.

The counseling profession, based on principles that are grounded in wellness, empowerment, and social justice, is particularly well suited to lead the mental health world in addressing sexuality. Although there are challenges and still much research to be done both related to best practices and infusing sexuality in counseling education, there is currently literature that aligns with the counseling postmodern constructivist approach, which is culturally sensitive and honors different worldviews. This ongoing omission by the counseling profession to address sexuality and provide the necessary education and training has resulted in limited understanding of what sexuality or sexual health is and how to effectively work with clients around these issues.

Sexuality impacts everyone in some aspect of their lives. Yet, despite the recognition of sexuality being fundamental to each person's life, throughout their development, inhabiting every culture, the mental health profession continues to avoid adequate research, education, and training in this critical area of the human experience.

There is an integrative and radical approach that embraces both a biopsychosocial model and a sex positive approach (Nimbi et al., 2021), which incorporates research, education, mental health, physical health, ethics, and culture, while incorporating a framework that highlights the importance of sexual health as well as sexual pleasure. A sex positive framework approach focuses on inclusivity, consent, and respect, as well as the intersectionality of all sexual expressions, orientations, genders and gender expressions, religions, ages, body shapes, abilities, and sizes. The strength of this holistic approach is the emphasis on education and training of medical and mental health providers, which includes examining their own cultures, values/beliefs, and biases. When counselors embrace this innovative approach that is culturally sensitive, celebrates pleasure, but also focuses on health, it aligns with the professional counseling values. This biopsychosocial model allows counselors not only to address sexuality-related issues but to foster sexual health (Russell, 2012). The World Health Organization's (WHO, n.d.) definition of *sexual health* is grounded in research that indicates physical, mental, and sexual health are integral to a person's overall well-being and quality of life. Despite research indicating a person's sexuality has an impact on their overall mental health (Anderson, 2013) and the critical role it plays in the human experience, counselors report discomfort and avoid addressing sexuality with clients (Dupkoski, 2012). In a study conducted by Haboubi and Lincoln (2003) of multidisciplinary health professionals, although 90% agreed that sexual issues should be part of holistic care, 86% had little or no training, and 94% were unlikely to discuss sexual issues with patients. This reticence, as well as overall lack of skills to respond to sexuality-related issues, has the potential to cause harm.

Professional Standards and Code of Ethics

A review of the professional ethics and standards for professional counselors reveals no clear expectations or guidelines regarding either the training or practice related to sexuality counseling. Neither the Council for Accreditation of Counseling and Related Educational Programs (CACREP, 2016) nor the National Board for Certified Counselors (NBCC, 2020), which establishes the standards for counseling programs and licensure exams throughout the United States, requires any training specifically related to human sexuality. CACREP does not explicitly require human sexuality coursework among the eight core curricular areas in the 2016 CACREP Standards that are applicable to all counseling education programs. Although the NBCC requires coursework in human growth and development, there are no definitive requirements for a course in human sexuality for National Counselor Certification. The *ACA Code of Ethics* (American Counseling Association [ACA], 2014) states that counselors are expected to practice in ways that (a) enhance human development, (b) recognize and respect all diverse aspects of clients, and (c) implement culturally appropriate strategies that encourage clients' individuality. Although sexuality in particular is not mentioned, it is clear that if a counselor is to adhere to ACA's ethical values, sexuality is a component that must be recognized and addressed. The call to be culturally sensitive to and respectful of clients' autonomy extends to their sexuality. The lack of adequate education and training, in addition to not having done the necessary self-reflection, is likely to result in a clinician pathologizing unfamiliar sexual behavior (Zeglin et al., 2018). Despite the recognition from researchers and academics alike that sexual health is integral to a counselor's role (Gray et al., 1996; Sansone & Wiederman, 2000), sexuality education and training at best remain ancillary to counselor education.

Call to the Profession: An Ethical Imperative

It has been over 40 years since Fyfe first challenged the counseling profession to respond to needs of individuals presenting with sexuality-related concerns. Fyfe (1980) wrote that "understanding human sexuality and its varied expressions is a necessary part of the agency counselor's role" (p. 150). He went on to outline a training model emphasizing the importance of providing comprehensive sexuality education for mental health professionals to meet the needs of clients. Miller and Byers (2010) stated that psychologists continued to lack adequate sex education and training and, therefore, did not feel competent in addressing or even initiating these discussions with clients. Over the years, the literature has spoken to the importance of mental health professionals obtaining knowledge of sexuality, but there remains a dearth of research on developing the competency of counselors in addressing sexuality-related issues with clients. Research has shown that counselors are uncomfortable with broaching the topic of sexuality with their clients, which inhibits their ability to provide effective care (Harris & Hays, 2008; Kazukaukas & Lam, 2009, 2010; Miller & Byers, 2010, 2012). However, when mental health professionals do receive education and training in sexuality, they feel more confident and are more likely to initiate conversations with their clients about sexuality-related issues (Harris & Hays, 2008). Yet, Dupkoski's (2012) review of the ACA and Association for Counselor Education and Supervision (ACES) Syllabus Clearinghouse found that less than 15% (57) of the 395 syllabi included the word "sex," and only approximately 1% (four courses) concentrated expressly on human sexuality.

Despite the importance of sexuality to mental health and well-being, most counselor education programs do not require human sexuality as a core course. When available, human sexuality courses are often offered as electives. So why is it that the counseling profession and counselor educators are unable to take the next step toward advancing the competency of the profession around human sexuality? It is ethically imperative that counselors have the ability to competently respond to clients with sexuality-related issues. The counseling profession is bound by the principles and philosophy it professes and should provide the necessary training and education to effectively respond to the needs of the communities we serve. As counselors, we must be willing with careful self-reflection to examine those obstacles that impede our moving forward.

Introduction of the Authors

As coauthors for this chapter, we were excited for the opportunity to share our experience teaching a human sexuality course in a counseling psychology department over the past 5 years. We have both worked in community mental health for over 25 years, coming to counselor education and academia the last 10 years. One of us has her doctorate in counselor education, is a licensed clinical professional counselor, and works full-time in a counseling psychology department as the director of clinical training; the other is a licensed clinical social worker and a certified addictions and other drug counselor who is full-time faculty in the social work department at a state university. We have been together for the last 25 years and legally married for 10 years. We like to tell people we have a "mixed marriage," because one of us is a counselor and the other a social worker. As a couple we were excited for an opportunity to teach human sexuality together. While having a married couple coteach a human sexuality class was probably unusual, we thought having a lesbian couple was undoubtedly groundbreaking. We are both openly queer, both personally and professionally, but coteaching as a couple, especially a human sexuality class, was certainly a different experience. So far, it has been universally well received. Students have specifically commented on course evaluations how much they appreciate the opportunity to observe a sexual minority couple teaching the course together.

In this chapter, we will examine some of the challenges impeding counselor education from moving forward in embracing human sexuality education and training of counselors. We will demonstrate how the counseling field is well positioned to provide leadership in educating and training around sexuality-related issues, not only within the profession but in the wider community as well. Last, we will introduce our framework for teaching human sexuality from a sex positive, postmodern feminist approach, offering examples of assignments and explaining how we have structured our course.

Challenges With Sexuality Training in the Field and the Classroom

There are several significant issues that hinder the adoption of human sexuality as part of the core curriculum in counselor education programs. When breaking them down, we came up with these key areas: (a) societal discomfort in dealing with sexuality issues is mirrored in the counseling profession, (b) human sexuality is a value-laden topic, (c) everyone is largely uneducated about basic human sexuality, and (d) the perception is that sexuality issues need to be referred to a specialist. Each of these issues brings its own plethora of problems and obstacles, but it is a professional responsibility to acknowledge and respond to the impact sexuality has on our client's lives and mental health. Although sexuality, as Schiller (1977) wrote, can be transformative, it is also capable of being both a uniting force and one that creates insurmountable rifts (Dupkoski, 2012).

Societal Discomfort Reflected in the Profession

In a world that is becoming increasingly more connected through social media, along with the myriad of confusing messages and information available online, conceptualizing and addressing sexuality has become even more complex (Ballam & Granello, 2011; Diambra et al., 2016; Giami, 2002; Kazukauskas & Lam, 2010). Even so, despite being bombarded daily with messages both implicitly and explicitly sexual, as a society, we in the United States avoid directly addressing sexuality in an education setting. Overall, the culture in the United States is largely ignorant regarding sexuality and views sex from a patriarchal, negative, and restrictive view (Harris & Hays, 2008; Stayton, 1998). Regarding open discourse, education, and skill training, human sexuality in the United States is still largely kept in the closet. Unfortunately, the counseling profession reflects society's repression of sexuality. There remains a great deal of ambiguity in the counseling field regarding education and training around sexuality, despite the empirical evidence indicating the importance of implementing human sexuality into the core curriculum (Bishop, 2001; Christensen et al., 1977; Collins & Sedlacek, 1972; Gray et al., 1989, 1996; Grove, 2009; Kirkpatrick, 1980; Russell, 2012).

Value-Laden Topic

Unlike other core courses in a graduate counseling program, such as a career or theories course, a human sexuality course comes with a host of challenges regarding the subject matter, eliciting strong feelings most often attached to religious beliefs and values. The human sexuality course is a minefield of topics that are most often avoided due to the discomfort and strong emotions/emotional opinions they provoke. Discussions of sexuality may be avoided by students who do not know how to engage in, and may actively avoid, topics that are controversial. This is not a course that only make students uncomfortable, but faculty and administration alike tend to veer away from either discussing or addressing sexuality as a part of the curriculum. Often, factors that influence either student, clinician, or faculty reluctance to engage in discussions around sexuality are related to their own experiences and messages while they were children and adolescents. Frequently, the reluctance has been influenced by culture and religious belief systems, as well as family and historical context. Everyone receives messages, sometimes overtly but often covertly, related to sex and sexual behavior. Sex and religion are two topics one is expected to avoid in polite society. In counseling sexuality education and training, both of these have to be addressed head-on if students are to be adequately trained and have the ability to navigate these issues effectively with their clients.

Lack of Knowledge About Sexuality

Historically, sex education in the United States has been met with opposition by social conservatives who "inflate the sense of danger" (Moran, 2000, p. 181) related to sex by focusing on teen pregnancy and sexually transmitted infections. According to Shapiro and Brown (2018), sex education across the United States is being insufficiently used and, in some instances, is even used incorrectly. Access to media, in addition to the standard methods for obtaining information regarding sex, has left adolescents with information that is often inconsistent, misleading, or even, at times, dangerous. When reviewing state laws, including the District of Columbia, regarding education standards, the Center for American Progress found there were only 11 states that mention terms associated with identifying health or unhealthy sexual behaviors such as "consent" (Shapiro & Brown, 2018). As a result, most adolescents move into adulthood with little or incorrect information regarding sexuality.

A counselor's willingness to address sexuality issues in treatment is impacted by several issues, the primary one being related to their own lack of knowledge about basic human sexuality. Insufficient information on the part of the clinician about human sexuality, which hampers their ability to provide adequate education for their clients, resulting in their perception of feeling incompetent, ensures they will not prompt clients to explore these issues (Risen, 2003). When we started teaching the human sexuality course in the counseling program at the graduate level, we had our own mistaken assumptions about what the students may know. We begin every class with students answering questions related to their own sex education, including where they obtained information. In cohorts that are predominantly millennial, they acknowledged having limited information about their own sexual anatomy and, generally, in a class of 15 to 17 students, only one or two students report having parents who openly talked and educated them about sex. One of our exercises is breaking students into groups and having them complete diagrams of male and female genitalia, both internally and externally. They are often amazed at how little they know. Despite access to the internet and resources never before available to past generations, students today entering the counseling field remain largely ignorant of human anatomy related to sexuality.

When establishing the Association of Counseling Sexology and Sexual Wellness, those that were engaged in promoting the need for an association to educate and advocate for sexuality issues within the counseling profession and larger community were often asked why there was a need for a separate group when the Society for Sexual, Affectional, Intersex, and Gender Expansive Identities (SAIGE) division already existed within ACA. This question itself is an indication of the need for greater education and expanded understanding of sexuality. Even highly educated individuals often use sexuality and sexual orientation interchangeably. The assumption is that if sexual behavior is not outside what is perceived to be the "norm," then it does not warrant discussion or examination. Although SAIGE is an important division and addresses critical issues specific to people who are oppressed and marginalized, there remains the need to address sexuality from a holistic perspective and to recognize the importance of researching, educating, and training about all aspects of human sexuality.

Misperception of Sexuality Issues Needing Specialists

Frequently, both students and seasoned clinicians shy away from addressing sexuality-related issues because of the misconception that any sexual issue requires someone with specialized training in the area of human sexuality. Although it is true that most counselor education programs do not require a human sexuality course, being able to respond to a client's needs around sexuality-related concerns does not require specialized training. Depending on severity, sexual disorders (similar to disorders such as posttraumatic stress disorder) may require the skills of a clinician with specialized training; however, competent counselors would be able to conceptualize most sexual issues integrating various theoretical approaches no differently than they would for a myriad of presenting concerns (e.g., psychodynamic, cognitive, client-centered). Relegating sex therapy as a specialty perpetuates the perception of sexuality as something that is forbidden to be addressed by other clinicians and further marginalizes sex therapy from other mental health treatment (Binik & Meana, 2009). Relying on professional ethics that require them to "practice within the boundaries of their competence" (ACA, 2014, Standard C.2.a.), clinicians will refer clients out due to discomfort or feeling as though they lack the necessary training when working in areas related to sexuality. Although this may at times be necessary, it also is a risk to disrupting the therapeutic process and further marginalizing a client with issues they may find difficult to discuss. When necessary, counselors should refer clients for medical consultation to determine if there is an additional medically related concern to the issue. However, more often, when clients inquire about sexuality-related issues, generally it is what we label as "sexual distress" as opposed to a diagnosable disorder or sexual dysfunction.

Counseling Profession Positioned as a Leader in Human Sexuality

The counseling profession is uniquely positioned to address issues related to sexuality both in the counselor's office and out in the broader community as an advocate for social justice issues. Constructivism has largely been embraced in the 21st century as a paradigm for the counseling profession (Cottone, 2007). Essentially, constructivism is a postmodern approach that maintains that there is no universal "truth" that can be revealed, but that truth or reality is created by society and individuals (Wilks, 2018). One of the trends at the turn of the century was recognition of the importance of viewing all individual issues within the social context in which they are embedded (McAuliffe & Eriksen, 1999). Social constructivism was also consistent with the multicultural movement in counseling and psychology, which emphasized the importance of respecting the individual's worldview and the social context with which they exist. As a result of the multicultural movement, the counseling profession has increased the standards for counselor education programs to include an integrated multicultural and social justice approach to the curriculum (ACA, 2014; CACREP, 2016). Diversity courses are required of all CACREP-accredited programs and state licensure (ACA, 2014). The Association for Multicultural Counseling and Development, a division of ACA, has been a leader in the mental health field in advocating for greater awareness of cultural biases and social privilege both within the field and in the greater community (Black et al., 2007; Hays et al., 2004; Sue et al., 1992).

However, most diversity course material that addresses sexuality focuses on sexual minorities within the lesbian, gay, bisexual, transgender, questioning, queer, intersex, asexual, and pansexual (LGBTQIA+) community, without consideration for other areas of diverse sexual expression and orientations that include people in the kink community (see Chapter 19) and people who identify as pansexual, demisexual, or asexual, as well as people who engage in polyamorous relationships (Sanabria & Murray, 2018; see Chapter 23). Nevertheless, the strong multiculturalism foundation in the counseling field, which has created a culture of examining implicit assumptions and biases as well as evaluative judgments of others' worldviews, has created the perfect groundwork for establishing leadership in the mental health field for sexuality education and training of clinicians, advocacy for social justice for persons marginalized based on their sexual orientations and sexual expressions, enhancing sexual development throughout the life span, and respecting each person's autonomy in expressing their sexual self without fear of oppression.

Counseling Sexuality Pedagogy

It is important when developing counseling sexuality pedagogy to be acquainted with the literature that indicates that competency in working with sexuality-related issues requires more than knowledge and skills but also comfort in broaching and addressing the topic with clients (Kazukauskas & Lam, 2010; Miller & Byers, 2012). This requires a comprehensive approach, being aware that most students enter the course with limited information regarding sexuality, along with a lifetime of misinformation and biases to move past.

As we mentioned before, we have now taught human sexuality in a counseling psychology department for the past 5 years, often offering it as many as three or four times a year. Of the courses we have taught, there is no other course that is as gratifying or challenging as the human sexuality course. The feedback from students has been universally positive with statements that this course was transformative for them. We do not imagine that this is due to our phenomenal teaching skills but rather how we have designed the course and the importance of the material. The unique experience both for ourselves and the students of having the opportunity to coteach a human sexuality course with your life partner has been an amazing one. Not everyone is able to coteach with their spouse, but we would always encourage instructors to think outside the box and be creative when approaching any course. Take a risk as it sometimes pays off for both the students and instructor alike.

Sex Positive Approach

The WHO in 1975 published the first international definition of sexual health that included the right to accurate information about sex and sexual pleasure; a capacity to enjoy sexual behavior in accordance with one's social and personal ethics; freedom from fear, shame, guilt, false beliefs, and other psychological factors that may inhibit sexual response and relationships; and freedom from organic disorders, diseases, and deficiencies that interfere with sexual and reproductive functions. Sex positivity is a strength-based theoretical framework that recognizes sexuality as a complex aspect of people's lives that is multifaceted and diverse and embraces multiple ways of knowing (Lewis, 2004). Consistent with counseling principles and values, the sex positivity framework emphasizes focusing on the well-being, happiness, and empowerment of those, who by virtue of their sexual orientation or sexual behavior, are marginalized and oppressed (Williams et al., 2015). Therefore, a sex positivity framework is most consistent and compatible with the counseling profession's philosophy, principles, and values.

When introducing sex positivity at the start of the course, we talk about sexual pleasure as something that can be enjoyed whether you believe sex is only for a man and woman in the sanctity of marriage or if you are polyamorous or pansexual. We have had students in our classes who are conservative Christian, Mormon, atheist, Hindu, Jewish (both Reformed and Conservative), pagan, Sikh, and satanist. By creating an environment where all views are valued and respected, we open a dialogue where students can explore a taboo topic while framing it within their values and beliefs. Initially, our own biases and assumptions were that, given we were teaching a graduate-level course, the students will have been sexually active. We were surprised early on when students disclosed that they were virgins, whether for religious, personal choice, or other reasons, resulting in our always making a point of normalizing virginity as well as asexuality from the beginning to ensure everyone feels heard and recognized.

Framing sex positivity not from a hedonistic free-for-all perspective but from a perspective of respect and dignity that celebrates sexuality—no matter what are an individual's orientation, values, beliefs, or sexual expressions—has been an effective framework for teaching a counseling sexuality course. From the onset, students who are less informed or come from a more conservative background feel seen and supported while challenged to think about sexuality somewhat differently.

Postmodern Feminist Approach

When we started teaching human sexuality, one of the first things we did was review syllabi from other counseling programs across the country. What we found was courses that largely focused on physiology and disease. While we felt there was importance in providing basic education regarding human sexuality, which we came to realize the more we taught the course how little the students knew about their own bodies and basic facts related to sex, we thought there were more important things to address in a human sexuality course in counseling. We already enthusiastically embraced the sex positive approach but felt that in developing our course we wanted to focus more specifically on the student's awareness of their own values and beliefs related to sexuality. We had been teaching the course for a couple of semesters when we came across an article, "A Postmodern Feminist Approach to Teaching Human Sexuality" (Baber & Murray, 2001), that articulated what we were trying to achieve in our course. Until that point, we had incorporated different speakers, activities, and assignments that were consistent with what we felt were important, but this article helped us recognize the importance of having a theoretical foundation. Using a postmodern feminist approach grounded our course in a framework that was consistent with the constructivist paradigm and, therefore, fit well with a counseling program. The postmodern feminist approach acknowledges the complexity as well as the fluid nature of sexuality. Additionally, this approach conceptualizes sexuality from a diverse perspective that emphasizes the importance of inclusion and attention to those whose experiences have been marginalized. A vital component of the course is to promote the development of critical thinking associated with current constructions of human sexuality and, most importantly, encourages students to take an inventory of their own biases, values, and beliefs regarding sexuality.

The postmodern perspective is essential when teaching the human sexuality course because of its emphasis on acknowledging historical context, variations among different cultures and groups, and the expectation that things change over time. Using feminist theory as part of the pedagogical framework brings a critical focus on attention to power differential and addressing the invisibility of marginalized groups (Baber & Murray, 2001). Adopting a postmodern feminist approach to teaching our human sexuality course, we established some primary goals for the course consistent with the framework, including (a) operating from a wellness-focused perspective, which challenges the pathologizing of alternative sexual behaviors and expressions that are outside of societal "norms"; (b) developing clinical knowledge and skills that students may immediately apply in their training experiences; (c) developing students' own sexual scripts to assist them in exploring their own sexual identity as well as creating a tool for establishing boundaries between their own and their clients values and beliefs; (d) encouraging critical thinking skills for approaching sexuality that emphasize inclusion; and (e) fostering the students' pursuit of their own sexual health. This could be obtained only through carefully establishing a learning environment whereby the students feel comfortable self-disclosing. One of the ways we have done that is by not asking students to share information that we ourselves are not willing to share as well. Also, students are never required to share anything they are uncomfortable with sharing.

As Baber and Murray (2001) pointed out, this type of approach is often criticized and perceived to be purely "hedonistic," whereby anything is acceptable and there are no limits or parameters on sexual behavior. When first introducing the framework, we have students identify and explore behaviors and beliefs clients may have that a mental health professional might not be able to tolerate, such as pedophilia or zoophilia. We then discuss situations where that might be tolerated; an example is working with an adult client who disclosed having desires to have sex with children but had not acted on the desires and wanting to work on controlling their behavior. We challenge them to think critically and distinguish between the monosexism in societal mores they have been indoctrinated with and alternative ways to view sexual behaviors. When discussing sex with animals, which is often identified as being a sexual behavior that is unacceptable with many of the students, one student disclosed living in a rural area where that was practiced. While it was not openly condoned, people were aware of it happening and people who engaged in the behavior were not prosecuted or socially ostracized. This was certainly surprising to numerous students but opened a dialogue around other cultures and how they view certain sexual behaviors differently. As instructors, we assert that not all behaviors are acceptable and highlight that there must always be consent. It is not acceptable if the person does not have the ability to consent, such as when someone is incapacitated or a child, or as is the case with an animal, does not have the ability to comprehend and consent.

Diversity

One of the fundamental aspects of the postmodern feminist approach as well as using a sex positive framework is a focus on diversity. This is inclusive of diversity in all aspects from race/ethnicity to religion, culture, age, physical abilities, sexual expression, sexual orientation, gender and gender expression, and all other identities someone may embrace. It examines the intersectionality of different diverse identities and how that may impact the therapeutic relationship as well as how the client's lived experiences may have been influenced by those identities. Discussions include exploring how different geographical areas in the country and across the world experience their sexuality. Care is taken to also review the differences across the life span and how historical context will greatly affect a client's experiences. An example is working with a lesbian client who is in her 50s versus one who is in her 20s. Their experience coming out to their families is likely to be distinctly different.

Sexual Identities and Sexual Scripts

Fine (1988) contended that the sex education in the United States is failing students because it does not focus on the development of the sexual self. For counseling sexuality pedagogy to be effective, it must facilitate students' exploration of their own sexual identity. As individuals, our sexual identity is complex and multilayered and includes different aspects such as physiology, sexual orientation, gender, and gender expression (Worthington et al., 2002). Having a clear concept of yourself as a sexual being and the ability to acknowledge the ways in which your culture, society, and current historical context have influenced your sexual identity is powerful and liberating. This is achieved through conscious and intentional self-explorative efforts, which can be facilitated in a course through reflective activities. The goal is to increase the student's self-awareness and improve comfort with their own sexual identity to reduce hesitancy in addressing sexuality-related issues with clients (Russell, 2012).

The postmodern feminist approach is a constructivist paradigm that operates from the assumption that sexuality is socially constructed through intricate scripting that is influenced by historical context, culture, social media, and other factors (Gagnon, 1990; Gagnon & Simon, 1973; Laumann & Gagnon, 1995; Laws, 1980; Simon & Gagnon, 2003). One of the ways we start working with students in the human sexuality class is to introduce them to the concept of sexual scripts (see Appendix 25.A: Sexual Scripts) at the beginning of the semester. *Sexual script theory*, which was developed by Gagnon and Simon (1973), describes sexual scripts as "blueprints" that provide parameters regarding sexual behavior related to whom someone will engage with sexually, as well as the where, how, and why (Atwood & Dershowitz, 1992).

According to Simon and Gagnon (1986), sexual behavior is guided by culture and both interpersonal and intrapsychic scripts. In our society today, through gender-reveal parties, even before birth, people are given messages about gender and gender expression and expectations of behavior based on biological sex assignment. Throughout our childhood and adolescence, messages are received regarding acceptable behavior toward members of the opposite sex, romantic partners, courtship, and how we perceive ourselves and our bodies.

Despite the mental health field's efforts to create distance from those we serve by giving them labels like patient, client, or consumer and pathologizing them with diagnoses, we still often find ourselves drawn to them in ways that would breach the therapeutic relationship. All of the professional code of ethics for mental health professionals, including counselors, social workers, psychologists, and marriage and family therapists, state clearly that sexual intimacy with a current client or client family member is prohibited. Mental health professionals are all told that engaging in a sexual relationship with a client is taboo. However, students are not given the tools for navigating those situations when they arise.

One of the things we always talk with students about is client attraction and how to best prepare for the day when they find themselves attracted to a client or when a client is attracted to them. We do not present it as though it may happen; rather, we let them know it is going to happen. As is often said in substance use work, "It's not the exception but the expectation." We talk about how the therapeutic relationship is an intimate one for both the client and the therapist. The client is often sharing things in session that they may have never told anyone before. If the therapist is doing things right, there is going to be transference, which often includes sexual attraction. It is inevitable. This is alarming and even frightening for students and new clinicians if they are not adequately prepared. Additionally, clinicians have times in their lives when they are vulnerable because of their own life circumstances. They may be going through a breakup or feeling particularly unappealing, or more simply, the client they are working with is someone who is attractive to them. As counselor educators, we feel an obligation to provide students with tools for navigating times in the therapeutic relationship when this happens. We talk about what this situation looks like and what we have done when it has happened in our own practice. We strongly emphasize the importance of consultation with other professionals for input and guidance, especially when these situations arise. By normalizing these attractions, students are more likely to seek support and assistance rather than feeling shameful and avoiding talking about it.

Having worked with students for many years, we frequently hear reports of instances where their supervisors have transferred clients away from the student if the client has expressed attraction to them or made sexual statements that have made the student uncomfortable. Rather than using this as an opportunity to educate and train the student, the supervisor chose to avoid the situation, which potentially caused harm to the client and gave the message to the student that the best approach to handling sexually charged situations with a client is avoidance. However, it is not surprising; research has shown that mental health professionals are uncomfortable addressing sexuality-related issues (Harris & Hays, 2008; Long et al., 2006; Rutter et al., 2010), which inhibits their ability to effectively treat and/or supervise whenever sexuality-related concerns arise (Kazukauskas & Lam, 2009, 2010; Miller & Byers, 2010, 2012).

By asking students questions about their family of origin regarding religious and spiritual values and beliefs related to sexuality, as well as when and where they first found out about sex, we find that students begin to think about how their views were shaped. During the first class, after providing an overview of sexual scripts theory, students are given the Sexual Scripts Questionnaire (see Appendix 25.A) to complete. We talk about how most sexual scripts are developed passively without much conscious thought as to how values and beliefs were developed. Additionally, for some students, although they may have discarded some beliefs or the values they grew up with—for example that premarital sex is sinful—they still operate from a script that labels this behavior as sinful. By reviewing the messages they were given while growing, and their current values/beliefs, they have an opportunity to "update" their script to better align with where they are as adults. Throughout the course, as part of their reflection paper assignment, they are encouraged to review their sexual script and reflect on whether they may be experiencing changes based on new information and/or experiences. During the last class, we have an open discussion with students about their reflective assessment of their sexual script and about whether change occurred as a result of their personal reflections and experiences in the course.

By reviewing their sexual scripts, students are proactively designing their own scripts and taking ownership. They are clearly defining their values and boundaries related to sexual behaviors, gender, and gender expression. We emphasize that students are permitted to have whatever values and beliefs they chose as individuals, but as professional counselors, they must adhere to the ethical code as a guide when addressing sexual concerns of clients. Ultimately, as a result of exploring their sexual script and creating boundaries within the script, students are better able to establish them with the clients in session. The ACA (2014) ethical values and principles of enhancing development throughout the life span, respecting diversity and people's worldviews, promoting social justice, safeguarding the integrity of the therapeutic relationship, practicing in a competent and ethical manner, respecting the autonomy of clients, and nonmaleficence and beneficence, demand that as counseling professionals, students must put the needs of their clients first.

Developing a Brave Environment and Maintaining Confidentiality

The responsibility for developing and providing a growth-promoting experience in a human sexuality course lies with both the students and the instructor. Class discussions can become fervent or spirited, and experiential activities can be empowering. Student experiences in the class may be positive, challenging, or even painful, so we always discuss this as an expectation at the beginning of the course. Since strong personal feelings may arise, the instructors make a concerted effort to create an environment for students to engage in the personal exploration necessary to address issues of sexuality honestly and openly. Students are asked to also take responsibility for maintaining such an environment. Although students are asked to disclose thoughts and feelings that are personal in nature, we remind students that they have control of what they will disclose in class. Students do not have to reveal any information—it is their choice. In addition, we consider information confidential that is disclosed in reflection papers, online discussions, or private conversations with the instructors. Information shared in the course should be considered confidential, but it cannot be guaranteed that other students will keep it so. Nevertheless, students are expected to maintain other class members' confidentiality and to respect their right to share personal information as they choose.

We remind students that everyone deserves civility, respect, and cooperation throughout the course. We state that it is important to remember that a wide range of sexual diversity exists and to not make any assumptions. Some students are virgins, and some have a lot of sexual experience; some are straight, others are gay, lesbian, or bisexual; some have conservative or religious values, and others have liberal or secular values; some are cisgender, transgender, nonbinary, or agender; some have experienced rape, sexual coercion, harassment, stalking, childhood sexual abuse, sexually transmitted infections, abortion, divorce, or other sexual traumas. We recognize that it is unrealistic to create a safe space given that for people of color and people from other marginalized and oppressed groups there is no space that feels altogether safe. What we do is openly discuss power differentials within the classroom. For example, as White instructors, we wield a great deal of power. We also talk about some of our struggles with assumptions and biases related to sexuality and what we have done to become more knowledgeable as clinicians. Although we are the instructors and have expertise in the area of sexuality, it is important the students see our process and how we have worked toward gaining the necessary skills to work effectively with clients on sexuality-related issues.

Per their feedback, we have found that students completing the human sexuality class have been emotionally impacted by the experience. Perhaps the course material is pushing students' intellectual boundaries, leading students to question received wisdom, challenging students to confront long-held biases and assumptions, clarifying conflicts between different ideological positions, or broadening their imagination. All of these are good things that the course should promote to stimulate learning. We always encourage feedback from the students throughout the course, especially if they have felt we have been insensitive or if a topic is particularly uncomfortable for them. Students are alerted to sensitive topics ahead of time.

Course Activities and Assignments

The type of assignments and activities included in the human sexuality course are especially important. In the following discussion, we present some key activities and assignments that we have found to be effective and meaningful for students.

In Vivo: Immersion Experience

The immersion experience has been identified by students as being the most transformative assignment/experience for them in the course. Students are required to choose from a list of activities, classes, plays, or events to attend in the area outside their comfort zone related to human sexuality. Fortunately, we teach in a large metropolitan area so there are ample opportunities and options for students to choose from, such as free or low-cost workshops offered by one of the area sex toy shops led by certified sex educators. Students are free to choose any experience or activity related to human sexuality and they are encouraged to bring along friends and significant others. By providing a wide range of choices and allowing students to choose the event/activity, the goal is to empower them to select something that will offer them a truly transformative experience. The students then write a reflection paper outlining their experience and reactions to it.

We have been amazed by student reactions and the positive results from this assignment. Our classes are filled with students from a wide range of racial/ethnic backgrounds as well as religious affiliations. At the outset of the class, we emphasize the importance of respecting wherever anyone is at regarding their beliefs around sexuality. We had one female Asian student who came from a conservative Christian background choose to attend a workshop on female orgasm at one of the sex toy shops in Chicago. As a debrief to the immersion activity, students are asked to share their experiences. This student described standing outside the shop beforehand using self-talk to gain the courage to go into the workshop. This student was an excellent student and highly motivated, so it was important for her to meet the spirit of the task. She was effusive in her description of the experience and how her discomfort and anxiety subsided after entering. She was both proud of herself for doing it but also felt she gained a lot from the experience as well.

Speakers

Throughout the time we have been teaching the human sexuality course, we have always had invited guest speakers. We try to select people who can speak from their own experiences, as that tends to elicit the best responses from students. We now have several people who are regulars each semester who have received excellent reviews from the students. Below is a list of some topics our speakers have addressed.

- *Transgender.* We have had a transman and transwoman speak together about their experience transitioning. Additionally, they are both comfortable in allowing students to ask any questions they may have about their experience. Students have reported that this is helpful to their understanding of the experience of transgender people and increases their comfort in working with the transgender population.
- *Sexual abuse.* An alumnus of our program who also is a survivor of clerical sexual abuse speaks from the perspective of both clinician and sexual abuse survivor. His presentation is always powerful as he has done a lot of his own therapeutic work and is comfortable talking about his journey toward healing.
- *Therapeutic use of sex toys.* Another alumnus of our class worked in a sex toy store. We asked them about the possibility of speaking in class, being careful to couch it in a therapeutic realm. We did not want it to digress into a sex toy party. The presenter has a background in applied behavioral analysis and working with

neurodivergent people, as well as using sex toys therapeutically. The goal is to assist students in gaining knowledge of how to use sex toys therapeutically in their work with clients.

- *Sex therapy.* We have had sex therapists who have been able to speak in our class. It is helpful in providing clarity between "sexual distress" and what might constitute a referral to a sex therapist. It also demystifies what a sex therapist does in sessions.
- *Puppy play.* We frequently attend different educational presentations related to sexuality, and our speaker on *puppy play*—which may or may not be sexual and is a subset of the BDSM or kink communities—was a presenter from an event we attended. He presents in puppy attire and is disarming in his ability to both charm and alarm students. Puppy play, which does not involve actual dogs, generally involves a human dressing up and taking on the role of a puppy or dog.
- *BDSM/kink.* An alumnus of our program is someone we call the "ambassador of kink." They were "raised" in the San Francisco BDSM community under the mentorship of Madame Cleo DuBois, who is the founder of the Academy of S/M Arts. Therefore, their perspective of BDSM and kink has a distinctly spiritual and healing aspect which is the BDSM culture in the San Francisco area. Given they have and still live in the BDSM community as well having been a sex worker, their message is both powerful and transformative.

Although we recruit speakers from the broader community, many of them tend to be alumni from our program or the university. We actively network within the BDSM, LGBTQIA+, and sexuality community in our area as a way to cultivate new speakers.

Case Vignettes, Role Plays, and Other Activities

Generally, in a 3-hour class, the first hour is devoted to lecture and introducing the week's topic, then the remaining time is spent in group discussion and group activities. Students have reported that discussions in small groups are especially beneficial as they feel less intimidated than when we talk as a larger group. Case vignettes have been a particularly powerful way to challenge student thinking when presented with situations outside their personal experience. Given the topic of sexuality and the student discomfort initially, early on it is helpful to do ice-breaking exercises that allow for brevity and lowering everyone's uneasiness. One favorite is to choose different terms related to sex and have the students write on the board all the names they have heard of related to it. We explain that, not just an exercise in exposing everyone to derogatory names for sex and body parts, it also is helpful for them to be aware of how different people may reference sex, their own body, and that of other people's bodies. This is often especially helpful for students who will be working with adolescents.

Conclusion

It cannot be denied that sexuality plays a significant role is every person's life. People are bombarded with sex through social media, popular music, film, and advertisements. However, as a society our culture is not effective at providing adequate education around sexuality, which has resulted in lack of knowledge and, worse yet, misinformation and even intentional dissemination of deceptive information related to sexuality. The training of counselors related to sexuality is not adequate to meet the needs of clients (Zeglin et al., 2018). There is evidence that clinicians who receive sexuality training and education are more confident and, as a result, more effective in responding to clients with sexuality-related issues (e.g., Haboubi & Lincoln, 2003; Hanzlik & Gaubatz, 2012; Harris & Hays, 2008; Juergens et al., 2009; Russell, 2012). Nevertheless, graduates leaving counseling programs today are not prepared to provide adequate care around issues related to sex and sexuality. As mentioned in Chapter 1, there are only two states, California and Florida, that require a human sexuality course for licensure; therefore, most counseling programs offer human sexuality only as an elective course. The 2014 *ACA Code of Ethics*, although not specific in directives related to sexuality, requires that in order to provide ethical care for clients, counselors must receive adequate education and training. This is the responsibility of counselor educators and the entire counseling community. The values (autonomy, nonmaleficence, beneficence, fidelity, veracity, and justice) that provide the foundation for counselors' ethical principles demand that the counseling profession meet the obligation and commitment to ensure all counselors are prepared to provide efficacious care around sexuality-related issues.

References

American Counseling Association. (2014). *ACA code of ethics*. https://www.counseling.org/resources/aca-code-of-ethics.pdf

Anderson, R. M. (2013). Positive sexuality and its impact on overall well-being. *Bundesgesundheitsblatt, Gesundheitsforschung, Gesundheitsschutz, 56*(2), 208–214. https://doi.org/10.1007/s00103-012-1607-z

Atwood, J. D., & Dershowitz, S. (1992). Constructing a sex and marital therapy frame: Ways to help couples deconstruct sexual problems. *Journal of Sex & Marital Therapy, 18*(3), 196–218. https://doi.org/10.1080/00926239208403407

Baber, K. M., & Murray, C. I. (2001). A postmodern feminist approach to teaching human sexuality. *Family Relations, 50*(1), 23–33. https://doi.org/10.1111/j.1741-3729.2001.00023.x

Ballam, S., & Granello, P. (2011). Confronting sex in the media: Implications and counseling recommendations. *The Family Journal, 19*(4), 421–426. https://doi.org/10.1177/1066480711417237

Binik, Y. M., & Meana, M. (2009). The future of sex therapy: Specialization or marginalization? *Archives of Sexual Behavior, 38*(6), 1016–1027. https://doi.org/10.1007/s10508-009-9475-9

Bishop, C. (2001). *Sexualia mundi*. Konemann.

Black, L. L., Stone, D. A., Hutchinson, S. R., & Suarez, E. C. (2007). The development and validation of the Social Privilege Measure. *Measurement and Evaluation in Counseling and Development, 40*(1), 16–32. https://doi.org/10.1080/07481756.2007.11909803

Christensen, E., Norton, J., Salisch, M., & Gull, S. (1977). An affective sexual awareness program for counselors. *Counselor Education and Supervision, 16*(3), 185–193. https://doi.org/10.1002/j.1556-6978.1977.tb01608.x

Collins, A., & Sedlacek, W. (1972). Counselor perceptions of sexual attitudes of female university students. *College Student Journal, 6*, 13–16.

Cottone, R. R. (2007). Paradigms of counseling and psychotherapy, revisited: Is social constructivism a paradigm? *Journal of Mental Health Counseling, 29*, 189–201. https://doi.org/10.17744/mchc.29.3.2125224257006473

Council for Accreditation of Counseling and Related Educational Programs. (2016). *2016 CACREP standards*. http://www.cacrep.org/for-programs/2016-cacrep-standards/

Dermer, S., & Bachenberg, M. (2015). The importance of training marital, couple, and family therapists in sexual health. *Australian and New Zealand Journal of Family Therapy, 36*(4), 492–503. https://doi.org/10.1002/anzf.1122

Diambra, J. F., Pollard, B. L., Gamble, R. M., & Banks, B. P. (2016). Teaching a human sexuality course: What are counseling students thinking? *American Journal of Sexuality Education, 11*(1), 76–91. https://doi.org/10.1080/15546128.2016.1141737

Dupkoski, W. (2012). Sexuality is universal: Implications for using a constructivist approach to sexuality training in counselor education programs. *VISTAS Online*, Article 12. https://www.counseling.org/knowledge-center/vistas/by-subject2/vistas-education-and-supervision/docs/default-source/vistas/vistas_2012_article_12

Fine, M. (1988). Sexuality, schooling, and adolescent females: The missing discourse of desire. *Harvard Educational Review, 58*(1), 29–53.

Flynn, K. E., Lindau, S. T., Lin, L., Reese, J. B., Jeffery, D. D., Carter, J., Baron, S. R., Abramsohn, E., & Weinfurt, K. P. (2015). Development and validation of a single-item screener for self-reporting sexual problems in U.S. adults. *Journal of General Internal Medicine, 30*(10), 1468–1475. https://doi.org/10.1007/s11606-015-3333-3

Fyfe, B. (1980). Counseling and human sexuality: A training model. *The Personnel and Guidance Journal, 59*(3), 147–150. https://doi.org/10.1002/j.2164-4918.1980.tb00519.x

Gagnon, J. (1990). The explicit and implicit use of the scripting perspective in sex research. *Annual Review of Sex Research, 1*, 1–43.

Gagnon, J. H., & Simon, W. (1973). *Sexual conduct: The social sources of human sexuality*. Aldine.

Giami, A. (2002). Sexual health: The emergence, development, and diversity of a concept. *Annual Review of Sex Research, 13*, 1–35. https://doi.org/10.1080/10532528.2002.10559801

Gray, L. A., Cummins, E. J., Johnson, B. P., & Mason, M. J. (1989). Human sexuality instruction in counselor education curricula. *Counselor Education and Supervision, 28*(4), 305–317. https://doi.org/10.1002/j.1556-6978.1989.tb01121.x

Gray, L. A., House, R. M., & Eicken, S. (1996). Human sexuality instruction: Implications for couple and family counselor educators. *The Family Journal, 4*(3), 208–216. https://doi.org/10.1177/1066480796043004

Grove, J. (2009). How competent are trainee and newly qualified counsellors to work with lesbian, gay, and bisexual clients and what do they perceive as their most effective learning experiences? *Counselling and Psychotherapy Research, 9*(2), 78–85. https://doi.org/10.1080/14733140802490622

Haboubi, N. H., & Lincoln, N. (2003). Views of health professionals on discussing sexual issues with patients. *Disability and Rehabilitation, 25*(6), 291–296.

Hanzlik, M., & Gaubatz, M. (2012). Clinical PsyD trainees' comfort discussing sexual issues with clients. *American Journal of Sexuality Education, 7*(3), 219–236. https://doi.org/10.1080/15546128.2012.707080

Harris, S. M., & Hays, K. W. (2008). Family therapist comfort with and willingness to discuss client sexuality. *Journal of Marital and Family Therapy, 34*(2), 239–250. https://doi.org/10.1111/j.1752-0606.2008.00066.x

Hays, D. G., Chang, C. Y., & Dean, J. K. (2004). White counselors' conceptualization of privilege and oppression: Implications for counselor training. *Counselor Education and Supervision, 43*(4), 242–257. https://doi.org/10.1002/j.1556-6978.2004.tb01850.x

Heiman, J. R. (2002). Sexual dysfunction: Overview of prevalence, etiological factors, and treatments. *Journal of Sex Research, 39*(1), 73–78.

Higgins, A., Barker, P., & Begley, C. M. (2006). Sexuality: The challenge to espoused holistic care. *International Journal of Nursing Practice, 12*(6), 345–351. https://doi.org/10.1111/j.1440-172X.2006.00593.x

Juergens, M. H., Smedema, S. M., & Berven, N. L. (2009). Willingness of graduate students in rehabilitation counseling to discuss sexuality with clients. *Rehabilitation Counseling Bulletin, 53*(1), 34–43.

Kazukauskas, K. A., & Lam, C. S. (2009). Importance of addressing sexuality in certified rehabilitation counselor practice. *Rehabilitation Education, 23*, 127–140. https://doi.org/10.1891/088970109805059137

Kazukauskas, K. A., & Lam, C. S. (2010). Disability and sexuality: Knowledge, attitudes, and level of comfort among certified rehabilitation counselors. *Rehabilitation Counseling Bulletin, 54*, 15–25. https://doi.org/10.1177/0034355209348239

Kirkpatrick, J. S. (1980). Human sexuality: A survey of what counselors need to know. *Counselor Education and Supervision, 19*(4), 276–282. https://doi.org/10.1002/j.1556-6978.1980.tb01626.x

Laumann, E. O., & Gagnon, J. H. (1995). A sociological perspective on sexual action. In R. G. Parker & J. H. Gagnon (Eds.), *Conceiving sexuality: Approaches to sex research in a postmodern world* (pp. 183–213). Routledge.

Laws, J. L. (1980). Female sexuality through the life span. In P. B. Baltes & O. G. Brim Jr. (Eds.), *Life-span development and behavior* (Vol. 3, pp. 207–252). Academic Press.

Lewis, L. J. (2004). Examining sexual health discourses in a racial/ethnic context. *Archives of Sexual Behavior, 33*, 223–234. https://doi.org/10.1023/B:ASEB.0000026622.31380.b4

Long, L., Burnett, J. A., & Thomas, R. V. (2006). *Sexuality counseling: An integrative approach.* Prentice Hall.

McAuliffe, G. J., & Eriksen, K. P. (1999). Toward a constructivist and developmental identity for the counseling profession: The context-phase-stage-style model. *Journal of Counseling & Development, 77*(3), 267–280. https://doi.org/10.1002/j.1556-6676.1999.tb02450.x

McCabe, M. M., Althof, S. E., Assalian, P., Chevret-Measson, M., Leiblum, S. R., Simonelli, C., & Wylie, K. (2010). Psychological and interpersonal dimensions of sexual function and dysfunction. *The Journal of Sexual Medicine, 7*(1), 327–336. https://doi.org/10.1111/j.1743-6109.2009.01618.x

Miller, S. A., & Byers, E. S. (2010). Psychologists' sexual education and training in graduate school. *Canadian Journal of Behavioural Science, 42*(2), 93–100.

Miller, S. A., & Byers, E. S. (2012). Practicing psychologists' sexual intervention self-efficacy and willingness to treat sexual issues. *Archives of Sexual Behavior, 41*, 1041–1050. https://doi.org/10.1007/ ssl0508-011-9877-3

Moran, J. P. (2000). *Teaching sex. The shaping of adolescence in the 20th century.* Harvard University Press.

National Board for Certified Counselors. (2020). *National certified counselor certification eligibility policy.* https://www.nbcc.org/assets/policies/ncc_certification_eligibility_policy.pdf#

Nimbi, F. M., Rosati, F., Esposito, R. M., Stuart, D., Simonelli, C., & Tambelli, R. (2021). Sex in chemsex: Sexual response, motivations, and sober sex in a group of Italian men who have sex with men with sexualized drug use. *The Journal of Sexual Medicine, 18*(12), 1955–1969. https://doi.org/10.1016/j.jsxm.2021.09.013

Risen, C. B. (2003). Listening to sexual stories. In S. Levine (Ed.), *Handbook of clinical sexuality for mental health professionals* (pp. 3–20). Brunner Routledge.

Russell, E. B. (2012). Sexual health attitudes, knowledge and clinical behaviors: Implications for counseling. *The Family Journal, 20*(1), 94–101. https://doi.org/10.1177/1066480711430196

Rutter, P. A., Leech, N. N., Anderson, M., & Saunders, D. (2010). Couples counseling for a transgender-lesbian couple: Student counselors' comfort and discomfort with sexuality counseling topics. *Journal of GLBT Family Studies, 6*, 68–79.

Sanabria, S., & Murray, T. L. (2018). Infusing human sexuality content and counseling in counselor education curriculum. *American Journal of Sexuality Education, 13*(2), 190–204. https://doi.org/10.1080/15546128.2018.1457461

Sansone, R. A., & Wiederman, M. W. (2000). Sexuality training for psychiatry residents: A national survey of training directors. *Journal of Sex & Marital Therapy, 26*(3), 249–256. https://doi.org/10.1080/009262300500084641

Schiller, P. (1977). *Creative approaches to sex education and counseling.* Association Press.

Shapiro, S., & Brown, C. (2018). *Sex education standards across the states.* Center for American Progress.

Simon, W., & Gagnon, J. H. (1986). Sexual scripts: Permanence and change. *Archives of Sexual Behavior, 15*(2), 97–120. https://doi.org/10.1007/BF01542219

Simon, W., & Gagnon, J. H. (2003). Sexual scripts: Origins, influences and change. *Qualitative Sociology, 26*, 491–497. https://doi.org/10.1023/B:QUAS.0000005053.99846.e5

Simons, J. S., & Carey, M. P. (2001). Prevalence of sexual dysfunctions: Results from a decade of research. *Archives of Sexual Behavior, 30*(2), 177–219.

Southern, S., & Cade, R. (2011). Sexuality counseling: A professional specialization comes of age. *The Family Journal, 19*(3), 246–262. https://doi.org/10.1177/1066480711408028

Stayton, W. R. (1998). A curriculum for training professionals in human sexuality using the sexual attitude restructuring (SAR) model. *Journal of Sex Education & Therapy, 23*, 26–32.

Sue, D. W., Arredondo, P., & McDavis, R. J. (1992). Multicultural counseling competencies and standards: A call to the profession. *Journal of Multicultural Counseling and Development, 20*(2), 64–88. https://doi.org/10.1002/j.2161-1912.1992.tb00563.x

Wilks, D. (2018). Twenty-first-century counseling theory development in relation to definitions of free will and determinism. *Journal of Counseling & Development, 96*(2), 213–222. https://doi.org/10.1002/jcad.12194

Williams, D. J., Thomas, J. N., Prior, E. E., & Walters, W. (2015). Introducing a multidisciplinary framework of positive sexuality. *Journal of Positive Sexuality, 1*, 6–11.

World Health Organization. (n.d.). *Sexual health topics.* https://www.who.int/health-topics/sexual-health

World Health Organization. (1975). *Education and treatment in human sexuality: The training of health professionals. Report of a WHO meeting* (Technical Report Series No. 572). https://apps.who.int/iris/handle/10665/38247

Worthington, R. L., Savoy, H. B., Dillon, F. R., & Vernaglia, E. R. (2002). Heterosexual identity development: A multidimensional model of individual and social identity. *Counseling Psychologist, 30*(4), 496–531. https://doi.org/10.1177/00100002030004002

Zeglin, R. J., Van Dam, D., & Hergenrather, K. C. (2018). An introduction to proposed human sexuality counseling competencies. *International Journal for the Advancement of Counselling, 40*(2), 105–121. https://doi.org/10.1007/s10447-017-9314-y

APPENDIX 25.A

Sexual Scripts

Everyone has values and beliefs around sexuality, which includes things such as gender roles and expression, sexual behavior, and sexual orientation. These are often based on how our family, especially our parents and/or primary caretakers, viewed these things. If you were raised in a particular faith or religion and/or if you participate in a religion as an adult, that may influence your values/beliefs around sexuality. Society and the historical time in which you grew up are also factors which shape your views about sexuality. Your perspectives and the guidelines that you follow related to sexuality are sometimes referred to as your "sexual script." It is helpful to have an understanding of not only where these values/beliefs come from but also how they impact you and your relationships.

It is also important to have an awareness of your sexual script as a clinician when working with clients. It is likely that you will work with clients who do not share the same values or beliefs that you do. According to *ACA Code of Ethics*, as a counselor, you need to have the capacity to work with clients and not impose your personal values, attitudes, and beliefs on them (ACA, 2014). As counselors, we must respect our clients' worldviews, especially when they are not consistent with our own.

Please answer the questions on the following pages as honestly as you feel comfortable. This is for your information only and will not be collected. It is up to you what you choose to share with the class/group.

Biological Sex/Gender/Gender Expression/Gender Roles

1. When you think about yourself as a male/female/nonbinary, who do you think influenced you most regarding your gender identity?

   ____

   ____

2. Are your views different now than they were when you were a child/adolescent?

   ____

   ____

3. Are your views different than your parents/family/culture?

   ____

   ____

4. Are your views influenced by your religious/spiritual beliefs?

   ____

   ____

Child/Adolescent

1. What sex were you assigned to at birth? ❑ Male ❑ Female ❑ Intersex
2. What did your family (parents, grandparents) tell you about being a girl/boy? Or did your family not pressure you to conform to binary gender roles?

   ____

   ____

3. Did you like to play with toys you were told were considered "appropriate" for your assigned sex (e.g., boys play with trucks, girls play with dolls)?

____

____

4. Did you ever feel like you were born in the wrong body? If you were assigned female at birth, did you ever wish you were a boy? If you were assigned male at birth, did you ever wish you were a girl? Or did you feel neither the boy nor girl labels felt comfortable to you?

____

____

5. Did you feel as though you had any say or choice in how you expressed your gender identity?

____

____

6. Did you dress in clothing you were told was appropriate for your gender (e.g., boys wear pants, girls wear dresses and/or "pretty things")?

____

____

7. Did other kids ever tease you because you were too "girly" if you were a boy? Or tease you for being a "tomboy" if you were a girl?

____

____

Adult

1. Do you think women should have careers?

____

____

2. Do you think there are some jobs a woman should not do?

____

____

3. Do you think it is okay for men to stay at home to take care of the children?

____

____

4. Do you believe that the husband is "the head of the house" and has final say about important decisions?

____

____

5. Do you think it is important for women to be mothers?

____

____

6. Do you feel comfortable in your gender expression? Would you like to be able to change the way you express your gender but are afraid of what others might think?

____

____

7. If you identify as nonbinary, do you feel supported by your family? Peers?

____

____

8. What is your current gender identity? (*check all that apply*)
   - ❏ Male
   - ❏ Female
   - ❏ Nonbinary
   - ❏ Female-to-Male (FTM)/Transman
   - ❏ Male-to-Female (MTF)/Transwoman
   - ❏ Genderqueer, neither exclusively male nor female
   - ❏ Genderfluid
   - ❏ Other: ________________

Sexual Orientation

1. Are your views about different LGBTQIA+ sexual orientations influenced by your religious/spiritual beliefs?
   ____
   ____
2. Are your views about the LGBTQIA+ community different than your parents/family/culture?
   ____
   ____
3. Has your view about the LGBTQIA+ community changed over time?
   ____
   ____

Child/Adolescent

1. How old were you when you were first attracted to someone in a romantic/sexual way? Who was your first crush?
   ____
   ____
2. Was that person the opposite sex or same sex as you?
   ____
   ____
3. People are different in their sexual attraction to other people. Which best describes your feelings? Are you:
   - ❏ Only sexually attracted to females
   - ❏ Mostly sexually attracted to females
   - ❏ Equally sexually attracted to females and males
   - ❏ Mostly sexually attracted to males
   - ❏ Only sexually attracted to males
   - ❏ It doesn't matter—you are sexually attracted to someone regardless of their biological sex, gender, or gender expression
   - ❏ I am not sexually attracted to anyone, but I am romantically attracted to males
   - ❏ I am not sexually attracted to anyone, but I am romantically attracted to females
   - ❏ I am sexually attracted to one sex but romantically attracted to the other
   - ❏ Other: ___________

4. Do you consider yourself to be:
   - ❑ Heterosexual/Straight
   - ❑ Homosexual/Gay or lesbian
   - ❑ Bisexual
   - ❑ Pansexual
   - ❑ Asexual
   - ❑ Questioning/Unsure
   - ❑ Queer
   - ❑ I don't believe in using labels
   - ❑ Other: ____________
5. Did you feel you had to "come out" to friends and family about your sexual orientation?

   ____

   ____
6. Do you have any close friends or family that identify as LGBTQIA+?

   ____

   ____
7. Are you uncomfortable around people from the LGBTQIA+ community?

   ____

   ____
8. What is your view of different sexual orientations, such as lesbian, gay, or bisexual?
   - ❑ I see it as being genetic and do not have a problem with it.
   - ❑ I believe it is a choice but don't have a problem with it.
   - ❑ I am not part of the LGBTQIA+ community but view myself as an ally.
   - ❑ I think it is fine for other people but don't want my children exposed to it.
   - ❑ I am okay with people being LGBTQIA+ but think marriage is between a man and woman.
   - ❑ I view any sexual orientation other than heterosexual as sinful.
   - ❑ Other: ___________

Sexual Behavior

1. How old do you think people should be before becoming sexually active?

   ____

   ____
2. How old were you when you first became sexually active? ____________
3. Is your answer different for women or men?

   ____

   ____
4. How do you view masturbation? Is it wrong?

   ____

   ____
5. Is your view about masturbation different for men and women?

   ____

   ____
6. Do you think it's okay for people to be sexually active prior to being married?

   ____

   ____

7. Do you believe someone should be in a committed relationship before becoming sexual with their partner?
____
____
8. What are your thoughts about monogamy? Do you think people who are in committed relationships should not have sex outside of their relationship?
____
____
9. What do you think about polyamory? This is when someone may have sexual/romantic relationships with more than one person at a time.
____
____
10. What are your views about engaging in sex simply for pleasure?
____
____
11. What are your views about pornography? Do you watch it yourself?
____
____
12. What are your views about people using sex toys?
____
____
13. Do you use sex toys?
____
____
14. What are your thoughts about people engaging in BDSM (bondage/dominance/sadomasochism)?
____
____
15. Do you engage in BDSM sexual behaviors?
____
____
16. Are your views about sexual behavior influenced by your religious/spiritual beliefs?
____
____
17. Is your sexual behavior consistent with your religious/spiritual beliefs?
____
____
18. Are your views about sexual behavior different than your parents/family/culture?
____
____

Please hold on to your answers over the course of the semester. We may ask you to reflect on your answers at different times throughout the class. At the end of the semester, we will have everyone revisit their answers to see if any of their views or answers to the questions have changed.

Index

Boxes, figures, and tables are indicated by b, f, and t following the page number.

A

C

(Continued)

G

(Continued)

J

K

L

M

(Continued)

T

U

V

W

X

Y

Z

www.ingramcontent.com/pod-product-compliance
Ingram Content Group UK Ltd.
Pitfield, Milton Keynes, MK11 3LW, UK
UKHW051928100926
8556IPUK00022B/1442

9 781556 203985